Foods That Changed History

Foods That Changed History

How Foods Shaped Civilization from the Ancient World to the Present

Christopher Cumo

An Imprint of ABC-CLIO, LLC
Santa Barbara, California • Denver, Colorado

Copyright © 2015 by ABC-CLIO, LLC

Library of Congress Cataloging-in-Publication Data

Cumo, Christopher.
  Foods that changed history : how foods shaped civilization from the ancient world to the present / Christopher Cumo.
      pages cm
  Includes bibliographical references and index.
  ISBN 978-1-4408-3536-0 (alk. paper)—ISBN 978-1-4408-3537-7 (ebook)
1. Food—History—Encyclopedias.   2. Agriculture—History—Encyclopedias.
3. Cooking—History—Encyclopedias.   4. Civilization—History—Encyclopedias.
I. Title.
  TX349.C86 2015
  641.3003—dc23   2015000810

ISBN: 978-1-4408-3536-0
EISBN: 978-1-4408-3537-7

19 18 17 16 15   1 2 3 4 5

This book is also available on the World Wide Web as an eBook.
Visit www.abc-clio.com for details.

ABC-CLIO, LLC
130 Cremona Drive, P.O. Box 1911
Santa Barbara, California 93116-1911

This book is printed on acid-free paper ∞

Manufactured in the United States of America

Contents

Alphabetical List of Entries

Topical List of Entries

Plant Based Foods

Apple
Banana
Beans
Bread
Breakfast Cereal
Cassava
Chickpea
Chocolate
Cinnamon
Citrus fruits
Coconut
Corn
Date
French Fries
Garlic
Hopping John
Lentils
Millet
Nuts
Oats
Olive and Olive Oil
Onion
Orange Juice
Palm Oil
Pea
Peanut
Peanut Butter
Pepper

Pineapple
Potato
Potato Chip
Rice
Rye
Sorghum
Soybeans and Their Foods
Sweet Potato
Tomato
Tortilla
Turnip
Vanilla
Watermelon
Yam

Animal Based Foods

Beef
Butter and Other Fats
Cheese
Chicken
Duck
Egg
Fish
Goose
Milk
Mutton and Lamb
Pork
Spam
Turkey

Preface

This encyclopedia, *Foods That Changed History: How Foods Shaped Civilization from the Ancient World to the Present*, aims to introduce students to the vast and trendy field of food studies. It is an important discipline that complements the study of global history, botany, animal husbandry, culinary traditions, and other fields. Within this field, this work aims to focus attention on the many foods that have shaped world history, attended the rise of monotheism and other religions, spurred the rise of civilizations, and forged culinary habits for centuries, if not millennia. Fish, for example, are tied to the canonical Gospels and have come to symbolize Jesus. In this context, they helped spur the rise of Christianity. The potato affected numerous fields of study: plant pathology, demography, a prelude to the Malthusian crisis, warfare, the decline of bread in northern Europe, and other developments. The Columbian Exchange has made the Andean potato a global staple in temperate zones. Sugarcane and coffee were the initial impetus for the rise of African slavery in the American tropics. This topic is full of perils, giving rise to racism and all the evils of slavery. Because blackness was conflated with slavery, a whole system of inferiority and exploitation attended the rise of slavery. Even a branch of pseudoscience emerged to try to prove the innate inferiority of Africans. In this case racism corrupted science, which was advertised to be objective. Mutton and lamb fueled the rise of Judaism and are the subjects of notable passages in the Old Testament, particularly the plagues upon Egypt that Exodus professes to record. The fig, apple, and banana may be at the core of the Genesis creation account, each acting as the putative "forbidden fruit," at least according to some scholars. One might multiply examples, but the point is that these foods and others had a disproportionate effect on the world. They shaped what we read and think. They have, in a real sense, shaped who we are as a species. Indeed, the study of food has shaped our own evolution and that of our close kin Neanderthals. Popular imagination views Neanderthals as having been crude and primitive. This stereotype could not be more wrong. They were creative, gifted, and intelligent people whose story is bound up in the rise of fishing among anatomically modern humans during about the last 40,000 years or so.

The scope of this encyclopedia covers a range of disciplines, geographies, and foods. The nearly 100 entries span a large range of foods from the fish, beef, chicken, and mutton and lamb of prehistory to the Coca-Cola of the modern era. This wide-ranging treatment necessarily covers all the habitable continents, from the first stirrings of wheat and barley culture in southwestern Asia some 10,000 years ago to the meteoric rise of hamburgers and hot dogs in modern America. These foods have left a deep imprint. Fish, a food of sustenance for the earliest humans, has led to overfishing and ecological crisis. The very fecundity of our food production and processing system has led to a global population of some 7 billion people, leading to the specter of a Malthusian Crisis, a danger that the Irish Potato Famine in the 1840s may prefigure. Such a large population only re-inforces the degree to which a prodigious food supply is essential to survival. Food is essential to all animals. We are the species that strains under the burden of the food supply, perhaps more than many other species. This was a struggle that British cleric Thomas Malthus predicted in the 18th century, and the problem has only worsened with the passage of time. Indeed, the Green Revolution, important as it was, has granted humans only a temporary buffer zone against the implacable limits of our food supply. Some dour scientists fear that some of the foods on which humans depend, rice being a good example, are near their biological limit in producing edible biomass. How, in such a context, will we derive more food to feed ever more people?

This encyclopedia has an alphabetical organization, an aid to readers who may easily find the foods of their choice. Each entry treats a single food in the context of how that food has changed history and performed the other functions outlined earlier in this preface. The treatment of each entry is chronological. Where possible, each subsection treats a way in which the food has shaped the world. The emphasis is not only on history, but also on botany, aquaculture, animal husbandry, social cohesion, competition for scarce resources, human evolution, and a variety of other disciplines. This encyclopedia is thus a multidisciplinary undertaking that relies on the humanities, the social sciences, and the natural sciences. Each entry closes with suggestions for further exploration: books, articles, and websites that enhance the reader's knowledge. *Foods That Changed History* begins with a list of entries arranged alphabetically, as mentioned above, along with a list of entries grouped in topical categories to help users identify entries on related topics. The encyclopedia has a timeline and an introductory essay that overviews how foods changed world history. The encyclopedia closes with a selected, general bibliography of print and electronic resources to support student research.

Introduction

The acquisition of food is basic to all life. Early in the tenure of life on earth arose green algae, some bacteria, and ultimately plants capable of producing food in the form of the sugar glucose by harnessing the energy of sunlight. These organisms combined sunlight, carbon dioxide, and water to yield this sugar. Almost all other life, including humans, depends on plants for food. This dependence is direct when a person eats a plant or part of a plant, say, a potato, which is an underground tuber of the potato plant. This dependence is a step removed when humans eat the herbivores that have in turn gotten their energy from plants, say, when people eat beef, pork, or any of a number of such animals.

We saw in the preface that our earliest forebears ate primarily plants, though they likely scavenged game when it was available. The pattern of eating meat seems to have become more important in our genus, *Homo*, which 18th-century naturalist Carl Linnaeus named. One thesis holds that meat enabled the brain in our genus to enlarge, a characteristic feature of humans. Indeed, Neanderthals, the greatest meat-eaters in our genus, appear to have had, on average, a brain slightly larger than our own. If meat paved the way toward human evolution, then it shaped our history in ways that are hard to overstate. The development of art, witnessed in the stunning paintings in the caves of Lascaux, France, and Altimira, Spain, testifies to the genius of the human brain. The human brain leveraged technology and agriculture to form the great civilizations that have become the hallmarks of human society. *Homo erectus*, we have seen, took another leap forward in mastering fire, which it used to cook meat, making more nutrients available for digestion. In a fundamental way, *Homo erectus* and Neanderthals were already human because anatomically modern humans interbred with them to yield fertile offspring. In a sense, then, one might argue that *Homo erectus*, Neanderthals and anatomically modern humans were really variants of the same species.

If meat played an important role in human evolution, one should not discount the importance of foraging for plants among the early hunter-gatherer societies. Roots; stems; leaves; flowers; fruits, including berries; and other plant structures were all part of the human diet. The human interest in plants, in their modification and eventual domestication, led to one of the monumental events in human prehistory, the rise of agriculture. Agriculture operated on two levels at the same time. On one level, humans domesticated and cultivated the plants that are at the forefront of the foods on which humans depend for sustenance. The grains rice, wheat, barley, oats, rye, millet, and sorghum rank high among the achievements of the first farmers. At the same time, and in other parts of the world, tubers and roots would be crucial to survival, with potatoes, sweet potatoes, yams, and cassava foremost among them. As a rule, the grains were domesticated at higher latitudes than the tubers and roots. On the second level, humans domesticated the livestock on which the world depends: sheep, pigs, cattle, and other large herbivores. These events were so close in time that they appear to have happened simultaneously. When the idea of domestication entered the human imagination, humans applied the principle to edible plants and animals. If modern humans have inhabited earth for the last 200,000 years—which appears to be a round figure that many physical anthropologists support—then the domestication of plants and animals occurred in a burst of time. Over only about 5,000 years, between about 10,000 and 5,000 years ago, people throughout the world domesticated plants and animals for food. The impetus in this direction appears to have begun in southwestern Asia, where the first farmers domesticated wheat, barley, peas, lentils, and chickpeas. The last three are legumes and were crucial to the human diet because they are protein rich, containing many of the essential amino acids that humans need to survive. Indeed, it appears that wherever grain culture took hold, the first farmers nearly everywhere likewise domesticated one or more legumes. The question, perhaps insoluble, concerns whether agriculture, once invented in southwestern Asia, spread to other regions of the world or was independently invented time and again. The assemblage of other crops in other regions of the world suggests an independent invention of agriculture over multiple regions of the world. This notion appears to be at the crux of the ideas of 19th-century French naturalist Alphonse de Candolle and 20th-century Russian agronomist Nikolai Vavilov. In this context, other important centers of agriculture, the new method of food production, arose in east and Southeast Asia. In these regions, particularly in the South, rice arose as the staple. Indeed, today rice provides more calories for more people than any other food. As in southwestern Asia, a legume, in this case soybeans, became an important complement to rice. Egypt and Europe, however, appear to be largely borrowers of southwestern Asian cultigens, with wheat and barley being important in Egypt and Europe. Like southwestern Asia, the people of Egypt and Europe grew these grains not only for food but to make beer, particularly in the case of barley. Rome, the great empire in the Mediterranean Basin, grew a large variety of crops including grains, legumes, vegetables, and fruit. First–century-CE Roman encyclopedist Pliny the Elder took pains to describe this diversity of foods. Among fruits alone the Romans knew and ate apples, apricots, grapes, figs, and dates. The Roman agricultural writers, namely Columella, appreciated the importance of legumes in rotation. The writer championed the chickpea in this regard. Among livestock, the Romans kept and ate pigs, sheep, cattle, chickens, and other poultry. The grape was the center of Roman life, making wine, the most potent beverage of antiquity. It quickly became associated with revelry and sexual prowess. The olive was the center of the Roman culinary experience. No meal, it seems, was complete without olive oil. Wherever the Romans went throughout the Mediterranean Basin they planted grapes and olives, so important was their culture throughout this region.

It is not enough to sketch the agriculture and culinary habits of portions of the Old World. The Americas were a separate experiment. The Amerindians, completely cut off from the Old World in the pre-Columbian era, had to develop their own suit of crops and livestock. To be blunt, the Amerindians did not have the cattle, pigs, and sheep to domesticate. In fact, when they came to the Americas perhaps 12,000 to 14,000 years ago (the date is fiercely debated and even earlier dates are given), the Amerindians hunted a rich fauna that included horses, mammoths, and sloths, but they all became extinct in the New World. Had the Amerindians hunted them to extinction? This seems unlikely for a Stone Age people with modest weapons. Even with modern chemistry, it seems impossible for humans to kill all dandelions. How could the Amerindians have wiped out a whole fauna? These large mammals provided a rich source of meat, and with it, protein. But once they were gone, these humans had to devise other means of attaining food. Though it was not the first choice, agriculture became the most viable option. As far as livestock are concerned, the Amerindians domesticated only the alpaca, the llama, and the guinea pig. The Amerindian crops were much more important. One thinks immediately of corn, a grain that yields more food per plant than any Old World grain, including rice. The grass has been so important that, during the Columbian Exchange, corn conquered Asia and large parts of Africa. Although it is the feed of livestock today in the developed world, it sustains life throughout the Old World. Even in the United States humans consume corn in the form of beef, pork, and other meats. Corn is thus, like rice, a world crop. The Amerindians also domesticated many varieties of beans in the genus *Phaseolus*. They are not the only beans in the world, but they are incredibly important as food. During the Columbian Exchange they replaced the fava beans of Europe and western Asia almost overnight. The American beans, like Old World legumes, are a rich source of protein and so have sustained the masses, often too poor to afford meat. In this sense, beans made it possible to sustain the plutocracies that had impoverished the masses because, even though poor, the masses could still eat protein in the form of beans and other legumes. The Americas also yielded the potato, whose effects on northern Europe, especially Ireland, are almost too numerous to list in this cursory introduction. The sweet potato, too, is an American crop that has rivaled and, in some cases, replaced the yam in Asia and parts of Africa. Yet another American food is cassava, a crop of great importance to large parts of Africa. The point is that the foods of the Americas did not languish at home. They vitalized the food habits of people throughout the world. Indeed, one can scarcely conceive of modern Europe without the potato or China without the sweet potato or Africa without cassava. These three American crops shunt aside the myopic focus on grains, important as they are. Much of the world subsists on a diet of tubers, roots, and legumes.

If the foods that agriculture made possible transformed the world, one must be cautious in evaluating them. In fact, the first farmers were almost certainly less healthy than hunter-gatherers. Dental and skeletal remains of early agriculturalists suggest notable dietary deficiencies. An overreliance upon grains may have been part of the problem, as no one grain can supply all dietary needs. Compounding the problem, and this was certainly evident in dynastic Egypt, was the tendency of the plutocrats to carry away much of the farmer's grain and other foods in what one might call a tax but was really more akin to theft. Deprived of much of their food, these early farmers had trouble meeting their dietary requirements. So in the short run, agriculture appears to have been a net loss, at least to those who grew the food that fed the plutocrats. In the long term, however, there appears to be no question that the surplus of food has helped humans thrive. For example, wherever humans adopted the potato, birthrates rose and the mass of people appears to have been healthy. Today, one cannot envision life without a plentitude of foods, at least in the developed world, though a new problem has arisen. In the developed world humans tend to be less active than their counterparts in, say, the 19th century. Today, people rely on the automobile instead of walking or bicycling. This sendentism would probably do no serious harm had humans cut their intake of food, but largely they have not. The results are obesity, some cancers, and cardiovascular disease. In a real sense, humans are on the brink of war with the foods they eat. Donuts, pizza, potato chips, french fries, and other junk foods are not sustenance. They provide empty calories and ought not to be eaten.

The classic tragedy on many levels is sugar. Sugar is devoid of any vitamins or minerals and has only the sugar sucrose. Its addition to breakfast cereals and almost all processed foods, for example, sugar is virtually guaranteed to expand one's waistline, but its flaws lie deeper. Initially the food of the peoples in the Old World tropics, sugar did not become widely available until European contact with the Americas. Italian Spanish explorer Christopher Columbus immediately recognized the value of the Caribbean islands to grow sugarcane. In 1493, less than a year after his epochal first voyage, Columbus planted sugarcane on the Caribbean island of Hispaniola (today Haiti and the Dominican Republic}. The plant spread throughout the American tropics during roughly the next two centuries, but the quest for sugar caused misery. The Amerindians had died from the Old World diseases to which they had no immunity. In their place, Europeans imported African slaves to toil on the sugar estates. It took little time for the connection to forge between blackness and mental and physical inferiority, laziness, deviance, and many other negative stereotypes, all of them untrue. Masters treated slaves inhumanely, in some cases feeding them too little to survive. The average slave in the Caribbean, according to one account, lived no more than 10 years from the date of importation. Sugar has thus come at a terrible cost. The connection between food and slavery existed elsewhere in the Americas, notably in the rice plantations in South Carolina and coastal Georgia. First U.S. president George Washington used his slaves to grow wheat, among other foods, and third U.S. president Thomas Jefferson employed slaves to grow a variety of foods, ever eager was he to try some new food plant.

Today we face perhaps our biggest challenge. As the world's population has surpassed 7 billion, it is increasingly difficult for scientists to determine how to increase crop yields still further. Eighteenth-century British cleric Thomas Malthus warned of the danger by which a population could outrun its food supply. The disaster of the Irish Potato Famine confirmed Malthus's ideas. Today we may face a new Malthusian Crisis with crops already near or at their maximum productivity and population still rising. Like petroleum, food is a limiting factor. The earth cannot continue to contain many more denizens. The food supply will not allow nearly infinite increase. In fact, we may be nearing the maximum carrying capacity of the earth. Perhaps humans will be forced to forgo much of their dependence on meat. The land given over to livestock will be needed to feed humans. Humans may need to rely more on fish, though overfishing is already a threat. Humans may need to plant more legumes and less grain to get the protein they need. Whatever the solution, our dietary habits must change. We will always depend on food, but the types of foods themselves must change.

Timeline

500,000 BCE	*Homo erectus* may have been the first hominid to drink tea.
100,000 BCE	Neanderthals may have been the first humans to consume soup.
45,000 BCE	Humans learned to fish and so added these vertebrates to the diet. Neanderthals never mastered the activity of fishing. Anatomically modern humans may thus have outcompeted Neanderthals for food.
12,000 BCE	The Natufians of southwestern Asia harvested wild wheat, barley, peas, lentil, and chickpeas.
10,000 BCE	Humans domesticated sheep to provide mutton and lamb. In this case animal husbandry may have predated plant agriculture. The domestication of the pig and cow followed, though as part of the Neolithic Revolution.
10,000 BCE	Humans drank the first beer. It is likely the world's oldest alcoholic beverage.
10,000 BCE	The people of Southeast Asia may have been the first to domesticate the chicken for meat and eggs.
8000 BCE	The people of southwestern Asia domesticated these food plants, marking the origin of agriculture as the method by which humans derived their foods, though one should note that the transition from hunting and gathering to farming was not sudden. In many regions of the world, including the Americas, the transition was quite gradual.
8000 BCE	People along the Yangtze River in China may have been the first to domesticate rice.
8000 BCE	The people of Brazil may have been the first to eat cassava.
7000 BCE	The peoples of the Andes Mountains in South America domesticated the potato.
7000 BCE	Humans made the first cheese, in this case from goat's milk.

7000 BCE	The people of New Guinea may have been the first to taste sugar.
6000 BCE	The Peruvians appear to have been the first to domesticate the common bean, those in the genus *Phaseolus*. Although the Old World has a small number of species of beans, *Phaseolus* beans have been a staple of humanity since the Columbian Exchange.
5000 BCE	The people of southern Mexico domesticated corn, whose progress toward what is today the United States would be slow.
4500 BCE	At the earliest, the people of West Africa domesticated African varieties of rice. These would become important in colonial America.
3000 BCE	The people of Brazil and the Caribbean islands ate peanuts.
3000 BCE	The Chinese began to eat soybeans, eventually producing a large number of foods from them.
2800 BCE	The Chinese domesticated the soybean.
1450 BCE	The Egyptians kept colonies of honeybees to produce honey.
1000 BCE	The peoples of South America ground peanuts into a paste, the forerunner of peanut butter.
800 BCE	The Phoenicians planted olive trees in Spain.
1 CE	Egypt, North Africa, Greece, and Rome subsisted on bread. Wine was the beverage of choice and olive oil was the staple dietary fat.
In 54 CE	Agrippina, the fourth wife of Roman Emperor Claudius, may have used toxic mushrooms to poison the emperor, opening the throne to her son, the violent and irrational Nero. Ironically, Nero would later kill his mother.
70–90 CE	The canonical gospels depict Jesus and his followers as either fishermen or consumers of fish. Fish became symbolically important in Christianity and governed dietary habits during Lent.
350 CE	Latin scholar and bible translator Saint Jerome named the apple the "forbidden fruit" in Genesis. The appellation, almost certainly false, has captured the imagination since.
In 1493	Italian Spanish explorer Christopher Columbus planted sugarcane on the Caribbean island of Hispaniola, now Haiti and the Dominican Republic. Within a century, sugar fueled a plantation economy that brutalized African slaves, leading to many of the evils that continue to torment Americans.
1513	The Spanish planted the first date palms in Cuba.
1640	The Spanish brought oranges and citrons to Puerto Rico.

1686	Sicilian entrepreneur Francesco Procopio de Coltelli may have been the first to sell ice cream in Paris, France, where he had relocated.
1690	African slaves brought African varieties of rice to coastal South Carolina, where rice became an important export.
1697	Spain introduced peanut butter to the people of Haiti.
1700	The people of Naples, Italy, may have been the first to taste pizza. It was and remains a food of the masses.
In 1747	Scottish physician James Lind proved that citrus fruits protect one against scurvy. Although citrus fruits are renowned for this quality, they are not alone. Pineapple, potatoes, and cabbage all protect against scurvy. Vitamin C, unknown at the time, provided this protection.
1765	Surveyor Henry Yonge planted soybeans as a curiosity on his Georgia farm.
1770	The fourth Earl of Sandwich in England may have invented the sandwich. British historian Edward Gibbon was particularly fond of this new food.
1792	The consumption of diseased rye bread may have precipitated the Salem Witch Trials in Massachusetts.
1809	French chef Nicolas Appert invented the process of canning, at the time bottling, foods, changing forever the methods of food preservation.
1845–1849	The potato crop failed in Ireland. About 1 million people starved and another 1.5 million fled Ireland. This event marked the last subsistence crisis in Europe.
1866	Gregor Mendel published his famous paper on pea hybridization, laying the foundation for the new science of genetics.
1886	American physician and pharmacist John Pemberton invented Coca-Cola.
1893	The U.S. Supreme Court issued its famed ruling that the tomato is a vegetable, despite its true status as a fruit.
1898	The U.S. Department of Agriculture funded the first expedition to Japan and China in search of new soybean varieties. These varieties would serve as the germplasm for all subsequent soybeans grown in the United States.
1900	American entrepreneur James Dole formed the Hawaiian Pineapple Company to ship canned pineapple to a global market.

1904	The Beech-Nut Company began selling peanut butter at the Saint Louis World's Fair.
1941–1945	Spam was a popular substitute for better cuts of pork.
1967	American scientists invented high fructose corn syrup, which competes with sugar as the sweetener of choice.
2014	Salsa outsells ketchup and is now the leading condiment in the United States.
2014	The world produces about 20 million tons of coffee beans per year, and coffee generates more revenue than any commodity other than petroleum.

A

Apple

The apple has long been an important fruit, first in Central Asia and then in Europe and the Americas. Today there may be several thousand apple varieties, but only about 20 are available in supermarkets in any number. These varieties constitute 90 percent of the apples that humans eat. The rest likely come from backyard orchards. The apple's aroma and flavor once set it apart, though today these qualities appear to be secondary to the apple's durability and longevity in storage; that is, the apple has suffered the fate of the tomato. Supermarkets sell unripe, insipid tomatoes with little nutrients because an unripe tomato stands up to rough handling and stores well. In these respects the grocer gives one what the grocer wants rather than what the consumer really wants. The modern apple is a creation of capitalism and its sidekick, agribusiness. In the Rosaceae family, the apple traces its lineage to Central Asia 4.1 million years ago. This family must have been one of the earliest families of flowering plants. In geological terms, flowering plants or angiosperms are among the most recent additions to the world's flora, though they have been remarkably successful.

The Forbidden Fruit

The forbidden fruit traces its origin to the first chapters in Genesis, which claim that God planted a garden in Eden, which he populated with the first creatures of all kinds, including the first man and woman. God instructed the humans to eat of the fruit of any tree except the tree of knowledge of good and evil. The serpent, however, gave the fruit to Eve, who ate it, sharing a portion with Adam. The temptation has been to link the serpent with Satan, though the text does not specify the serpent's identity. Moreover, the Old Testament does not mention Satan until the book of Job. Much scrutiny has focused on the forbidden fruit, with scholars suggesting the fig, banana, and apple as possibilities.

The apple is an ancient fruit. In the fourth century CE St. Jerome named it the forbidden fruit in Genesis. (Cosmin Constantin Sava/ Dreamstime.com)

Apples and Evolution

In 1859, British naturalist Charles Darwin ignited a controversy when he published *On the Origin of Species*. In the United States evolution remains controversial, though one may see its fingerprints everywhere. The apple is a good example. Early in its evolution, the fruit tempted herbivores to eat an apple whole. The animal swallowed the seeds, but stomach acids did not impair them. Rather, the animal, on its trek from feeding ground to feeding ground, excreted the seeds after about one day, and sometimes less for birds. These seeds, covered in excrement, came with a built-in fertilizer. The stomach acids activated the seeds for germination. The apple thus coevolved with birds and mammals, which served as seed-dispersal machines. An apple itself is a seed-dispersal package, and its scent and flavor drew many birds and mammals to it. Apple trees thus ensured the survival of their progeny and in this way illustrate how evolutionary biology works.

Apple and Religions

Given the apple's importance as food, it is not surprising that the fruit became central to the religions of antiquity. The Greeks believed that the goddess Aphrodite coveted apples, and the Romans devoted a goddess, Pomona, to ensuring the abundance of the apple harvest. The foundation story in Genesis has garnered the most attention given the prominence this story holds for Judaism, Christianity, and Islam. The text is straightforward. God permits the first humans, Adam and Eve, to eat the food of any tree but the tree of knowledge of good and evil. A serpent tempts Eve astray. Some people believe the serpent to be Satan, but the Old Testament does not mention Satan until the book of Job. The serpent promises that eating the fruit from this forbidden tree will make Eve akin to a goddess. Reassured, Eve eats the fruit, finding it tasty, and offers it to Adam. Aware of their disobedience, God banishes the two from the garden, telling them that they must labor for their food and that they will one day die.

This story is among the most famous in world literature, but it never specifies the forbidden fruit. Unwilling to tolerate ambiguity, humans have tried to fill in the blank. The Orthodox Church fastened on the fig as the forbidden fruit. This selection has a certain logic. After they ate the fruit, Adam and Eve, recognizing that they were naked, covered themselves in fig leaves, so figs must have grown in the garden. Some Islamic traditions likewise point to the fig. The problem, however, is that the putative presence of figs in the garden does not prove that they were the fruits of the tree of knowledge of good and evil. Another Islamic tradition favors the olive, and there is every reason to suppose that it was grown in western Asia at

Saint Jerome

Born about 347 CE, Saint Jerome lived during an era when imperial Rome was in decline and the Catholic Church was emerging as an important religious, political, social, and economic institution. A priest, theologian, linguist, and historian, Jerome devoted much of his life to translating scripture into Latin, the language of the Roman world. While a student in Rome, he devoted himself to philosophy, but in Syria he claimed to have had a vision of God that led him to Christianity. As an interpreter of scripture, Jerome marked the apple as the "forbidden fruit" in Genesis. The idea is almost certainly wrong but has persisted to the present.

the time Genesis was written. Other, more recent suppositions have favored the banana or pomegranate. The banana has gained favor on the grounds that its leaves were more substantial than fig leaves and so would have made better garments, skimpy as they were, for Adam and Eve. The banana, however, is a tropical fruit and would not have grown in western Asia. The pomegranate is a better climatic match, but there appears to be no other evidence in its favor.

All these suppositions have ceded ground to the apple. In the fourth century, Saint Jerome, a Christian translator of and commentator on the Bible, was the first to suggest the apple. The guess seemed inspired. The Latin for apple, *malus*, means both "apple" and "evil." Being the fruit of what Jerome assumed to be Satan, the apple must have been the forbidden fruit. Curiously, neither Jews nor Muslims accepted this tradition, but it has resonated throughout Western Christianity. Indeed, from an early date Christian art depicted Adam and Eve with an apple, a tradition that even the German Renaissance master Albrecht Dürer upheld. The success of this hypothesis is strange given that the apple tree is a temperate tree that needs a period of dormancy during winter, when temperatures must be cold. The climate of the Levant, if indeed it is the putative place of the Garden of Eden, does not provide sufficient cold during winters to have favored apple culture at the time Genesis was written. Jerome must have focused on the widespread cultivation of the apple in Europe rather than its apparent absence in the Levant. Thanks to Jerome, the apple has become one of the cornerstones of Christian belief and for that reason has echoed throughout history. Perhaps because of the apple's association with Christianity, it has come to have many meanings: desire, danger, reproductive vigor, and immortality. The last association is strange because the Genesis account holds that Adam and Eve died because of their disobedience to God.

The Apple Conquers the World

In the 1920s, Russian agronomist Nikolai Vavilov was the first scientist to pinpoint Central Asia as the cradle of the apple. But Vavilov had the misfortune to run afoul of Soviet dictator Joseph Stalin because Vavilov had first come to prominence with the support of Leon Trotsky, who Stalin viewed as a rival. When Trotsky fled the Soviet Union, Stalin had him murdered in 1940 in Mexico. That year he imprisoned Vavilov, who died three years later, probably from starvation and exposure. Only after the fall of the Soviet Union did Western scientists learn about Vavilov's research, confirming his insight that the apple had arisen in Central Asia.

The first apples probably bore little relation to today's varieties. The first apples were small and sour, much like today's crab apples. Cross-pollination, however, led to genetic diversity, with some apples small and others larger. From the outset, humans likely selected for size, flavor, and aroma. These traits were difficult to control, however, because cross-pollination leads to a diversity of types, just as humans are diverse because we outbreed, to use the jargon of science. Only in Roman times did humans latch onto a solution. By grafting the most promising apple branch onto the rootstock of an apple tree or a related fruit tree, one could be sure of getting the best apples. The apple tree must have been among the first plants to be grafted. Thanks to the apple, humans were advancing the young science of horticulture.

Even in antiquity, the apple was on the march, conquering, in addition to Central Asia, China, parts of western Asia—especially Persia (today Iran)—Iraq, maybe Egypt, Greece, and Rome. Pharaoh Ramses the Great (Ramses II) claimed to have planted apple trees in his orchard, but doubts persist. Egypt does not have cold enough winters for apple trees to become dormant. The Etruscans and Romans were particularly avid about growing apple trees. To these people, no orchard was complete without apple trees. The Romans planted apple trees throughout Europe. One might think of the Roman Empire as the creation of an agricultural edifice throughout Europe, North Africa, Egypt, and western Asia. The apple played a large role in the advancement of Roman civilization on three continents.

In antiquity and the Middle Ages, Europeans found an important new use for the apple. Like any fruit—the grape is the example par excellence—the apple may be fermented into alcohol because yeast naturally resides on its skin. The alcohol derived from this process was known as cider. Because fermentation occurs naturally, any apples allowed to sit out will produce cider. Until the 20th century and the invention of refrigeration, all apple juice turned to cider. The process of refrigeration, however, halts the process of fermentation so that apple juice remains apple juice. Accordingly, one must distinguish between alcoholic cider ("hard" cider) and nonalcoholic cider (just cider). This distinction, of course, did not apply in antiquity and the Middle Ages. Hard cider was an important drink because, like wine, the alcohol killed pathogens, so that hard cider was safer to drink than water, which was subject to bacterial, fungal, and viral contamination. The deadly disease cholera is an example of a disease caused by a waterborne bacterium. The people who drank hard cider were safe from cholera and other waterborne diseases. Hard cider must therefore have lessened mortality and increased longevity, though by how much is difficult to know. Even in the American colonies hard cider was popular. The colonists were much more likely to drink hard cider than wine. Even today hard cider remains an important beverage in the temperate zones.

During the Columbian Exchange, the apple conquered large regions of temperate America. Canada and parts of North and South America grew apple trees. Apart from the Columbian Exchange, the Dutch planted apple trees in South Africa. The British planted apple trees in Australia, Tasmania, and New Zealand. In the 20th century a second Columbian Exchange saw apple varieties from the

United States spread to China, Korea, Japan, India, and Pakistan. Today, China and the United States are big producers. India yields a harvest twice as large as that of the United Kingdom. Argentina, Brazil, and Chile are important exporters. Today, Washington, New York, and Michigan produce most American apples.

Further Reading

Browning, Frank. *Apples*. New York: North Point Press, 1998.

Ferree, D. C., and I. J. Warrington, eds. *Apples: Botany, Production and Uses*. Cambridge, MA: CABI, 2003.

Hughes, Meredith Sayles. *Tall and Tasty: Fruit Trees*. Minneapolis: Lerner, 2000.

Janik, Erika. *Apple: A Global History*. London: Reaktion Books, 2011.

Morgan, Joan, and Alison Richards. *The Book of Apples*. London: Ebury Press, 1993.

Seabrook, John. "Annals of Agriculture: Crunch," *The New Yorker*, November 21, 2011, 54–64.

B

Banana

Although the casual observer might consider a banana plant a tree, botanists classify it a perennial herb. The banana is the world's largest herb, growing as tall as 30 feet. It is the world's largest fruit crop and the fourth leading crop, trailing wheat, rice, and corn. A crop of the tropics, the banana will not grow at high latitudes. Farmers cultivate the banana in Florida but, perhaps because of the latitude, it is not grown on a large scale there. Instead, farmers grow the banana in Southeast Asia, western Asia, China, India, Pakistan, Bangladesh, several Pacific Islands, Africa, the Caribbean, and Central and South America. An indigene of Southeast Asia, the Columbian Exchange brought the banana to the Americas in the 16th century. In much of Asia, Africa, and the Pacific, small farmers raise bananas for local consumption, whereas growers in the Caribbean and Central and South America export much of their fruit to the United States, Canada, and Europe. Americans and their counterparts in the rest of the developed world eat the banana as dessert, whereas it is a staple in the developing world. A single banana plant yields three or four harvests in its life. Six months after it flowers, a banana plant yields mature fruit. In total, a banana plant needs eight to 10 months to grow from seedling to maturity. Bananas remain green as long as they are on a plant. As soon as they are picked, however, they begin to ripen. During ripening they convert starch into fructose. A green banana has 1 percent fructose, whereas a ripe banana has 80 percent sugar. Once picked, a banana releases ethylene gas, a chemical that hastens ripening. The banana is a source of carbohydrates, potassium, vitamin C, and vitamin B_6. In some regions of the world, manufacturers make bananas into chips, flour, and puree.

Origin and Diffusion

In Asia and Africa, people describe the origin and importance of the banana in myth. Notorious in the creation story in Genesis is the forbidden fruit. Saint Jerome

An Old World indigene, the banana has become a staple export in Latin American countries. Much of the produce goes to the United States. (Lunamarina/Dreamstime.com)

thought the fruit was the apple, a belief that lingers today, though another tradition identifies the banana as the forbidden fruit. The Koran populates Eden with banana plants. Some Arab scholars consider the banana the "tree of paradise." In the 18th century, Swedish naturalist Carl Linnaeus named the banana *Musa paradisiaca*, meaning the "banana of paradise." Some believe that, after eating the banana, Adam and Eve clothed themselves in banana leaves. The belief that they used fig leaves may be inaccurate because people confused the banana and the fig. Alexander the Great, for example, called the banana a fig. The author of Genesis may have known of the banana, which may have been grown in the Near East. Wherever Eden is thought to be, farmers today grow the banana in Jordan, Egypt, Oman, and Israel.

In India, the banana has religious significance. Indian mystics meditate beneath banana plants. According to one tradition, the banana is the incarnation of Lakshmi, the goddess of wealth, beauty, and wisdom. At an Indian wedding, the groom gives the bride a banana as a symbol of fertility. In India, the banana is the subject of Hindu art. In the Vedic tradition, a banana grove is home to the monkey god Hanuman. India grows roughly 17 million tons of bananas per year, 20 percent of the global total. India's production is thrice that of Ecuador, the second leading producer. India grows the banana for local consumption, whereas Ecuador produces for export. The people of Ecuador eat less than 2 percent of the country's bananas. In India, banana chips are the most popular snack. Indians even eat fried banana peels with black-eyed peas. As unappealing as it may seem to Westerners, Indians make bananas into ketchup. In New Guinea, farmers use the banana in rainmaking ceremonies. Africans include the banana in one of their creation accounts. Kintu, the first human, married Nambi, the daughter of Gulu, the creator god. Her brother, unhappy that she had married a mortal, expelled the couple from Eden. Leaving paradise, Kintu and Nambi carried a banana root, presumably for planting, in their wandering. Some scholars believe Uganda was the African Eden. So important is the banana to Uganda that people sometimes use it as money. A farmer, for example, might repay a loan with bananas. Ugandans eat a special variety of banana at the birth of twins, and another to mark the passing of kin. A husband or wife might eat a particular variety to encourage his or her spouse to be faithful. Another variety, Ugandans believe, increases sperm production. Uganda produces 11 million tons of bananas per year, a figure that computes to more than 500 pounds per person per year. This amount is 20 times more than the per capita consumption in the United States. In some Ugandan villages, farmers produce 970 pounds of bananas per person per year. Although this figure seems large enough to encourage exports, Ugandan farmers grow bananas for local consumption.

So central is the banana to the concept of food in Uganda that the word *matoke* means both "banana" and "food." On Samoa, *mei'a* means "banana." In New Zealand and on Easter Island, *maike* means "banana." The Hawaiian *mai'a* means "banana." The people of Indonesia, the Philippines, Malaysia, and New Guinea render banana as *pisang*. The Papua *pudi* and *fud* both mean "banana." *Buti* means "banana" on the Solomon Islands. The people of Fiji call the banana *vud*. In Tonga the banana is *feta'u*, and on Tahiti, *fe'i*. Hindus term the banana *kalpatharu*, meaning "virtuous plant." The English word for banana derives from the Arabic *banan*, meaning "finger," because each banana in a bunch is a finger.

The banana originated in Southeast Asia. Wild bananas are inedible, leading one to wonder why the ancients selected them for eventual domestication. The people who took an interest in these wild bananas selected for seedlessness and flavor. Wild bananas arose in southern China, Southeast Asia, and India. As early as 7000 BCE, the people of New Guinea ate the banana and may have been the first to cultivate it. Around 5000 BCE, people throughout Southeast Asia began cultivating the plant. In antiquity, the banana spread to Samoa, New Zealand, Hawaii, Easter Island, Indonesia, the Philippines, Malaysia, New Guinea, India, Taiwan, southern China, and Borneo. Around 300 CE, Indonesians brought the banana to Madagascar, from which it spread to East Africa. The fact that many African bananas are descended from Pacific cultivars suggests a second introduction. In 650 CE, Arabs brought the banana to the Middle East. At first, European explorers did not know what to make of the banana, often confusing it with the plantain. In 1350, one European explorer found the banana in Sri Lanka. In 1482, the Portuguese found bananas being grown in Sierra Leone, Liberia, and Gambia. Around 1500, the Portuguese planted the banana in the Canary Islands. In the late 16th century, travelers observed the banana in the Nicobar Islands and India.

Some scholars speculate that the banana arrived in the Americas before Columbus's voyages. One school of thought holds that bananas from West Africa reached the Americas ahead of the Genoese explorer. Another school of thought traces the banana's putative trek across the Pacific to the west coast of South America. The first mention of the banana in the Americas dates to 1516, when Spanish missionary Tomás de Berlanga introduced it to Santo Domingo (today the Dominican Republic), marking the advent of banana culture in the Caribbean and possibly in all the Americas. From Santo Domingo the banana spread to the rest of the Caribbean and to Central and South America. In Central America, planters have established large estates, especially in Ecuador, Colombia, Honduras, Guatemala, Costa Rica, and Panama.

Planted in the Caribbean from the 16th century, the banana became an export only in the 19th century. In the 1860s, the United States began to import bananas from Jamaica. Planters, sensing an opportunity to profit, converted abandoned sugarcane estates to banana plantations. In the 20th century, United Fruit Company monopolized the shipping of bananas from the Caribbean to the United States. On Saint Lucia, farmers converted hilly terrain from sugarcane to banana. The Dominican Republic grew banana and coffee. On Grenada, farmers raised banana and nutmeg. In 1902, the eruption of Mount Pelée on Martinique covered sugarcane plantations with ash. Some farmers replanted their land to banana. Between 1987 and 2002, banana exports on Martinique rose from 191,140 tons to 341,720 tons. The latter figure totaled 40 percent of the island's exports. Martinique ships most of its bananas to France, Italy, and the United Kingdom. Since 1950, bananas have been the leading export on Saint Vincent. In 1981, bananas totaled 72 percent of the island's exports. On Guadeloupe, the banana harvest increased in the 1990s, rising 30 percent in 1991 alone and another 13 percent in 1992. In the latter year, the harvest tallied 163,470 tons, 122,430 of which went to export. In 2002, a drought worsened the effects of 2000's Hurricane Debby, decreasing production to 127,320 tons.

In Central Africa, people ferment bananas into beer. In Uganda, the variety Mbidde is used to make beer. In Zaire, the variety Makandili serves this purpose. In Zaire, farmers plant bananas and coffee. In Burundi, growers intercrop the banana with taro, beans, peas, and cabbage. In Rwanda, farmers grow the banana and sweet potato. So important is the banana in Rwanda that it adorns the 20-franc coin. In some areas, farmers intercrop bananas with cacao. In this system, the banana provides income during the four or five years during which cocoa matures. When cacao is mature, farmers cut down their banana plants for mulch. Today,

Cameroon, Coté d'Ivoire, the Canary Islands, and Israel export bananas to Europe. The Philippines, adopting varieties from Latin America, began exporting bananas in the 1970s and today exports them to Japan, the Middle East, and Hong Kong. Bananas total half the value of exports in the Philippines, Dominica, Grenada, Saint Lucia, Saint Vincent, Martinique, and Guadeloupe.

The Banana and the Forbidden Fruit

The banana, to a lesser degree than the apple, has shaped religious attitudes as the putative forbidden fruit of the creation story in Genesis, the first book of the Old Testament. It is interesting to note that the apple was not the obvious choice at first. The bible does not specify the forbidden fruit, leaving it to the imagination. The supposed first humans Adam and Eve knew only that God prohibited them from eating the fruit from the tree of knowledge of good and evil. Because Adam and Eve realized their nakedness after eating the forbidden fruit, they covered themselves with fig leaves. It was logical, therefore, to think that the tree of knowledge of good and evil must have been a fig tree, and the fruit the fig. One wonders whether the fig tree was grown in the Garden of Eden at the time of the writing of Genesis. The location of this garden is not easy to pinpoint. Genesis remarks initially that the tree is in the east, but later is more specific in pointing to four rivers, only two of which are known to moderns, the Tigris and the Euphrates Rivers. Their mention places Eden in Mesopotamia (today Iraq). The fig tree must have been grown in Iraq, but it has a defect: its leaves are not adequate to cover a person's private parts. This defect led to the assertion that the banana was the forbidden fruit because its leaves were adequate to cover Adam and Eve. But the banana has two defects of its own. First, it is not a tree but an herbaceous plant, and Genesis clearly specifies a tree. Second, and more serious, is the fact that the banana is a tropical plant that could not have been grown in Iraq. In the fourth century CE, Christian theologian and biblical translator Saint Jerome settled on the apple as the forbidden fruit. A Latin scholar, Jerome may have played upon the Latin words for evil, *malus*, and for apple, *malum*. Their resemblance may have led Jerome to link the forbidden fruit with the apple. The consensus, however, disputes Jerome. The apple was not grown in Iraq at the time Genesis was written. Nevertheless, the apple has come down to modernity as the forbidden fruit, enshrined prominently in Western art. It is the iconic image of sin and temptation.

The Business of Bananas and Imperialism

As the United States expanded its economic system to Latin America, it used the banana to create fortunes. In this context, the banana shaped the history of the

Americas and the prominence of American capitalism and imperialism. In 1885, Boston Fruit, now Chiquita, formed to ship bananas from the Caribbean to the United States. Because bananas are perishable, Boston Fruit was the first company to ship them in refrigerated compartments. In New Orleans arose Standard Fruit to supply bananas to the South. Because Boston Fruit and Standard Fruit depended on the volume of sales to generate profit, they priced bananas cheaply. In the 19th century, bananas were half the price of apples, and around 1900 Americans could buy a dozen bananas for 25 cents. This price fetched only two apples. The inexpensiveness of bananas encouraged Americans to buy them, and consumption rose from 15 million bunches in 1900 to more than 40 million bunches in 1910. Although it dipped in the 1940s, per-person consumption of bananas has risen 43 percent in the United States since 1970. Buying bananas throughout Latin America and the Caribbean, the United States nonetheless imports most of its bananas from Ecuador.

In Central America, cattle rancher Minor C. Keith, building lines in Panama, Guatemala, Honduras, Nicaragua, Colombia, and Ecuador, planted bananas alongside the tracks. Initially, bananas fed railroad workers, but Keith came to understand that he could ship the surplus to the United States and so supply the American Southwest with them. In 1899, Keith merged with Boston Fruit to create United Fruit Company. This conglomerate grew bananas on land the size of Connecticut. United Fruit was an early investor in Cuban bananas, owning 300,000 acres of bananas and sugarcane. As United Fruit grew in size and wealth, it gained influence in the Caribbean, in Central and South America, and in the United States. When aroused to action, the United States used force to compel recalcitrant government to do the bidding of United Fruit. In 1912, the United States invaded Honduras, forcing the government to concede to United Fruit the right to build railroads and grow bananas. Depending on cheap labor, United Fruit was hostile to labor activism. In 1918, U.S. troops, acting at the behest of United Fruit, crushed strikes by banana workers in Panama, Colombia, and Guatemala. In 1925, U.S. soldiers crushed another banana strike in Guatemala. United Fruit was equally ruthless toward competitors, buying them or bankrupting them by undercutting their prices. By the late 1920s, United Fruit was worth more than $100 million, had 67,000 workers, owned 1.6 million acres and counted banana estates in 32 countries. Workers did not share this prosperity. At the peak of operations, laborers worked up to 72 hours with little respite, harvesting bananas and loading fruit on ships. They had no access to toilets, could not unionize, and were seldom paid cash. Instead, they received script, which they could redeem only at United Fruit stores, whose prices were high and which sold products from the United States rather than locally produced goods. Always eager to increase sales, United Fruit hired physicians to approve the practice of feeding bananas to infants, knowing that mothers did the grocery shopping. United Fruit advertised the combination of corn flakes with sliced bananas as the ideal breakfast. The company put coupons for free bananas, paid for by cereal manufacturers, in cereal boxes.

United Fruit's actions in Colombia precipitated the banana massacre. In 1899, the year of its founding, the company acquired its first banana plantation in Columbia. To its dismay, labor became restive in the early 20th century. In October 1928, 32,000 banana workers, seeking better working conditions, went on strike. Their demands seem moderate. They wanted medical care, the use of a toilet, payment in cash rather than script, and classification as employees rather than independent contractors so they could enjoy the protection of Colombia's labor laws, weak though they were. Rather than negotiate, United Fruit denied that its workers were discontent. The strikers would not relent, and on December 5, 1928, Columbia's government, surely under pressure from United Fruit, declared martial law. Soldiers fired on workers after they had attended a Catholic mass on Sunday, killing more than 1,000 of them.

Events in Guatemala were no more reassuring. In the early 20th century United Fruit established its first banana plantations and from an early date seems to have dominated the weak Guatemalan government. The government required its people to labor 100 days per year on banana estates, a system of forced labor that was too common in the Americas. If United Fruit loathed workers it also appears to have disdained the government, refusing to pay taxes on the land it owned. The growth of a middle class in Guatemala in the 20th century raised the people's consciousness. Educated, the middle class understood that United Fruit was exploiting the country. They resented the fact that the company ran Guatemala as a banana plantation. Indeed, banana companies owned 4 million acres, 70 percent of Guatemala's arable land. In 1944, schoolteachers went on strike. Shaken, the government legalized unions but barred banana workers from joining them. The fall of one government led to the rise of Jacobo Arbenz, who founded a liberal government. Arbenz demanded that United Fruit pay taxes and give up some of its land so that the people might farm as they wished. Sympathetic to United Fruit and branding Arbenz a communist, President Dwight D. Eisenhower ordered the Central Intelligence Agency (CIA) to overthrow the government. Using misinformation, the CIA created confusion in Guatemala. Convinced they were on the verge of defeat, military leaders refused to muster their troops against the CIA. Arbenz fled Guatemala. United Fruit had made the world safe for the banana.

Further Reading

Charrier, Andre, Michel Jacquot, Serge Hamon, and Dominique Nicolas, eds. *Tropical Plant Breeding*. Enfield, New Hampshire: Science Publishers, 2001.

Eagen, Rachel. *The Biography of Bananas*. New York: Crabtree Publishing, 2006.

Grossman, Lawrence S. *The Political Ecology of Bananas: Contract Farming, Peasants, and Agrarian Change in the Eastern Caribbean*. Chapel Hill: University of North Carolina Press, 1998.

Jenkins, Virginia Scott. *Bananas: An American History*. Washington, DC: Smithsonian Institution Press, 2000.

Koeppel, Dan. *Banana: The Fate of the Fruit that Changed the World*. New York: Hudson Street Press, 2008.

Roche, Julian. *The International Banana Trade*. Boca Raton, FL: CRC Press, 1998.

Wiley, James. *The Banana: Empires, Trade Wars, and Globalization*. Lincoln: University of Nebraska Press, 2008.

Beans

The term "bean" is used too casually. The seed that develops from the flower of a coffee tree is called a bean, though it has no claim to this distinction. A true bean is a legume, a member of the Fabaceae, or Leguminosae, family. A legume has special properties. Its roots are a marvel of evolution. The primary gas in the atmosphere is nitrogen, an important plant nutrient. However, no plant root can absorb gaseous nitrogen. Plants need help from a special class of bacteria known as nitrifying bacteria. Legumes, like beans, make special accommodations for these bacteria. Their roots contain nodules that are safe havens for nitrifying bacteria. These bacteria congregate inside the nodules, where they are safe from predation. The relationship is symbiotic because the root nodules provide safety and the bacteria convert gaseous nitrogen into nitrate or ammonium ions, both forms of nitrogen that legume roots readily absorb. The absorption of nitrogen is critical in allowing legumes to form nitrogen-carbon bonds (polypeptide bonds) that allow the plant to assemble amino acids into proteins. This process explains why beans and other legumes are such good sources of protein. Being legumes, beans are related to a number of important food plants, including peas, chickpeas, lentils, peanuts, cowpeas, and the livestock fodder alfalfa, clover, and vetch.

Protein for the Masses

One may derive protein from animals and plants. As civilizations arose with the development of agriculture and livestock raising, hierarchies arose. The elites—those with money and privilege—could afford meat and derived their protein accordingly. But the masses, often poor, could not always afford meat, fish, and other sources of animal protein. They had to subsist on plant proteins, and here beans

Kidney Bean

A member of the species *Phaseolus vulgaris*, the kidney bean is one of many American beans. Those accustomed to red kidney beans may be surprised that a white variety, prevalent in Italian cuisine, also exists. Even the red beans are not consistent in coloration, with some varieties darker than others. Because the red kidney beans look something like miniature kidneys, the name has stuck. Chili often contains red kidney beans. Red kidneys are prominent in Louisiana's cuisine, paired with rice. The people of India and Pakistan have also incorporated the kidney bean into their cuisines.

and other legumes came to the fore. Beans were especially important because they were a better source of protein than grains, tubers, and roots. In fact, the combination of beans and a whole grain is an ideal source of complete protein. A dish of brown rice and beans, for example, is abundantly nourishing.

There are several species of beans native to the Old and New Worlds. Historically, the most influential beans were those that evolved in the Americas. One suspects that very early in the development of agriculture in the New World, the Amerindians cultivated the three sisters: corn, beans, and squash. Again, one notes the coupling of a whole grain, corn, with a legume, beans. The addition of squash provided additional minerals so that the Amerindians must have been well-nourished as a rule, even in the absence of animal protein, though it is evident that the Native Americans hunted and fished to supplement their intake of protein. Beans were thus the staff of life in the Americas long before the arrival of Europeans. As elsewhere, beans provided the Amerindians with protein for the masses. The American tradition of coupling beans with corn remains at the heart of Amerindian culture. Mexicans use beans and corn in a variety of ways, and their food habits have influenced the cuisine of the United States.

In 1753, Swedish naturalist Carl Linnaeus (also known as Carl von Linné) put these American beans in the genus *Phaseolus*, though he erroneously thought they had originated in India. *Phaseolus* means "boat shaped," a fitting name given that the pods of these beans resemble tiny boats. In fact, if one examines several other legumes (the pea is a good example) one sees that the pods do resemble small boats. Several legumes, therefore, share this feature in common, though only the beans of the Americas are in the genus *Phaseolus*. These American beans have become emblematic of beans everywhere, thanks to the Columbian Exchange, which spread *Phaseolus* beans throughout the world. The familiar kidney (both red and white), pinto, black, green northern, navy, scarlet runner, green, lima, and hundreds more, are all *Phaseolus* beans. Some people—and this may be a European custom—eat beans young when the pod is still tender and so may be consumed with the beans intact in the pod. Many, though by no means all, American beans are in the species *Phaseolus vulgaris*, which, loosely translated, means nothing more than "common beans," meaning beans that are well known. This species may have originated in Central America.

As noted earlier, the Amerindians played an essential role in founding bean agriculture. The Peruvians were probably the first to cultivate beans, showing an early interest in the lima bean, around 6000 BCE. Probably independently, the people of Mexico began growing beans about 1000 years later. Bean culture did not reach what is today the eastern United States until about 2500 BCE. There, sickquatasch, what the Spanish mistook for succotash, emerged as an important bean dish for the masses. The lima is the bean of choice in preparing this dish. The Cherokee and the Maya made a type of cornbread with beans, again coupling beans with a whole grain. Black beans appear to have been an important food to these people. Wherever one looks, one sees that beans were the foundation upon which the Amerindians of many nations built their civilizations. The natives of the Caribbean were no different. In Jamaica cooks made kidney beans with rice and coconut milk, though this cuisine must postdate the arrival of Spanish Italian explorer Christopher Columbus because rice and coconut are not native to the Americas. Cubans made black beans with rice and pork, a dish derived from the Moors of Spain and known as *Moros y Cristianos*. Throughout the Caribbean, people ate kidney beans with coconut and thyme. Again, these are all post-Columbian developments.

In 1493, Columbus witnessed the culture of haricot beans, another type of *Phaseolus* bean, in Cuba. Spanish conquistador Hernán Cortés likewise came across the cultivation of *Phaseolus vulgaris* in Mexico. Other Europeans made similar finds. Because these beans resembled (though not closely) the fava bean of the Europeans, the European arrivals to the New World quickly recognized the importance of these new beans. In 1493, Columbus brought American beans to Spain. Europeans adopted these beans more quickly than they did the tomato, potato, and other American crops. Indeed, Europeans may have assumed that American beans were a variant of fava beans; strictly speaking this is not true, though they are all legumes. In the early 16th century, Europeans began growing American beans in preference to fava beans, perhaps because of the high yield of *Phaseolus* beans and their greater varieties of textures and flavors. Italy acquired American beans in 1528, using white kidney beans, known as cannelloni beans, in making minestrone. The adoption of American beans was thus rapid and, in their new environs, *Phaseolus* beans continued to nourish the masses, whether they be Italian, Spanish, or another ethnicity. As they had in the New World, *Phaseolus* beans fulfilled their destiny as protein for the masses in the Old World. American beans were on their way to becoming a source of protein for commoners world-wide. Moreover, *Phaseolus* beans were easier to prepare than fava beans and quickly surmounted them in importance.

In their rise to world dominance, *Phaseolus* beans were not always used for good. The slave trade corrupted American beans. Because Africans were familiar with Old World beans, they were willing to eat American beans on their journey to the New World. Slavers favored these beans because they knew that American beans were nourishing and so stood a good chance of keeping the slaves alive until they reached their destination. A monotonous diet of beans cannot have been the sole sustenance of slaves because beans are deficient in vitamin C. Slaves should have contracted scurvy aboard ship, but the fact that they did not points to other foods.

Old World Beans and the Masses

Pre-Columbian Europe, Asia, and Africa knew nothing about American beans. Rather, they relied on beans of the species *Vicia faba*, better known as fava beans. Fava beans may have originated in Africa, though they may have been domesticated in western Asia, probably about the same time as the domestication of peas. Resembling large lima beans, favas were a staple in Iran, North Africa, and other parts of the Mediterranean Basin. Egypt, Palestine, Greece, Assyria, and Phoenicia all adopted fava beans. Not surprisingly given the history of American beans, fava beans filled the same niche. They were the source of protein par excellence of the masses.

Perhaps more than any other people, the Romans embraced fava beans. The species name *faba*, derives from the claim of the Fabian family, an ancient patrician family, that they were the first to cultivate fava beans in Rome. One may doubt the accuracy of this boast, but it is worth scrutiny. In claiming to be the first bean farmers in Rome, the Fabian family, though elite, claimed humble origins. They had arisen to greatness because of their adoption of piety, self-reliance, thrift, and hard work, all rural values. The Fabian family chose fava beans as their symbolic food because of these beans' importance to the Roman economy. The Fabians acted as had the illustrious Piso family in claiming their origins as pea farmers.

Throughout Europe, as in the Americas, the more meat one ate the fewer beans one consumed. Humans seem to have a biological predisposition for favoring meat. But meat was expensive in Europe so that only the elites could afford it, as noted earlier. The masses ate fava beans, peas, lentils, and chickpeas. Accordingly, as one's consumption of beans increased, one's ingestion of meat decreased, again for economic reasons. In Europe as in the Americas, beans sustained the masses. The absence of beans and other legumes would have threatened the masses with malnourishment and perhaps starvation, so important were beans in the diet. Remember that ordinary people did the real work of farming and other occupations that made civilization possible. The elites were idle, and one suspects that commoners could have gotten along well on their own. The fate of beans amid Europe's class divisions was clear. First-century-CE Roman agricultural writer Columella considered beans suitable only for the poor. They were not sufficiently refined for the patricians, of whom he was a member. In Europe, therefore, the association of beans with poverty stigmatized beans.

No such stigma existed in Asia. In India, in particular, commoners and elites ate beans. The tendency toward vegetarianism only raised the importance of beans. In other regions of Asia, notably China, Korea, and Japan, the soybean was an important food. Although the soybean is a world crop it will not receive treatment here. It has its own entry, which examines its worldwide importance.

Further Reading

Albala, Ken. *Beans: A History.* Oxford: Berg, 2007.

Denny, Roz. *Beans.* Des Plaines, IL: Heinemann Library, 1998.

Hughes, Meredith Sayles. *Spill the Beans and Pass the Peanuts: Legumes.* Minneapolis: Lerner, 1999.

Johnson, Sylvia A. *Tomatoes, Potatoes, Corn, and Beans: How the Foods of the Americas Changed Eating around the World.* New York: Atheneum Books, 1997.

Sumner, Judith. *American Household Botany: A History of Useful Plants, 1620–1900.* Portland, OR: Timber Press, 2004.

Beef

Beef has a long history and may be bound up with the pace of human evolution. At the same time, in modernity, beef has emerged as just another commodity. To be sure, it has also become more than a commodity. It may be a symbol of American exceptionalism and is at the heart of the modern global economy. The tensions between employer and employee that are so stark today had their advent in the factory system of which the hamburger stand was a part.

Beef and Human Evolution

In an era before the rise of animal husbandry, humanity's forbearers hunted or scavenged meat from the ancestors of cows. This beef, or protobeef, supplied vital

Young Masai herders herd and protect their cattle, a food staple, in Tanzania, Africa on February 9, 2014. (Aleksandar Todorovic/Dreamstime.com)

nutrients and calories, particularly in the form of essential fatty acids. Our ancestors appear to have expanded this activity at about the time one can quantify increases in brain size. In fact the nourishment from beef may have allowed the hominid brain, which demands many calories and nutrients, to enlarge. Human evolution may therefore have resulted from a preference for beef. By one account, species of *Australopithecus* began eating beef about 3 million years ago. The intersection of cows and early humans in Ethiopia is not coincidence. Early humans ate these cows, making Ethiopia perhaps a cradle of humanity. Matters have changed little in Ethiopia with the passage of time. The Masai continue to herd cattle and eat beef. The Masai believe that the gods gave them cattle and taught them to eat beef. In fact, the Masai also believe that the gods desire them to possess all the world's cattle. From their origins, humans seem to be genetically programmed to hanker for beef and find it much more satisfying than a steady supply of food plants. Perhaps evolution programmed us to salivate in this way because, in a food-scarce world, beef represented a calorie-dense food.

Beef in the Greco Roman World

Given the propensity of early and modern humans to eat beef, it is curious to gauge its status among the Greeks and Romans. The experiences of these people are not trivial. Classical Greece invented or refined philosophy, science, architecture, drama, sculpture, and religions. The Romans, though initially thought a backward people, built one of the world's great empires. The Greeks preferred and ate much more fish than beef. Much the same can be said about the Romans, who preferred fish, chicken and other birds, and pork to beef. The Roman chef Apicius wrote little about beef. Curiously, the rise of Christianity in the Roman world appears to have introduced other attitudes toward beef. According to the canonical Gospels, a son asked his father for his share of the inheritance. Spending it, he returned home repentant. The father celebrated his son's return by serving him meat from a calf. Presuming the calf to have been a young cow, the father must have served beef at this feast. Yet beef never arose in Christianity to the status that fish and wine have attained.

Beef and Nomads

At the origin of agriculture and animal husbandry, a farmer kept his own cattle. As herds grew, the farmer had to devote more of his or her land to grazing. As herds increased still further, a shepherd had to migrate with cattle to summer and winter pastures. Gradually the farmer became increasingly sedentary while the shepherd became a nomad. The nomad had his food, in the form of cows, always with him, and he came to depend on cattle for beef, milk, and cheese. These nomads herded their cattle on the Eurasian steppe with the aid of horses. Excellent horsemen with their herds as their supply line, these nomads could be ferocious warriors. At times these warriors united to form a fast and formidable force. Beef thereby shaped warfare. These warrior nomads played some role in the decline of the Roman Empire, but perhaps the most well-known eruption of the nomad occurred when the Mongols over-ran large parts of Asia, Russia, and Eastern Europe. The Mongols did not concentrate solely on destruction. Their unity ushered in a period of relative peace that allowed the Silk Road to flourish. Marco Polo was able to travel unmolested from Italy to China because of the Mongol peace. The Mongols had founded an empire partly on beef.

Beef in America and the West

The ubiquity of beef appears to have altered the Western world in fundamental ways. In the Americas beef was plentiful because of the policies of the Europeans who colonized the New World. They brought cattle with them, importing so many, which reproduced so quickly, that Europeans and their descendants quickly lost track of them. The cows went feral, carving out large tracts of grassland in Argentina and the American West. It became a duty and a chore to kill and eat the surplus

at many suburban-
e demand for corn
e in corn, and now

have invented the
a bit more compli-
sandwiches. These
wned British histo-
ording his first en-
g beef sandwiches.
ef. Yet, in an era of
swer was a patty of
other place for this
amburg introduced
he hamburger they
a path toward com-
ese were the attri-
fact, they are the
helped the United
ntroduction of new
ped define America.
took root. The ham-
s a quick sandwich
t many workers also
to eat something on

n, consumption, and
n 1916 to convert a
ry hamburger identi–
instructions for prep-
work for him at low
Here arose the man–
d together the entire
hburger, just as every
ger helped create the
or this quality's ubiq–
te Castle. Additional

nous dictum holds that cheap
idea behind this quip is that
m in the United States, could
ey did not need to revolt to be
rs possible to assert that the
ion, but because beef is calo-
se of obesity in the West. As
are of fewer calories per day,
mption of beef. The result is
circumstance has created a
an environment of surplus
y humans were wise to eat
longer works in a sedentary,
gy adapted to a food-scarce

t

and pork created the meat-
first in Cincinnati and then
Great Plains. Meatpackers
g workers next to nothing.
author Upton Sinclair in-
rvations were the founda-
le. Sinclair hoped the book
kers, and his lurid description. President Theodore
hen the Republican Party
ded action. The result was
d and Drug Act in 1906.
ral government.

e grasslands of the Great
o depend on cheap corn.
an to allow them to range
ass only in the first year.
rn, which prompted them
grass. (Strictly corn is a

grass, but here the term is used to mean the ordinary grasses th
ites regard as weeds.) The feeding of corn to cattle increased th
and was one factor that led farmers in the Midwest to specializ
corn and soybeans, creating the Corn Belt.

The Hamburger

Texas, Wisconsin, New York, and Connecticut all claim to
hamburger about 1880. This is untrue, and the real story is
cated. By the 1760s, the British and French were eating beef
were not hamburgers but rather used thin cuts of steak. Reno
rian Edward Gibbon delighted in eating beef sandwiches, rec
counter in 1762. By about 1800, Americans, too, were eatin
American tearooms sold a variety of sandwiches, including be
tooth decay, people wanted something easier to chew. The an
ground beef. Hamburg, Germany has as good a claim as any
innovation. In the 19th century, German immigrants from H
the hamburger to Americans. If Americans did not invent
knew how to market it. The hamburger thus put America on
mercialization, mass production, and mass consumption. T
butes of the meatpacking and automobile industries. In
characteristics of the American experience. The hamburge
States transition to a lifeway that has quickened with the
technology and advertising. In this sense, the hamburger hel
The hamburger also influenced the industrial era in which it
burger found a place in the factory system, serving worke
during their short lunch breaks. Not only was lunch brief, bu
lived too far from home to return there for lunch. They had
the spot, and the hamburger seemed the perfect solution.

The potential of the hamburger for widespread distributi
ease of preparation persuaded Kansan J. Walter Anderson
shoe shop to a hamburger joint. He specialized in making eve
cal, quickening cooking time, and formulating a single set of
aration. Now he could hire anyone without experience to
wages. McDonald's would not lose sight of these advantages
tra of standardization and scientific management that knitt
economy. Every hamburger was a replica of every other har
Model T was a copy of every other Model T. The hambur
drive toward standardization and at the same time benefit f
uity in the economy. The Anderson model produced Whi

efforts streamlined the menu over which a customer would not anguish. Serve a customer quickly, the model dictated, and send him or her on the way to make room for the next customer. Profits were tied to the volume of sales, a classic spin-off of capitalism.

White Castle had set the standard, and in 1937, brothers Richard and Maurice McDonald established what would become McDonald Brothers Bar Drive-in in 1940. This went on to become the popular McDonald's franchise. Noting that hamburgers accounted for 80 percent of sales, the brothers slashed the menu and advertised to families rather than teens, whom they thought prone to violence. The brothers switched from glass containers to plastic, to avoid breaking items. They automated wherever possible and paid workers poorly. Indeed, low wages have become standard in the global economy. McDonald's refused to bargain with union representatives and so crushed labor. McDonald's also opposed increases in the minimum wage and the extension of benefits to workers. In all these cases, McDonald's paved the way for the global economy. The result of low wages and poor working conditions was high turnover. It is not unusual for McDonald's to hire six people per year to fill a single opening.

Further Reading

Edge, John T. *Hamburgers and Fries: An American Story*. New York: G. F. Putnam's Books, 2005.

Rimas, Andrew, and Evan D. G. Fraser. *Beef: The Untold Story of How Milk, Meat, and Muscle Shaped the World*. New York: William Morrow, 2008.

Smith, Andrew F. *Hamburger: A Global History*. London: Reaktion Books, 2008.

Beer

Originating about 10,000 BCE, beer is likely the oldest alcoholic beverage. The secret of brewing beer may lie in an accidental discovery. The first humans to harvest barley, and probably wheat as well, must have saved seeds to last through lean times. Any seeds exposed to moisture in storage began to sprout. The beginning of the germination of barley seeds is known as malting. The process of malting was all-important because it signaled the release of enzymes that converted the starch in barley seeds into sugars. Yeast that had gathered on these malted seeds fermented these sugars into alcohol. The Sumerians of what are today Iraq and Iran appear to have been the first to discover what must have seemed a magical process. The Sumerians, then, must have invented beer, a drink that may be the most widely

Villagers at a beer festival in the village of Klais in Bavaria, Germany.
(Tim Graham/Corbis)

consumed alcoholic beverage in the world today, though one may wonder whether wine might make a similar claim. Wine remains central to Mediterranean culture, and the benefits that humans derive from beer and wine often overlap.

Beer and the Rise of Agriculture

Because beer is so old, some scholars believe that the desire for beer prompted humans to settle down and cultivate barley. Wheat, peas, lentils, and perhaps chickpeas were domesticated soon after. The invention of beer, therefore, may have been the impetus behind the origin and development of agriculture. If this link is correct, then beer has changed the world in a momentous way. The rise of agriculture was the precondition to the rise of civilizations. Agriculture made it possible for people to gather in steadily larger communities. Because agriculture created a surplus, though not a large one initially, not everybody had to till the fields. Urban specialists arose: merchants, artisans, and the first manifestations of a literati. These specialists created civilization, though, again, they cannot have been numerous at the outset. By the time of Jesus, however, Rome had 1 million inhabitants, a testament to what a small food surplus could create. Even at the height of its grandeur Rome had a food surplus of only about 10 percent, according to historian Lynn White. To maintain its population Rome had to be ruthless, commandeering grain from Sicily and Egypt. So important was Egypt as a source of grain that Rome's emperors administered it as their own private property.

The confluence of science with agriculture in the early modern era made possible ever-larger surpluses. The crops of the New World, the potato in particular and also corn, yielded more calories per acre than the crops that were native to the Old World. Populations grew rapidly in modernity. Nations like Ireland grew by several million in only a couple of centuries. Better varieties of rice buoyed the population of East Asia. This agricultural revolution, if one may be permitted to use the phrase, has allowed humans to increase to about 7 billion worldwide today. If agriculture made such gains possible, then beer, the stimulus behind the rise of agriculture, deserves credit for changing the world in a way that would be difficult to overstate.

Beer and Sanitation

In the era of modern sanitation, humans take clean drinking water for granted. This was not always true. Throughout much of history, drinking water could be suspect. As human populations grew and humans settled in one place with their livestock, human and animal waste became problematic. Once allowed to pollute the water, feces were capable of spreading harmful microbes throughout the water. Cholera is an example of a waterborne disease that has stalked humanity into modernity. Indeed, in parts of Africa it remains a lethal disease. The rise of killers like cholera puzzled and frightened humans. They had no germ theory of disease and knew nothing about the existence of pathogens.

Fortunately, humans, perhaps through a process of trial and error, learned that alcoholic beverages were safe to drink even when the water was polluted. As the oldest alcoholic beverage, beer must have been bound up with this discovery. Accordingly, humans drank beer throughout the day without fear of contamination. Beer was safe to drink because the alcohol killed the pathogens in water. Mediterranean lands made the same discovery with wine. In fact, any alcoholic beverage should be a sanitary drink. Because of beer's abiotic properties it must have saved countless lives over millennia. In this context, beer changed the world by holding bacteria and other noxious microbes at bay.

Beer and the Development of Writing

Before the era of the written word, humans had difficulty passing knowledge from one generation to the next. Oral traditions had to suffice in place of detailed records of events and phenomena. The Sumerians appear to have invented writing sometime before 3000 BCE. Among the first Sumerian records were recipes for beer. Beer thus appears to have stimulated the development of writing. In this context beer's contribution to the world is difficult to summarize neatly. Writing marked the development of literature. The *Epic of Gilgamesh*, which refers to beer repeatedly, may be the oldest product of literature. The influence of writing on religion has been enormously important. Without writing there would be no Bible, no accounts of Jesus, no establishment of Judaism, Christianity, and Islam in the West and western Asia. The same is true of Hinduism and Buddhism. So important is writing in this context that many people literately interpret their scriptures. This fundamentalism, if one may call it that, has led religion to clash with science, at least in the West, where fundamentalism and evolution are very far apart.

The rise of writing has led to the establishment of an incomparable canon of literature. Greek philosopher Plato's dialogues still occupy the apex of philosophy. Through his treatises, Plato's pupil Aristotle made important contributions to science. English playwright William Shakespeare's works represent the zenith of drama, though the more modern works of Norwegian playwright Henrik Ibsen and American dramatist and Nobel laureate Eugene O'Neill continue to resonate with readers and theatergoers alike. In the 19th century, Russian novelists Fyodor Dostoyevsky and Leo Tolstoy penned some of the world's great novels. German philosopher Friedrich Nietzsche overturned many of humanity's most cherished ideas. One might lengthen the list still further, but the point is that writing is one of the core human inventions, and it may have stemmed from the desire to bequeath knowledge about beer from one generation to the next.

Beer, Religion, and Sex

The Sumerian goddess Ninki ensured that the masses would have abundant beer. She was also the goddess of fertility and eroticism. In this context, Ninki would be a kind of proxy for later developments in Greece and Rome, where Dionysus and Bacchus, respectively, were the gods of wine, revelry, intoxication, and sexual excess. In the case of beer, and later wine, humans made the connection between alcohol, intoxication, and the weakening of sexual inhibitions. For this reason, beer was the drink that men and prostitutes shared at brothels, and that men and women shared at bars. Beer was the sexual lubricant that brought people together. Beer and its goddess made sex a sacred activity in which everyone should participate. Sex was a healthy, normal activity. One may note the contrast between this attitude and puritanical Christianity. Primarily through the writing of North African bishop Augustine of Hippo, Christianity adopted a view that sex was an evil action. It was the act that passed the original sin of Adam and Eve to all their descendants. The Sumerians clearly disagreed. The Sumerians had their beer and an uncomplicated, guilt-free attitude about sex. In this sense it seems that Christianity, not beer, altered the world by making sex a sin, especially outside marriage.

Beer and the Spirit of Democracy

The rise of civilizations led to social and economic stratification in which the elites owned more and had more power than commoners. This invidious distinction has been a mournful hallmark throughout history. In Rome, the patricians held power. The plebeians were impotent. German economists Karl Marx and Friedrich Engels wrote scathing attacks against the chasm between rich and poor, yet even the communist revolutions in Russia and parts of Asia did not bridge the divide between rich and poor. Today the minimum wage is 28 cents in Vietnam, a nation that once claimed the allegiance of the masses.

In this context, beer has been a kind of elixir. Its inexpensiveness allowed the masses to indulge in it. Beer was a communal drink to be shared among family and friends. It was the egalitarian beverage par excellence. Even the nobles drank beer. Eighteenth-century Prussian king Frederick II (known as Frederick the Great), disturbed at the widespread consumption of coffee, reminded his subjects that his parents had raised him from childhood on beer. Coffee was not a suitable drink for Prussians. They believed their greatness owed much to their centuries-old consumption of beer. In this sense, beer has been powerful enough to become a symbol of a nation and its people. Prussia was one of the founding states of modern Germany, a place where beer remains the national beverage.

Beer and Warfare

Perhaps beer's least-favorable status is its admixture with warfare. The Vikings must have been among the first to stress this connection. Avid drinkers, the Vikings stored their beer in the skulls of their enemies. These skulls served as crude beer glasses. The Viking afterlife centered on Valhalla, a sacred hall for the warrior elite. A cursory glance at some of German composer Richard

Wagner's operas reveals that a Viking killed on the battlefield gained immediate access to the afterworld. The Valkyries came to the battlefield to carry the dead to Valhalla, where the slain warriors drank beer in eternal fellowship and in confirmation of their bravery. Muslims hold similar views of the afterlife, though devoid of alcohol. Beer was the beverage of the Americans who fought in Vietnam. American director Francis Ford Coppola's movie *Apocalypse Now* featured a colonel who dispensed beer to his soldiers for destroying a village. Perhaps because beer lessens inhibitions it gives rise to the destructive, irrational forces that govern so much of human behavior. In this case, perhaps beer is not a desideratum.

Beer, the Industrial Revolution, and the Contemporary World

During the Industrial Revolution, the scale of beer production and consumption increased. It became the drink of factory workers and other urbanites. After a long day at the factory, workers gathered in pubs to share a round of beer. With the arrival of something approximating a leisure class in the 20th and 21st centuries, beer guided the impulse to recreation and athletics. Brewer Budweiser sponsored Major League Baseball. Several beer companies sponsor the National Association for Stock Car Auto Racing (NASCAR), and for a long time beer has been at the center of festivities at U.S. football games. It was fashionable to drink beer, which was a symbol of youth, vigor, athleticism, and, again, sex. Brewers have advertised on television, particularly in the context of the promotion of sports. Football players advertise a brand of beer in hopes of creating a large following of admirers. Some athletes promote the flavor of full-bodied beers, whereas others tout the benefits of light beers. Perhaps because humans, particularly in the West, are relatively inactive and obese, light beer would be a better option, though the removal of beer from one's diet might better please physicians.

Further Reading

Dineley, Merryn. *Barley, Malt and Ale in the Neolithic*. Oxford: BAR International, 2004.
Smith, Gavin D. *Beer: A Global History*. London: Reaktion Books, 2014.

Bread

There are eight categories of wheat: hard red winter, hard red spring, hard white winter, hard white spring, soft red winter, soft white winter, soft white spring, and

Bread has been a staple for perhaps 10,000 years, at least in the Old World. The canonical Gospels elevated bread to a symbol of Jesus. (Michael Flippo/Dreamstime.com)

durum. Not all eight are suitable for making bread. As a rule, the harder the wheat (and durum is the hardest) the less often it is used to make bread. The soft wheats, however, are fine for making breads, cookies, and cakes. The hard spring and winter wheats may also be used to make bread. Rye is also a good bread grain. Wheat and rye are suitable for making bread because they contain gluten, a protein that causes kernels to adhere, making it possible to form dough. Although one might find oat bread at the supermarket, oats do not make an ideal bread. Oat bread is only possible because its maker combines oat flour with wheat flour to obtain a mixture with sufficient gluten.

The earliest wheats to be cultivated were einkorn and emmer, neither of which sufficed to make bread. These wheats were suitable only for making porridge. Neither type is grown today, and the modern classification of wheat omits them. Although bread has nourished many groups of humans for millennia, it is not nutritionally superior to the potatoes and sweet potatoes of the Americas. The primary defect of wheat is its incomplete aggregate of essential amino acids. The remedy, as the people of western Asia and Europe discovered, was to combine bread with legumes—chickpeas, peas, and lentils are Old World examples—which supply a better balance of amino acids.

Bread in Antiquity

The cultivation of club wheat as early as 10,000 years ago supplanted einkorn and emmer. For the first time, humans had a wheat suitable for making bread. At first humans made and ate an unleavened bread. During these early centuries confusion existed, and still exists, about the status of durum. As noted earlier, it is not truly suited for making bread, though some scholars have wondered whether prehistoric people made unleavened bread from durum. The momentum of nutrition may support this idea because, as the hardest wheat, durum has the highest protein content. Apparently the Bedouins of Arabia still eat unleavened bread, though the category of wheat is difficult to pinpoint.

The Egyptians may have been the first to make leavened bread. They understood the importance of bread in maintaining a stable society. Accordingly, the Egyptians stored extra wheat so that they would have bread even during famine. One notes the reliance on bread in Eurasia and Egypt. Bread was so important in Egypt that one could use it as currency. The rise of Greece and Rome heralded a separation between bread and money. Coins supplanted bread as currency. The Greeks and Romans thought of bread strictly as food. Only the arrival of the potato in Europe would challenge this hegemony. To the extent that bread changed the world, it did so partly by sustaining the populations of Europe, western Asia, Egypt, and North Africa. Dynastic Egypt appears to have rested on a foundation of bread. In this sense, bread concretized the division between elites and commoners. Elites ate bread, but the poor often subsisted on porridge. Bread also hardened gender lines. The husband might work the field, but if the family was to have bread, the wife had to make it. One assumes that she passed on this chore to her daughters.

One cannot say, however, that bread lengthened the lifespan of humans in antiquity. Death before age 30 was common. One who reached age 40 had likely outlived his or her contemporaries and perhaps even his or her children. Yet disease, rather than bread, might have been the cause of the brevity of life in the ancient world.

As the example of Egypt suggests, bread may have been the glue that held together human societies in antiquity. The Romans, alert to the need to keep the masses content, distributed free bread to the inhabitants of the city. This could not have been an easy task, given that at the time of Jesus the city—possibly the world's largest to that date—had 1 million residents. In Greece and Rome, bread was important enough to shape religion. Because wheat was the source of bread, the Greeks created Demeter, the goddess who guaranteed the bounty of the wheat crop. In Rome, Ceres served the same purpose. There can be no doubt of bread's importance to Rome. Excavations at Pompeii have revealed many ovens in which the Romans baked bread. Second-century-CE emperor Trajan understood the importance of bread to the stability of the empire, distributing it to Egypt when famine threatened. The longevity of the empire owed much to the supply of bread. In this regard, Rome assigned Sicily and Egypt the task of supplying wheat so that the bread supply would never be in doubt. Bread, therefore, made possible the glory of the empire.

One should exercise caution in extrapolating from these examples to assume that bread was the staff of life everywhere. There may be some truth to this assertion in parts of the Old World, but until the Columbian Exchange, the Amerindians appear to have done well without wheat or bread. Depending on their location, the Native Americans ate corn, beans, squash, tomatoes, peppers, peanuts, potatoes, sweet potatoes, and cassava. The arrival of wheat and bread in the New World would change its history.

The Middle Ages and Modernity

Even in England, bread was not a staple until the 11th century, though thereafter one would have trouble thinking about the English without the consumption of bread. Curiously, the English grew rye, but they preferred wheat to rye bread. During the period of Anglo Saxon ascendancy the English asked much from their women. They worked the wheat fields and baked bread at home. In this context, bread was a source of oppression. Its seems curious that England came so late to bread given that it was part of the Roman Empire as early as the first century CE. One wonders about nutrition given that the English preferred the softest wheats, those with the least protein, for their bread. As elsewhere, the English demanded white bread. In an era before modern dentistry tooth decay was common, impeding people from chewing fibrous brown bread even though it was much more nutritious than white bread.

Bread was a barometer that measured the oscillation of people between plenty and famine. In the 12th century a brief interlude of warm weather contributed to a plentitude of bread and a consequent increase in population. By contrast, the 14th century was a demographic disaster. Between 1314 and 1317, cold weather and heavy rain doomed the wheat crop. Bread was in shortage. Famine killed people and weakened the survivors. Given these horrors, the paucity of bread must have sowed the seeds of the Black Death, which may have claimed half Europe's population and an unknown number of Asians.

The 16th-century arrival of the potato might have challenged bread's supremacy, but for a variety of reasons Europeans only cautiously adopted the potato, and then only in Northern Europe. Well into the 18th century, for example, the British preferred bread to potatoes. By one account the average Brit ate between 1000 and

1800 grams of bread per day. The average loaf weighed about 900 grams, suggesting that some Brits ate as much as two loaves of bread per person per day. This evidence suggests that bread, at least in some regions, more than held its own against the nutritionally superior potato.

The politics of bread, as Great Britain played it, crippled Ireland. The British ruthlessly exploited the Irish, taking all their grain as rent, which could have been made into bread for the masses. This system worked only because the Irish adopted the potato. Rarely have one people so depended on one food. The potato famine between 1845 and 1849 deprived the Irish of their staple. Even then the Irish might have survived had British landlords let them keep their grain for making bread. Britain's refusal condemned 1 million Irish to starvation. Another 1.5 million fled Ireland. Seldom have the politics of bread done so much damage.

Bread also destabilized France. Had France adopted the potato as rapidly as one physician counseled, France might not have descended into chaos. As it was, the French relied on bread, and when the grain harvest failed in the late 1780s, the price of bread rose above the level that the masses could afford. The ensuing bread riots swept aside the French monarchy, the guillotine dispatching both king and queen. Similar events cascaded out of control in Russia. Although Russia had rapidly adopted the potato, its dependence on bread was still strong. In the crucible of World War I and faltering harvests, bread, too, became unaffordable. Russia repressed the initial demonstrations, but revolutionary Vladimir Lenin was able to use the tumult that high bread prices had caused to topple the czar and create what was to have been a communist state, though it never approximated the ideals that German economist Karl Marx and British-German economist Friedrich Engels had upheld.

In the United States, bread took a different course. The colonial plantings of wheat in New England were not spectacular, but when wheat moved west to the Great Plains in the 19th century, yields soared and the price of bread halved between 1877 and 1886. Perhaps socialism and communism never gained a foothold in the United States because cheap bread kept the masses content. Although industrial workers faced horrible wages and working conditions, they could still afford cheap bread.

The discovery of vitamins in the early 20th century struck white bread like a lightning bolt. Nutritionists demonstrated that the milling of wheat kernels removed the vitamin-rich bran and germ. Aside from calories, white bread has no value. Whole-grain wheat bread became the standard of excellence. Physicians pointed to white bread as a culprit in the increase in obesity and diabetes. Paradoxically, supermarkets continue to sell white bread, and consumers continue to ingest it. Perhaps humans do not learn their lessons well.

Bread and Monotheism

Bread was central to the rise of Judaism and Christianity. Numerous passages in the Old and New Testaments refer to bread. In this context, the use of the term "corn" in some biblical translations causes confusion. "Corn" was once used as a generic term to refer to any type of grain, but modern usage confines the term to maize, a grain native to the Americas. Because the biblical writers could not have known about the Americas, they could not have known about corn. The people of the Old and New Testaments did not eat corn bread. Indeed, corn is not ideal for making bread. Instead, the people of the Bible ate wheat bread. The New Testament references to bread are telling because they almost always occur in connection with Jesus's ministry. The canonical Gospels, for example, report that Jesus multiplied five loaves of bread and two fish, distributing the excess to the hungry people who had come to hear him preach. Bread assumes particular importance in the retelling of the Last Supper. According to these Gospels, Jesus asked his apostles to eat the bread they shared in remembrance of him. Jesus is said to have instructed his apostles that in eating this bread they were really consuming his flesh. This language suggested to the Romans that Christians were cannibals and may have led to persecution, though many Christians do not realize that this persecution was sporadic. The Romans never attempted to exterminate Christianity. In the 13th century, Italian cleric Thomas Aquinas, borrowing the categories of Aristotle, revealed how it could be possible to eat Jesus's flesh when consuming bread. Ordinarily the substance—what something is—is immutable. Bread is bread. But by the miracle of the eucharist, God transforms bread into the flesh of Jesus even though the flesh continues to taste like bread. This process, Aquinas averred, was transubstantiation, meaning that the substance, not the appearance, of bread had changed.

The Lord's Prayer invoked God's help in securing the people their "daily bread." The church encouraged the baking of bread on Good Friday in the belief that such bread was lucky. Christians made special types of bread to commemorate the feast days of the church's many saints. Christmas, Lent, and Easter also demanded their own carefully prepared breads. The church asked parishioners to give bread to the poor. Bread even became a source of demarcation. Whereas the Catholic Church believed that Jesus had eaten unleavened bread at the Last Supper, the Orthodox Church maintained that the bread must have been leavened, though neither church could marshal decisive evidence. In the 16th century, the rise of Protestantism reignited the furor over what type of bread Jesus had eaten.

Further Reading

Marchant, John, Bryan Reuben, and Joan Alcock. *Bread: A Slice of History*. Gloucestershire: The History Press, 2008.

Rubel, William. *Bread: A Global History*. London: Reaktion Books, 2011.

Breakfast Cereal

Many nutritionists claim that breakfast is the most important meal of the day. Over time and throughout the world there has been much variation in what people eat for breakfast. The inventor of breakfast cereals, American physician John Harvey Kellogg believed that many people ate too much meat, eggs, and other animal products for breakfast. A vegetarian, Kellogg wished to promote a breakfast of whole grains as an antidote to the over-on meat and meat products. The raising of nutritional standards and health consciousness motivated Kellogg. It appears ironic that breakfast cereal companies have departed from this sentiment, offering products that substitute sweetness for nutrients. A 20th-century invention, breakfast cereals are latecomers to the roster of foods. The people of south, east, and Southeast Asia have cultivated rice for millennia. By contrast, Americans have chomped down on breakfast cereals for only a century.

Breakfast before Breakfast Cereals

Prior to the invention of breakfast cereals, many Americans in the South, both black and white, ate corn grits for breakfast. Oatmeal was popular among Scottish and Irish immigrants. The tendency to settle for a bowl of rice porridge remains common in China. People in Iran and Turkey still eat wheat porridge. South Africans subsist on a variety of breakfast preparations of corn. For those who could afford a richer diet, breakfast might include eggs, bacon, ham, sausage, milk, cheese, fried potatoes, pancakes, butter, maple syrup, coffee, orange juice, or tea. Such fare was filling and was suited to a time when work required vigorous labor. Quite simply, the burning of many calories required a calorie-dense diet.

Lucky Charms

General Mills debuted Lucky Charms, a popular breakfast cereal, in 1964. The main ingredients are oats and tiny, semihard marshmallows. Like many foods, Lucky Charms has a cartoon character in the form of a leprechaun, a part of Irish folklore, as its mascot. The leprechaun offers the cereal to television viewers, but they will not find any of his gold.

Into the 20th century, however, innovations like the automobile lessened the strenuousness of daily life. A lighter breakfast seemed desirable.

The Advent of Breakfast Cereals

At the turn of the 20th century, American physician and surgeon John Harvey Kellogg believed that breakfast fare was short on fiber and too high in fat. A vegetarian since age 14, Kellogg took charge of the renowned Battle Creek Sanitarium in Battle Creek, Michigan. Its visitors included President Abraham Lincoln's widow Mary Todd Lincoln, President Warren G. Harding, aviator Amelia Earhart, automaker Henry Ford, and dramatist George Bernard Shaw. Early on, Kellogg advocated the truism that prevention of disease was far superior to treatment once illness struck. He promoted exercise, outdoor activity in the presence of sunlight, and a healthy diet. His pursuit of health through the invention of breakfast cereals came from all the right motives. From the outset, Kellogg aimed to create a product that required no preparation, easing a woman's household duties. He first invented something akin to a biscuit of whole wheat, oats, and cornmeal. Kellogg named the product granula and then granola, but success was not immediate because the biscuit was difficult to chew. Kellogg's answer was always to simplify, converting the biscuit into thin flakes that were easy to chew.

Even then, Kellogg's rise to fame was not meteoric. The efforts of his more pragmatic brother Will Keith Kellogg were necessary for success. Will shrewdly added sugar to his brother's formulas. Here was the connection between the sugar empire of tropical America and the rise of a breakfast cereal industry in Michigan. Sugar revolutionized breakfast cereals. No longer were they the austere foods of health-conscious adults but rather under the purview of children (and adults) who desired sweetness above all else. Breakfast cereals thus shaped history by transforming breakfast from a meal of diverse foods to the fulfillment of the human craving for sweetness, a deep biological longing. Again, in a calorie-sparse environment in which early humans evolved, the craving for sugar must have helped humans survive, but today, in a calorie-dense environment, this craving no longer benefits humans. Today the Kellogg empire is worth $13 billion.

Breakfast Cereals Today

Kellogg's, Post Foods, and Ralston Foods, all cereal makers, have their headquarters in John Kellogg's Battle Creek, Michigan. Every year these companies host a cereal festival known as the World's Longest Breakfast Table. The companies serve free cereal to anyone who wants a bowl. Many brands are on display: Cocoa Pebbles, Lucky Charms, Corn Pops, Raisin Bran, Corn Flakes, Frosted Flakes, and innumerable others. At least for the people of Battle Creek, breakfast cereals are a local food, though one that has been industrialized in imitation of the meat-packers and automakers.

Breakfast cereals shaped history by promoting economies of scale, mass production, and mass consumption. The accent is on the rise of a culture of consumerism and conspicuous consumption. Part of the success of breakfast cereals lies in branding. Tony the Tiger, Toucan Sam, and Count Chocula invite consumers to fill their breakfast bowls with their products. The choice of Count Chocula is particularly interesting because it must derive from the stories about Count Dracula, a historical figure who Irish author Bram Stoker immortalized in the novel *Dracula*. The real-life Dracula, also known as Vlad Tepes, was a Romanian prince of unspeakable barbarism. Somehow Count Chocula has managed to dissociate himself from this connection to the real Dracula. In a sense, Count Chocula has shaped history by remaking a bloodthirsty tyrant into a playful image.

Today about 20 percent of American adults and one-third of children eat breakfast cereals. The sale of these foods has become a $10 billion-per-year industry in the United States alone. In food sales, breakfast cereals trail only soft drinks, milk, bread, salty snacks, beer, wine, and cheese. It is difficult to believe that breakfast cereals boast higher earnings than coffee and tea. Few other foods can match the diversity of breakfast cereals. A casual survey of the cereal shelves at Walmart reveals a dizzying number of brands, each competing for market share. The average Kroger store displays 215 different brands of breakfast cereal compared to 120 types of soft drinks, 94 brands of bread, 128 kinds of crackers, and 34 brands of peanut butter. The United States, Canada, the United Kingdom, and Australia have 6 percent of the world's population but eat more than half the globe's breakfast cereals.

Can Marketing Go Hand in Hand with Nutrition?

Cereal makers tout their products as nourishing and low fat. Yet one should reflect on the fact that the milling of the grains in breakfast cereals strips away nutrients. The companies add sugar, as Will Kellogg had, increasing the number of calories. Conscious of their trespasses, these companies add back the vitamins they had eliminated in the first place. The effect may be akin to eating vitamin-fortified white bread, though in recent years cereal makers have insisted that they use whole grains. This assertion is difficult to verify because cereal makers are so secretive about their formulas that they will not allow the public or journalists to tour their factories.

Yet cereal makers are adept at advertising the wholesomeness of their products. In an effort to capture the attention of health-conscious consumers, cereal makers advertise their products as part of a back-to-nature golden age in America, reminiscent of a time when nature was unspoiled and the United States was a land of small farmers who Thomas Jefferson had mythologized as the core of what it meant to be an American. Breakfast cereals have shaped history by recovering the Jeffersonian notion of a mystical, rustic, natural America of wholesome vigor. Grape-Nuts, for example, has long touted its wholesomeness.

Reality does not appear to square with this mythology. Most consumers do not know that, because a box of cereal may linger at the warehouse and store nine months before purchase, many of the vitamins may have degraded by the time the cereal is eaten. Cereal makers may add 75 percent of the recommended daily allowance of vitamin C to a box of cereal in hopes that 30 percent will last to the day of consumption. Moreover there is no consensus about the safety of dyes and other colorings. Contrary to advertising, many cereals lack the fiber that most health-conscious Americans would expect from a "whole grain" product. Neither do the marshmallows in Lucky Charms have any nutritional value, though they remain popular with children and many adults. Some nutritionists believe that the sugar spike one experiences from eating cereals may contribute to the epidemic of diabetes. The added calories from sugar must exacerbate the problem of obesity.

Because these are processed foods, breakfast cereals are easy to digest, requiring the body to expend few calories. For a person who does not exercise vigorously, as most Americans do not, the reduction in calories needed to digest cereals compounds the problem of inactivity. As early as the 1970s, a civil engineer-turned-nutritionist in President Richard M. Nixon's White House labeled breakfast cereals "empty calories." This assessment is surely true for the many brands of heavily sweetened cereals. Cereal makers retorted that at least cereal eaters were not consuming donuts for breakfast.

Cereal makers have responded by adding more protein, sometimes in the form of soy protein, to address recent research that soy protein may lower the risk of heart disease. These companies have launched a "heart healthy" campaign, asserting that Cheerios and other oat cereals reduce the risk of heart disease and may lower cholesterol. Others think premature the association between soy protein and a reduction in the risk of heart disease. Breakfast cereals are convenient but they may not win many accolades from dieticians.

Further Reading

Anderson, Heather Arndt. *Breakfast: A History*. Lanham, MD: Rowman & Littlefield, 2013.

Warner, Melanie. *Pandora's Lunchbox: How Processed Food Took over the American Meal*. New York: Scribner, 2012.

Burrito

Often considered Mexican food, the burrito differs in a dramatic way from the taco, the tortilla, the enchilada, and other traditional Mexican foods. The standard Mexican fare is based on corn flour, not surprising given the long importance of corn to the Americas. The burrito, however, is made from wheat flour. The Amerindians did not know about wheat because it was an Old World plant. Though corn and wheat are closely related, both being grasses, they were separated by continents before European contact with the Americas. Only during the 1490s did the Amerindians learn about wheat, and even then, tropical America was unsuited to growing wheat. The burrito was thus a post-Columbian development. In this sense, despite its association with Mexico, the burrito is not strictly a traditional Mexican food. One might think of the burrito as a Mexican European hybrid or perhaps as a Mexican afterthought. As such, the burrito is not a tortilla, which is the basis of almost all Mexican foods. The burrito is wrapped into a sphere to hold its ingredients. It is almost always steamed or grilled rather than fried, and so it is soft, unlike the taco or enchilada. The term *burrito* means "little donkey." It is possible that men who rode donkeys ate a food to which the term burrito was later applied. Perhaps *burrito* acquired its name because the packs that donkeys carried resembled the wrapped foods that would acquire the name *burrito*.

An Array of Ingredients

One might consider the burrito an adopted food of Mexico. Mexicans tend to eat burritos with beef and beans, both good sources of protein. The burrito in this case is a mix of New World beans and Old World beef. In this sense, it is helpful to understand the burrito as a composite food. In addition to beef and beans, a burrito may have rice, lettuce, salsa, guacamole, cheese, and sour cream. Again, these foods combine New and Old World traditions. With all these ingredients, a burrito may be calorie dense. This quality was appropriate in an era when people led strenuous lives and worked arduous jobs, but the modern sedentary person in the developed world is apt to become obese on such a rich diet.

History

As we have seen, it is difficult to trace the burrito to the Amerindians because they did not have wheat, though Native Americans ate corn tortillas that encased ingredients similar to those of a burrito. Doubtless the Amerindians had their own equivalent of the taco and enchilada, but the burrito is a stretch. That said, the

Amerindians had a culinary relationship with beans that spanned millennia, and they surely ate beans inside a wrapped tortilla. In this sense the Amerindians had something akin to a burrito. The Native American tortilla might contain chili peppers, tomatoes, mushrooms, squash, and avocados. This was vegetarian fare. The mushrooms were native to the Old and New Worlds and are not plants but fungi. All the other ingredients derive from plants only found in the Americas before the Columbian Exchange brought them to worldwide prominence. The pueblo dwellers of the American Southwest appear to have eaten tortillas with meat and beans. The meat must have come from guinea pigs or perhaps dogs because the cow, pig, and chicken did not appear in the Americas until the Columbian Exchange, though some controversy attends the chicken.

The burrito might have originated in northern Mexico in the 19th century and in that sense may be classified a Mexican food. The region grew wheat and so must have been the source of wheat flour for making a thin flatbread that would be the basis of a burrito. A Mexican culinary dictionary from 1895 may contain the first Spanish-language reference to the burrito. This dictionary, however, confusingly identified the burrito as a type of taco, which it cannot be because the grains and preparation differ. A legend claims that, in the early 20th century, one Mexican food vendor sold the burrito, which he kept warm by placing it on the back of a donkey. Some folk historians point to this story as the origin of the term *burrito*, but this cannot be the case because the term was coined no later than 1895. In the 1940s, another street vendor reputedly sold the burrito to poor children, calling them his burritos. The name is thought to have stuck, but again there is the problem that the term burrito is at least as old as 1895. The 20th century is too late to be the source of the word. In the 1930s, restaurants in southern California were the first in the United States to serve burritos. In 1934, historian Erna Fergusson published the *Mexican Cookbook*, which contains the first English mention of, and recipe for, a burrito.

Variations on a Theme

The burrito is a culinary staple in the northern Mexican province of Chihuahua. The Mexican burrito differs from the American burrito, being thinner and at times less calorie dense. It may have meat or fish, potatoes, beans, rice, cheese, or chile relleno and may be eaten for breakfast, lunch, and dinner. Again, one notes the combination of New and Old World foods. By contrast, southern Mexico appears to have little interest in the burrito, probably because the region does not grow wheat. Some Mexicans call the burrito "wheat flour tacos." This language confuses more than clarifies because a burrito is not a taco. Again, one notes the contrast between wheat and corn flour.

The people of San Francisco have been eating burritos since the 1960s. There, burritos are produced on an assembly line. In this context, the burrito shaped history in its adoption of the assembly line that American meatpackers had pioneered in the 19th century (actually it was a disassembly line) and that American automaker Henry Ford adopted in the early 20th century. In San Francisco, the popular ingredients include beef, rice, steamed or boiled beans, sour cream, and onion. In 1961, Febronio Ontiveros, owner of The Lighthouse restaurant, claimed to have served the first burrito in San Francisco. He also claimed to have been the first to have added rice, sour cream, and guacamole to the burrito. San Francisco is headquarters to several chain restaurants that sell burritos.

San Diego claims to favor a less caloric burrito, sticking to the basics of beef, cheese, and salsa. As a rule, the San Diego burrito contains fewer ingredients than is traditional in San Francisco. San Diego also departs from the assembly line methods that remain prominent in San Francisco. The burrito appears to have come to San Diego in the late 1960s. Several taco houses sold them along with other Mexican foods. By 2000, one chain restaurant alone had 60 outlets that served burritos in San Diego. The city claims to have invented the "California burrito" in the 1980s. The California burrito is far from the austere food one might expect of San Diego, containing beef, french fries, cheese, cilantro, sour cream, onion, and guacamole. Known as "fusion food" because of the combination of beef and french fries in Mexican cuisine, this pairing is not much different than what McDonald's offers. Some San Diegans substitute chicken or shrimp for beef.

Because of its large Mexican population, Los Angeles is difficult to classify. The Los Angeles burrito may contain fried beans, beef or chili, cheddar cheese, and rice. Los Angeles also features a burrito of just beans and cheese. Another variant includes beans and chili pepper sauce. Some people in the city of angels eat burritos with nothing more than beef. Los Angeles even offers a hot dog wrapped in a burrito. Still others favor soy sauce, bringing the culinary traditions of East Asia to Los Angeles. The sushi burrito is another Asian American fusion food.

The breakfast burrito appears to be an American innovation, with scrambled eggs, potatoes, onion, and bacon. Other ingredients may include chili and cheese. In the 1980s, McDonald's introduced its own breakfast burrito, featuring sausage and eggs. In the 1990s, other fast food restaurants followed this example.

Taco Bell popularized the burrito worldwide. It promotes three options. The Beefy Fritos Burrito has beef, Fritos corn chips, rice, and nacho cheese sauce. The Smothered Burrito-Shredded Chicken contains chicken, rice, beans, chipotle sauce, cheese, and sour cream. The Cheesy Bean and Rice Burrito includes beans, rice, nacho cheese, and jalapeno pepper sauce.

Further Reading

Arellano, Gustavo. *TACO USA: How Mexican Food Conquered America*. New York: Scribner, 2012.

Pilcher, Jeffrey M. *Planet Taco: A Global History of Mexican Food*. Oxford and New York: Oxford University Press, 2012.

Taco Bell. "Burritos." Accessed September 26, 2014. www.tacobell.com/food/burritos.

Butter and Other Fats

Butter and ghee may be produced from the milk of a few domesticated animals, though the cow is most important. Humans derived both foods, butter in western Asia and butter and ghee in what are today India and Pakistan, in prehistory. They must have played a role in the rise of the first civilizations in these regions and so have helped shape the world. Margarine is another important fat, but vastly different from butter and ghee. Whereas butter and ghee are animal products, margarine is a composite of what are called vegetable fats. Margarine is a product of the

Butter, ghee, and later margarine have been important sources of dietary fat for humans. There are health risks, however, from ingesting too much saturated fat. (Fortyforks/Dreamstime.com)

Butter versus Margarine

Butter had been the chief dietary fat of many people for centuries, but in the 19th century margarine burst upon the scene. Incensed dairymen and dairywomen believed that margarine masqueraded as butter and did not believe that a blend of vegetable oils was as wholesome as butter. These men and women lobbied their state legislatures to promote truth in labeling so that margarine could not pretend to be butter. In fact, in the 1910s, University of Wisconsin scientist Elmer V. McCollum demonstrated that butter, but not margarine, contained a new nutrient, later named vitamin A.

Industrial Revolution. In a sense, history shaped the origin and development of margarine.

Butter and Ghee

Both butter and ghee derive primarily from the milk fat of cows. The difference is the fat content. Butter has about 82 percent fat, whereas ghee is 99 percent fat. Ghee is obviously the more calorie dense of the two, ounce for ounce. The fraction that is not fat is water, in both butter and ghee. Because of the importance of milk fat in butter and ghee, the first requires brief attention. Milk fat may be processed into a variety of saturated fats, including butter, ghee, cream, and cheese. Worldwide, butter is the most coveted fat, surpassing animal lards of all types, including those of cattle, pigs, sheep, and chickens. The flavor of butter captivates many people, and butter is used as a spread and in baked and fried foods. Butter has some 500 fatty acids, more than any other type of fat. Butter may be made from the milk of goats, sheep, and camels, but the cow is the global powerhouse in the production of butter. Among the cow's products, it is worth noting that butter is about 82 percent fat, cheese 30–50 percent fat, cream 30–45 percent fat, and milk about 2–4 percent fat, though it is possible to buy skim milk devoid of fat. This list makes obvious that, ounce for ounce, butter is the most calorie-dense milk fat that a cow produces. Butter also contains salt. Because humans crave fat, salt, and sugar, butter, having two of the three, must always have enticed humans. The production of butter is not complicated. One simply churns cream. Worldwide, humans consume about 7 million tons of butter per year. India and Pakistan, the leading consumers of ghee, are also the leading consumers of butter, though Europe, especially France and Germany, is not far behind.

Depending on a cow's diet, the flavor may vary worldwide. There is no variation in flavor in the United States because of the uniformity of what cows eat: grass in the first year and corn thereafter. The corn may be supplemented with soybean meal, a good source of protein. In parts of the developing world, cows are allowed to eat grass throughout warm weather, being confined only in winter. This practice yields seasonal differences in the flavor of butter. By weight, butter is more than 80 percent fat. Because of butter's antiquity and its ability to satisfy humankind's taste buds, states and nations protect butter by forbidding margarines or oil-butter blends to advertise themselves as butter. In short, the addition of other fats to butter or the deletion of any of butter's many fatty acids disqualify the product from being butter. Any product with less than 80 percent fat cannot be labeled butter, though Europe has variants of what would otherwise be butter that contain 60–62 percent fat or 39–41 percent fat. Europeans define the first as "three-quarter-fat butter," and the second as "half-fat butter." In the United States, products may claim to be "light butter" if they are no more than 40 percent fat. "Reduced butter" must be less than 20 percent fat.

Some oils, soybean oil for example, are frequently combined with butter, but this blending must occur before chemists hydrogenate soybean oil, to supply the most healthful product. From the perspective of consumers, butter-oil blends have two benefits. Butter-oil blends, depending on the oil, are more healthful than butter. Moreover, butter-oil blends are easier to spread than butter. Palm oil is also combined with butter, and perhaps provides an even more nutritious product, given palm oil's vitamin composition.

The high saturated fat content in butter suggests that the spread should not be a staple in the diet. Butter is also a source of trans fats and cholesterol, neither desirable in the diet. Butter is also deficient as a spread. Taken directly from the refrigerator, butter is too solid to spread on toast or another bread product. It must be lightly heated or allowed to warm to room temperature to serve as a spread. Butter and cocoa butter from the pod of the cacao tree must have similar melting points because both will melt in the human hand. As a healthful product, butter cannot boast many achievements, though it is less processed than margarine. Consumers tend to prefer the flavor of butter to that of margarine.

Humans must have derived butter, and also ghee, in prehistory as they transitioned from hunter-gatherers to livestock and crop raisers. This was not an instantaneous transition, but took millennia to occur worldwide. In the Americas, for example, the dearth of domesticated animals precluded the making of butter. Rather, the cow cultures of western Asia must have been among the first to make butter. These people created the first civilizations. Butter must have played a role in the origin of these civilizations, not only in western Asia but also in Egypt, Greece, and Rome. In this context, butter was probably a beneficial food because it was calorie dense in an era that required arduous work. By virtue of the absence of labor-saving devices, humans must have burned more calories than the sedentary people who populate the modern West. The consumption of butter must have been appropriate to replenish these calories.

As noted earlier, ghee has a higher fat content than butter and is geographically distinct from butter. Ghee is a fat of Asia, particularly India and Pakistan, where butter is the fat of Europe and the United States. It is worth emphasizing that India and Pakistan continue to consume butter in addition to ghee. Ghee has a higher melting point than butter and so is favored in the tropics. With 99 percent milk fat, ghee is the most potent fat derived from milk. A prehistoric food, ghee helped form the civilizations of the Indus River valley. Even in the tropics, ghee may store six to eight months without fear of rancidity.

Margarine

Compared to the antiquity of butter and ghee, humans have made margarine, a combination of "vegetable" oils, for only about a century. One might note that not all oils in margarine are true vegetable oils. Soybean oil, for example, is an oil derived from the seed of a legume. The impetus for the development of margarine came in the 19th century when people throughout Europe and the United States began moving from farm to city, abandoning the tradition of making butter. A new product to satisfy the nascent industrial era was needed. The cycle of boom and bust, omnipresent in industry, haunted agriculture too, and by the late 1860s butter was in shortage in Europe's burgeoning cities. With butter in shortage, its price increased beyond the means of the poor. France had experienced a similar though more serious crisis when high bread prices lead to the French Revolution in the 18th century. The high price of butter would not likely have sparked revolt because butter was not a staple. But France reacted nonetheless, offering a prize to anyone who could invent a substitute for butter. In 1869, French chemist Hippolyte Mège-Mouriès patented what Americans know as margarine, claiming the prize. Margarine was thus a product of the Industrial Revolution and so shaped history along with this epochal series of events.

Margarine was cheap, as the French government had hoped, but the early variants were not flavorful. Some governments required margarine to be white so consumers would not mistake it for butter. Yet margarine has matured and now claims to be a healthy alternative to butter, having less cholesterol, saturated fat, and trans fat. Some margarines have less fat than butter. The oils that compose margarine are typically soybean, rapeseed, canola, sunflower, cottonseed, palm, palm kernel, and coconut. Peanut oil might have been another possibility, but it does not store well. Some of these oils may be hydrogenated to their detriment. Salt, preservatives, and vitamins may be added to margarine. Margarine contains about 30–40 percent solid fat and the rest liquid oils. These proportions allow margarine to spread well even at the 4°C that is normal for a refrigerated food. In this respect, margarine is the superior spread.

Further Reading

Gunstone, Frank D. *Oils and Fats in the Food Industry*. Oxford: Wiley-Blackwell, 2008.
Gunstone, Frank D., ed. *Vegetable Oils in Food Technology: Composition, Properties, and Uses*. Boca Raton, FL: CRC Press, 2011.

C

Cake

It is difficult to define a cake except to say that it is the sweet centerpiece of a celebration, though the idea of a cake may be larger and more diverse than this attempt at definition. Some tentative points merit mention. A cake is not just bread, though both may be made of wheat flour. A cake is also not a brownie, a muffin, a cookie, a biscuit, a scone, a pastry of some type, or pudding, though all may be sweet. Despite the name, a pancake is not synonymous with a cake. It is more difficult to include or exclude cheesecake as a cake. It seems unnecessary that a cake contain chocolate in the way that chocolate chip cookies must have chocolate as a leading ingredient. In fact, a chocolate cake may not actually contain chocolate.

Origins and Religious Importance

The antiquity of cake is in dispute, with some food historians looking deep into the past and others claiming cake to be a more recent invention. Archeologists point to evidence for the origin of cake in the earliest civilizations in western Asia, Egypt, and China. Yet the sweet, soft, spongy item that many people know as cake may have appeared as recently as the 18th century. The first "cake" may have been

---

Birthday Cake

It is traditional to celebrate the birthday of a young person with a cake. The cake is usually caloric with its icing, eggs, and plenty of sugar throughout the food. It is customary to mark one's age with the number of candles. Blowing them out with a single breath of air is said to ensure good fortune or to ensure that a wish comes true. As one ages, the desire for such displays fades. Who wants a birthday cake with 50 candles?

crushed, moist, cooked grain. One may object that the absence of sugar, honey, or another sweetener disqualified these foods from being cakes. The Romans made something akin to cheesecake. Because it contained honey, one may be more confident in defining this food as cake.

The Egyptians made several types of cakes, considering them the food of religious festivals. Here, one glimpses a prefiguring of the association between cake and Christmas, between cake and the putative birth of Jesus. The Egyptian cakes must have been especially sweet, containing both honey and dates. Indeed, the Egyptians may have made a syrup from dates, adding yet more sweetness to the cake. They gave some of these cakes to goddess Isis, perhaps the most important deity in Egypt and the Mediterranean world. Isis appears to prefigure the rise of Christianity because she is the goddess who resurrected her slain brother and husband Osiris. Jesus was clearly not the first resurrection god. To affirm the connection to femininity, the Egyptians often made cakes in the shape of the female genitalia. This practice was also common in Syracuse, Sicily, a Greek colony before Roman conquest. Sicilians associated cake with the goddesses Demeter and Persephone, both Greek deities that had roots in Egypt. The cake and the gods and goddesses of the Mediterranean Basin may have their origin in Egypt. It was common at this stage to add milk to cake, though this practice must have hastened the decay of cake by encouraging the growth of harmful bacteria. In the second century BCE, Roman agricultural writer Cato the Elder listed several types of cake. Because he tended to confine himself to what he regarded as important, like viticulture and the making and selling of olive oil, the cake must have been important to the Romans.

The Middle Ages and the Early Modern Era

In the Middle Ages, Britain made gingerbread, though one does not ordinarily classify it as cake. The use of honey may tempt one to call gingerbread a cake of sorts, though the addition of pepper, saffron, cinnamon, and ginger may argue otherwise. These expensive spices made gingerbread a food of the elites. The attempt to trace the origin of cake to the making of bread appears to be counterproductive. Bread lacks the sweetness that seems essential to a cake. Not content with mere honey, Europeans in the late Middle Ages and early modernity added cream, butter, and eggs to flour, a food that the modern critic may confidently classify as cake. During this period, the people of England and Northern Europe often coupled cake with beer, a pairing that may seem odd today. In this context, cake was part of entertainment and eroticism. The Puritans reacted against these associations and, in 1592, England attempted to ban the making and eating of cake. The attempt doubtless failed. Easing its position, England allowed the consumption of cake at funerals, Christmas, and Good Friday. Here, again, is the merging of cake with Christianity. By the early modern era, Europeans had coupled cake with cocoa, a tasty combination that reinforced the importance of chocolate in Europe, and of the Columbian Exchange, which brought chocolate from the Americas to Europe. Also important in this regard was the rise of sugar as an ingredient in cake. Before the discovery of the Americas, Europeans had little access to sugar. The peopling of tropical America with European masters and African slaves changed matters. Sugarcane, which Italian Spanish explorer Christopher Columbus had planted in the Caribbean in 1493, led to the creation of a sugar empire in the Americas. With an abundance of sugar flowing from the Americas to Europe, the sweetener became an increasingly important ingredient in cake. The Columbian Exchange also brought vanilla from the Americas to Europe, giving cake a new flavoring.

Toward the Modern Cake

Into the 18th century, British North America and Europe paired cake with coffee. Here was another manifestation of the importance of the Columbian Exchange. An Old World tree, coffee, found a home in the American tropics. It was perfectly suited to the sugarcane empire because coffee thrived at the slight elevations upon which sugarcane could not be grown, leaving the lowlands free for the grass. Sometime in the 18th century, cake makers abandoned yeast, firmly separating cake from bread. The use of the oven brought the modern cake into being. By 1780, the oven was ubiquitous to the making of cake. The use of beaten eggs allowed cakes to rise without yeast. Cake recipes of this era called for one pound each of butter, sugar, and flour, and eight eggs. By the end of the 18th century, potassium carbonate was the raising agent of choice, though bicarbonate of soda soon showed its superiority. By 1850, baking powder had supplanted all other raising agents, though one should note the presence of bicarbonate of soda in it. In the 17th and 18th centuries arose the practice of icing a cake with ever more sugar. Today, buttercream or whipped cream are often the icings of choice.

Cake and the French Revolution

According to some accounts, when French queen Marie Antoinette learned that the masses could not afford bread, she may have instructed them to eat cake. The story may be apocryphal, but it reveals much about France on the eve of the French Revolution in 1789. The queen seems to have been ignorant of the fact that the masses could never afford wheat bread, or cake for that matter, and so subsisted on rye bread. In the years before the revolution, the rye harvest had failed, pricing rye bread, like wheat bread and cake, above the means of ordinary French people. The status of the potato complicated matters. Although a French physician and pharmacist had advocated its cultivation as early as the 1770s, agricultural transitions often take long to accomplish. The French did not adopt the potato on a large scale as the Irish were doing. Had the French adopted the potato rapidly, the bread crisis might have led nowhere. As it was, the failure of the rye harvest caused bread riots in French cities, as they would in early 20th century Russia. In both cases tragedy ensued. The out-of-touch French monarchs lost their heads to the guillotine, ushering in the Reign of Terror in which many French people, notably chemist Antoine Lavoisier, lost their lives. Using the revolutionary fervor to his advantage, French commander Napoleon Bonaparte rose to emperor and plunged all of Europe into war. In some circles, cake coupled with ignorance symbolizes all that went wrong in revolutionary France.

Cake and Symbolism

The status of cake is ambiguous. It seems unlikely that anyone will starve for want of cake, and yet it has amassed an important symbolism. Cake is a symbol of birth and for this reason is a staple at any birthday celebration, particularly among children. It is unclear when people adopted candles on a cake to enumerate the years a child had lived, but it is evident that the cake with candles emerged as a marker of time. This marking of time must have been important in an era when child mortality was high. The cake also symbolized excess as a concoction of sugar and fat. Although one need not eat cake from a nutritional standpoint, humans are biologically predisposed to crave salt, sugar, and fat. Because cake provides two of the three, the cake may seem like a necessity. Yet it is possible to assert that a cake is entirely superfluous. One can live a full life without eating cake and without fear of nutritional deficiency. Were it not for the eggs in cake, one might be tempted to dismiss it as junk food, as empty calories in the way that one might dismiss sugar itself. The cake marks milestones in human life. Is it possible to have a wedding without an elaborate cake? Is it possible to celebrate Christmas without a cake? The answer to the latter is important because it marks the union of the cake with Christianity. If cake symbolizes birth, in this context it celebrates the birth of Jesus, though most theologians doubt that Jesus was born December 25. Rather, Christianity co-opted a pagan festival that marked the winter solstice and, with its passing, the triumph of light over darkness. Because the canonical Gospels, particularly John, equate Jesus with light, it was fitting to associate him with the passing of the winter solstice. The cake's symbolism far outweighs its contribution to the diet. In fact, one might assert that the cake is excess alone. Being layer upon layer of flour, eggs, sugar, and fat, a cake symbolizes decadence.

Further Reading

Humble, Nicola. *Cake: A Global History*. London: Reaktion Books, 2010.

Canned Foods

It is neither possible nor desirable to attempt to consume an entire harvest in a brief period. The difficulty is that fresh foods perish due to the multiplication in them of harmful bacteria. The concept of microorganisms, bacteria for example, was unknown to prehistoric people, but they understood the dangers of rotten foods. Accordingly, methods of preservation have preoccupied humans for millennia. Early advances came from salting or dehydrating foods. Salted fish is a good example of this progress in food preservation. In its own way, the processing of milk into cheese likewise creates a durable product that remains edible long after the milk from which it was derived has soured. Canned foods are a much more recent innovation, but they have gained enormous importance. For the first time it is possible to preserve foods not merely from season to season but for years and even decades.

The French Achievement

French research was at the core of the invention of the technique of canning, though the initial medium was glass rather than a metal can. In 1795, France, in the midst of a war against many other European nations and still in the throes of the French Revolution, understood that its army and navy needed rations that would store well. French emperor Napoleon Bonaparte, a gifted military leader, in particular understood this need and is alleged to have remarked that an "army marches on its stomach." French commanders were alert to the dangers of scurvy and other diseases of nutritional deficiency, though the science of nutrition had yet to develop. These generals knew that food must be safe, to use a modern lexicon, from harmful bacteria.

At the time the French army and navy subsisted on salted meat and bread, probably made from rye. That year (1795) the French government, with Napoleon at its head, offered 12,000 francs to anyone who could devise a new and better method of food preservation. Although he needed 14 years, French chef Nicolas Appert invented the process of canning, at the time bottling, goods. He worked on the premise of boiling food. Although there was, as noted earlier, no knowledge of microorganisms at the time, in boiling the food, Appert killed any bacteria that might have been present. He then sealed the food in an airtight, vacuum container, in this case glass with a cork. This method was as close to antiseptic as could be devised at the time and ensured that these foods would last not days or weeks, but years and decades. In recognition of his achievements, in 1810 France awarded Appert the 12,000 francs it had promised. Napoleon was particularly grateful to Appert for his invention. That year, Appert published the first book on canning, which was widely translated and read throughout Europe. Many people copied Appert's methods, claiming the invention as their own.

The United Kingdom and the United States Come to the Fore

In 1813 the British were the first to actually can food, using tin as the metal container of choice. Canned foods were now a reality. As had France, the United Kingdom gave the army and navy rations in these tin cans. By 1818, civilians, soldiers, and sailors could choose among a variety of canned foods: meats, vegetables, and soups. Here was a revolution in the consumption of foods that shaped daily life and the food habits of Europeans and Americans in just a few short decades. In 1815, Russian explorers charted new territory in the Arctic thanks to a supply of canned foods. Canned foods were thus on the cutting edge of new advances in the human understanding of geography.

In 1817, British immigrant William Underwood established the first canning operation in the United States. His first efforts in New Orleans, Louisiana, had fizzled, but he managed to establish the first cannery in Boston, Massachusetts. Soon his business included customers in South America and east Asia. In New York City other innovators began canning seafood: salmon, lobster, and oysters. By the 1840s, canned seafood and tomatoes were popular with Americans, not in combination, but in separate cans. In the 1850s, American entrepreneur Gail Borden was the first to condense and can milk. The American Civil War witnessed the expansion of canned foods as the rations of Union and Confederate soldiers and sailors. After the Civil War, the pace of urbanization and industrialization quickened. The Americans who lived in cities and toiled in factories did not always have access to the freshest food and came instead to subsist on canned foods. The Industrial Revolution was thus a revolution in the quantity and availability of canned foods. Railroads shipped these foods across the country, from the West to the large cities along the eastern seaboard. Ohio, Indiana, Illinois, and California led the way in canning fruits. California is curious in this context because it was and remains known for its fresh fruits, vegetables, and nuts. Florida, intent on processing its citrus into juice, did not participate vigorously in the canning revolution for some decades.

Canning came to resemble the economies of scale, mass production, and mass consumption that characterized the rise of the meatpacking industry and that would later define the automobile industry. Canned foods helped lead to the rise of consumerism, a product of American capitalism. Canned foods thus shaped the modern world by promoting the principles of global capitalism. Canners were aware that not everyone liked canned foods. Canned peas, for example, were apt to be mushy and insipid. Canners responded by shortening the cooking time in hopes of retaining as much flavor as possible. As canned foods were going through their growing pains, growth was nevertheless rapid. In 1872, Chicago's meatpackers began to can pork and beef. Three years later, New Orleans began canning shrimp caught in the Gulf of Mexico. In 1878, Alaska began to can salmon. In 1892, in an iconic development that remains part of America's culinary history, Hawaii began canning pineapple, the fruit that Italian Spanish explorer Christopher Columbus had favored above all else. In the late 19th century and through the 20th century the world witnessed a rapid increase in the consumption of canned soups. In 1870, the United States had fewer than 700 soup canneries, but by 1900 the number had mushroomed to nearly 2,000.

At the same time, canners mechanized the processing of food, removing the apricot seed by machine before canning the fruit. The new processes quickened the pace of canning and cut costs—again, tenets of global capitalism. The world wars heightened the demand for canned foods. During World War I, for example, the U.S. Army bought three-quarters of the nation's canned salmon and 40 percent of all canned tomatoes. By 1921, Florida had finally caught up with the national mania for canned foods, offering canned grapefruit segments and even canned orange juice. That decade, the United States began canning baby foods. After World War II, physicians and dieticians touted the nutritional quality of canned foods. Not surprisingly, the canning industry was eager to seek these endorsements, asserting that the process of canning removed no, or only a small fraction of, vitamins. Canners touted canned foods, depending on the food, as good sources of the B vitamins; vitamins A, C, and D; iron; calcium; phosphorus; and protein. Yet, after World War II, canned foods faced increasing competition from frozen foods. Canned peas, to return to that example, could not compete with frozen for flavor and nutrients.

Canning has benefited farmers in important ways. The canning industry ensures a dependable outlet for farm produce. Canners even buy crops before planting to ensure, among other things, the stability of farm income. With canned foods the farmer no longer feared the glut of harvest and its destabilizing vacillations in prices. Canning, by keeping the harvest for years, eliminated that annual glut and buoyed farmers' income. Canned foods have thus arisen as an essential component of agribusiness, an important sphere of the global economy. By the 1970s, U.S.

canners bought the equivalent of 4 million acres of food, mostly fruits and vegetables. Today, the United States processes roughly 90 percent of all tomatoes; 75 percent of olives; and more than half of the harvest of asparagus, sweet corn, and peas. The sweet corn market cannot be massive because almost all U.S. corn feeds livestock, especially pigs and cattle. Among fruits, the United States cans 70 percent of apricots, about 65 percent of pears, and more than half the peaches. About 99 percent of tuna, 90 percent of sardines, and 85 percent of salmon is canned, though the market for frozen salmon seems poised to grow rapidly. Canners have long established a close relationship with the agricultural sciences, funding many research projects. Canned foods benefit the grocer by accounting for some 15 percent of all food sales. With allowances for hyperbole, canners compare their foods with fresh foods for flavor and nourishment.

Further Reading

Communications Services. *The Canning Industry: Its History, Importance, Organization, Methods, and the Public Service Values of Its Products.* 6th ed. Washington, DC: National Canners Association, 1971.

Hawkins, Richard A. *A Pacific Industry: The History of Pineapple Canning in Hawaii.* London: I. B. Tauris, 2011.

Newell, Dianne, ed. *The Development of the Pacific Salmon-Canning Industry: A Grown Man's Game.* Montreal: McGill-Queen's University Press, 1989.

Cassava

A perennial shrub in the Euphorbiaceae family, cassava, like the sweet potato, develops from a root. It does not produce tubers, notwithstanding the tendency of one scientist to refer to cassava as a tuber. Accordingly, cassava is not closely related to the potato. Like sugarcane and several other plants, cassava is propagated from sections of stem. The Tainos of Hispaniola (now the island of Haiti and the Dominican Republic), who greeted Spanish explorer Christopher Columbus in 1492, called cassava *casabe* or *cazabe*, which the Spanish misunderstood as "cassava." The Tupi-Guarani Amerindians of the Amazon River valley called cassava *tapioca* and used the pulp from the root in pudding. So important is cassava that the people of Ghana, Togo, and Benin know it as *agbeli*, meaning, "there is life." Other names for cassava include *manioc, manioca, mandioca,* "Brazilian arrowroot," and "yucca." The scientific name *Manihot esculenta* refers only to cultivated varieties of cassava. No wild varieties of this species exist, suggesting that cassava

Cassava is an important root crop throughout the tropics. An American indigene, cassava is now prominent throughout tropical Africa and Asia. (Suryo/Dreamstime.com)

has long been in cultivation. Cassava is low in fat, cholesterol, and sodium. It has vitamin C and manganese. One hundred grams of cassava contain 550 calories, 30.5 grams of carbohydrate, and two grams of fiber.

Origin and Diffusion

Cassava shaped history first as a staple of the Amerindians and, after the Columbian Exchange, the peoples of the Old World, especially Africa. A New World cultigen, cassava may be descended from the wild *Manihot flabelifollia*. One school of thought places the origin of cassava south of the Amazon River in Brazil. Another school of thought proposes broadly that cassava originated in Mexico and Central and South America. From this region, cassava spread to the Caribbean at an early date. The Amerindians of Brazil cultivated cassava as early as 8000 BCE, a date that makes the root among the oldest crops. One authority holds that humans began growing cassava as early as 7000 BCE. This antiquity draws strength from the observation that humans may have domesticated vegetatively propagated crops before seed crops. As early as 1827, one researcher posited Brazil as the region where cassava culture began. By 6600 BCE, farmers were growing cassava in lands along the Gulf of Mexico. The Tupi-Guarani grew cassava about 3000 BCE in Colombia and Venezuela. The Peruvians began to grow cassava about 2000 BCE. The Mexicans were growing cassava by the time of Christ. From antiquity, cassava was grown intensively in northern and eastern Brazil, southern Brazil and eastern Paraguay, Colombia, Cuba, Haiti, and the Dominican Republic. Not everyone accepts a date of great antiquity. Those who hold out for a later period assert that the most ancient fragments of cassava date only to 600 CE in El Salvador.

The Maya, who may have cultivated cassava first in the Yucatán peninsula, and the Aztecs cultivated different types of cassava. The Maya grew sweet varieties, which had little hydrocyanic and prussic acid, toxins that can be fatal if ingested. Because sweet varieties had few toxins, they were safe to eat. The Maya may have eaten cassava raw or cooked. The Aztecs, on the other hand, grew bitter varieties. These had high concentrations of toxins and so were lethal if not prepared properly. To remove the toxins one may grate the root, allowing the liquid to drain. Alternatively, one may soak cassava in water for five hours, a process which allows the enzyme linamarase to degrade the toxins. A third option is to ferment cassava in water for several days, a process that renders the toxins harmless.

By the 15th century, the people of Mexico, Central and South America, and the Caribbean cultivated the root. The Tainos brought cassava to the attention of Columbus, preparing cassava bread for him. The Spanish thought the bread, which in the absence of yeast was not leavened, insipid, ranking it well below wheat bread. Cassava bread, whatever one thought of its taste, could be stored as long as two years without a loss in quality. Cassava bread was a staple of commoners. The Amerindians issued it as a ration to soldiers. Some Amerindians ate unprocessed cassava to kill themselves so that they would be free of Spanish oppression.

Notwithstanding the judgment of Columbus and his party, cassava, once adopted by the Spanish and Portuguese, spread throughout the tropics of the Old World. In the 16th century, the Portuguese brought cassava from Brazil to Africa, using it to feed slaves aboard ship. The root quickly became a staple in Cameroon, Gabon, the Republic of the Congo, and Angola. In the 18th century, the Portuguese introduced cassava to the island of Reunion and from there to Madagascar, Zanzibar, and India, while the Spanish planted it in the Philippines and Southeast Asia. Thailand quickly emerged as an exporter. By 1850, cassava was widespread in Africa and Southeast Asia. By 1900, farmers everywhere in the tropics grew cassava.

Cassava in the 21st Century

In 2002, Africa was the largest producer of cassava. Asia ranked second, and South America occupied third place. Asia boasted the highest yield per acre, and Africa, the lowest. In 2008, the leading producers were Nigeria, Thailand, Indonesia, and Brazil. Nigeria, the Republic of the Congo, and Tanzania produce the majority of Africa's cassava. In East and West Africa, less than half of the harvest goes to make flour and pellets. The leading exporters are Thailand, Vietnam, Indonesia, and Costa Rica. Thailand, Vietnam and Indonesia account for the majority of the world's exports in the form of starch and pellets. Worldwide, 80 countries, all of them in the tropics, grow cassava. As a source of calories cassava ranks third, behind rice and corn, in the tropics. Cassava ranks second to corn in tonnage. In southern China, cassava ranks fifth in tonnage behind rice, sweet potato, sugarcane, and corn. Unable to meet demand through domestic production, China imports cassava from Vietnam and Thailand. China converts a portion of its harvest to ethanol, much as the United States converts corn to ethanol, a practice that may increase demand for the root. Brazil harvests the majority of the Latin American crop. Brazil, Colombia, Cuba, Haiti, Paraguay, Peru, and Venezuela produce virtually all Latin American cassava. According to one authority, cassava yields more calories per acre than any other crop, though this honor may belong to sugarcane. Cassava may be the world's least expensive "source of starch." Today, the root supplies one-sixth of the daily calories of the people of Madagascar, Ghana, Nigeria, Liberia, the Republic of the Congo, Uganda, Tanzania, and Mozambique. In Ghana and Nigeria, per-person consumption of cassava has increased in the last 40 years, whereas consumption has declined in the Congo, Tanzania, and Uganda.

Intolerant of frost, cassava is grown between 30° north and 30° south and at elevations no higher than 6,000 feet above sea level. Cassava needs a temperature between 64°F and 77°F and two to 200 inches of rain per year. Tolerant of acidic and alkaline soils, cassava may be grown in soil with a pH between 4 and 9. Cassava yields best in sandy loam. High humidity favors the growth of roots. Because cassava tolerates low rainfall, it is a famine food, supplying calories and some nutrients when other crops fail. Some Africans eat cassava every day, some-times at breakfast, lunch, and dinner. In Africa, nearly half of the population eats cassava as the primary food. One might question whether cassava deserves to be a dietary staple. Seventy percent water, the dry matter of the root is carbohydrate, 64–72 percent of it starch. The root has only 1–2 percent protein, an amount that compares poorly with the protein in legumes and grains. Cassava has vitamin C and calcium, but little thiamine, riboflavin, and niacin. So deficient is cassava in iodine that women in the Congo who eat primarily the root develop goiter. After the harvest, roots begin to rot within two days, making it imperative that they be processed or eaten quickly. Perhaps because cassava has toxins, is vulnerable to insects and diseases, deteriorates rapidly unless processed and has little protein, researchers have not lavished the money on the root that corn and soybeans have received. Cassava, unlike corn, has few uses aside from the feeding of humans. The people of Africa eat most of the harvest. Less than 10 percent goes to livestock and industry. Industry uses cassava starch in the manufacture of clothes, adhe-sives, packaging material, food products, pharmaceuticals, and batteries. In Africa as elsewhere, corn, rather than cassava, feeds livestock. In an effort to increase the use of cassava as livestock feed, Nigeria refused to import corn in 1985. In the 1980s, high grain prices led Europeans to import cassava from Asia and Latin America to feed livestock. After 1992, the decline in grain prices caused European stockmen to jettison cassava for corn.

Small farmers grow most cassava, using it for their own sustenance. Most cas-sava, destined for the dinner table, never enters the market. Farmers who grow corn and cassava do not harvest cassava unless corn yields poorly. In this circum-stance, farmers harvest cassava to stave off hunger. Farmers may leave cassava in the ground as long as four years without a loss in quality. In the Republic of the Congo, farmers have adopted cassava because of its drought tolerance. Cotê d'Ivoire, Ghana, and Uganda grow sweet varieties of cassava whereas the Congo, Nigeria, and Tanzania grow bitter varieties. Most cassava varieties are bitter, per-haps because they are more resistant to insects and disease than sweet varieties. Today, high-yielding cultivars increase yields 40 percent over traditional varieties.

Some farmers fallow cassava land, especially where population is sparse. Throughout Africa, farmers grow cassava in preference to yams. It competes well with millet, banana, and yams. In West Africa, farmers intercrop cassava with yams. In Nimbo, Nigeria farmers plant yams, corn, and melon in April and cassava in June. After the harvest, farmers fallow the land three years. In Uganda, banana is the primary crop, and cassava, secondary. Farmers intercrop cassava with corn, beans or peas, millet, and sesame. They plant cassava in March, harvesting it in November. Fallowing the land four months, they replant it to cassava. Where the soil is poor, farmers plant cassava rather than banana. Throughout the tropics, farmers intercrop cassava with beans, peas, soybeans, mung beans, peanuts, banana, plantain, rice, millet, sorghum, yam, and sweet potato. In the Congo and Tanzania, people eat cassava leaves as a vegetable, though they must be cooked to destroy the toxins. Leaves have more protein than the root, as well as vitamins A and C, calcium, and iron. Despite these nutrients, Ugandans consider the leaves a food of the poor and so will not eat them. Although cassava is a subsistence crop, it has grown in importance as a cash crop in recent years. In Africa and South America, middlemen buy cassava from farmers, transport it to market, and sell it for profit. In India, Brazil, and Nigeria, women do much of the work of tending cassava. In Nigeria, half of all working women are cassava farmers, though they earn little money. Whereas men clear the land, plow it, and plant cassava, women weed the land, harvest the roots, and process them. Men prefer to take wage labor rather than to grow cassava. Women's contribution to the cultivation of cassava is especially large where it is a subsistence crop. Men do more work where cassava is a cash crop. Cassava's popularity may be ebbing. As its price has increased, the poor have had to buy cheap rice.

Cassava is a staple in the cuisine of several people. Rwandans combine cassava and beans. Liberians make *gari foto* from cassava, onion, tomato, and egg. *Fufu*, another Liberian dish, combines cassava, vegetables, and meat or fish. The people of Thailand coat fish, shrimp, or squid with cassava starch, frying the dish. In Kerala, India, cassava and fish are a popular combination. Cassava bread is widespread throughout the Caribbean. Puerto Ricans make *chili de yucca* from cassava and beans. Guatemalans make cassava soufflé. Peruvians combine cassava, cheese sauce, and chili peppers. Colombians make *yucca frita* by frying slices of cassava, much as Americans make fries from the potato.

Further Reading

Charrier, Andre, Michel Jacquot, Serge Hamon, and Dominique Nicolas. *Tropical Plant Breeding*. Enfield, NH: Science Publishers, 2001.

Food and Agriculture Organization. *The World Cassava Economy: Facts, Trends and Outlook*. Rome: Food and Agriculture Organization, 2000.

Hillocks, R. J., J. M. Thresh, and A. C. Bellotti, eds. *Cassava: Biology, Production and Utilization*. New York: CABI Publishing, 2002.

Hughes, Meredith, and Tom Hughes. *Buried Treasure: Roots and Tubers*. Minneapolis: Lerner Publications, 1998.

Khachatourians, George G., Alan McHughen, Ralph Scorza, Wai-Kit Nip, and Y. H. Hui, eds. *Transgenic Plants and Crops*. New York: Marcel Dekker, 2002.

Nweke, Felix I., Dunstan S. C. Spencer, and John K. Lynam. *The Cassava Transformation: Africa's Best-Kept Secret*. East Lansing: Michigan State University Press, 2002.

Cheese

Cheese derives from milk. Its invention appears to have been a necessity, given the fact that fresh milk did not store well in the era before pasteurization and refrigeration. Bacteria would multiply to unsafe levels in milk. In hot weather, milk might last only a few hours before being lost to contamination. A more durable and semipermanent product was necessary. The answer may have come from serendipity. The storage of milk in the gut of an animal extracted after a kill brought milk into the presence of the enzyme rennet. This enzyme and others like it cause milk to solidify into cheese, exactly the durable product that humans sought. Cheese had another advantage over milk. Some people, mainly adults, cannot digest the sugar lactose in milk because their bodies do not produce the enzyme lactase. These people cannot drink milk, but they can eat cheese because the body can digest it without the presence of lactase. Mozzarella and provolone were particularly important in this regard. As a rule, the longer cheese is aged, the more digestible it is. Cheese arose to prominence as an important source of protein and calcium, though it has a large amount of saturated fat. With its advantages, it is no

A derivative of milk, cheese is an important source of protein, calcium, and dietary fat. Many brands are available to meet consumer preferences. (Ariadna De Raadt/Dreamstime .com)

surprise that cheese became a global food that shaped the rise and fall of civilizations.

The Origin, History, and Importance of Cheese

Perhaps 9,000 years ago, goat's milk might have been the source of the first cheese. This invention may have occurred in the Zagros Mountains in northwestern Persia (today Iran). Sheep and cattle followed in other parts of western Asia, also serving as sources of cheese. In China and other parts of east Asia, the water buffalo was the source of cheese. Arabia derived cheese from camels. Europe and India may have been early adopters of cheese, though the case of India is questionable. By 4000 BCE, dairy farming and cheese making were important in large areas of Eurasia. From an early date, the Egyptians may have put cheese in tombs, probably in the belief that the dead would need such food in the afterworld. Upper and Lower Egypt each had their own preferences about what type of cheese was worthy of consumption. Egyptian hieroglyphs are probably the earliest written accounts to mention cheese, perhaps about 3000 BCE. A little later, the Sumerians of southern Mesopotamia (what is today part of Iraq), compiled written accounts of cheese. Cheese appears to have been an item of trade in Iraq. The Sumerians made about 20 types of cheese. In these accounts it is important to note that cheese was one of the foods that led to the rise of the first civilizations in Egypt and Iraq.

Some cheeses were known for their smell, others for their shape, texture, and color, and still others for their flavor. The Akkadians, another people of western Asia, may have compiled the first cookbook to include recipes for cheese. The Hittites also had a variety of cheeses and seem to have been most concerned about the shape, texture, and color in classifying cheeses. They may have been the first, though by no means the last, to regard cheese as a food for soldiers. The Greeks had cheese, though the oldest written accounts date only to roughly 1600 BCE. The Greeks raised little cattle and so derived cheese from sheep and goat's milk. In the fourth century BCE, Greek philosopher Aristotle took a scientific interest in the process of making cheese. In Roman antiquity, the Greek island of Crete emerged as a cheese exporter. Perhaps even more important in this regard was Roman Sicily. Sicilian cheese was also derived from goat's milk. The Romans thought of cheese as a luxury for the patricians, though Roman taverns appear to have served cheese to the masses. Perhaps from this fact arose the association between cheese and wine, an essential beverage at every Roman tavern. The Roman Empire provided the stability, ships, and roads that fostered trade in cheese and other foods, notably wine and olive oil. In the empire, Italy, Portugal, Spain, Anatolia, and Asia Minor (today Turkey), Greece, Gaul (today

France), North Africa, Egypt, and the northern provinces all produced cheese. The Romans provisioned their army with cheese as the Hittites had. Even during Roman antiquity, the parts of northern Europe outside the empire produced cheese to trade with Rome. Eastern Europe and Russia were large cheese producers in antiquity.

China was not a large cheese producer or consumer. The Chinese thought of cheese as a food of the uncivilized nomads to the north. The Chinese were civilized and so did not eat a barbarian food. Today, Southeast Asia and India consume little cheese. Central and southern Africa produces and consumes little cheese. Before European contact, cheese was unknown in the Americas and Australia. Ethiopia and Somalia, perhaps inheriting the cheese-making tradition from Egypt, produce and consume cheese. One should note the large culinary role that cheese has played throughout history. Among other foods, the cheeseburger and the sandwich in general, pizza, and macaroni and cheese could not exist without cheese. These foods have become worldwide staples thanks to cheese.

Cheese and the Decline of Rome

Sedentary people and nomads have long had cheese, which has been particularly important to nomads. Traveling with their herds, these nomads had ready access to milk, and thus cheese. Because it is durable and portable, cheese made possible vast migrations by these peoples. Early on, the tradition developed that horsemen would carry cheese with them. These horsemen made a ferocious army. They could eat cheese on horseback or whenever they dismounted. These cheese-eating nomads had an enormous effect on the rise and fall of civilizations.

Rome provides an example. The empire had made possible a period of relative peace that fostered trade and the exchange of ideas. But by the end of the second century CE Rome was increasingly beset by these nomads, many of them originating in the Asian steppe. For the purpose of defense, Rome had to raise ever-larger armies, but this practice was costly. Like many civilizations before and since, Rome funded its armies by raising taxes. Then as now, the tax burden fell disproportionately on those least able to afford it: the small farmers who kept the empire afloat. Many abandoned their land to escape taxes, worsening Rome's plight. With the decline in arable land, Roman food production fell, contributing to the empire's decline. In desperation, Diocletan (a typical emperor in having first been a general), moved to fix the peasant family on the land by making it illegal for a farm worker to leave the land on which he or she toiled. The cheese-eating nomad had thus been a factor in the rise of serfdom, a situation akin to slavery that would haunt Europe during the Middle Ages and Russia into the 19th century. Ultimately, by the fifth century, these nomads carved up the empire, which ceased to exist, leaving a Europe that was smaller, more rural, and beholden to the Christian church for some semblance of order.

Cheese and the Rise of the Mongol Empire

At its zenith, the Mongol Empire was the world's largest contiguous empire, stretching from the Sea of Japan in the east to the Carpathian Mountains in the west. This empire began to take shape in the 13th century, when the cheese-eating nomads of Mongolia and Turkic peoples, also nourished on cheese, allied, laying a foundation for an army of skilled horsemen as had occurred during the late Roman Empire. In the early 13th century, Mongol leader Genghis Khan furthered the process of unification, creating the Great Mongol Nation. Under his leadership, the Mongols conquered Ningxin and Gansu provinces in China, taking the rest of northern China in 1211. By 1216, little of China remained independent from Mongolia. Meanwhile, in 1209, a second Mongol army turned to Central Asia. Taking these lands, the Mongols absorbed Muslims into their growing empire. What are today Afghanistan, Iran, and parts of Iraq all fell to the Mongols. Although Genghis Khan could be ruthless, his real interest appears to have been the advancement of trade. Armenia and Georgia fell to the assault of his second son, Ogodei. The Mongols over-ran Russia in pursuit of the armies of Hungary and Poland. By the mid-13th century, what was left of southern China had fallen to the Mongols. Baghdad, Iraq, and Aleppo and Damascus, Syria, capitulated. Ultimately, Egypt forced the Mongols out of Syria, and in the east the Mongols failed to capture Japan. By taking Syria (today Turkey), the Mongols had an outlet to the Mediterranean Sea, long important in trade.

Warfare was only part of the Mongol achievement. These nomads brought writing to Mongolia, laid a foundation for the rise of the Ottoman Empire in Turkey, and encouraged the formation of cities in Central Asia. The Mughal Empire in India was an offshoot of the Mongol Empire. By virtue of its size, the Mongols promoted trade and spread ideas throughout Eurasia. As Rome had earlier, the Mongols provided the stability essential for vigorous commerce. This trade included the migration of printing, gunpowder, and the blast furnace west from China. The Mongols promoted the sciences of astronomy and medicine. They promoted Buddhism, taking particular interest in religious developments in Tibet. By the 16th century, Mongolia was a Buddhist land. The Mongols were also interested in Islam and Christianity, even inviting the pope to send theologians to instruct them in the precepts of Christianity. Perhaps shortsightedly, the pope refused. If cheese had laid the groundwork for the destruction of Rome, it had allowed the Mongols to soar, though like all empires, that of the Mongols was fleeting.

Further Reading

Dalby, Andrew. *Cheese: A Global History*. London: Reaktion Books, 2009.

Chicken

Chicken has been an important food for perhaps the last 12,000 years. At the same time, the chicken has been a religious symbol, a circumstance that would emanate from Southeast or perhaps southwestern Asia to Africa and, through the slave trade, to the Americas. Africans played an important role in developing the culinary and religious context of the modern chicken. One often thinks of a white man, Colonel Sanders, as the king of fried chicken, when it was actually an African American dish before it attracted attention from whites. There is controversy over the nutritional value of fried chicken, though physicians and nutritionists often tout the value of baked or grilled chicken. Chicken appears to be a food of choice among bodybuilders and other athletes.

Origins as Food and Religious Symbol

From the outset, the chicken was not just an edible item. It was a symbol for a variety of polytheistic religions. As a religious symbol, the chicken would exert great influence in shaping the world from antiquity almost to the present. For all its importance, the chicken's evolutionary roots are not entirely clear. British naturalist Charles Darwin traced the chicken's ancestors to the Red Jungle Fowl of Southeast Asia, and there is support for this view. Those in Darwin's camp pinpoint the domestication of the chicken in Southeast Asia to between 7500 and 5000 BCE. There is an older tradition, however, that favors southwestern Asia as the domesticator as early as 10,000 BCE. A third option might be to suppose independent domestication in each region, a position that would give southwestern Asia priority. The southwestern Asia scenario fascinated the Greeks, who believed that Persia (today Iran) was the source of the chicken. Accordingly, the Greeks called the chicken the "Persian bird."

In this thinking, as well as in a religious context, the chicken was important to Persia. Mithras, the Persian sun god, who would take on additional influence among the mystery cults of the Greco-Roman world, was the protector of chickens. Zoroastrianism, a Persian religion that influenced Christianity, held that the chicken was a divine animal that protected one against evil. Some Zoroastrians likened chickens to angels. In this context one may note that Zoroastrianism created many of the spiritual beings that would populate Christianity. There is some tendency, for example, to see in the evil god Ahriman the precursor of Satan, though to be fair, Satan appears to have been a Hebrew creation.

Perhaps in the first or second century CE the Egyptians began eating chickens. By then, Egypt was part of the Roman Empire, making it tempting to wonder whether Rome had given Egypt the chicken. Other scholars place the chicken in Egypt much earlier. Curiously, given the chicken's widespread religious symbolism and the Egyptian fascination with religion, the Egyptians did not regard the chicken as a divine bird. It was fit only for eating. The pyramid builders ate chicken as part of their compensation. The ancient Egyptians may have eaten some 20 million chickens per year.

The Greeks may have been the first to subject the chicken to scientific inquiry, creating a sort of poultry science that would influence the United States, where the U.S. Department of Agriculture, the land-grant universities and the agricultural experiment stations all studied chickens with the aim of creating a creature with ever larger breasts. Greek philosopher Plato was interested in the chicken's biped locomotion, which he compared to bipedalism in humans. His pupil Aristotle pioneered the study of chicken embryology. Yet the chicken remained important as a religious symbol. At the end of Plato's dialogue the *Phaedo*, Socrates, on the point of death, asks a friend to sacrifice a cock to Aesculapius, the god of health, perhaps in hopes of gaining immortality. If this interpretation is true, it marks a watershed in Plato's thought. The Socrates of an earlier dialogue, the *Apology*, appears to have been an agnostic who thought that an afterlife might or might not exist, but the Socrates of the *Phaedo* emerges as a man of both faith and reason. Either Socrates or Plato changed his mind between the two dialogues. Another possibility is that in the *Apology*, Plato sought to capture Socrates's thought as faithfully as possible. By the Phaedo, however, Plato had become more intent on expressing his own ideas rather than those of Socrates. Images of chickens were chiseled on tombs, again as a symbol of the afterworld. The chicken played other roles in Greece. It symbolized fertility and eroticism, much the place that wine and the god Dionysus held in the Greek imagination.

The Romans may have acquired the chicken from Etruria in the north. Like the Greeks, Persians, and many other ancients, the Romans believed the chicken to be sacred. The Romans may have originated the tradition that a wishbone could grant the wish of a person with the good fortune to break off a larger part of the bone. For all the religious symbolism of Greece, Persia, and Rome, Christianity, which arose during the high empire (200 BCE—200 CE), drained the chicken of religious content. In its place were fish, bread, and wine.

Whatever their role in the domestication of the chicken, the people of Southeast Asia believed that the bird was divine. They thought the chicken could predict the future, perhaps because of a cock's reliability in announcing the coming of dawn. The Arabs, Greeks, Phoenicians, and Romans all delighted in eating chicken.

From the outset, then, the chicken shaped the world as both food and religious symbol. The thought that the chicken was divine, however, does not quite square with the fact that it could be killed or die from any of a variety of causes.

The African and African American Context

In an African and African American context the consumption of chicken may be inseparable from the tradition of frying foods. This tradition may predate the arrival of Africans in the Americas and may instead be part of West African traditions before European contact. Africans would take this West African tradition to the New World. It is possible that the Arabs introduced the chicken into West Africa sometime before European contact, meaning the coming of the Portuguese to sub-Saharan Africa in the early modern era. Since antiquity, North Africa was part of Mediterranean commerce and has shared a different fate than sub-Saharan Africa. It seems likely that the Arabs from North Africa took the chicken south. The introduction may date to about 1000 CE. In West Africa as well as in the Americas, the consumption of fried chicken was a social event. The consumption of fried chicken was a way of affirming one's African roots.

West Africans told religious myths about chickens in the way that the Hebrews mythologized the "forbidden fruit." The Yoruba of Nigeria believed that the god Oduduwa used chickens to transmit messages to humans. Unlike Europeans and Asians, West Africans had no interest in cockfighting because such behavior devalued an animal with a putatively religious pedigree. West Africans had been fond of other birds as well, but the chicken took precedence over these lesser birds. Images of chickens emblazoned architecture and served as art in much the way that potato flowers would in 18th-century France. West Africans sacrificed chickens to their gods, a practice that must have been nearly ubiquitous, though in the Americas, humans turned to human sacrifice. Because elites owned chickens, they possessed a superior source of wisdom than was available to commoners. Through chickens, the elites had direct access to the gods, a benefit commoners did not share.

In culinary terms, West Africans combined chicken and rice. One thinks of rice as an Asian plant, but one must remember that a subspecies of rice is native only to Africa, and that it was this rice that Africans ate. Fried chicken remains important in West Africa. In fact, West Africa may have been the cradle of fried chicken because the region was awash in vegetable oils of many types. Yet, at least in African American circles, chicken tended to be fried in lard rather than vegetable oils, leaving the connection to West Africa uncertain. In fact, the use of lard for frying chickens remained an African American tradition into the 1970s. If the chicken was the food of elites, there appears to be paradoxical evidence that every West African household owned chickens, just as every 19th-century Irish household owned a pig, or perhaps a milk cow. The Irish owned chickens as well.

Chickens were important to the slave economy in the Americas. Masters gave slaves, many of them women, the task of raising, slaughtering, and preparing chickens for the white elites. As slaves made the transition to Christianity, the African American minister emerged as a person of special regard. From an early date, then, fried chicken was part of the African American-Protestantism complex. African Americans steeped in this tradition refer to the chicken as the "Gospel bird." In the African American South, fried chicken was a staple of Sunday dinner in the way that church service was obligatory on Sundays. From the time of slavery grew the tradition of inviting the minister to the home of a congregant to enjoy a dinner of fried chicken. Fried chicken was important as a staple of slaves, and later freed persons, and part of African American identity. These dinners were special occasions. The minister, who often had little money, at least had the good fortune of commandeering the best pieces of chicken for his plate. The family that had invited him, especially the children, were left with little chicken to claim as their own. The religious hierarchy of African American society dictated these terms. In this way grew the association between fried chicken, Sundays, and the ministry. The chicken dinner was a way of respecting the minister as the representative of God. Racist whites lumped African Americans with chicken.

As African Americans came north for industrial jobs during the 20th century, they settled in cities, where chicken was less common, so they may have eaten less chicken. But this was not necessarily so. African Americans turned to street vendors for fried chicken the way that many Americans turned to street vendors for hamburgers and hot dogs. The street vendor who sold fried chicken was usually a black man, whose clientele was multiracial. African Americans who established restaurants served fried chicken, though this number would likely have been larger had white bankers been willing to lend blacks money. This injustice remains today. These restaurants, in keeping with tradition, featured fried chicken on Sundays. Black churches also served fried chicken during fundraisers in the way that Italian Catholic churches held spaghetti and meatball fundraisers. Some African American restaurants have been prominent in their mastery of fried chicken: Ezell's in Seattle, French's in Houston, The Golden Bird in Los Angeles, and Harold's in Chicago. Note the importance of northern cities like Chicago and Seattle. Asian Americans and Latinos have embraced African American fried chicken. At first soul food, fried chicken has been a signature dish in America.

Further Reading

Miller, Adrian. *Soul Food: The Surprising Story of an American Cuisine, One Plate at a Time.* Chapel Hill: The University of North Carolina Press, 2003.

Percy, Pam. *The Complete Chicken: An Entertaining History of Chickens*. New York: Crestline, 2011.

Smith, Page, and Charles Daniel. *The Chicken Book*. Athens: The University of Georgia Press, 2000.

Chickpea

A legume, chickpea (*Cicer arietinum*) is in the family Fabaceae, or Leguminosae, and the genus *Cicer*. *Cicer* has some 40 species, many of them perennial, but the cultivated chickpea is an annual. Of *Cicer*'s species, only *Cicer arietinum* is cultivated. Chickpea is of two types. Kabuli has large, light-colored seeds, whereas desi contains small, dark seeds. Kabuli is native to the Mediterranean Basin and western Asia. Desi is native to India and eastern Asia. Despite its name, the chickpea is not a pea, though it shares with peas a round shape. The chickpea may be more closely related to beans than peas. One account holds that chickpea derives its name from the seed's resemblance to a chicken's head. Chickpea is also known

A legume, the chickpea is an important source of protein. Because it is an edible seed, the chickpea may be consumed or saved for next year's planting. (Sever180/Dreamstime.com)

Columella

Born about 4 CE, Lucius Junius Moderatus Columella ranks among the great agricultural writers in history. His 12-volume treatise, *On Agriculture*, has been consulted from antiquity to the present. He may have been a native of Spain and served in the Roman army, likely as an officer. Upon retirement, he bought a large estate, devoting the rest of his life to the study of agriculture. This was not a peculiarity. Rome had always valued its farmers for their piety, hard work, and thrift. To be a great Roman was to be a great farmer. Columella explored every aspect of farming, focusing attention on the maintenance of soil fertility. He ranked the dung of various animals for their value in improving soils, and he was among the early advocates of legumes for their role in maintaining fertility. In this context, he was an early advocate of the chickpea and lentil, both as foods and as soil improvers. He died about 70 CE. So little is known about his life that even the dates of his birth and death are contested.

as garbanzo bean. The word "chickpea" may derive from the Italian *ceci*. The Arabs know chickpea as *hamaz*, Ethiopians as *shimbra*, Turks as *nohund* or *lablebi*, Indians as *chana*, and the people of Latin America as *garbanzo*, from which garbanzo bean must derive. Chickpea is related to beans, soybeans, peas, lentils, clover, and alfalfa.

Origin and History

A crop of the temperate zone and subtropics, chickpea was first eaten in Syria in the eighth millennium BCE and in Turkey about 7500 BCE. These dates may represent the gathering of chickpeas from the wild rather than their culture. The discovery of chickpeas in Damascus, Syria, dating from the seventh millennium BCE, in an area apart from the geography of wild chickpea, implies that Syrians brought chickpea to Damascus, cultivating it there. This early date of cultivation makes chickpea among the oldest crops, and for that reason it has shaped the history of the Levant and western Asia in general. Humans domesticated it about the time that they began cultivating wheat and barley. From an early date, chickpea must have been an important source of protein given the relative paucity of the nutrient in grains. One authority believes, however, that southwestern Turkey, rather than Syria, was the site of chickpea domestication. The chickpea was abundant during the Bronze Age (fourth to second millennium BCE). In Bronze Age Israel, Jordan, and Jericho, the presence of large seeds suggests human selection and cultivation. By the Bronze Age, people in Greece (including Crete), Egypt, Ethiopia, Mesopotamia (present-day Iraq), India, and Pakistan grew chickpea. By the third millennium BCE, the people of what is today southern France were growing chickpea.

In the ninth century BCE, the Greek poet Homer regarded chickpea as food and medicine. In ancient Rome and India, chickpea was likewise food and medicine. The ancients ate chickpea after dinner as a snack, taking it with a beverage. In this context, the Greek philosopher Plato mentioned chickpea in the *Republic* as a snack. First-century-CE Roman encyclopedist Pliny the Elder called chickpea the "pea of Venus," perhaps referring to its aphrodisiac properties. His contemporary, the agricultural writer Columella, took the chickpea more seriously. He encouraged his readers, all of them likely large landowners, to plant chickpeas. He understood two points in favor of the chickpea. First, Columella understood that there was a large market for chickpeas. They could be sold in bulk to the masses. In this sense, the chickpea shaped history and daily life as a good source of protein for commoners, who did not always have access to meat or fish. Columella also understood that chickpeas somehow enriched the soil. He knew that a crop that followed chickpeas in rotation yielded better than a crop that was grown on fallowed land. No one then knew the principal of nitrogen fixation, but one did not need this knowledge to appreciate the value of chickpeas, and any legume, in rotation with other crops. In boosting yields, the chickpea must have helped sustained agriculture at a time when farming was largely a subsistence activity, and in this way it helped shape the Roman Empire.

Perhaps in the context of the assertion that the chickpea was an aphrodisiac, Galen, physician to second-century-CE Roman emperor Marcus Aurelius, asserted that chickpea increased sperm production. Galen thought that chickpea was more nutritious than beans and caused less flatulence. Here, too, Galen promoted the chickpea as food of the masses. Galen mentioned that the ancients ate chickpea in soup and with milk, and ground it into flour. The ancients salted and added dried cheese to whole chickpeas. They ate chickpea raw or roasted, much as Americans eat roasted peanuts. The Romans regarded chickpea as an important food of the poor. To call someone a "buyer of roasted chickpeas" was to say that he was poor.

In the Middle Ages, Europeans retained the ancient conviction that chickpea was food and medicine. Italian and Spanish cookbooks included recipes for chickpea. On Fridays, Jews cooked a stew with chickpea, eating it on the Sabbath. After 1492, the Spanish Inquisition, intent on apprehending Jews, took the consumption of chickpea as evidence of Jewishness. In the eastern Mediterranean Basin, people ground chickpea into flour, making it into flat cakes. The French made a type of pancake from chickpea. In South and western Asia people made hummus, a popular dish that featured the chickpea as the main ingredient. Here, as in Rome, chickpeas were the food of the masses, again shaping history and daily life by giving people a cheap but nourishing source of protein.

In the 16th century, the Spanish and Portuguese brought chickpea to the Americas. In the 18th century, merchants carried kabuli chickpeas along the Silk Road from the Mediterranean to India. In the 19th century, Indians brought desi chickpeas to Kenya. Today, the United States grows kabuli for export to Europe. Mexico also harvests kabuli, much of it for export. Afghanistan grows chickpea in the provinces of Takhar, Kunduz, Herat, Badakhshan, Mazar-Sharif, Smangan, Ghazni, and Zabal. Afghans grow kabuli and desi without irrigation, rotating them with wheat. The Chinese cultivate chickpea in the provinces of Xianjiang, Gansu, Qinghai, Inner Mongolia, Yunnan, Shanxi, Ninjxia, Hebei, and Heilongjiang. In India, farmers plant chickpea on one-quarter of land devoted to legumes. Chickpea totals nearly half of India's legume harvest. After beans, chickpea is the most widely grown legume for human consumption. Ideal for semiarid regions, chickpea tolerates drought better than do soybean and pea. Today nearly 50 nations cultivate chickpea. By one estimate, the Mediterranean Basin, including North Africa, the Middle East, and India, produce two-thirds of the global harvest of chickpea. Another estimate holds that India produces four-fifths of the world's chickpeas. In this sense the chickpea is a world crop.

Nutrition and Consumption

Although people in the developed world eat only the seed, in the developing world people eat the seed and leaves. The seed contains protein, fiber, calcium, potassium, phosphorus, iron, and magnesium. Chickpea leaves contain more calcium, phosphorus, and potassium than spinach or cabbage. The leaves also have iron, zinc, and magnesium. In the temperate zone, people couple chickpea with grain, and in the tropics, with roots and tubers, to pair protein and carbohydrates.

Worldwide, the Turks eat the most chickpeas. Whereas chickpea consumption has declined in Pakistan, it has risen in Myanmar, Jordan, and Iran. The people of India, Pakistan, and Bangladesh grind chickpea into flour known as *besan,* combining it with wheat flour to make roti or chapati. The people of the Indian subcontinent eat chickpea leaves in addition to the seeds. They eat young chickpea pods the way Westerners eat young pea pods. Stockmen in this region of Asia feed chickpea to their animals. Growing desi, India imports kabuli from Mexico, Australia, Iran, and Turkey, and desi from Myanmar. In India, the chief regions of chickpea consumption are Punjab, Harayana, Rajasthan, and western Utter Pradesh.

Of the chickpeas that Americans eat, half is whole chickpea, much of it canned. Americans consume 30 percent of their chickpeas in soup. Mexicans consume whole chickpeas from cans. In the United States and Mexico, people eat whole chickpeas in salad and stew. Peruvians eat chickpea with rice or vegetables. The faithful of the Ethiopian Coptic Church eat chickpea as a substitute for fish during the months of fasting. Again, chickpeas made up for the protein deficit that would have resulted from abstinence from fish. Ethiopians combine chickpea with soybean and wheat to make *faffa*, a food for children. The people of Sudan and Egypt eat chickpea during Ramadan, combining it with sesame oil, salt, onion, chili pepper, garlic, and baking powder. Tunisians boil chickpea, adding salt and pepper. In the Middle East, as noted earlier, people eat hummus, a dish of mashed chickpea, and also consume chickpea in salad and soup. Israelis prefer kabuli to desi. They eat chickpea with rice and meat or roast it as a snack. Iraqis boil and roast chickpea, add it to soup, and eat it raw. Syrians consume three-quarters of their chickpeas as hummus. Iranians cook kabuli with rice. Afghans combine chickpea and meat and eat roasted chickpea with dried fruit. Like Israelis, Afghans prefer kabuli. The Chinese fry chickpea, salt it, and eat it as a snack. They also bake and boil chickpea, serving it with rice. The people of Myanmar substitute chickpea for soybean, making a kind of tofu.

Further Reading

Albala, Ken. *Beans: A History*. Oxford: Berg, 2007.

Columella, Lucius Junius Moderatus. *On Agriculture*. Cambridge, MA: Harvard University Press, 1979.

Maiti, Ratikanta, and Pedro Wesche-Ebeling. *Advances in Chickpea Science*. Enfield, NH: Science Publishers, 2001.

Saxena, M. C., and K. B. Singh, eds. *The Chickpea*. Wallingford, UK: CAB International, 1987.

Yadav, S. S., R. J. Redden, W. Chen, and B. Sharma, eds. *Chickpea Breeding and Management*. Wallingford, UK: CAB International, 2007.

Chili

Chili is a mysterious food whose origins are not entirely clear. Its origins are almost surely Mexican, but it is now a dish primarily of white Americans. Once a simple dish of beef and pepper, chili is now tied to the kidney bean of American renown, and often to the chili pepper, another American food plant. Chili is thus a food of the Columbian Exchange, with beef and pepper from the Old World and the kidney bean and chili pepper from the Americas. In this respect, chili is a polyglot food, and has risen in importance partly because of its mixed heritage.

San Antonio

As shown, chili's origins may be a bit murky. It seems possible that it originated in what is today Texas but was then *Tejas*, part of northern Mexico—at least those Mexican lands north of the Rio Grande. San Antonio, Texas may be the place of origin, and certainly was vocal in promoting chili. San Antonio may have been the national capital of chili before 1880. Although the date of invention is obscure, it must have been sometime in the 1870s, perhaps some three decades after Texas joined the United States. This entrance to the United States did not automatically make Texas white. The state still had and has a large number of people of Mexican descent. White Texans and the state's Mexican inhabitants knew the meal as *chile con carne*, though now it is known simply as "chili."

Initially a dish of beef and pepper, chili now contains the kidney bean, a member of the genus *Phaseolus*, the world's most important source of beans. One may also add American chili peppers to enhance spiciness. Americans who visited Texas in the late 19th century were eager to sample a bowl of chili. In the 19th century, large stretches of Texas were given over to rangeland for grazing cattle. In this environment, what could be more natural than to create a dish featuring beef as the main ingredient? Chili thus shaped history as a marker of the Texas economy. One might note that the Amerindians knew nothing about beef. Only after European contact did the Spanish import cattle into the Americas. The abundance of cattle, not only in North America, led Americans to consume large quantities of beef. In many respects, the United States remains a nation of beefeaters. One need only witness the success of McDonald's to verify this fact. So plentiful was beef in the 19th century that Texans regarded it as ubiquitous as water. In Texas, women tended to make and sell chili. The more attractive the woman, the more customers she enticed. These women tended to sell chili at lunch and at dusk, when cattlemen came in from the grasslands. Chili provided a quick meal to busy people, serving the same function as the hot dog and hamburger; in this way it shaped history as a food of the bustling masses. Some vendors hired musicians to attract attention.

Chili was a holdover of Mexican lifeways and of people who were not sure that they wanted to be part of the United States, whose nascent industries seemed to threaten the agrarian ways of a prideful past. Writers who visited San Antonio were struck by this nostalgia for the past. It seemed to some that the Mexicans of the 19th century still inhabited the 17th century. Chili asserted a sense of pride and a celebration of the past, even if it was a novel food in the 19th century. Yet Texas was changing. Mexican cuisine, including chili, was attracting Americans of European ancestry to Texas. Demographics were changing in a region still attached to its Mexican roots. If chili was a Texas food, Mexicans, remembering the days when Texas was part of Mexico, embraced the food as authentic Mexican cuisine. Mexicans ate the spiciest chili and drank the bitterest coffee, according to critics, though this criticism had no effect on the restaurants that grew up near the Alamo to sell chili to tourists. Many of the Mexicans who prepared chili claimed descent from the Aztecs, surely in an effort to impress tourists. Their real lineage, however, probably traced to Spain or West Africa, given the frequency of inter-breeding among Native Americans, Spanish, and Africans. This is an important point because, even in the United States, though the taboo was strong, people of European and African ancestry interbred. In this context, chili was a food that brought people together. Some Americans, ensnared in gender and ethnic biases, dismissed the women who cooked and served chili as primitive. Even American author Stephen Crane was unkind in his estimation of these women, describing only the young as beautiful. As for the aged, he considered them ugly. Americans with an open mind and open eyes confessed their attraction to these women, calling them "chili queens."

The 1893 World's Columbian Exposition

One account holds that the Texas delegation to the 1893 World's Columbian Exposition in Chicago opened the San Antonio Chili Stand, attracting worldwide notice. The curious were only too eager to eat a bowl of chili. At last, chili had risen to fame, though if chili had really been invented a little before 1880, then its rise to eminence must have been rapid. Given the magnitude of this event, it is curious that no contemporary accounts exist of the San Antonio Chili Stand. San Antonio's two newspapers were silent, though they described the exposition in detail. Surely they would not have overlooked the stand. Likewise, newspapers in Chicago said nothing about the San Antonio Chili Stand. It seems, therefore, not to have existed but to have been a creature of later legend. Indeed, the official cookbook of the exposition includes a Texas recipe for almonds and other ingredients but mentions nothing about chili. Only in 1927 did the legend begin, spurred by Texas tax commissioner Frank Bushick. His name seems thoroughly European, but it is not known whether he had any Mexican ancestors. More importantly, did Bushick have any knowledge of the World's Columbian Exposition that was unavailable in 1893? It is entirely possible that the San Antonio Chili Stand was "invented" after the fact. Rather, Bushick was an up-and-coming businessman who wanted to promote San Antonio in particular and Texas in general. The legend of The San Antonio Chili Stand must have been Bushick's way of promoting both San Antonio and chili. Chili must have been an important food to have garnered this attention.

In fact, the exposition may have been less important than one might imagine. Chili had become something of a national dish before the exposition. Restaurants in several states served chili in the 1880s. That decade, newspapers in Washington,

DC and Hawaii (Hawaii was not yet a state) praised chili, recommending it to their readers. In 1889, the Paris World's Fair featured canned chili, which must have been shipped from the United States to France. The Chicago company Libby, McNeil and Libby took credit for showcasing canned chili at this world's fair. Even if there was no San Antonio Chili Stand at the 1893 exposition, it seems certain that a number of canners advertised chili there. If San Antonio was the innovator, Chicago appears to have emerged as the national publicist of chili. By the 1890s, the kidney bean had become a staple in chili. During the depression between 1893 and 1897, many Americans lost work and could afford little food. Some historians rank this depression and not the Great Depression as the worst in American history. Chili fit the bill during lean times because it was nutritious and inexpensive.

San Antonio Again

Ironically, San Antonio turned against chili, or at least against its makers, about 1890. Mayor Bryan Callaghan erected several buildings near the Alamo, evicting the vendors who had sold chili. He had no patience with what had become a Chicago food. Defiant, the vendors crept back to the Alamo, daring to sell chili without a license. In the 1930s, San Antonio required vendors to register with the health department, convinced that they harbored disease. Fearing contagion, the mayor required them to serve chili in screened tents. If the screening inhibited the penetration of mosquitoes and flies it was useless to prevent the spread of pathogens, and so was misguided policy from the standpoint of epidemiology. Patrons, of course, did not wish to venture into these tents, and by the end of World War II, the chili queens were gone. What had once been a Mexican food is now the tidbit of whites, who likely devour it without full knowledge of its origins and colorful past.

Further Reading

Arellano, Gustavo. *TACO USA: How Mexican Food Conquered America*. New York: Scribner, 2012.

Pilcher, Jeffrey M. *Planet Taco: A Global History of Mexican Food*. Oxford and New York: Oxford University Press, 2012.

Chocolate

A recent food with paradoxically deep historical roots, chocolate is closely related to the Amerindian beverage cocoa. Both are products of the cacao tree, an American indigene. The chocolate familiar to Americans, Europeans, and Asians comes in

A cocoa farmer uses a machete to open a pod of raw cocoa for inspection on a cocoa plantation in Kumasi, Ghana. This raw product becomes the chocolate made in Switzerland and other confection-producing nations before export around the world. (David Snyder/Dreamstime.com)

bars and other treats. It is solid and packed with milk and sugar. In this sense, chocolate is a world product and has been important in the industrialization of food production, mass production, and mass consumption. In these attributes chocolate borrowed much from American meatpackers and automakers. Chocolate is a democratic treat, an inexpensive, rich combination of fat and sugar, both of which humans appear biologically to crave. If chocolate is part of human biology, it is also part of the advertising wizardry of U.S. capitalism. It has conquered Easter and Valentine's Day and become a favorite among children.

Origins and Early Importance

Chocolate is a product of the cacao tree, which is native to tropical America. Most trees grow very near the equator. Year-round warmth and moisture are essential to the tree's success. Chocolate is derived from the seeds of cacao trees, which the pods yield. These seeds are confusingly called "beans," but they bear no relation to true beans, which are all legumes. The Amerindians did not make chocolate, but rather the beverage cocoa, from cacao seeds. The potion contained chili peppers, which added a kick to the beverage. This spiciness struck Italian Spanish explorer

Christopher Columbus as bitterness. He sampled the drink in 1492 but confessed his dislike of it. About 1550, Italian adventurer Girolamo Berzoni had a similar encounter, though his reaction was not quite the same as Columbus's. Berzoni agreed that cocoa was too spicy, yet he admitted that it was a refreshing change from the monotonous consumption of water. Cocoa, according to Berzoni, had some pleasurable qualities and did not intoxicate one.

As is true with chocolate, the cacao seed, pulverized, is the source of cocoa. In this sense, one might argue that the Amerindians invented chocolate, or at least its precursor. Typically, cacao seeds must be fermented, a process akin to the production of alcoholic beverages, dried, roasted and pulverized. Although cacao originated near the equator, the Olmecs further north in Mesoamerica may have been the first to cultivate cacao for the purpose of making cocoa. Building on Olmec traditions, the Maya likewise made cocoa. In this context, cocoa, and later chocolate, were never as important as Amerindian staples like corn, beans, potatoes, sweet potatoes, and cassava, but they were essential to Amerindian lifeways, tracing their roots deep into Amerindian prehistory. The Maya held chocolate in special regard and may have been the first to call cacao the "chocolate tree." The Maya appear to have placed chocolate, or something akin to it, in tombs in the way that many ancients, like the Egyptians, put other foods in tombs. This act must have been a ceremonial and religious undertaking in which the Maya believed that the dead needed chocolate in the afterlife. So important was chocolate that the Aztecs demanded cacao seeds as tribute. This circumstance must have been necessary because the Aztecs, occupying the cool highlands of Mexico, could not grow tropical cacao trees for their own needs. Along with corn kernels, cacao seeds served as currency throughout Mexico and Central America. For example, a cotton garment cost about 100 cacao seeds during the brief tenure of the Aztecs.

The Secret is in the Seed

Chocolate is made from one of three types of cacao seeds. Criollo derives its name from the Spanish word for "indigenous." The criollo seed comes from trees grown in Mesoamerica. Enthusiasts prize the seeds as the most flavorful. The criollo seed yields a pleasant aroma and delicate flavor. Because the yield is low, criollo beans account for only 7 percent of the world's cacao beans. The criollo tree grows principally in Venezuela, Mexico, Nicaragua, Guatemala, Colombia, Trinidad, Grenada, and Jamaica. Given its high quality and dearth, the criollo seed is expensive.

The forastero seed derives from the Spanish word for "foreign." The tree that bears these seeds originated in the Amazon River basin. The Portuguese introduced forastero trees into the African island of São Tomé, from where it spread to West Africa. Having been transplanted into Africa, forastero produces most of the continent's cacao seeds. Growers also derive forastero seeds from Brazil and other parts of South America, Central America, and the Caribbean. Forastero is a fast-growing tree with greater hardiness and a higher yield than criollo. Although forastero produces the majority of the world's cacao harvest, it cannot claim the quality of criollo. Forastero seeds have a strong, bitter flavor and an acidic aroma, and so are often blended with other cacao seeds. The forastero seeds produced in Ecuador are higher in quality than most forastero seeds.

The trinitario seed derives from a tree that hybridized without human aid on the island of Trinidad. Trinitario trees are hybrids of criollo and forastero trees, both of which were planted on Trinidad. Trinitario seeds have a high fat content. These seeds account for about 7 percent of the world's cacao seeds. Grown in Central and South America, Indonesia, and Sri Lanka, the trinitario tree yields the highest quality cacao seeds in Trinidad.

The European Interlude

In the 16th century, Europeans acquired cacao seeds from Central and South America and began planting trees in the Old World tropics, with Indonesia receiving the first planting about 1520. The 16th century was an important moment in the evolution of chocolate. Europeans, establishing sugarcane plantations in tropical America, now had their own source of sugar, which they added to sweeten chocolate. Once the source of a bitter beverage, chocolate now tugged at Europe's sweet tooth. At the same time, consumption of cocoa declined in Europe through competition from coffee and tea, two other tropical products. In the 19th century, the true chocolate pioneers in the Netherlands, the United Kingdom, Switzerland, and later the United States began to manufacture chocolate bars. In 1875, the Swiss were the first to add milk to chocolate.

In the late 18th century, revolutions in the Caribbean endangered the supply of cacao seeds to the Old World, where consumption fell. Chocolate colonialism was under assault. The British naval blockage of France during the Napoleonic Wars decreased the import of cacao seeds into the continent. The 20th century marked the advent of the chocolate box, which contained assorted chocolates. The accent was on combination with other flavors, in deviation from Milton Hershey's experiments with chocolate in the United States. These boxes were part of the story of mass production and mass consumption, a theme almost as old as capitalism itself. Companies like Cadbury built their reputation and fortunes on boxed chocolates. In the 20th century, women and children became the primary consumers of chocolate at a moment when chocolate manufacturers were hiring women. This marked the sublimation of women, with them as laborers and men as supervisors. The chocolate workforce in France, the United Kingdom, Germany, and later the United States, became primarily female.

Women doubtless proved attractive because they commanded on average less pay than men. This differential remains a problem in modern America.

Chocolate and Forced Labor

With foment in tropical America, European colonists planted cacao trees in Africa and parts of Asia, especially Indonesia, and coerced labor to work on the new cacao estates. By 1910, the African island of São Tomé was the world's largest producer of cacao seeds. Today, Côte d'Ivoire and Ghana produce 70 percent of the world's cacao seeds. Europeans associated the blackness of chocolate with the blackness of the labor force. Chocolate had taken on racial overtones. Germany and Belgium knew one chocolate product as the "Negro kisses."

The Race to the South Pole

Chocolate may even have played a role in the race to the South Pole. Because it is calorie dense and because the effort to reach the pole was strenuous, explorers took chocolate as a ration. British explorer Robert Falcon Scott allotted each member of his team 4,430 calories, including 24 grams of chocolate, per day. The allowance was not enough. Scott's party reached the South Pole only to find that the Norwegians had beaten them. Exhausted and beset by terrible weather, Scott and his entire party perished on the return journey. Norwegian explorer Roald Amundsen allocated each member of his expedition 4,560 calories per day, including five times more chocolate than Scott and his men ate. Fortified with chocolate, Amundsen and his team were the first to claim the South Pole.

Triumph in America

In the 1820s, the Baker Company, founded by American chocolatier Walter Baker, began making chocolate and, in the process, creating the brownie. Baker also made chocolate cakes, with other baked goods following later. In 1893, Pennsylvania caramel maker Milton Hershey began manufacturing chocolate bars. So successful was this venture that by 1900 Hershey had abandoned caramel to concentrate all his business acumen and assets on chocolate. He benefited from his early reputation, forged by carmel, as a quality candy maker. Living in a dairy-rich region of the Keystone State, Hershey had easy access to milk, another worldwide food, for his chocolate bars. In 1907, Hershey created the Kiss, doubtless founded on the belief that chocolate was an aphrodisiac and a symbol of romance and fertility. He applied the methods of mass production and standardization that had resonated with the meatpacking and automobile industries. Every Hershey bar was cloned, with the same size and flavor. The same was true of Kisses. Like automaker Henry Ford, Hershey tamed the market for chocolate by building an economy of scale that offered inexpensive chocolate. As others had done before him, Hershey created a company town for his workers, though a more benevolent one than its predecessors. A fourth-grade dropout, Hershey grew to champion education and established schools for his workers and their children. As oil would for John D. Rockefeller, chocolate made Hershey an important philanthropist of the 20th century. Thanks to Hershey, chocolate was a food for the public good. It became a symbol of stewardship and an antidote for the harshness of American capitalism.

In 1930, Ruth Wakefield, owner of the Toll House Inn in Massachusetts, created the chocolate chip cookie, known as the Toll House cookie. By 1939, she had partnered with Nestle to mass-produce chocolate chips much as Hershey mass-produced chocolate bars and Kisses. These uses of chocolate are today foreign to the South American region where the cacao tree had arisen. For these people chocolate remains a spicy treat devoid of milk and sugar.

Further Reading

Bailleux, Nathalie, Herve Bizeul, John Felswell, Regine Kopp, Corby Kummer, Pierre Labanne, Christna Pauly, Odile Perrard, and Mariarosa Schiaffino. *The Book of Chocolate*. Paris: Fiammarion, 1995.

Beckett, Stephen T. *The Science of Chocolate*. Cambridge: RSC, 2008.

Coe, Sophie D., and Michael D. Coe. *The True History of Chocolate*. London: Thames and Hudson, 1996.

Foster, Nelson, and Linda S. Cordell. *Chilies to Chocolate: Food the Americas Gave the World*. Tucson, University of Arizona Press, 1992.

Moss, Sarah, and Alexander Bodenoch. *Chocolate: A Global History*. London: Reaktion Books, 2009.

Off, Carol. *Bitter Chocolate. The Dark Side of the World's Most Seductive Sweet*. New York: The New Press, 2006.

Presilla, Maricel E. *The New Taste of Chocolate: A Cultural and Natural History of Cacao with Recipes*. Berkeley, CA: Ten Speed Press, 2001.

Young, Allen M. *The Chocolate Tree: A Natural History of Cacao*. Gainesville: University Press of Florida, 2007.

Chop Suey

The phrase "chop suey" may derive from the Mandarin *za sui* or perhaps the Cantonese *shap sui*. If one considers the Cantonese variant, *shap* means "to mix together," a reference to the mix of ingredients that comprises chop suey. In both Mandarin and Cantonese, *sui* may be translated as "odds and ends," giving one the sense that chop suey is an eclectic combination of ingredients. Chop suey is among the authentic foods of China. Some journalists have lauded it as the "national dish" of China, though this may be hyperbole. In the 19th century, Chinese immigrants brought chop suey and other foods to the United States. Chop suey succeeded first along the East Coast, and from there it migrated to the Midwest. Curiously, it conquered the West Coast last even though California was the destination of Chinese immigrants.

The Introduction of Chop Suey into the United States in the 19th Century

Chinese cuisine did not receive an ovation when it entered the United States about 1840. Part of the problem stemmed from racism, the original sin that the Europeans committed when they populated the Americas. History textbooks do a good job of suggesting the fury and depth of white racism against African Americans. Less well known is the racism that confronted Asian Americans. As a brief note, we are stuck with the term "racism" as a historical artifact even as the term "race" draws criticism from biologists who do not believe that humans differ sufficiently in their genes to warrant racial categories. Even though the plight of Chinese Americans has received less attention than that of African Americans, California erupted in riots against the Chinese newcomers. Even President Theodore Roosevelt warned about the dangers of the "yellow peril." With the Chinese under suspicion, their food could not at first get a fair hearing. Moreover, Chinese cuisine was suspect because it was foreign. Yet the United States has done well to embrace the cuisines of other immigrant groups. The hamburger is as American as it is German, and spaghetti and meatballs are more than the exclusive preserve of Italians or Italian Americans. They are an American food.

The same has happened to Chinese food. As early as the 1850s, small numbers of Americans were familiar with chop suey, among other Chinese foods. The Chinese had much to do with moving Americans toward this transition. Chinese Americans planted gardens with Asian vegetables as they began to remake their environment into something that suited their culinary tastes. Each Chinese American family prided itself on having its own chop suey recipe. Americans were slow to gain familiarity with this new food, mispronouncing it as "chop soly" or "chow chop sui."

Chop suey often contained bacon and other cuts of pork, chicken, mushrooms, bamboo shoots, onion, and pepper, all Old World ingredients, though species of mushrooms are also native to the Americas. Other possibilities included duck, beef, turnip, black beans, yams, peas, and string beans. The black and string beans and peas are all legumes and so are good sources of protein. The black and string beans, but not peas, are native to the Americas, suggesting that chop suey, when it arrived in the United States, did not confine itself to the familiar foods of the Old World. Some Americans, usually journalists, believed that chop suey was China's national food, but others have protested such a grandiose label. Perhaps China is too large and diverse to herald a single food as its national dish.

Chop suey rose to prominence during what American author Mark Twain described as the Gilded Age, a time when a very few businessmen amassed colossal fortunes. They spent money with abandon on jewelry, real estate, oceangoing vessels, clothes, and food. Some of these plutocrats retained the belief that French cuisine was ever fashionable, but others departed from the norm and were willing to try other cuisines, including Chinese. These millionaires ate chop suey. For them it was fashionable to eat chop suey with tea, another putatively oriental food. The adventurous ate chop suey with rice liquor, an alcoholic beverage popular in China and what would become Southeast Asia, especially Vietnam (Under French rule, the region was known as French Indochina.). Chop suey came of age in New York City, whose Chinatown influenced the culinary habits of European Americans. In San Francisco, Mongolian immigrants ate chop suey, though the city, and California at large, were tardy in coming to appreciate chop suey.

The Chinese and Chinese Americans tend to fry the ingredients of chop suey, imparting a greasy texture and taste to the dish. In the United States, chop suey has been more a fad than an essential part of the nation's cuisine. It is not the hamburger or hot dog of Chinese cuisine. Americans tend to reduce the number of ingredients, though not by much. Americans tend to focus chop suey on the main ingredient of pork or chicken. Other ingredients may include bean sprouts, onion, celery, bamboo shoots, and water chestnuts. Americans tend to overcook these ingredients, leaving one an indistinct, insipid dish that does not truly satiate. Chop suey, at least in the 19th century, was often served over a plate of polished rice, even though Americans should have known that brown rice has many more nutrients than white rice. The vegetables suggest that chop suey is a nourishing food, though the white rice and lard in which the dish is fried may tempt one to believe that chop suey has too much fat and too many calories in general. The use of fish would appear to have been an appetizing addition. While it was sometimes incorporated into chop suey in the 19th century, fish is not a common ingredient today.

In the 19th century, Chinese Americans identified with chop suey the way that Bostonians hankered for baked beans. That century, chop suey was a food of China and Hong Kong. When Chinese dignitaries visited the United States, Americans were astonished to learn that they did not eat chop suey. Perhaps chop suey was not China's national dish after all. The *Brooklyn Eagle* nonetheless urged Americans to eat chop suey, sensing that the United States was in the midst of a mania for all things Chinese. Another newspaper, however, reported the "queer foods" that the Chinese ate. (The meaning of "queer" then had nothing to do with gay and lesbian studies.) At the height of popularity. Chinese American restaurants were known as "chop sueys." Many Americans thought of chop suey as a type of stew, but it was really more akin to a stir-fry.

The 20th and 21st Centuries

The early 20th century witnessed a period of rapid reconfiguration of Chinese foods to make them more pleasurable to European Americans. It became popular to eat chop suey with a platter of Saratoga chips (potato chips). In some circles, rice was on the way out. Instead, restaurants served chop suey on a plate of noodles. This was hardly a move away from authenticity because the Chinese likely invented noodles sometime before the 13th century. Unlike rice, noodles consist of a special type of wheat known as durum. Durum is the hardest wheat with the highest quantity of protein and so is a good dietary choice.

Some Americans thought of chop suey as a food of African Americans and the poor, though this view appears to have been conjecture. Nonetheless, journalists linked African Americans and Chinese Americans, both inferior races. The early 20th century was a terrible time in the history of racial and social relations, and so for chop suey as well. The eugenics movement, strong in the United States, the United Kingdom, and Germany, was a rehashing of old racial attitudes. Eugenicists secured the passage of laws forbidding intermarriage between blacks and whites, lest blacks pollute the racial purity of whites. These ideas drew on old stereotypes of black women and men as unable to control their libidos. By nature, it was believed, they forced themselves on white men and women who were too immature to understand that such overtures were dangerous to the survival of the white race. In Philadelphia, Race Street passed through Chinatown. This language was probably no accident. Chop suey thus became code for the old racial attitudes that the new eugenics movement had unleashed.

Nonetheless during the early 20th century chop suey grew in popularity along the East Coast. Artists and academics ate chop suey at Chinese restaurants, feeling that they had reached the pinnacle of sophistication. With chop suey established on the East Coast, a movement toward the Midwest was natural and probably inevitable. Among Midwestern cities, Chicago and St. Louis were probably the earliest adopters of chop suey. Asian restaurants offered not only chop suey but foods more in line with Midwestern tastes: corned beef, egg sandwiches, and potato salad. One could thus visit a Chinese restaurant without eating anything remotely

Chinese. In this way, chop suey and other Chinese foods made headway with European Americans. American author Theodore Dreiser took interest in Chinese foods, describing several dishes, though one is left to wonder whether any of them were chop suey. By the 1920s, chop suey was a staple in Chicago; St. Louis; Kansas City, Missouri; and Minneapolis. This was progress for a food that had invaded the corn kingdom.

Curiously, the West Coast, where the Chinese immigrants had disembarked, was the last region of the United States to welcome chop suey. San Francisco, borrowing the language of race, depicted chop suey as a food of African Americans and Irish immigrants. As in the Midwest, chop suey had to accommodate American tastes. The restaurants that served chop suey also sold ham and omelets. Where chop suey became part of the culinary fabric of the United States, Americans came to appreciate it as an inexpensive, filling, and putatively exotic food. The Far East had come to the United States in a bowl of chop suey.

Further Reading

Coe, Andrew. *Chop Suey: A Cultural History of Chinese Food in the United States.* Oxford: Oxford University Press, 2009.

Cider

There is confusion over the use of the terms "cider" and "hard cider." Some writers use "cider" as shorthand for "hard cider," but one must draw a distinction. Hard cider is an alcoholic beverage made from apple juice. For millennia, hard cider was all humankind knew because over time and at room temperature all apple juice ferments. In essence, there was then no distinction between hard cider and cider. This reason must have caused people to conflate the two. The 20th century, with the era of refrigeration, changed all this. Refrigerated apple juice did not ferment. This marked the beginning of the era of cider and the consumption of a nonalcoholic beverage made from apple juice. Cider and hard cider are no longer synonyms. Because of the importance of hard cider over millennia, this entry will focus primarily on it, using the term "cider" to mean hard cider.

Europe

The preparation of hard cider is straightforward. One need only crush apples to obtain juice. Allowed to sit, this juice grows cloudy and, over a few weeks,

In the era before refrigeration all cider contained alcohol and so was an important adjunct to beer and wine, though the alcohol content of cider (now known as hard cider) could not match the potency of spirits. The cider that one buys from the grocer on Halloween does not contain alcohol. (Václav Psota/Dreamstime.com)

ferments. For millennia in Europe, the primary use of apples was to make hard cider rather than to serve as fresh fruit. Hard cider has about half the alcohol of wine and was a safe drink in an era when drinking water was suspect. Before the advent of the chlorination of water, the liquid could harbor the cholera bacillus or other harmful microbes. Indeed, cholera was frequently fatal. The alcohol in hard cider, on the other hand, killed microbes and so was safe to drink. For this reason people drank hard cider as the beverage of choice in northern latitudes rather than water. One could always mix hard cider with water to be sure of having sufficient quantities to drink.

No one is certain where or when hard cider originated. When Roman patrician and military leader Julius Caesar invaded Britain in the first century BCE he found the Celts making hard cider from crab apples. By tradition, then, the Celts are credited as the first people to make hard cider. The Celts established hard cider as the beverage of choice in southwestern Britain, northwestern France, and northern Spain. Because the apple is a temperate fruit, hard cider was unknown in the tropics and subtropics, where sugar was the basis for rum. The northernmost regions of the globe grow apple trees where the climate is too cold for grapes, and thus wine. The ease of making hard cider encouraged its spread. Although hard cider could be consumed as is, it was sometimes transformed into brandy or frozen into applejack, both of which had considerably more alcohol than hard cider. The hangovers from applejack were, however, severe.

Aside from the Celts, the Romans discovered other people in northern Europe who made hard cider. Some Romans, probably a minority, preferred hard cider to wine. The Romans experimented with making hard cider from pears, but this was not really hard cider. Caesar and the emperors who followed him were often partial to hard cider, according to one writer, though wine appears to be more prevalent in Roman literature. The status of the apple grew. Over time the Romans cultivated more than 20 varieties of apple for use fresh or as hard cider. Biblical scholar Saint Jerome coined the word *sicera* to describe the beverage, which we translate into cider.

As Rome fragmented in the fifth century CE, Christian monasteries and the Muslims (Moors) in Spain perpetuated the tradition of making hard cider. The Moors derived new varieties of apples for fresh use and hard cider. Hard cider was not new to Spain, as the indigenous people had made hard cider for centuries. The Moors merely elevated apple culture. Indeed, it is possible that Spain may have been the earliest region in Europe whose people consumed hard cider. Frankish emperor Charlemagne believed hard cider to be a valuable commodity. He ordered peasants to plant apple trees and labored to enlarge the trade in hard cider. Despite these efforts the peasants of northern France preferred beer to hard cider until the 11th century, when the Normans made hard cider popular in France and England. By the 16th and 17th centuries, all of France consumed hard cider, a curious circumstance given France's reputation for producing wine. French agricultural societies promoted the production and consumption of hard cider. In this context, these societies sponsored contests to determine who could best make hard cider. Every French farmer had his own apple orchard and made hard cider and brandy. The

Calvados region of northern France gained renown for the quality of its cider and brandy. In the 19th century the spread of an aphid devastated grape growers and winemakers, further shifting the tide toward hard cider. By the 1860s, France alone had 4 million apple trees. Today, France is the world's largest producer of cider. The consumption of cider shaped history because of the alcohol it contained. This alcohol killed microbes, making an abiotic beverage that was safer to drink than water, which, before the advent of modern water treatment plants, could be contaminated with cholera, dysentery, and other waterborne diseases. In an era before machines supplemented human muscles, one might drink cider throughout the day without fear of excessive intoxication and a diminution in one's job performance. The slight buzz from the consumption of cider throughout the day must have diminished the sensation of fatigue in an era when work was physical and exertion heavy.

From the Middle Ages the English vacillated between hard cider and beer. As indicated earlier, the Normans increased interest in hard cider. In the 15th and 16th centuries, however, the arrival of hops to England boosted the brewing of beer, so that hard cider lost favor for a time. Curiously, English Protestants (Anglicans) preferred hard cider to beer. As in France, English farmers favored the apple and hard cider as ways to diversify and increase income. In this era, employers allotted hard cider as part of laborers' pay, a practice that ended only in 1878 when Parliament outlawed it. The shortage of wood in England further tilted the balance toward hard cider because, unlike beer, hard cider does not require heat to make. England also emphasized domestic production of hard cider so it would not be dependent on French wine or German beer. In the 18th century, one novelist estimated that the port of Exeter exported 1 to 2 million gallons of hard cider per year. Quasi-religious rites urged farmers to sprinkle apple trees with hard cider and leave a few apples on each tree for pixies to eat, in the belief that the tree gods kept away evil spirits. During the Industrial Revolution, farmers moved to the city. The quality and quantity of hard cider declined, though demand remained robust. With the Industrial Revolution, the making of hard cider became a large-scale enterprise. The practice arose of adding water to hard cider, diluting flavor and alcohol. Some makers stored hard cider in lead tubs, poisoning consumers. Given these circumstances, beer made a comeback.

America

English settlers brought apples and hard cider with them, and by the American Revolution 10 percent of New England's farmers had a cider mill on their property. In early America, hard cider was the beverage of choice. Some Americans consumed hard cider with every meal. Second president John Adams believed that hard cider promoted longevity and consumed it every morning. For a time, hard cider was akin to currency and could be traded for clothes or other items. Hard cider was even used to pay tuition.

The 17th and 18th centuries marked the apogee of hard cider in America. Because of its antimicrobial properties, hard cider was to America what wine had been to ancient Rome. New Jersey enjoyed the highest reputation for the quality of its hard cider. In 1810, Essex County, New Jersey, yielded nearly 200,000 barrels of hard cider. George Washington and Thomas Jefferson, other U.S. presidents, grew their own apples and made their own hard cider. Jefferson was particularly eager to serve the best hard cider at Monticello. As it had in England, the Industrial Revolution caused a decline in the quantity and quality of hard cider. Immigrants brought beer to the United States, which replaced hard cider as the national beverage. In the 19th century, poet Ralph Waldo Emerson appreciated a glass of good hard cider. John Chapman (Johnny Appleseed) may have planted apple trees to further the production of hard cider.

In the 19th century, the temperance movement attacked hard cider and other alcoholic drinks. At the prodding of temperance advocates, some farmers cut down their apple trees. Whereas in 1899 the United States had produced 210 million liters of hard cider, by the beginning of Prohibition in 1919 production shrank to 50 million liters. Prohibition gave rise to nonalcoholic cider, giving the term its current meaning. The end of prohibition did not restore hard cider to prominence. Today, however, the demand for hard cider is rising worldwide, including in the United States.

Further Reading

Janik, Erika. *Apple: A Global History*. London: Reaktion Books, 2011.

Proulx, Annie, and Lew Nichols. *Cider: Making, Using and Enjoying Sweet and Hard Cider*. North Adams, MA: Storey Books, 1997.

Cinnamon

An ancient spice, cinnamon has been coveted throughout its long history. The spice is added to rolls, cookies, pudding, pie, quick bread, chutney, stew, and curry. In sales, cinnamon ranks second only to pepper in the United States and Europe. People have called cinnamon the "spice of life" because of its importance. In the family Lauraceae, cinnamon is the dried inner bark of the tree *Cinnamomum verum*. Although Americans tend to lump cinnamon with cassia, the two are not synonymous. Indeed, in the United States the sales of cassia exceed those of cinnamon.

Because of its long association with Sri Lanka, the spice is known as Ceylon cinnamon (the island of Ceylon is today Sri Lanka) or Sri Lankan cinnamon. The genus *Cinnamomum* derives from the Greek *kinnamon* or *kinnamomon*, meaning "sweet wood," an appropriate name given cinnamon's origin in the bark of the cinnamon tree. The Greek terms may in turn derive from the Hebrew "quinamom." The Malayan and Indonesian *kayamanis* likewise mean "sweet wood," and it is possible that *kayamanis* may be the source of the Greek and Hebrew words. The Dutch *kaneel*, the French and Italian *canella*, and the Spanish *canela* trace their lineage to the Latin *canella*, meaning "small tube" or "pipe," a reference to cinnamon quills. Because of its antiquity and ubiquity, the word cinnamon appears in a large number of languages.

Origin and History

Cinnamon was part of the spice trade that coaxed Europeans to explore vast reaches of the globe and, in the late 15th century, to discover the Americas. In this context, cinnamon is difficult to overvalue. The discovery of the Americas led to the Columbian Exchange, whereby diseases, plants, and animals crossed both ways across the Atlantic and Pacific Oceans. The new diseases from the Old World extirpated the Amerindians. European settlers, devoid of indigenous labor, imported Africans to work the sugarcane, rice, indigo, tobacco, coffee, and cotton estates in the New World. Europeans treated Africans as an inferior grade of human at the same time that white masters raped their female slaves. The Europeans and their descendants created a racism that has plagued the Americas ever since. African Americans continue to be under assault from white police officers.

The genus *Cinnamomum* originated in the mountains of the Western Ghats and southern India. From an early date, the people of Sri Lanka cultivated cinnamon, and the tree has been synonymous with the island. Its trade was early a part of Indian Ocean commerce. The Egyptians used it in embalming the dead. About 1500 BCE, the pharaoh Hatshepsut dispatched five ships to Punt, land along the coast of the Red Sea, to acquire spices. The ships returned with cinnamon and other spices. Cinnamon trees may not have been grown in Punt, leading one to speculate that this region of Africa obtained the spice from Asia. As early as the second millennium BCE, the people of China and Southeast Asia may have exported cinnamon from Indonesia to Madagascar along what one authority terms the "cinnamon route." It seems possible that from Madagascar cinnamon was traded along the eastern coast of Africa, arriving in Punt and from there to Egypt.

In addition to the Egyptians, the Hebrews valued cinnamon. It may be possible that the Hebrews learned about cinnamon during their captivity in Egypt. So important was the spice that, according to the author of Exodus, God told Moses to prepare "an oil of holy anointment" from cinnamon, cassia, and myrrh. The Song of Solomon mentions cinnamon as being among "the chief spices." The early Christians also knew about cinnamon, its being mentioned in Revelation.

One authority believes that cinnamon was more valuable than gold in antiquity. Certainly it was a luxury that only the wealthy could afford in Greece and Rome. First-century-CE Greek physician Dioscorides regarded cinnamon as a medicine, recommending it as a diuretic. According to him it improved sight, digestion, and the function of the intestines and kidneys; freshened breath; aided women during menses; rendered snakebites harmless; and soothed the stomach. Dioscorides recommended a mixture of cinnamon and honey to remove blemishes from the skin. Given its cost, one wonders how widely it was used as medicine.

The Greeks did not acquire cinnamon directly from Asia but instead relied on the Phoenicians. More generally, the people of the Mediterranean basin depended on the Phoenicians and Arabs to supply cinnamon from India and presumably Sri Lanka. Also active in the cinnamon trade were the Sabians of Arabia, who might have supplied cinnamon to Egypt. If this is true, Hatshepsut must have gotten cinnamon from Arabia rather than Punt. In the fourth century BCE, Greek botanist Theophrastus confirmed the availability of cinnamon in Arabia. According to Greek geographer Strabo (64 BCE-23 CE), cinnamon trees were so numerous in Arabia that people used their wood as fuel.

At first the Romans relied on the Arabs for cinnamon, but it must have remained costly. It is said that first-century-CE Roman emperor Nero flaunted his wealth by burning a year's supply of cinnamon at his wife's funeral. One authority doubts this story. Nero would not have burned cinnamon wood because it yields no fragrance. Rather, he might have burned *Cinnamosma fragrans*, a tree of the eastern coast of Africa and Madagascar. Building a maritime empire, the Romans bypassed the Phoenicians and Arabs, trading for cinnamon directly with India. In the late empire, Constantinople (now Istanbul) acquired cinnamon from Sri Lanka. With the decline of Rome, the Arabs reasserted control of the cinnamon trade.

In antiquity, the people of the Mediterranean basin appear to have been unsure of the location of cinnamon trees. The Arabs told the story of the Phoenix, a bird from "a distant land" that made its nest in a cinnamon tree. Flapping its wings fast, it ignited the tree. The fire consumed the bird, but it was reborn in the flames. Apparently because the Phoenix consumed cinnamon trees in fire, the spice was rare and expensive. In this way the Arabs, by referring to "a distant land," concealed the location of cinnamon trees.

Intent on uncovering the location of cinnamon trees, European explorers searched Asia. Italian adventurer Marco Polo (1254–1324) found cinnamon trees on the Malabar Coast of India. By the 13th century, the East Indies emerged as the center of the cinnamon trade. In Asia, the Chinese traded cinnamon much as the Phoenicians and Arabs had in the Mediterranean. In the Middle Ages, physicians used cinnamon to treat cough, chest pain, headache, poor digestion, and flatulence.

By discovering an oceanic route to India in 1498, Portuguese explorer Vasco da Gama enabled Europeans to obtain cinnamon directly from Asia. Eclipsed, Arab trade in cinnamon declined. In place of the Arabs arose the Portuguese, who monopolized the cinnamon trade in the 16th century. Yet the Portuguese had no interest in reducing the price of cinnamon, leading other Europeans to resent them. In an effort to break Portugal's monopoly, Dutch explorer Cornelius van Hartman arrived in the East Indies in 1596. In time, the Dutch wrested control of the cinnamon trade from Portugal. In 1658, the Netherlands conquered Sri Lanka, gaining control of the source of cinnamon. Although the Dutch promoted the cultivation of cinnamon, they were no more eager than the Portuguese to reduce prices. The Netherlands exported only a portion of the harvest. In years of surplus the Dutch destroyed cinnamon to keep it off the market. In 1796, Britain took Sri Lanka, and with it the cinnamon trade, from the Netherlands. The United Kingdom established large plantations on Sri Lanka, cultivating 40,000 acres by 1850. The British planted cinnamon trees in India as early as 1798. Additional plantings followed on the Seychelles islands, Madagascar, and the Caribbean. By 1867, Sri Lanka exported nearly 1 million pounds of cinnamon per year. During World War II, Japan occupied the Dutch East Indies, causing a decline in the cinnamon trade.

Production, Cultivation, and Commerce

Today, cinnamon production is concentrated in western and southwestern Sri Lanka. The island is the leading producer of cinnamon. Also important as producers are the Seychelles islands, Madagascar, and India. In Sri Lanka, cinnamon is a crop of small farmers. Harvested in their second or third year, cinnamon trees remain productive for 30 or 40 years. Farmers harvest cinnamon two or three times per year. A tree of the tropics, cinnamon grows in many soil types. In Sri Lanka it does well in the sandy soil of Kadirana, Ekola, and Ja-ela, and in the loam and lateritic soil of Kalutara, Galle, and Matara. The best quality comes from trees grown in the sandy soil of the Negambo district. The tree flourishes between 68°F and 86°F with 50 to 100 inches of rain. Sri Lankan farmers grow eight cultivars, a number that seems small compared to the large number of cultivars of strawberries and several other plants.

The Department of Export Agriculture of Sri Lanka recommends the application of urea for nitrogen, rock phosphate for phosphorus, and muriate of potash for potassium to the soil. In a tree's first year it should receive 175 pounds of fertilizer per acre, in its second year 350 pounds per acre, and in its third, 525 pounds per acre. Where magnesium is deficient the farmer should apply dolomite at 440 pounds per acre. Farmers fertilize cinnamon trees every six months. Sri Lanka yields 300 pounds of cinnamon per acre, whereas Madagascar yields 210 to 250 pounds per acre.

The quintessential export commodity, 94 percent of the cinnamon crop is exported. London, Amsterdam, and Rotterdam are the centers of the cinnamon trade. Japan, Australia, India, Mexico, the United States, the United Kingdom, Germany, the Netherlands, and Colombia, among other nations, import cinnamon. The United States is the world's leading importer, followed by India. Japan, the United States, and Australia import cinnamon from Sri Lanka. Mexico imports more cinnamon than any other spice.

Further Reading

Ravindran, P. N., K. Nirmal Babu, and M. Shylaja, eds. *Cinnamon and Cassia: The Genus Cinnamomum.* Boca Raton, FL: CRC Press, 2004.

Citrus Fruits

Citrus fruits are known worldwide as a good source of vitamin C. These fruits were among the first that humans used to combat scurvy, a disease of dietary deficiency. The use of citrus fruits for this purpose made possible long-distance sea voyages, journeys that had either been impossible or had caused so much death that they should not have been undertaken. Citrus fruits thus furthered commerce between widely scattered peoples. Citrus fruits were not alone in bringing these benefits. Potatoes, pineapple, and cabbage, among others, were also very valuable as sources of vitamin C. Citrus fruits have also had great economic importance. South Florida, California, and Brazil, all New World recipients of Old World crops, reap billions of dollars from the citrus industry annually.

Origin and Economic Importance

Citrus fruits are native to the Old World tropics and subtropics. Citrus fruits come from trees that reach about 30 feet in height, though some are shorter. A fecund

All citrus fruits except the grapefruit originated in the Old World tropics. Valuable sources of vitamin C, citrus fruits made it possible for long voyages in the age of sail. (Luboš Chlubný/ Dreamstime.com)

tree may yield 60,000 flowers, though only about 600 will bear fruit. Unable to tolerate drought or frost, citrus fruits, like sugarcane, need year-round tropical conditions. India was among the early cultivators of citrus trees, excepting the grapefruit, which is a New World fruit. By about 4000 BCE, the Persians had cultivated oranges and lemons. Before 300 BCE, Greek conqueror Alexander the Great found these trees throughout Persia (today Iran). Although Alexander died in western Asia, his troops may have returned to Greece with orange and lemon seeds or seedlings. By 200 BCE, the people of Palestine were growing citrus fruits. From the eastern Mediterranean, citrus trees spread throughout the rest of the basin, whose warmth benefited the trees. Greek botanist Theophrastus, Greek physician Dioscorides, Roman poet Virgil, and Roman encyclopedist Pliny the Elder all mentioned citrus culture in the Greek and Roman worlds. In all of these cases citrus fruits appear to have been important in ancient Asia and Mediterranean Europe.

The real citrus empire, however, was to take shape in the Americas rather than the Old World. The Spanish brought oranges and citrons to Puerto Rico about 1640, and later to Saint Augustine, Florida. In the 18th century, the Spanish planted orange groves in what was then part of northwestern Mexico and is today southern

Grapefruit

The grapefruit is a happenstance of nature to which the Columbian Exchange contributed. The parents of the grapefruit are likely the sweet orange and the shaddock, both ancient, Old World fruits. Europeans planted both in the Caribbean. The orange had long been the more popular of the two. Many people considered the shaddock a sour fruit. Apparently, on Jamaica, the two hybridized without human aid to yield the grapefruit, the only citrus fruit that may claim a New World origin. The grapefruit is now an important fruit in Florida and California.

California. By the 1880s, citrus groves were numerous in this region. Brazil was also an early convert and an important orange grower. As is true of South Florida, Brazil's oranges go chiefly to make juice, a worldwide beverage. By contrast, California's citrus crops are eaten fresh. Coca-Cola, McDonald's, Sunkist, Florida Fruit, United Fruit, and Sucocitrico own citrus groves in California, Arizona, Florida, or Brazil. The United States and Brazil are the world's centers of citrus culture. Worldwide, the tropics and subtropics have 1 billion citrus trees. These areas produce about 100 million tons of citrus fruits per year, only about 10 percent of which is consumed fresh. In Florida alone, the sale of citrus fruits and juice tops $9 billion per year. Each American drinks about six gallons of orange juice per year. In the quest for sweetness, some manufacturers add corn syrup, high fructose corn syrup, or beet sugar to orange juice. This practice is common in Brazil, though the attempt to hide these ingredients is illegal. This attempt stems from the desire to convince consumers that orange juice is 100 percent pure.

Citrus Fruits and Scurvy

We live in an era that has conquered scurvy, and so we seldom reflect on the fact that the disease was once prevalent and hideous. Symptoms include fatigue, pain and sensitivity throughout the body, purple spots on the skin (with these spots being most pronounced below the waist), swollen gums, and loose teeth. Without treatment, death is certain. When scurvy held sway it was and remains a disease of dietary deficiency. A poor diet deficient in fruits and vegetables causes scurvy. Such deficiencies prevailed aboard ships in the age of sail. The longer the voyage, the greater was the torment. Scurvy was routine. Consider as just one example the British attempt in 1740 to circumnavigate the globe, as Spanish mariner Ferdinand Magellan did in the 16th century. Magellan himself, killed during the voyage, did not succeed, but the crew who survived completed the journey. The British fleet commanded six ships with 2,000 men. Within seven months scurvy had set in.

Sunkist

Sunkist Growers Inc. boasts 6,000 citrus growers in California and Arizona. Sunkist growers produce more citrus fruits in general and more oranges in particular than any other cooperative in the United States. As a group, Sunkist growers own more land than almost any other landowner in California. Sunkist prides itself on fresh produce and is the largest seller of fresh citrus fruit in the United States. By contrast, most of Florida's oranges go to produce juice. Sunkist traces its roots almost to the beginning of citrus culture in California. During the 1880s, growers began to organize themselves into cooperatives. The Southern California Fruit Exchange became active in 1893, growing into Sunkist in 1908. Best known for its oranges with the signature Sunkist label, Sunkist has partnered with other large agribusiness firms over the years.

Two of the ships returned before rounding the southern tip of Africa because the disease had so weakened the crew. A third ship was lost at sea. Of the remaining three, 626 of the 961-member crew died of scurvy before reaching Africa. By the return to Britain in 1744, more than 90 percent of the crew had succumbed to scurvy. Many other voyages too numerous to name suffered similar tragedies.

Given this background, it seems surprising that Britain was willing to suffer such losses. As early as about 1500 CE, Arab and Portuguese mariners were probably the first to adopt citrus fruits as an antiscurvy agent. (Among citrus fruits, the grapefruit is not mentioned in this context, since it did not arise until a chance hybridization occurred in the Caribbean in the 18th century.) Although this finding was empirical, no one then knew why citrus fruits were effective. This discovery would await the 20th century. One should note that the use of citrus fruits to stave off scurvy was only practical on tropical voyages. Citrus fruits, like many other foods, are perishable. Even if one began a voyage in the temperate zone with citrus fruits on hand, the supply would be depleted without hope for replenishment, since citrus trees will not grow in the temperate zone; they will not tolerate frost. Yet long distance temperate-zone voyages were possible with the potato, a temperate tuber crop. A medium potato has half a day's serving of vitamin C, the antiscurvy agent. Because citrus fruits are perishable, a ship must stop periodically in the tropics to harvest new oranges, lemons, citrons, limes, and the like. This need led to the practice of planting citrus trees near tropical harbors to ease the task of harvesting and storing citrus fruits. The Jesuits in Brazil may have been the first to undertake these systematic plantings. Although the mind fastens on citrus fruits as the antiscurvy agent par excellence, it was not the only alternative, not even in the tropics. Pineapple, potatoes (as noted earlier), cabbage, and other fruits and vegetables all have important levels of vitamin C.

Among mariners, Portuguese explorer Vasco da Gama may have been the first of great renown to provision his ships with citrus fruits. By the 17th century, lemons and oranges were part of the foods that Dutch sailors ate. That century, at least one British captain gave sailors two spoonfuls of lemon juice per day with promising results. In this context it seems strange that the British navy was so slow to grasp the benefits of citrus fruits. Well into the 18th century, British ships regularly suffered 50 percent mortality because of the absence of citrus fruits. In the 18th century Denis Diderot, the French intellectual behind *Encyclopédie*, pointed out that, as early as the time of Greek philosopher Plato, Greek scholars knew of the benefits of citrus fruits. Part of Britain's backwardness may have stemmed from the fact that Portugal, eager to maintain a competitive advantage over other nations, did not share its knowledge of citrus fruits with its rivals. Yet Britain began to take note when 18th-century Scottish physician for the Royal Navy, James Lind, proved that citrus fruits protected one against scurvy. In 1747, he performed a classic clinical trial aboard ship, giving a group of sailors one lemon and two oranges per day while another group received no such supplementation. The citrus group remained healthy whereas the others developed scurvy. Even then, the British navy dragged its feet. Only in 1795 did it require ships to give sailors a daily ration of lime juice. Accordingly, British sailors were known as "limeys." Whereas the Royal Navy Hospital had 1,500 cases of scurvy in 1780, the number plummeted to only two in 1806.

The acceptance that citrus fruits worked led scientists to wonder why. The answer eluded them for more than a century after the British navy mandated the consumption of lime juice. Scientists first focused on isolating chemicals from the peel of citrus fruits, a misguided action. No more successful was a focus on citric acid. Only in 1927 did Hungarian professor Albert Szent-Györgyi isolate from oranges, lemons, and cabbage what he called "Groningen reducing agent." The editor of the journal to which Szent-Györgyi sent his findings renamed the chemical "hexuronic acid" to signal that it contained six carbon atoms in a type of arrangement that is common among organic molecules. Here the European line of inquiry appeared to end. American scientists came to the fore. In the 1910s, Wisconsin agricultural scientist Elmer V. McCollum was the first to discover and publicize the existence of vitamins with his landmark discovery of vitamin A. Other scientists took up the crusade to find additional vitamins. Americans were pragmatic, understanding that the discovery of the antiscurvy agent would command a Nobel Prize in chemistry, or perhaps in medicine or physiology. As it turned out, both would be awarded. In 1931, University of Pittsburgh professor Charles Glen King discovered and named vitamin C as the antiscurvy agent. He proved that vitamin C was what Szent-Györgyi's editor had called hexuronic acid. King published his results in *Science*, among the leading scientific journals worldwide, in 1932. He omitted Szent-Györgyi's contributions to this discovery, an unprofessional action that offended the Hungarian, who moved swiftly to publish his work anew in *Nature*, a prestigious British scientific journal. In 1933, Szent-Györgyi renamed the molecule "ascorbic acid," an appellation that has held true to the present. In 1937, the Nobel Prize in physiology or medicine went to Szent-Györgyi because his work had predated that of King in the same way that British naturalist Charles Darwin's work preceded that of British naturalist Alfred Russell Wallace, meaning that the scientific community recognized Darwin as the originator of the theory of evolution by natural selection. King lost the accolades of a lifetime. A second Nobel Prize, this one in chemistry, went to two other researchers for their description of vitamin C's structure.

One riddle remains. Since the discovery of vitamin C, scientists have learned that a large number of animals synthesize the vitamin in the body and so do not need an external source of it. This situation is akin to the fact that humans exposed to sufficient sunlight do not need an external source of vitamin D because the body, in the presence of sunlight, manufactures vitamin D on its own. The puzzling fact, however, is that humans are among the few species that cannot manufacture their own vitamin C. Perhaps the answer is bound up in the circumstances of human evolution. As Darwin understood, humans evolved in Africa, apparently in a region rich in berries and other fruits with vitamin C, though citrus fruits were not part of the ancestral patrimony. In an area awash in vitamin C, there was presumably no selective advantage for a hominid to synthesize its own vitamin C.

Further Reading

Carpenter, Kenneth J. *The History of Scurvy and Vitamin C*. Cambridge: Cambridge University Press, 1986.

Laszlo, Pierre. *Citrus: A History*. Chicago and London: The University of Chicago Press, 2007.

Coca-Cola

An American soft drink, Coca-Cola has become both product and hallmark of global capitalism. Today Coca-Cola may be the world's most widely distributed commodity, being sold in more than 200 countries, though coffee and tea ought to be able to make similar claims. Coca-Cola has grown into a symbol of Western

An iconic soft drink, Coca-Cola is an American favorite, and a long-time leader in advertising. (Bettmann/Corbis)

civilization and become a giant among advertisers. Coca-Cola has accomplished much for a beverage that is at least 90 percent sugar and water. How could such a simple formula conquer the world? This entry attempts to answer that question.

Origins and Importance

Coca-Cola arose during the 1880s at the height of the Gilded Age. The period was one of adulation of the wealthy. Many Americans believed in steelmaker Andrew

Pepsi Cola

In 1893, North Carolina native Caleb Davis Bradham invented the beverage "Brad's Drink": carbonated water, sugar, kola nut, and vanilla, a recipe not dramatically different from that of Coca-Cola. In 1898, Bradham renamed the beverage Pepsi Cola, which would soon grow to rival Coca-Cola, a position Pepsi maintains to the present. In 1902, the entrepreneur created the Pepsi Cola Company. That year, Bradham began advertising in newspapers. In 1923, Bradham bankrupted Pepsi when his investments in sugar plummeted, leading a Wall Street banker to buy the company.

Carnegie's "Gospel of Wealth." In an era before the income tax, a few Americans (one thinks immediately of Cornelius Vanderbilt and John D. Rockefeller), amassed colossal fortunes. Beneath them was a huge mass of ambitious entrepreneurs who sought to invent the next product to command dizzying profits. Among them was John Pemberton. He had earned a medical degree and, after medical school, studied pharmacy so that he was both physician and pharmacist.

Pemberton came of age during the era of patent medicines. Most of them were useful and some were harmful, but Americans on the lookout for a cure for some malady or another bought them in large amounts. Pemberton set his sights on developing a new medicine, but he wanted more. He wanted a medicine that would serve as a beverage so that he could make sales in a number of niches. The official history of Coca-Cola states that Pemberton developed a novel product, but this is propaganda rather than truth. The truth, however, does not discredit Pemberton, but shows him to have been a careful reader who knew how to use up-and-coming ideas. In the course of his reading, Pemberton came upon the work of Sigmund Freud, a Viennese physician who was among the founders of psychiatry and psychology. In 1884, Pemberton read an article by Freud on the benefits of cocaine. Freud advertised cocaine for its ability to dispel depression and to increase the libido. At a distance, Pemberton became a disciple of Freud. The drug, which comes from the leaves of the coca plant, was then unregulated. At the same time, Pemberton read reports that the people of Peru chewed coca leaves, a practice they claimed to lengthen life. Even Pope Leo XIII chewed coca leaves in the belief that they were the source of longevity. Here at last was a real medicine, thought Pemberton. Reading other reports, Pemberton concluded that cocaine was useful in breaking morphine addicts of their addiction. He seems not to have known that cocaine is more addictive than morphine. Not only was it used as medicine, cocaine could be marketed as an aphrodisiac that would be sure to sell handsomely if packaged correctly.

In addition to cocaine, Pemberton added to his new medicine and beverage an extract (really caffeine) from the kola nut, which he named the Coca and Cola Nut. Because both cocaine and caffeine are stimulants, Pemberton evidently wanted his new product to give people a boost of energy. In fact, energy came directly from this new product because Pemberton put sugar in it, though he later switched to saccharin. Sugar was another world commodity that changed the world in profound ways. In this case it became the prime additive of the emerging soft drink industry. Pemberton also added an extract from diarriarra, a plant of tropical America, Texas, and California, because of its reputation as an aphrodisiac. Obviously the human libido was much on his mind. Clearly Pemberton thought of his new product as a lustful stimulant. These ingredients would horrify the modern medical mind, but in the era of patent medicines, Coca-Cola was not at all outlandish.

Whatever medicinal qualities Pemberton wished to promote, he had his eye on the soda fountain industry. Indeed, by 1886, the year Pemberton invented Coca-Cola, more than 300 other brands competed for sales at the nation's soda fountains. Because Pemberton's home of Atlanta, Georgia, was at the center of the soda fountain industry, he could hardly have ignored it. Pemberton surveyed the many brands noting that they were fruity treats: orange, lemon, lime, and so forth. In contrast, Pemberton sold a beverage that had no connection to these other drinks. Accordingly, Coca-Cola stood out from the crowd and quickly won partisans. If Pemberton had borrowed his ingredients and ideas from other people, he nonetheless marketed something that was not just another run-of-the-mill beverage.

Pemberton also quickly came to appreciate the importance of advertising. He noted that Dr. Pepper, another successful beverage, put out an ad with an illustration of a nude woman frolicking in the ocean. Only a wave covered the area between her legs. The titillation of such ads provoked Pemberton to pour money into advertising, and it has been advertising, perhaps more than anything else, that contributed to Coca-Cola's success. Pemberton thus found his way in an era when chocolatier Milton Hershey spent almost no money on advertising, believing that the best advertisement was a Hershey wrapper lying on the ground. Pemberton and his successors elevated Coca-Cola to what one historian regards as the "secular communion drink." This may be hyperbole because Coca-Cola does not take on any of the religious associations that wine does. If Coca-Cola can claim to be secular, it cannot claim the antiquity of wine. Coca-Cola was a drink of industrial America. Wine had helped build the Greco-Roman world. At the same time, Coca-Cola, according to advertisers, represented all that was clean, fresh, and vital about the United States. One did not need to try to create some concoction of soda fountain drinks to taste something novel. One needed only to drink Coca-Cola.

Coca-Cola also had the benefit of being the beverage of democratic America. If the rich drank a prized vintage of wine, and the masses drank beer, all Americans nonetheless shared a passion for Coca-Cola.

One also finds in Coca-Cola the profits on which American capitalism depends. By one estimate, the ingredients in a glass of Coca-Cola cost 1.5 cents, but this same glass cost Americans 5 cents. Another estimate put the cost of ingredients at half a cent, meaning that each sale was a tenfold markup. Profits of this magnitude captivated Americans then as now. Although Pemberton had first experimented with Coca-Cola wine, he quickly abandoned alcohol, attuned as he was to the gathering might of the temperance movement. Coca-Cola was thus the perfect beverage for sober-minded Americans.

Pemberton appears to have ignored an 1866 medical report, which may have been the first of its kind to reveal that cocaine was more addictive than morphine. Pemberton apparently decided that all foods and medicines posed some risk. In this context, he thought it worthwhile to preserve cocaine in his formula. He decided that cocaine posed fewer risks than morphine, opium (of which morphine is a derivative), or tobacco. Pemberton never veered from his belief that cocaine promoted mental and physical vigor. Most of all, Pemberton saw Coca-Cola as his path to America's pantheon of millionaires. He maintained a fervent belief in American author Horatio Alger's tales of rags to riches, a fiction for all but the luckiest Americans. In this context, one theology professor holds that Americans do not make wealth. They inherit it.

In circumstances that remain murky and disturbing, Asa Candler, the brother of a successful lawyer, acquired Pemberton's formula in the late 1880s, seeking, as Pemberton had, to climb to the lair of the gods. Like many Americans, he pursued wealth. Everything else was superfluous. Born into poverty, Candler ever after sought to distance himself from his childhood. Here, again, one sees Coca-Cola functioning within a purely capitalistic framework.

Worldwide Ascent

From the outset, Coca-Cola was not merely a product of capitalism and of ambitious men. It changed the world as a pioneering advertiser. By 1900, Coca-Cola was a phenomenon. Yet sober-minded Americans began to question the beverage's reliance on cocaine, the drug Pemberton had rationalized. Many critics saw in cocaine the devious side of capitalism. By addicting its drinkers to Coca-Cola, the beverage would never witness its sales flag. A coalition of ministers and scientists began to attack Coca-Cola. By the early 20th century, American chemist and federal employee Harvey Wiley, who enjoyed a reputation as a careful, impartial scientist, turned against Coca-Cola. With his support, Congress, in 1906, passed the

Pure Food and Drug Act. In the wake of this defeat, Coca-Cola dropped cocaine and saccharin from its formula and returned to its mantra that the beverage was wholesome and pleasurable. By the Great Depression, Coca-Cola was the popular beverage of choice. Even the repeal of prohibition in 1933 did not blunt Coca-Cola's success. It had become, to use a modern phrase, "too big to fail." By 1935, Coca-Cola was the most expensive stock on the New York Stock Exchange. Coca-Cola also advertised itself as the beverage of the cinema, opening a new market for the drink. Coca-Cola was among the first companies to advertise on radio. The Great Depression also appears to have given American soft drink Pepsi new life, and it became Coca-Cola's steadfast rival.

At the end of World War II, Coca-Cola entered a new age of prosperity. Whereas most European overlords retreated from empire, Coca-Cola had the money to colonize the world, thus changing it. Coca-Cola executives toured Saudi Arabia, the United Kingdom, Egypt, Mexico, and Brazil, introducing the beverage in the process. As in the United States, the lure of Coca-Cola was too great to resist. In effect, Coca-Cola was helping to create and advance a global economy. Coca-Cola thus shaped the world by helping to create the modern global economy. Coca-Cola is as responsible as any food for the rise of globalism. Perhaps coffee and tea are the only items more deserving this assessment. Coca-Cola rapidly conquered Europe and South America, where sales soared. The beverage had immediate but transitory success in China. When communist leader Mao Zedong prevailed over U.S.-backed General Chiang Kai-shek in 1949, the communists nationalized Coca-Cola's facilities.

Undeterred, Coca-Cola returned home to advertise on television, a presence it retains today. In 1950, Coca-Cola began an advertising blitz on Thanksgiving, associating the holiday season between Thanksgiving and New Year's Day as a special time to enjoy Coca-Cola. Not surprisingly, sales continued to surge, and Coca-Cola broadened its appeal by jumping from the mom-and-pop stores of its youth to the chain supermarkets that thrived in suburbia. In the 1960s, Japan opened its doors to Coca-Cola, not surprising given the close commercial ties between Japan and the United States. At the same time, Coca-Cola targeted its ads to African Americans. If Coca-Cola were to be the universal drink, it would need to convert Africans and their descendants, whether in the United States or elsewhere.

Yet problems arose. In the late 1960s and throughout the 1970s, Arab nations, angered at U.S. support of Israel, boycotted Coca-Cola. A global beverage, Coca-Cola was now caught up in geopolitical crises. Nutritionists joined the malcontents, wondering whether a beverage of primarily sugar and water had any value. Was not this another case of empty calories? Did not sugar, and thus Coca-Cola, cause tooth decay?

Buffeted as it was, Coca-Cola remained in frenetic motion. Making a second entry into China, Coca-Cola also became the beverage of choice in the Soviet

Union, now Russia and its former satellites. Such came in Portugal, Egypt, Yemen, and Sudan. Yet Coca-Cola was not immune from the Great Recession of 2008. If it was too big to fail, it was not too big to falter. Its stock fell. As gasoline prices rose, people had less disposable income and bought less Coca-Cola. Yet Coca-Cola dodged these blows, sponsoring the Beijing Olympics in 2008. The beverage did not benefit fully from this endorsement because China was massacring people in Tibet and arming Sudan. In the 21st century, Coca-Cola has received renewed scrutiny from nutritionists. A force for profit, it is not clear today that Coca-Cola has become a force for good.

Further Reading

Pendergrast, Mark. *For God, Country & Coca-Cola: The Definitive History of the Great American Soft Drink and the Company that Makes It*. 3rd ed. New York: Basic Books, 2013. ·

Coconut

A palm tree, coconut (*Cocos nucifera*) is grown in Asia, the Pacific Islands, Africa, and Latin America. A member of the Palmae family, coconut is widely cultivated between 20° north and 20° south. Near the equator, farmers grow coconut as high as up to 3,000 feet of elevation, though they rarely plant it in large numbers above 900 feet. In Jamaica, coconut is planted no higher than 350 feet. A coconut palm may live more than 100 years, remaining productive for 60 years. Traditional varieties begin flowering in their fifth or sixth year. Ripening on the palm, a coconut requires one year to mature. The word "coconut" derives from the Portuguese term for monkey because the Portuguese thought a coconut resembled a monkey's head. Because of its importance, the coconut is known as the "tree of life," the "tree of abundance" and the "tree of heaven." Eighty grams of coconut contain 283 calories, 37.6 grams of water, 2.7 grams of protein, 12.2 grams of carbohydrates, 7.2 grams of fiber, 285 milligrams of potassium, 90.4 milligrams of phosphorus, 25.6 milligrams of magnesium, and 11.2 milligrams of calcium. Coconut milk and coconut water also provide nutrients. Coconut oil, having only calories, is devoid of nutrients.

Origin and Diffusion

One scholar admits that the origin of the coconut is unknown, though scientists are eager to put forward hypotheses. In the 19th century, scholars proposed an origin

The coconut has long been an important source of nourishment throughout the tropics, though the tree does not grow inland. The coconut is nearly ubiquitous on several Pacific islands. (Rrab1972/Dreamstime.com)

in Central or South America. Hypotheses that place the origin of the coconut in the Old World appear to be the current fashion. One authority favors Malaysia or Indonesia. Various authorities have proposed India and Melanesia. A coconut-like fossil dating between 15 and 40 million years ago may point to the desert of Rajasthan, India as the place of origin. Nevertheless, several scientists dispute an Indian origin of the coconut. Melanesia is a candidate because, according to one scientist, it supports a large population of insects that feed on coconut, implying that it has long been part of the flora of the islands. The coconut dates to 3400 BCE in Melanesia, predating human settlement. If the coconut did not originate in Melanesia, some mechanism must be invoked to explain its transit to the islands. New Zealand is also a candidate for the origin of the coconut, bearing a 15-million-year-old fossil. The Malaysian hypothesis makes clear that the coconut may have originated in Southeast Asia. An Eocene fossil of a coconut, *Cocos sahnii*, places the putative origin in the western Indian Ocean. Fossils along the northern coast of Papua New Guinea may place the origin of the coconut there. Archaeologists have found one fossil of a coconut with a human skull, permitting the inference that humans were using the coconut in Papua New Guinea by 4500 BCE, a date that

Melanesia

Melanesia comprises several islands near Australia in the Pacific Ocean. Four countries are part of Melanesia: Papua New Guinea, Fiji, Vanuatu, and the Solomon Islands. The region lies within the tropics. Indeed, New Guinea lies on the equator. The people who settled Australia (and their identity is in dispute), about 50,000 years ago, colonized Melanesia by about 30,000 years ago. Some scholars believe that sometime after settling these islands these aborigines began harvesting coconuts. The coconut thus may have arisen in Melanesia.

likely preceded cultivation. One scholar puts the origin of the coconut at the Lord Howe Rise-Norfolk Island Ridge of Gondwanaland 15 million years ago.

Whatever its origin, the coconut has dispersed as far west as the Seychelles islands and as far east as the Line Islands. The question of how the coconut got to these regions has not been answered. One authority asserts that ocean currents could not have taken the coconut far because it will not germinate if it has been in water more than a few days. In the absence of diffusion by ocean currents, humans must have carried the coconut wherever they went. According to this hypothesis, Polynesians, Tamils, and Arabs spread the coconut throughout the tropics of the Old World. When Europeans migrated into the tropics they became agents of diffusion. Between 1499 and 1549, the Portuguese carried the coconut from the Indian Ocean around the Cape of Good Hope to the Cape Verde Islands, and from there to the Caribbean and Brazil. After 1650, the Spanish took the coconut from the Philippines to Central and South America.

Another authority invokes ocean currents as the mechanism of diffusion, noting that salt water, absorbed by the husk, must induce dormancy. The coconut germinates slowly when placed in salt water and more rapidly when immersed in fresh water. Thick-husked coconuts float best and so must have drifted great distances in the Pacific and Indian Oceans. Assuming that the coconut originated in Asia or the Pacific Islands, it spread, possibly by ocean currents, to Australia, Africa, and the Americas, though these vast distances appear to have been difficult to traverse without human aid.

Coconut Agriculture and the Uses of the Coconut

Early humans must have prized the coconut as a source of water that required no tools or digging to obtain. As coconuts washed ashore, humans who dwelled along the coast must have gathered them, an action that surely predated cultivation. As early as 1000 BCE, humans cultivated the coconut on the Malabar Coast (now Kerala) of India, a region that is known as the "land of the coconut." By the time of Christ, the people of Sri Lanka were growing coconut. The beginning of coconut agriculture therefore postdated the rise of agriculture in the Old and New World. Today, among tropical nations, the Philippines, India, Sri Lanka, Malaysia, Indonesia, and the Pacific Islands, all within 1,000 miles of the equator, produce the majority of coconuts. These fruits sustain the people of the tropics and so have shaped their history and daily life.

In many regions of the tropics, coconut has long been a crop of small farmers, who planted the palm near homes and in gardens. In this respect, coconuts have shaped the local economy by boosting agriculture. Small farmers account for more than 80 percent of acreage in the Philippines, where the average coconut farm is five acres. In India, the average size is less than one acre. Minimizing their reliance on a single crop, farmers plant coconut with sweet potato, cassava, corn, sunflower, and pumpkin. In Jamaica, farmers grow coconut and banana, and, in the Seychelles islands, coconut, cinnamon, and vanilla. The small farmer relies on coconut as a cash crop and as sustenance. Every part of the palm has value. Coconut leaves are used to construct roofs, walls, mats, and mattresses. The trunk yields furniture. Coconut meat yields food, feed, and oil. Coconut cake—the portion of copra, the dried kernel of a coconut left after the oil has been extracted—is fed to cattle and chickens. Coconut sap yields a sugary substance and vinegar. The husks are made into rope and the shell into charcoal. The roots are used as dye and medicine. Coconut oil yields lubricant, soap, laundry detergent, margarine, and nondairy creamer, and is burned for light and fuel. Most coconut oil is used in cooking. In the 19th century, the United States and Europe derived oil and soap from coconut. By 1900, the coconut was used to make margarine. The demand for copra spurred exports, which rose from 385,000 to 800,000 tons between 1910 and 1925. Exports exceeded 1 million tons in 1935 but slowed thereafter, reaching 1.5 million tons only in 1975. Coconut is popular as food and oil in the Philippines, Indonesia, Papua New Guinea, Sri Lanka, India, and Malaysia.

Important as coconut oil is, it faces competition from soybean and palm oils. The rapid expansion in soybean acreage in the United States and South America in the 20th century increased the supply and decreased the price of soybean oil. The same dynamic occurred with palm oil because the cultivation of the oil palm increased in Malaysia and Indonesia in the 20th century. According to the World Bank, the production of one ton of coconut oil costs $320 to $400 in the Philippines, whereas the production of one ton of palm oil costs $200 to $220 in Indonesia. Faced with this reality, consumers use vegetable oils in preference to coconut oil, resulting in stagnant demand for the latter. Since 1980, the consumption of coconut oil has grown less than 1 percent per year. What demand there is the Philippines meets, exporting 75 percent of the world's coconut oil. The Philippines is the largest producer of copra and oil. One-third of the islands' population, 18 million people, depends on the coconut for income.

Further Reading

Banzon, Julian A., Olympia N. Gonzalez, Sonia Y. de Leon, and Priscilla C. Sanchez. *Coconut as Food.* Quezon City, Philippines: Philippine Coconut Research and Development Foundation, 1990.

Green, Alan H., ed. *Coconut Production: Present Status and Priorities for Research.* Washington, DC: The World Bank, 1991.

Piggott, C. J. *Coconut Growing.* London: Oxford University Press, 1964.

Coffee

Today more than 100 countries in the tropics and subtropics grow coffee, producing 18.7 million tons of beans annually. Worldwide, coffee generates more revenue than any commodity other than petroleum. Coffee grows in partial shade or full sun. It needs moderate rainfall evenly distributed throughout the year, altitudes no higher than 6,000 feet, temperatures between 60°F and 70°F, and the absence of frost. Because it is a crop of the tropics and subtropics, coffee must be grown at altitude to achieve moderate temperatures. Although there are more than 20 species of coffee, two are cultivated above all others: *Coffea arabica* and *Coffea canephora var. robusta*. Of the two, arabica has superior flavor and aroma and so commands a higher price. Arabica grows best at altitudes of 1,500 to 6,000 feet, whereas robusta is grown from sea level to 3,200 feet. Worldwide, 70 percent of the coffee harvest is arabica and the rest, robusta. Comparatively cheap and with twice the caffeine of arabica, robusta has found its way into instant coffee and blends, whereas arabica is marketed in specialty coffees. Arabica is more susceptible to disease and more intolerant of poor soils. Robusta tolerates higher temperatures and humidity but suffers more acutely from frost. Farmers have grown arabica at least since the 16th century and robusta since roughly 1850. Arabica is widely grown in East Africa and Central and South America, whereas robusta, an indigene of Uganda, has sunk roots in West Africa and Southeast Asia. Brazil is the world's largest arabica producer, whereas Vietnam is the largest grower of robusta. Robusta claims half the coffee market in Britain, one-third in Italy, and one-quarter in the United States. Today, Brazil,

Although coffee originated in the Old World, one might argue that it has had the most lasting effects in the Americas, where it complemented sugarcane and propped up the slave system. (Pablo Caridad/Dreamstime.com)

Vietnam, Indonesia, Colombia, and Mexico are the leading coffee growers. Worldwide, farmers plant 25 million acres to coffee. At 9.7 million acres, South America claims a plurality of this land. Coffee occupies 5.5 million acres in Asia, 5.1 million acres in Africa, and 4.7 million acres in Central and North America.

Coffee, the Coffee Shop, and Globalism

Coffee gave rise to a new institution, the coffeehouse, today known as the coffee shop. Once a phenomenon in Europe, the coffee shop has spread worldwide, doing its part to remake the global economy. Globalism would exist without coffee, but, because it is so essential to the modern economy, one would have difficulty making sense of the vast connections throughout the global marketplace without it. It would be fair to say that coffee did not create globalism but instead was an important precursor by creating its own global networks of trade. Indeed, coffee was among the first commodities to achieve worldwide importance as an item of commerce. Coffee was thus an important commodity of the nascent and modern global markets. In its rise to prominence, coffee has conquered the world, spreading, among other places, to Hong Kong, Mexico City, Dublin, Rio de Janeiro, Tokyo,

Folgers

In 1850, the Pioneer Steam Coffee and Spice Mills formed in San Francisco, California. In 1872, entrepreneur James Folger bought the company, renaming it in his honor as J.A. Folger & Co. His timing was right because San Francisco was then in the midst of a coffee boom, establishing itself as the port through which South America shipped coffee into the United States. The company grew so popular that it enticed Procter and Gamble to buy it in 1963. In 2008, Procter and Gamble toyed with the idea of making Folgers a Cincinnati, Ohio-based spin-off, but later that year Orrville, Ohio, giant the J. M. Smucker Company bought Folgers. Folgers offers a number of grades of coffee. Success has come at least partly through television advertising. Since the 1980s, Folgers has sponsored the National Association for Stock Car Auto Racing (NASCAR).

Sydney, New Delhi, and Johannesburg. The modern airport can scarcely be envisioned without a multitude of coffee shops.

The rise of coffee shops has been so successful partly because they amplify the human need for a social gathering place. True, the tavern operates on the same principle, but it tends to intoxicate its patrons. In contrast, the coffee shop promotes sobriety and conviviality. The coffee shop has become a place for study, conversation, and relaxation, though of course too much coffee is likely to make one jittery. The coffee shop has long been important and is now the fastest-growing segment in the restaurant industry. McDonald's, for example, promotes itself as a purveyor of quality coffee. Thanks to this union among coffee, the coffee shop, and the larger restaurant industry, coffee sales have risen steadily since 2000. Coffee appears to be the beverage of the 21st century.

Coffee and Islam

Whereas bread and fish have been important in the rise of Judaism and Christianity, Islam early fueled the consumption of coffee. Because the Koran forbids the consumption of alcohol, Muslims had to turn elsewhere. Coffee increasingly became the beverage of choice, perhaps because its caffeine kept the faithful alert during their daily routine of prayers. By the 16th century, coffee had conquered Muslim western Asia, including Arabia, and North Africa. Muslim merchants became rich selling coffee to Europe. Here arose one of the central tensions in the coffee trade. The Muslims commanded tropical lands suitable for the cultivation of coffee trees. The peasants and landless laborers who toiled to grow coffee received scant reward for their efforts. Pay was uniformly low. Yet the Muslim

Islam

Islam traces its origins to Arabia. In pre-Islamic times, the people of Arabia were poly-theists. In 570 CE, Mohammad ibn Abdullah was born in Mecca (in what is today Saudi Arabia). His childhood was difficult, but at age 25 he married a wealthy woman. Wealth doubtless gave him time for contemplation. In the early seventh century, believing that he had had visions from the Archangel Gabriel, Mohammad founded Islam, the last of the three monotheistic religions. He channeled these visions into the holy book of Islam, the Koran. In the Koran, Mohammad forbade his followers from drinking alcohol because it deflected their attention away from Allah, the one god. Instead, his followers, Muslims, turned to coffee, which helped them stay awake during night prayers.

merchants turned around to sell coffee to prosperous Europeans at high prices. From an early date, then, coffee widened the socioeconomic chasm between rich and poor, with elites enjoying coffee at the expense of the poor who grew it. To put matters another way, the temperate zone benefited—one might say unfairly—from tropical products. In some ways, then, coffee fostered a widening of the gap between the temperate zone and the tropics; one rich, the other poor. Coffee was not the sole cause of this problem. Sugarcane and tea also played important roles in this regard.

Coffee, the Americas, and Race

This tension between elite and peasant, between temperate zone and tropics, may have reached its nadir in the Americas. If sugarcane was first to conquer tropical America, coffee was not far behind. From the outset, sugarcane and coffee trees made an ideal combination that resulted in a kind of sugar-coffee plantation complex. Sugarcane, the quintessential tropical crop, did well in the hot lowlands. Although coffee is likewise a tropical commodity, the tree does not prefer maximum heat. Rather, the tree thrives at low elevations, exactly the land least suited to sugarcane. A planter could thus plant both sugarcane and coffee because the two did not compete for the same land.

As with sugarcane, coffee encountered a problem at the outset of its tenure in the Americas. The planter could not rely on Amerindian labor because the Native Americans died in horrific numbers from European and African diseases to which they had no immunity. To meet this labor shortage, the planter turned to Africa, thus creating the detestable slave trade and the institution of slavery.

The enslavement of Africans, first in the Caribbean and then throughout tropical America and what would become the southern United States, created a host of problems that haunt the Americas to the present. Africans did all the manual labor that attended the cultivation of coffee. They were treated as robots, bereft of rights and dignity. Quickly, whites branded Africans as inferior in every way, creating the new and still-unresolved evil of institutional racism. Many biologists today deny that humans can be divided into races, but this notion was foreign to the coffee estates of tropical America. The taint of race and racism polluted the Americas. Racism contaminated the ideas of first U.S. president George Washington and, more importantly, of third U.S. president Thomas Jefferson. In the 19th century, South Carolina physician Samuel Morton devoted his life to measuring skulls in an attempt to prove that blacks had smaller brains than whites and so must be less intelligent. Slavery and racism plunged the United States into a disastrous civil war. If coffee did not invent slavery, it did much to cement the notion of race with the status of inferiority. This was the dark side of coffee, a part of its history that its advocates would prefer to forget. In this way, coffee changed the world for the worse.

Coffee and Imperialism

From a rather primitive continent in the Middle Ages, Europe emerged in the early modern era as an imperial power. Although coffee did not invent imperialism, it quickened the pace. The Spanish, English, French, Dutch, and Danes all rushed to establish coffee estates in the Caribbean. The Dutch planted coffee trees throughout Southeast Asia, Indonesia perhaps being the jewel in the Dutch coffee crown. This relentless land grab had consequences, broadening the scope and destructiveness of warfare as each European nation sought to strip its rivals of their coffee colonies. Plenty of times England landed armies in the French Caribbean, where yellow fever and hurricanes prevented them from assaulting the French. The French returned the favor many times, with neither side able to develop generals who knew how to win wars in the deadly tropics. If the rivalries among European nations predated the rise of coffee as a world crop, coffee nonetheless intensified these rivalries to the detriment of all. Imperialism was also a feature of the coffee-slave complex, for without slaves, who would tend the coffee estates that dotted Europe's tropical colonies? In this context coffee fueled the slave trade, as European nations, notably Portugal and Spain, jockeyed to supply slaves to the New World's insatiable coffee plantations. Here, again, the rivalry to control the slave trade brought colonial powers to blows. Like sugar, coffee became a symbol of imperialism, particularly of its wasteful and destructive tendencies. This, too, was part of coffee's dark history. Again, the link between coffee and imperialism changed the world for the worse.

The Drug of Choice

When one considers that worldwide consumption of coffee may exceed 400 billion cups daily, one must concede that caffeine, an ingredient in coffee, must be the world's most widely used drug—in this case, a stimulant. Although more than 60 plants contain caffeine, including tea, coffee is the most conspicuous. Caffeine may have arisen as an evolutionary adaptation to a cruel world, protecting coffee trees from several pests, pathogens, and fungi. From an early date, it has been difficult to determine whether humans have preferred coffee for its flavor and aroma or because they craved caffeine. Perhaps both alternatives are right. One thesis holds that the human desire for caffeine predisposed people to drink coffee. As humans formed societies, at least in the tropics, they planted coffee trees to meet their desire for caffeine. In this regard humans, coffee, and caffeine may all have coevolved. One suspects, for example, that humans selected coffee beans with a high caffeine content. In this case, one should note that the coffee bean is not a true bean. Although both are seeds, the true bean is a legume, whereas the coffee bean is not. Tantalizing is the possibility that humans and coffee trees arose in Ethiopia. In this case humans, coffee, and caffeine must have a long evolutionary association. One wonders to what degree coffee and caffeine shaped human evolution.

Coffee and the Internet

Coffee did not invent the Internet, but it has increased the Internet's appeal. Coffee has achieved this result by stroking the social sensibility in humans. As discussed earlier, the coffee shop has long been a gathering place. Now many coffee shops worldwide offer free or low-cost Internet access. One is not limited to face-to-face interaction, but can interact with others through the worldwide reach of the Internet. Skype introduces a new level of intimacy at the cyber coffee shop. The local coffee shop has become a portal to the rest of the world. In this regard, coffee has again conquered the world, remaking it in coffee's image. In this way, coffee brings people together in ways that transcend geography. Coffee, the source of so much misery for so many people, can now boast of positive outcomes. The amplification of coffee as a glue that holds people together in turn holds much progress, as well as suggests the growing interconnectedness of coffee and technology. In this respect, coffee appears to humanize technology and so may be a source of good. Coffee is valuable in helping create a virtual universe and so, apart from other reasons, should be even more important in the future.

Further Reading

Allen, Stewart Lee. *The Devil's Cup: A History of the World According to Coffee*. New York: Ballantine Books, 2003.

Luttinger, Nina, and Gregory Dicum. *The Coffee Book: Anatomy of an Industry from Crop to Last Drop*. New York: New Press, 2006.

Pendergrast, Mark. *Uncommon Grounds: The History of Coffee and How It Transformed Our World*. New York: Basic Books, 1999.

Tucker, Catherine M. *Coffee Culture: Local Experiences, Global Connections*. New York and London: Routledge, 2011.

Wild, Antony. *Coffee: A Dark History*. New York: W. W. Norton, 2005.

Cookie

By one definition, a cookie is a small, sweet cake. This definition seems odd given that one thinks of a cake as soft and moist. Although some cookies fit these criteria, others are hard and comparatively dry. The chocolate chip cookie, for example, can be either hard or soft, depending on the maker. The chocolate chip cookie, to be authentic, must include chocolate, one of the most important foods native to the Americas. Chocolate derives from the cacao tree, which is an indigene of South America. The cookie is a perennial snack food. In this context, one may classify it among roasted peanuts, potato chips, ice cream, candies of many types, and crackers. Housewives once specialized in the production of cookies for the home, and some still do. But multinational corporations are apt to make the most cookies. Certainly they are a premiere item in Walmart and other grocers. One thinks of the cookie as a food that fits in the hand and so is portable in the same way as are the hot dog and hamburger. Indeed, it is often possible to buy cookies where one buys sandwiches. Subway is an example.

Famous Amos

A U.S. Air Force veteran, Wally Amos worked as an agent for the William Morris Agency. To recruit celebrities, he sent them a package of home-baked chocolate chip cookies. He distributed packages to friends as well. They enjoyed the cookies so much that friends encouraged Amos to start his own cookie company. Following their advice, Amos opened a cookie stand, Famous Amos, in Los Angeles, California, in 1975. In its first two years the stand sold nearly $1.5 million in chocolate chip cookies. The Kellogg Company now owns the right to make Famous Amos cookies.

Origins

The cookie may have originated as a small piece of batter put into an oven to gauge the temperature. This must have come at a moment when thermometers did not exist. One thesis holds that the Persians (now Iranians) invented the cookie in the seventh century CE. This invention must have come at the moment of the Muslim conquest of Persia, though it is not certain that Islam influenced the invention of the cookie. The Muslim Arabs (Persians are not Arabs) may have contributed to the cookie because their vast trade network gave them access to sugar, the perfect ingredient to sweeten the cookie. Sugar has long been an enormously important food, first in the Old World tropics and later during the Columbian Exchange in the New World tropics. By incorporating sugar and sometimes chocolate, the cookie was an important item that shaped history and the demand for these world foods. The Arabs probably bought sugar from southern India, though Southeast Asia is also a possibility. During the Columbian Exchange, sugar became more readily available and must have lowered the price of cookies. The Persians appear to have discovered sugar in India by the sixth century CE, but there is no evidence that they made cookies then.

The Spread of the Cookie

By the 14th century in Paris, France had a number of street vendors who sold cookies. Renaissance cookbooks in Europe contained several recipes for cookies with different ingredients. In the late 16th century, cookies were popular in Great Britain. Recipes called for sugar, flour, several spices, and egg yolks. This is a simple but caloric cookie. In an era when people were more active, the addition of extra calories probably did no harm and may even have benefited those with labor-intensive jobs. The problem lies in the inactivity of moderns. People still enjoy cookies but are not always active enough to burn the extra calories. Coupled with a lack of exercise, the result, and cookies are not the lone culprit, is obesity. It does not help that cookies contain sugar and fat because humans innately crave these foods, adding to the temptation to overeat.

The cookie maker did not master his or her craft overnight. An apprenticeship to a master chef was necessary to prepare one to bake quality cookies. These apprenticeships tended to last years. This model differs from current practices, in which machines make cookies and the investment of human capital and skills is minimal. Even those who pride themselves on their ability to make good cookies often follow a recipe. There is no need for ingenuity or forethought. By the Renaissance, the cookie maker was adept at adding extra ingredients like butter and oils from several sources. Cookies tasted even better but were even more fattening. At the same time, it was not unusual to combine three pounds of flour with one-and-a-half pounds of sugar. In this case, sugar represented one-third of a cookie by weight. Such a cookie must have been extremely sweet.

The United States

The cookie was unknown to the Amerindians, as was sugar. They managed well without the cookie, demonstrating that it was, in a sense, a superfluous food rather than a necessity. The Columbian Exchange changed matters. The English, Dutch, and Scots brought cookie recipes to what would become the United States. Over time, there would be no dearth of sugar as the Europeans erected sugar plantations in tropical America. These estates were productive but terribly exploitive. They overworked and abused captive Africans, who had no rights and could not refuse to labor under such brutal conditions. In time, blackness was the metaphorical equivalent of original sin. It marked one as inferior in every respect. To the extent that cookies, and sweets of all kinds, were a factor in this hellish system, they bear some responsibility for the evils of slavery.

Cookies appear to have been particularly valued in the American South. Every housewife knew how to make good cookies to serve her husband, children, and guests. Cookies were thus an item of hospitality as well as a comfort food. Immigrants from all parts of Europe and Asia brought their own cookie recipes to the United States, so that the country must have thousands of recipes that no single cookbook could compile. The rise of trade with Polynesia for coconut and with Florida and California for oranges opened new avenues for cookie makers in the 19th century. The advent and spread of electric refrigerators in the 1930s and 1940s made easy the storage of perishable cookies. The availability of the refrigerator stemmed from the New Deal commitment to electrify the countryside. People on farms and in cities alike could buy an electric refrigerator, which must have expanded the purchase and storage of cookies. Strictly speaking, though, hard cookies without egg yolk did not need refrigeration.

The Variety of Cookies

Initially imported from Britain, what are today animal crackers are really a type of simple cookie. These "Animals," as they were called in the 19th century, were popular with children and became a staple of circuses. Their renown was tied to American entertainer P. T. Barnum and for years they were known as "Barnum's Animals." They came in the shape of lions, bears, and other exotic creatures that were a staple of the circus. The appellation "crackers" made these cookies

"Barnum's Animal Crackers," a name that has stuck. Adults ate animal crackers with a glass of cocoa, a product derived from the cacao tree.

The Italians who came to the United States brought several types of cookies with them. Biscotti may be the best known, at least in the United States. The word *biscotti* means "twice cooked," though the phrase might be better rendered "twice baked." Those accustomed to the sweetness of sugar or chocolate chip cookies may be disappointed upon encountering biscotti. It is a hard, long cookie that has a hint of spices but very little sugar. For some Americans, biscotti is an acquired taste. Biscotti traces its roots to a type of biscuit that the Romans made in the second century CE. This biscuit predated the invention of cookies, and it may be that biscotti is among the oldest cookies. Biscotti follows the Roman tradition of a low-moisture biscuit that will store well, given that the Romans lived in an era without refrigeration. Bakers who have desired a sweeter cookie have altered the traditional recipe for biscotti by adding chocolate and honey.

By one account, the chocolate chip cookie accounts for half of all cookie sales in the United States. This cookie was an innovation of the Great Depression. In 1937, Massachusetts housewife Ruth Wakefield invented the chocolate chip cookie by adding chunks of chocolate to her batter. Because she worked at the Toll House Inn, these cookies became popular as the Toll House cookies. Two years later, Betty Crocker publicized Wakefield's cookies nationwide. Overnight, the cookie became a sensation. With Wakefield's permission, Nestle printed the Toll House recipe on the back of every pack of chocolate bars. Nestle agreed to give Wakefield a lifetime supply of its chocolate chips for her own use. In 1997, some 20 years after Wakefield's death, Massachusetts declared the chocolate chip cookie its state cookie, a posthumous honor.

The Nabisco company credits Philadelphia innovator James Mitchell with inventing the Fig Newton, another popular cookie. By definition, the cookie must include figs, originally the fruit of an Old World tree that withstands aridity. The Columbian Exchange brought the fig tree to California. The tree itself may have religious significance, and the fruit are very sweet without the addition of sugar. Mitchell converted the interior of the fig into a type of jam, which he enveloped in a flour shell. The cookie is soft, filling, and quite sweet. Another account credits Florida innovator Charles Roser with inventing the Fig Newton around 1892. This account claims that Roser sold his recipe to Nabisco for $1 million, the equivalent of about $20 million today. Nabisco denies this claim.

Further Reading

"The History of Cookies!" The Kitchen Project: Food History. Accessed February 14, 2015. www.kitchenproject.com/history/cookies.htm.

"History of Cookies." What's Cooking America. Accessed February 14, 2015. Whatscookingamerica.net/history/cookiehistory.htm.

Corn

Also known as "maize" and "Indian corn," corn is an annual grass related to sugar-cane, sorghum, teosinte and tripsacum. The latter two are not cultivated for food. In the 18th century, Swedish naturalist Carl Linnaeus placed corn in the genus *Zea*, meaning "wheat like grass," and in the species *mays*, a transliteration of "maize." In turn, "maize" derives from the Taino word *maiz*, meaning "life giver." A world crop grown in more varied climates and soils than any other grain, corn is cultivated in all tropical and temperate locales from 58° north to 40° south. So important is corn to the United States that it is grown in all 50 states. Corn is adapted to a range of growing conditions, and can survive in areas with as little as 10 inches of rain per year and as much as 400 inches yearly.

Corn cob fossils from the Joya de Ceren archaelogical site at the new facilities of the Joya de Ceren museum in San Juan Opico, El Salvador. Corn is an ancient crop that is still grown extensively today. (LUIS GALDAMEZ/Reuters/Corbis)

Hybrid Corn

An American achievement, hybrid corn has been among the great successes of applied science. Its foundation dates to the work of Austrian monk Gregor Mendel in hybridizing pea plants, the results of which he published in 1866. By then there was already great interest in corn breeding. The subject fascinated British naturalist Charles Darwin, though the real strides would be made in the United States. At the agricultural experiment stations, the land-grant universities, and the U.S. Department of Agriculture, much interest surrounded the breeding of corn from the late 19th century. The crucial breakthrough came in 1909 when American geneticist George Harrison Shull, inbreeding corn over several generations, came to the insight that he had created a number of pure lines, similar to the varieties of peas that Mendel had used. Crossbreeding these pure lines would cause hybrid vigor or heterosis, a desirable trait that would manifest in higher yield, stout stalks that would not lodge, drought tolerance, and in some cases resistance to insects or diseases. Several breeders followed Shull, and by the 1940s nearly every American corn grower planted a variety of hybrid corn. The rapidity of this success was remarkable.

Unlike several other crops, corn is not primarily a food for humans. Worldwide, farmers feed three-quarters of their corn to livestock. In the United States, corn growers feed an even larger portion to livestock. One bushel of corn yields 15 pounds of beef, 26 pounds of pork, and 37 pounds of chicken. Humans thus consume corn secondhand.

The corn that livestock and humans do not eat is converted into an astonishing variety of products. Chemists convert corn into syrup, sugar, glue, and ethanol. Mayonnaise, soap, paint, and insecticides contain corn oil. Peanut butter, chewing gum, soft drinks, vegetables, beer, wine, crackers, bread, frozen fish, hot dogs, and corned beef all have corn syrup among their ingredients. Derivatives of corn are found in cough drops, toothpaste, lipstick, shaving cream, shoe polish, detergents, tobacco, rayon, leather, rubber tires, urethane foam, explosives, and latex gloves. A product in baby food and embalming fluid, corn attends life from birth to death. One ear of corn contains 75 calories, 15 grams of carbohydrate, two grams of protein, one gram of fat, and two grams of fiber. Corn is a source of vitamin C, vitamins B_1 and B_5, folic acid, phosphorus, and manganese.

American Origins

Despite intensive research, scholars do not agree on where and when corn originated. The outstanding feature of corn is its dependence on humans for survival.

No species of corn is wild. Rather, corn perpetuates itself only with human aid. The husk that surrounds corn binds the kernels (seeds) so tightly that they cannot disperse. Were an ear of corn to fall to the ground, the seeds would germinate so close together that they would die from overcrowding. This state of affairs suggests that humans have cultivated corn many millennia.

In the 19th century, French botanist Alphonse de Candolle proposed that corn originated in Colombia, from which it spread to Peru and Mexico. From Peru, de Candolle believed, corn diffused to South America and the Caribbean, and from Mexico, to North America. In the 1920s, Peruvian archeologist Julio Tello dismissed the idea that corn originated in Colombia. Rather, he believed, the people of Peru and Mexico independently domesticated corn. In 1939, American botanist Paul Mangelsdorf proposed a variety of wild pod corn, now extinct, as corn's ancestor. Pod corn differs from corn in having a husk for each kernel. This early corn hybridized repeatedly with teosinte, a process that increased the size of corn's ears. This hybridization may have been accidental. Humans may have grown corn near fields of teosinte. This hypothesis is most plausible if corn originated in Mexico, where a species of perennial teosinte grows. Because corn cross-pollinates it might have readily hybridized with teosinte. Alternatively, humans may have purposefully crossed early corn and teosinte to obtain hybrids (a process different from the production of hybrid corn). Mangelsdorf believed that humans first propagated corn in both Mexico and South America. Others propose Central America as the cradle of corn. American agronomist Hugh Iltis thinks that corn derived from a perennial teosinte and that corn evolved rapidly in size, possibly by mutation.

Archeologists have found the oldest fossilized corncobs in the Tehuacan Valley, suggesting that corn originated in Mexico about 7,000 years ago. Subsequent excavations in New Mexico turned up corncobs as old as 5,600 years. From Mexico corn must have migrated north throughout North America as de Candolle thought. From Mexico corn spread to Colombia around 5,000 years ago and to Peru around 4,000 years ago. Mangelsdorf is surely right in supposing that the Amerindians took corn wherever they migrated. Wherever migrants made contact they likely exchanged varieties of corn, hybridizing them in the process.

Before 1492, the indigenes of the Americas grew corn from Canada to Chile. So important was corn to the Amerindians that it was believed to have come from the gods. The Maya believed that the god Oze Hunahpu, who defeated the Lords of Death, gave them corn. The Inca believed that the god Manco-Poca, the son of the sun, gave humans corn. The Totenae of Central America received corn from the goddess Tzinteatl, the wife of the sun. The Aztecs looked to the goddess Xilonan and the god Quetzalcoatl for corn. The Pawnee believed that the Evening Star, now known as the planet Venus, gave them corn.

Probably using recurrent selection, the Amerindians developed the principal types of corn: flint, dent, flour, pop, and sweet. Because cob size increased with time, the Amerindians must have selected plants with large ears, though they may have eaten the best corn and saved only the less desirable kernels for planting.

The Amerindians did not plant corn in isolation. The Peruvians grew corn and potatoes. The natives of North America planted the three sisters: corn, beans, and squash. This triad of plants is nourishing and agriculturally sound. Beans provide protein that corn lacks and take full advantage of sunlight by climbing the corn stalks. Squash, covering the ground with its leaves, chocks out weeds and helps soil retain moisture. Despite the absence of knowledge of nutrition, the Amerindians were nonetheless perceptive enough to soak corn in alkali water, which liberates the niacin that is otherwise unavailable for digestion. The Amerindians prized corn for its rapid maturation, its meager demand for labor, and its longevity in storage. The indigenes understood that corn, unlike other crops, need not be harvested when ripe. By one estimate, the Amerindians devoted 20 hours of labor per bushel of corn.

Corn was the staple of New World civilizations. Indeed, it made civilization possible in the Americas. The Maya erected their civilization on a foundation of corn. Human sacrifice was part of corn culture for the Maya, who fertilized their fields with the blood of sacrificial victims. So central to Mayan civilization that its failure was surely catastrophic, the corn crop may have declined sharply in the ninth century CE, abruptly truncating the civilization. One hypothesis holds that a disease spread by insects killed large numbers of corn plants, causing famine. Unable to recover, the Maya abandoned their cities.

Corn and Demography

Columbus's discovery of the Americas transformed corn from a hemispheric to a world crop. He may have first seen corn on October 14, 1492, on the Caribbean island of San Salvador. A few days later he saw in the Bahamas what he called *panizo*, Italian for "millet." Because millet had not yet been introduced to the New World, Columbus must have been mistaken. Instead, he likely saw corn. On November 5, he dispatched two men to reconnoiter Cuba. They returned with corn, calling it *maiz*, as the indigenes did.

Recognizing its value, Columbus brought corn back to Spain in 1493. Within 25 years it spread throughout the Mediterranean basin. Within 50 years it was grown worldwide. So ubiquitous did corn become, and so quickly, that some people forgot that it was a native plant of the Americas. In the 16th century one French botanist called corn "Turkish wheat," in the mistaken notion that corn had originated in Turkey. Confusing it with millet, the Portuguese called corn *milho*, which derives from *milhete*, meaning "millet." Because of this confusion, Portuguese writers posited Asia as the home of corn. Later generations of Chinese were sure that corn had originated in China.

Despite their ambivalence toward corn, the Chinese grew it in bulk upon their adoption of the crop from the Portuguese in 1516. A surplus of corn made possible the population expansion that began in the 17th century. Thanks to corn, China's population quadrupled in the eighteenth and nineteenth centuries. Farmers grew corn in Manchuria, the Yangtze delta, the mountains of Yunan and Szechwan and southwestern China. Today, corn totals 22 percent of all crops grown in China.

In Africa, corn became the food of the masses and of the slave trade. Because Africans would eat corn aboard the slave ships, it became their staple, along with beans. Because corn has vitamin C, it must have saved Africans from scurvy, though mortality during the transatlantic voyage remained appalling. Corn was thus complicit in the evils of the slave trade. In Africa, people grew corn with millet. Because corn yielded more food than Africa's traditional crops, people turned to it for sustenance. Corn, cassava, and sweet potatoes, perhaps more than any other assemblage of crops, fueled Africa's dramatic population increase that began in the 16th century and accelerated in the 19th century. Perhaps corn has become too successful because Africa has outrun its food supply and depends on the West, the United States in particular, for perhaps 30 percent of its grain. Part of the problem was the late arrival of the Green Revolution in Africa. The varieties of hybrid corn that have been so successful in the United States since the 1920s have only recently made their way to Africa.

The Hybrid Corn Revolution

Among the great achievements of applied science, the development of hybrid corn marks an important confluence between science and agriculture that changed the world. The new science of genetics was at the core of this revolution. Austrian monk Gregor Mendel had founded the science as a result of his work hybridizing pea plants. The American geneticist George Harrison Shull realized in 1909 that if he inbred corn, a naturally cross-pollinating plant, he could separate it into types. Each type would be similar to a variety of peas, and by crossing them a breeder would hybridize corn as Mendel had hybridized peas. Hybridization allowed breeders to derive corn with heterosis or hybrid vigor. Heterosis was not a new phenomenon. Humans had known for millennia that the mule, a hybrid between the horse and donkey, has greater vigor than its parents. In corn, heterosis might give plants high yield; resistance to diseases, insects and drought; stalk strength; or some combination of desiderata.

Although simple in concept, the breeding of hybrid corn occupied plant breeders for a generation. The problem lies in the reproduction of corn, a plant that cross-fertilizes rather than self fertilizes, as do many other grains. The tassel, having the pollen, and the silk, having the ovule, are far apart on corn, and wind wafts pollen from one plant to another. To inbreed corn, the first step in producing a hybrid, a scientist or farmer or someone familiar with the anatomy of a corn plant must cover the tassel and silk to prevent their cross-pollination. When the tassel is full of pollen, a scientist gathers it to place on the silk of the same plant. The process of inbreeding yields homozygous lines of corn that breed true, as does a variety of peas. In perverting the natural process of crossbreeding, inbreeding attenuates corn, producing scrawny ears with little seed. This small sample provides a breeder enough seed to make a cross on a tiny parcel of land but not enough to produce hybrid seed on the scale that farmers needed for their fields. As long as the yield was small, hybrid corn remained an interesting phenomenon rather than a business venture. In 1917, however, Connecticut agronomist Donald F. Jones obtained large amounts of seed by crossing four inbred lines over two generations.

Accustomed to saving a portion of their corn crop for next year's seed, farmers did not buy hybrids in large numbers in the 1920s. The drought of 1934 and 1936, however, proved the superiority of hybrids. In arid lands farmers saw their varieties of corn wither, whereas hybrids survived. This demonstration won over farmers. Between 1933 and 1943 the percentage of corn acreage planted to hybrids leapt from one to 90.

Hybrid corn aided the spread of technology. The old varieties of corn were difficult to harvest because they did not stand straight, but bowed under the weight of ears. With stronger stalks, hybrids stood erect and were easily harvested by the mechanical corn picker. The mechanical harvester spread throughout the Corn Belt after World War II. Today, almost no corn is harvested by hand.

In the 1940s, scientists discovered genes that made corn produce no pollen. Using these male sterile lines as the female plant, breeders crossed them with normal plants to obtain hybrids. Although the use of male sterile lines simplified the work of breeding corn, scientists did not fully appreciate their susceptibility to disease. The southern corn leaf blight, a fungal disease, struck the U.S. corn crop in 1970 and 1971. Some farmers along the Mississippi and Ohio Rivers lost their entire crop. Science had not been able to save the corn crop from catastrophe.

In the late 20th century, traditional breeding ceded ground to genetic engineering. In the 1970s, scientists learned to extract genes from one organism and insert them into another, an achievement with obvious applications to agriculture. In 1997, the agrochemical company Monsanto inserted into corn genes from the bacterium *Bacillus thuringiensis* (Bt) that code for the production of a toxin to the European corn borer, a pest of corn since 1917. Bt corn allowed farmers to use less insecticide, a practice that saved money and helped the environment. Yet, in 1999, scientists at Cornell University charged that Bt corn pollen killed monarch butterflies, stirring up a debate over the role of genetic engineering in agriculture that continues today. Despite the furor over genetic engineering, the future of corn, as was true of the past, is surely tied to the progress of science.

Further Reading

Fussell, Betty. *The Story of Corn*. New York: Knopf, 1992.

Mangelsdorf, Paul C. *Corn: Its Origin, Evolution and Improvement*. Cambridge: Harvard University Press, 1974.

Smith, C. Wayne, Javier Betran, and E. C. A. Runge. *Corn: Origin, History, Technology and Production*. Hoboken, NJ: Wiley, 2004.

Warman, Arturo. *Corn and Capitalism: How a Botanical Bastard Grew to Global Dominance*. Chapel Hill and London: The University of North Carolina Press, 2003.

Corn Syrup and High Fructose Corn Syrup

Corn was first used as a sweetener when scientists began to extract glucose from corn. Glucose is a sugar abundant in plants and a primary product of photosynthesis, though less sweet than sucrose (what is conventionally known as "crystalline sugar" or just "sugar") or fructose, an important sugar found in fruits such as grapes, peaches, plums, cherries, and many more. Corn syrup is a sweet, viscous liquid made from cornstarch. High fructose corn syrup (HFCS) is a bit more complicated. Glucose and fructose are isomers. That is, they have the same chemical formula ($C_6H_{12}O_6$) but different arrangements of these atoms, so that they have different properties. Before the 1950s there was no way to convert one to the other, but in 1957 Illinois scientists Richard Marshall and Earl Kooi isolated an enzyme that converted glucose to fructose, setting the stage for the development of HFCS. The problem was that the enzyme was poisonous. Japanese researchers quickly solved the problem by finding a nontoxic enzyme that converted the glucose in corn into fructose, creating the first edible HFCS. In 1967, the United States marketed the first brand of HFCS.

Corn Syrup

The use of corn syrup as a sweetener increased in the late 19th century and throughout the 20th century, displeasing growers of cane sugar who believed that their sweetener was the only pure and "natural" sweetener. This opposition created a rivalry between corn and sugarcane growers. The contest between corn syrup and cane syrup, a viscous liquid derived from the sugarcane plant, pitted two giants in the food industry against one another. The outcome was not immediately certain. Sugarcane growers in the Deep South were vigorous opponents of corn syrup, but they were not especially numerous or well funded. In antebellum America, Louisiana had been an important sugar and cane syrup producer, but by the 20th century Louisiana sugar was in decline. If sugarcane remained important in south Florida, as it is today, oppressive labor conditions discouraged the recruitment of workers. To be sure, Hawaii was and is the sugar and cane syrup empire in the United States, but it was not always united with the interests of Florida growers.

Ranged against them were the more-united and better-funded corn growers of the American Midwest, an area known as the Corn Belt, though soybeans have for decades been an important crop in this region. Corn was king in the United States, and corn growers understood that corn syrup could enrich them by providing another avenue for their product. Corn was not just a livestock feed. It was the source of sweetness. Because corn syrup was cheaper than sugar or cane syrup, it gave corn growers a critical edge. The appeal of sugar now hinged on aesthetic considerations. Only where it was important to showcase the appetizing appeal of sugar crystals—in cookies, for example—did sugar have a clear advantage over corn syrup. But, wherever aesthetics did not dominate, corn syrup more than held its own against sugar. In this context, corn syrup became critical to the beverage industry, flavoring soft drinks, a position that HFCS would strengthen in the 1970s and 1980s.

For this reason sugar growers saw threats everywhere. In the 20th century the Interstate Sugar Cane Growers Association launched a propaganda war against corn syrup. The upshot of this war came down to the assertion that corn syrup was somehow unnatural and foreign. It lacked the wholesomeness and goodness of sugar. These claims ignore the fact that both sugar and corn syrup lack any nutrients. Both are nothing more than empty calories, a circumstance that does not seem natural in either context. Yet in many ways cane sugar growers and marketers adapted to the new terrain by mixing corn syrup with cane syrup. Even the mixing of the two was unnatural to the most vigorous cane sugar proponents.

Both sugarcane and corn growers wanted these products labeled so that consumers had the information to decide whether they wanted the item. The Georgia legislature went further, outlawing the addition of corn syrup to cane syrup, again on the grounds that corn syrup was somehow impure. Meanwhile, in the Midwest and throughout the north, corn syrup manufacturers were distributing corn syrup to households, to give the occupants a real taste of sweetness. They also distributed free corn syrup at the 1904 Saint Louis Centennial Exposition. The U.S. Department of Agriculture (USDA) established quality standards against which various brands of corn syrup would be measured, upgrading these standards in 1951. The USDA also promoted the establishment of a corn syrup canning industry. Into the mid-20th century, corn syrup was sometimes paired with maple syrup to create a super-sweet treat. The Food and Drug Administration (FDA) required that the product be labeled so that one would not conclude that one was buying a product with pure corn syrup.

At other times, corn syrup was mixed with glucose and fructose. Interestingly, the brand Pure Georgia Cane Syrup was actually 15 percent corn syrup. The federal government sued and secured a conviction of the brand for misleading consumers. Another brand with 20 percent corn syrup suffered a similar fate. The worst offender of "pure" cane syrup was more than 45 percent corn syrup. Dixie Maid, Cross Roads, and Sunnyland all contained corn syrup. Nigger in de Cane Patch, an offensive name, promoted itself as "NOT a blend of corn syrup and other cheap products," making clear its low opinion of corn syrup. These deceptive practices led to a sharp rebuke from consumers. Understanding the source of this anger, the FDA required manufacturers to list all ingredients in descending order of importance. By the mid-1930s, the United States consumed roughly 1 billion pounds of corn syrup per year, much of it in soft drinks, confectionaries, and table syrups. In these examples, corn syrup and HFCS shaped history by emerging as alternatives to sugar, an ancient and important sweetener.

High Fructose Corn Syrup

At the time HFCS was first marketed, in 1967, it was possible to convert about 15 percent of corn's glucose into fructose. Sales began to soar after 1970, with HFCS being used to sweeten soft drinks, baked goods, pickles, salad dressings, and other syrups. By 1980, HFCS flavored ice cream and ketchup. By then, HFCS was sufficiently enriched with fructose to be, ounce for ounce, as sweet as sugar.

By using other enzymes to convert the glucose in corn into fructose, several companies developed their own brands of HFCS. Much of this activity occurred in Iowa and other Corn Belt states. Even sugar makers invested in the manufacture of HFCS to diversify their product line. With so much HFCS on the market, sugar seemed to be an afterthought. In the 1980s, Congress ended subsidies to cane growers, though beet sugar producers have been relentless in hounding Congress to retain subsidies on their product. Perhaps the situation is akin to the subsidies to the oil industry, whose support from the government has also been questioned.

As early as 1974, Coca-Cola announced that Sprite, Mr. Pibb, and Fanta had 25 percent HFCS. Royal Crown Cola and Canada Dry released similar figures. By 1980, Coca-Cola was 50 percent HFCS. Four years later, the figure stood at 75 percent. In 1983, Pepsi had 50 percent HFCS. HFSC thus made the soft drink industry viable in the late 20th and early 21st centuries. Consumption leapt among Americans. In 1974, the average American consumed four pounds of HFCS per year. By 1987, the number had mushroomed to 129 pounds. In the context of such consumption, nutritionists warned that HFCS was a cause of obesity. Many causes factor into the rise of obesity in the United States and other developed countries. Lack of exercise and the absence of strenuous labor are causes, but so, too, are calorie-dense foods like HFCS and other sweeteners. HFCS has become so important that it is now part of a public health crisis.

Further Reading

Warner, Deborah Jean. *Sweet Stuff: An American History of Sweeteners from Sugar to Sucralose*. Washington, DC: Smithsonian Institution Scholarly Press, 2011.

D

Date

A palm tree that produces sugary fruit, the date palm (*Phoenix dactylifera*) is among the oldest cultivated trees. The people of Israel and Arabia knew the date palm as *tamar*, from which the Portuguese derive *tamara*. The English *date*, the French *datte*, the German *dattel*, the Spanish *datel*, and the Italian *dattile* derive from the same source. The genus name *Phoenix* may derive from *phoinix*, Greek for "date palm." The Greeks may have associated the date palm with date-producing civilization Phoenicia, from which *phoinix* may be derived. The species name *dactylifera* is Latin for "finger bearing," an apparent reference to the resemblance of clusters of dates to fingers. The genus *Phoenix* has 12 species. A ripe date is 60 percent sugar. The ancients fermented dates into wine because of their sugar content. The date has little protein and fat, just 2 percent of each. The date has iron, magnesium, potassium, phosphorus, calcium, copper, boron, cobalt, fluorine, manganese, selenium, zinc, and small amounts of vitamin A, vitamin B_1, vitamin D, riboflavin, and fiber. Date palm leaves were once used to make baskets, roofs, mats, and rope. Egyptians still use date palm leaves to make rope. The wood was used to build houses. In this context, the date palm and its fruit shaped history in a variety of ways.

The Date Palm and Its Fruit

The date is a staple in the Middle East and Saharan Africa, much as rice, wheat, and the potato are staples in other regions of the world. The date palm is dioecious, bearing male and female flowers on separate trees. If a palm is planted from seeds, the offspring, as one might expect, are half male and half female. To the grower this is wasteful because only half the palms, the females, can bear fruit, and the male trees, shedding abundant pollen, are more numerous than is necessary to pollinate the females. In the 1970s, growers planted palms in a ratio of one male to

An Arab street vendor sells fresh dates at a bazaar in Medina, Saudi Arabia. Dates are a staple breakfast food for Muslims around the world. (Ahmad Faizal Yahya/Dreamstime.com)

forty or fifty females. Today the ratio is one to 100. Some growers do not plant male trees, but rather buy pollen each year to satisfy their needs.

A palm yields small clusters of flowers in spring. Because insects do not pollinate the flowers, they are not showy. Wind pollinates the date palm, though since antiquity humans have hand-pollinated it to increase the yield. Having flowered in spring, a palm is ready to harvest in late summer or early autumn. In California, the harvest spans November to February. If planted from a shoot, a palm needs four years to bear fruit. If planted from a seed, a palm needs eight to 10 years to mature. A palm may grow to 100 feet and live 200 years. The grower who wishes to gather shoots must strip a palm of fruit. The grower who wishes to harvest an abundant crop of dates must remove several shoots. (Removing all shoots will prevent a tree from issuing forth new shoots in subsequent years.) A palm will not produce abundant fruit and shoots simultaneously.

A plant of the desert, the date palm is unusual in tolerating saline soil. Rain may damage dates, so an arid climate is best. The date palm needs full sun and arid conditions, but it is not drought tolerant. From antiquity, humans have irrigated date palms, building irrigation canals or digging wells to tap water underground. The requirement of irrigation made the palm a labor-intensive crop from its earliest days. The planting of a palm was also labor intensive. The grower selected a sucker or shoot from an elite tree, a practice that allowed him or her to be certain of the traits of the new plant and to know its sex. Digging a hole eight feet deep, he added five feet of a mixture of loose soil and manure. Planting the shoot in a hole that was now three feet deep, he was able to cultivate the palm in partial shade. As it grew, the grower filled the hole with soil until he reached the surface of the ground.

There are hundreds of varieties of dates, classified as soft, semidry, and dry. A palm tree yields 100 to 300 pounds of dates per year. Although a tree of the desert the date palm tolerates temperatures below freezing. Americans and Europeans consider the date a dessert and import it from the Middle East and North Africa. In 2007, the world produced 7.6 million tons of dates. Egypt was the leader with 1.4 million tons. Iran ranked second with 1.1 million tons, Saudi Arabia was third with 1 million tons, the United Arab Emirates placed fourth with 832,000 tons, and Pakistan ranked fifth with 614,000 tons. The United States was not a leading producer.

The ancients attributed health benefits to dates. First century CE Roman encyclopedist Pliny the Elder believed that the date treated chest pain and cough, and strengthened a person weakened by a long illness. Other ancients used the date to treat anxiety, kidney ailments, and stomach problems. Mohammed (570–632 CE), the founder of Islam, counseled nursing women to eat dates in the belief that the fruit helped them lactate. Mohammed believed that dates protected one from "poison and treachery." Other Arabs believed that the date cured fever, impotence, and other maladies. Oil from the seeds is used in soap and cosmetics. Dates were thus central to the rise of Islam and Arabic culture.

Origin and History

An Old Word domesticate, the date palm has left fossils in the Mediterranean basin dating to the Eocene epoch. No wild palm exists, suggesting the antiquity of cultivation. Wild palms once grew in the region of the Dead Sea, inhabiting lands with brackish water where no other plants lived. According to one authority, humans may have first encountered the date palm in the lower valley of the Tigris and Euphrates Rivers in ancient Sumer. Its cultivation dates to 4000 BCE in Sumer. Another authority shifts the origin of date cultivation to Arabia around 6000 BCE, from which it spread to Mesopotamia (now Iraq). Ancient Jericho had so many date palms that it was known as the "City of the Palms." In ancient Babylon, landowners leased land with date palms to tenants in exchange for half the harvest. Babylonians planted date palms at a density of 50 trees per acre. In the 18th century BCE, the law code of Babylonian king Hammurabi set the fine for cutting down a date palm at 15 ounces of silver, surely a prohibitive amount for the average person. The Babylonians interplanted date palms with sesame, grain, and clover. The delta of the Tigris and Euphrates Rivers is today home to some 5 million date palms. In warfare the victors, notably the Assyrians, cut down the date palms of the conquered.

From Mesopotamia the date palm migrated to North Africa. The Egyptians cultivated it by 3000 BCE. In the Eighteenth Dynasty, Egyptian art depicted Pharaoh Thutmose I offering dates to the gods. Today, Egypt has some 10 million date palms. Around the time of Christ, North Africans cultivated the date palm in the Sahara Desert, terming the date the "bread of the desert." Travelers across the desert carried a bag of dates as food for both humans and camels. In Algeria, farmers intercropped the date palm with the orange, apricot, nuts, and vegetables. From Mesopotamia, the date palm spread to Greece and Rome. The Romans planted date palms in Spain 2,000 years ago. Under Muslim rule, the date palm became widespread in Spain.

In 1513, the Spanish attempted to plant the date palm in Cuba, but the Amerindians killed the plants. This act did not deter Spanish soldier Rodrigo de Tamayo, who founded the town of Datil, meaning "date," where he planted date palms and tobacco. The palms did not thrive in Cuba, which is today not an important producer. In the 16th century, Spanish explorer Hernán Cortés introduced the date palm to Mexico. The Spanish attempted to grow it in Florida, but the climate was too humid. In the 18th century, Spanish missionaries planted date palms, derived from Mexican stock, near San Diego, California. In the 19th century, farmers tried again to grow the date palm in Florida, but by the 1830s these efforts had failed. In 1857, rancher J. R. Wolfskill planted date palms in the Sacramento River Valley in California. These trees began bearing fruit in 1877. In the 1860s, farmers planted date palms in Yuma, Arizona. These trees began to yield dates in the 1880s. In 1890, the U.S. Department of Agriculture (USDA) gathered shoots from Egypt, Algeria, and Arabia, planting them in New Mexico, Arizona, and California. In 1900, the USDA made a second introduction of date palms in Arizona. In 1903 and 1907, farmer Bernard Johnson introduced the date palm to the Coachella Valley in California. In 1912, Johnson made additional plantings in Yuma, Arizona. By then, Arizona had more date palms than California. Between 1913 and 1923, U.S. farmers sent plant explorers to the Middle East and North Africa to find the best varieties of date palm. After 1913, plantings in the Coachella Valley made California the leading date producer in the United States. Since 1921, the Coachella Valley has hosted an annual Date Festival in February, attracting 250,000 visitors from the United States and Canada.

In the 20th century, the date was so popular in California that merchandisers sold date shakes and date ice cream. In the 1960s, however, some growers sold their land to real estate developers. Other growers planted citrus to diversify their income. The growers who survived capitalized on consumers' desire for natural foods. Growers boasted that they did not spray their trees with insecticide, use synthetic fertilizers, or add preservatives to dates, because they keep for months if stored at low temperature. By the 1970s, the Coachella Valley had 220,000 date palm on 4,400 acres. The rest of the United States had 260 acres of date palm. In 2004, California totaled 4,500 acres of date palm. The rest of the United States totaled fewer than 450 acres.

Further Reading

Barreveld, W. H. *Date Palm Products*. Rome: Food and Agriculture Organization, 1993.

Musselman, Lytton John. *Figs, Dates, Laurel, and Myrrh: Plants of the Bible and the Quran*. Portland, OR: Timber Press, 2007.

Popenoe, Paul. *The Date Palm*. Miami, FL: Field Research Projects, 1973.

Simon, Hilda. *The Date Palm: Bread of the Desert*. New York: Dodd, Mead and Company, 1978.

Zaid, Abdelouahhab, ed. *Date Palm Cultivation*. Rome: Food and Agriculture Organization, 2002.

Duck

Humans have likely eaten ducks for at least 6,000 years. The Chinese likely domesticated the aquatic bird, though other sources point to Egypt. Partly because of the way it is bred and raised, the duck is not a low-calorie food. For a type of poultry, it has a surprising amount of fat and cannot compete with the chicken or turkey for producing lean meat. The duck has shaped history primarily in East Asia, where it is an important protein source, even if for centuries it was a food of the affluent. Its importance in Asia contrasts with the comparative neglect in the West, where beef, pork, chicken, turkey, and fish are all more significant as protein sources. Duck has none of the religious significance, at least in the West, when one compares it to the role that fish play in the canonical Gospels, or the role that the fig, banana, or apple may play in our interpretation of Genesis as the putative forbidden fruit.

Origins and Domestication

The wild mallard is the ancestor of nearly all varieties of domestic ducks today. Unlike the chicken and turkey, the duck is an aquatic bird. Accordingly, ducks have webbing between their toes, doubtless an evolutionary adaptation to aquatic life. The domestic duck is too heavy to be an apt flier. Many cannot fly at all. The question of domestication has not been settled. It is clear that the Chinese made clay figurines of ducks about 4000 BCE. Ducks must have been important to the Chinese, almost certainly as food. This does not prove domestication at this point, though if the Chinese did not domesticate the duck at that date they must have hunted and trapped it. In either case, duck was part of Chinese cuisine from an early date. Others point to ancient Egypt. A 14th-century BCE carving depicts the pharaoh Akhenaten, a bold reformer in many respects, sacrificing ducks to a god. Knowing his preference for monotheism, Akhenaten must have sacrificed the duck to the sun god. This gesture strongly suggests that the Egyptians ate ducks. A parallel is the example of the Hebrews, who both ate lamb and sacrificed it to their god Yahweh. In this context, the duck must have played some role in shaping monotheism and, for this reason, must have shaped history. Why else would the Egyptians have domesticated the duck, assuming that they did domesticate it, if not for food?

Southeast Asia must have been another pioneer, eating ducks before 500 BCE. The Romans were not far behind Southeast Asia and were avid consumers of duck. First–century-CE Roman agricultural writer Columella urged farmers to raise ducks, both to meet their own needs and to sell at the local market. For Columella, then, the duck was both sustenance and income. Aside from Columella, other agricultural writers in Europe did not mention the duck until the ninth century CE. At that time, the duck was a food of necessity and a means by which tenants paid their landlords. In the West, the duck is a tertiary bird. Most Europeans and Americans prefer chicken and turkey. In terms of cost, duck cannot compete with chicken or turkey. East Asia retains a preference for duck. Although chicken is still an important food, many Asians prefer duck.

The Duck in Commerce and Dining

The leg meat has a stronger flavor than the breast. One experiences a similar phenomenon with turkey. In 2007, the world produced nearly 4 million metric tons of duck. Eighty-four percent of this total came from Asia, 83 percent of it being from China alone. The Vietnamese and Indonesians raise ducks primarily for eggs. Indeed, a female duck may be as fecund as a hen. The duck egg, at more than 90 grams, is much heavier than the chicken egg, which seldom eclipses 65 grams. The duck egg is about 50 percent egg white, 35 percent yolk, and 15 percent shell. The duck egg is nutritious, containing several vitamins, notably A and D. Recent attention paid to the importance of vitamin D can only propel the duck egg to greater renown. Duck eggs, however, lack vitamin C. The bad news is that the

duck egg has more than twice the cholesterol of the chicken egg. All the cholesterol resides in the yolk, as is true of any avian egg.

The Role of the Duck in Nutrition

Duck is a fine source of protein, and in parts of Asia it is the primary source of
protein. In this context, duck has shaped history and daily life. The knock against
duck is that it is too high in fat. Duck is far more fattening than fish, chicken, or
turkey. By weight, duck is 39 percent fat, 12 percent protein and 49 percent water.
The amount of fat fares particularly poorly against several species of fish that contain either no fat or 1 percent fat. The high fat content comes as much from the
science of duck breeding and the process of raising ducks. Scientists concentrate
on breeding ducks that grow very rapidly and so may be butchered in a matter of
weeks. These ducks, fed to hasten growth, are still juveniles despite their large
size. As juveniles, they retain lots of "baby" fat. As juveniles they also have purely
developed breasts. This scientific wizardry is anything but. It is at odds with what
the consumer wants. The consumer desires a small, lean duck with appreciable
breasts, rather than the large, fat, small breasted duck that scientists and growers
produce. Having perfected the fat duck, scientists are pivoting in the face of criticism and are now attempting to breed a lean duck with notable breasts. But these
ducks will probably take longer to grow and may cost more at the grocer. One
wonders whether consumers will get what they want in the end.

Pekin Duck or Peking Duck?

There is confusion in the terminology of ducks. For example, "Pekin" and "Peking"
duck are not the same. Pekin duck is a breed that may well have originated in
China. It is the most popular duck eaten in the West and is generally served with
plum sauce. Peking duck, however, is a Chinese dish that must take its name from
Peking, the city that is now Beijing, the capital of China. Because Peking had long
been the capital of dynastic China, Peking duck must have been a special dish.
Initially, only the emperor and his advisors had the privilege of eating Peking
duck, now known as "Beijing" duck given the change in the capital's name. Peking
duck is roasted duck upon thin layers of pancakes, a sauce containing noodles, and
sliced green onions. Traditionally the chef wraps the duck in one or more pancakes. The Yuan Dynasty of the Mongols may have pioneered Peking duck in the
13th or 14th century. In the 16th century the earliest Chinese restaurant to serve
Peking duck opened for business. Because a restaurant profits only by serving lots
of food, one might suppose that Peking duck had become a mass commodity. But
this seems untrue. Into the 18th century Peking duck remained a food of the elites.

It was then a food of scholars and poets. The Chinese enjoyed coupling duck with pork. The Romans would do much the same. In 1926, Peking had nine restaurants that specialized in preparing Peking duck. In Beijing today, the Quanjude Restaurant may be the world's largest specialist in Peking duck. The establishment can serve 5,000 Peking duck meals per day.

The Duck in the Americas and Australia

Americans consume more than 100 million pounds of duck per year, an impressive figure in a nation not known for its consumption of duck. Indiana is the leading producer of ducks in the United States, followed by California, Pennsylvania, Wisconsin, and New York. The United States raises nearly 4 million ducks per year for domestic consumption. Duck production in Texas appears to have coincided with its admission to the United States in 1845, though production would not expand until the 20th century. At first, the duck, like the chicken, was part of the small farm. Growers raised enough to supply their needs with perhaps a small surplus to sell at the local market. As late as 1890, ducks were an afterthought, as Texas raised more chickens, turkeys, and geese than ducks.

Whereas the duck has a long culinary history in Asia, Australia is a latecomer but is making rapid strides. Only in the 1970s and 1980s did duck production begin to soar. Australians roast, braise, or barbecue ducks, much as Americans apply the same cooking methods to beef. Australia raises more than 8 million ducks per year and the continent eats about 18,000 metric tons of duck per year. Ninety-five percent of ducks supply the domestic market, with the rest exported to Asia.

Further Reading

Damron, W. Stephen. *Introduction to Animal Science: Global, Biological, Social, and Industry Perspectives*. 5th ed. Boston: Pearson, 2013.

Scanes, Colin. *Fundamentals of Animal Science*. Australia: Delmar, 2011.

Dumplings

An old food, the dumpling appears to have originated in China. It can be a simple food, being no more than a boiled or steamed piece of dough of a consistency akin to bread. In addition, the dumpling may be fried, to the detriment of consumers who do not need the extra fat. The dumpling, almost infinitely variable, is part of the world's cuisines and in this context has shaped the culinary habits and daily lives of people throughout the globe. A piece of dough may not be inherently appetizing, but the beauty of the dumpling is that one can add many other foods to it. Meats like pork, beef, and mutton may be part of a dumpling. A dumpling may contain fish or other seafood. It may contain a variety of vegetables and fruits. The apple dumpling is particularly appealing in the United States, though the plum dumpling is no less popular in other parts of the world. In this context, the dumpling may be a savory or sweet food. It may serve as breakfast, lunch, or dinner. It may be the main course, a side dish, or dessert. The question is not what one can do with a dumpling but rather what can one not do with a dumpling? It is as variable as the human imagination.

Origins

The origin of the dumpling may be obscure, but what evidence exists seems to point to China. According to legend, a man who must have lived in northern China invented dumplings during the Han dynasty (circa 200 BCE–200 CE). One year he took a long trip, returning to his village in winter amid frigid weather. He observed that many of his neighbors suffered frostbite, particularly on the ears. In an effort to help them, he filled dough with mutton, beef, and medicinal herbs. Distributing them to his neighbors, he invited them to eat the dumplings to keep them warm. Despite the antiquity of this legend, the word "dumpling" was not in common use until about 1600. About the same time, the Germans coined their own word for a dumpling, making difficult the assignment of credit for this new terminology. This language came very late given the antiquity of the dumpling. The Roman chef Apicius wrote the first recipe for a dumpling in the first century CE. He recommended that cooks make dumplings with sausage and celery. Another recipe called for dumplings with roasted pheasant, to which Apicius added salt and pepper. Both recipes remain part of Europe's cuisine, a testament to Apicius's enduring legacy and, in general, of the enduring influence of Rome. Because of Apicius's influence, some authorities credit Rome with inventing the dumpling, though, again, China probably deserves this credit. Dynastic China did not differ much from Rome, favoring dumplings with various types of meat and vegetables. In China, dumplings were an important ritual food that one ate at the end of one year and the beginning of the next. Akin to bread, dumplings may have arisen as part of the cuisines of many separate communities. The dumpling may be as simple as a small ball of boiled or steamed dough. The masses ate these dumplings simply to satisfy hunger. In a culinary sense, these dumplings must have been no more flavorful than a slice of bread. More elaborate dumplings must have existed from an early date. The Italian dish ravioli is an example of a dumpling. One might fill dumplings with other foods. A notable Italian example is gnocchi, which contains potato. Gnocchi must have been a late invention. The potato, in Europe since the 16th century, only began to come to the fore in the 18th century. Perhaps Italians grew potatoes during the winter, when temperatures were cool and rainfall adequate. It is also possible that Italians traded for potatoes with parts of northern Europe.

The Dumpling in Several Iterations

Peasants appear not to have been particular about the grain with which to make a dumpling, though durum wheat flour was probably ideal for this purpose. After the Columbian Exchange, wheat of other grades, oats, barley, rye, and corn might all have been used. The dough might contain legumes like peas, peanuts, chickpeas, lentils, and beans, especially the *Phaseolus* beans of the Americas. Over time, dumplings have been more important in the diet of northern Europeans than of those in the south. In the United States, dumplings are apt to contain chicken and are frequently served for lunch or dinner, especially on Sunday. Nutritionists tend to regard dumplings as full of starch and, depending on the meat, fat. Dumplings are often calorie dense, though an apple or plum dumpling ought to be nourishing. The tendency in some countries, including the United States, to cover dumplings with gravy only adds extra calories, many of them in the form of fat.

Dumplings around the World

Dumplings have shaped history as a worldwide phenomenon. Europeans, Americans, the Chinese, and Japanese are not alone in favoring dumplings. The people of Ghana make a dumpling (*fufu*) from cassava. The people of Nepal and Brazil have their own variants. It is common in Europe and parts of Asia to fill dumplings with pork or beef, cabbage, and onions. In parts of Africa and the Caribbean, people stuff dumplings with plantains or cocoyams. Ethiopians make dumplings (*tihla*) from barley. South Africans make dumplings with fruits, adding cinnamon and a type of custard. Another South African recipe calls for dough, milk, butter, and cinnamon again. In Italy, people envision dumplings on a grand scale. We have seen the importance of ravioli and gnocchi. Ravioli may contain beef, cheese, spinach, seafood, and mushrooms. Norwegians make several types of dumplings, favoring pork, especially bacon. Pork dumplings are also popular in Sweden, though the dough may be either flour or potato. Swedes boil their dumplings. Germans, Hungarians, Austrians, and the people of the Czech Republic and Slovakia boast a number of dumplings. These peoples are loyal to their local recipes. Eggs and durum flour are central to the dumplings of this region. Some dumplings, put in soup, contain liver. Other dumplings, in Germany and nearby countries, like Italy's gnocchi, feature potatoes. Other dumplings, being large, resemble a loaf of white bread. The Poles, Ukrainians, and Russians pride themselves on making dumplings that resemble the ravioli of Italy. Russians are content with beef and pork dumplings, though in other cases fish or mutton fits the bill. The Poles put sour cream on their dumplings. Americans often add brown sugar, caramel, or cinnamon to apple dumplings. Americans and Mexicans may make dumplings from corn flour. The people of Barbados flavor dumplings with cinnamon and nutmeg, both popular spices in the Caribbean. Pork and plantains also serve as ingredients, often topped with gravy. Jamaicans fry, boil, and roast dumplings. Wheat or corn flour is common in Jamaica. These dumplings are stuffed with salted fish, especially the kidneys and liver of mackerel. In Jamaica, dumplings are popular at breakfast. As one might expect, Peruvians make dumplings from potatoes. Beef, pork, chicken, onions, and garlic are important ingredients, though one might also add peanuts, raisins, olives, and eggs.

Further Reading

Butler, Stephanie. "Delightful Delicious Dumplings." Hungry History. Accessed September 28, 2014. www.history.com/news/hungry-history/delightful-delicious-dumplings.

"The History of Dumplings." The Kitchen Project. Accessed September 28, 2014. www.kitchenproject.com/history/dumplings.

E

Egg

One associates the egg with the hen or female chicken, but the egg is much older. Strictly speaking, an egg is the female gamete or sex cell of a large number of organisms. The human female produces eggs, one per month while fertile, but the egg is still much older. Insects, having a tenure of hundreds of millions of years on earth, produce eggs—at least the female does. In many cases, the production of insect eggs harms humans. The female mosquito must suck blood from a bird or mammal for her eggs to be fertile. In the case of malaria and yellow fever, mosquitoes have done humans great harm. Even plants bear an egg of sorts, known as the ovum, the female gamete, in the stigma of the flower. The stigma in turn is part of the pistil. Aside from bacteria and other such organisms, the egg is the dominant means of reproduction from insect to human. It is valuable because it ensures the genetic diversity of a species.

The Origin of Egg Cuisine

It is difficult to know when humans began eating eggs. The moment probably came early in human evolution, but written records are quite recent. In the ninth century BCE, the Assyrians, a people of western Asia, were the first to write an egg recipe. Assyrian king Ashurnasirpal celebrated banquets that included various egg dishes. The Greeks preferred peacock and goose to chicken eggs. Throughout the Mediterranean Basin, almost every household owned chickens and ate eggs. The Chinese preferred duck eggs but nonetheless were avid consumers of chicken eggs. The Chinese began eating duck eggs at least as early as 2000 BCE. By about 246 BCE, the Chinese constructed egg incubators that could hold 56,000 eggs each. The Romans appear to have eaten both chicken and ostrich eggs. The egg was the appetizer of choice in Roman antiquity. In the first century BCE, Roman poet Horace described the progress of a banquet from egg to apple, with the egg being

Eggs, commonly from hens, have been an important source of nourishment and income for centuries. Women and children commonly tended chickens and were responsible for collecting eggs. At market, eggs often provided these women and children a ready source of cash. (Dvmsimages/Dreamstime.com)

the appetizer and the apple being the dessert fruit of choice. Elaborate feasts of this kind were the province of the patricians, as was true of the Assyrian aristocracy. The plebeian masses made do with simpler fare. Eggs thus marked one's status and so were important in social history. Roman soldiers kept chickens so they could have eggs and poultry. In the Middle Ages and early modern era, preference for chicken eggs increased as people began to fear that duck eggs caused bad breath. Even then, duck eggs were considered suitable only for men. The egg was thus a mark of gender as well as status, and so was important in social history.

The Egg and Potato in Ireland

Legend holds that the Irish invented a dish of bacon and eggs, among the most versatile of breakfast foods even today. According to one account, a wife was frying bacon for her husband when a pregnant hen flew into the home. She dropped her egg precisely in the pan. It broke and the woman continued cooking the bacon with the addition of an egg. Her husband liked the dish so much that he told the local monks about it at the monastery where he worked. Soon Ireland's monks were eating bacon and eggs at every breakfast. Egg consumption appears to have been high in Ireland before the coming of the potato.

The potato, among the most important products of the Columbian Exchange, appears to have changed matters. The masses came to subsist on potatoes, opening a new use for the egg. Although the masses continued to keep chickens, they no longer ate the eggs but rather sold them, desperate as they were for any income with which to pay rent. Indeed, eggs appear to have generated one-fourth of all income for the poor. The over-reliance on the potato led to one of history's most harrowing events, the Irish Potato Famine in the 1840s. Perhaps a more nutritionally balanced Ireland might have weathered this crisis.

The Egg, Cuisine, and Art around the World

Before the arrival of the potato, Europeans appear to have eaten large quantities of eggs. Only bread was more ubiquitous in the diet. In France, a bishop could command 50 eggs from each town in his diocese. The egg also appears in the 16th-century art of Flemish painter Hieronymus Bosch. Bosch's work may bewilder the modern viewer and is often notoriously difficult to interpret. One painting centers on a broken egg. In the middle are a group of townspeople reading a single book. Beside them and within the egg are two desolate trees bereft of leaves. The rendering leaves one uneasy. What is the purpose of the egg and why is it broken? What text are the people reading? It might have been the Bible given Bosch's preference for religious themes. Why are the trees so stark? Indeed the egg and the trees appear to be more symbols of death than life.

Seventh-century Buddhist Japan forbade the consumption of meat and chicken from April to September, but the faithful could eat eggs during this time. Still, some Buddhists believed in the existence of a special hell for egg eaters. In this context, and centuries later, one wonders whether Bosch's characters are in a kind of hell. Japan's openness, reluctant as it may have been, to China and Europe after 1500 witnessed an increase in egg consumption. By the late 18th century, Japanese cookbooks listed more than 100 recipes for eggs.

Western Asia, Egypt, and North Africa often paired eggs with meat. From antiquity to modernity, eggs were the festive food of elites. French emperor Napoleon Bonaparte prized himself as a competent omelet maker. The egg thus served not only to mark gender, but status as well, and in this sense shaped history. So ubiquitous has the egg become that one food historian doubts that any cuisine would exist without the egg.

The Egg and Religion

Humans have eaten many types of eggs over the millennia, but the hen's egg has been the focus of Christianity. By the fifth century CE, the Christian church, which would become the Catholic Church during the Reformation, linked the egg with the resurrection of Jesus. This is a mysterious connection because the canonical gospels do not mention that Jesus was fond of eggs. Indeed, the foods that appear to have drawn his attention were fish, bread, and wine. There is no record of any preference for chicken, let alone the egg. Nonetheless, because of the association between the egg and Jesus's resurrection, Christians developed the practice of eating eggs on Easter. The Church harnessed this tradition to its own practices, requiring that Christians not eat eggs during Lent, the 40 days that precede Easter. Lent was to be a time of fasting, when one eschewed meat for fish. Only Easter had the power to reinstate a diet of eggs. In the 16th century, however, the Council of Trent reversed course. While affirming the centrality of the egg to the resurrection of Jesus, the council allowed Christians to consume eggs during Lent. No longer was it a forbidden food of sorts. Within and without Christianity, the egg came to symbolize the beginning of time, life, wisdom, strength, vitality, procreation, and death. Some of these associations seem odd. The beginning of time must have occurred at the Big Bang more than 13 billion years ago. At that moment there was no egg and no life. The beginning of life also does not coincide with the egg, because bacteria, among the first life, did not and do not now produce eggs. Because the egg may mark the beginning of life for a sexually reproducing organism, its connection to death seems strange. Yet Bosch may have played upon this theme.

The Egg and Bodybuilding

The egg does not have a close affinity with any sport other than perhaps bodybuilding. Because the bodybuilder seeks to sculpt the physique, displaying large muscles and little body fat, he or she spends hours in the gym attempting to build muscles. The bodybuilder, in addition, seeks to craft a diet that will minimize fat. In this quest the egg has assumed importance—but not the entire egg. The egg contains the white, that portion of the egg that is liquid before cooking, and the yolk. The bodybuilder does not value both equally. He or she eschews the yolk, even though it contains many nutrients, because of its fat and cholesterol. Bodybuilders eat only egg whites. Indeed the egg white appears to be the food most central to the bodybuilder's diet. Bodybuilding no longer appears to be a sport with a mainstream appeal. The days when Arnold Schwarzenegger and Franco Colombu were the face of bodybuilding are long past.

The Egg, Agribusiness, and Fast Food

The egg has become a capitalist commodity. The notion of small farmers gathering eggs in the morning, once true, is now fiction. Agribusiness controls the production and distribution of eggs. As a commodity eggs have infiltrated the menu at McDonald's and Denny's. McDonald's serves the Egg McMuffin: egg, ham, and cheese between two halves of a muffin. The product is uniform and probably not all that healthy. The experience of eating an Egg McMuffin is the same in San Francisco as in Baltimore. Denny's has stuck to the Irish tradition of serving bacon with eggs. Again, the combination is probably unhealthy. The egg has become one of a handful of foods that has made fast food popular, palatable, and standardized. An Egg McMuffin has no more diversity than did the Model T. The egg has adapted to the modern world of commodification and capitalism.

Further Reading

Toops, Diane. *Eggs: A Global History*. London: Reaktion Books, 2014.

Enchilada

Like the taco, the enchilada derives from corn flour, with corn being the great American grass that sustained the Amerindians the way that wheat and rye bread sustained Europeans and rice sustained south, east, and Southeast Asia. Because the enchilada uses corn, it is an important food with deep American roots. The modern enchilada is a tortilla wrapped around a variety of ingredients in which meats play a prominent role. The use of Old World beef and pork made the enchilada a food with truly international roots. It was a product of the Columbian Exchange. Depending on who one asks, the enchilada is or is not an authentic

Mexican food. To be sure, its modern incarnation displays less of its Mexican roots than one would assume.

History and Significance

According to tradition, one made an enchilada with the sauce of chili peppers, giving the food a sharp bite. As shown, the enchilada is a New and Old World hybrid, containing perhaps corn, chili peppers, beans, potatoes, beef, pork, cheese, vegetables, and possibly seafood. The corn, chili peppers, beans, and potatoes were all American indigenes. The beef, pork, and cheese were Old World contributions to the enchilada. In this sense, it is difficult to specify the enchilada as a purely Mexican food. Rather, it is an international food, given the breadth of its potential ingredients. To the chili pepper sauce one often added tomatoes, another American food. The word *enchilada* means, simply, "to enhance with chili peppers."

It seems possible that the Maya of southern Mexico and Guatemala may have made something akin to an enchilada, though they did not have access to beef and pork because these were Old World foods. The date of this protoinvention appears to be lost to history. likely the Maya stuffed their enchiladas with fish rather than meat. Another thesis holds that the Aztecs invented the enchilada. By the time of European contact the enchilada was popular throughout Mexico, though the Spanish would introduce beef and pork fillings to give the enchilada a distinctly European cast. By then, the enchilada was a popular street food because it was portable to an extent, though perhaps not as much so as the taco. The coming of the factory and farm system to California made the enchilada a staple lunch food because it was quick and relatively easy to prepare. It shaped history in this regard because it latched onto the Industrial Revolution, catering to farm and factory, and to office workers who had only a brief respite for lunch. Some Mexican Americans regard the enchilada as a food of American tourists to California or the American Southwest rather than as an authentic food. Indeed, Mexicans and Mexican Americans tend to regard the enchilada as a simple food and tend not to lavish it with the many ingredients that European Americans think necessary.

Many types of enchilada recipes call for beef, pork, or chicken, all unknown to the pre-Columbian Amerindians. Recipes often call for chili pepper sauce, cheese of various kinds, sour cream, lettuce (as with the taco), olives, onions, salsa, and cilantro. Again, one detects a mix of New and Old World foods. Indeed, no limits really bind the enchilada. One may pile it with whatever ingredients one wishes. The enchilada is as limitless as one's imagination. Costa Rica, Honduras, Nicaragua, Guatemala, and Mexico all have their own enchilada recipes. In fact, each region of Mexico brags that its recipes surpass those of anywhere else.

The Spanish who colonized southern California in the 1760s had begun the tradition of eating enchiladas, but the meaning of an enchilada was shifting. Whereas the Amerindians had not used meat but instead fish, the Spanish wrapped their enchiladas in beef and pork, bringing the cow and pig to the fore and in the process introducing these livestock to the Americas as part of the Columbian Exchange. California was then part of Mexico so it was natural to modify and consume putatively Mexican foods. California would become a U.S. state only in 1850, in the aftermath of the Mexican-American War. In the 18th century, the Spanish and Native Americans ate what was evolving into Mexican cuisine. To eat an enchilada was to acknowledge one's Mexican culinary roots. It was a statement of one's allegiance to Mexico and was therefore significant as a quasi-political food.

Food historian Andrew F. Smith recalls the enchilada as a childhood treat, though he thought of it as Spanish fare because a stigma was attached to Mexican food. Poor people ate Mexican food whereas those with a refined palate ate Spanish foods. Smith admits, however, that he disliked the greasiness of Mexican enchiladas fried in fat. Indeed, the enchilada is calorie dense. This fact was not problematic in an era when people were active and had arduous work. In today's sedentary developed world, calorie-dense enchiladas only contribute to the problem of obesity. In this sense, one might be tempted to regard the enchilada as "junk food." Certainly it is fast food. Frying foods was a European tradition. Before European contact the Americans did not fry foods of any kind but began to do so only under European tutelage. As an antidote to fried foods, one may bake or grill an enchilada. An anonymous cookbook from 1831 may contain the earliest Spanish-language recipe for an enchilada.

In 1876, the First Congregational Church in Marysville, Ohio, published a Mexican cookbook to which Anson Safford, the governor of Arizona territory (Arizona was not yet a state) contributed a recipe for an enchilada. This was likely the first English reference to, and recipe for, an enchilada. Safford proclaimed the enchilada a national dish, every bit as American to the people of the Southwest as pumpkin pie was to New England. Throughout the rest of the 19th century, American cookbooks tended to refer to the enchilada as a Spanish dish. In 1896, the U.S. Army published its own enchilada recipe, which called for chili pepper sauce, cheese, and onions. It is difficult to know what meats the Army used, perhaps canned rations of some type. In the 1920s, some Americans were experimenting with making enchiladas with two tortillas, what must have been a filling meal.

Modernity

According to one thesis, the enchilada is among Mexico's contributions to fast food. In the guise of independent restaurants, street vendors, and chain restaurants, the enchilada provides a quick but filling meal. At the same time, the enchilada became a restaurant staple beyond the world of fast food. In 2010, El Torino, a restaurant that capitalized on the enchilada's popularity, took root near Angel Stadium in Anaheim, California, to sell enchiladas to baseball fans. In this respect, the enchilada is part of the regional lore of baseball, whereas in the Midwest Americans tend to eat hot dogs at baseball games. The enchilada thus represents a departure from the hot dog and so has shaped history, recreation, and daily life in the West and Southwest. The enchilada, along with chiles rellenos, burritos, tacos, and guacamole, arose as the staples of Mexican and Mexican American foods. One could not have a proper Mexican meal without an enchilada.

Throughout southern California these restaurants prospered, attracting customers who liked the food even if they could not pronounce it. In Los Angeles, Olvera Street, among the city's oldest roads, became the headquarters of Mexican restaurants and street vendors. Along this road, cooks made the enchilada into a staple of southern California. Indeed, Los Angeles trails only Mexico City as the largest Mexican city and may be the largest consumer of enchiladas. The restaurants on this street specialize in making enchilada platters, nachos, and tequitos. Perhaps the leading restaurants in this context are El Paso Inn, El Rancho Grande, and La Golondrina. All have served enchiladas since the 1920s, an important period in the history of southern California because of the large influx of Mexican immigrants who had fled instability in Mexico.

Further Reading

Arellano, Gustavo. *TACO USA: How Mexican Food Conquered America*. New York: Scribner, 2012.

"Enchilada." Gourmet Sleuth. Accessed September 22, 2014. www.gourmetsleuth.com/articles/detail/enchiladas.

Hernandez, Ruben. "The Enchilada: A Tradition that Transcended Conquest, Borders, and Culture." Accessed February 15, 2015. Latinopm.com/features/the-enchilda-14844.

Pilcher, Jeffrey M. *Planet Taco: A Global History of Mexican Food*. Oxford and New York: Oxford University Press, 2012.

Smith, Andrew F. "Tacos, Enchiladas and Refried Beans: The Invention of Mexican-American Cookery." Paper presented at "Cultural and Historical Aspects of Foods–Yesterday, Today, and Tomorrow," symposium, Oregon State University, Corvallis, OR, April 1999. Accessed September 22, 2014. Web.archive.org/web/20070718154326/http://food.oregonstate.edu/ref/culture/mexico_smith.html.

Zeldes, Leah. "Eat This! Enchiladas, Mexican Comfort Food." Dining Chicago. Accessed September 22, 2014. www.diningchicago.com/blog/2010/11/10/eat-this-enchiladas-mexican-comfort-food.

F

Fish

The 19th-century practice—witness the scientific treatises of Swiss American ichthyologist Louis Agassiz—of using fish in the singular and fishes in the plural has ceded ground to the almost-universal tendency to employ the term *fish* as both singular and plural. This essay follows the modern convention. Fish were among the earliest animals to have evolved in the water. The primeval ocean appears to have been the birthplace of fish, meaning that the first fish could live only in saltwater. Later, some fish evolved the capacity to live amid very little brine. These are the freshwater fish. Fish are cold-blooded animals with fins and a tail to propel them through the water. Many fish have scales, as do reptiles, but some fish, catfish for example, lack scales. Humans tend to think of fish as the inhabiters of relatively shallow water, but even the darkest, deepest parts of the ocean contain fish, though apparently not in great numbers. Because of the darkness, these fish have evolved their own source of illumination. Even if humans wished to eat these fish, the likelihood appears slight because of the depth and pressure of the ocean, virtually excluding humans from this region.

Fish Changed the World Even before the Rise of Homo sapiens

The consumption of fish has changed the world in a variety of ways. Fishing arose as an essential activity long before the appearance of anatomically modern humans. All our ancestors and humans themselves evolved in Africa. The first hominid to leave Africa, *Homo erectus*, crossed the Sinai peninsula on its way east to Java, the largest Indonesian island. The point of emphasis is that *Homo erectus*, not surprisingly given its initial ignorance of the existence of Java, did not take the most direct route to the island but rather hugged the southern coastline of Asia. *Homo erectus* thus had the ocean as a constant companion. The ocean could not have served as a source of potable water because it

One can scarcely overstate the importance of fish. They shaped our evolution and have become a worldwide symbol of Jesus. Fish are prominent in the canonical Gospels. (Zhangjinsong/Dreamstime.com)

was brine. Instead it must have been a source of nourishment, providing fish and shellfish. It seems difficult to believe that *Homo erectus* could have survived its trek through Asia without the protein-rich diet that fish provided. Fish thus changed the world by making possible the first hominid settlements outside Africa.

The Possible Role of Fish in the Competition between Neanderthals and Anatomically Modern Humans

No less momentous was the rise of anatomically modern humans about 200,000 years ago in Africa. Like *Homo erectus*, some anatomically modern humans left their homeland, about 40,000 years ago, venturing east into Asia and north and west into Europe. They were not the first arrivals to either continent. *Homo erectus*, as noted, predated them in Asia, and Neanderthals (sometimes rendered Neandertals), a species of human remarkably akin to anatomically modern humans, reached Europe millennia before the latter. Anatomically modern humans came with an advantage. With sharpened sticks they speared fish in Europe's rivers and lakes. Remarkably adaptable in so many ways, Neanderthals

Jesus of Nazareth

It is difficult to find the historical Jesus. Decades after his death, a number of anonymous authors wrote accounts of Jesus's life. The early church rejected most of them as heretical, accepting only the four known as Mark, Matthew, Luke, and John. The names do not record the author because no one knows who wrote these gospels. These gospels, canonical and noncanonical, vary in their details. Some even dispute Jesus's birth narrative, wondering why, if he was truly born in Bethlehem, several of the gospels refer to him as "Jesus of Nazareth." The peculiar story of his birth in the canonical Gospels leaves one with the impression that Jesus had no human father. Almost nothing appears to be known about Jesus' childhood, though the Infancy Gospel of Thomas (not related to the canonical Gospels) describes his childhood as one of mischief and malevolence. As an adult, Jesus appears to have assumed the role of teacher, assembling a small number of disciples and preaching a ministry in Galilee. His teaching, in apparent defiance of Jewish and Roman authority, led to his crucifixion. The canonical Gospels insist that Jesus rose from the dead, but the heretical Gospel of Thomas mentions no resurrection. Some of the Gnostic texts imply that the resurrection was symbolic rather than a literal event. For our purposes, it is important to remember that Jesus recruited fishermen as his followers and is said to have eaten fish after his resurrection. Fish have become a symbol of Jesus in the modern world.

never acquired this technique. The abundance of fish bones in anatomically modern human encampments and their absence in those of Neanderthals suggests that the former had an additional source of protein that the latter lacked. Perhaps this advantage gave anatomically modern humans a survival and reproductive edge over Neanderthals. During the next 12,000 years or so, anatomically modern human populations grew, whereas Neanderthals retreated. Fish might therefore have played some role in the extinction of Neanderthals about 28,000 years ago. Their demise must have been a world-changing event. Neanderthals, with a brain even larger than that of modern humans, were highly intelligent. They exchanged technologies with anatomically modern humans during their time together. The two might even have interbred. The loss of Neanderthals cost anatomically modern humans their closest relative in the animal kingdom. Humans are alone to solve their own problems. Without Neanderthals, modern humans have no one else to consult about the dangers of climate change, the proliferation of warfare, and the ubiquity of poverty. They have no one with whom to share knowledge and aspirations, or with whom to commiserate. The world may have changed for the worse with the loss of Neanderthals.

Tuna

A relative of mackerel, tuna is among the most widely consumed fish. It may be purchased as frozen fillets or as disarticulated flesh in cans. Canned tuna is among the most widely consumed fishes in the United States. The majority of tuna comes from the Pacific Ocean, the Indian Ocean, and the Mediterranean Sea, in that order. The catch was plentiful between the 1930s and 1960s, but as the amount of tuna caught steadily increased, the population of tuna has had difficulty adapting. Overfishing is now the scourge of the tuna industry and of all fish. Some environmentalists believe that because of human voracity, the tuna population may be near extinction.

Fish in Antiquity

Much attention has focused on the role of agriculture and animal husbandry in the creation of civilization. But fish can scarcely have been less important. The first civilizations clustered along rivers that provided a bounty of fish. The ascent of civilization in western Asia centered on the populations along the Tigris and Euphrates Rivers. The Hebrews, who would emerge as among the first proponents of monotheism, fished in the eastern Mediterranean Sea and in inland lakes. The Egyptians sustained themselves on fish from the Nile River and the Mediterranean Sea. The emerging civilizations in what are today India and Pakistan drew sustenance from the fish in the Indus and Ganges Rivers. The Chinese gathered along the Yellow and Yangtze Rivers, which supplied abundant fish. The people in southernmost China gathered fish from the South China Sea. There appears not to have been a time when China did not rely on fish. Indeed, the Chinese may have invented aquaculture: the raising of fish in artificial ponds or other bodies of water. China's population had apparently exceeded the supply of fish gathered by traditional means, prompting the development of aquaculture to supplement the supply of fish.

As noted, the consumption of fish was important to the people of the Levant and Egypt, but one should not neglect the rest of the Mediterranean Basin. The people of North Africa depended on fish for sustenance. If anything, the Roman conquest of North Africa, and later, Egypt, increased the demand for fish and the intensity of fishing in the Mediterranean Sea. Fishing was particularly important in Greece because much of the land was poorly suited for agriculture. In Italy, the Etruscans (perhaps of Greek origin), and later the Romans, likewise depended on fish. Although farming was more important in Rome than in Greece, the demand for fish was robust. Like the Chinese, the Romans turned to aquaculture to augment the supply of fish from the Mediterranean Sea, and also from lakes and rivers, notably the Tiber. As elsewhere, the ancients believed fish to be an important source of nourishment for all social classes. In Rome, plebeian and patrician alike consumed fish. Several notables and emperors appear to have been partial to fish. Julius Caesar, who perverted the office of dictator, was sure to take extra helpings of fish at the banquets he attended. This practice was pronounced on occasions when the fish was improperly prepared or otherwise unsatisfactory, because Caesar wished in this way to thank his hostess for her work in preparing the feast. Through fish, Caesar found favor with many women.

In the Americas, the supply of fish appears to have been particularly abundant. The Amerindians had not only enough to feed themselves but also to use as fertilizer, putting a fish into each hole into which they deposited a seed. The consumption of fish was not merely an end in itself but an essential part of agriculture. Indeed, the lifeways of the Native Americans appear difficult to understand without an appreciation of the central role that fish played in both the cuisine and the agriculture.

Fish and the Rise of Monotheism

Fish also appear to have been important in the rise of monotheism. Hebrew dietary laws did permit the consumption of fish, but it was an offshoot of Judaism, Christianity, that elevated fish to the status of a religious symbol. Fish played a prominent role in the canonical Gospels. According to them, Jesus recruited fishermen as his first apostles. Among them, Peter would emerge, according to Christian tradition, as the first pope. According to the Gospels, Jesus multiplied two fish and distributed them, along with bread, to the hungry people who had gathered to hear him preach. Upon his resurrection, Jesus was said to have appeared along the coastline, observing his apostles who had returned to their vocation. Learning that they had caught nothing, Jesus instructed them to cast their nets yet again. The catch was so large that they had trouble securing it. At once they recognized the man as Jesus. The Gospel according to John holds that Jesus appeared suddenly to his apostles. Convinced that he was a ghost, the apostles feared him. To prove that he was not a ghost, Jesus ate a piece of fish. The emerging Christian church made fish a symbol of Jesus, counseling its followers to forgo meat on Fridays and eat fish instead. During Lent—the 40 days before Easter—Christians were to eat fish every day. Particularly pious Christians ate fish nearly every day throughout the year. For this reason fish became a staple in the diet in the age of faith. In recent decades, however, these strictures have loosened. The Catholic Church no longer expects Catholics to eat fish every Friday and every day during Lent. Indeed, American playwright and Nobel laureate Eugene O'Neill did not mention fish in his masterpiece, *Long Day's Journey into Night*, about an Irish Catholic family. Yet the fish has lost none of its symbolism. People of faith emblazon outlines of fish on the back of their automobiles, and many Christians are adamant that the Gospel stories of fish are true.

Fish in Modernity

In modernity, fish have lost none of their importance. Some people do not consider pizza complete without anchovies. Fish remain a staple in the diet of east Asians. The Chinese, Filipinos, Japanese, Thai, Vietnamese, Indonesians, Malaysians, and the people of Laos and Myanmar are avid consumers of fish. In fact, modern medicine has taken note of this dietary trend, remarking that fish are an important source of protein and omega-3 fatty acids. A diet of fish may contribute to the longevity that many Asians enjoy. The contrast between a fit and trim Thai nourished on fish and an obese and moribund American engorged with hamburger and sausage has led physicians in the West to despair. Indeed, several government agencies encourage Americans to eat more fish and less meat in hopes of stemming the tide of obesity.

Unfortunately, improper preparation vitiates this advice. Possibly of African origin, the frying of fish adds too much fat and too many calories to what is otherwise an important food. Long John Silver's, McDonald's, Wendy's and other fast food restaurants shamefully fry fish, and the British appear to be addicted to a diet of fried fish and chips. By contrast, Asians are less likely to fry fish. Food preparation clearly matters when one determines to extract the maximum nutrients and the minimum fat from fish. Americans have a particularly paradoxical attitude toward their cuisine. They continue to fry fish but, at least since the 1940s, have demanded leaner cuts of pork. Americans and Europeans would do better not to fry fish or add creamy, calorie-laden sauces, and to eat more unadorned fish and less pork.

Further Reading

Fagan, Brian M. *Fish on Friday: Feasting, Fasting, and the Discovery of the New World.* New York: Basic Books, 2007.

Gagne, George P., and Richard H. Medrano. *Fish Consumption and Health.* Hauppauge, NY: Nova Science Publishers, 2009.

Miller, Adrian. *Soul Food: The Surprising Story of an American Cuisine, One Plate at a Time.* Chapel Hill: The University of North Carolina Press, 2003.

French Fries

Their origins mysterious, french fries are an amalgam of an American food and European cooking techniques. The potato, the source of french fries, is native to

Thomas Jefferson

Born April 13, 1743, Thomas Jefferson has attracted attention as a statesman. He was among the founding fathers of the United States. He wrote the Declaration of Independence, acted with Congress to buy the Louisiana Territory from France, and founded the University of Virginia. Yet his rhetoric outshone his personal life. The man who wrote about equality owned slaves, among them Sally Hemings, the woman who bore him children. As a slave, she could not refuse Jefferson's advances, so that one must conclude that the sex was nonconsensual. Apart from the luminous and sordid events of his life, Jefferson was an amateur gardener who grew many crops and trees. Among the early advocates of the tomato and potato, Jefferson touted french fries as a flavorful dish. In vigorous health most of his life, Thomas Jefferson died July 4, 1826, 50 years to the day of the signing of the Declaration of Independence.

the Andes mountains in South America, but the people of this region appear not to have cut and fried their potatoes, for good reason. Rather, once introduced and accepted in Europe, a process that took time, the potato became the subject of culinary experiments in frying. No one appears to know who invented french fries and when. They began to grow in popularity in the 19th century. By the 20th century, french fries were a staple of the fast food industry, perhaps better known as the junk food industry, especially in these times of sedentism.

The New World Contribution

The Andes grew several tubers. A tuber is a swollen underground stem, not a root. Of the Andes tubers only one, the potato, came to worldwide renown. Even though these peoples grew potatoes for millennia they do not appear to have fried them. There may be a number of reasons for this omission. One possibility seems to be that the Amerindians had no convenient source of plant oils for frying. A brief survey of American food plants before the Columbian Exchange reveals the presence of several plants that were good sources of starch—the potato itself, the sweet potato, corn, cassava, *Phaseolus* beans, and some others—but inadequate sources of oils. Nor did the Native Americans have numerous livestock from which to derive lard for frying. True, game might have yielded lard, but wild animals tend to be leaner than livestock as a matter of course. Probably the biggest detriment to frying potatoes or any other food was the absence of pots and pans in which to fry foods. This defect made frying, if conceptually possible, factually unlikely if not impossible. This does not minimize the American achievement. The Amerindians contributed the potato without which the french fry would not exist.

The European Contribution

Throughout most of its history, Europe knew nothing about the potato. The masses got by on a diet of turnips, vegetables of several sorts, bread (both wheat and rye, though rye bread was the staple of the masses), peas, lentils, and chickpeas. On the whole, this diet had the potential to be nourishing, particularly if the vegetables contained vitamin C. To this mix of foods would come the potato, but it was not an instant part of European cuisine. Europeans had never seen a food quite like the potato. Physicians, recognizing a resemblance to the deadly belladonna, warned that potatoes were poisonous. Others thought that potatoes caused leprosy, a hideous disease. Until the 18th century, few people ate potatoes, but during that century interest in them quickened. A French physician and soldier, imprisoned in Prussia during a war between France and Prussia, subsisted on potatoes for several years. He did not languish, and upon his release credited the potato with his robust health. He devoted the rest of his life to promoting the nutritiousness of the potato. Throughout Northern Europe, especially Ireland, farmers converted their spare acres, and there were not many, to potatoes because they provided more calories per unit space than any other food.

The potato had taken hold, setting the stage for the invention of the french fry. The debate, and it may be insoluble, centers on whether France or Belgium invented the french fry, though the date of this invention appears to be lost to history. One tradition holds, sensibly enough, that the French invented french fries. Another tradition holds that the Belgians invented the french fry. American and British soldiers stationed in Belgium during World War I mistakenly called the food french fries because the Belgian soldiers, from whom they acquired the habit of eating fries, spoke French.

This conjecture does not seem plausible. One might suggest an earlier date. In the 1780s, Thomas Jefferson, among the founders of the United States, was a U.S. minister to France. He dined with the elites of French society. Among the foods that they introduced to him were thinly sliced fried potatoes. They impressed Jefferson. Upon his return to the United States—the French Revolution had forced him to evacuate Paris—he became the third U.S. president. As early as 1802, the second year of his presidency, Jefferson served these fried potatoes to White House guests. When queried about the source of this novel food, Jefferson responded that he had acquired a taste for the fries in France. Thus began the American interest in french fries. Jefferson also became enamored of potatoes, growing them in his garden at Monticello.

Fast Food and Junk Food

If the potato was a South American achievement and the french fry a French innovation, then the United States excelled in marketing this new food. The hamburger was an Old World innovation, but in the New World it needed a food to accompany it. The potato chip, another product of the potato, was one possibility, but in the 20th century arose the coupling of hamburgers and french fries. No one appears to know who first made this pairing, but it has been enduring. Fast food restaurants, particularly in the United States, sell burgers and fries as a matter of course. One need only examine the experience of McDonald's to grasp this phenomenon. McDonald's aggressively markets its Big Mac, cheeseburger and other variants of the hamburger with a ubiquitous side of fries. McDonald's does not even bother to call them french fries. It is enough to pigeonhole them as just "fries." The coupling is so omnipresent that one feels that one cannot order just a hamburger. One must also have fries. The meal is incomplete without these fries. Together a Big Mac, french fries, and a Coke, the dietary triad of McDonald's, supply fat, salt, and sugar. How is one to resist given that humans are biologically predisposed to crave all three? French fries are thus a staple of the fast food industry such that the average person probably cannot conceive of a time when they were not part of the menu. In this context, the french fry has shaped history by helping to build the fast food empire that looms over the United States and other parts of the developed world. Whether this is truly an achievement is another matter.

But french fries are not just fast food. One might, after all, microwave a small potato for three minutes and call the product fast food. French fries are junk food. Although partisans of the junk food industry will commend french fries as a source of vitamin C, they are so immersed in lard or oil that they are not healthy. They contain too much fat. Too much of this fat, in turn, is saturated or trans fat. In an era before mechanization, especially the automobile, people led active, often strenuous lives. Work was arduous. Even in the era of the bicycle one needed to exert oneself to get to work. Today, too many people, especially in the developed world, are inert. Yet they eat as their active progenitors had. The result is obesity, some cancers, and cardiovascular disease. The french fry has shaped history as junk food, as a component of an unhealthy lifestyle. This, too, is not much of an achievement.

The Antidote to the French Fry

Americans and people of other nations might do best by foregoing the french fry, replacing it with whole foods. Rather than eat a serving or two of french fries, one might eat a small packet of dry roasted peanuts, a nutritious legume. True, the peanut also has fat, but most of it is unsaturated. None of it is trans fat. Even a pinch of salt on roasted peanuts will not approach the amount of salt in a single serving of french fries. French fries are so unhealthy because they are processed food. Try a small baked potato instead. Eat the whole potato, including the skin, for maximum nutrients. The point is to eat whole natural foods, which are the antithesis of the french fry. The french fry clearly satisfies cravings. In all other respects, it is an unwholesome food. Still, one cannot ignore the french fry's popularity. Like it or not, the food is important.

Further Reading

Johnson, Sylvia A. *Tomatoes, Potatoes, Corn, and Beans: How the Foods of the Americas Changed Eating Around the World*. New York: Atheneum Books, 1997.

Meltzer, Milton. *The Amazing Potato: A Story in Which the Incas, Conquistadors, Marie Antoinette, Thomas Jefferson, Wars, Famines, Immigrants, and French Fries All Play a Part*. New York: HarperCollins Publishers, 1992.

Reader, John. *Potato: A History of the Propitious Esculent*. New Haven, CT: Yale University Press, 2008.

Rodger, Ellen. *The Biography of Potatoes*. New York: Crabtree Publishing, 2007.

Salaman, Redcliffe. *The History and Social Influence of the Potato*. Cambridge: Cambridge University Press, 1985.

Frozen Food

Frozen foods are not as novel as one might think. Their history sinks roots deep into the past in cold climates. For example, the Inuit of the Aleutian Islands and other parts of Alaska have long frozen fish to preserve it. The peoples of Russia and Siberia have acted similarly. In these instances, one simply left food outside to freeze it. Freezing, like canning, has the advantage of lengthening the period during which food may be stored. The preservation of food was essential in a world in which calories were sometimes in shortage. In this sense, frozen foods, by having a long shelf life, shaped history and daily life. Frozen foods are also important because they approximate the flavor and nutrition of fresh produce, though this point may be overdrawn. Frozen foods also make some foods available to people who, because of geography, would not be able to obtain them. An example is frozen seafood, which makes fish and other aquatic foods available to people who do not live near a body of water. Of course, canning serves a similar function.

Origins

As shown, frozen foods have a long history, though modern events have shaped the process of freezing. In 1875, for example, frozen foods became more widely

Frozen foods preserve nutrients and flavor better than do canned foods. Even so, the flavor of frozen foods does not quite match the taste of fresh produce from the garden. (Niloo138/Dreamstime.com)

available when scientists discovered that the mechanical evaporation of ammonia, a gas, caused food in contact with the expanding gas to freeze. This process occurs because any gas will cool its surroundings upon expansion. This is simply the principle of refrigeration. In several respects, one may rank frozen foods ahead of canned foods. Consider the pea. Canned peas are apt to be mushy and insipid. Texture and flavor are wanting. Frozen peas, by contrast, have superior flavor, color, and texture. They are far crisper than canned peas. Partisans believe that frozen peas approximate the flavor and nutrition of fresh peas. To some extent this contention is true, though it is likely that no method of preservation equals the flavor of fresh garden peas. The real value of frozen foods would become apparent only in the 1930s and 1940s, when two events occurred in the United States. First, during the Great Depression, the New Deal (President Franklin D. Roosevelt's response to the depression) electrified large areas of the United States, especially the countryside. Now millions of Americans had access to electricity, which was essential to the refrigerators and freezers that were becoming widespread, especially during the 1940s. The freezer was so important because it allowed homeowners for the first time to store frozen foods. It is important to note, despite its value, that freezing is not always desirable. Chocolate and peanuts, for example, store well without the need to freeze them.

Clarence Birdseye

Born December 9, 1886, in Brooklyn, New York, Clarence Frank Birdseye II attended Amherst College until he could no longer afford tuition. A taxidermist as young man, Birdseye dabbled in the sciences, serving as a naturalist and entomologist in various state agencies. An assignment in Canada stoked his curiosity in the making of frozen foods. Conducting his own experiments, Birdseye froze fish to –40°C. Thawing them later, he was unable to distinguish the taste from fresh fish. In 1925, Birdseye formed the General Seafood Corporation in Massachusetts. Four years later, he sold the business for $22 million to Goldman Sachs. Birds Eye Frozen Food Company, a spin-off of what had been renamed the General Foods Corporation, remains a leader in the frozen food market. Birdseye died of a heart attack on October 7, 1956.

Frozen Legumes

Legumes are an important type of seeds that add protein to the diet. They have been important to the human diet for millennia but have been frozen only since the end of the 19th century. Like peas, beans are often frozen, though in this case flavor does not decline precipitously when one cans beans instead. Great northern beans, navy beans, and several others have excellent flavor, frozen or canned. In this instance, freezing and canning are complementary processes. Frozen lima beans, for example, are traditionally prepared without cooking them, an omission that appears to be at odds with the canning of these beans. Before freezing, workers must wash and blanch the beans. As a rule, two types of lima beans are suitable for freezing. Beans (all beans are seeds) with a thin seed coat fall into this category. Henderson, Bush, and Thorogreen varieties satisfy this criterion. Second are lima beans with a comparatively thick seed coat. Remember that a thick seed coat is not that thick. Evolution constrains the thickness of the seed coat because the bean must be able to germinate a new plant if it is to pass its genes to the next generation, the desideratum of evolution. The varieties Baby Potato, Baby Fordhook, Fordhook, and Evergreen satisfy this criterion, though the name Baby Potato is misleading in applying to lima beans rather than to the true potato. The confusion is likely old and probably derives from the fact that lima beans and potatoes are both native to the Andes mountains in South America. Yet there is no mistaking the difference. The lima bean is a legume and is related to all other beans in the American genus *Phaseolus*. The potato, on the other hand, is a tuber. The plant is related to tomato, peppers, and tobacco. Manufacturers also freeze butter beans, though again confusion may result because butter beans are just lima beans. In these instances names deceive more than inform.

Frozen Vegetables

Frozen vegetables are also popular, but a vegetable is not easy to define. Strictly, a vegetable should be the vegetative part of a plant, namely the leaves, though other foods over time became known as vegetables: legumes, carrots, broccoli, tomatoes, and several other foods. Brussels sprouts are a good example of a true vegetable that may be frozen. The spherical bundle of leaves is washed, sometimes cut, and blanched before freezing. The flavor of frozen brussels sprouts is excellent, though again it does not quite equal fresh garden produce. The freezing of corn opens another avenue toward controversy whereby some authorities hold that frozen sweet corn is a vegetable. Only when the kernels are dried and fed to livestock is corn truly a grain. This distinction ignores that corn, like wheat, barley, rye, oats, millet, and sorghum, is a grass. Corn is sometimes frozen on the cob, though it is more likely to be cut off the cob prior to freezing. Among the true vegetables, beet, collard, mustard, and turnip greens are all available from the grocer's freezer. There is even the possibility of buying frozen dandelion greens. Even though American author Henry David Thoreau favored dandelion greens, it is hard to imagine that there is much demand for them in the United States. Okra is another popular frozen food. Often labeled a vegetable, okra is really a seedpod. The pod encases white seeds in much the way that fruits, the tomato for example, encases seeds. The grower must take care to pick pods young because older pods become tough, fibrous, and nearly inedible. The manufacturer ideally freezes only young pods, though it is possible for an occasional old pod to be frozen, to the displeasure of the consumer. French fries are often frozen for home use, though it is a considerable stretch to call them vegetables.

Frozen Fruits

A large number of fruits may be frozen for their flesh or juice. Apples, apricots, berries, and citrus fruits form just the beginning of a long list. Frozen apples cannot compare in quality and nutrition to fresh apples. The problem is that the skin is removed from apples before freezing, with the result that many nutrients are lost because the nutrients are in the skin just beneath it. Sugar may be added to apples before freezing, furnishing unwanted calories. Frozen apricots may likewise be sweetened. This process strikes one as odd given that apples and apricots are naturally sweet and need no inputs of sugar prior to freezing. The seeds are removed from both apples and apricots before freezing. In the case of apricots and similar fruits, the seed is known as the stone or pit. Among berries, blackberries, raspberries, dewberries, loganberries, youngberries, blueberries, and strawberries are all frozen, though not every member of this list is, by the standards of botanical nomenclature, a true berry. Cherries, their stones removed, are also available as a frozen fruit. Citrus fruits are well represented by their juice. Frozen orange juice, known as frozen concentrate, is enormously popular in the United States. Frozen lemon and grapefruit juices also have a market. Manufacturers also freeze lemonade. Another popular frozen juice comes from pineapple.

Frozen Seafood

Fresh seafood decays rapidly. Freezing is an important method of preservation, making seafood available to people some distance from bodies of water, fresh or saline. Safety and sanitation must be strict, given several cases in which frozen fish have contained toxic bacteria in the genera *Salmonella* and *Staphylococcus*. Ironically, the danger comes from human contact with the fish during processing and freezing. Frozen seafood may store several months. This achievement is not monumental given the expectation that canned salmon or tuna, for example, will outlast its frozen counterpart. It is also true that canned tuna generates more revenues than the sale of frozen tuna in the United States. Fish may be frozen with the addition of minimal ingredients. In other cases, fish may be battered and fried before freezing. From the perspective of health one should choose frozen seafood with minimal processing. One may choose from an array of frozen seafood: shrimp, oysters, tuna, salmon, tilapia, cod, smelt, walleye, perch, and other fish. The selection of canned seafood is much less broad.

Further Reading

Hui, Y. H., Paul Cornillon, Isabel Guerrero Legaretta, Miang H. Lim, K. D. Murrell, and Wai-Kit Nip, eds. *Handbook of Frozen Foods*. New York and Basel: Marcel Dekker, 2004.

G

Garlic

Among the oldest cultivated plants, garlic produces a bulb made of cloves. The cloves are swollen leaves. Garlic rarely flowers or produces viable seeds, probably because humans selected against these traits. Instead, the farmer or gardener propagates garlic by planting cloves. As a rule, the larger the clove, the larger will be the forthcoming bulb. In the 18th century, Swedish naturalist Carl Linnaeus named garlic *Allium sativum*. *Allium* is Latin for "garlic" and *sativum* means "cultivated." Garlic derives from two Anglo-Saxon words: *gar*, which means "lance," and *leac*, which means "herb." Garlic is therefore the herb with cloves in the shape of a spear or lance. Garlic is related to onion, leek, shallot, and chive. Despite its name, elephant garlic is a leek rather than a true garlic.

Folklore and Mythology

From Romania arose the iconic use of garlic as protection against vampires. In *Dracula*, Irish novelist Bram Stoker assigns physician Abraham Van Helsing the task of protecting the vulnerable Lucy from Dracula. True to the beliefs of Romanian folklore, Lucy wears a necklace of garlic to deter Dracula. Van Helsing rubs garlic on the windows and door of Lucy's room to prevent Dracula from entering the room. Lucy might have rested peacefully but for the interference of her mother. Revolted by the odor, she removes the garlic, ensuring Dracula's triumph. Both mother and daughter die, and Van Helsing, convinced that Dracula has made Lucy a vampire, ends her nightly search for blood by packing garlic into her mouth and cutting off her head. Dracula, repulsed by garlic, will have no more power over her. The superstitious in Romania put garlic in the mouths of corpses suspected of being vampires to ensure that they would not rise from the grave. Another folk belief recommended the placing of garlic in the coffin of a corpse to ensure

Garlic may be linked to ethnic identities given the bulb's prominence in Italian cuisine. Medical authorities appear to appreciate the health benefits of garlic. (Viktoriat/Dreamstime .com)

that it would decompose and not become a vampire. In this context, garlic has formed part of the iconic literature of modernity.

Because garlic gives off an odor akin to sulfur, some people have associated it with the fire of hell. In ancient Etruria, in Italy, according to one account, people sacrificed boys to the goddess Mania. The magistrate, Junius Brutus, convinced the Etruscans to spare the boys, sacrificing garlic instead. Mania apparently accepted garlic and did not visit evil on Etruria. One Islamic myth holds that Satan, after having tempted Adam and Eve, left Eden on two feet. Garlic sprouted where his left foot had trod, and onion germinated in the print of his right foot. Having issued from Satan, garlic must not have been a suitable plant for humans. A Hindi myth likewise hints at an unsettling origin of garlic. According to this myth, the demon Rahu stole a vase containing the elixir of immortality. Determined to retrieve the liquid, the god Vishnu captured Rahu, but not before he drank it. In anger, Vishnu cut off Rahu's head. From the liquid that dripped to the ground, perhaps a mixture of blood and the elixir of immortality, emerged a garlic plant.

The Greeks, holding a belief similar to Romanian lore, wore necklaces of garlic to fend off evil. They put garlic bulbs at their doors to keep demons from entering the home. Ninth-century-BCE Greek poet Homer credited garlic with saving Greek king Odysseus from goddess Circe. His shipmates had no garlic to protect them, and so Circe turned them into pigs. The Egyptians believed garlic

Dracula

Drawing on Romanian legend, Irish author Bram Stoker conceived of Dracula (based on the historical figure Prince Vlad Tepes) as the supreme vampire, the undead who can only be satisfied with blood. The story opens with British lawyer Jonathan Harker on his way to Transylvania to close a real estate deal with Count Dracula. At his castle Harker encounters the count and observes his bizarre behavior as he is imprisoned, with his reason shaken by fear. When he escapes, Harker returns to London, but not before the count, who has drunk the blood of Harker's friend Lucy Westera. Lucy rises from the grave a vampire, and Abraham Van Helsing must convince Harker and his friends to stake Lucy's heart and decapitate her. Once accomplished, the group turns to Dracula, chasing him back to Transylvania, and killing him in the process. Since its publication in 1897, *Dracula* has retained its place as a horror classic. Innumerable films have been made of the novel, though many are not true to Stoker's storyline.

protected one from harm. Perhaps for this reason, the pharaoh Tutankhamun's tomb contained six garlic bulbs. A European folk belief held that a horse fed garlic would not have nightmares. The superstitious put necklaces of garlic around a horse's neck to deter trolls from injuring it. A necklace of garlic likewise was believed to protect cows from trolls who wished to steal their milk. The superstitious placed garlic near the opening of a snake's hole to prevent it from exiting. Worn around the neck, garlic, some believed, protected the wearer from witches, werewolves, demons, and the evil eye. Superstitious parents hung garlic over a crib to prevent fairies from stealing their baby. According to tradition, grandmothers would give garlic to newborns to protect them from evil spirits.

Origin and History

Garlic is native to southern central Asia, where it grew wild in the Tien Shan and Pamir-Alai mountains. Originating in an extreme climate, garlic tolerates hot, dry summers and frigid winters. To avoid the worst effects of hot weather, garlic, nourished by water from snowmelt, matured in late spring. Dormant during summer, garlic has thick skin to retain moisture. More than 10,000 years ago, nomadic hunter-gatherers may have planted garlic. Because the bulb is light and stores well, it might have been among the provisions of these nomads. From an early date, people used garlic to flavor other foods and to preserve meat and vegetables. Garlic's antimicrobial properties made it possible to store food for long periods. Because garlic has a strong flavor it disguised the taste of rancid meat and fish. The nomads of Central Asia may have traded garlic with India, Egypt, and other parts of the Mediterranean Basin. In this way, these regions may have acquired the habit of cultivating garlic. The Egyptians valued garlic so much that 15 pounds of the plant were worth one slave. The Egyptians made clay models of garlic bulbs more than 5,000 years ago, putting them in tombs. In other instances, the Egyptians put garlic into tombs. The practice was apparently not confined to Tutankhamun. Egyptian overseers fed garlic to laborers, including those who built the pyramids, to maintain their strength. Although the Egyptians used garlic as food, medicine, and in religious rites, it never appeared on tomb paintings. One writer believes this omission was due to the fact that the Egyptians did not regard garlic as a sacred plant. The Romans, who were not fond of garlic's odor, called the Egyptians "the garlic eaters." Similarly the Hebrews were "the stinking ones."

According to one school of thought, the Chinese began cultivating garlic during the Han dynasty. Nineteenth-century French botanist Alphonse de Candolle favored an earlier date. The Hsia Calendar mentioned garlic 4,000 years ago, a reference that may point to the cultivation of the bulb. The Greek dramatist Aristophanes mentioned garlic. The Roman patricians, we have seen, disliked garlic, but soldiers and laborers ate it because it fortified one with strength, stamina, and courage. Archeologists have found garlic in Pompeii, evidence of its consumption in this city.

In the 14th century, Alfonso XI, king of Castille and Leon, evidently had a low opinion of garlic because he forbade knights from eating it. In the 15th century, Queen Isabella the Catholic disliked garlic so intensely that she would not eat plants that had been grown near garlic. The British, unenthusiastic about garlic, thought it a food suitable only for Mediterranean people. Others were not so negative. By the 16th century, the consumption of garlic was so widespread, at least among commoners, that the phrase "garlic eater" referred to an ordinary person. The Finns, Icelanders, Irish, Norse, and Scots flavored butter with garlic.

In Africa, garlic protected one from mosquitoes and crocodiles. Middle Easterners regarded garlic as an aphrodisiac. A groom pinned a clove to his lapel to ensure a productive night with his new bride. The Amerindians of the Pacific Northwest believed that garlic could rid them of an unwanted lover. The person who wished to be free of his encumbrance put pins in a garlic bulb, placing it at the intersection of two roads. The unwanted lover who walked over the garlic lost interest in him.

Health

Three cloves of garlic have just 13 calories, no fat or cholesterol, and more than 200 vitamins, amino acids, enzymes, and minerals. With vitamins A, C, and the B complex, garlic has calcium, magnesium, potassium, zinc, iron, selenium, germanium, and sulfur. In one study, people who ate garlic lowered their cholesterol 28 percent. Garlic may reduce blood pressure. Because it has antibacterial properties, garlic may protect one from lung infections. Research suggests that garlic may protect against stomach, colon, and skin cancers. Possibly effective against heart disease, garlic may retard the aggregation of platelets in blood vessels.

The Egyptian medical text the *Codex Ebers*, dating to 1550 BCE, listed 20 garlic remedies to treat several ailments, including headache and throat tumors. According to a first-century-CE Indian medical text, garlic improved the function of the eyes, heart, joints, and muscles. Fourth-century-BCE Greek philosopher Aristotle believed garlic was a stimulant. First-century-CE Greek physician Dioscorides thought garlic useful in treating a large number of ailments. Galen, physician to Emperor Marcus Aurelius, praised garlic as a "heal all." During the plague of 1665, people wore garlic necklaces to protect them from contagion. Physicians carried garlic in their pockets in the belief that it counteracted the effect of bad air, the putative cause of plague. In 1772, according to one account, thieves in Marseilles, France, dug up the corpses of plague victims to steal their grave goods. Washing themselves in a mixture of garlic and vinegar and sprinkling the solution around their homes, they never contracted the disease. In 1858, French scientist Louis Pasteur demonstrated the antibacterial properties of garlic. During World War I, physicians put garlic to good use, applying its juice to wounds to prevent infection.

In Nepal, people use garlic oil to treat cough and pneumonia. Indians combine an extract of garlic and honey to treat bronchitis. In Oman, people crush garlic, rubbing it into the scalp to treat dandruff. They use garlic to treat colic, diarrhea, and diabetes. Boiling garlic in water, the people of Oman also inhale the steam to treat tuberculosis. Pregnant women in Mexico eat garlic to ease the delivery of their children. The Chinese use garlic to treat bites, boils, the common cold, dysentery, lead poisoning, nosebleed, and whooping cough. The people of Venezuela consume garlic to slow heart palpitations; stimulate the function of the liver, kidneys, and bladder; cure hemorrhoids, headache, neuralgia, depression, hysteria, insomnia, and varicose veins; relieve constipation, rheumatism, and gout; and decrease the amount of uric acid in the body.

Further Reading

Coonse, Marian. *Onions, Leeks, and Garlic: A Handbook for Gardeners*. College Station: Texas A&M University, 1995.

Engeland, Ron L. *Growing Great Garlic: The Definitive Guide for Organic Gardeners and Small Farmers*. Okanogan, WA: Filaree Productions, 1998.

Meredith, Ted Jordan. *The Complete Book of Garlic: A Guide for Gardeners, Growers, and Serious Cooks*. Portland, OR: Timber Press, 2008.

Midgley, John. *The Goodness of Garlic*. New York: Random House, 1992.

Platt, Ellen Spector. *Garlic, Onion, and Other Alliums*. Mechanicsburg, PA: Stackpole Books, 2003.

Thacker, Emily. *The Garlic Book*. Canton, OH: Tresco Publishers, 1994.

Woodward, Penny. *Garlic and Friends: The History, Growth and Use of Edible Alliums*. Cincinnati, OH: Hyland House, 1996.

Goose

The goose is not an easy animal to classify. Some authorities place geese into species, but this appears to be more a taxonomic than a biological category. Strictly speaking, a species is all the organisms that can interbreed to yield fertile offspring. If two animals can interbreed but cannot yield fertile offspring then they are separate species by definition. A good example is the relationship between the horse and donkey. The two may interbreed to yield the mule, but because the mule is sterile the horse and donkey are rightly separate species. A more infamous case concerns Neanderthals. Modern humans tend to equate them with primitive characteristics, yet genetic evidence reveals that all humans have Neanderthal DNA. This can only be true if modern humans interbred with Neanderthals to yield fertile offspring. We are not, strictly speaking, a separate species from Neanderthals. The same is true of goose "species." Because these species can interbreed to yield fertile progeny, they are not really separate species at all.

Origin and Domestication

The goose is fascinating in having inhabited all continents excluding Antarctica long before the Columbian Exchange. There appears to be no way to know exactly where the goose originated. Other species contrast with this worldwide status. The soybean, for example, was confined to China before it spread to Europe and, with the Columbian Exchange, to the Americas. Cattle, sheep, pigs, and chickens were unknown in the Americas before the Columbian Exchange. The turkey was unknown in the Old World before the Columbian Exchange. One might multiply examples, but the point is that the goose appears novel in having migrated throughout the world without human assistance.

According to one thesis, the goose is among the earliest domesticated animals, perhaps trailing only the dog and sheep. Yet there appears to be little evidence for this conjecture. If one puts the date of domestication at about 1000 BCE in Egypt, one must conclude that the goose was a latecomer, trailing a number of other species, among them the dog, sheep, pig, cow, goat, and chicken. Others push Egypt's domestication of the goose to 3000 BCE, but even this is not an early date when one surveys the antiquity of animal husbandry. Among poultry, the goose seems never to have been as important worldwide as the chicken, turkey, or duck. Even if not the pinnacle in the food hierarchy, the goose has fed humans for at least 3,000 years and so has shaped history and daily life.

Because the goose inhabits both cold and hot climates, one might expect people everywhere to have specialized in goose production. But in historic times Asia and Europe were the principal producers. It is possible that Asia and Europe domesticated the goose independently. If this is true, and it is also true that Egypt domesticated the goose, one must count three separate acts and places of domestication. The European goose derives from the wild greylag goose, whereas the Asian goose traces its lineage to the swan goose. Again these "species" can interbreed to yield fertile offspring. Canada, the United States, South America, Egypt, Hawaii, India, Central Asia, Australia, and Papua New Guinea all eat local varieties of geese. Parts of Africa may do so as well, but this tradition may stem from Egypt. China alone consumes the meat from more than 20 varieties of geese.

The goose appears to have been important both as a source of food and religious mythology in Rome. As the Hebrews ate lamb and sacrificed it to their god, Yahweh, the Romans ate goose and sacrificed it to Juno, the primary goddess and wife of Jupiter. In Roman antiquity, the encyclopedist Pliny the Elder and the poet Horace collected goose recipes and gave advice about how to raise geese for domestic use and for market. In the 19th century Frankish king Charlemagne commanded all farmers and stockmen to raise geese for their own sustenance and for market. This command appears to have been nothing more than a continuation of Roman policies.

The Role of Selective Breeding

In the 19th century British naturalist Charles Darwin called attention to the role of selective breeding in shaping domestic animals and plants. This was certainly true of the goose. At first, humans almost certainly hunted geese the way that they hunted wild cattle and pigs. At some date, though the time is disputed, humans, probably in Egypt, began keeping geese in cages or pens of some type. As has been true of much of the history of agriculture, the Egyptians were not satisfied merely to keep and eat geese. They wanted larger, meatier animals, and with this in mind began breeding the largest males with the largest females to yield large offspring. In this way, the Egyptians gained two immediate advantages. First, they derived a meatier, more caloric goose to eat. The goose is a high-calorie meat because it contains much fat and so is akin to duck. This fat is not marbled in the flesh but is subcutaneous. It can therefore be removed, though the extra effort probably deterred many people in antiquity from doing so. Also, living strenuous lives, humans would have welcomed extra calories to match the rate at which people burned them. The second advantage that came with greater size was the deterrence of predators. Geese could look after themselves without too much attention. The same cannot be said of the chicken. Nonetheless, large geese, unlike turkeys and domestic ducks, remain capable fliers.

The United States

As late as the 19th century, some Americans ate goose in preference to turkey during holidays. Since then, the goose has fallen from favor. The goose is not a principal source of nourishment in the United States. America produces many more chickens, turkeys, and ducks than geese. To gain a sense of proportion, one might consider that China produces about 4 billion geese per year as well as a large number of goose eggs. The United States, by contrast, produces only about 178,000 geese per year. In the United States, Texas is the leader with a production of more than 14,000 geese per year. Minnesota, South Dakota, Wisconsin, and Michigan are also important producers. Some authorities add California to the list, but absent figures it is difficult to know where California ranks. According to the U.S. Department of Agriculture, the average American eats less than one-third of a pound of goose per year.

The Developing World

In parts of the developing world, small farmers raise geese as among their chief sources of protein. In this case, the goose makes daily life possible. These farmers favor geese because of the ease of care and because geese take up comparatively little space and can forage for their own food. In some cases, geese provide an important source of cash for otherwise impoverished peasants. Geese are also popular in the developing world, as we noted earlier, because they were large enough to deter predators. Moreover, geese needed less attention than did chickens. Geese have also adapted well to captivity. The drawback, of course, is the high fat content. One may partly alleviate this problem by roasting a goose, as one roasts a duck, to allow some of the fat to drip from the bird. In southern China, farmers tend to raise two essential commodities: rice and geese. Despite the prominent layer of subcutaneous fat, the meat itself is comparatively lean. It is possible to strip away the fat, but the resulting lean meat strikes many as less flavorful.

Roasting is one process that will allow the household to reduce the fat from goose meat.

Mythology and Religion

The Egyptians believed that before the universe existed, space was devoid of everything except a female goose. At the beginning of time, she laid an egg from which hatched the entire universe, including earth and humans. The story has a certain "Big Bang" element to it, though is much less well-known in the West than the Genesis story of creation. The Egyptians believed that the god Amun took the form of a goose. The Egyptians also associated the goose with the god Osiris and the goddess Isis. The cult of Isis would shape religions, including Christianity, throughout the Mediterranean world. The goose symbolized the love that Isis and Osiris shared as wife and husband and as sister and brother. This love may have had an erotic component, though eroticism was not on display as prominently in Egypt as in Rome. The Greeks associated the goose with Aphrodite, the goddess of love. Here the connection between the goose and eroticism is secure. The Romans placed geese in the temple of Juno. According to legend, about 390 BCE, geese in this temple squawked so loudly that the Romans awakened in the early morning to discover that a barbarian army from Gaul (today France) was approaching the city. Arming themselves quickly, the Romans defeated the Gauls. The geese had sounded the alarm just in time to avert disaster. Christians named Saint Martin of Tours as the patron saint of geese because Martin had hidden in a barn with geese to avoid an appointment as bishop. He longed instead for the simple life of a hermit. The geese betrayed him and the crowd elevated him to bishop. The ancient peoples of northern Europe associated geese with their warrior elites. The Celts buried geese with prominent soldiers as confirmation of their heroism.

Further Reading

Damron, W. Stephen. *Introduction to Animal Science: Global, Biological, Social, and Industry Perspectives*. 5th ed. Boston: Pearson, 2013.
Scanes, Colin. *Fundamentals of Animal Science*. Australia: Delmar, 2011.

H

Honey

The honeybee produces honey from the nectar and pollen it derives from flowers. Honey is a mix of glucose and fructose. Glucose is the fundamental sugar that plants produce from photosynthesis. Fructose is a sugar found in fruits: apples, pears, peaches, plums, apricots, grapes, citrus, dates, figs, and many others. It is surely the world's oldest sweetener, originating long before humans began to derive sugar from the sugarcane plant. In this sense, one cannot overstate the degree to which honey must have shaped the rise of civilizations. Because the honeybee may be 100 million years old, it seems reasonable to suppose that, as it coevolved with flowering plants, it has produced honey for many millions of years. By contrast, sugar has arisen as a food only during the last 10,000 years or so.

Honey is in a sense a prehuman commodity, when one considers that humankind's ancestors ate it. *Homo habilis, Homo erectus* and perhaps even the Australopithecines before them ate honey. If so, honey must have been an African food before it conquered the world. This claim makes sense when one turns to the antiquity of honey in Egypt in northeastern Africa.

Honey in Historic Times

The people of Egypt and Arabia may have been the first to keep bees for honey. Egyptian funereal art depicts people keeping bees and sampling honey. The earliest evidence of this art dates to about 1450 BCE. By this date, the Egyptians made clay structures for bees, stacking one atop another. They collected honey in clay pots, so that by this date beekeeping and honey making were quite advanced. Indeed, Egypt's connection to honey is at least 5,000 years old. Honey was associated with pharaohs and the nobility. Honey and the honeybee symbolized civilization and, in a real sense, were a foundation upon which the early civilization of Egypt and southwestern Asia arose. Honey was also a symbol of eroticism,

Honey must have been humanity's first sweetener. Even with competition from sugar, corn syrup, high fructose corn syrup, and other sweeteners, honey holds its own. (Justin Skinner /Dreamstime.com)

sexuality, love, and death. This is a strange sequence. The union of eroticism, sexuality, and love makes sense and was a common theme surrounding many foods and beverages. One need only consider wine by comparison. The association with death, however, is mysterious. What has death to do with eroticism, sex, and love? Honey also symbolized power, order, magic, and truth. Perhaps no other ancient food had so many associations.

Honey and Terrorism in Yemen

Infamous terrorist Osama bin Laden recruited many followers from Yemen's bee-keepers and honey makers, young men who wanted glory through membership as a warrior elite. One wonders whether bin Laden would have succeeded without his honey men. In this context, honey, thanks to bin Laden, changed the world, plunging the United States into two dismal wars in Iraq and Afghanistan and sharpening the divide between the Muslim East and the Christian West. Bin Laden also sold honey to finance his operations. In 2001, the year of the fateful World Trade Center attack, the U.S. Central Intelligence Agency (CIA) identified the honey trade as Al

Qaeda's principal source of income. Yemen honey companies Al Shifas and Al Nur supported Al Qaeda. In retaliation, the United States froze their assets in U.S. banks. The United States considers both companies terrorist organizations. Indeed, Al Nur was among the first to recruit soldiers to fight the United States in Afghanistan.

It is difficult to reconcile this view of Islam and its relation to honey with the more benign outlook that had prevailed earlier in Yemen's history. Yemeni Muslims consider honey the food of the blessed. Yemenis believe that honey is a gift from Allah. Perhaps for these reasons Yemeni honey is expensive. Yemeni beekeepers feed bees sugar, an unusual and ahistorical diet that makes sugar the creator of honey when honey, as shown, predated sugar by many millennia. One local woman compared Yemeni honey to dates in flavor, though others believe that honey is much sweeter than dates.

Australia and Honey

In the Southern Hemisphere, Australia has emerged as an important honey producer and exporter, ranking sixth worldwide in honey production. The island continent exports one-third of the 30,000 metric tons of honey it produces per year. Honey is also an important import. Australia encourages imports by not putting a duty on them. In contrast, other countries place a tariff on Australian honey that nearly triples its price. One would not think Australian honey could compete in the world market. Australia has about 9,600 beekeepers and honey makers. The continent has four major honey makers: Capilano, Beechworth Honey, Wescober, and Leebrook Farms. The British settlers were the first to keep bees in Australia, with 1822 marking the date of introduction. In this sense, beekeeping and honey making are recent activities in Australia and can claim none of the antiquity of these activities in Egypt and Yemen. Yet, in another sense, honey itself is older in Australia. When humans first reached Australia about 40,000 years ago, a comparatively late date when one considers the tenure of Africa, Asia, and Europe, they found a wild species of bee that produced honey. They did not, however, domesticate this bee, and it is uncertain how important honey was to these earliest human inhabitants of Australia.

Borneo

Borneo is an island in Southeast Asia directly on the equator. It is a patchwork of nations, including Indonesia and Malaysia. Borneo is important in the history of honey because it must represent the collecting of honey in its embryonic state, given that the people of Borneo simply collect honey, never bothering to have domesticated the wild bee that produces it. This wild bee is native to the tropics and cannot endure cold weather. It is ideal for tropical Borneo. The people of Borneo believe that these bees carry the souls of the dead to the afterworld. Because of Borneo's practices and beliefs, it must resemble the conditions millennia ago when humans had not yet learned to tame the honeybee. In this context, Borneo honey must be akin to a living fossil of honey in its earliest manifestation. To the people of Borneo honey is part of a rustic life. They may plant crops, harvest rubber, fish, and collect honey. In the Indonesian part of Borneo, five species of wild bees exist. Indonesia produces several types of honey, each with a distinctive flavor. By the third century CE, Borneo exported honey to China. The ancients of Borneo believed that honey connected one to the spirits in the forest. These people collected honey at night when bees were less likely to sting. Beekeepers used smoke to calm the bees, though if they were not careful a hive might burst into flames. Borneo sells most honey locally. Often water laden, its quality is not always high. Much of the harvest falls in January and February with a secondary collection during the dry season. The January-February harvest is the larger. The people of Borneo believe that when fish begin swimming upstream the harvest is near. As a rule, the flavor of Borneo honey is intense.

China

China is the global behemoth, producing and exporting more honey than any other nation. China has about 140,000 beekeepers and honey makers. The average beekeeper has some 200 colonies of bees. The country produces roughly 150,000 metric tons of honey each year. Yet China has its problems, feeding its bees antibiotics, which the bees impart to the honey. Because some of these antibiotics treat rare but serious infections, they may not be in the food supply. China has tried to beat international authorities by sending its honey through Turkey and several nations of Southeast Asia to disguise its origin. As much honey as China makes, it also imports the sweetener to satisfy the appetites of a growing middle class. Foreigners suspicious of China deride its honey as contaminated and substandard. Curiously, the Chinese consider the honey industry part of agriculture, ignoring the Roman distinction between agriculture and apiculture. Advertising is also a problem. Some Chinese companies market their brand of honey as high protein when it is not. Clearly communism has surrendered to a market-oriented, fiercely competitive capitalism.

The United States

The honeybee is not native to the Americas. Not until European contact were the Amerindians aware of it. Europeans imported the honeybee into all regions of the Americas during the Columbian Exchange. The English established honeybees in

Jamestown, Virginia, in 1621. Because these bees tended to move ahead of European settlement, third U.S. president Thomas Jefferson noted that Native Americans knew of the approach of Europeans before their arrival. Philadelphia, Pennsylvania, luminary Benjamin Franklin adored honey, dividing the Americas into tropical regions that yielded sugarcane and a northern temperate zone that produced honey, believing that God approved this division. In the North the bee was the laborer. In the tropics the slave was the worker. Because honey did not have the taint of slavery, Franklin preferred it to sugar. In 1850, the United States made 15 million pounds of honey. Ten years later, the figure surpassed 23 million pounds, with a value of nearly $7 million. In the 19th century, Italian immigrants brought the Italian honeybee to the United States. Well adapted to cold weather and very productive, this bee laid the foundation for modern apiculture in the United States. From the outset, the U.S. Department of Agriculture (USDA) funded research on the bee with the aim of increasing production and on honey with the aim of making it sweeter still. As in so many cases, the relationship between the USDA and honey was part of a large narrative of the interaction between science and the food industry. For that reason, honey is important in U.S. history. The federal government rationed sugar during World Wars I and II and funded beekeepers to produce more honey to satisfy America's sweet tooth. With the end of sugar rationing in 1946, the demand for honey fell. To keep prices from declining, the USDA bought surplus honey for export to U.S. troops overseas. In the 1980s, inflation caused U.S. honey prices to rise, making the sweetener too expensive to compete on the global market. At home, honey benefited the baking industry because, unlike sugar, honey moistens baked goods.

Further Reading

Chaline, Eric. *Fifty Animals that Changed the Course of History*. Buffalo, NY: Firefly Books, 2011.

Pundyk, Grace. *The Honey Trail: In Pursuit of Liquid Gold and Vanishing Bees*. New York: St. Martin's Press, 2008.

Warner, Deborah Jean. *Sweet Stuff: An American History of Sweeteners from Sugar to Sucralose*. Washington, DC: Smithsonian Institution Scholarly Press, 2011.

Hopping John

Sometimes rendered "hoppin' John," hopping John is a variant of the traditional and now ubiquitous dish of rice and beans. Given the antiquity of rice culture in

The Legend of Hopping John

Hopping John is a dish of rice and beans that legend holds to be the invention of a poor African American man with a limp. The limp led to his designation as "Hopping John." As with many legends, little is known about this man, who may or may not have existed. Presumably his name was John, and presumably he was a southerner born in the age of segregation.

southern Asia, it is tempting to trace this dish to China and Southeast Asia. The bean must have been the mung bean or perhaps the soybean, which Chinese lore described as one of the five sacred grains. Actually, the soybean, like all beans, is a legume rather than a grain. Had the Chinese examined the roots closely, they probably would not have described the soybean as a grain. Hopping John, however, comes from a different tradition. It combines African and American foodways, though the bean in question is subject to debate.

From Africa

The Portuguese probably introduced American beans to Africa, particularly West Africa, in the 16th century. These beans were and are part of the genus *Phaseolus*, the world's most important source of beans. As such, *Phaseolus* beans have revolutionized cookery as they have spread around the globe. The roots of hopping John may not, however, reside in *Phaseolus* beans, though they were surely incorporated into the dish after the 16th century. Rather, the roots of hopping John may lie in the black-eyed pea. The black-eyed pea may cause confusion because it is not really a pea. The true pea is a western Asian cultigen and among the first food plants to be domesticated. It formed the basis of Austrian monk Gregor Mendel's famous experiments in heredity that established the science of genetics. Rather, botanists classify the black-eyed pea as a bean, though it is not in the genus *Phaseolus* and so is not an American bean. The people of West Africa have grown black-eyed peas since the sixth century BCE. Even today, West Africa harvests about 90 percent of the world's black-eyed peas.

The other part of the equation is rice. Again, it is tempting to suppose that the Chinese or some other East Asians brought Asian rice to Africa, and this transfer would eventually occur. But from a very early date Africa had its own rice, now classed as a subspecies of Asian rice, though at an early date Asian and African rices were a continent apart. For one accustomed to the long grains of polished, white Asian rice, African rice is distinct and of two types. One is a short, white kernel and the other a long, red grain. There was thus no mistaking African rice for Asian rice. The prevalence of black-eyed peas and rice in West Africa led ship captains to feed slaves these foods on the transatlantic crossing to the Americas. In this sense, hopping John sustained the slave trade to the misery of Africans.

An African American Dish

The Americas had no indigenous varieties of rice and so the Amerindians knew nothing about the grain. Since the 19th century, historians have confirmed that Africa, rather than Asia, first introduced rice into the Americas. Much attention has focused on South Carolina, where a slave-master dynamic arose, with the slaves providing the muscle and knowledge of growing African rice to profit their masters. One should not neglect the Caribbean and the Louisiana Territory, first under Spanish rule, then French, and after 1803 part of the nascent United States. In both the Caribbean and Louisiana slaves grew African rice.

The combination of black-eyed peas and African rice formed the first iteration of hopping John in the Caribbean, Louisiana, South Carolina, and many regions of the American South in general. Much of the Caribbean, on the other hand, substituted red kidney beans (there is a white variant) for black-eyed peas. Cuba, however, preferred to serve black beans with African rice. Both kidney beans and black beans are, of course, *Phaseolus* beans. The beans, whether black-eyed peas, kidney beans, or black beans, were enormously important as a source of protein, particularly among the masses who were too poor to afford meat. In this sense, hopping John propped up what is now called the income inequality that was and is a chasm between rich and poor. Hopping John shaped history by enabling the masses to survive and to obtain protein from what was close to a vegetarian existence. Beans were ideal in a world before the era of refrigeration. They are deceptively easy to grow and, perhaps more importantly, can be stored dry for long periods. Only after boiling them in water is their consumption necessary or indeed desirable. At minimum, the rice provided carbohydrates, which were incredibly important in an era in which African Americans did strenuous farm work every day of their lives. Whether rice provided additional benefits is open to question. A grain of brown rice, with bran and germ intact, is an important source of vitamins, containing A and several B vitamins. Unfortunately, most Americans, and Asians for that matter, seem to have eaten polished or white rice. The process of milling rice deprived it of the bran and germ and so denuded it of vitamins. In this context, rice was not an ideal source of nutrients, though most people appear to prefer white rice to brown.

One legend conveys the importance of hopping John to African Americans. One woman who reputedly dined on nothing but hopping John died at an old age.

Knowing her love for hopping John, a family member placed a bowl of the dish before her nose while she lay in the coffin. Had she stirred at the aroma, everyone would have known that she was alive still. The fact that she did not move confirmed the conclusion that she was truly dead. Hopping John thus marked one's identity as an African American and combined the foodways of Africa and the Americas. Hopping John brought the peoples of these continents together as Europeans tried to divide and conquer on the putative basis of race. The term "race" is used here in a guarded sense, as several biologists no longer believe that humans have sufficient genetic variability to justify the division of people into races, which are literally subspecies.

From the Civil War to the Great Depression, the American South was in economic malaise. While industry roared in the North, peons and tenants eked out a living in the South. In a context in which the masses, black as well as white, were poor, hopping John spread across ethnicities so that poor whites were as likely to eat it as poor blacks. At times, and these occasions must have been infrequent, cooks added meat to hopping John, though this was a luxury that was often beyond the grasp of ordinary people. Pork was the desired and attainable meat, shared among neighbors at the time of butchering. Often, African Americans made do with the worst and fattest cuts of pork. This act of sharing strengthened solidarity within the African American community. Hopping John forms one of the pillars of Southern cuisine and would be a component of soul food. Like turkey, hopping John arose in the South to symbolize the holidays. New Year's Day was and is a festival of ham, hopping John, greens, stewed tomatoes, and cornbread. With gluten free diets in fashion today, Southern cooking provided an early example. One legend traces the tradition of serving hopping John on New Year's Day to a crippled South Carolinian who began selling hopping John on January 1, 1841. Perhaps during these festive occasions, people were apt to combine rice, black-eyed peas, bacon, and salted pork of another kind. This combination must have enhanced the appetite because the dish had fat and salt, two items that humans crave. The black-eyed peas in combination with bacon or other salted cuts of pork give the dish a creamy, pleasurable flavor.

In New Orleans, people favored red kidney beans over black-eyed peas. One might consider this dish a variant of traditional hopping John, though it remains important. This dish may have varied with the addition of sausage, pork shoulder, ham, pickled meats, and possibly pig tails. The days of slavery had taught African Americans to subsist on the least desirable parts of a pig because the best cuts went to the master's family. This dish may be cooked all day with little attention and so was often prepared on wash day, when African American women would have been too absorbed with other chores to attend closely to the preparation of a meal. Whereas rice fueled the slave empire in South Carolina, sugarcane was the scourge of black Louisiana. In this variant of hopping John, red kidney beans were important but not essential. When other beans were cheaper, the substitution was automatic. Inexpensiveness rather than allegiance to a particular bean was the criterion of preference. African American residents of New Orleans used smoked sausage flavored with garlic to enhance the meal. They may have also added onions, green peppers, celery, more garlic, and parsley. The meal was comfort food.

A third variant of hopping John is the Cuban combination of black beans and African rice. The dish is as much a lesson in history as a nutritious item. The Muslim Arabs, in the early Middle Ages, swept through North Africa and crossed the Mediterranean Sea, where they conquered the southern portions of Spain. The Spanish invoked the authority of Catholic Christianity to launch a crusade of sorts to recapture the rest of Spain from the Arabs, known as the Moors. The conquest was complete in 1492, the year of Italian Spanish explorer Christopher Columbus's first voyage. As the Moors and Spaniards coexisted throughout much of the Middle Ages in places like Spain and Sicily (though Sicily is a more complicated example), so the Cuban mixture of black beans and African rice creates a successful dish. Black beans and rice may have included vinegar or chili peppers. Common ingredients included onion, New World pepper (which comes in several colors when fully ripe), and garlic.

Further Reading

Albala, Ken. *Beans: A History*. Oxford: Berg, 2007.

Janer, Zilkia. *Latino Food Culture*. Food Cultures in America, edited by Ken Albala. Westport, CT: Greenwood Press, 2008.

McWilliams, Mark. *The Story behind the Dish: Classic American Foods*. Santa Barbara, CA: Greenwood Press, 2012.

Roahen, Sara. *Gumbo Tales: Finding My Place at the New Orleans Table*. New York: Norton, 2008.

Sauceman, Fred W. "Beans." *Foodways*. Edited by John T. Edge. Vol. 7 of *The New Encyclopedia of Southern Culture*, edited by Charles Reagan Wilson. Chapel Hill: University of North Carolina Press, 2007. 119–20.

Hot Dog

The hot dog is not merely a type of sausage. It is, certainly in the United States, the most popular sausage. In 1971, a General Motors executive, asked to list what Americans prized, answered "hot dogs, baseball, apple pie and Chevrolet." Notably, the hot dog headed this list, coming even before Chevrolet, the type of

People line up at a characteristic fast food hot dog stand near the Museum of Modern Art in New York. Fast food mobile stands are very popular all over Manhattan. (Stefano Armaroli/ Dreamstime.com)

automobile that the executive surely meant to promote. To eat a hot dog is to engage in an American ritual that brands one as an American as perhaps no other food does. At its origin, the hot dog was an assemblage of meat encased in part of the gut of a slaughtered pig or cow. Stuffed vegetables as a form of encasement probably predated the hot dog, which cannot claim the antiquity of such staples as rice, wheat, barley, and corn. Even renowned tubers and roots like potatoes, sweet potatoes, yams, and cassava are older than hot dogs. Although the emphasis is on meat, hot dogs now contain fish or plant protein. Derivatives of soybeans may also be present, probably because soybeans are a good source of protein.

In many ways, hot dogs and sausages in general use the beef, pork, and chicken that are not suitable for fine cuts of these meats. (Even the U.S. Department of Agriculture classifies chicken as meat.) Also important is the shape of a hot dog. No one has trouble differentiating between a hot dog and a slice of bologna even though the two products may have identical ingredients. The meat in a hot dog is ground, as is the beef patty known as hamburger. The hot dog eschews utensils and is meant to be eaten in a bun, almost always of white bread, held in the hand. It is probably a stretch to call a hot dog a sandwich, though some food historians define it as such.

Origins

Although a hot dog is a sausage, the invention of sausages may still hold some mystery. Astonishingly, in the late Paleolithic era (the Old Stone Age), humans may have hit upon the idea of encasing meat in part of the gut of a butchered animal. If this account is true, then the sausage, at perhaps 20,000 years old, traces its roots to prehistory, though the hot dog is a later offshoot. Although the people of several ethnicities spanning the globe were quick to adopt the sausage, the invention of the hot dog traces its roots to Europe, a surprising fact given the tendency of Americans to identify it as an American indigene. Although Greek poet Homer and later Roman chefs mentioned sausage, the origin of the hot dog is not a Mediterranean achievement. At the time, pork was the ingredient of choice in sausage. Sausage appears to have had ties to the rise of Christianity, being a traditional item for consumption on Easter, though Christianity traced its culinary and religious roots to wine, bread, and fish.

The Hot Dog and American Exceptionalism

The first evidence of the hot dog came from the German kingdoms of the Middle Ages. Frankfurt made the first frankfurters, a common European name for the hot dog. The tradition spread to Austria, where the Viennese appear to have coined the term "wiener" for the nascent hot dog. The Germans who immigrated to the United States brought hot dogs with them during the rise of American industry. From the outset, there was nothing fussy about the hot dog. It was a lunchtime staple, like the hamburger, for factory and retail workers. The lunch break was brief and workers demanded a quick meal, a need the hot dog satisfied. By this time most workers lived too far from home to return to it for lunch, further entrenching the need for a quick meal. The hot dog thus became a staple of the working class. There may be reason to claim that the hot dog shaped history by solidifying the culinary preferences of ordinary Americans and so helping to create a national sense of identity. Unpretentious, the hot dog was the perfect egalitarian fare for a nation that claimed to be a democracy, even though the United States has often veered in the direction of plutocracy. To eat a hot dog was, and is, to be an American. The hot dog itself was not the sole prime mover in this context. The hot dog bun celebrated Americans' peculiar adoration of white bread. In the milling of white bread, the nutrient-rich bran and germ are lost, leaving a flour devoid of nutrients. To eat white bread is to ingest empty calories, as is the case with sugar. Yet this is just what Americans want. Research suggests that even cockroaches will not eat white flour, but nothing appears to deter Americans. The putative solution, after the discovery of vitamins in the early 20th century, has been to add them to white bread and pretend it is nourishing. In this context, one is tempted to rate the hot dog and bun as nothing more than high-fat, low-nutrient junk food. Yet the hot dog seems to have transcended such a lowly status.

The Rise of the Hot Dog and the Meatpackers

Because of the strong connection between immigrants, particularly those from Germany, and the hot dog, these immigrants almost single-handedly founded the meatpacking industry. Companies like Mayer, Swift, Armour, and Hormel made their livelihood from the hot dog and other processed meats. They had operations throughout the Midwest, where the pig was the ingredient of choice in the hot dog. These meatpackers also used beef, using the railroads to transport cattle from the grasslands of the Great Plains to their stockyards. The hot dog was thus a catalyst for the rise of huge businesses, enormous profits, and substandard wages and working conditions. The hot dog did not invent these conditions, but it certainly benefited from them. The hot dog is important because it helped immigrants emulate American capitalism and create their own economies of scale. American consumers relished their hot dogs but were indifferent to the fate of workers, much as coffee drinkers do not appear to empathize with the workers in the tropics who earn next to nothing. The hot dog and several other foods thus have the peculiar habit of shielding consumers from the excesses of capitalism that in some other universe would be glaring. A socialist funded by socialists, American author Upton Sinclair in 1905 investigated the meatpacking industry, hoping to unmask its exploitive nature. The result of his labors, *The Jungle*, made vivid the misery of workers, but readers disappointed Sinclair. Instead of focusing on workers, readers reacted against the filth of the meatpacking industry and demanded reforms. Even President Theodore Roosevelt may have read *The Jungle*. He and Congress acted in 1906, passing the Meat Inspection Act and the Pure Food and Drug Act. The hot dog had thus expanded the role of the federal government, an expansion that many conservatives have critiqued over the decades.

The Hot Dog Comes of Age

In 1893, a Tennessee newspaper coined the phrase "hot dog" for the frankfurter and wiener. In April 1901, the New York Giants (now the San Francisco Giants) appear to have been the first major league baseball team to sell hot dogs. Because the day was cold, attendees ate hot dogs partly to stay warm. Although baseball vendors sold peanuts, gum, cigars, soft drinks, and ice cream, the hot dog quickly surpassed them as baseball's iconic food. If Americans live and breathe football today, baseball was once the national pastime, and the association with the hot dog was consequential.

No trip to a baseball stadium was complete without sampling a hot dog with mustard. Over the years it has been possible for northeastern Ohioans to eat many hot dogs at Cleveland Indians games. Fans have fond memories of the food, though the Indians have been a lackluster team during much of the last four decades. The Indians, and presumably other teams, celebrate "dollar dog nights," when they sell each hot dog for $1. By contrast, in 1906, a hot dog cost just 5 cents. Visiting the United States at the height of the Cold War, Soviet premier Nikita Khrushchev attended a baseball game and ate a hot dog. Photographs from the event suggested that the premier enjoyed himself a great deal. Hot dogs were also a popular food at bicycle races, which created a sensation in the late 19th and early 20th centuries.

The hot dog paved the way for other immigrant foods: chop suey, chow mein, and spaghetti and meatballs. In this sense, the hot dog was the pioneer immigrant experience. The others followed in imitation. Of the other arrivals, not even spaghetti and meatballs appear to rival the hot dog in popularity. The hot dog lies at the core of the American culinary experience. Jewish immigrants who observed dietary laws refused to eat pork and so demanded all-beef hot dogs. By the 1930s, all-beef hot dogs were the leading item in Chicago's cuisine, thanks to the city's Jewish immigrants. German Jews added mustard to their hot dogs, a staple condiment at the ballpark. The Greeks added garnishes. New Yorkers created the chili dog. Mexican immigrants favored hot dogs wrapped in bacon. Texans may have been the first to fry hot dogs. The hot dog converted Asian immigrants, who appreciated its flavor. The hot dog is thus bound up in the immigrant experience. In its making, the hot dog was a product of the machine age and so central to the American experience and industrialization. The hot dog was also part of the tradition of a meat-eating people. Europeans who visited the United States commented on the amount of meat in the form of hot dogs and other commodities that Americans ate.

The hot dog was also important as an American export to the rest of the world. The hot dog, in this context, was part of American imperialism, which itself appears to be an extension of American culinary traditions and capitalism. From the United States, the hot dog migrated north to Canada and south to Mexico. From Mexico, the hot dog has spread throughout Central and South America. In Europe, the hot dog may well have radiated from Germany, though even Germans use the phrase "hot dog." In Asia, the Chinese and Koreans are avid hot dog consumers. Curiously, despite strong trade links between Japan and the United States, the hot dog is not popular in Japan. Yet it is no overstatement to say that the hot dog has conquered the culinary world.

Further Reading

Kraig, Bruce. *Hot Dog: A Global History*. London: Reaktion Books, 2009.

I

Ice Cream

Ice cream is a global phenomenon. It is difficult to find people who dislike it, though lactose intolerance may pose a problem for some. With plenty of fat and sugar, ice cream triggers the human craving for both. Satisfying these cravings causes the brain to emit chemicals that heighten pleasure. That is, the brain on ice cream contributes to a feeling of well being. In this sense, the biology of craving and ice cream's ability to satisfy it have shaped history and daily life. Ice cream pleases not only the taste buds but also the eye. In this context, ice cream has an aesthetic quality. All these attributes make ice cream popular among children and adults. This ability to span generations likewise shapes daily life and social history. A celebratory food, ice cream is central to any birthday party. What cake or pie is complete without a scoop of ice cream? The dessert conjures memories of childhood and a sense of nostalgia. Both traits are significant in the creation of memory and longing, and in this sense shape the dynamics of each life. The ice cream truck is part of summer in the United States, whereas vendors deliver ice cream by bicycle in Vietnam. Ice cream is the staple of celebration and fun in general. The dessert has emerged as a global giant and is part of the mass production and mass consumption model that is at the heart of American consumerism, an important corollary of capitalism.

Origins among the Elite

At its origins, ice cream was a luxury. Its transition to a food of the masses is an important dynamic in social history. China may have developed a forerunner of ice cream, but food historians usually credit Europe with its invention. Italy, France, and England were all early pioneers. In this context, ice cream, traveling from Europe to the Americas, was part of the Columbian Exchange. In the United States, Americans regard ice cream as something of a national dessert, rivaling

Ice cream is a festive and comfort food. What child's birthday party is complete without it? (Og-vision/Dreamstime.com)

even apple pie. For some people, a slice of apple pie is incomplete without a scoop of vanilla ice cream. Italian immigrants played an important role in bringing ice cream to North America. Italian Americans sold ice cream as a street food in New York City. In this sense, ice cream may be the world's most popular street food, rivaling even the hamburger and hot dog. Flavors abound, but some are misleading. Aztec chocolate ice cream has nothing to do with the Aztecs, who had no way to make ice cream. Living in a warm climate they could not have had access to ice as a primitive means of refrigeration.

During the Tang Dynasty, which coincided with the early Middle Ages in Europe, the Chinese ate a frozen milk treat, a possible forerunner of ice cream. It was probably neither as appealing nor as sweet as ice cream, being full of odd ingredients. One legend, though untrue, holds that 13th-century Italian adventurer Marco Polo brought ice cream from China to Italy. From another historical direction came the Arabs, who during the Middle Ages drank what would later be known as sherbet. This, too, was not ice cream. Italians, perhaps under Arab influence, added fresh peaches and raspberries to sherbet. In the 17th century, Italy began to combine cream, milk, sugar, and ice, marking the birth of ice cream. As with sherbet, the Italians added fresh fruit to this novelty. Some food historians point to this development in Naples, which also may have invented pizza and

Häagen-Dazs

Although its name evokes a European aura, Häagen-Dazs is really an American product, the creation of entrepreneurs Reuben and Rose Mattus of the Bronx, New York City. In 1961, they began selling vanilla, chocolate, and coffee ice cream. The first Häagen-Dazs shop opened in Brooklyn, New York City, in 1976. As do many food makers, Häagen-Dazs has abandoned sugar as a sweetener in favor of corn syrup and high fructose corn syrup, though the company takes pride in introducing very few artificial ingredients. Ice cream may be the company's most notable product, but the form can vary from a pint of ice cream to a packet of ice cream bars. Sorbet, frozen yogurt, and gelato all compete for market share, offering consumers of Häagen-Dazs a variety of choices.

spaghetti and meatballs. Lemon, strawberry, and chocolate ice creams were all popular with Italy's elites. In 1686, Sicilian entrepreneur Francesco Procopio dei Coltelli may have been the first to sell ice cream in Paris, France, where he had relocated. The clientele drew its members from the elites. French emperor Napoleon Bonaparte, French authors Voltaire, Victor Hugo and Honoré de Balzac, and American scientist and statesman Benjamin Franklin all dined at Il Procope. In 1771, a Naples cookbook contained the first written recipe for ice cream. By one line of thought, ice cream was elitist because it was expensive, partly because sugar was expensive. Yet this reasoning does not appear to coincide with the trend in sugar production. By the 18th century, the moment when ice cream was invented, sugar production was rising on the slave plantations in tropical America. If anything, sugar prices should have fallen during this century. European ice cream makers added vanilla from the Americas to create perhaps the most popular flavor.

The Trend toward Mass Consumption

In North America, ice cream was immediately popular in New York City, Philadelphia, and other eastern cities. An ambassador to France in the 1780s, Thomas Jefferson acquired a taste for ice cream. Back in the United States, Jefferson, partial to vanilla ice cream, served the dessert to his guests at Monticello. First U.S. president George Washington did likewise at Mount Vernon. Though Jefferson and Washington served the treat, they surely do not merit credit for having made it. Ice cream was arduous to make in the 18th century, and the task must have fallen to their slaves. One wonders whether they were able to eat what they had worked so hard to make. New York City probably invented the ice cream parlor, which may not have differed from Il Procope. No July 4 celebration was complete without ice cream, suggesting the democratization of ice cream in the United States, perhaps as early as the end of the 18th century.

Like Italians, Americans were fond of adding fruit to the dessert. One recipe called for the addition of 12 fresh apricots, though it is not clear how large was the volume of ice cream necessary to accommodate a dozen apricots. Other recipes called for lemon and strawberries, just as Italians had done. Ice cream spread into the interior of the United States, where inns served it to guests. Cincinnati, Ohio, and West Chester, Pennsylvania, emerged as centers for the manufacture of ice cream. In the 19th century, the United States pioneered the use of machines that reduced the labor necessary to make the dessert. Between the end of the American Civil War and the beginning of the Great Depression, consumption of ice cream was particularly robust. Americans served ice cream at soda fountains. While Italians continued to make ice cream in small batches by hand, the United States arose as a mass producer of the dessert. It was as American as the Model T and apple pie. Drug stores, department stores, and railroads all sold ice cream. It was not unusual for a drug store or another establishment to sell 100 gallons of ice cream per day in the early 20th century.

The emergence of the ice cream sundae may trace its origins to the prohibition against ice cream soda, a liquid, on Sundays, on the grounds that the drink was too frivolous for a day of religious importance. If Americans could not drink ice cream soda, perhaps they would try a novelty: ice cream with chocolate sauce and whipped cream. The question of who invented the sundae is unresolved. One account credits a drug store worker in Ithaca, New York; and another, the owner of an inn in Two Rivers, Wisconsin. Buffalo, New York; New York City; and Evanston, Illinois, have issued similar stories. Over time, toppings multiplied to include hot fudge and strawberry sauces, marshmallows, caramel, nuts, candies, and a variety of fruits, notably the cherry on top. Another favorite is the banana split. The traditional version contains a whole banana and three scoops of ice cream: vanilla, chocolate, and strawberry, though other variants are possible. One might choose among chocolate, strawberry, and pineapple sauces, though the combination of all three is popular.

By the early 20th century, vanilla, strawberry, and chocolate ice cream had established themselves as the great trio. Neapolitan ice cream, of course, included all three flavors in a single serving. In the 20th century, the cone, initially patterned after a waffle, emerged as the carrier of ice cream, making the treat portable in the way that the bun made the hot dog and hamburger portable. France and the United Kingdom claim to have invented the cone, though decisive evidence eludes one. In Saint Louis, Missouri, the cone made its American debut at the 1904 World's Fair to acclaim. By 1924, Americans consumed 245 million cones per year. One could no longer doubt that ice cream had become a food of the masses. On the eve of the Great Depression, Americans ate 365 million gallons of ice cream per year. The advent of the refrigerator and freezer, widely purchased during the 1940s, ignited a new burst in ice cream consumption. Essential to this development was the spread of electricity into rural areas during the New Deal. No longer did one need go to a restaurant to buy ice cream. One could buy a quart or a gallon from the emerging supermarkets, store it in the freezer and enjoy the dessert whenever one wished. In these decades, corn syrup and high fructose corn syrup emerged to challenge sugar as the sweetener in ice cream. Other innovations followed, including the popular Eskimo Pie and Klondike bar. The ice cream bar, positioned on a stick like the corn dog, accentuated the portability of ice cream. Soft serve ice cream, a staple at McDonald's, has gained adherents worldwide.

Further Reading

Weiss, Laura B. *Ice Cream: A Global History.* London: Reaktion Books, 2013.

K

Ketchup

In 1831, an anonymous author noted that ketchup "indicates a sauce of which the name can be pronounced by everybody but spelled by nobody" (Smith, 2001, 6). This reflection appears true, given that ketchup may be rendered "ketchup," "catchup," or "catsup." Each variant has its partisans, but the term "ketchup" will be used here, as the most common of the three possibilities.

The Strange Origins of Ketchup

To Americans accustomed to supermarkets filled with bottles of red ketchup, it seems odd that ketchup initially had nothing to do with tomatoes. This is striking because the tomato is an indigene of the Americas, native to South America but possibly domesticated in Central America, though South America remains a possibility. The British and French claim the invention of ketchup, but not tomato ketchup. The British and French claimed the invention of a fish sauce that they named ketchup. Food historian Andrew F. Smith debunks this myth, tracing the origin of fish sauce to the Romans, who called theirs *garum*. The Romans applied *garum* to nearly every food imaginable. *Garum* could not have contained tomatoes because the fruit was unknown in the Old World until the Columbian Exchange. If the Romans had their fish sauce, the Chinese and Japanese had their soy sauce. The use of such sauces was a global phenomenon well before humans turned to the tomato in large numbers. Even into the early modern era Europeans neglected the tomato as an ingredient in ketchup. In the 17th century, the English turned to the Americas for an ingredient for ketchup, choosing, of all things, the kidney bean. This American bean, one of many in the genus *Phaseolus*, was a substitute for the soybean of Asian cuisine. The English also made ketchup from mushrooms, fish (again) and other seafood, and walnuts.

The Heinz Company

In 1869, American entrepreneur Henry John Heinz founded the H. J. Heinz Company in Sharpsburg, Pennsylvania, though headquarters have since moved to Pittsburgh. Although Heinz focused first on horseradish, it quickly determined that ketchup would generate greater profits. Henry Heinz incorporated the business in 1905, serving as the first chairperson of the board of directors. The company's profits were robust in the 1980s. Between 1981 and 1991, the annual return on investment was nearly 30 percent. The company made millionaires nearly overnight, among them the wife of Secretary of State John Kerry.

The Tomato's Rise to Prominence

Americans of European descent were slow to appreciate the tomato for a variety of reasons. Mexicans had no such qualms, using tomatoes to make salsa. Perhaps this use of the tomato inspired the development of tomato ketchup (hereinafter simply "ketchup"). In the 18th century, Americans made ketchup in New Jersey, which was popular in parts of Canada. Ketchup quickly sank roots in Louisiana, which was successively owned by Spain, France, and finally the United States, thanks to the landmark Louisiana Purchase in 1803. The first written recipe for ketchup in the United States dates to 1812. Early recipes prided themselves on the thickness of the ketchup, though surprisingly few spices were used in an era when spices were taken in quantity. The British published their own ketchup recipes throughout the 19th century.

During the 19th century, the distinction between tomato sauce and ketchup was not large. Ketchup tended to be spicier than tomato sauce, but the prominence of the tomato made both items similar. Ketchup also tended to be partly fermented, which would have produced alcohol, which was not a product in tomato sauce. The addition of sugar to ketchup was then unknown. Certainly the first ketchups were less calorie dense than their modern equivalents because of the initial absence of sugar. In the 19th century, the United States and Britain were avid ketchup consumers, with ketchup cookbooks in wide circulation. During that century ketchup was the condiment of choice in the British Empire.

As a condiment, ketchup added color and flavor to other foods. Today there is no consensus about whether ketchup or mustard is the proper condiment for a hot dog, or even a hamburger, though ketchup is popular in both cases. McDonald's serves burgers and fries with ketchup. In this context, ketchup shaped culinary and social history by raising the profile of McDonald's. In fact, french fries and ketchup seem to be an inseparable tandem. Again, the combination of the potato (in this case sliced and fried) and ketchup has shaped culinary and social history. In the 19th century, ketchup was even used to flavor some types of fish, haddock and cod being popular in this regard. At times, one might add ketchup to soup, stew, or hashes.

As ketchup matured in the 19th century, it moved in the direction of spiciness. In addition to the tomato, ketchup might contain cloves, pepper, ginger, and mace. Chili peppers were sometimes added, perhaps in deference to the success of salsa, which in the 21st century dethroned ketchup as the preferred condiment in the United States. Ketchup might also contain garlic, onion, shallot, horseradish, and even mustard. Was the intent to flavor foods or overwhelm the taste buds? Moreover, one wonders whether ketchup of this stripe conveyed the flavor of tomatoes, which may have been overpowered.

About 1850, a U.S. cookbook printed the first recipe for ketchup that included sugar. The United States had crossed the culinary Rubicon. Ketchup has not been the same since. As the years passed, manufacturers added increasing amounts of sugar to ketchup. In turn, manufacturers added more vinegar to ketchup in an attempt to balance sweetness and sourness. Some food critics have noted that the addition of too much sugar and vinegar detracted from the flavor of the tomatoes, which was presumably what drew consumers to ketchup in the first place. Why eat ketchup that did not taste of tomatoes? The cheapness of sugar, thanks to the high production of sugar in tropical America, accelerated the trend toward sweetness. One witnesses the same phenomenon with breakfast cereals. At first, ketchup was more a homemade product than a manufactured good, though this state of affairs did not persist into the 20th century.

The Rise of Commercialization

By the first decade of the 20th century most Americans bought ketchup rather than made it. The rise of commercial ketchup predictably featured sugar, vinegar, and salt in quantity. These ingredients were no accident. Humans crave sugar and salt, and the more of these ingredients that ketchup could give them, the more desirable the product. In this sense, ketchup shaped history by catering to our biological predispositions. Although the manufacture of ketchup has been an important part of the 20th century, U.S. companies began to make ketchup as early as the 1830s. The average two-pound bottle held about 25 processed tomatoes. The Deep South was an early buyer of the first commercial brands. By the 1850s, nearly every major city in the United States had a ketchup factory. Profits were not assured. In winter and spring, at least in the north, no one had access to fresh tomatoes so ketchup was expensive. During the summer, manufacturers, awash in tomatoes and in competition with rivals, had to lower their prices.

Ketchup manufacturers, as in other industries, aimed for standardization. Every bottle of ketchup needed the same flavor and texture, just as every Big Mac had to taste the same. This drive toward standardization is a fundamental feature of American capitalism. After the American Civil War, manufacturing consolidated in Maine, Maryland, Missouri, and Minnesota. By 1910, New York City; Rochester, New York; Detroit; Chicago; Philadelphia; Cincinnati; and parts of California had emerged as ketchup manufacturers. California, of course, was also noted for making salsa. The 20th century marked the apex of ketchup as the national condiment. Campbell's, an early canner of soups, boasted of making ketchup from only giant Beefsteak tomatoes to guarantee maximum flavor. There appears to be no record of how many Beefsteak tomatoes went into a single bottle of Campbell's ketchup. In the 20th century, Heinz came to the fore as an important ketchup manufacturer. Its fortunes have bolstered the careers of several prominent Americans, notably former U.S. senator and current secretary of state John Kerry. Like Chevrolet, Heinz introduced a variety of brands at a range of prices. The aim was to entice the public to buy the more expensive brands as a marker of status and conspicuous consumption, both hallmarks of American capitalism. By 1905, Heinz was the chief U.S. producer of ketchup. By 1909, sales neared $3 million per year. Heinz erected factories throughout the Northeast and Midwest. An early exporter, Heinz shipped ketchup to the United Kingdom, Australia, New Zealand, South Africa, South America, continental Europe, Japan, and China. Ketchup was popular enough in Canada to entice Heinz to open a factory in Ontario in 1909.

Then, as now, sugar drove sales. Today at least one-third of ketchup's calories come from sugar. By contrast, mustard is much less caloric. Today, a single ketchup factory may process more than 2,000 tons of tomatoes per day. Given the popularity of yellow tomatoes among the Amerindians and Italians, it seems strange that all ketchup is made from red tomatoes, though perhaps yellow ketchup would blur the distinction between ketchup and mustard. The adulteration of ketchup and other foods motivated U.S. Department of Agriculture (USDA) chemist Harvey Wiley to craft what Congress would pass in 1906 as the Pure Food and Drug Act. In expanding the powers of the federal government, ketchup has shaped American history.

Further Reading

Smith, Andrew F. *Pure Ketchup: A History of America's National Condiment.* Washington, DC and London: Smithsonian Institution Press, 2001.

Kool-Aid

The history of Kool-Aid is enmeshed with the myth of the American Dream, in which a young man with few resources has an idea for a product, perseveres when others might have quit, and becomes a multimillionaire. In this sense, Kool-Aid reinforces what Americans like to believe about themselves and the upwardly mobile country in which they live. In reality, the gap between rich and poor has widened to a chasm and the notion of upward mobility seems naïve to some. Kool-Aid is also important because of the control it gave the consumer. One could buy Kool-Aid to which one added sugar or Kool-Aid that did not need sugar, depending on one's preference. Even in the case of sugar, the consumer could choose to add less than the packet recommended to produce a beverage comparatively light in calories. By contrast, no real flexibility exists with, say, Coca-Cola (often simply known as "Coke"). One buys and drinks a can or bottle as is. In this sense, Kool-Aid goes further in empowering the consumer.

Kool-Aid as a Symbol of the American Dream

One might trace the symbolic inspiration for Kool-Aid to 19th-century American author Horatio Alger. Alger published a number of novels in which a penniless young man, through hard work, courage, and luck, amassed great wealth, scaling the ladder to the American Dream. It can be argued that the notion of a fluid society open to the ascent of young men and women of talent and drive did not really exist, even in Alger's day. Yet one can pick examples that seem to echo Alger's core belief. Iowa-born Edwin E. Perkins appears to be the kind of man Alger had in mind. Born toward the close of the 19th century, Perkins spent an itinerant childhood between Iowa and Nebraska. Always restless and in search of new opportunities, his family had little money. When it settled in Nebraska, the family had only a farmhouse made of sod to inhabit. The property had no indoor plumbing and the nearest source of water was a two-mile trek away.

Although he did not quit school, Perkins, at age 11, began to work at a general store to supplement the family's income. At the outset, a new product, Jell-O, intrigued him. Perkins wondered whether he might make a beverage with similar chemicals. In the 1920s, Perkins established the Perkins Chemical Company. His first inspiration was to create a fruity soft drink, Fruit-Smack, in an era when Coca-Cola and Dr Pepper were the big players. Because he sold Fruit-Smack through the mail, the bulk of a bottled beverage was a drawback. He needed something compact and light and aimed to create a powder of chemicals that approximated the flavor of Fruit-Smack. The consumer would need only add water and, as it turned out, sugar, to prepare an instant drink. One wonders whether the rapidity with which one might make tea or instant coffee inspired Perkins.

In 1927, making a powder of the sugar dextrose, citric and tartaric acids, artificial fruit flavors, and food coloring, Perkins created Kool-Aid. The original flavors were raspberry, cherry, grape, lemon, orange, and root beer. Strawberry is a contentious item, with some historians believing it to have been among the original flavors whereas others insist that it was a later addition. The product did not initially blow away the competition. Grocers were skeptical. Many preferred to sell Coke and other established products rather than a strange new powder. With the coming of the Great Depression, Perkins found his opportunity. Halving his price per packet to 5 cents, he positioned Kool-Aid as the inexpensive alternative to soft drinks. Sales soared. Between 1931 and 1937, the income from Kool-Aid leapt from less than $400,000 to more than $1.5 million. As early as 1931, Perkins began advertising on radio, in magazines and newspapers, and on billboards. Comic strips featured the Kool-Aid Kid. The product expanded beyond the United States when Kool-Aid began to sell in Canada in 1938 and in Mexico and Cuba in 1951. Two years later Perkins sold the Kool-Aid franchise to General Foods, the maker of Jell-O.

Further Reading

Adams County Historical Society. 2002. "History of Kool-Aid." In "Kool-Aid Days." Accessed October 1, 2014. Kool-aiddays.com/history.

"The History of Kool-Aid." Hastings Museum. Accessed October 1, 2014. Hastingsmuseum .org/exhibits/kool-aid/the-history-of-kool-aid.

Robertson, Caisey. "A Brief History of Kool-Aid." Mental Floss, Inc. Accessed October 1, 2014. Mentalfloss.com/article/50278/brief-history-kool-aid.

L

Lentils

An annual legume, lentils were among the first plants that humans domesticated. Like all members of the Fabaceae family, lentils bear their seeds in pods. Like beans, lentils feed the poor, possibly averting famine in years that the grain crop fails. India is the leading producer of lentils at 800,000 tons per year, a figure that is more than half the world's output. Even so, India is not self-sufficient but must import lentils from Turkey. Although its yield has fallen in recent years, Turkey produces 600,000 tons of lentils per year. Canada is the world's largest exporter, selling 280,000 tons of lentils per year. Lately Australia has grown as an exporter. The big importers are Colombia, Spain, Belgium, and Italy. One cup of lentils contains 229 calories, molybdenum, manganese, iron, phosphorus, copper, potassium, folic acid, thiamine, protein, tryptophan, and fiber.

Prehistory and Antiquity

Humans gathered wild lentils of the species *Len orientalis* before domesticating them. As early as 11,000 BCE, Greeks cooked lentils, but they may not yet have cultivated them. Between 9000 and 8000 BCE, the Syrians harvested wild lentils, though, again, this activity predated their cultivation. Under human aid, wild lentils gave rise to the cultivated species *Lens culinaris*. By one account, about 10,000 years ago, women, gathering lentils in the wild in the Near East, saved the largest seeds from the most vigorous plants. This early use of lentils suggests that they shaped history and daily life as a source of protein for the masses, who did not always have access to meat or fish. They planted these seeds and then, being nomads, followed the caravan routes to various destinations. Upon returning months later, they had lentils ready to harvest. Repeating this process over many generations, humans selected for lentils that did not shatter. Unable to disperse seed, lentils now depended on human intervention for survival. The cultivated lentil also

197

Lentils come in a variety of colors. This is not surprising given the diversity of colors of potatoes or tomatoes. Much of human history has witnessed a diminution in this diversity. (Mk74/Dreamstime.com)

differed from its wild counterpart in having large seeds and a thin seed coat that made lentils easier to digest. Plant stalks were sturdy, allowing lentils to grow without support. Doubtless, humans prized lentils because they yielded well on marginal land. As a winter crop, lentils provided food in spring, when other sources of food were scarce.

As nomads and hunter gathers settled down in the first villages, they came to depend more on lentils and less on meat for protein. Again, this development is significant because it suggests that lentils were the chief source of protein in western Asia. In the Fertile Crescent, the likely place of origin of lentils, humans also domesticated wheat and barley and from an early date may have rotated lentils and grains. The ancients understood that lentils enriched the soil—though they were ignorant of the process of nitrogen fixation—and so followed lentils with a grain. Lentils thus raised the productivity of the soil, a fact of importance given the near-subsistence level of farming in antiquity. Lentils had a dual use, feeding livestock in addition to humans. Livestock produced manure, further enriching the soil. Lentils and grains provided an adequate diet. They are complementary foods, each supplying amino acids that the other lacks. Lentils and other crops provided more calories per unit of land than did meat from grazing livestock. The surplus of calories fed an expanding population, fueling the growth of cities and the rise of civilization. Humble though they are, lentils helped lay the foundation of Western civilization.

The first evidence of the cultivation of lentils comes from Jarmo, Iraq, where farmers grew the legume as early as 7000 BCE. The Greeks grew lentils by 6500 BCE. Turkey and Iraq traded lentils by 5000 BCE, evidence that they must have relied on agriculture to yield a marketable surplus of lentils. By 5500 BCE, farmers throughout Europe grew lentils. Between 3000 and 1000 BCE, farmers grew lentils in the Danube River valley. By then lentils were cultivated as far north as Britain, as far south as Ethiopia, and as far east as India. Lentils were then unknown in the Americas. Egyptians grew lentils before 3000 BCE. In their religion, Horus, the god of lentils, ensured a bountiful harvest. The Egyptians regarded lentils, and probably other plants as well, as a symbol of resurrection. In antiquity, Egypt reputedly grew the best lentils. Some people believe that Egypt still holds this distinction. Alexandria was the center of the lentil trade and the port through which merchants shipped lentils to Rome. As elsewhere Egyptians grew lentils, which do not need irrigation, in arid lands and on marginal soil. Egyptians put lentils in tombs to feed the dead on their journey to the afterlife. Archeologists have found lentils in predynastic tombs and below pharaoh Zoser's pyramid. The fact that lentils were among the food in a pharaoh's tomb suggests that the wealthy ate lentils. In Sumeria, where farmers planted lentils, chickpeas, wheat, barley, and millet, the pattern of consumption diverged from that of Egypt. As the gulf between classes widened, the rich confirmed their affluence by consuming meat. Abundant and cheap lentils fed the poor. Given this state of affairs it is not surprising that ancient cookbooks did not devote much space to lentils. The first written recipe for lentils dates to 1600 BCE. Even then, the recipe includes meat, which may have been the main dish. The lentils were to be cooked in beer.

The people of India, many of them vegetarians, cultivated lentils. So important were they that one Indian proverb held that "Rice is god, but lentils are my life." The Old Testament makes several references to lentils, the most notable being in Genesis. Brothers Jacob and Esau represented competing lifeways. Esau, the hunter, returned home hungry one day to find Jacob, the farmer, enjoying a bowl of lentil soup. Esau asked for a bowl of soup but Jacob complied only when Esau agreed to sell him his birthright. Lentils had triumphed over meat. Prophet Ezekiel ate a type of lentil bread, though it is not clear that he enjoyed the bread. Old Testament prophets warned against the unnatural mixture of lentils and grains. This warning taught a larger lesson, reminding the Hebrews not to intermingle with other people to the point of losing their identity and faith. Lentils were thus bound up with the rise of monotheism in antiquity, another significant feature.

The Greeks had a low opinion of lentils, regarding them as fit only for the poor. One Greek saying held that "He became a rich man and suddenly he no longer likes lentils." Greek physician Galen believed lentils could cause elephantiasis and liver problems, produce black bile, damage eyesight, and inflame the spleen. Others believed that eating lentils with pickled meat thickened the blood. Yet Greek philosopher Zeno apparently ate lentils. To a degree, the Romans shared the Greek distrust of lentils. One Roman medical authority held that lentils were hard to digest and so made one sluggish. In this context, theologian Isidore of Seville suggested in the sixth century that the word "lentil" derived from the Latin *lentus*, meaning "slow." Not all Romans shared this opinion. Consumption of lentils was so great that, as shown earlier, Rome had to import them from Egypt. In the second century BCE, agriculturalist Cato the Elder valued lentils as a medicine. All classes ate lentils during the Republic, and only in the Empire did patricians stigmatize them.

The Middle Ages and Modernity

In the Middle Ages, Arab physician Averroes warned that lentils caused depression, weakened vision, and vitiated sexual impulses. Taking a similar view, Arab Haliabbas worried that lentils caused depression, mania, elephantiasis, cancer, and bad dreams. Italian physician Antonius Gazius, having read the Arabs, recommended that people eat lentils only when they had no other food. The absence of lentil recipes from medieval cookbooks suggests that lentils were not an important food in the Middle Ages. It is not certain that lentils did well in cold, wet northern Europe, leading one to wonder how familiar Europeans were with lentils. This state of affairs is surprising for a food that was so central to the ancients.

The stigma against lentils persisted in modernity. In the 17th century one Italian wrote, "In general lentils are only eaten by the lowest of the low." Yet this stigma may have been waning. As early as the 16th century French surgeon Ambroise Paré believed lentils could cure smallpox. Marie de Sevigne, a friend of King Louis XIV, ate lentil soup, recommending lentils grown in Nantes as the best. Partial to the lentils of Nantes, King Louis XV named them "the queen's lentils" for his wife, Marie Leszczynska, a native of Poland, where lentils were prized. During the bad harvests of the 1780s, lentils spared many French men and women from starvation. With the system of food distribution in crisis during the French Revolution, people subsisted on lentils.

In the 18th century, a French priest planted lentils in the Saint Lawrence River valley, teaching the Iroquois to grow them. By 1774, farmers in Virginia cultivated lentils. Thomas Jefferson grew them at Monticello. During World War I, a missionary gave lentils to a farmer in Washington, and by the 1930s they were an important crop in this state and in Idaho. In the 1970s, farmers in western Canada grew lentils for export. Today, the people of India grow and eat more than 50 varieties of lentils. The average Indian eats some five pounds of lentils per year, whereas the average American eats less than one-quarter pound of lentils per year. In India people eat lentils with oil, ginger, chili peppers, cilantro, and cumin. In southern India, people eat lentils, brown sugar, cardamom, coconut milk, and butter during the rice festival of Onam. In northern India people eat lentils, onions, and chili peppers during the Hindi festival of Holi.

Further Reading

Albala, Ken. *Beans: A History*. Oxford: Berg, 2007.

Hughes, Meredith Sayles. *Spill the Beans and Pass the Peanuts: Legumes*. Minneapolis: Lerner Publications, 1999.

Macaroni and Cheese

Macaroni and cheese is a compound dish. Though the ingredients may be numerous, in its simplest form two ingredients are necessary. Cheese is a byproduct of milk, usually cow's milk. Macaroni is a generic name for pasta, which derives from wheat, but not just any type of wheat. Macaroni uses the hardest class of wheat, durum. Because durum wheat has more protein than any other kind of wheat, macaroni, and macaroni and cheese, are more nourishing than bread. Macaroni and cheese arose as a dish among medieval Europeans. Initially a food of the elites, it became more widely consumed, though not immediately, in the American colonies. The confluence of African American and Italian American foodways in the United States made macaroni and cheese a food with the potential to spread among large numbers of Americans. Today, it is an integral part of the American culinary experience.

Macaroni and Cheese and European and European American Cuisine

As early as the Middle Ages, Europeans ate macaroni and cheese. From the outset, it was the food of monarchs and aristocrats. England's King Richard I and Queen Elizabeth I both ate the dish. Macaroni and cheese remained a favorite among Europe's nobility well into the 18th century, when upper-class European Americans, eager to emulate Europe's elites, dined on macaroni and cheese. The important connection between macaroni and cheese and elitism shaped third U.S. president Thomas Jefferson's culinary aspirations. While U.S. minister to France in the 1780s, Jefferson acquired a taste for macaroni and cheese from his aristocratic hosts. He also came to enjoy french fries, serving both dishes to guests when he returned home to Monticello in Virginia. Jefferson even imported a machine from Naples, Italy, the world's macaroni capital, to make noodles. Jefferson, of

An important comfort food, macaroni and cheese, once the sustenance of African Americans, is now popular among whites. The dish is wholesome and nourishing. (Joshua Resnick/Dreamstime.com)

course, expected his black slaves to cook the dish for him. He first settled on James Hemings, the brother-in-law of Sally Hemings, Jefferson's mistress, for this task. Jefferson took both Hemingses to Paris, where James apprenticed to a renowned French chef to teach him to prepare macaroni and cheese properly. The job soon fell to female slaves Edith Fosset and Frances Hern. When elected president, Jefferson brought Fosset and Hern to the White House to prepare macaroni and cheese and other treats for him. Jefferson served macaroni and cheese at White House gatherings, though not everyone liked it. In 1802, Protestant minister Manasseh Cutler privately expressed his disappointment, though he did not state the reasons for his dissatisfaction.

American elites wanted the finest ingredients, importing their cheese from Italy rather than relying on America's emerging dairy industry. One may observe from the outset that macaroni and cheese was as much status symbol as food. It marked a line of demarcation in a society in which the elites had enormous egos and fortunes. Macaroni and cheese thus shaped history because of what it conveyed about class. Parmesan cheese was the proper ingredient and could only be obtained from Italy. In the early 19th century, however, the popularity of macaroni and cheese widened beyond European and American plutocrats, as ordinary people began to find the food intriguing. Europeans and Americans began to rely less on Italy for parmesan cheese, turning increasingly to local dairymen for cheese. The Italian aura of macaroni and cheese began partly to dissipate, though Italian immigrants would have much to say about the relationship between macaroni and cheese and ethnicity. Given the prominence of cheddar cheese in making macaroni and cheese today, it seems surprising that Europeans and Americans took so long to use it for this purpose. Cheddar cheese appears to have sunk roots in England before America. American dairymen were slow to make cheddar cheese, perhaps unaware of its potential as the cheese of choice in making macaroni and cheese. Even then, the North produced far more cheddar cheese than the South. Around the middle of the 19th century, Rome, New York, established the first factory for making cheddar cheese. By 1862, the United States was exporting cheddar cheese to Europe, with Britain being the big buyer. It appears likely that the South used local varieties of cheese.

No less important than cheese was the acquisition of durum wheat. At midcentury, this posed a problem for Americans because the leading wheat states, Ohio and Illinois, could not grow durum. Only with the opening of the Great Plains after the American Civil War did farmers discover that North Dakota and Minnesota were ideal for growing durum wheat. Parts of Canada are likewise suitable for durum. In parts of the South, the preparation of macaroni and cheese became an elaborate event, calling for durum wheat, cheese, cream, eggs, and meat. This was no side dish but a full meal, nutritious and calorie dense.

Macaroni and Cheese and African and African American Cuisine

Macaroni and cheese appears to have been unknown to the people of West Africa before the era of European contact. This absence may stem from the fact that the people of West Africa were not dairymen and dairymaids. The situation in North Africa must have been different. The people of North Africa, long in contact with southern Europe, likely borrowed macaroni and cheese from Italians. But because many African Americans trace their lineage to West Africa rather than North Africa, the latter must remain on the margins of this story. Europeans probably brought macaroni and cheese to the people of West Africa in the 16th century. In retrospect, it is surprising that macaroni and cheese had any influence on West Africans and African Americans, given that neither people initially favored cheese. Cheese was much more widespread in the diets of white Europeans, European Americans, and Asians. To the Mongol army, for example, cheese was indispensable.

In the American colonies, macaroni and cheese was closely associated with African Americans, particularly black women who cooked for their families and white elites. From the outset, then, macaroni and cheese was a food simultaneously of white elites and poor black slaves. In this sense, macaroni and cheese shaped history by crossing racial and economic divides. Nonetheless, the dish's association with African Americans led it to have the status as an ethnic food that it only began to shed in the 20th century. In this sense, macaroni and cheese was a democratic food even in an undemocratic America where women and blacks could not vote and most blacks were slaves.

Macaroni and cheese is at once a dish of rich and poor. It is a food for special occasions, a comfort food, a convenience food, and a side dish to enhance the main course. It has been served in African American restaurants in South Florida as a side dish to the main course of lasagna. It is part of a larger love affair that Americans have with pasta. At first the connection between macaroni and cheese was tenuous. "Macaroni" was just the generic name of any type of pasta from Italy, though "spaghetti" must have asserted its own identity early on. African American slaves, not having a strong dairying tradition, bought cheese from local stores for use on special occasions like Christmas and the Fourth of July, and must have combined it with macaroni.

It is clear that from an early date black women made macaroni and cheese for white elites, but did they prepare it for their own families? The answer must be yes, because in the South, as was true of America at large, cuisines crossed racial and ethnic divides. Perhaps one should say, simply, ethnic divides, because many biologists believe that humans cannot be divided into races.

The Great Migration in the 20th century brought African Americans to cities where they encountered Italian immigrants. The two traded macaroni and cheese recipes as the dish forged cross-cultural ties among different ethnicities. This experience enriched the appreciation for macaroni and cheese among both African Americans and Italian Americans. This occurrence was the sort of melting-pot experience so typical of the culinary experiences and experiments in America. Immigrants from southern Italy who had been too poor to afford macaroni and cheese in Italia found the food more plentiful and cheaper in the United States. If they did not inhabit the same neighborhoods, blacks and Italians nevertheless lived near one another, facilitating the exchange of culinary traditions including macaroni and cheese. The black-Italian alliance in the North forged macaroni and cheese into an ethnic food with the potential to radiate among large numbers of Americans. This alliance included parts of the South, particularly New Orleans, which African Americans and Italian Americans both inhabited. In fact, by 1850 New Orleans trailed only New York City in the size of its Italian American population. The use of Sicilian labor on Louisiana's sugar estates elevated the profile of macaroni and cheese and of the Italians and African Americans eager to eat it.

By 1900, macaroni and cheese was becoming increasingly a food of the poor. In the early 20th century, home economists at the land-grant universities championed macaroni and cheese as a nutritious, affordable food, though they still tended to classify it as an African American and Italian American food. In a sense, though now widely popular, macaroni and cheese has never quite shed its ethnic origins. Cookbooks aimed at African Americans heightened the profile of macaroni and cheese. The Harlem Renaissance was partly a food awakening with the city's embrace of macaroni and cheese. Harlem was also a stronghold of Italian Americans, who doubtless played a role in the rise of macaroni and cheese in this ostensibly African American city. By the Great Depression, macaroni and cheese was solidly the food of African Americans, Italian Americans, and the white middle class. In the 1930s, Kraft Foods began selling macaroni and cheese throughout the United States. To ease preparation, Kraft canned the product, at last ensconcing macaroni and cheese as a convenience food. Today the simplicity of preparation makes macaroni and cheese widely popular.

Further Reading

Miller, Adrian. *Soul Food: The Surprising Story of an American Cuisine, One Plate at a Time*. Chapel Hill: The University of North Carolina Press, 2003.

Milk

One often thinks of milk as the product of cows, but a broader perspective is necessary. Any female mammal that is lactating as a result of having given birth produces milk. Milk is not specific to a single species but rather to all species of mammals, including humans. Humans may be unique, however, in using other mammals to supply milk. The cow is the queen in this regard, but goats have also been important. The ancients understood the diversity of milk producers well. Milk was the liquid of the goddesses of antiquity. It made the Netherlands an international power in the early modern era. Its connection with the rise of dairy science, perhaps first articulated in the Netherlands, continues today.

Milk in Antiquity and Its Role in Religions

The cow was an early domesticate and a part of the nascent discipline of animal husbandry. The cow gives humans more than milk, though milk has long been important to the rise of civilizations and their religions. Milk was not always

The Turkana, a nomadic pastoral Nilotic people, live in the harsh semi-arid desert and raise camels, sheep, and goats for their survival. The Turkana rely on their animals primarily for their milk and meat. (Wendy Stone/Corbis)

healthy before the era of pasteurization because it could harbor pathogens. Even pasteurized milk will degrade because pasteurization does not kill all microbes. According to one thesis, cows transmitted the terrible disease smallpox to humans. We have paid a price for milk.

In ancient India the cow was sacred. Some Hindus believed that milk granted one immortality, a claim that is more hyperbole than real. Milk was an important beverage in ancient Egypt and in its religions. According to the people of West Africa, the gods created the universe from a single drop of milk. The Norse believed that the first humans drank milk from a sacred cow. Dionysus, better known as the Greek god of wine, also favored milk. There is tension here between the intoxicating eroticism of wine and the mundane world of milk. The Hebrews believed that their god, Yahweh, gave them a land of "milk and honey." The reality is that Israel is a semiarid swath of the globe. The premiere goddess Isis, important in the religions of Egypt and the mystery cults that spread throughout the Mediterranean world, was the protector and dispenser of milk. In Egyptian religion, Isis gave humans milk from her own breasts. She nursed pharaohs' children and commoners alike. Here, the tension between wine and milk

Holstein-Friesian Cattle

The Holstein-Friesian cow, known as the Holstein cow in North America and the Friesian cow in Europe, is a cow prized for its milk. The breed is native to Europe, possibly to the Netherlands. Its black and white coloration identifies the breed. Virtually anyone who has toured a dairy farm has seen Holstein-Friesian cattle. The animals are specialists in converting the grass on which they graze into biomass, including a profusion of milk. In southern Europe, however, many people use the breed as a source of beef, indicating the variability in its use. At maturity, a Holstein-Friesian cow may weigh almost 1,300 pounds.

is resolved. The scantily clad Isis has beautiful breasts and is an object of eroticism. This conjunction of the mundane and the erotic gains strength from the fact that Isis dispensed phalluses to her followers. The phallus was the symbol of her brother and husband, the god Osiris, who lost his penis during his murder and dismemberment. Faithful Isis restored her husband to life, pointing the path toward Christianity, in which a god may be killed and yet rise from the dead. In an indirect way, milk seems to have been important in the development of Judaism and Christianity, an assertion that will gain strength in passages that follow. The connection to Judaism may be a bit tenuous because not all Jews believe in an afterlife, but those who do insist that Yahweh will raise the righteous at the end of time. Jesus may have had similar apocalyptic ideas. Egyptians placed jars of milk at the tomb in which Osiris was said to have been buried. Every day these jars were replenished. The Great Mother, sometimes identified with Isis, appears to have been a popular goddess among several ancient peoples. Her large breasts lactated for all humanity. One Greek goddess, Artemis of Ephesus, outdid Isis and the Great Mother in having several breasts with which to nourish humans. The people of what are today Iraq and Iran had a number of milk goddesses. In some sense, one might identify Mary as a milk goddess who nourished Jesus. Yet this notion dismayed the men who led the Christian Church. Moreover, Jews were uncomfortable with the notion of a milk goddess. Jews believed that one could not represent God. They thought of God in masculine terms, so the idea of a milk goddess was wrong on several counts. The Romans did not have such hang-ups. Their goddess Juno was a milk goddess whose milk was thought to have created the Milky Way galaxy. Perhaps there is a parallel here between Roman and West African beliefs. Christian leaders, however, persisted in their criticism. The milk goddesses were really cows in the guise of a human female, and therefore repugnant. God was philosophical and abstract, not a woman allowing all humanity to suck her breasts. Worse were the goddesses who offered their breasts to all animals, not merely humans. Mary had nursed Jesus not with milk but with the word of God. Yet, into the Middle Ages, art depicted Mary and Jesus in the same setting and positions that Isis and a pharaoh's child had assumed. The beliefs about Isis, if anathema to authorities, were never far from the popular imagination. One last connection to antiquity is crucial to the foundation of Rome. According to legend, a female wolf nursed the abandoned brothers Romulus and Remus, both of whom played a role in founding Rome. In part, the story has a Cain-and-Abel element because Romulus killed Remus. From the Roman perspective, the story amplifies the toughness and survival skills of Rome's founders. One of the world's great empires arose from the story of a lactating wolf.

Milk and Modernity

By modernity, the Dutch had arisen as the archetypes of milk consumers and cow raisers. The Dutch succeeded partly because of their eagerness to apply the latest science to an emerging dairy industry. This scientific perspective took root throughout Europe and the United States. In the latter, the U.S. Department of Agriculture (USDA), the land-grant universities, and the agricultural experiment stations labored to advance dairy science into the model of the applied sciences. Milk may have had much to do with the rise of the Dutch as a commercial people. Milk also appears to have shaped Dutch Protestantism, which encouraged the scientific inquiry that was important to every dairyman and dairymaid. This spirit of scientific inquiry may have fueled the Dutch contributions to the scientific revolution of the 16th and 17th centuries. Other Europeans who toured the Netherlands commented on the widespread availability of milk, cheese, and butter, and on the ubiquity of dairy farms. In some sense, the Netherlands was a nation of small dairy farms, a perspective that may have influenced third U.S. president Thomas Jefferson, who believed that America would be strong as long as it remained a nation of small farmers. The availability of milk and its by-products may have helped the Dutch population expand in the 17th century, though one suspects that the potato must have played a role in this demographic transformation. Milk was so abundant that it was cheap enough to nourish the masses. The keeping of cows benefited Dutch agriculture in other ways. Their manure enriched soils, causing crop yields to increase. Indeed, into the 20th century, American scientist Charles Thorne promoted manure as the best fertilizer.

Into the early modern era, Puritanical men tried to convince women not to nurse babies but rather to prefer cow's milk. This advice was mistaken, given the number of antibodies that human milk supplies an infant. There was a tendency among these men to see mother's milk as a forbidden fruit, a source of conflict and shame. The Enlightenment brought new dignity to breast feeding, challenging the supremacy of cow's milk.

In the 19th century, German chemist Justus von Liebig promoted the scientific study of milk and the furthering of research in dairy science. In the Americas, milk was abundant. Introduced into the Americas, cows became ubiquitous, even becoming feral on the pampas of Argentina and on the grasslands of the Great Plains. The amount of milk that could be derived from so many cows was staggering. Milk also became safer that century when French microbiologist Louis Pasteur invented the process of pasteurization, though it is a mistake, we have seen, to think that pasteurization kills all pathogens. Even today milk has a "sell by" date to alert consumers not to buy expired milk. If the American colonies had small dairy farms, by the 19th century consolidation prevailed, creating economies of scale that mimicked the rise of industrial capitalism. Yet it is possible to overstate the importance of milk in the 19th century. Soldiers in the American Civil War drank far more coffee than milk. Civil war generals appear not to have learned from the Mongols that if an army kept herds of cattle it could have its own supply of milk, cheese, butter, and meat. Perhaps armies had grown too large to make the Mongol experience relevant. By the 1860s, condensed milk was an early product to be canned, an emerging technology that transformed the way people ate and thought about food. Nonetheless, consumers preferred fresh milk. The Civil War was part of a larger battle between coffee and milk in the 19th century. After the Civil War, the USDA and other agencies strove to restore the popularity of milk by promoting its nutrients, safety, and wholesomeness. Into the 20th century, milk consumption increased in the United States and Canada. The rise of chocolate in Europe, the United States, Japan, and other regions of the world gave milk new prominence. American chocolatier Milton Hershey owed his success partly to being in a dairy-rich region of Pennsylvania. Ice cream further increased the demand for milk.

Milk and the Discovery of Vitamin A

The nutritional importance of milk stimulated Wisconsin agricultural scientist Elmer V. McCollum to study it closely. He fed one group of rats milk fat and another group margarine, noting that in every case the first group flourished while the second grew poorly and ultimately died. By way of digression, Wisconsin taxpayers would not have appreciated what seemed to be experiments on an undesirable animal rather than serious agricultural research. McCollum concluded that milk fat must contain a new kind of nutrient, which he called vitamin A. The discovery created a new branch of nutrition virtually overnight, as scientists scrambled to identify other vitamins. The study of nutrition had entered its era of maturity, thanks in part to milk.

The 20th and 21st Centuries

Despite McCollum's epochal work, there remained an urban-rural divide. Americans who inhabited the countryside were far more likely to drink milk than were urbanites. By requiring milk, breakfast cereals did much to narrow this gap, particularly among children. Milk became indispensable to the morning routine. No less important was the imbalance of supply and demand. Since the late 19th century the production of milk outpaced demand, so that through the Great Depression milk was too cheap not to buy. In this context it is uncertain how much dairy science helped dairymen because it taught them to produce more milk at the very time that the oversupply of the liquid caused prices to fall. Science was exacerbating the problems of agriculture, including the overproduction of milk. This episode serves as a corrective. Science is not always progressive, and in many ways the situation has not improved, at least not for producers. By 2009, milk was cheaper than at any time since the Great Depression.

Further Reading

Valenze, Deborah. *Milk: A Local and Global History*. New Haven, CT and London: Yale University Press, 2011.
Velton, Hanna. *Milk: A Global History*. London: Reaktion Books, 2010.

Millet

An annual grass, millet is a crop of arid and semiarid Africa and Asia. Like other grains, millet is a member of the Gramineae family. Millet is not a single species but rather a complex of species, a group of related grains. Among the types of millet are pearl, proso, and finger, which farmers grow for food; forage, foxtail, and Japanese, both of which serve as forage; and several other lesser millets. Farmers in Africa and Asia grow millet primarily for food, whereas their counterparts in Australia and the Americas raise millet principally for forage. In 1753, Swedish naturalist Carl Linnaeus described two species of millet. By 1950, botanists had added more than 100 species to this list. Millet is 5.8 to 20.9 percent protein, a range of figures that compares well with the protein content of other grains. In addition to protein, millet contains fiber, starch, thiamine, calcium, phosphorus, iron, zinc, manganese, phytate, linoleic acid, oleic acid, palmitic acid, stearic acid, linolemic acid, palmitoleic acid, riboflavin, and potassium. A nutritious grain, millet nourishes pregnant and lactating women and children.

A Food of Warm, Arid Regions

Where the climate is warm, farmers may plant millet as a spring or autumn crop, though most millet is sown in spring. Having a large root system, millet extracts the maximum water and nutrients from the soil. Millet yields better in light soil than in heavy clay because the roots do not penetrate the latter. Millet even grows well in sandy soil, which is notorious for its lack of water and nutrients. Being more than a good crop for sandy soil, millet does well in infertile soil in which other crops would fail. Of course, the best yields are in fertile soil, but good soil goes to higher-value crops like corn and rice. In India and Africa, farmers grow millet on alfisol soil. Tolerating slightly acidic to slightly basic soils, millet grows in soils with a pH between 6.2 and 7.7. Millet will grow with as little as 10 inches of rain per year whereas sorghum must have at least 14 inches of rain per year. During dry periods, millet, closing its stomata periodically, transpires little water. Although millet tolerates low rainfall, sporadic and inconsequential rain that evaporates quickly may form a hard outer layer in the soil. Seeds that germinate in this hard crust may not penetrate it and so may not emerge. As a rule, the harder the crust the fewer millet seedlings emerge. Because millet matures in as little as forty-five days. farmers may plant it where another crop has failed. This strategy means that farmers will likely plant millet late, when the weather is hot and dry, conditions that millet tolerates better than many other crops.

Tolerating a range of temperatures between 50°F and 115°F, millet, like sorghum, grows best between 91°F and 93°F. Able to grow in moderately saline soils, millet will not tolerate a high concentration of salt in the soil. Photosensitive, millet needs between eight and 12 hours of daylight to flower. Although 14 to 16 hours of daylight delay flowering, millet grows best with 16 hours of daylight. Millet needs long days for the formation of tillers and leaves. Because of the requirement for long days, millet grows better in temperate zones than in the tropics.

Needing a warm soil, millet is planted two to three weeks later than corn. In Korea, farmers sow millet around April 30. In Bikaner, India farmers plant millet in mid-July to coincide with the onset of summer rains. In Coimbatore, India, millet is planted in mid-September. Of the three chief plant nutrients—nitrogen, phosphorus, and potassium—millet generally does not need applications of potassium. Farmers plant and fertilize millet in a single operation, applying all the phosphorus and half the nitrogen in one dose. A second application—the other half of the nitrogen—follows later. Farmers spray the second application of nitrogen on the leaves, a peculiar practice given that nitrogen is absorbed through the roots. Applied alone, phosphorus does not increase yields and so must be applied with nitrogen. Farmers may apply nitrogen up to 185 pounds per acre and phosphorus up to 53 pounds per acre. Higher applications will not increase yields. The application of fertilizer is wise given that so much millet is grown on poor land.

Stockmen grow foxtail millet for hay. Others pasture livestock in millet fields. Like rice, millet will regenerate so that stockmen, removing their animals, may harvest millet after it matures. Millet is not ideal for pasturage, however, because livestock tend to uproot the plant when feeding on it. In addition to its use as livestock feed, farmers feed millet, usually as a corn-millet mix, to chickens. Research has shown that millet nourishes chickens better than do rice and wheat. In the United States, some millet is used as bird feed.

As is true of other crops, scientists worry that millet has become genetically uniform. To promote diversity, scientists have collected wild species and neglected varieties. The International Crops Research Institute for the Semi-Arid Tropics in Kenya and Niger has collected more than 16,000 varieties of millet. The Tropical Agronomy and Food Crops Research Institute in Burkina Faso has collected germplasm since 1961. The International Crops Research Institute has, since 1971, amassed its gene bank and, since 1981, the Food and Agriculture Organization has collected wild and cultivated millets. In 1981, scientists collected 284 samples in Ghana; in 1989, 555 samples in Togo; in 1991, 1,270 samples in Namibia; and in 1992, 682 samples in Yemen.

Origin and Diffusion

Scholars do not agree on the place and time of millet's origin. Even the continent of origin is a matter of dispute, with some authorities pointing to Africa and others to Asia. In the Africa-first camp are those who assert that, because Africa has the greatest diversity of wild species, it must be the homeland of millet. Using this reasoning, Russian agronomist Nikolai Vavilov, in 1949 and 1950, identified Ethiopia as the place of origin. One school of thought traces the domestication of millet to the Mande of the Niger River valley, who first cultivated millet between 5000 and 4000 BCE. Others reject this view because this area then had a wet climate, making it implausible that a drought-tolerant crop would have arisen there. In 1971, American agronomist Jack Harlan proposed the area between western Sudan and Senegal as the region where farmers domesticated millet. Another hypothesis fingers the southern edge of the Saharan highlands as the place where farmers domesticated millet between 3000 and 2000 BCE.

Those who favor Asia as the center of millet culture point to millet's antiquity as an Asian crop. Some scholars believe that farmers in east Asia grew millet as early as 8000 BCE, making it among the oldest cultivated plants. One authority believes that Chinese farmers began growing millet about 8300 BCE. Another writer believes farmers in China began to raise millet around 6500 BCE. Even this comparatively late date may predate the cultivation of rice, barley, and wheat in east Asia. The priority of millet may mean that people in northern China and Korea ate more millet than rice in prehistory. So important was millet to China that in 2700 BCE one text listed it among the five sacred grains. As early as 2000 BCE, the Chinese were making noodles from millet. By then, millet had spread to other regions in Asia, being grown in Japan after 4000 BCE and in Korea as early as 3500 BCE.

Given the diversity of locales where farmers grew millet in prehistory and antiquity, it may have been domesticated independently in several areas over time. Whether millet arose in Africa or Asia, it diffused to other regions of the globe. According to the Asia-first school of thought, millet migrated from China to lands along the Black Sea by 5000 BCE. Those who advocate the origin of millet in West Africa trace its spread to East Africa, the Sudan, and India by the time of Christ. By 3000 BCE, Europeans were growing millet, though it became widespread only around 1000 BCE. In the Middle Ages, people ate millet in porridge and flatbread. So popular was it that people may have eaten more millet than wheat. Only in 1849, did U.S. farmers begin to cultivate millet, though never on a large scale. In the United States, as in other places, millet had to compete with sorghum for acreage in arid lands. In the United States, North Dakota, South Dakota, Colorado, and Nebraska grow proso and foxtail millet for feeding livestock. In the American Southeast, livestock graze fields of pearl millet.

Today, farmers raise millet from Senegal to Ethiopia, and in Spain, northern India, southern Arabia, Pakistan, Bangladesh, Argentina, and the United States. Several countries in southern Asia—southern India, Myanmar, Sri Lanka, Thailand, Laos, Cambodia, the Philippines, and Indonesia—raise millet. Indeed, southern Asia harvests 60 percent of Asia's millet. India produces nearly all of southern Asia's millet. Smaller harvests are recorded in Mexico, northeastern Brazil, and Bolivia. Among the specialty millets is finger millet, which farmers grow in Uganda, Kenya, Ethiopia, Tanzania, Zimbabwe, India, and Nepal.

Of the types of millet, pearl millet totals half the world's production. Farmers grow finger millet at altitude, where the climate is cooler, in Africa and Asia. The people of these continents use finger millet as food and to make beer. The developing world, especially countries in Africa and Asia, produces 94 percent of the world's millet. Small farmers produce almost all the world's millet, consuming it or trading it locally. Millet is therefore a subsistence rather than a market crop. By most measures, millet is a minor crop. Farmers grow it on only a small percentage of the world's grain land. Millet accounts for less than a very small portion of the world's grain output.

In 2007, India was the world's leading producer of millet, followed by Nigeria, Niger, China, and Burkina Faso. The United States was not a leading producer. The Chinese eat congee, a millet porridge. The people of Niger eat congee with fried onions. Millet porridge is also popular in Russia and Germany. Kenyans make porridge from millet, milk, banana juice, and sugar, serving it hot for breakfast or lunch. Nigerians eat porridge made from millet, sugar, and salt. In India, people make porridge from millet and buttermilk. They also serve millet with sauce, dal, pickles, chutneys, buttermilk, curd, and vegetables. A similar recipe calls for millet, pickles, chutneys, dal, and vegetable sauce. In some countries (Kenya is an example), people eat millet with milk as a breakfast cereal. Cooks make millet into thin strips, which they fry. In the United States, muffins and multigrain bread may contain millet. The Russians, Indians, and Kenyans make stew with millet, meat, and vegetables. Ethiopians make stew with meat, a legume, and vegetables. In India, one recipe calls for millet, greens, and lemon or orange slices, and another includes millet, fried onions and garlic, rice, chickpeas, dal, groundnuts, salt, grated coconut, and coriander. In West Africa, people eat couscous, a dish of millet with ground baobab, peanut paste, okra, and sauce or milk. In Nigeria, a recipe includes millet, bean cake, onion, tomatoes, chili peppers, spinach, salt, and pepper. The Russians eat millet porridge with milk and sugar. In the Sudan, people make millet pancakes, serving them with vegetables, a legume, meat, and soup. The Chinese eat millet with beans, sweet potatoes, and squash. In Taiwan, people brew millet into beer. In Nepal, people distill millet into the liquor *rakshi*. In Romania and Bulgaria, people ferment millet into the beverage *boza*. Some people eat millet in tortillas, rice soup, and cookies. Given millet's importance in Africa and parts of Asia, the grass has shaped the history of these continents and the daily lives of their people.

Further Reading

Dendy, David A. V. *Sorghum and Millets: Chemistry and Technology*. Saint Paul, MN: American Association of Cereal Chemists, 1995.

Leslie, John F., ed. *Sorghum and Millets Diseases*. Ames: Iowa State Press, 2002.

Lupien, J. R. *Sorghum and Millets in Human Nutrition*. Rome: Food and Agriculture Organization, 1995.

Maiti, Ratikanta, and Pedro Wesche-Ebeling. *Pearl Millet Science*. Enfield, NH: Science Publishers, 1997.

The World Sorghum and Millet Economies: Facts, Trends and Outlook. International Crops Research Institute for the Semi-Arid Tropics and Food and Agriculture Organization, 1996.

Molasses

Molasses is a by-product of making sugar from the pith and juice of the sugarcane plant, one of history's most influential plants. Molasses is not simply an iteration of sugar. The differences are important. Sugar is pure sucrose. As such, it contains about four calories per gram, so one does derive energy from it, but nothing else. Sugar contains no nourishment of any kind and for that reason may be considered the essence of junk food. It is empty calories any way one examines it. Molasses, having some sugar, likewise has calories and is sweet. But unlike sugar, molasses has important vitamins and minerals, though no protein. A reasonably nourishing food, it cannot be the staff of life because of the absence of protein. Other foods such as fish or meat must complement it. Because molasses has food value it may be fed to livestock and in this sense is more versatile than sugar, though the human craving for sugar makes it a versatile product in its own right and in world cuisines. Molasses may also be fermented and then distilled into rum, a beverage with a higher alcohol content than wine, the most potent drink known to antiquity and the Middle Ages.

The Sugarcane Empire

Molasses was part of the sugarcane empire that the Europeans who followed Italian Spanish explorer Christopher Columbus founded in tropical America. The Caribbean islands and Brazil were long prominent members of the empire. Not only sugar, but also molasses and rum were abundant in tropical America. Molasses would begin to play an important role in the Caribbean and in North America in the 17th century. In 1627, the English began to settle the Caribbean island of Barbados. Within a decade, Barbados was planting sugarcane and importing African slaves. Ten years later, Massachusetts Bay Colony governor John Winthrop came to realize that molasses could be an important commercial commodity. He understood that, because England and Barbados were so smitten by molasses and sugar, cane planters devoted virtually every acre to the tropical grass. In other words, the English did not grow enough food for themselves and their slaves. Here, Massachusetts solved the problem by exporting food, primarily fish and cattle, to feed Barbados. The English and Africans would, of course, need to slaughter the cattle for beef. Massachusetts sent horses to Barbados to power sugar mills, though masters would not allow slaves to use horses to plow land. Rather, slaves had to make do with hoes to break ground and weed the soil. This arduous work kept slaves in a perpetual state of exhaustion, too tired, masters believed, to foment rebellion. Yet the fact that masters underfed their slaves led to the very rebellions that white Europeans claimed to fear. Massachusetts also sent Barbados timber to make buildings and barrels. In exchange the colony received sugar, molasses, rum, and money. First U.S. president and Virginia plantation owner George Washington also traded with Barbados, sending slaves, fish, and wheat flour in exchange for molasses, rum, and tropical fruits of various kinds. From New York came iron, bricks, and boilers for use on the sugarcane estates, again in exchange for molasses, sugar, rum, and money.

In North America and the Caribbean (sometimes known as the West Indies), the English used molasses to flavor whole wheat bread, gingerbread, Indian pudding, and pies of various types. Molasses was thus part of the culinary history of early America. Second U.S. president John Adams favored pudding made from corn and molasses. Washington believed that Virginia rivaled Massachusetts in the consumption of molasses. New Englanders may have flavored baked beans with molasses, sometimes adding lard. This recipe marked a union of Old and New World foods during that intense period of globalism known as the Columbian Exchange. It also seems possible that baked beans and molasses were not a popular dish until the 19th century. Indeed, the earliest written record of baked beans and molasses dates only to 1847. The thought that this recipe dated to the Amerindians must be untrue. Although the Native Americans had beans, they could not have had molasses before European contact because sugarcane is an Old World crop.

Molasses appears to have been a marker of class. The rich ate it, though not often. In contrast, the masses appear to have eaten molasses every day. They often consumed it in beer, another commingling of Old and New World foods. Because the alcohol content was low, the masses could drink in quantity without fear of severe intoxication, though they must have gone through the day with a slight buzz. Perhaps this state of mind lightened the burden of work. This habit also suggests that Americans did not think of alcohol as an evil before the rise of the temperance movement. The United States taxed alcohol and molasses to derive income before the institution of an income tax in the early 20th century.

Because sugar was still a luxury in 17th-century America, molasses was the food of necessity of the masses. One 17th-century estimate put the consumption of molasses among New England fishermen at 30 gallons per year, again in the form of beer or corn bread. In 1872, a newspaper reported that the poor fed children molasses and bread, leading to unsanitary conditions because the children put their sticky hands on walls, floors and objects. These molasses spots attracted many flies. Poor adults tended to consume molasses, bread, and tea. Physicians did not like this state of affairs, warning that molasses could cause tuberculosis (an untruth). Early America believed that molasses was fit for prisoners and the institutionalized poor. Famed British scientist Benjamin Thompson (Count Rumford) liked the idea, recommending it to the English penal system. Third U.S. president Thomas Jefferson fed slaves molasses, corn bread, and pork fat. In the 1890s, the U.S. Department of Agriculture (USDA) pinpointed these poor rations as the cause of malnourishment among African Americans in Alabama. In the 1920s, an American physician pointed to molasses as the cause of pellagra. He was on the right track in seeking a dietary explanation, but the real culprit was corn rather than molasses.

Molasses and Congress

In 1789, molasses was the cause of what we today call congressional gridlock. That year the first Congress convened to determine how to pay the debts from the American Revolution and, more broadly, how to raise revenues in an environment in which Americans loathed the idea of an income tax. The natural idea was to turn to a tariff. Congress was intent on imposing a 4-cents–per-gallon duty on molasses from the Caribbean. Massachusetts' delegates rose in opposition. Dependent on cheap molasses to make rum, they would not countenance the thought of paying more money for molasses. These delegates were certain that European governments in the Caribbean would retaliate with tariffs on American products, making it difficult for Massachusetts to export fish. After nearly six months' debate Congress imposed a 2.5-cent duty per gallon on molasses, less than it had originally wanted. Congress also enacted a tariff on sugar and rum, in effect declaring war on the sugarcane plant.

In 1791, the success of the Haitian rebellion cut sugar and molasses production on the former French colony of Saint-Domingue. Saint-Domingue became Haiti and it along with the Dominican Republic comprises Hispaniola, the Caribbean island on which Columbus initially landed in October 1492. With an increase in molasses prices, Alexander Hamilton, the first U.S. Secretary of the Treasury, advised American distillers to use homegrown grains, not foreign molasses, an interesting position for a man who had been born in the Caribbean.

An American Commodity

Merchants packed molasses in barrels, using a utensil to scoop out the amount a customer requested. By the early 20th century, molasses was sold in packages convenient for serving to families. About 1908, a Louisiana manufacturer was the first to sell canned molasses. As with other foods, advertisers touted the benefits and inexpensiveness of molasses. Molasses was a meal stretcher, a food that helped stave off the hunger that was omnipresent to the poor. Canners trumpeted the antiseptic quality of molasses, asserting that it was among the safest foods that mothers could feed children. The brand Aunt Dinah featured a black woman, doubtless a mother who worked hard to feed her family. Aunt Dinah must have appealed to African American consumers, probably women. Another brand, Trixy, featured a gorgeous black woman who doubtless targeted an audience of black men. Grandma's Old Fashioned Molasses featured an elderly white woman and must have appealed to a different audience.

Further Reading

Warner, Deborah Jean. *Sweet Stuff: An American History of Sweeteners from Sugar to Sucralose.* Washington, DC: Smithsonian Institution Scholarly Press, 2011.

Mushrooms

The term "mushroom" derives from the French *mousseron*. In the *Grete Herball* of 1526, scientist Peter Treveris rendered mushroom as *musherom*. For centuries in the West, scientists and philosophers thought of mushrooms as plants. The ancients understood that mushrooms lacked roots, but this insight did not stop them from classifying mushrooms as plants. The Greeks and Romans understood that mushrooms lacked seeds, but this knowledge did not dissuade them from characterizing mushrooms as plants. In the fourth century BCE, Greek philosopher Aristotle assigned mushrooms to the plant kingdom. In the 18th century Swedish naturalist Carl Linnaeus, perhaps misled by Aristotle, categorized mushrooms as

Mushrooms have long fascinated humans. Once considered plants, mushrooms are really fungi. Mushrooms do more than complement the main dish. The quality of protein is excellent and other nutrients abound. (Michael S. Yamashita/Corbis)

Agrippina

A wealthy Roman woman, Agrippina the Younger was the great-granddaughter of Emperor Augustus, the fourth wife of Emperor Claudius, and the mother of Emperor Nero. Men were drawn to her beauty, though her tendency toward cruelty and amorality made her a difficult person. The depraved emperor Caligula was among the first to feel her wrath and might easily have executed her for treason. Her survival owed much to Caligula's assassination. She married but never loved Claudius. Ambitious for her son Nero, Agrippina plotted Claudius's death as she had Caligula's. Accounts vary, but one tradition holds that Agrippina poisoned Claudius with toxic mushrooms in 54 CE, securing Nero as emperor. In 59 CE, Nero, after an unsuccessful attempt to drown his mother, had his soldiers execute her. In turn, the senate condemned Nero to death, and he killed himself.

plants. In the East, this mistaken view was a tenet of agriculture and science. In 1313, Chinese scholar Weng Cheng devoted a chapter to mushrooms in the *Book of Agriculture*. Not everyone made the connection between mushrooms and plants. The Amerindians of Mochiacan in Mexico understood that mushrooms were not plants and this view has prevailed. Mushrooms lack roots, stems, leaves, and chlorophyll, making them poor candidates for inclusion in the plant kingdom. Scientists now classify mushrooms as fungi and group all fungi in their own kingdom, the Kingdom Myceteae or the Kingdom Fungi. Yet the association between mushrooms and plants has not been abandoned in all quarters. Mushrooms have a cell wall akin to that of plants. Two mycologists consider "mushroom science" to be a branch of agronomy. Indeed, the language of agriculture permeates the culture of mushrooms. The people who tend mushrooms are farmers, and the cultivation of these fungi occurs on farms. More broadly, the fact that humans cultivate mushrooms for food links them to agriculture. As late as 1941, Cornell University horticulturalist Liberty Hyde Bailey listed mushrooms as a cultivated plant. More recently, one scholar has written that fungi and therefore mushrooms are "a large group of plants." Their association with plants makes mushrooms a proper subject of an encyclopedia of cultivated plants.

Folklore, Origin, and History

In Europe, the superstitious have long associated mushrooms with fairies and witches. Europeans referred to mushrooms as "fairy clubs," "fairy stools," "witches' butter," and "witches' spittle." In India and Afghanistan, people know the field mushroom as a "fairy's cap." European folklore attributed magical powers to mushrooms, perhaps because some of them cause hallucinations. The Talmud mentions mushrooms, though not in a flattering light. In some cultures, people used mushrooms in religious ritual and divination. In the Americas, mushrooms are part of folklore. The people of Belize, Honduras, and Guyana believe that little spirits inhabit the forest. When rain falls at night these spirits open their umbrellas to avoid getting wet. They disappear in the morning, before any person can detect them, leaving only their miniature umbrellas as a sign of their presence. This story explains why mushrooms are in the shape of tiny umbrellas and why they appear near moisture, and it accounts for the rapidity with which they appear. In parts of Africa, people believed that mushrooms harbor the souls of the dead. The Orotch of Siberia believed that the dead are reborn as mushrooms on the moon. Some Amerindians and Europeans believed that a shooting star created a mushroom on the spot where it fell. The Greeks, Romans, Maya, and Filipinos all believed that lightning created mushrooms on the spot it struck. Like the belief in fairy umbrellas, the notion that shooting stars and lightning created mushrooms accounted for their sudden appearance. According to one Greek myth, Sisyphus, the founder of Corinth, populated the city with people who had arisen from mushrooms.

According to one definition, mushrooms are "macrofungi," large enough to be seen and suitable for picking by hand. The ancestor of mushrooms arose 438 million years ago, and mushrooms have been part of the fossil record for 300 million years. Mycologists have identified 14,000 species of mushrooms, though ten times this number may exist. The fact that gorillas also eat mushrooms may suggest that mushroom eating is part of the lifeway of primates. The fact that several Cro-Magnon sites, Lascaux for example, were in areas rich in mushrooms may indicate that humans gathered them, perhaps for several reasons, from an early date. These early humans may have gathered mushrooms for food, medicine, and as hallucinogens and tinder. Indeed, Otzi, the remains of a 5,000-year-old man discovered in the Italian Alps, was carrying bracken mushroom at the time of his death. This mushroom was used to start fires in Europe until the invention of matches. Otzi carried two other types of mushroom, perhaps to use as medicine.

The Chinese have eaten mushrooms for 7,000 years, and the Japanese have consumed them for 2,000 years. In this context, mushrooms have shaped history, cuisine, and daily life. By 3000 BCE, the people of east Asia gathered wild mushrooms rather than cultivated them. The first written account of mushrooms dates to the third century BCE from China. Around 600 CE, the Chinese were the first to cultivate mushrooms. The Chinese first cultivated the species *Auricularia auricula* on logs. About 800 CE, the Chinese began to cultivate the species *Flammulina velutipes*, and around 1000, *Lentinula edodes*. This third species is today the chief mushroom grown in Asia. China and Japan grow mushrooms for export to the United States and Europe. So enthusiastic are they about mushrooms that the Chinese refer to them as the "elixir of life." In addition to the Chinese, the ancient Greeks, Romans, Egyptians, and Mexicans ate mushrooms as a delicacy and used them as medicine. The Greeks believed that mushrooms gave soldiers strength. The Pharaohs prized mushrooms for their flavor and texture. The Romans ate mushrooms on festive occasions. In Rome, the elites ate mushrooms. Emperor Nero proclaimed mushrooms the "food of the gods." One especially prized mushroom was known as "Caesar's mushroom." The Aztecs ate mushrooms, and the people of Central America consumed them for their hallucinogenic effects. The Chinantecs and Mazatec of Mexico grew mushrooms on horse manure. Some Amerindians carved stones in the shape of mushrooms, putting them in tombs. Some Hindus considered mushrooms unwholesome and so did not eat them. From an early date, therefore, mushrooms were a global food.

Medieval cookbooks included recipes for mushrooms, though in the 13th century German theologian Albertus Magnus found a new use for the mushroom *Amanita muscaria*, claiming that it could kill flies. Interest in mushrooms grew during the Renaissance, and in 1564 Dutch physician Hadrian de Janghe wrote the first pamphlet, spanning 13 pages, on mushrooms. In 1597, British herbalist John Gerard, perhaps aware that some mushrooms were poisonous, warned against their consumption. In 1601, Dutch physician and botanist Carolus Clusius published the first monograph on mushrooms. *A Brief Inquiry into Fungi Found in Pannonia* described twenty-five types of mushrooms. In the 18th century, Italian scientist Pietro Antonio Micheli discovered that mushrooms arise from spores, a finding that solved the long-standing problem of how mushrooms were propagated. Micheli demonstrated that no mushrooms grew in the absence of spores and that they always grew in the presence of spores. This work was an early critique of spontaneous generation.

Europeans eat mushrooms, though according to one authority the British and Dutch are not avid consumers. Italians favor the oyster mushroom. Mushrooms no longer enjoy renown in Greece. The Greeks believe mushrooms are fit only for commoners. The people of Eastern Europe and Russia regard mushrooms as a meat substitute for the poor. Mushrooms are grown in Slovakia, Poland, Hungary, Lithuania, Estonia, Latvia, and Finland. The French and Italians eat mushrooms fried or baked and in soup or stew. Europeans eat canned mushrooms of the species *Gyromitra esculenta*, though this mushroom causes allergy in some. In the West, people use mushrooms to flavor the main dish. In Southeast Asia and Japan, people eat mushrooms every day. Mushrooms are unpopular in some regions of Latin America, perhaps because the descendants of the Spanish and Portuguese dislike them. The Amerindians of these areas, however, eat mushrooms.

In 1993, American scientist Mitchell Sogin created a sensation when he wrote that mushrooms are more closely related to humans than to plants. Both mushrooms and humans depend on plants for sustenance whereas plants manufacture their own food.

Nutrition, Medicine, and Toxicity

Mushrooms contain protein, lipids, phosphorus, potassium, sodium, calcium, magnesium, copper, zinc, iron, manganese, molybdenum, cadmium, thiamine, riboflavin, vitamin C, and niacin. This nutritional profile has doubtless benefited the health of those who consume mushrooms. Mushrooms are between 0.6 and 3.1 percent fat. More than 70 percent of this fat is unsaturated, making mushrooms a healthy choice. Mushrooms contain only 1.75–3.63 percent protein by weight, a much lower percentage than beans or other legumes, and lower even than grains. Yet mushrooms have twice the protein of asparagus and cabbage, four times more protein than oranges and 12 times more protein than apples. What protein mushrooms lack in quantity they have in quality. Many species have all nine essential amino acids. By contrast, most legumes and grains lack at least one essential amino acid.

The Chinese have used mushrooms as medicine for thousands of years. During the Ming dynasty, physician Wu Shui wrote that the donko mushroom, *Lentinula edodes*, increased stamina, cured the common cold, improved circulation, and reduced blood pressure. Some 700 species of mushrooms have medicinal value. The polysaccharides in mushrooms—some 660 species have these compounds—may combat cancer and may stimulate the immune system. *Lentinula edodes* may protect one against influenza. This species may lower cholesterol and may lessen the side effects of chemotherapy and radiation treatment, diminishing pain and reducing hair loss in chemotherapy patients. In 1994, the market for medicinal mushrooms totaled several billion dollars. The figure rose in 1999. In Bohemia, lumberjacks eat mushrooms on the advice that they protect against cancer. Asia and Europe account for nearly the entire market for medicinal mushrooms, whereas North America tallies a very small fraction.

Some mushrooms, providing no nutrients, are poisonous. Luckily, very few mushroom species are poisonous. Of these some species are lethal. Greek dramatist Euripides and Greek physician Hippocrates understood that some mushrooms were poisonous. Greek botanist Theophrastus, Roman encyclopedist Pliny the Elder, and Greek physicians Galen and Dioscorides drew a distinction between edible and poisonous mushrooms. The Romans may have used toxic mushrooms to poison people. The emperor Claudius may have died from mushroom poisoning. If this is true, then mushrooms changed history by bringing to the throne the violent and often irrational Nero, a much worse emperor than Claudius had been. In the Middle Ages, Arab physician Avicenna mistakenly thought that mushroom poisoning could be cured. People who have ignored the dangers of eating toxic mushrooms sometimes lost their lives. In 1767, French organist and harpsichordist Johann Schobert joined a friend and physician in an excursion to collect mushrooms in the countryside. Selecting several specimens, the doctor assured Schobert that they were edible. They took the mushrooms to a chef, asking him to prepare them. The chef refused, saying that the mushrooms were poisonous. A trip to a second restaurant yielded the same result. Growing angry, Schobert and the doctor went to the musician's home to prepare the mushrooms. The chefs were right, however, and the mushroom soup that Schobert prepared killed him, his wife, all their children but one, and the physician.

Further Reading

Chang, Shu-Ting, and Philip G. Miles. *Mushrooms: Cultivation, Nutritional Value, Medicinal Effect, and Environmental Impact.* Boca Raton, FL: CRC Press, 2004.

Flegg, P. B., D. M. Spencer, and D. A. Wood. *The Biology and Technology of the Cultivated Mushroom.* New York: John Wiley and Sons, 1985.

Kaul, T. N. *Biology and Conservation of Mushrooms.* Enfield, NH: Science Publishers, 2002.

Morgan, Adrian. *Toads and Toadstools: The Natural History, Folklore, and Cultural Oddities of a Strange Association.* Berkeley, CA: Celestial Arts, 1995.

Schaechter, Elio. *In the Company of Mushrooms: A Biologist's Tale.* Cambridge, MA: Harvard University Press, 1997.

Singer, Rolf, and Bob Harris. *Mushrooms and Truffles: Botany, Cultivation, and Utilization.* Koenigstein, Germany: Koeltz Scientific Books, 1987.

Stamets, Paul. *Mycelium Running: How Mushrooms Can Help Save the World.* Berkeley, CA: Ten Speed Press, 2005.

Stamets, Paul, and J. S. Chilton. *The Mushroom Cultivator: A Practical Guide to Growing Mushrooms at Home.* Olympia, WA: Agarikon Press, 1983.

Mutton and Lamb

Mutton and lamb, both types of meat, derive from the sheep. Mutton is the product of an adult sheep, whereas lamb meat comes from a lamb. The U.S. Department of Agriculture (USDA) classifies any sheep over two years old as an adult. The lamb is a juvenile and must be no older than two years. The USDA further classifies lambs into three categories. The hothouse lamb is less than three months old and less than 60 pounds. The spring lamb is between three and seven months old. The full-fledged lamb, which the USDA refers to simply as a lamb, is between seven months and two years old and weighs between 110 and 130 pounds. The USDA assigns grades to lamb: prime, choice, good, and utility.

Mutton, Lamb, and Monotheism

Mutton and lamb were crucial in the diet of the ancient Hebrews, the possible originators of monotheism. So important were mutton and lamb that they could approach the divine. Sheep and lambs were the primary sacrificial animals to the Hebrew god, Yahweh (sometimes rendered Jehovah). If mutton and lamb were good enough for humans to eat, then these meats would please Yahweh. One senses this sacrificial purpose in parts of the Old Testament, part of the Jewish scriptures. Genesis tells the story of Abraham and Isaac. The Hebrews believed that all Hebrews descended from Abraham, making him the patriarch of this people. According to Genesis, Yahweh called Abraham to sacrifice his son Isaac. Nineteenth-century Danish philosopher and theologian Soren Kierkegaard puzzled over a command that would have made Abraham the murderer of his son, but the story does not end badly. While Abraham prepared to kill Isaac he spotted a ram (a male sheep) entangled in a thicket. Abraham instead sacrificed the sheep, pleasing Yahweh.

Lamb plays an enormous role, according to Exodus, in the Hebrews' escape from Egypt. Apparently the Hebrews had journeyed to Egypt in search of work, but were instead enslaved. They resented their captivity and longed for freedom. At this juncture Moses came to the fore. He was an enigmatic figure. His name is surely Egyptian and not at all Hebrew. Moses must have been Egyptian by birth but possibly a convert to Judaism. Through his interaction with Yahweh, Moses decided to strike Egypt with a series of calamities. The Egyptians bore them all but the last, when Moses told each Hebrew family to sacrifice a lamb. Perhaps the family ate the meat, but the important point is that they painted the lambs' blood on their doors. That night the angel of death did not enter any home with lamb's blood on the door, striking only Egyptian households and killing the firstborn son in each Egyptian family. When the morning revealed this tragedy the pharaoh, likely Ramses the Great (Ramses II), granted the Hebrews permission to leave. He later recanted his decision but by then the Hebrews had fled.

Lamb plays a curious role in the New Testament. Whereas the fish is the symbol of the canonical Gospels, the lamb—a slaughtered but resurrected lamb—symbolizes Jesus in the book of Revelation. The book is strange in relating nothing about Jesus's life. It is a sequence of visions that purport to chronicle Jesus's future doings. As the slaughtered lamb, Jesus holds a sword in his mouth, a strange image, with which he will kill his enemies and usher in a new world. Jesus the lamb is thus concerned with the world not as it is now but as it will be at the end of time. In this sense, Revelation may harken back to the canonical Gospels, which portray Jesus as someone who anticipated the imminent end of the world, at least in the early Gospels, like Mark. Mutton and lamb are thus important because they shaped the rise of Judaism and Christianity.

The Practice of Eating Mutton and Lamb

In prehistory, humans must have hunted sheep before they domesticated them. Because sheep were abundant in western Asia, they must early have supplied an important source of the protein and calories necessary to sustain the robust lives of Stone-Age hunter-gatherers. As foods, mutton and lamb dominated the Old World in prehistory, antiquity, and the Middle Ages. In the Americas, the story was very different. Because sheep were unknown in the Americas before the Columbian Exchange, the Amerindians did not eat mutton and lamb. After the dog, the sheep was the next animal to be domesticated and so gave humans a steady supply of mutton and lamb. These foods were essential to the economy of prehistoric and ancient western Asia and the Mediterranean Basin. In some cultures—namely, what are today Israel and Greece—mutton and lamb played a large role in the diet. In ancient Rome, however, pork was the meat of choice, though mutton and lamb remained important. A diet of mutton and lamb in part made it possible for humans to settle in villages and ultimately to build the first civilizations. In this context, mutton and lamb shaped history in important ways.

The domestication of sheep for mutton and lamb is a source of contention. One line of thought holds that humans domesticated sheep as early as 9000 BCE. Another camp sees this date as the beginning but not the completion of domestication, arguing that domestication took millennia and was not complete until about 7000 BCE. At the end date, humans were breeding sheep for greater mass. That is, humans wanted sheep that yielded more mutton and lamb. By about 3000 BCE, mutton and lamb were available throughout Europe, North Africa, Egypt, the Levant, and western Asia in general.

Toward the Present

In the 16th century the Spanish introduced sheep, and therefore mutton and lamb, into South and Central America. The British, French, and Dutch brought mutton and lamb into North America, though it seems likely that the Spanish introduced these foods into Mexico, leaving what would become the United States and Canada to the British, French, and Dutch. Sheep herds ballooned in places like the pampas of Argentina. Europeans and Argentines hunted these herds and ate large quantities of mutton and lamb. As Americans moved west, they brought sheep into the Great Plains. The desire for mutton and lamb conflicted with farmers' desires to convert the Great Plains into a vast wheat belt. The problem was that the desire for mutton and lamb would precipitate a crisis because sheep graze grasses down to their roots, denuding patches of land. With no native grasses to hold the soil in place, the Great Plains were on the precipice of an ecological disaster. The dearth of rain in the 1930s was the proximate cause of the giant dust storms that plagued the decade. The desire for mutton and lamb shaped the tragedy of the Dust Bowl, one of the great disasters in American history.

Today, mutton and lamb are popular throughout the Muslim world and in Australia, New Zealand, the Caribbean (sometimes known as the West Indies), and India. The worldwide trend, however, is toward decline, as mutton and lamb do not compete well against beef, pork, and chicken. In 2006, the world produced about 14 million metric tons of mutton and lamb. Though the number seems impressive, it pales in comparison to the 61 million metric tons of beef that the world produced that year. In 2006, China yielded about 5 million metric tons of mutton and lamb. Also important were India, Australia, Pakistan, Iran, New Zealand, the United Kingdom, the Sudan, Turkey, and Spain, though all trailed China by a large margin. As late as 1906, the United States had as many as 50 million sheep, but by 2006 the amount had fallen to just over 6 million sheep. Because American stockmen have always raised sheep for meat, with wool being an afterthought, the decline in numbers stems from the fact that Americans do not eat much mutton or lamb. By 2006, mutton and lamb accounted for less than 5 percent of the meat that Americans consumed. The modern mutton and lamb producer often raises sheep almost as a hobby, deriving much of his or her income from a job in a nearby town or city. In the United States, Texas and California are the leading producers of mutton and lamb. The Great Plains and the West in general remain important mutton and lamb producers. In the present United States, mutton and lamb trail beef, pork, chicken, and, surely, canned tuna. Worldwide, mutton and lamb are likely to cede ground to beef and pork. In the United States, mutton and lamb comprise less than 1 percent of farm income. Mutton, lamb, and wool fetch about $460 million per year. It is difficult to specify mutton and lamb income alone because the USDA tabulates its figures to include wool in the aggregate rather than as a separate commodity. The average American eats less than one pound of lamb per year. It is hard to imagine that the consumption of mutton can be larger. In fact, the U.S. mutton and lamb market is superfluous in the sense that America could fill its small need for these meats through imports alone. Mutton and lamb are more important in the diet of people in the developing world than in the developed world. In the developing world, stockmen raise sheep in small herds and so sell small quantities of mutton and lamb. But the income from these sales may be enough to lift people out of poverty.

Further Reading

Chaline, Eric. *Fifty Animals that Changed the Course of History*. Buffalo, NY: Firefly Books, 2011.

Damron, W. Stephen. *Introduction to Animal Science: Global, Biological, Social, and Industry Perspectives*. 5th ed. Boston: Pearson, 2013.

Scanes, Colin. *Fundamentals of Animal Science*. Australia: Delmar, 2011.

N

Nuts

Nuts are among the few foods appreciated over time and geography. Wine, beef, bread (particularly white bread), and several other foods have had their detractors. Nuts, however, have remained popular throughout history. To be sure, a critic might condemn nuts for their high fat content, but this fat is unsaturated. In fact, it is the same fat that is found in fish: omega-3 fatty acids, which have long been thought beneficial against cardiovascular disease, cancer, and other ailments. When humans think of wholesome foods, they often consider nuts in this category.

What Is a Nut?

The definition of a nut seems straightforward. A nut is a drupe, a type of fruit, though it has none of the sweet pulp that surrounds the seeds of what humans are accustomed to call fruits: the peach, pear, tomato, apricot, cherry, apple, watermelon, plum, grapes, and many others. Note that the breeding of seedless grapes or oranges does not diminish their status as fruits. In this respect, the designation of nuts as fruits seems odd, though it is botanically correct. In the 18th century, Swedish naturalist Carl Linnaeus (his name is sometimes rendered Carl von Linné) defined a nut as a seed encased in a "hard skin." One might argue that the encasement is more of a shell than a skin.

Nonetheless it is easy to become confused about what is and is not a nut. Peanuts and Grape-Nuts are good examples of inaccurate names. The peanut, despite its name, is neither a pea nor a nut. It is a legume closely related to the pea, another legume. Grape-Nuts is a type of breakfast cereal that bears no relation to grapes or nuts. Neither grapes nor nuts are ingredients in this cereal. Rather, Grape-Nuts are primarily kernels of barley, a grass that bears no relation to nuts. Obviously we cannot always take names at face value. The person who wishes to

Werner Weber harvests walnuts in his plantation in Ettenheim, Germany. Weber owns about 250 old walnut trees and collects the ripe nuts with seasonal workers. The nuts are cleaned, dried, and sorted into three sizes before they are sold. (AP Photo/Winfried Rothermel)

contemplate "soy nuts" makes the same error. Soy nuts are really soybeans, and soybeans are, like the peanut, a type of legume. Because of this confusion, some botanists have abandoned the term "nut," insisting that it has become so broad and misused as to be devoid of meaning.

Professor Ken Albala retains the term, asserting that nuts are products of a tree. This partial definition excludes peanuts and soybeans and the other legumes with which humans have had an intimate relationship, but it does not rule out oranges, grapefruits, lemons, apples, peaches, and a large number of other fruits. Here, Albala draws the important distinction that a nut must have a hard shell, an assertion that excludes peaches and all the other fruits listed above. Nuts must be edible, a partial definition that excludes very few foods, and they must be crunchy. Again, the criterion of crunchiness may be too broad because it does not exclude Grape-Nuts or granola. But taken together, all parts of Albala's definition appear to hold.

The Origin of Nuts in the Human Diet

It is difficult to know when and where humans began eating nuts, but the origin must have been many millennia ago, well before the advent of agriculture. By

Peanuts versus Nuts

Despite its name, the peanut is not a nut but rather a legume, and so is related to peas, beans, chickpeas, lentils, clover, and vetch. Nuts, in contrast, botanically speaking, are fruits grown on trees rather than on a vine. Both are nourishing, containing protein and essential fatty acids. Peanuts are a single species, but there are numerous species of nuts. Peanuts are native to only South America, whereas various species of nuts may be found in both Old and New Worlds. Nuts appear to have been cultivated before peanuts.

necessity, then, the consumption of nuts must have been part of the hunter-gatherer past of humans. Some experts contend that humans, when they turned to gathering food, selected nuts and berries as the first foods. This diet must have been healthy because the earliest human remains show no sign of dental decay. Nuts therefore shaped the world by being among the first foods that nourished humans. If they did not give rise to civilization, nuts nonetheless made possible the survival of a species that might otherwise have become extinct. One has the sense that we would not be here today without the nuts that fortified our ancestors.

Acorns might have been the first food of the Amerindians who settled the Americas perhaps 12,000 to 14,000 years ago, though some hold out for an even earlier date. Prehistoric Europeans also ate acorns. In the second century CE, Galen, physician to Roman emperor Marcus Aurelius, wrote about a famine that caused the poor to devour their pigs for sustenance. When conditions did not improve, they turned to acorns, making acorn soup with honey and milk, though how and where they got milk during famine is unclear. From this experience Galen concluded that nuts are as nutritious as grains. In fact, in some ways, nuts are more nutritious. They are a better source of protein and of vitamin A and some B vitamins. In the 16th century a French writer, underscoring what was already known, noted that acorns were the first food of humans.

If the acorn was an important nut of the temperate zone, the coconut was an important tropical nut. The tree is ubiquitous along the shorelines of the tropics, especially on the many tropical islands of the Pacific Ocean. Like the acorn, the coconut was esteemed for its nutrients and was known as the "tree that provides all the necessities of life." Coconut water and milk contain an ideal balance of electrolytes to replenish those lost through sweat. The people of Southeast Asia long ago added coconut milk to their diet. Again, the coconut serves to remind the reader that nuts were a primary means of sustenance before the rise of agriculture.

Nuts after the Rise of Agriculture

Even since the rise of agriculture, nuts have remained important. We have noted their nutritional value. Not only are they rich in omega-3 fatty acids, but also many nuts are important sources of vitamins and antioxidants. Some nuts are rich in vitamin A. The hazelnut has folate, a B vitamin. Pistachios contain lutein for the maintenance of healthy eyes. Since antiquity, physicians have been consistent in affirming that nuts are nourishing. Because they are eaten with little processing, they give one the sense of eating a wholesome food in an era of prepackaged, chemically adulterated foods. Nuts are the antidote to the processed foods industry and for this reason are important. One need sample only a few nuts to appreciate their value.

The kola nut is an important stimulant because it contains caffeine. Native to West Africa, the kola nut has been part of the diet for millennia. West Africans chew the nut to gain what appears to be a boost of energy. Actually, however, caffeine contains no calories, so the person who chews a kola nut does not gain energy in terms of calories but rather a stimulant that increases alertness and stamina. These properties are important, perhaps not to the building of civilizations, but to the workaday world where concentration and continual exertion are necessary. In this fundamental sense, nuts shaped history. The kola nut made history as one of the ingredients in the original formula of Coca-Cola, the soft drink that has become a worldwide commodity along with such important beverages as coffee and tea. Muslims chew kola nuts during a fast because the caffeine keeps them alert and does not stimulate the appetite. In this sense, the kola nut is a quasi-religious food and so it is important in the tradition of monotheism. Other Africans have incorporated the kola nut into their religions. In addition, the kola nut is a wedding food in many parts of sub-Saharan Africa. The people of Southeast Asia chew the betel nut to derive a similar effect, though one worries that the nut may cause cancer. Accordingly, the nut is not swallowed.

Another nut, nutmeg, was one of the spices that anchored the lucrative spice trade. The desire for this spice and others fueled Europe, a small inconsequential continent, to explore the rest of the world. This impulse led to the European discovery of the Americas and to the momentous changes that followed in the wake of Italian Spanish explorer Christopher Columbus's voyages. The rise of sugarcane, slavery, racism, industrialism, and imperialism all came from this burst of European expansion, fueled initially by the spice trade. Nutmeg, then, is a nut of great consequence. The Dutch found it in Indonesia, declaring a monopoly on its sale. In the Americas, Europeans planted nutmeg on the Caribbean island of Grenada, which is today the world's leading producer of the nut.

Pecans and corn syrup, both world foods, are the prime ingredients in pecan pie. Cashews are a tropical nut indigenous to equatorial Brazil, the home of pineapple, cacao, cassava, and the coca plant. The people of Sri Lanka tell a story in which God created the universe and all life except the cashew tree. Satan felt that something was amiss, so he created the cashew tree. This story implies that there is something mischievous about cashews, but this sentiment does not resonate with Americans, who can buy them in any Walmart anywhere in the United States. In the 16th century, the Portuguese encountered the cashew tree in Brazil. The nut quickly became part of the Columbian Exchange as the Portuguese planted the tree in Mozambique, Goa, southeastern India, and Malaysia. The Spanish planted cashew trees throughout the Philippines. Today, Nigeria, India, and Vietnam are the world's leading producers.

Pistachios were first a snack food in Iran, from where the United States imported the nut. In the 20th century, production surged in California. No longer did the United States need to import pistachios from Iran. In 2011, the United States banned pistachio imports from Iran, though one cannot imagine that the announcement had any effect because California had long ago driven Iran from the U.S. market. The pistachio is one of many foods that have made California one of the world's great agricultural producers. In building an empire in California, the pistachio has grown in global importance and in this way has shaped history. Like cashews, pistachios can be bought at any Walmart in the United States. Today California is the world's leading producer of pistachios, almonds, and several other nuts.

Further Reading

Albala, Ken. *Nuts: A Global History*. London: Reaktion Books, 2014.

Oats

An annual grass, oats are the sixth most widely grown crop, trailing corn, rice, wheat, barley, and sorghum. At first people grew oats for food, but their suitability as feed led farmers to raise them principally for livestock. Three-quarters of cultivated oats are of the species *Avena sativa*. These are either white or yellow oats, depending on the color of the grain. Farmers plant white oats in April or May, harvesting them in July or August. Farmers in Argentina grow *Avena byzantine*, also known as red oats. Most oats are sown in the spring. Because oats do not tolerate frigid weather they are a winter crop only where winters are mild. The red oats of Argentina are winter oats. Farmers grow spring oats between 35° and 50° north, though they grow winter oats at lower latitudes, between 20° and 40° north.

Oats in Antiquity and the Middle Ages

By one account, oats arose as a weed in the wheat and barley fields of northern Germany. Another tradition holds that oats originated in the eastern Mediterranean and Near East, where farmers first grew them about 2000 BCE. A third hypothesis, noting the diversity of oat species, posits the origin of oats in the Canary Islands, the Mediterranean, the Middle East, or the Himalayan Mountains. A fourth hypothesis suggests that oats arose in the islands of the South Pacific, though this idea has fallen out of favor. As early as 8600 BCE, the people of Syria were consuming oats, though oat cultivation probably came later. The people of southern Jordan ate oats around 7000 BCE and possibly cultivated them as well. In Moldavia and the Ukraine, farmers grew oats as early as 4700 BCE.

By the end of the second millennium oats had spread throughout Europe as the climate cooled and grew wetter. Sometime in antiquity, oats spread to Egypt, surely from other lands of the eastern Mediterranean. From Turkey, oats migrated to Greece in early antiquity. Familiar with oats, Greek physician Hippocrates

An ancient crop, oats were originally a staple in northern Europe, though they have since spread to many other temperate regions. Oatmeal is a healthy breakfast food. (Dave Reede/AgStock Images/Corbis)

believed in the fifth century BCE that they had value as a medicine. In the fourth century BCE, Greek botanist Theophrastus characterized oats as "wild or uncultivated," leading one to suppose that he was unaware of its status as a crop. Relying on this evidence, French botanist Alphonse de Candolle asserted in the 19th century that the Greeks did not cultivate oats in antiquity, though others have challenged this view. In the first century CE, Greek physician Dioscorides believed oats relieved coughs and dried oily skin. The Hebrew may not have grown oats in antiquity, for the Bible does not mention them. There is little evidence that humans grew oats in Britain as late as 1000 BCE, where they may have appeared as a weed in spelt fields. One authority dates the cultivation of oats in Britain to the second century BCE. Another scholar dates the arrival of oats in Britain to the invasion of the Vandals in the fourth century CE, but the historical record does not support this idea. By 100 BCE, farmers were growing oats in Germany, Denmark, and Switzerland, where they cultivated them alongside emmer. In the first century CE, farmers in northern Europe raised oats alongside beans, barley, and flax.

In the second century BCE, Roman agricultural writer Cato did not list oats as a fodder crop, leading one to wonder whether the Romans took full advantage of the crop. In the first century BCE, Roman poet Virgil referred to oats as a weed, suggesting that the Romans, at least the elites, had a low opinion of the grass. In the first century CE, Roman agriculturalist Columella mentioned oats but did not give them much space. In the first century CE, Roman encylopedist Pliny the Elder recognized the value of oats in feeding livestock. Given to erroneous beliefs, Pliny held that barley could transmute into oats in wet climates and soils. Barley that had been dormant too long in the soil might germinate as oats, believed Pliny. In the fifth century CE, theologian Jerome, who apparently thought little of oats, denigrated his opponent, British scholar Pelagius, as an oat eater.

The Romans promoted the cultivation of oats in Britain from the first century CE. Farmers grew oats near encampments of Roman soldiers, suggesting that oats must have fed troops and cavalry horses. This impression gains strength from the fact that, in the second century CE, emperors Trajan and Hadrian imported oats from northern Europe to Britain to feed the cavalry. Trajan and Hadrian must have taken this step because Britain was not self-sufficient in oats. Nevertheless Britons grew enough oats to pay the grain tribute to Rome.

In the eighth century CE, farmers in France grew oats, spelt, and barley. By the 13th century, oats had emerged as a secondary crop in Denmark, trailing rye and barley. The Danes grew oats on unmanured land distant from the village. They regarded oats as suitable only for infertile soils. In northern Europe, farmers raised oats as a spring crop. As a rule, oats yielded less than rye and barley and, as in Denmark, farmers confined the grain to poor soils, exacerbating the problem of low yields. Oats were nonetheless an important crop. In the 12th century, the Count of Flanders, facing famine, forbade the brewing of oats to preserve the crop for human consumption.

In the Middle Ages, by one estimate, oats were the fourth most widely cultivated crop, following wheat, barley, and rye. During this time, oats emerged as the staple of the Scots and so helped shape history and daily life in northern Europe. By the 13th century, and probably earlier, oats were the principal crop of Scotland. The Scots fed oats to sheep and also ate oats as food. In northeastern France, farmers grew oats in a three-year rotation, growing oats in the first year and wheat in the second, and fallowing land in the third. Because farmers did not manure their oats, yields were half that of wheat. In medieval Britain, farmers rotated oats with wheat or barley and fallow. In Scotland, farmers grew oats for two years, followed by barley. Other fields were sown to oats and pasture grasses for livestock.

From the first century CE, the climate cooled in northern Europe and soils became more acidic. Farmers who could no longer raise barley and wheat grew oats instead. The wet, cold climate of the ninth and tenth centuries ceded ground to warm summers between 1250 and 1300. After 1300, temperatures gradually declined, and in this environment oats thrived. In the 14th century the estates of Sussex, England, recorded good harvests. Poorer land, for example the Kent Marshes, was fallowed two years between oat crops. On poor land, farmers grew oats in preference to other grains. In the 14th century, oats were the principal crop in Kent and East Anglia. In medieval Britain, tenants, as they had under Rome, paid rent in oats. Using oats to feed their horses, landlords kept large stables. The fact that even peasants owned horses made essential the growing of oats.

In medieval Britain, oats may have been the most widely grown crop. Records from isolated estates confirm this impression. In 1211, one manor of the Bishop of Winchester yielded thousands of quarters of oats, and lesser amounts of wheat and barley. In 1296, the Earl of Lancaster's Great Sutton Manor harvested hundreds of quarters of oats, and lesser quantities of rye and wheat. In other instances, oats produced a harvest much larger than that of wheat, suggesting that oat acreage was large. In the Middle Ages, farmers grew principally yellow oats, whose grain could be easily removed from the husk. Demand for yellow oats must have been strong because they fetched the same price as wheat. The yield of oats was large on the best land. In 1300, Romney Marsh, England, recorded even larger yields, though an estate in East Kent recorded only a small harvest. Between 1370 and 1399, Lullington Manor, England, yielded several bushels per acre, whereas between 1376 and 1393, Alceston Manor recorded a slightly smaller yield per acre.

Oats were not the leading crop everywhere. Between 1283 and 1348, the Bishop of Winchester's 14 manors yielded more barley than oats and wheat. Fluctuations in weather appear to have affected oats less than other grains. In 1315 and 1316, the Bishop of Winchester saw his wheat yield decline, whereas the oat yield held constant. In 1339 and 1346, wet springs and dry summers caused wheat yields to decline but oat yields appear to have been uniform. In the late Middle Ages, oat yields increased and the wheat harvest decreased, evidence that may point to the possibility that farmers grew oats on good soils whereas they had earlier grown them on marginal land. From an early date, the British distinguished oats by color. They thought the black oats of Westmoreland suitable only for horses. Red oats yielded the best oatmeal and white oats were made into bread and pottage.

Yet as the demand for beer increased some farmers switched from oats to barley. In some instances, clover and other legumes replaced oats in rotation. Nevertheless, oats held their own on the land of Thierry d'Hirecon in Artois, France, where oats were the principal spring crop in the 13th century.

The Fate of Oats in the New World and Beyond

In 1516, the Spanish introduced oats to the island of Hispaniola (now Haiti and the Dominican Republic), probably to feed their horses. One scholar believes that English settlers cultivated oats on Roanoke Island in 1585 and 1586. In 1602, traveler Bartholomew Gosnold planted oats on Cuttyhunk Island near Martha's Vineyard. English settlers were growing oats in New Hampshire and Massachusetts in the 1610s. As early as 1622, farmers grew oats in Newfoundland. In 1626, the Dutch in Manhattan exported oats to the Netherlands. By the 1640s, farmers grew oats throughout New England, though they were not as important as corn, wheat, barley, peas, and rye. By 1650, oats were widespread in New England and by 1660 were grown in Maryland and Virginia. In 1682, farmers grew oats along the Ashley River near Charleston, South Carolina. Initially a spring crop, by the 1750s American farmers were planting oats in the fall as a winter crop. In 1768, Virginia exported oats to the Caribbean. In the 1780s, the enterprising George Washington grew 400 to 500 acres of oats. In the early 19th century, the Spanish introduced oats to the Pacific coast, though before 1840 most oats were grown east of the Mississippi River. In 1839, Virginia, Kentucky, and Tennessee produced a minority of the U.S. oat crop, and as late as 1860, the South produced an even smaller amount of the nation's oats. In the late 19th century, farmers in the West and western Canada were raising large oat crops.

In the United States, the largest oat producers are Iowa, Minnesota, South Dakota, and Wisconsin. Today, oats are grown in Central Asia, Europe, and North America. Smaller amounts of oats are raised in Argentina, Australia, New Zealand, North Africa, and South Africa. Oat production has decreased worldwide in recent years as mechanization has increased. Moreover, the preoccupation with yield has hurt more modestly yielding oats. Once grown in rotation, oats have fared poorly in schemes that emphasize one or a small number of crops. Whereas in the early 20th century farmers had grown oats in the American Midwest, they now prefer corn in rotation with soybeans. Throughout the twentieth century farmers in the U.S. replaced oats with soybeans. This trend accelerated with the diffusion of the tractor. The tractor made it possible for farmers to forgo the horse. Without the need to keep horses, farmers no longer had to grow oats to feed them. Oat acreage declined accordingly. In Canada, farmers devoted their energy to growing high value crops of wheat, barley, and canola. They raised oats almost as an afterthought, planting them late because they were too busy to tend to them earlier. Oat production decreased from 54 million tons in the 1960s to 27 million tons in 2005. Despite this decline, oat production has increased in Russia, Australia, Sweden, and Finland.

Oats as Food

In the first century CE, Pliny reported that the people of Germany and of the Oones Islands in the Baltic Sea consumed oats. Oats must have bulked large in the diet in the Middle Ages and modern era. In 1800, 40 percent of people in Great

Britain did not eat wheat bread and instead subsisted on oats, other grains, and potatoes. Throughout Europe, commoners ate oat or barley bread when wheat bread was expensive. Between 1806 and 1808, the town of Lancaster imported tens of thousands of quarters of oats but far less wheat, leading one to assume that people ate oats in preference to wheat. Some urbanites disdained oats as "vulgar" and "coarse," but their defenders esteemed oats as the food of hardy yeomen and outdoor laborers. Indeed, throughout Wales and Pennine Manor people ate oat bread in preference to wheat bread. Eating up to one stone of oats per week, some Scots ate oatmeal at every meal. In Scotland and Ireland, people ate oat porridge, oatcakes, brewis (oats with broth), biscuits, pudding, muffins, and bread. In the 18th century, the Scots increased their consumption of oats as they decreased their intake of meat. In the 18th century, Scottish economist Adam Smith warned against the consumption of oats, asserting that they produced weaklings and homely people. Yet, in Scotland, even the gentry ate oats, though the food was more deeply ingrained in the diet of commoners. Throughout Europe, commoners ate oatmeal bread and the poor subsisted on oats in gruel and soup. In 1740 and 1741, oat prices more than doubled after the failure of the potato crop in Ireland. The poor were forced to visit soup kitchens for oatmeal soup. In northern Britain, people ate oats, potatoes, and milk. In 1795 the average family in Westmoreland, Great Britain, spent much of its income on oatmeal. By contrast, it spent just a few percent of its income on meat and a bit more on potatoes. In the 19th century, poor factory workers subsisted on oats, potatoes, wheat bread, and cheese. Even the well-to-do ate oats, but only at breakfast along with fish, eggs, tea, or coffee and toast. During the potato famine, English landlords exported oats from Ireland, contributing to the misery of the masses. Whereas oats had sustained them during the 18th-century crisis, the crop was sold abroad during the calamity of the 1840s. In the 19th century, the demand for oats to feed humans declined. Increasingly, urbanites ate wheat bread rather than oats. After 1850, wheat bread was the staple in Wales and northern Britain. After 1875, wheat bread was commonly consumed even in Scotland and Ireland.

In America, colonists ate oats with milk and maple syrup. Judging from 19th-century cookbooks, the absence of recipes for oats suggests that they were not a popular food. In 1859, the cookbook *Cookery As It Should Be* advised the sick and frail to eat oats. As this advice suggests, oats were easier to find in the pharmacy than in the grocery store. This state of affairs began to change in the late 19th century. German immigrant Ferdinand Schumacher, known as the "oatmeal king," promoted the addition of oatmeal to the diet. Manufacturers began to advertise oats as a healthy breakfast cereal. Consumers identified with brand names, the most popular being Quaker Oats. Oatmeal is today the most popular breakfast cereal in the United States. Today, oats are an ingredient in baby foods, pastes, and even pasta. Oat protein is an additive in some beverages. In recent years, manufacturers, keen to advertise the health benefits of their products, have added oats to bread. Although oats are comparatively high in protein they have little gluten, the protein that gives dough its stickiness, and so are not ideal for making bread. Oat breads usually contain 20 to 30 percent oats, whereas multigrain breads have only 5 to 15 percent oats. In addition to bread and other products, granola bars containing oats are popular in Japan.

Today nutritionists tout the value of oats. The possible health benefits of oats may be shaping dietary habits of people worldwide in the temperate zones. With 15 percent protein, oats exceed barley, wheat, corn, and rice. Oats are a source of the minerals manganese, magnesium, calcium, zinc, and copper. In addition, oats have 14 percent of the recommended daily allowance of thiamine, 10 percent of pantothenic acid, and smaller amounts of other vitamins. Since the 1960s, research has reported that the consumption of oats lowers one's cholesterol. One early study documented an 11 percent decline in cholesterol in people who ate oats just three weeks. When the study participants returned to their old diet their cholesterol increased, reinforcing the insight that oats should be a regular part of the diet if one is to receive long-lasting benefits from them. Although regular whole grain oats reduce cholesterol, the greatest benefit derives from the consumption of oat bran. Between 1980 and 1993, scientists conducted 37 studies of the cholesterol-lowering properties of oat bran. Only two of these studies failed to document a reduction in cholesterol. Moreover oats may reduce the incidence of colon cancer. Diabetics benefit from the consumption of oats because a meal of oatmeal increases glucose levels less than a meal of many other foods. By stabilizing glucose levels, oats help diabetics manage their affliction. The media have made much of these benefits, and health-conscious consumers began to add oats to their diet. Between 1984 and 1988, the Dutch doubled their consumption of oats. In 1988 and 1989, Americans more than doubled their intake of oats.

Further Reading

Hughes, Meredith Sayles. *Glorious Grasses: The Grains*. Minneapolis: Lerner Publications, 1999.

Marshall, H. G., and M. E. Sorrells, eds. *Oat Science and Technology*. Madison, WI: American Society of Agronomy, 1992.

Webster, Francis H., ed. *Oats: Chemistry and Technology*. St. Paul, MN: American Association of Cereal Chemists, 1986.

Welch, Robert W., ed. *The Oat Crop: Production and Utilization*. London: Chapman and Hall, 1995.

Olive and Olive Oil

The olive and olive oil were important in the ancient Mediterranean and western Asia. The grandeur of Greece and Rome arose from three pillars: olive oil, wine, and bread. Many of Rome's patricians traced their wealth and power to the olive. General and dictator Julius Caesar was particularly fond of olive oil and General Septimius Severus rose to emperor thanks to the fortune that he and his family had derived from olive oil. In modernity, people have not forgotten the importance of olive oil. The fashionable Mediterranean diet features olive oil at its core and is changing the way humans eat and think about food.

The Characteristics of Olives and Olive Oil

Olive oil is the only worldwide oil to be extracted from a fruit rather than a seed. The fruit in this case is the olive. By contrast, soybean oil, another global product, derives from the soybean, the seed of arguably the world's most important legume. As a rule, olive oil is easier to extract than seed oils because one need only press olives, whereas laborious chemical processes are necessary to extract oil from

The olive has for millennia been the staple source of dietary fat for the peoples of the Mediterranean Basin. The Romans in particular carved a commercial empire out of olive oil and wine. (Gandolfo Cannatella/Dreamstime.com)

seeds. This holds true of the extraction of soybean oil, though soybeans too were once pressed to yield oil.

The source of olive oil is the olive, a fruit of a tree or shrub native to the Mediterranean Basin and western Asia. One of the great contributions to Mediterranean civilizations, the olive thrives in hot semiarid conditions in which many other important trees, citrus for example, cannot survive. The tree may yield progeny in two ways. First, the tree yields suckers that will mature into trees of their own. Pineapple is an example of this phenomenon. Because a sucker grows into a clone of the parent, the danger of genetic uniformity is omnipresent. One may consider the Irish Potato Famine to appreciate the perils of genetic uniformity. Second, an olive yields a seed that grows into a new tree. Containing this single seed, the olive is a drupe, like the cherry, apricot, plum, peach, and nectarine. In this context, the oil in an olive may be an evolutionary adaptation that lured herbivores to consume it, seed and all. When the animal excreted the seed it was covered in excrement, serving as a built-in fertilizer. The seed was thus ready to germinate. In this instance, then, sucker or seed may propagate the olive. Only propagation by seed ensures genetic diversity. Flowering trees like the olive are important because they shaped the scientific study of the means of reproduction and seed dispersal.

Origin and Early Foodways

Probably in the Paleolithic era (the Old Stone Age), humans first began to eat wild olives, though they did not domesticate the tree until the Neolithic era (the New Stone Age). From an early date, the cultivation of the olive was widespread in Spain, southern Gaul (today Mediterranean France), North Africa, Greece, and Palestine (today Israel). The Romans would boast of having given the olive as a gift to the people of the Mediterranean Basin when in fact olive culture was widespread before the rise of Rome. What the Romans did was intensify olive culture, particularly in North Africa. The three pillars of Mediterranean civilizations were the foundation of Rome's grandeur. According to Roman accounts, Julius Caesar was especially fond of olive oil, ordering second helpings of it at the banquets he attended as a way of thanking the matron of the home for inviting him to dinner. In the Mediterranean world no meal was complete without olive oil. Olive oil was the chief fat in the Mediterranean diet. Curiously, given its importance in the diet, olive oil may have first served as skin lotion, being eaten only later.

Through human selection, olive trees came to produce olives with high oil content. Despite the importance of Greece and Rome, Palestine may have been the early center of olive culture. Indeed, the Hebrews memorialize the olive in the story of the great flood. According to Genesis, God decided that humans were so evil that he must destroy them, though he preserved a small remnant of life in an ark while a flood killed everything else. When the flood began to recede, the boat's proprietor, Noah, sent a dove in search of land. The bird returned with an olive branch. The olive thus signified the return of peace and the rejuvenation of life. From an early date, the Egyptians placed olive oil in tombs, perhaps thinking that the dead needed the oil in the afterlife. Pharaoh Ramses the Great (Ramses II) bragged of planting olive trees throughout Egypt.

So versatile was olive oil that in addition to food the Greeks used it as fuel, lotion, a contraceptive, a detergent, a preservative, a pesticide, a perfume, and in several medicinal concoctions. In the ancient Mediterranean Basin, as the Greek example underscores, olive oil had the importance that petroleum does worldwide today. Greek philosopher Plato held his Academy, perhaps the first institution of higher learning, in an olive grove. Greek dramatist Sophocles echoed the Greek belief that the olive was a divine gift. The goddess Athena had planted the first olive tree in Athens. Plato's pupil Aristotle believed that anyone who cut down an olive tree deserved death. Athenian law mandated that its citizens collectively could cut down no more than two trees per year. Revenues from olive oil exports fueled the Spartan army and so furthered the grim pursuit of warfare.

Olives and Olive Oil in Modernity

Today Greeks eat more olive oil than anyone else, at 21 liters per person per year. People on the Greek island of Crete consume some 50 liters of olive oil per year. Behind Greece, Italy ranks a distant second at 13 liters per person per year. Despite widespread publicity in recent years that olive oil is a nutritious fat, the average American eats less than one liter per year, though these numbers have been on the upswing since the 1980s. Olives, once a symbol of peace, have been an instrument of economic war. In the 21st century, particularly after 2005, Israeli soldiers have uprooted millions of olive trees in the West Bank, depriving thousands of Palestinians of their livelihood. In this context is it surprising that so much animus exists between Jews and Palestinians? In the Levant, then, olives have been a weapon and in this context have shaped this sensitive part of the world.

In modernity as in antiquity, olives and olive oil are the sources of fortunes. If Septimius Severus rose to emperor thanks to his family fortune in olive oil, modern industrial agriculture treats olives and olive oil as the queen of profits, the creator of massive wealth. Olive oil from Italy appears to have a magical allure and is coveted worldwide as is no other vegetable oil, though strictly the olive is not a vegetable but rather a fruit. In the olive one glimpses the centuries of conflict between olive oil in the Mediterranean Basin and lard in northern Europe. Here again the olive is a source of tension. Today olive oil is so ubiquitous that Walmart sells several brands of it.

Olive Oil and the Mediterranean Diet

Olive oil may be responsible for a dietary revolution that is changing the world. After World War II, American epidemiologist and physician Ancel Keys observed that people who consumed olive oil were less susceptible to cardiovascular disease than lard-loving Americans. Surprisingly, this phenomenon holds true even when Mediterranean people eat more fat than Americans. Because olive oil does not contain saturated fat or cholesterol, it is a healthy fat. Keys began a crusade, urging that Americans and northern Europeans adopt a Mediterranean diet of olive oil, fish, bread, fruit, vegetables, and pasta, along with some dairy products and wine. Keys's views came at a difficult moment. During the 1970s, the U.S. Congress and U.S. Department of Agriculture (USDA) declared war on fat of any kind. Even olive oil was not safe from criticism. Yet many scientists did not budge, insisting that olive oil was a healthy fat. Even more, it has proven difficult to link the consumption of fat to heart disease, cancer, and obesity. The last point seems counterintuitive given that fat has twice the calories by weight as carbohydrates or protein.

In Keys's work lies the origin of today's Mediterranean diet, which features olive oil at its core. Curiously, this Mediterranean diet may not actually exist because the peoples of the Mediterranean world are not homogeneous but have their own culinary traditions. In fact, the Islamic parts of the eastern Mediterranean, like Turkey, and of North Africa, like Libya, consume more animal fat than olive oil. What today's nutritionists call the Mediterranean diet is relevant only to Greece, southern Italy, and Spain. If olive oil has succeeded, it has done so because of the tensions between opposites, between good and bad fats. Olive oil is good. Lard, butter, cheese, and whole milk are bad. Once fats were branded in this way, triumph crowned olive oil. In the 1980s, the tomato was added to the list of food that comprised the Mediterranean diet. In retrospect, it seems surprising that this connection was not made earlier. One should note that the Mediterranean diet is plant-based rather than erected on an edifice of meat. In the Mediterranean diet, fish appears to serve as the primary source of protein. In the Mediterranean diet, the olive is important not only for its cardiovascular benefits but as a source of vitamin E. Americans are participating in this diet. Between 1982 and 1994, the consumption of olive oil nearly quadrupled in the United States.

Further Reading

Bartolini, Giorgio, and Raffaella Petruccelli. *Classification, Origin, Diffusion and History of the Olive*. Rome: Food and Agriculture Organization, 2002.
Bitting, K. G. *The Olive*. Chicago: Glass Container Association of America, 1920.

Food and Agriculture Organization. *Modern Olive Production*. Rome: Food and Agriculture Organization, 1977.

Lanza, Fabrizio. *Olive: A Global History*. London: Reaktion Books, 2011.

Mueller, Tom. *Extra Virginity: The Sublime and Scandalous World of Olive Oil*. New York and London: W. W. Norton, 2012.

Train, John. *The Olive Tree of Civilization*. Woodbridge: Antique Collectors' Club, 2004.

Onion

A perennial bulb grown as an annual, the onion is a member of the Amaryllis family and is related to garlic, leek, shallot, and chive. The species name, *Allium cepa*, may derive from the Latin *cepa* or *caepa*, meaning "onion." It is also possible that onion derives from the Celtic *cep*, meaning "head," probably a reference to the shape of the bulb. From the Latin or Celtic are derived the Polish *cebula*, the Spanish *cebolla*, the Italian *cipolla*, the Czech *cibula*, and possibly the Scottish *sybo*. In the first century CE, Roman agricultural writer Columella referred to the onion as *unionem*, the source of the French *oigam* and the English *onion*. The Dutch called the onion *ui*, and the Germans, *zwiebel*. The Chinese *yang cong* means "foreign onion" and may refer to the fact that the onion is not indigenous to China. The Greeks knew the onion as *bolbos*, from which derives the word "bulb." From *bolbos* the Romans derived *bulbus*. It appears, therefore, that the Romans had two words for onion: *unionen* and *bulbus*. The onion is 86 percent water, 11 percent carbohydrates, 1.4 percent protein, 0.8 percent fiber, and 0.2 percent fat, and has vitamins A and C, niacin, riboflavin, thiamine, and calcium. As a seasoning, onion trails only butter, salt, and pepper. The onion is grown worldwide in the subtropics and temperate locales. In addition to the common onion, gardeners grow the ever-ready onion, the potato onion, and the tree onion.

Origin and History

The wild ancestor of the onion is extinct, suggesting the antiquity of cultivation. One authority believes that it is no longer possible to pinpoint the origin of the onion. Another places its origin in Iran, western Pakistan, Turkestan, Uzbekistan, and Mongolia. An Islamic legend holds that Satan, after tempting Adam and Eve, left Eden. In the print of his right foot grew an onion. Where his left foot trod grew a garlic bulb. With such a diabolical origin, one wonders whether the onion was fit for consumption. Yet it has a long history as a food plant. Humans may have cultivated the onion as early as 5000 BCE. The Egyptians began growing the onion

Like garlic, the onion is receiving renewed scrutiny for its health benefits. The tendency to refer to onion as a vegetable obscures the fact that it is a bulb. (Ivonne Wierink/Dreamstime.com)

about 3200 BCE. In the fifth century BCE, Greek historian Herodotus remarked that the Egyptians spent 1,600 silver talents (worth $30,000 today) on onions, garlic, and radishes to feed the pyramid builders. The elites of Egypt included onions in their feasts. Regarding it as a sacred plant, the Egyptians offered the onion to the dead at funerals by 2800 BCE. Placing onions on altars, the Egyptians offered them to the gods during religious rites. They entombed onions with the dead, placing them in the thorax, the pelvis, and the ears; near the eyes; and on the soles of the feet. Egyptian tomb paintings included the onion, probably because it was a sacred plant. Egyptian priests did not eat onions during religious festivals, perhaps because they were sacred. It is also possible that religious law forbade priests from eating onions during certain times of the year. The Egyptians believed that onions had a soul, a belief that second-century-CE Roman poet Juvenal mocked.

The Hebrews apparently encountered the onion during their captivity in Egypt. Exodus recorded the complaint that the Hebrews had only manna to eat in the wilderness. They yearned for the onions and other vegetables that they had known in Egypt. Greek physician Hippocrates (460–377 BCE) knew of the onion, though his knowledge may have been secondhand if it is true that only in the mid-fourth century did the army of Greek conqueror Alexander the Great introduce the onion from Egypt to Greece. Alexander adopted the Egyptian belief that the onion gave one strength and courage, and so he fed it to his soldiers. First-century-CE Greek physician Dioscorides and fifth-century Irish cleric Palladius were also familiar with the onion.

In the 1490s, Spanish Italian explorer Christopher Columbus introduced the onion to the Caribbean town of Isabella. Following the Spanish, European immigrants brought varieties of onion to the New World. In the 17th century, the Iroquois cultivated onions in New York. In 1634, American author William Wood wrote that the people of Massachusetts grew onions. The dehydration of onions, which reached a commercial scale during the U.S. Civil War, made available onion flakes, onion powder, onion salt, onion rings, and onion dip. Manufacturers added onion to instant soup, tomato sauce, and ketchup. The Brazilians used onion as a spice. Hondurans used it as an herb. Outside the Americas, Filipinos, like many other people, used onion to season food. In Africa, people used onion to repel insects, believing it effective against moths and mosquitoes.

Health

Like oats and garlic, onion is shaping dietary habits as its nutritional value comes to the fore. A first-century-CE Indian medical text, the *Carake-Semihita*, recommended the onion as a diuretic. According to the author it improved digestion and the function of the eyes and heart, and treated rheumatism. Yet Indians thought onions were not a proper food for holy people. Brahmans, Buddhists, Hindu widows, and Jains did not eat onions. The ancients used onions to treat cough, the common cold, croup, wounds, boils, pimples, ulcers, sores, hemorrhoids, rheumatism, gout, epilepsy, worms, asthma, tuberculosis, and other maladies. In the 16th century, British herbalist John Gerard reiterated several of these uses. He believed that onions could treat obesity and baldness. Gerard recommended that a person who was losing his hair should stand in the sun while rubbing onion juice on the scalp to stimulate the hair follicles. In his most enthusiastic vein, Gerard wrote: "it [the onion] is cherished everywhere in kitchen gardens." Yet Gerard tempered his enthusiasm, complaining that onions caused headache and flatulence, injured the eyes, and made one groggy. It is difficult to know what effect his pronouncements had on the English. Demand apparently exceeded supply in England, which imported onions from Spain. In 1877, the U.S. Dispensatory of Medicine remarked that onion oil aided digestion, treated bronchitis, and functioned as a diuretic.

The Greeks believed that the onion was an aphrodisiac, a belief that persisted in Britain into the early modern era. In ancient Thrace in southeastern Europe, the guests at a wedding gave onions to the bride and groom to ensure their fertility. Some people believed that onions remove freckles. Chileans believed that the onion was a stimulant. In the Bahamas, people rubbed onion juice on the chest to relieve congestion. It was believed that, placed in the shoes, onions cured the common cold. The people of Trinidad boiled an onion in water, inhaling the steam to treat cough, the common cold, and tuberculosis. In the Yucatan, people mashed onions, using them to treat scorpion and spider bites. In Curacao, people put the neck of an onion in an ear to treat earache and ringing in the ears. They used onion peels to disinfect rooms. The Chinese ate peeled onion fried in peanut oil to relieve constipation. They used onion juice to treat spider bites and protect plants from diseases. One herbalist believed that onions stimulate the appetite and help one fall asleep at night. Herbalists used onions to treat bronchitis. Onion soup was reputed to treat infections of the chest. Home remedies enlisted the onion to treat anemia and infections of the stomach and urinary tract. Onions were grated and rubbed on joints to treat rheumatism. Rubbed on insect bites, onions reduced pain and inflammation. Despite these putative benefits, the onion may cause heartburn.

Further Reading

Brewster, James L. *Onions and Other Vegetable Alliums*. Wallingford, UK: CABI, 2008.

Comin, Donald. *Onion Production*. New York: Judd, 1946.

Coonse, Marian. *Onions, Leeks, and Garlic: A Handbook for Gardeners*. College Station: Texas A&M University, 1995.

Griffith, Linda, and Fred Griffith. *Onions, Onions, Onions*. Shelburne, VT: Chapters Publishers, 1994.

Jones, Henry A., and Louis K. Mann. *Onions and Their Allies: Botany, Cultivation, and Utilization*. New York: Interscience Publishers, 1963.

Moon, Rosemary. *Onions, Onions, Onions*. Buffalo, NY: Firefly Books, 2000.

Platt, Ellen Spector. *Garlic, Onion, and Other Alliums*. Mechanicsburg, PA: Stackpole Books, 2003.

Rabinowitch, Haim D., and James L. Brewster, eds. *Onions and Allied Crops*. Boca Raton, FL: CRC Press, 1990.

Rogers, Mara Reid. *Onions: A Celebration of the Onion through Recipes, Lore, and History*. Reading, MA: Addison-Wesley, 1995.

Woodward, Penny. *Garlic and Friends: The History, Growth and Use of Edible Alliums*. Cincinnati, OH: Hyland House, 1996.

Orange Juice

Extracted from the orange, a citrus fruit native to the Old World tropics, orange juice is often portrayed as a health food. It is rich in vitamin C, potassium, and some antioxidants. Its detractors, however, assert that one would do better by eating an orange rather than drinking its juice, because in eating an orange one gets the fiber of which the juice alone is bereft. Sometimes loaded with sugar, orange juice may be more caloric than an orange, but to the extent that one drinks orange juice as part of a healthy diet, orange juice may be shaping the diet and daily life by promoting a wholesome lifestyle and eating habits. Oranges and orange juice are, we have seen, rich in vitamin C, thiamine, riboflavin, niacin, pantothenic acid, vitamin B_6, folic acid, calcium, iron, magnesium, phosphorus, potassium, and zinc. One serving of orange juice has 12 percent of the recommended daily allowance of folic acid. The body that is nourished by oranges and orange juice readily absorbs iron. In addition to vitamins and minerals, oranges contain antioxidants that may protect against cancer. The consumption of oranges and orange juice lowers a person's cholesterol and may reduce the rise of stroke. Yet fresh orange juice loses 70 percent of its vitamin C in seven hours. The freezing of juice to make concentrate destroys some of the antioxidants. Some manufacturers compromise the nutritional value of orange juice by adding corn syrup or beet sugar. These ingredients sweeten orange juice but they also add unwanted calories. The consumption of too much orange juice of this kind may cause obesity.

Orange Juice Shapes the Americas

Although the orange is an Old World fruit, it may exert its greater influence in the Americas. It seems possible that, centuries ago, people in the Old World tropics might have squeezed and drank juice from oranges. The problem is that the earliest evidence for orange juice dates to 18th-century North America rather than from the Old World. At its origins, orange juice was part of a movement toward citrus fruits. The American colonists were partial to citrus fruits, especially oranges, lemons, and limes. It is curious to omit grapefruits, which were the only citrus fruit to have an American pedigree, having arisen as a sport in the Caribbean islands, possibly Jamaica. The Caribbean islands of Bermuda and the Bahamas exported citrus fruits to North America, which then had no tropical or subtropical lands of its own to grow citrus trees. Because of the cost of transit and the perishability of the fruits, only the affluent could afford citrus, which was available only from January to June. In 1742, an advertisement in a Massachusetts newspaper called attention to the availability of orange juice for $1 per gallon, then a high price.

In 1821, the United States bought Florida from Spain and erected a citrus empire. Yet prices remained high because of transit costs. In 1850, the United States admitted California as a state, adding a new citrus empire in the West. The United States finally had its tropical, subtropical, and Mediterranean climates necessary to sustain citrus culture. Yet the maturation of these empires would take time. Because of high shipping costs, most California and Florida oranges were eaten fresh locally. The proliferation of railroads by the 1880s lowered rates, allowing shipping throughout the United States. The rapid plantings of new orange trees caused a glut of oranges and orange juice by 1900. The rise of Sunkist in 1908 led to an expansion in the market for orange juice. By 1914, Sunkist had orange juice vendors throughout the United States. Restaurants began to serve orange juice as a standard beverage, often for breakfast. Sunkist adopted the slogan "Drink an Orange." The company promoted the wholesomeness and health benefits of orange juice and contracted grocers to carry it. Sunkist advertised orange juice on radio, in schools, on subways and trolleys, and in cinema and magazines. The company appealed to science to bolster its claims that orange juice, full of vitamin C, was good for drinkers.

Orange Julius stands sold orange juice throughout the United States on the eve of the Great Depression. Between 1920 and 1940, the consumption of orange juice tripled in the United States. By 1935, orange growers sold 2 million cans of orange juice per year. In 1940, the average American drank 7 gallons of orange juice per year. During World War II, the demand for metals forced orange juice makers to turn to frozen concentrate. Yet not all Americans liked the taste or color. Concentrate then had little aesthetic appeal. During the war, orange growers also developed powdered orange juice, to which one simply added water. In this form, orange juice nourished American soldiers, sailors, and marines, and those of our allies. After the war, Minute Maid turned to frozen concentrate that tasted and looked better than earlier variants. By 1960, the United States consumed 5 billion pounds of frozen concentrate.

During the 20th century, orange growers processed an ever-larger fraction of their harvest into orange juice. In the early 20th century, pasteurization killed the bacteria that might have otherwise made orange juice unsafe. Trucks brought orange juice to northern and midwestern markets, expanding the reach of orange growers. In the aftermath of the Spanish flu, the last great pandemic to engulf the United States and the rest of the world, mothers wanted to give their children food and drink that would ward off contagion. When physicians recommended orange juice these mothers bought copious quantities of the liquid. Health-conscious Americans appreciated the benefits of orange juice. By the 1920s, orange juice had become a popular breakfast beverage. By then orange juice came chiefly from Florida, which produced the juiciest oranges. California, in contrast, produced oranges with less juice that were sold as fresh produce. In 1950, half Florida's orange crop went to juice, whereas in California the figure was one-quarter. The United States processed several percent of oranges into juice in 1934, the figure rose to more than half of all oranges worldwide in 1953.

This increase owed much to the baby boom. The post-World War II increase in the birthrate spurred the consumption of orange juice. Parents who had been reared on orange juice fed it to their children in turn. In the 1940s, manufacturers began to make orange juice from frozen concentrate. Between 1945 and 1960, the consumption of orange juice tripled in the United States. In 1999, the average American drank several gallons of orange juice. To keep pace with this consumption, a factory can produce several hundred gallons of orange juice per minute. The beverage nets billions of dollars in revenue per year in the United States. Brazil is the world's largest producer of orange juice, totaling the majority of the world's output. Coca-Cola buys juice from Brazil, selling it under the Minute Maid label. Anxious to prevent Brazil from gaining too large a share of the market, Florida growers convinced Congress to impose a tariff on Brazilian juice in the early 21st century. The wealthiest Brazilian planter, Jose Cutrale, responded by purchasing orange trees in Florida, thereby circumventing the tariff. With land in Brazil and Florida, Cutrale has millions of orange trees. Florida and São Paulo, Brazil, total nearly all the world's production of orange juice. Brazil grows twice the number of oranges that Florida does. Because labor is cheap, growers in São Paulo employ tens of thousands of workers to pick oranges by hand. The mechanical tree shaker is not widespread. São Paulo reaps several billion dollars in revenue annually from the sale of orange juice. The people of the United States, Denmark, Honduras, the Philippines, Jamaica, and Trinidad and Tobago drink orange juice at breakfast. Today about 95 percent of U.S. oranges go to make juice.

Further Reading

Hamilton, Alissa. *Squeezed: What You Don't Know about Orange Juice*. New Haven, CT: Yale University Press, 2009.

Hyman, Clarissa. *Oranges: A Global History*. London: Reaktion Books, 2013.

Laszlo, Pierre. *Citrus: A History*. Chicago: University of Chicago Press, 2007.

McPhee, John. *Oranges*. New York: Farrar, Straus and Giroux, 2000.

Patil, Bhimanagouda S., Nancy D. Turner, Edward G. Miller, and Jennifer S. Brodbelt. *Potential Health Benefits of Citrus*. Washington, DC: American Chemical Society, 2006.

Smith, Andrew F. *Drinking History: Fifteen Turning Points in the Making of American Beverages*. New York: Columbia University Press, 2013.

South America, Central America, and the Caribbean, 2007. London: Routledge, 2006.

Train, John. *The Orange: Golden Joy*. Easthampton, MA: Antique Collectors' Club, 2006.

Wilson, Ted, and Norman J. Temple, eds. *Beverages in Nutrition and Health*. Totowa, NJ: Humana Press, 2004.

Organic Foods

Organic foods are grown without chemical inputs. Such foods may not be genetically modified. Under the conditions of modern agribusiness, most foods do not qualify as organic. Some partisans portray organic foods as a fresh, new approach to agriculture, when the current interest in these foods is a recrudescence rather than a novelty. Although the current state of affairs has deep roots, it would be incorrect to suppose it a worldwide revolution. There are significant regions of the world where conventional agriculture and conventional foods prevail. Despite interest in organic foods, most U.S. farms produce food with the assistance of synthetic chemicals and genetically engineered (GE) crops and livestock. The real organic revolution was the Neolithic Revolution itself. The foods of prehistory and most of history were all organic. There was no notion that food production could be otherwise.

The Origin and Importance of Organic Foods

The trend toward organic foods is and is not a recent phenomenon. It is not, because throughout almost their entire tenure on earth, humans, and the hominids that predated them, ate foods harvested or raised without the application of synthetic chemicals. Such technologies did not exist and no one foresaw them. These foods were organic by definition. If humans lacked synthetic fertilizers, they had manure from a variety of animals (including humans), which was valued by Chinese, Egyptian, and Roman antiquity. In fact, the Roman agricultural writers were advocates of manure, comparing the value of that from various animals, including birds. If humans had no herbicides, they leveraged their labor to weed the soil, arduous but necessary work. If humans had no pesticides, they had to gamble that locusts or other pests would not devour their crops. In Exodus, the Hebrews concretized the fear of insect damage to crops. Although humans were at the mercy of nature, the harvest of organic foods was large enough to free a small portion of the population to engage in other pursuits. This move toward specialization led to the rise of the first civilizations. Chinese civilization arose from the bounty of rice. Andean civilizations arose from the fecundity of the potato. One might multiply examples, but the point is that organic foods made possible the rise of civilizations throughout the world. In this respect one can hardly overstate the importance of the organic food revolution, which was the original Neolithic Revolution. Yet the production of organic foods had limits. Even at the height of the Roman Empire the surplus of food was never above 10 percent of the harvest, a fact that confined 90 percent of the population to the farm. Rome managed to mushroom to 1 million inhabitants by the time of Jesus, but this was only possible because Rome commandeered the grain harvest from Sicily and Egypt to secure its population in the capital.

The Movement away from Organic Foods

The small surplus that organic agriculture made possible tempted educated people, many of them scientists or gentlemen farmers, to speculate about ways to boost food production. Early efforts focused on the keeping of more livestock to produce more manure, but this idea was still squarely within the compass of organic agriculture and the production of organic foods. In the 19th century, however, these intellectuals made decisive strides away from organic foods. In the 1840s, German chemist Justus von Liebig was among the first to promote the use of synthetic fertilizers, emphasizing the importance of fertilizers with the big three: nitrogen, potassium, and phosphorus. The first synthetic pesticides also dated to the 19th century, but their effectiveness was limited. Most were arsenic compounds, arsenic being a lethal element. An insect would only succumb to arsenic if it ate a part of foliage sprayed by arsenic compounds. Where arsenic did not adhere to leaves or other structures, predatory insects could feed all day without ill effect. The problem was particularly acute for insects, usually larvae, that burrowed into a plant, penetrating to a depth arsenic compounds did not reach. The depredations of the European corn borer were a manifestation of this problem.

In the 20th century came the crucial breakthroughs, the triumph of food produced with synthetic chemicals. Unlike the previous generation of insecticides, DDT, in widespread use in the 1940s, killed on contact. Insects no longer needed to ingest the poison to die. Merely touching a foot on a plant structure sprayed with DDT was enough to kill the insect. The U.S. Department of Agriculture (USDA), the land-grant universities, and the agricultural experiment stations all championed DDT as a superior insecticide. These agencies sprayed barns with DDT, allowing an astonished public to tour them without the presence of any insects. The public concluded that DDT was magic and that the new breed of chemists had magical powers. Even more deadly pesticides followed the release of DDT. The 20th century also witnessed the rise of a new generation of herbicides, though until the biotechnology revolution the danger remained that herbicide drift might injure or kill a crop plant. The 20th century also witnessed a takeoff in the use of synthetic fertilizers and the technologies to deliver them. The late 20th and early 21st centuries brokered a new merging of science and technology with the advent of biotechnology. Again, one might multiply examples, but one example should suffice. The American agrochemical company Monsanto manufactures the herbicide known as Roundup. A broad-spectrum herbicide, Roundup killed weeds of all classes. Its nature as a broad-spectrum herbicide led to the danger that it could kill crops as well. In the late 20th and early 21st centuries, Monsanto solved the problem by engineering corn, soybeans, sugar beets, and other crops that metabolized Roundup and accordingly did not die from it. Farmers could now spray their fields with abandon, compounding the problem of over-reliance on synthetic chemicals. The Green Revolution and biotechnology revolution depended on synthetic chemicals and genetic manipulation on a scale that was new in human history. With a population of 7 billion people, earth seems to be locked into this system of production because it appears to be the only way to sustain such huge numbers of people. This type of agriculture and the food it produces, now known as conventional agriculture, may be the only way to avert the Malthusian crisis.

The Recrudescence of Organic Foods

Because conventional agriculture is neither biologically nor environmentally neutral, critics emerged in the 20th century to attack it. The DDT miracle was short lived as scientists quickly noted the phenomenon of insect resistance. This phenomenon was an evolution adaptation that British naturalist Charles Darwin might have predicted were he alive. It seems surprising that scientists were initially so Pollyannaish about DDT when they should have seen the inevitable. In her influential book *Silent Spring*, American biologist Rachel Carson in 1962 galvanized the public's attention about the dangers of conventional agriculture, particularly its use of synthetic chemicals. Perhaps more than anyone before her Carson made clear the dangers of human reliance on conventional foods. The activists who followed her advocated the abandonment of these agrochemicals and instead focused on the production of organic foods. The over-reliance on these chemicals has produced ecological crises. In 2014, for example, the runoff of fertilizers, herbicides, and pesticides created a toxic mixture in Lake Erie. Able to feed on these chemicals, algae multiplied in the lake. They produced a toxin that entered the water supply to Toledo, Ohio, making the water unsafe to drink for two days. Near-panic ensued as stores sold out their stocks of bottled water. These agro-chemicals also contaminate groundwater. The over-reliance on synthetic fertilizers has led farmers to deplete the soil of organic matter, robbing it of its natural fertility.

Genetic engineering has caused alarm as well. GE corn known as StarLink created controversy. In the 1990s, Monsanto derived the first of its genetically engineered corns, known as Bt corns, resistant to the European corn borer. Problematically, some Bt lines are effective against only the first brood of the European corn borer. Farmers in states like Iowa, where first and second broods are both omnipresent, did not grow these Bt lines. To their credit, Bt lines give greater protection against insects than insecticides had. Yet this fact did not pre-vent controversy. In the United States and Europe the infamous StarLink contro-versy wrecked one Bt line of corn. The cautious U.S. Environmental Protection Agency (EPA) refused to approve StarLink for human consumption because of fears that it might irritate the stomach, approving StarLink only to feed livestock. Because the vast majority of corn feeds livestock rather than humans, this ruling did not disconcert corn growers. In 2000, however, reports surfaced that Kraft Foods had used StarLink, probably inadvertently, to make taco shells, prompting the EPA to order a recall. StarLink was now infamous. Monsanto stopped selling it. Simply put, Americans and Europeans do not trust GE foods.

As farmers began to sell organic foods in the 1980s, consumers responded. By the 1990s, the market for organic foods had increased 20 percent per year in the United States. Because organic food requires much labor to substitute for chemicals, it tends to command a high price, making it the food of affluent peo-ple. The masses in the developed world continue to rely on conventional foods. One's education and income are the best predictors of organic food consumption. The high price of organic foods may lure farmers to move in the direction of or-ganic food production. Organic foods now compete with conventional foods for space on the grocer's shelves. The absence of GE foods from the lexicon of or-ganic agriculture tempts Americans and Europeans, already suspicious of GE foods, to welcome organic foods. Moreover, surveys reveal that Americans prefer the taste of organic foods. Nowhere is this truer than with the tomato. Conventional agriculture yields a hard, durable, green sphere that is artificially reddened but contains few nutrients and no flavor. Organic tomatoes, by contrast, are vine rip-ened to the peak of nutrients and flavor. Locally grown organic produce is diffi-cult to resist even if it is more expensive. If the United States is a leader in the organic food movement, Europe, Japan, New Zealand, and Australia are all on board.

Small farmers in the developing world are not easy to classify. Necessity demands that some produce organic foods because they cannot afford chemical inputs. Others, however, do grow GE rice or corn, disqualifying them from being organic producers. As a rule, the smaller the farm, the more likely it is to produce organic food.

Further Reading

Lumpkin, N. *Organic Farming*. Ipswich, UK: Farming Press, 1990.

Valenzuela, Hector. "Organic Food." In *Encyclopedia of Food and Culture*. Vol. 3. Edited by Solomon H. Katz. Detroit: Thomson and Gale, 2003, 21-24.

P

Palm Oil

Palm oil derives from the oil palm, an equatorial tree that is seldom cultivated above 10° latitude north and south. The tree is prolific, being among the flora's best sources of oil. In fact, no other crop yields as much oil per unit of land than oil palm. Palm oil is often classified as a vegetable oil, vegetable in this case serving as a catchall world. Strictly speaking, palm oil does not derive from a vegetable but rather from the fruit of the oil palm. In a similar way, soybean oil is also not a vegetable oil but the oil from a seed. The oil palm is among a rare class of trees that yields two oils: palm oil, as discussed, and palm kernel oil. Palm oil may be unique in containing both saturated and unsaturated fatty acids. Nutritionists warn against the consumption of saturated fats. Palm oil is prized for its range of uses, being suitable for making soap, candles, margarine, shortening, cooking oils, salad dressing, creamer for coffee, and other products. Bread, biscuits, confectionaries, pastries, ink, and cosmetics may contain palm oil. Palm oil is not simply empty calories but rather contains vitamins A and E, the first an important nutrient given its shortage in the developing world where the oil palm is grown. The body will absorb all fat-soluble vitamins, including A, E, and D, in the presence of palm oil.

The Margarine Controversy

Margarine is a comparatively recent food. For millennia, humans had consumed butter as a chief dietary fat. Dairy farmers, who depended on butter sales for part of their livelihood, confronted a crisis in the early 20th century with the arrival of margarine. Margarine is not an animal fat, like butter or ghee, but rather a composite of "vegetable" oils. Palm oil is ideal for making margarine and so was early and often used for this purpose. Dairy farmers objected that the makers of margarine tried to pass off their product as a butter substitute when it did not have the prosperities of

Palm oil derives from the oil palm, a tree of the tropics. This image, deriving from Malaysia, gives one a glimpse of the tree's importance to tropical Asia. (Tan Kian Yong/Dreamstime.com)

butter. They insisted on strict labeling of margarine so that consumers could easily tell that the product was not butter. In many cases, margarine makers were eager to comply, noting that butter was purely saturated fat whereas palm oil margarine was partly unsaturated fat. Moreover, as we have seen, palm oil has important nutrients, though one may make the same claim for butter or ghee. The point palm oil margarine makers wished to emphasize was that palm oil was in no way nutritionally inferior to butter or ghee.

The Dynamic between Palm Oil and Soybean Oil

Not only did palm oil compete with butter and ghee, but it also locked horns with soybean oil in a competition between two very different worlds. An acre of oil

Oil Palm

The oil palm, the source of palm oil, is a tree of the Old World tropics. Its cultivation is intensive in Southeast Asia. As a rule, land that is suitable for rubber trees is also fine for oil palm. The tree is often a crop of small farmers and so diversifies income, in some cases providing the majority of a farmer's cash. In this case palm oil is a cash crop, whereas the farmer may tend to subsist on rice. Some authorities regard the oil palm as an ecologically friendly crop because the tree absorbs much carbon dioxide and emits oxygen.

palm produces about 10 times the oil as an acre of soybeans, so from the outset palm oil has been more abundant, particularly in the tropics. Palm oil was the product of tropical Africa and Asia, though the Columbian Exchange widened its appeal to tropical America. Soybean oil, on the other hand, was the product of the temperate zone, particularly in the developed world. Countries like the United States have a large stake in obtaining consistent and large profits from soybean oil. The soybean plant itself is one of the pillars upon which farmers in the American Midwest built the Corn Belt. Coming from different regions of the world and with different properties, palm oil and soybean oil have had to compete for market share in the global economy. The advantage appears to go to palm oil, which does not need to be hydrogenated, as soybean oil must, to increase shelf life. Accordingly, as a rule, palm oil may be stored longer than soybean oil.

Is Palm Oil Just Another Excuse for Junk Food?

About 90 percent of the world's palm oil is processed to make edible fats. Palm oil is a basic ingredient in frying oils and so is used to fry potato, corn, and tortilla chips; crackers; cookies; pastries; donuts; french fries; and some noodles. It is added to ice cream and mayonnaise. Palm oil is ideal as a frying agent because it tolerates the high temperatures necessary to fry foods. Potato chips fried in palm oil may store six months before purchase. As a frying oil, palm oil is sometimes blended with sunflower oil. Palm oil may be added to whipped cream and "diet" and "specialty" margarines. Palm oil shortening is suitable for making bread and other baked goods, though one wonders why the oil obtained from the wheat germ does not suffice to make bread without additional calories. Palm oil is also used to make vanaspati, the principal dietary fat of western Asia, India, and Pakistan, and in this case competes with ghee. In this case, palm oil is hydrogenated and so supplies a fat that cannot claim the best nutritional properties. Vanaspati, not surprisingly, melts between 37°C and 39°C, the melting point of palm oil. Palm oil also competes with cocoa butter, a product of the cacao tree, another equatorial tree.

The perpetuation of potato chips and other calorie-dense foods is shaping history, though not for the better. The problem in the developed world is that too many people eat too much of these foods, which deserve the label of junk food. At the same time, the inhabitants of the developed world rely on the automobile and labor-saving devices to ease the burdens of life, becoming more sedentary in the process. One survey suggests that only about 3 percent of Americans get 20 minutes of exercise three times per week. The consumption of so many calories and the expenditure of so few are causing a health care crisis. Heart disease, diabetes, and obesity have compromised the health of many. One cannot put all the blame on palm oil, but in its widespread use in the preparation of junk foods, it deserves part of the blame.

Palm Oil in the 21st Century

In 2007, Malaysia, Indonesia, Nigeria, Coté d'Ivoire, Colombia, Thailand, Papua New Guinea, and Ecuador were the leading producers of palm oil. Malaysia and Indonesia totaled 80 percent of global production. Palm oil has surpassed even soybean oil in its use as an edible oil. Acre for acre, oil palm produces three times more oil than coconut and 10 times more oil than soybeans. Palm oil is the dietary fat of Africa and Southeast Asia, as olive oil is the fat of the Mediterranean basin.

Once regarded with suspicion because it contains saturated fat, palm oil is today deemed a healthy fat. Palm oil helps the body absorb vitamins D, E, and K, and the elements calcium and magnesium. Palm oil contains neither trans fat nor cholesterol. Palm oil may protect one against heart disease and cancer, including breast cancer, and premature aging. It may reduce blood pressure and lower the incidence of arteriosclerosis.

According to one authority, palm oil improves blood circulation and stabilizes the amount of sugar in the blood, combating diabetes. Palm oil strengthens bones, teeth, lungs, the immune system, the eyes, and the liver. Palm oil may improve the function of the brain and so ward off Alzheimer's disease. In addition to containing antioxidants, palm oil has more vitamin E and beta-carotene than any other food.

Further Reading

Charrier, Andre, Michel Jacquot, Serge Hamon, and Dominique Nicolas. *Tropical Plant Breeding*. Enfield, NH: Science Publishers, 2001.

Fife, Bruce. *The Palm Oil Miracle*. Colorado Springs, CO: Piccadilly Books, 2007.

Gunstone, Frank D. *Oils and Fats in the Food Industry*. Oxford: Wiley-Blackwell, 2008.

Gunstone, Frank D., ed. *Vegetable Oils in Food Technology: Composition, Properties, and Uses*. Boca Raton, FL: CRC Press, 2011.

Hartley, C. W. S. *The Oil Palm*. New York: Longman Scientific and Technical, 1988.

Piggott, C. J. *Growing Oil Palms: An Illustrated Guide*. Kuala Lumpur, Malaysia: Incorporated Society of Planters, 1990.

Pancakes

Pancakes have been versatile over the years and may include a range of ingredients. They have been particularly popular in Europe since antiquity and in the Americas likely for some time, because the Amerindians appear to have made a food akin to pancakes in the pre-Columbian period. Africans, forcibly taken to the American South and other parts of the Americas, also ate pancakes, so that the food became a marker of ethnicity. In their ingredients, pancakes, at least early in their history, marked class and manifested conspicuous consumption. Pancakes have emerged as a breakfast food and so have shaped dietary habits and daily life for millions of Americans and Europeans. Pancakes have become part of agribusiness with giants like Eggo making them.

Origins

It is difficult to pinpoint the origin of pancakes, though it seems clear that they were not initially a breakfast food. Rather, one wrapped a pancake around sausage. The sausage, in turn, might have been attached to a stick, eaten much like a modern corn dog. In fact, the two foods must have resembled one another. The Greeks made pancakes with wheat flour, probably from whole wheat, wine, and milk.

Maple Syrup

The derivation of syrup from maple trees is an important part of the New England economy. Vermont is among the leading producers. The product is sugary and so a condiment for many foods. By tradition, pancakes are often drizzled with maple syrup. The richness of the flavor does not require the addition of sugar, corn syrup, or high fructose corn syrup. Maple syrup is also used on waffles.

Once mixed, the Greeks fried the pancake in olive oil, the ubiquitous cooking oil of the ancient Mediterranean Basin. Finally, the cook covered the pancake in honey, which was then more common than sugar. Only with the establishment of sugarcane plantations in the American tropics would sugar become plentiful. In this context, the Greeks made pancakes a breakfast food, a designation kept today. Not all Greeks approved. Galen, the second-century-CE Greek physician to Roman emperor Marcus Aurelius, thought pancakes undermined one's health.

Modernity

There is little evidence of the place of pancakes during the Middle Ages, but the early modern era is another matter. By this period recipes had become more elaborate and calorie dense. Such elaboration was satisfactory in an era when people still did arduous work. But excess calories are a scourge in the modern developed world in which people are too inert to need so many calories. One 16th-century recipe called for a pint of heavy cream, four or five egg yolks, sugar, and flour, probably wheat. Once the ingredients were whipped into a batter, the cook, presumably a housewife, added ginger and cinnamon, frying the pancake in butter and beer. Another recipe, this one dating to 1615, called for less shock and awe. The author substituted water for milk or cream and cut the egg yolks to two or three. The recipe called for three spices: mace, cloves, and nutmeg. Spices then were expensive and their use must have restricted pancakes to the affluent. Today a democratic food, pancakes in the early modern era must have been confined to the elites. One cannot imagine that commoners could afford to eat them. Once the housewife had prepared the pancake, the 1615 recipe called for a sprinkling of sugar on top. Again, sugar may have been a marker of class. The American sugar estates were not yet in full stride, and in the early 17th century sugar must still have been expensive. The use of spices and sugar therefore marked pancakes as a food of conspicuous consumption, a theme throughout history.

The emphasis in early modern Europe and North America was on thin, probably crisp, pancakes that the consumer could layer one upon another. The American colonists excelled at making these pancakes, which were the fashion in the way that gluten-free foods are in vogue today. Most American recipes took inspiration from English cookbooks, so that the English colonists considered pancakes almost as a native food in a land where the Amerindians had relied on corn and other foods that Europeans initially thought strange. The colonists tended to use little flour but their pancakes, heavy on eggs, milk, cream, and butter, were far from austere. In 1747, the American cookbook *The Art of Cookery* championed the thin pancakes light on flour and heavy on eggs and dairy products. Other cookbooks of the 18th century highlighted similar recipes. One called for the making of an

"Indian" pancake. The author certainly did not take inspiration from the people of the Indian subcontinent. The emphasis must have been on Native American food-ways, though it is difficult to detect any Amerindian influence on her recipes. One might note variants in spelling in the 18th century, with recipes for "pan cakes" and others for "pancakes." One recipe for "Indian Slapjack" did indeed call for corn flour, though it does not seem possible to know how popular corn pancakes were among all Americans. One has the sense that people of European descent clung to wheat flour. The descendants of Africans ate several foods, including pancakes, based on corn. In this context, pancakes must have marked differences in ethnicities. The term *ethnicity*, rather than *race*, is used here to reflect current thought in biology.

In fact, Native Americans may have made something akin to pancakes from corn in the pre-Columbian era. The Algonquian of eastern North America were innovators in making pancakes from a variety of types of corn. Their influence on English culinary habits is difficult to pinpoint. In the American South and among African Americans pancakes were known as "johnnycakes" and "hoecakes." The latter name derived from the apparent resemblance between a thin pancake and the thin edge of a hoe, the part that worked the soil. The hoe was a ubiquitous, and probably despised, agricultural implement. In large parts of the Americas, slaves had no access to plows but were forced to break ground with hoes. The masters devised such arduous work to keep slaves in a state of near exhaustion, too weak to be able to foment rebellion. One account holds that African Americans fried pancakes on the blade of a hoe. The name "johnnycakes" is obscure, though it dates to the 1730s. In the South, slave cooks, many of them women, made hoe-cakes for their masters' families. Military leader and first U.S. president George Washington had slaves prepare his hoecakes with butter and honey. Through African American influence, therefore, the plantation elites took pleasure in corn pancakes.

Washington preferred pancakes for breakfast and he was not alone. By the 19th century pancakes had become a breakfast staple, as had been true in ancient Greece. Buttermilk pancakes were especially popular. Nineteenth-century cooks added baking soda to leaven flour, creating a thick pancake that replaced the thin, crisp imitator. The thick pancake has been a culinary staple since. These 19th-century recipes sometimes omitted eggs, long a centerpiece of pancake recipes. That century, the blueberry pancake came to the fore. This was an American innovation, given the importance of blueberries to the New England economy. Though not part of New England, New Jersey emerged as a significant producer, upon which cooks could draw in making blueberry pancakes. Given the importance of blueberries in North America, it seems surprising that not until the late 19th century did any cook combine them with other ingredients to make pancakes. In 1879, American author Sarah Chauncey Woolsey wrote the children's book *Eyebright*, which may contain the earliest reference to blueberry pancakes. Of course, these pancakes must have predated publication of the book. Otherwise, Woolsey would have had nothing to describe. Since the late 19th century, breakfast menus throughout the United States have featured blueberry pancakes and a great deal more. Blueberry pancakes were initially difficult to prepare. The careless or hasty mixture of blueberries into pancake batter would have crushed the blueberries, forcing the juice to turn the pancakes blue. To avoid this fate the cook had to be patient, carefully and slowly mixing the soft berries into the batter. As a breakfast staple, pancakes of all kinds have shaped dietary habits and daily life.

In the 20th century, new forces were at work. Attention turned to the breakfast habits of men. The austere breakfast of coffee and toast no longer sufficed. Bacon and eggs might be acceptable but at the same time were often not filling enough. Pancakes filled the void and gave men a diversion. On Saturday and Sunday it was now their turn to make pancakes for the family. The wife, with a brief respite from cooking, could luxuriate in the pancakes her husband had prepared. The husband no longer was the caricature of a man's man who ate steak all day. He could find his role by helping his wife without being effeminate. Some male authors went further, suggesting that pancakes had helped make breakfast the proper domain of the husband and father.

Further Reading

Albala, Ken. *Pancakes: A Global History*. London: Reaktion Books, 2008.
Anderson, Heather Arndt. *Breakfast: A History*. London: Rowman & Littlefield Publishers, 2013.

Pasta

The primary ingredient in pasta is durum wheat, which has a fascinating history of its own. Grown throughout the drier regions of the Mediterranean Basin in antiquity, it was cultivated in southern Italy by the first century CE. The first plantings may date to the reign of Emperor Vespasian, the builder of the Colosseum. Durum wheat is the hardest grade of wheat and so does not make an ideal bread. It seems possible that the ancients of southern Italy made a bread from durum wheat or ate it as porridge. It was not then a source of pasta because ancient Italy knew nothing about pasta. In this context, durum wheat had special significance as the wheat that

An Italian woman from Bari makes pasta, a food that is important in many areas of the world. If Italians claim it as their own, Americans seem no less eager for it. (Gunold Brunbauer/Dreamstime.com)

supplied more protein than any other type of wheat, of which the U.S. Department of Agriculture (USDA) recognizes a number of grades.

The chief use of durum wheat is in the making of noodles, what one commonly refers to as "pasta," or perhaps "macaroni." A quick glance at the grocer's shelves reveals a wide variety of pasta. One historian has tabulated more than 20 types. Perhaps the most notable is spaghetti: long rods of pasta, the diameter of which varies by the manufacturer. Because the diameter varies, there are a number of variants of spaghetti, angel hair for example. Americans and Italian Americans tend to believe that no meal of spaghetti is complete without meatballs. Such a meal is nourishing, providing protein, fat, carbohydrates, vitamins, especially the B vitamins, and several minerals. It is also calorie dense and should be eaten in moderation. Pasta tends to be yellow because the endosperm of durum wheat flour is yellow, though red varieties of durum wheat exist. Whole durum wheat pasta is gaining ground among the health conscious. This pasta has a much browner appearance than traditionally milled varieties of durum wheat.

Despite much fanfare among Italians and Italian Americans, it is hard to credit Italy with the invention of pasta. Sometime before the 13th century CE the Chinese appear to have invented durum wheat noodles, the source of pasta. The transit of

Durum Wheat

Durum wheat is the hardest and most nourishing category of wheat. It has more protein than any other wheat. It does not make an ideal bread but is better for making noodles and pasta. Canada and the United States are important producers. In the United States one might find durum fields in Minnesota and North Dakota. Durum may have been a latecomer to agriculture. The people of southwestern Asia planted emmer, einkorn, and bread wheats before they came upon durum. This wheat is interesting in that is has double the number of chromosomes of other wheats, making it a polyploid. Durum wheat must be an ancient hybrid.

this food to Italy appears to have been an achievement of the Mongol empire. Because the empire controlled lands along the eastern Mediterranean Basin, the Mongols had an outlet onto the Mediterranean Sea. The Romans had been among the first to extend trade networks from the eastern Mediterranean to Sicily and the Italian mainland, so that Italy must have early acquired pasta from the Mongols, likely in the 13th century.

An Italian Food

In Italy no food is less expensive and more plentiful than pasta. For centuries, pasta has rivaled pizza as the archetypal Italian cuisine. Italy recognizes pasta of two types. The more popular is dried pasta, that is, noodles made with the addition of water. Anyone who has eaten a short length of uncooked spaghetti can attest to the dry texture. On the other hand, one may make pasta with eggs as a substitute for water. Known as fresh pasta, it contains egg protein and a number of vitamins and minerals. It is the more nourishing and calorie-dense type of pasta but will not store well because harmful bacteria multiply in the egg admixture. Even refrigeration will permit storage only a few days. In some countries the name "macaroni" substitutes for "pasta." Both black and white Americans know macaroni and cheese. Despite the name, it is still just a variant of pasta. Italians likely coined the term *maccherone*, meaning "macaroni." In the 19th century, the word "pasta" came into widespread use. According to Catholic cardinal Giacomo Biffi, Italy gave the world two commodities, pasta and Christianity, though, strictly speaking, Christianity appears to have arisen first in the Greek-speaking eastern Mediterranean Basin. The tradition of naming the apostle Peter the first pope in Rome must account for the cardinal's declaration.

By the 17th century, pasta had become a food of monarchs and commoners. This circumstance arose because of Italy's disunity. The peninsula, disunited since the fragmentation of the Roman Empire by the fifth century CE, would not reunite until the 1870s. During this long period of division, other nations conquered parts of Italy, a fact that exasperated Italian writer and famed author of *The Prince*, Niccolò Machiavelli. These foreigners in Italy adopted Italian cuisine and culture. For example, French king Ferdinand I, wanting to appear a man of the people, ate spaghetti in the restaurants of Naples. Here, as elsewhere, the poor and rich mingled to an extent, both sharing an appetite for pasta. In this sense, pasta may have been a more democratic food than pizza, which appears to have confined itself to Naples' poor. Elsewhere pasta's synonym "macaroni" could be a term of derision for a non-Italian who mimicked Italians in fashion and food. The American phrase "Yankee Doodle" may have a similar meaning.

By the 1860s, as the example of Ferdinand I suggests, pasta was fashionable among the French nobility, particularly among those who were ambassadors to various Italian cities. Accordingly, a feast called for stracchino and gorgonzola cheeses from Lombardy, parmesan cheese from Parma, wine from several districts of Italy, and Sicilian oranges. The final course of the meal would be a large bowl of pasta, whose culinary roots may trace to Naples. Naples was therefore a second home to pasta and a home to pizza. In short, pasta has become the symbol of the people of Italy and those who aspire to the refinements of Italian culture and cuisine. Yet there is no consensus that pasta was a staple of just Naples. Sicily's tradition of eating pasta appears at least as old as that of Naples. Sicilian women made pasta for their fishermen husbands to eat aboard ship. Genoa also has a long tradition of making pasta. Italian Spanish explorer Christopher Columbus, heir to this tradition, ate pasta on his voyages to the Americas. In this sense, pasta crossed the Atlantic Ocean at the very beginning of the Columbian Exchange. The need of a durable food on such long voyages meant that Columbus and explorers like him could take only dried pasta with them. Fresh pasta would not last.

Columbus and the Europeans who followed him reinvented pasta. Before contact with the Americas, there could be no tomato sauce because the tomato was unknown in the Old World. A South American fruit that grows on a vine, the tomato came to Spanish attention in the 1520s and was part of the cuisine of southern Italians by the 1540s or 1550s. The making of tomatoes into sauce gave pasta its archetypal ingredient. Although it is possible to make pasta with other sauces, wine-based sauces for example, tomato sauce remains at the zenith of a proper meal of pasta. In the same way the *Phaseolus* beans of the Americas remade pasta. Many types of American beans may be added to pasta. The most popular appears to be a white kidney bean, the ingredient of choice in making what is now an Italian favorite. These are not minor alterations, but essential changes in how people thought of pasta and the nourishment they derived from it. The tomatoes supplied vitamin C, and the beans are an excellent source of protein. In fact, one might assert that a simple dish of pasta and beans is at least as nourishing as the more calorie-dense spaghetti and meatballs.

An International Dish

The very nature of the durum wheat used to make pasta suggests something of its international character. Putative Italian durum wheats may have more genes from Russian wheats than from Italian wheat plants, if such things exist. For all its fanfare, Italy is not a large producer of durum wheat. Italy imports durum for making pasta from Minnesota, North Dakota and parts of Canada. If one wishes to trace the origins of today's pasta to their ingredients, one would necessarily find a large American component from the durum grown in Minnesota and North Dakota to the tomatoes of American origins. The lesson is that pasta has never been just an Italian food. It has shaped the world because of its receptivity to the foods of both Old and New Worlds. Nonetheless, pasta maintains its status as an ethnic food. It is not quite as "American" as the hamburger, hot dog, or fried chicken. Even so, pasta is a composite food with a decidedly American contribution. The adventurous may appreciate the diversity of foods that may be served with pasta: cheeses of several types, the ubiquitous tomato sauce, beans, bacon and other types of pork, eggs, garlic, onion, chili and sweet peppers, pepper, salt, olives, wine, anchovies, plums, pumpkin, bilberries, currants, figs, lobster, frogs' legs, and walnuts. Clearly, pasta is a food with few limits. In this diversity, pasta is among the most notable foods of the Columbian Exchange, containing ingredients from several regions of the world. Pasta is an international food.

Further Reading

Cecla, Franco La. *Pasta and Pizza*. Chicago: Prickly Paradigm Press, 2007.
Dickie, John. *Delizia!: The Epic History of the Italians and Their Food*. New York: Free Press, 2008.
Kostioukovitch, Elena. *Why Italians Love to Talk about Food*. New York: Farrar, Straus and Giroux, 2006.

Pea

An annual flowering plant, peas, grown from the subtropics to cold climates, are the most geographically and climatically variable legume. Despite this adaptability, peas yield best in cool weather. Like other legumes, peas are a member of the

Clarence Birdseye experimenting on different vegetables, including the ever-popular peas and carrots, to determine the effects of the various stirring speeds and air velocities on the food. These are factors important in developing the dehydration process which, Birdseye predicted, would make dehydrated foods as popular as the quick-frozen products. (Bettmann/Corbis)

Fabaceae or Leguminosae family. The word *pea* derives from the Old English *pease*, from which also derives *pease porridge*. Although *pease* is a singular noun, the English came to think of it as plural because it contained the letter "s." Accordingly, the singular became "pea." Farmers and gardeners grow peas for their seeds and sometimes for their pods. From *Pisum sativum* scientists have bred peas with edible pods. These peas, known in French as *mangetout*, meaning "eat all," may be eaten pods and seeds. Among these peas are snow peas, which are often eaten in stir-fries, and sugar snap peas. Snow peas are picked and eaten when the seeds are immature, whereas sugar snap peas are eaten when the seeds have matured. In addition to *Pisum sativum*, farmers grow *Pisum arvense*, field peas, as feed for livestock. As a livestock feed, pea protein supplements soy protein.

The flavor of peas deteriorates after picking. The grocery store may claim to have fresh peas, but they are at least three days old and no longer at the peak of flavor. Around 1900, growers began to can peas in an effort to preserve flavor. After cooking peas for twenty minutes, growers canned them, though this method of preservation leaves peas mushy and tasteless. More successful has been the practice of freezing peas, a method that American innovator Clarence Birdseye pioneered in 1920. Because consumers want peas at the peak of flavor, growers freeze them within three to four hours of picking. With this method, peas are boiled briefly to kill parasites and then frozen to 0°F. Frozen peas retain color, texture, and flavor. Between the 1950s and 1970s, demand for frozen peas increased rapidly, as Americans craved a convenience food and as they came to own freezers. Growers first froze peas in fish freezers, making the seaports the center of this industry. As frozen peas have become popular, the demand for canned peas has declined, notably since the 1930s. Today, growers freeze 65 percent of peas. Like other legumes, peas are nutritious. Two-thirds of a cup of peas has as much protein as a large egg. In addition to protein, peas contain vitamin A, thiamine, riboflavin, niacin, pantothenic acid, vitamin B_6, folic acid, vitamin C, calcium, magnesium, phosphorus, potassium, and zinc.

Origin and Importance

Wild peas are native to the Mediterranean Basin and the Near East, though the place of their domestication is contested. One school of thought asserts that farmers first cultivated peas in Central Asia and Ethiopia. A second school of thought points to India as the place of origin. Indian farmers, this line of reasoning holds, domesticated peas from a wild ancestor that is now extinct. A third school of thought believes that farmers began to grow peas in the Near East about 10,000 years ago. If this hypothesis is correct, peas are among the most ancient crops and were domesticated around the same time as lentils, barley, and wheat. This Neolithic Revolution gave people a dependable source of protein in peas and lentils and a source of carbohydrates in barley and wheat.

Peas were a staple in antiquity and the Middle Ages. In this era—before botanists bred sweet peas—peas made a nourishing but bland diet. Peas were not flavorful, in part because people dried them before consumption so that they would store. Commoners, unable to afford meat, derived their protein from peas and lentils. They made peas into soup and porridge. The rhyme "pease porridge hot, pease porridge cold, pease porridge in the pot nine days old," suggests that people ate peas day after day. Their reliance on peas was acute during years when the grain harvest was poor and the price of bread high. Peas shaped history because they enabled the poor to survive when most foods were priced too high. In benefiting those who might otherwise starve, peas were an important famine food.

The Romans ate pease porridge. The patrician family Piso (Julius Caesar's wife Calpurnia was a Piso) took its name from peas, declaring that its ancestors had been pea farmers. Although it may seem peculiar that a wealthy family would claim a humble origin, one should remember that the Romans prized the virtues of thrift, self-reliance, hard work, and piety, and believed that these values originated in the countryside. The Piso family chose to identify with peas as a way of claiming that its members embodied rural values. The pea was thus central to the success of the Roman Empire. Roman recipes called for the combination of peas and meat. Because commoners seldom ate meat, these recipes suggest that the affluent ate peas. Gourmet Marcus Apicius devised a recipe for peas, sausage, meatballs, pork, pepper, lovage, oregano, dill, onion, coriander, garum, and wine. Medieval recipes combined peas, almonds, and various spices. Scandinavians ate peas and pork. Pea soup, known as *aertsoppa*, was ubiquitous in Sweden. Pea soup was *gula aerter* in Denmark, *harnekeitto* in Finland and *arwtensoap* in the Netherlands. Another indication that the affluent ate peas comes from the fact that Eric XIV, king of Sweden, ate pea soup. His brother John, lacing pea soup with arsenic, killed Eric in 1577.

Peas were unknown in the Americas until 1493, when Christopher Columbus introduced them to Hispaniola (now the island of Haiti and the Dominican Republic). In the 16th century, the Spanish brought peas to Mexico and Florida. In 1608, one year after the colony's founding, colonists planted peas in Virginia. In 1629, peas, probably in a separate introduction, were grown in the Massachusetts Bay Colony. In the 1670s, a food shortage in the Carolinas reduced the colonists to subsisting on one pint of peas per person per day. This ration, though it was not generous, averted starvation. Thomas Jefferson declared fresh peas his favorite vegetable and cultivated them as early as 1767 at Monticello. Planting 30 varieties, Jefferson competed with his neighbors to determine who could harvest the earliest peas.

In the 17th century, some Americans ate peas three times daily. Martha Washington's *Booke of Cookery* included a recipe for pease porridge and pea soup with mint. *The Virginia House-Wife* recommended the cooking of peas with butter and mint. It detailed a recipe for pea soup with celery and for pease pudding with pork. In 1841, Sarah Josephe Hale's *The Good Housekeeper* included a recipe for soup with peas and spinach, and for peas and lettuce. New Englanders ate peas with corned beef, thyme, and marjoram. Cooks added pearl ash to old peas to soften their seed coat. Perhaps the most unusual and unappetizing use of peas comes from Amelia Simmons' *American Cookery* (1796), which advises bakers to substitute peas for apples and other fruit in pies.

Peas and the Rise of Genetics

The pea shaped the world by being the experimental plant on which Austrian monk Gregor Mendel founded the science of genetics in the 19th century. At the outset, Mendel had no commitment to the pea but rather testcrossed a number of species. During this initial testing, the pea came to the fore for a number of reasons, perhaps the most important being the unambiguity of results. For example, a pea plant may be tall or short. The cross between a tall and short plant will be either tall or short. In practice, the progeny from the first cross are always tall, as will become clear later. Because the progeny are either tall or short, Mendel had no difficulty determining from where these offspring acquired the trait. To underscore the importance of this phenomenon, consider the ambiguity among humans. Cross a tall human, usually a man, with a short one, usually a woman. The children are not usually tall or short but intermediary in height. Plus, humans display a slight sexual dimorphism. These facts make it much less easy to ascribe the height of a human to the stature of either parent. Both parents seem to contribute some hereditary particles (genes) to determine the height of a person. Skin complexion and perhaps intelligence may be other examples of what one might call blended inheritance, though strictly the phrase is out of favor.

An exacting experimentalist, Mendel began his crosses with peas in 1856. It is important to note that the pea is naturally a self-fertilizing plant, so that Mendel, in every cross, had to remove the pollen from what he designated as the male plant and dust it on the stigma of the so designated female plant. The pea had already been the subject of experiments by British gentleman farmer Andrew Knight, and this work appears to have intrigued Mendel, but in the end he charted an independent course. In 1856, Mendel bought 34 varieties of peas displaying a range of characteristics. He testcrossed these varieties, finding 22 that segregated into the simple traits under his scrutiny. Mendel used the subsequent experiments in an attempt to trace the heredity of at least seven traits, among the most important being whether offspring present a smooth or wrinkled seed coat. Today, people eat only peas with smooth seed coats because of aesthetic appeal. The second trait was whether the pea was green or yellow. Today, only green peas are served. As shown, the third major trait was height. Mendel found, for example, that the cross between tall and short pea plants yielded all tall progeny, in what he called the first filial generation, the F_1. It was as though the trait for shortness had disappeared. Self-fertilizing, the F_1 yielded an F_2 generation in which the missing trait reappeared. Here Mendel made a decisive contribution to the new science of genetics. He classified a trait as either dominant or recessive. Tallness was dominant and shortness recessive. Further, when a dominant gene paired with a recessive gene in a plant the dominant trait always masked the recessive trait. A pea plant with one pair of the dominant gene will always be tall, but a plant with one pair of the recessive gene will always be short. As shown, the heterozygous coupling is always tall. From his work Mendel reached two other fundamental conclusions. First, he derived the concept of segregation. Consider the heterozygous pairing Tt, with T being the dominant trait of tallness and t being the recessive trait of shortness. These traits segregate, by which Mendel meant that an offspring might receive a T from one parent and a t from another. TT and tt segregations are also possible. Third, Mendel posited the law of independent assortment, by which he meant that a gene for each trait is inherited independent of a gene for any other trait. Strictly, this is incorrect. Genes come in bundles known as chromosomes. The chromosomes, rather than the genes, sort independently. Mendel published his results in 1866, but his work was ahead of the times. Only in the 20th century would biologists flock to this new science. Thanks to the pea, genetics has transformed the world, undergirding the hybrid corn revolution, the Green Revolution, and the rise of biotechnology. Someday humans are likely to cross an ethical chasm by cloning a person, work that Mendel surely never foresaw but which his experiments with peas have helped make possible.

Further Reading

Albala, Ken. *Beans: A History*. Oxford: Berg, 2007.

Hughes, Meredith Sayles. *Spill the Beans and Pass the Peanuts: Legumes*. Minneapolis: Lerner Publications, 1999.

Mayr, Ernst. *The Growth of Biological Thought: Diversity, Evolution, and Inheritance*. Cambridge, MA: Harvard University Press, 1982.

Sumner, Judith. *American Household Botany: A History of Useful Plants, 1620–1900*. Portland, OR: Timber Press, 2004.

Peanut

Neither a pea nor a nut, the peanut, a perennial legume related to the pea, chickpea, lentil, beans, alfalfa, and clover, has several names. The Inca called the peanut *ynchia* or *inchia*. The Tainos of Hispaniola (now the island of Haiti and the Dominican Republic) referred to the peanut as *mani*, a name the Spanish appropriated. The Gedda of West Africa knew the peanut as *nguba*, from which may have arisen the slang term "goober." Another tradition holds that the Bantu word *nguber* is the source of the term "goober." The Aztecs called the peanut *tlalacachuafl*, meaning "the chocolate bean that grows underground." This linkage between the

Originally a legume of South America, the peanut has conquered large parts of the world. Africa is an important producer. This woman demonstrates the value of peanuts in northern India. (Edwardje/Dreamstime.com)

peanut and chocolate implies that the Aztecs combined these foods. The pre-Columbian people of Brazil called the peanut *manobi*. In the 17th century, Dutch physician Willem Piso referred to the peanut as *mandubi*, perhaps borrowing this term from the Amerindians. A member of the Fabaceae family, the peanut is also known as "the pygmy nut," "the pig nut," "the monkey nut," "pinder," "pinda," and "the Manilla nut." Some people call the peanut "the groundnut" and "the earth nut" because the pod matures underground. Finally, scientists know the peanut by the name *Arachia hypogaea*.

Scientists believe that the ancestor of the peanut bore pods above the soil but may have evolved an underground habit to protect peanuts from grasshoppers, locusts, and other predators. The modern peanut plant bears flowers low on the stem. Once fertilized, the flowers produce pods on the stems known as pegs. The pegs hang near the ground and enter the soil, where the pods mature. The peanut is 43–52 percent oil and 25–32 percent protein. A calorie dense food, one pound of peanuts has as many calories as two pounds of beef, 1.5 pounds of cheddar cheese, and 36 eggs. A nutritious food, the peanut has protein, oil, niacin, folic acid, fiber, magnesium, vitamin E, manganese, and phosphorus. It has small amounts of calcium and copper.

Planters Nut & Chocolate Company

Italian immigrant and Pennsylvania resident Amedeo Obici began his career selling fruits, expanding to peanuts when he bought a peanut roaster. His early years were itinerant as he searched for the best market for his peanuts. Calling himself the peanut specialist, Obici in 1906 partnered with another Italian immigrant, Mario Peruzzi, the two co-founding Planters Nuts. In 1908, the name changed to Planters Nuts & Chocolate Company. In 1960, a small company bought Planters, which later merged with Nabisco. In 2000, Kraft Foods bought Planters.

Origin in the Americas

The peanut is indigenous to South America, which has 29 species of the legume. One hypothesis puts its origin in Bolivia, which has the largest number of wild species. Another hypothesis traces the peanut's lineage to the land bounded by Brazil, Bolivia, and Paraguay. About 3000 BCE, the people of Brazil and the Caribbean cultivated the peanut. Between 1800 and 1200 BCE, the Peruvians first grew the peanut. The ancient Peruvians ate peanuts as a snack, just as Americans do today. Around 700 CE, the Chimu of Peru painted images of peanuts on pottery and must have grown the crop earlier. The Nazca of Peru also painted images of peanuts on pottery. The pre-Columbian people of Peru put peanuts in tombs, perhaps intending them as food for the dead. In the second millennium CE, the Inca and the people of the Bahamas grew the peanut. The Aztecs cultivated the peanut and may have used it to treat swollen gums. The peoples of the Americas may have traded the peanut and carried it with them as they migrated throughout Central and South America and Mexico. From its earliest days, the peanut sustained the masses as a cheap source of protein, serving the same function as beans in the Americas and the chickpea, lentil, and pea in the Old World. In this way, peanuts shaped history and daily life.

In the early 16th century, Spanish priest Bartolomé de Las Casas, working in Hispaniola, may have been the first European to encounter the peanut. He wrote the first European description of the plant.

Africa and Asia

In the early 16th century, the Portuguese transferred the peanut from Brazil to Africa, particularly West Africa, the source of slaves for the New World sugarcane, coffee, rice, indigo, tobacco, and cotton plantations. By the 1560s, the peanut was widespread in West Africa. Within a century, the peanut was so widespread that many Africans forgot that it was not an indigene of the continent. Africans welcomed the peanut because of its ease of cultivation, though this point is disputed, and its nutritional value. As in the Americas, the peanut in Africa represented an inexpensive source of protein for the masses. In this way, the peanut has shaped history and daily life in Africa. The people of Ghana combine peanuts and cassava, yams, and plantains, a relative of the banana. The people of Mali make a peanut stew that includes chicken, okra, tomatoes, and sweet potatoes. The peanut, tomato, and sweet potato were all American introductions to Africa. In Zimbabwe, as in the United States, people roast peanuts, eating them with salt. Ethiopians make a stew of peanuts and chili peppers, eating it with rice or millet cakes. Kenyans make a stew of peanuts and beans, consuming it with corn pudding. The people of Malawi and Zambia make a dish of peanuts and tomatoes, both American crops. The people of Mali eat fried peanut cakes. The people of Mozambique prepare a dessert of peanuts, egg yolks, and sugar, commonly eaten as pudding. Indonesians combine peanut sauce with meat and rice. They make the sauce from peanuts, ginseng, chili peppers, garlic, lime, shrimp, and shallot.

Portugal introduced the peanut into India. In 1530, the Spanish carried the peanut from Peru to Spain and Malaysia. In 1565, the Spanish introduced the peanut to the Philippines. Indonesia, China, and Japan all embraced the peanut. The people of Southeast Asia grind peanuts to make a sauce for rice, meat, and vegetables. They also eat peanuts with chili peppers or with coconut milk, lime juice, and vegetables of many kinds. In 1690, the Dutch introduced the peanut to Indonesia. In the 17th century, the Chinese adopted the peanut. The peanut must have quickly become a food for the masses, though its success bothered Gonzalo Fernández de Oviedo y Valdés, governor of Hispaniola, who declared it fit only for slaves, children, and commoners. He denigrated its "mediocre taste" and found it suitable for people "who do not have a fine taste." Indonesia and Thailand, both part of Southeast Asia, skewer meat covered with peanut sauce. Indonesians place peanut sauce on a salad of cooked vegetables. On Java, the largest island of Indonesia, people fry peanuts and rice. They also serve rice with ground peanuts and coconut. The people of southern India add ground peanuts to curry sauces. They also eat whole peanuts as Americans do, though the concept of the peanut as a snack food does not appear to resonate with Indians. The Chinese stir-fry vegetables, chili peppers, and peanuts. Indonesians also make wafers of chopped peanuts, eat boiled peanuts with chili sauce, and put chopped peanuts on salad. Malaysians make a sauce of peanuts and coconut milk, pouring it on vegetables. The Thai prepare a salad of roasted peanuts and papaya, and use chopped peanuts in several dishes. The Vietnamese combine peanuts and vegetable roots. Vietnamese children eat boiled peanuts at breakfast. The Chinese use peanut oil for frying, and fry peanuts in peanut oil. Alternatively they boil peanuts, eating them in stir-fries. The Chinese make candy from ground peanuts and sugar. Indians eat a type of trail mix of peanuts and other legumes. They use peanuts in curries, stews, and soups.

Throughout Africa and Asia, peanut oil is the cooking oil of choice. With little saturated fat, peanut oil may be relatively benign, though the addition of extra calories to a meal is a concern among sedentary peoples, particularly in the developed world. By contrast, Americans use little peanut oil, probably because it does not store well.

Back to the Americas

After 1600, African slaves introduced the peanut to North America. This was a circuitous and curious route, being essentially two Columbian Exchanges, the first from the Americas to Africa and Asia, and the second from Africa to North America, what would become the American South. This transit is puzzling because it does not posit a direct transfer of the peanut from South America to North America. If this thesis is true, then the peanut did not take the obvious route, as corn did, into North America. Peanuts and beans were the rations on slave ships. The peanut, not by its own choice, empowered the slave trade and so propped up slavery, an important but undesirable effect on history. Not everyone accepts the Americas-to-Africa-and-back-to-the-Americas route. Alternatively, the peanut may have migrated from the Caribbean to North America, perhaps without the aid of slaves. As a worldwide crop, the peanut has inspired a multinational cuisine. The people of Peru, Bolivia, and Ecuador make the peanut into a sauce, combining it with eggs, cheese, olives, chili peppers, and spices and using the sauce to flavor potatoes. Brazilians eat chicken stew with a sauce of peanut and coconut milk. Americans have recipes for peanut soup, peanut brittle, and peanut crust pies. They boil peanuts in the shell in salt water.

The United States

Enthusiasm for the peanut produced a crisis. The end of World War I allowed the United States to re-establish the peanut trade with South America, Asia, and Africa. In 1920, imports flooded the United States and peanut prices fell. Anxious peanut growers approached Congress for help. Among the supplicants was Alabama agricultural chemist George Washington Carver, whose testimony helped persuade Congress to pass a tariff on peanut imports. Carver's conversion to the peanut had not been dramatic. He credited a white woman with stimulating his interest in the legume. She had planted thousands of acres of cotton but lost the crop to the boll weevil. She turned to Carver for an alternative and for help marketing peanuts. Turning his attention to the peanut, Carver conducted a series of experiments on peanuts as hog feed. These experiments were not revolutionary. Stockmen had fed peanuts to hogs for many years. Nevertheless, this work marked an important stage in Carver's career, for he had shrewdly selected a crop whose importance was dawning on the nation. The South's oil mills that had crushed cottonseed could now derive oil from peanuts. Sharecroppers grew peanuts as a cash crop and as food. Whites employed blacks to pick peanuts and to work in factories that produced peanut butter. The South in general and African Americans in particular would benefit from Carver's work. During a long, productive career, Carver developed more than three hundred uses for peanuts, among them flour, cake, feed, shoe polish, pickles, rubber, coffee, vinegar, punch, cough syrup, and face cream. In making his case for the peanut, Carver even touted its use in treating polio. The American Medical Association did not endorse this claim and Carver admitted that he had not proven the efficacy of the peanut as a treatment for polio. More appropriately, Carver urged farmers to grow the peanut because, as a legume, it fixed nitrogen in the soil and so helped them combat the bugaboo of American agriculture: soil exhaustion.

In 1941, the year that marked America's entry into World War II, the federal government declared the peanut an essential crop. In response to wartime demand, the U.S. peanut harvest increased sharply between 1940 and 1945. Under the federal farm program that evolved during the 20th century, farmers sold a portion of their peanuts to the federal government and exported much of the crop. The rest satisfied domestic demand. In 1990, Americans consumed the majority of the harvest as peanut butter. They ate one-quarter of the crop as shelled or salted nuts and a little more than one-fifth as candy. Presently, Americans eat the vast majority of the peanut harvest. The rest is crushed into oil or set aside as seed and livestock feed. Today, Georgia grows nearly half of all U.S. peanuts. Three-quarters of Georgia's peanut crop are sold to make peanut butter. Peanuts generate millions of dollars for the state's farmers. Former president Jimmy Carter rose to prominence partly because he used his occupation as a peanut farmer to convince Americans that he embodied the rural values of diligence, thrift, piety, and honesty.

Popular during much of the 20th century, peanuts suffered a setback in the 1990s. The demand for peanuts fell as many Americans branded them fattening. Reports of allergies to peanuts and even of deaths for their consumption led nervous administrators to reduce or eliminate peanuts and peanut butter from school lunches. Between 1982 and 2002, as demand for peanuts ebbed, competition from cheap imports intensified, and the trend toward the consolidation of farms in fewer hands caused the number of peanut farmers in the United States to decline by half. Yet the peanut is enjoying a revival. Weight Watchers and the

American Diabetes Association tout the nutrition of peanuts. In 2002, the average American ate several pounds of peanuts, a larger quantity than many other nations can boast.

The combination of peanuts and chocolate mixes saltiness and sweetness in a way that many people cannot resist. An early peanut candy, Reese's Peanut Butter Cups sold for a penny per cup in 1928. Other peanut candies followed, including Baby Ruth and Snickers. In 1991, in the midst of the Gulf War, Mars Incorporated put a Snickers bar in every U.S. soldier's ration for Thanksgiving. Reese's, Baby Ruth, Snickers and other peanut candies are favorites of children who trick or treat on Halloween. In the United States, candy makers use one-quarter percent of the peanut harvest. Today, peanuts are ubiquitous. One may eat them at a baseball game or on a flight to Dallas, Cincinnati, or hundreds of other destinations.

Further Reading

Hughes, Meredith Sayles. *Spill the Beans and Pass the Peanuts: Legumes*. Minneapolis: Lerner Publications, 1999.

Johnson, Sylvia A. *Tomatoes, Potatoes, Corn, and Beans: How the Foods of the Americas Changed Eating around the World*. New York: Atheneum Books, 1997.

Krishna, K. R. *Peanut Agroecosystem: Nutrient Dynamics and Productivity*. Oxford: Alpha Science International, 2008.

Smart, J. *The Groundnut Crop: A Scientific Basis for Improvement*. London: Chapman and Hall, 1994.

Smith, Andrew F. *Peanuts: The Illustrious History of the Goober Pea*. Urbana: University of Illinois Press, 2002.

Smith, C. Wayne. *Crop Production: Evolution, History, and Technology*. New York: John Wiley and Sons, 1995.

Peanut Butter

The primary ingredient in peanut butter is the peanut, a legume from South America. The Amerindians of South America and Mexico deserve credit for inventing peanut butter, though West Africa seems to have played an independent role in making peanut butter, having acquired peanuts from Spanish or Portuguese merchants. Many Americans like to think of the United States as the home of peanut butter, but this is an ahistorical idea. Nonetheless, the United States played and continues to play an important role in making and selling peanut butter, which has now grown into an international food.

Jif

Known for its peanut butter, Jif introduced both creamy and crunchy peanut butters in 1958. In 1974, Jif introduced an extra crunchy brand, and in 1991, a low-salt and sugar variety. In 1994 came a brand with less fat. In 2014, Jif introduced the first whipped peanut butter. Procter & Gamble owned the company until 2001, when the J. M. Smucker Company purchased Jif. Jif currently markets 10 different brands of peanut butter.

Origins and Importance

About 3,000 years ago, the Amerindians of South America ground peanuts into a paste. It did not spread as easily as do modern types of peanut butter, but the Native American product was surely a forerunner of peanut butter if not peanut butter itself. In fact, there appears to be no reason not to credit these Amerindians with the invention of peanut butter. Later, the Aztecs as well made peanut butter. The patenting of peanut butter would come much later with apparent disregard for the achievements of the Americas' indigenes. Thanks to the Columbian Exchange, the people of West Africa were making peanut butter in the 16th century. The historians of peanut butter likewise neglect the contributions of these Africans. The people of West Africa ate peanut butter with honey, a food that must have been wholesome, flavorful, and calorie dense. In an era of strenuous activity, it made sense to eat peanut butter and honey. In this regard, peanut butter must have shaped the history and daily lives of West Africans. Where calories were scarce one could rely on peanut butter.

During the American Civil War Confederate soldiers ate ground peanuts as porridge, though this was not exactly peanut butter. Early accounts of the peanut and peanut butter suggest that they did not move north from South America to North America, but rather west from West Africa to North America. This is a circuitous route and begs the question of why a simple northern migration apparently did not occur. Peanut butter and roasted peanuts in general have an alluring aroma and flavor. Despite the popularity of peanut butter in the United States and parts of Africa, Australia, and Asia, the spread has not conquered all of Europe. This oddity may be a cultural artifact of life in Europe because Americans of European ancestry enjoy peanut butter.

The Typology of Peanut Butter

Peanut butter may be made from four types of peanuts. Of these four, runners are the most prevalent in peanut butter. This circumstance is curious, given that some experts in the making and marketing of peanut butter regard this peanut as bland. Peanut butter manufacturers buy runner peanuts from farms in the Carolinas and Virginia, with a small supply coming from western Texas. Two other types, Virginias and Spanish peanuts, were once common in peanut butter, but runners have dethroned them. As late as 1945, Virginias and Spanish peanuts held their own as ingredients in peanut butter, but the story today is different. The trend toward runners should be familiar to anyone who knows something about capitalism. Runners are cheap and on that basis alone command the market for peanut butter. This circumstance may not benefit the consumer because Spanish peanuts are regarded as sweeter than runners. The fourth type, Valencias, are seldom grown in the United States and have never exerted much influence on the makers of peanut butter. Because runners are bland, even insipid, peanut butter makers resort to the addition of sugar and salt to add the flavor that runners lack. This is a powerful mix of fat from peanut oil, and the added salt and sugar. Humans crave all three, making peanut butter irresistible for many. Simply put, peanut butter satiates the biology of craving. As with McDonald's foods and the Model T, standardization is essential in the making and marketing of peanut butter. Every jar of a brand of peanut butter must have the same consistency, flavor, and aroma. Because runners are uniformly bland, they guarantee this consistency. Runners are also in favor because they yield more peanuts and more peanut butter than the other three types of peanuts. The yield of runners contributes to their inexpensiveness, the trait that gave them renown in the first place.

Peanut Butter in the United States

In the United States, Americans began eating peanut butter in the 1890s. Nutritionally, the decade marked an important juncture, as people began to clamor for wholesome, natural foods. Peanut butter fed this desire. The peanuts were roasted and ground into a smooth texture. Grinding released the oil from the peanut, which has a large oil content, very little of it saturated. The peanut oil rose to the top of the can or jar and had to be stirred into the rest of the peanut butter. No additional oils or other fats then marred peanut butter. Oils were not then hydrogenated, so that peanut butter was a wholesome and nourishing, if calorie-dense, food. Peanut butter is perhaps the great American snack food, the peanut butter and jelly (or jam) sandwich being a staple of a child's lunch. In this way, peanut butter shaped the history and daily life of the masses. Between the 1890s and 1920s, peanut butter had no sugar and only a little salt to enhance flavor. The 1920s to the 1960s marked a less wholesome era, when manufacturers introduced hydrogenated oils into peanut butter. These oils no longer needed to be stirred and so made spreading peanut butter easier, but they added too much fat to peanut butter. Since the 1970s, natural peanut butter has recrudesced. In 1935 debuted the first peanut butter with the addition of partly ground peanuts to give the product a crunchy texture. The J.M. Smucker Company of Orrville, Ohio, continues to make crunchy peanut butter in addition to smooth and creamy peanut butter. Smucker's peanut butters have no additional oil and sugar and only a little salt. Early peanut butters were canned. Jars prevailed after World War II. Today, jars or plastic are standard.

As discussed earlier, the health movement of the 1890s led to the early prominence of peanut butter and attracted the affluent, who ate it at spas. American physician John Harvey Kellogg, a health fanatic and gifted self-promoter, claimed to have invented peanut butter in about 1895, depriving the Amerindians of their due. Under Kellogg's tutelage, housewives ground their own peanuts for making peanut butter. He believed that peanut butter was a better and more wholesome source of protein than meat. For all his devotion to the peanut, Kellogg also tried to make a spreadable paste of almonds and perhaps was not aware that the peanut, unlike the almond, is not a nut. Under Kellogg's spell, President Warren G. Harding, aviator Amelia Earhart, actor Johnny Weissmuller, and automaker Henry Ford all ate peanut butter. The Vegetarian Food and Nut Company sold peanut butter, surely furthering the erroneous connection between peanuts and nuts. Vegetarians early turned to peanut butter as a source of protein. As a protein source, peanut butter became an inexpensive food of the masses, just as the chickpea, pea, and lentil had been in antiquity and the Middle Ages. In sustaining the masses, peanut butter has helped shape history and daily life, as have these other legumes. At the same time, peanut butter was winning recognition as a snack food that conscientious mothers could serve their children. Companies began selling peanut butter and potato chips, pretzels, and crackers, all aimed to build peanut butter's profile as a snack food. Among Americans, midwesterners are the leading consumers of peanut butter per person, a surprise given that the peanut is not a midwestern crop but rather a Southern one. In 1904 at the Saint Louis World's Fair, Beech-Nut company began selling peanut butter, reinforcing the erroneous stereotype. Known for its ketchup, Heinz made its early reputation with peanut butter, entering the market in 1909. In the early 20th century, the boll weevil devastated cotton. Enterprising growers switched to peanuts, adding to the renown of the peanut and peanut butter. In this regard, the boll weevil changed American history by causing an increase in the availability of peanuts and peanut butter. American agricultural chemist George Washington Carver arose as a promoter of peanuts and peanut butter. Partisans even credit Carver with inventing peanut butter. This was no truer of Carver than Kellogg.

Peanut Butter Goes Global

As the United States stationed troops abroad during the world wars and after World War II, the military fed them peanut butter. In this way the product became an international commodity. Germany, India, Canada, Mexico, Japan, Saudi Arabia, South Korea, the United Kingdom, Hong Kong, Singapore, and the United Arab Emirates all import peanut butter from the United States. Per person, Canada is the leading consumer of peanut butter. Canadians eat peanut butter on toast for breakfast. The Netherlands ranks second, with the United States managing to hold onto third place. Australia makes its own peanut butter and claims to have the world's oldest peanut butter company. Haitians flavor peanut butter with chili peppers. Spain claims to have introduced peanut butter to what is now Haiti in 1697, during its brief tenure as what would become the jewel in the crown of France's sugar empire. Haitians also eat peanut butter with melons of various kinds. The Dutch advertise peanut butter as the food of soccer players, an important connection in a nation that idolizes the sport. Elsewhere in Europe, France, Italy, and Greece eat very little peanut butter. The product is not popular in Eastern Europe and Russia. Nigeria and South Africa, however, are avid consumers. Peanut butter is popular in Southeast Asia, especially Indonesia. In fact, the Netherlands may have acquired a taste for peanut butter from Indonesia, which was once the Dutch East Indies.

Further Reading

Hughes, Meredith Sayles. *Spill the Beans and Pass the Peanuts: Legumes*. Minneapolis: Lerner Publications, 1999.

Krampner, Jon. *Creamy and Crunchy: An Informal History of Peanut Butter, the All-American Food*. New York: Columbia University Press, 2013.

Smith, Andrew F. *Peanuts: The Illustrious History of the Goober Pea*. Urbana: University of Illinois Press, 2002.

Smith, C. Wayne. *Crop Production: Evolution, History, and Technology*. New York: John Wiley and Sons, 1995.

Pepper

A tropical plant, the pepper plant is not exceptional by tropical standards. It has no flashy, large flowers and no mesmerizing aroma. The plant produces small berries that when picked dry, wrinkle and turn black. This phenomenon gives pepper the

The Spice Trade

Europeans were eager participants in the Spice Trade. Because important spices like pepper were found only in Indonesia, Europeans had to travel some distance to buy them. An overland route was feasible but long, to contact Indian or Chinese merchants to purchase these spices. Moreover, the Chinese were not always willing to trade with foreigners. Another solution was to allow Arab middlemen to get the spices, though prices were high, a position that was intolerable once Istanbul fell to the Muslims in the 15th century. Portugal circumvented the Muslim monopoly by rounding the southern tip of Africa while Spain sent Italian Spanish explorer Christopher Columbus west in hopes of reaching Asia. Spices fueled all this activity and helped usher in the modern world.

alternate name of "black pepper." Each berry contains one seed, the peppercorn, which is the source of pepper. The spice played an enormous role in shaping the world.

Origins

Pepper appears to be native to southern India, though it early spread to what Europeans would call the Spice Islands, which are now part of Indonesia. A tropical plant like sugarcane and citrus fruits, it cannot endure frost. Contrary to European beliefs, pepper did not grow on trees, but on a herbaceous plant, technically a vine. Its confinement to India and obscure islands was one reason that Europeans were so energetic in seeking it and thereby changing the world.

The Romans may have been the first European people to use pepper to enhance a meal. Roman gold coins found in India support the assertion that Rome traded directly with India for pepper. The Romans thought of pepper as a spice and a medicine, in the belief that it could cure aches and pains. It was the aspirin of Roman antiquity. The Romans also used pepper to treat coughs, fever, or snakebite. Although pepper was important to the Romans, it never rivaled bread, ·wine, and olive oil as the staples of Roman life. As a spice, pepper ranked with cloves and cinnamon among the Romans. First-century-CE Greek physician Dioscorides who served Emperor Nero touted pepper's medicinal value. Greece, southern China, and southern India also embraced pepper. Indian physicians came to conclusions similar to Dioscorides's, adding that pepper aided digestion and improved appetite. Ironically, pepper may have hastened the decline of Rome in the fifth century CE. Early that century the Goths, a Germanic tribe from the Balkans, invaded Italy from the north, besieging the city of Rome for the first time in more than 400 years. Unlike during the Punic Wars, Rome's allies did not aid the city. Bereft of support, it fell to the Goths, who looted it for gold, silver, and pepper.

Into the Middle Ages, European elites claimed pepper as their own, and it appears that they had much greater access to it than did the masses. In 1439, one pound of pepper cost two days' wages for a worker in England. The masses simply could not afford pepper. Pepper was so valuable that it was literally worth its weight in gold and silver. Pepper had a dark side, as the Dutch and English bought opium from western Asia to trade for pepper in China. In this way, China acquired an addiction to the dangerous narcotic. Legend supposes that medieval people used pepper heavily to disguise the rancidity of rotting meat, but this assertion appears to be untrue. The popularity of pepper in the Middle Ages may have stemmed from the nobility's inordinate fondness for meat. The elites held fowl in special regard because they believed that birds soared near God.

The Early Modern Era

The Indonesian island of Sumatra was long a source of pepper. In the early modern era, Sumatra was the world's largest exporter of pepper, though today coffee has replaced it. Pepper satiated the palate the way sugar does today. Pepper amassed wealth for Venice, which plied the Mediterranean Sea and overland routes to acquire pepper from Asia and then sell it to the rest of Europe. In the 15th century, about 80 percent of Europe's pepper came through Venice. Europeans came to associate pepper with the biblical story of creation. The Garden of Eden must have been in the east and must have been the original source of the pepper that Asia sold Europe. In the early modern era, it was possible to buy a home with pepper, so valuable was it. Cinnamon, nutmeg, and cloves may have been more valuable ounce for ounce than pepper, though Europeans used about eight times more pepper than the other spices, so that pepper had a much greater potential for aggregate profits. Pepper heightened the rivalry between England and the Netherlands, with both nations competing for control of the pepper trade in the Indian Ocean.

The Role of Pepper in the Discovery of the Americas

Europeans had long sought pepper from parts of Asia, especially south and Southeast Asia. Crisis arose in the 15th century CE when Muslim warriors conquered Constantinople (now Istanbul, an important city in Turkey). This conquest allowed the Muslims to close the overland and Mediterranean Sea routes by which Europeans had acquired pepper and other spices. With the Muslims now in command of pepper, they could set the price as high as they wished, squeezing Europe. Portugal on the westernmost edge of Europe felt the price increase most acutely. The Portuguese wondered whether they might be able to circumvent the Muslim monopoly by sailing south. Initial prospects looked grim. Ptolemy, the ancient Greek geographer and astronomer, understood, as all Greek intellectuals did, that the world was a sphere. He correctly positioned Africa between Europe and Asia, though he did not believe that Africa had a southern tip. Rather, he thought that southern Africa simply circled the globe from north to south in a belt of land. Africa therefore could only be crossed by land.

By the 15th century, however, some European intellectuals were willing to challenge Ptolemy, thinking him outdated. Among this new breed of Europeans was Portugal's Prince Henry the Navigator. He wished to test the premise that Africa had no southern tip. The prince sent a series of explorers down the western coast of Africa to determine whether Ptolemy had been right. These voyages posted many obstacles, most of them conceptual. For example, Europeans understood that the further north one went, the colder the climate. It seemed reasonable that if one went far enough south one would encounter boiling seawater and land afire. These Portuguese sailors falsified such beliefs and the expeditions continued. Finally, a ship commanded by Bartholomeu Dias was blown off course. When calm resumed, Dias realized that he had sailed south and then east. He had rounded the southern tip of Africa, known as the Cape of Good Hope. His men were too frightened to go forward, so Dias returned to Portugal. Explorer Vasco da Gama completed the voyage, sailing south from Portugal, rounding the southern tip of Africa, and sailing northeast to India. Portugal had bypassed the Muslims and at last had its own access to the pepper trade.

At the same time the Chinese, who sold spices throughout Asia, wanted a sea route through which to sell spices in Europe. The Silk Road had served the function of trade as a land route, but it was too slow in a maritime era. Between 1405 and 1433, China dispatched Admiral Zheng He on a number of expeditionary voyages. Wide-ranging in his search, He visited islands in the South Pacific and then went west to the Persian Gulf and Africa. He had the technology and talent to have gone further, perhaps even to the Americas. Yet China truncated his voyages in 1433. Politics had intervened as conservative Confucian scholars came to the fore. They thought trade with foreigners was beneath the dignity of the Chinese people, and that China should look inward to reach its destiny. These scholars promoted agriculture and internal improvements. Out of touch with much of the rest of the world, China would eventually fall behind in economic and technological developments.

Meanwhile Portugal's success had sharpened its rivalry with Spain. If Portugal had sailed east to find pepper, might it be possible to venture west? On this point the temptation was to believe Ptolemy, whose map of the world suggested that the distance between Western Europe and East Asia was comparatively short and so feasible to cross by sea. No one, certainly not Ptolemy, had dreamed that two continents stood in Spain's way to east Asia. Italian Spanish explorer Christopher Columbus, a vigorous proponent of a westward crossing, finally secured money from Spain for his voyage. He landed not in India, China, or any other part of Asia, but on an island in the Caribbean Sea. He had come upon the Americas, though he refused to believe that he had never set foot in Asia. The Europeans who followed Columbus came to understand the import of his discovery. The rejoining of the Old and New Worlds by sea—what had begun as a search for pepper—changed the world forever. The Amerindians, never having been exposed to the diseases of the Old World, had no immunities and so died in the millions. With little native labor in the Americas, the European masters of these new lands imported African slaves to toil on the new sugarcane plantations in tropical America. Here, for the first time in history, arose the differentiation of people as slave or free based on race, though one should add that some biologists doubt the validity of any notion of race. The racism that grew out of the slave system has complicated the subsequent development of the Americas, particularly the United States, where poor African American communities haunt relations between whites and blacks. The discovery of the Americas also made possible the transfer of plants and animals from one hemisphere to the other. Pigs, cows, horses, wheat, sugarcane, coffee, and many more came from the Old World to the New, and corn, tomatoes, potatoes, cassava, peanuts, beans, sweet potatoes, and many more came from the New World to the Old. The search for pepper thus shaped the world in ways that are difficult to overstate.

The Pepper Trade and the United States

When the United States entered the pepper trade in the early 19th century it had no foothold along the Pacific Ocean. Rather, merchants made long voyages across the Atlantic and Indian Oceans to acquire pepper from India and Indonesia. The leader in this trade, Massachusetts, stood at the westernmost destination of this trade route. Despite the length and cost of these voyages, Massachusetts's merchants were able to sell pepper for eight times the price they had paid for it. In 1831, pirates attacked a U.S. merchant ship near Sumatra. President Andrew Jackson, a former general and a bellicose man, dispatched a warship to Sumatra, the first U.S. military venture in Southeast Asia. This foray would form the template for later involvement in Hawaii, the Philippines, and even Japan after the end of World War II. In the 18th and 19th centuries the United States may have spent 17 million silver dollars for pepper from Sumatra. In the age of sail, these long voyages could be perilous. The role of citrus fruits, pineapple, and potatoes was well known by the 19th century, but deaths from these voyages were numerous. Hunger, diseases, storms, and drowning claimed many U.S. sailors in their quest for pepper.

Is Modern Medicine Embracing Pepper?

Today, physicians are fastening fresh eyes on pepper's medicinal qualities. Scientists and doctors in the United States, the United Kingdom, and Italy are studying pepper's potential in reducing inflammation and killing pathogens and cancer cells. Other uses may evolve to include a potential insecticide in keeping with organic farming. Pepper may have antioxidant and analgesic properties. It may treat skin disorders. Pepper may even fight depression and obesity. Japanese researchers believe that pepper may have value in treating pneumonia. They also wonder whether the aroma of pepper might help smokers quit their addiction. The Chinese have long believed that pepper may treat epilepsy. In this respect, research is focusing on children with epilepsy. The Chinese also believe that pepper may enhance the properties of other medicines, requiring, for example, a smaller dose of an antibiotic to treat an infection. A compound in pepper, pipertine, may treat epilepsy, high blood pressure, asthma, tuberculosis, and possible acquired immunodeficiency syndrome (AIDS). To date, the U.S. National Library of Medicine has compiled a list of some 300 peer-reviewed papers on the efficacy of pepper in treating various ailments.

The Present

India and Indonesia remain leading pepper producers, though Brazil and Africa also play an important role. In Southeast Asia, pepper production has spread from Indonesia north to Vietnam. Today, Vietnam supplies about 30 percent of the world's pepper. The world produces about 640 million pounds of pepper per year. The United States imports most of its pepper from India. Yet a fungus in the genus *Phytophthora* (the genus of microbe that destroyed Ireland's potato crop in the 1840s) now threatens pepper.

Further Reading

Civitello, Linda. *Cuisine and Culture: A History of Food and People*. Hoboken, NJ: John Wiley and Sons, 2011.

Shaffer, Marjorie. *Pepper: A History of the World's Most Influential Spice*. New York: St. Martin's Press, 2013

Pineapple

A perennial herb, pineapple is a crop of the tropics and subtropics. Americans associate the fruit with Hawaii, though the islands are past their heyday in pineapple production. The Tupi-Guarani of South America called pineapple *nana*, meaning "excellent fruit." Nana is the root of the genus *Ananas* and the Spanish word *anana*. A member of the Bromeliaceae family, all species of pineapple are in one of two genera: *Ananas* and *Pseudonanas*. *Ananas* contains the five species *Ananas bracteatus*, *Ananas fritzmuelleri*, *Ananas comosus*, *Ananas eretifolius*, and *Ananas ananassoides*. *Pseudonanas* has only the species *Pseudonanas sagenarius*. Pineapple is 80–85 percent water, 0.4 percent protein, 0.5 percent ash, 0.1 percent fat, and 12–15 percent sugar, of which 5.9–12 percent is sucrose, 1–3.2 percent glucose, and 0.6–2.3 percent fructose. One hundred grams of pineapple contain 2.5 to 4.8 milligrams of folic acid, 200 to 280 milligrams of niacin, 75 to 165 milligrams of pantothenic acid, 69 to 125 milligrams of thiamine, 20 to 88 milligrams of riboflavin, 10 to 140 milligrams of vitamin B_6, 0.02 to 0.04 milligrams of vitamin A, and 10 to 25 milligrams of vitamin C. In addition to nutrients, pineapple contains the enzyme bromelaia, which reduces inflammation.

American Origins and the European Quest for Empire

The pineapple likely originated near the equator in what is today Brazil. This appears to be the region that yielded the cacao tree and the coca plant, both of which would become important worldwide, though in the case of coca not for the best

Hawaii

Polynesians from nearby islands as well as Tahiti settled the Hawaiian Islands as early as 1500 BCE, though the Tahitians may have arrived some 500 years later. In 1778, British captain James Cook was the first European to view Hawaii, though his experience was not fortuitous because he died on the big island about a year later. Its influence growing throughout the 19th century, the United States claimed the Hawaiian Islands as a U.S. territory in 1898. Sugar and pineapple were and are important to the economy.

reasons. Before the era of European conquest, the pineapple had spread from Brazil to Guiana, Colombia, and many parts of Central America and the Caribbean. Indeed, Italian Spanish explorer Christopher Columbus first came upon pineapple in 1493, on what are today the Caribbean islands of Guadeloupe, which have had longstanding ties with France rather than Spain. The natives of Guadeloupe ate pineapple fresh or roasted them over a fire. They even made a type of wine from pineapple juice, a surprise to the Spanish who associated wine only with the grapevine. The Spanish who followed Columbus delighted in eating pineapple and in writing about it for a European public eager to learn of the flora and fauna of the Americas. In this context, the pineapple shaped history as a symbol of exoticism and a fruit of enchantment. Puzzlingly, Europeans seemed initially unaware that the pineapple would not tolerate frost and so could not be grown in Europe or North America.

With the Columbian Exchange, the pineapple invaded the tropics worldwide: Hawaii and other tropical islands in the Pacific Ocean, tropical islands in the Atlantic Ocean, and Asia and Africa. Throughout the tropics, pineapple was often grown alongside sugarcane. Sugar was frequently used to sweeten pineapple, though from the standpoint of sweetness, this act was superfluous. The pineapple did not need additional sweeteners, though sugar arose as an important ingredient in lengthening the duration of storage.

The pineapple was first a luxury because transit from the tropics to Europe was expensive in the age of sail. In this respect, pineapple was much like sugar, a commodity of privilege before it became an item of the masses. Its status as a luxury irritated British philosopher David Hume, who lamented that he could not form an opinion about pineapple because he could not find one to taste. From the outset, pineapple was a dessert fruit, a status it shares with the apple and many other fruits.

Once Europeans formed some sense of the demand for pineapple, they carved out estates in tropical America as they had for sugarcane and coffee. They quickly learned that land that favored sugarcane was equally suited for pineapple. In this regard, pineapple changed history as a symbol and object of empire, of conquest, riches, and exoticism. Pineapple was the fruit of colonialism. Portugal, France, the Netherlands, and England all sought to carve out pineapple estates in the tropics. South and Central America and the Caribbean were the first sites of the pineapple empire. By 1700, the pineapple had conquered the tropics worldwide, thanks to European desires for empire.

The Queen of Fruits in Hawaii and the Rise of Pineapple Capitalism

According to one thesis, British mariner James Cook may have introduced the pineapple to Hawaii, though others favor a later Spanish introduction. By the 19th century sugar, and secondarily, pineapple, emerged as cash crops. Americans had first tried to grow pineapple in South Florida without much success, turning thereafter to Hawaii, whose ideal climate and rich volcanic soils made it the perfect region for pineapple culture. So eager for wealth from sugar and pineapple was the United States that it established a naval base at Pearl Harbor in the 1880s. In 1893, the United States overthrew the Hawaiian government and in 1898 annexed Hawaii. The United States was building its own pineapple empire. It appears important as well that the United States conquered the Philippines, islands on which pineapple could be grown, during and immediately after the Spanish-American War. Hawaii supplied California with pineapples, particularly after the gold rush when California's population swelled.

In 1900 American entrepreneur James Dole, initially toying with the idea of establishing coffee trees on Hawaii, settled on pineapple as the source of what would become an immense fortune. That year he formed the Hawaiian Pineapple Company, now Dole, carving out a huge plantation on the island of Oahu. His chief innovation was to can pineapple, which could now be enjoyed anytime by any consumer. Dole established a cannery in Wabiewa so he could export pineapple worldwide. Determined to minimize costs, he paid laborers only $12 per month at a time when Ford Motor Company paid workers $5 per day. By paying so little, Dole undercut the cost of growing pineapple in Florida. By 1921, Dole was the largest and wealthiest landowner in Hawaii, though when labor costs rose he transferred operations to the Philippines. By 2000, Hawaii, no longer the center of pineapple culture, totaled just 2 percent of global output. Today, farmers grew pineapple throughout the tropics and subtropics: Thailand, the Philippines, China, Brazil, India, the United States, Vietnam, Mexico, Indonesia, South Africa, Colombia, Malaysia, Kenya, Costa Rica, Singapore, Ghana, Cotê d'Ivoire, Taiwan, and Zaire. Thailand, the Philippines, and Brazil are the leading producers.

Pineapple plutocrats put their money in intensive cultivation and in paying workers poorly, following the business model that has made American capitalism a worldwide success. Pineapple thus helped point the United States and the rest of the world in the direction of the modern global economy, in which global forces put downward pressure on wages and working conditions. Pineapple has changed the world by helping make possible the global economy.

The Pineapple and Scurvy

Scurvy is seldom thought of today, but it was once a lethal disease. It threatened life wherever the diet was too poor to permit the consumption of fruits and vegetables. Much attention has focused on the historical role of citrus fruits in preventing and treating scurvy. Citrus fruits deserve this renown, but less attention has focused on pineapple, which, like citrus fruits, is a tropical fruit rich in vitamin C, the antiscurvy agent. In the 18th century, European mariners, British explorer James Cook foremost among them, recognized the importance of pineapple in the diet of sailors. These mariners supervised the planting of pineapple suckers near the harbors in the tropics to ease the harvest and storage of pineapples. Because pineapples, like citrus fruits, are perishable, a voyage through the tropics required a ship to make several stops to ensure that sailors had enough fresh pineapple to eat. In this context, the importance of the pineapple was confined to the tropics. One could not undertake a voyage through waters in the temperate zones in the expectation of harvesting pineapples along the way, because the pineapple, as noted earlier, will not tolerate frost. Fortunately, the potato may be used for such voyages because it, too, is an important source of vitamin C.

The Pineapple as the Forbidden Fruit

The creation story in Genesis has become a classic tale in the West. It has been part of the foundation upon which would arise the great monotheistic religions: Judaism, Christianity, and Islam. The story makes clear that the first humans, Adam and Eve, could eat from any tree in Eden except from the tree of knowledge of good and evil. The two disobey and are cast out of Eden, though men have been too eager to focus the blame on Eve. Curiously, the story does not specify the fruit, allowing the imagination to run wild. Readers, religious people, and scholars have had no shortage of suppositions. Some have favored the fig. Others point to the banana. The most popular suggestion came from Christian theologian and biblical translator Saint Jerome. He chose the apple. In the 17th century, England's King James I offered his own suggestion, the pineapple. Like many of the earlier suggestions, the pineapple was a poor choice. Because it will not grow outside the tropics, it could not have grown in Eden if one assumes that Eden was somewhere in western Asia, perhaps in the Levant.

Further Reading

Bartholomew, D. P., R. E. Paull, and K. G. Rohrbach, eds. *The Pineapple: Botany, Production, and Uses.* Honolulu: University of Hawaii at Manoa, 2002.

Beauman, Fran. *The Pineapple: King of Fruits.* London: Chatto and Windus, 2005.

O'Connor, Kaori. *Pineapple: A Global History.* London: Reaktion Books, 2013.

Okihiro, Gary Y. *Pineapple Culture: A History of the Tropical and Temperate Zones.* Berkeley, CA: University of California Press, 2009.

Salunkhe, D. K., and S. S. Kadam. *Handbook of Fruit Science and Technology: Production, Composition, Storage, and Processing.* New York: Marcel Dekker, 1995.

Pizza

An indigene of Naples, Italy, pizza was one of the many by-products of the Columbian Exchange, specifically of the migration of the tomato from tropical America to southern Italy. From Naples, pizza spread only gradually throughout Italy, a slowness that may hinge on several factors. Italian immigrants brought pizza to the United States in the late 19th century, where the food took on a greater variety of forms amid the American obsession with experimenting with ethnic cuisines. Perhaps the fundamental transformation of pizza has been its standardization and mass marketing, traits that have long characterized the American and now global economies.

Italian Origins

Pizza appears to have originated in Naples in the 18th century. There was then no Italy but rather a fragmented peninsula, with rival European powers each claiming their own piece. Italian author and political theorist Niccolò Machiavelli had complained about this problem in the 16th century, but only in the 19th century would

Originally a food of the poor in Italy's slums, pizza has emerged as a world food. It's popularity in the United States is difficult to overstate. (Viktor Pravdica/Dreamstime.com)

Italy unify. Its fragmented character in the 18th century must at least partly explain why pizza was so slow to expand from its Neapolitan roots.

Pizza's early history is bound up with that of the tomato. A product of the Columbian Exchange, the tomato was cultivated in southern Italy as early as 1564. The Columbian Exchange was a momentous event that transformed forever the biota of the world. In many parts of Europe people were suspicious of the tomato, noting its resemblance to the toxic belladonna. Many people, particularly those in northern Europe, would not eat tomatoes at first, but the fruit's reception seems to have been much better in southern Italy. No one can be sure when the tomato was added to pizza, but by the early 19th century, if not earlier, the people of Naples were arranging tomato slices on pizza the way one might eat a slice of tomato on a hamburger. The use of tomato sauce would come later, but it seems an essential ingredient in the United States today.

Pizza's early history seems to be bound up with durum, the hardest species of wheat with the highest protein content. Several lines of evidence point to durum. First, southern Italy was well suited to the cultivation of durum wheat. Second, although durum wheat does not make an ideal leavened bread, the people of Naples used a flatbread that could easily have been made from durum as the foundation of their pizza. Third, there was an early connection between pizza and pasta. Pasta is made from durum wheat, strengthening the suggestion that it was used to make pizza as well. In fact, the vendors who sold pasta in and around Naples were the first to sell pizza.

Even though the Spanish occupied Naples in the 18th century, and even though Spanish soldiers stationed in Naples ate pizza, there is no evidence that pizza was an early Italian export to Spain. In fact, very few European outside Naples knew about pizza. In the early 19th century, French author Alexandre Dumas came across pizza while touring Naples and other parts of southern Italy. His accounts gave the French their first taste of pizza. Dumas noted that pizza was primarily a food of the poor. Because they were too poor to afford cooking utensils, these people had to buy pizza daily from street vendors. The original pizza was primarily bread because the people of Naples needed something filling to eat. Dumas wrote that the poor subsisted on watermelon in summer and on pizza in winter. Like potatoes and peas, then, pizza was a food of the masses and so made possible an expansion in population. Yet corn played a greater role in population expansion in southern Europe, and the potato had its effects in the north. At the outset, the variety was not extravagant. One could buy pizza with slices of tomato, pizza with oil, pizza with animal fat, pizza with fish, or pizza with cheese. Cheese pizza was not initially popular because it tended to be more expensive than the alternatives.

Even in the early 20th century, pizza was nothing like a world food. The fascists who ruled Italy hoarded the wheat crop to be sure of having enough bread on hand. They believed that wheat flour diverted to the making of pizza was wasteful and so discouraged the consumption of pizza. Only after World War II did pizza begin to spread beyond Naples in its conquest of the Italian peninsula.

Pizza in the United States

In the United States, pizza was part of the immigrant experience. Italian immigrants brought pizza to the United States in the late 19th century, where it quickly became a symbol of the Italian American experience. Pizza became a way of asserting one's Italian heritage. It was a staple food in the Little Italy neighborhoods that Italian Americans carved out in America's cities. New York City was the first home of the American pizza, but wherever Italians spread they took pizza with them. Soon a rivalry developed between thin and thick crust pizza, with Chicago championing thick pizza, and New York City, thin crust. This rivalry transcended the important but still nascent sports rivalries between cities. One could argue about many things in America, including what city made the best pizza. Like spaghetti and meatballs, pizza became an Italian American gift to the United States. Both have risen to the status of a comfort food.

Robust progress came after World War II. Americans, with more leisure time, visited restaurants more often and bought more pizza. Pizza became a celebratory food. College students feasted on pizza at parties and so the food became part of the postwar college experience, shaping the lives of innumerable young men and women. As a celebratory food, pizza became the food that Americans ate on Sundays while they watched their favorite football teams. It soon became the takeout food of the Super Bowl. It accompanied the TV dinner as the staple of the stay-at-home crowd.

In a large sense, pizza has become the quintessential American food. Per capita, the United States consumes more pizza than any other nation. As a nation, America eats more than 1 billion tons of pizza per year. Only the hamburger rivals these figures. Americans spend more than $1 billion on frozen pizza per year. An eclectic food, pizza underscores the regional diversity of the United States. People in New Haven, Connecticut, put clams and oregano on their pizza. Duck and goat cheese are the toppings favored in Hollywood, California. Unlike the original pizzas of Naples, Hollywood pizza is not cheap. Pineapple and Canadian bacon are the toppings of choice in Hawaii.

The range of toppings reinforces what some historians call the American tendency toward food experimentation and the tendency to embrace and manipulate ethnic cuisine. Despite variation, the chains, notably Pizza Hut and Domino's, have attempted to standardize pizza the way automaker Henry Ford standardized the automobile and McDonald's standardized the hamburger. The McDonald's analogy is particularly apt because the labor model is identical and is a distillation of the American experience with capitalism. The objective of maximizing profits comes at the expense of diversity and labor. The pizza employee, like his or her McDonald's counterpart, occupies the lowest rung on the ladder of employment. Pay is at or near minimum wage; the toil, unrelenting and repetitive; the benefits and pension, nonexistent. The person who takes such a job holds it only long enough to find something better. Turnover is high; job satisfaction, low; and loyalty, unknown.

The American Midwest, the land of corn and soybeans, was the cradle of the pizza chains. Pizza Hut traces its roots to Kansas, and Domino's hails from Michigan. The founders were not Italian American and were more devoted to profits than to pizza. They favored thin crusts because they reduced the cost of buying flour. They added more cheese than was typical of Italian pizzas to enhance fat and flavor. Fresh ingredients were expensive enough to eschew all the while that executives touted the freshness of their pizzas. Americans, in a land of abundance, wanted many toppings, so the chains complied. The older of the two giants, Pizza Hut, opened in 1958, claiming 310 stores within the next decade. As with McDonald's, Pizza Hut targeted middle class families with disposable incomes and plenty of mouths to feed. By 1977, Pizza Hut had 3,400 restaurants worldwide. That year PepsiCo, a giant conglomerate, bought Pizza Hut for $300 million. Pizza Hut entered food courts to offer express service to affluent teens armed with mom's credit card. Pizza Hut even combined with Taco Bell to create joint restaurants in a move that looked much like a merger. To counter Domino's, Pizza Hut entered the delivery market. This proved hazardous, for the rush to deliver pizzas on time risked lives. By the 1980s, delivering pizza was as hazardous a job as becoming a miner or working in heavy construction. Capitalist to the core, Pizza Hut was not shy about courting communists, opening the first pizza store in China in 1988. Two years later a store followed in Russia, though communism was already in retreat. Even more successful was Pizza Hut in Poland. Polish franchises were rich enough to buy their counterparts in Russia. Italy, however, has not succumbed to Pizza Hut. The franchises have failed to find customers. Nevertheless, by 2005 the United States had more than 8,000 Pizza Huts, and 90 other countries claimed more than 4,000 franchises. Even India has Pizza Hut restaurants.

Domino's opened in 1960 and became so profitable that the owners were able to buy the Detroit Tigers in 1983. Here was the marriage between pizza and baseball, though it is premature to predict the demise of the hot dog. The hot dog seems destined to remain baseball's signature food. By 1983, Domino's had more than 1,000 stores in the United States and Canada. Like Pizza Hut, Domino's targeted families. The first to enter the delivery business, Domino's at one time promised a free pizza if one did not receive it within 30 minutes. The entrance into the delivery business signaled how closely the pizza industry was tied to the automobile. The automobile made possible new levels of convenience in the pizza industry. Apart from Pizza Hut and Domino's, Chuck E. Cheese's also caters to families, but the real emphasis appears to be on raising a generation of children to become gastronomically dependent on pizza.

Further Reading

Helstosky, Carol. *Pizza: A Global History*. London: Reaktion Books, 2008.

Pork

Pork is a category of meat derived from the pig. For much of prehistory and history pork had abundant fat because the pig accumulated fat as it aged. In recent decades, however, consumers have demanded leaner cuts of pork. The dietary change owes much to the automobile, labor-saving devices, health concerns, and the science of livestock breeding.

Pork and Population

For at least 7,000 years, humans have eaten pork. This transition appears to have begun in Asia with the people of western Asia and China. It seems possible that this development was independent in each region rather than a borrowing from one society to another. From these nascent events pork is today the most widely

Berkshire Pig

The Berkshire pig originated in Britain, and by the 19th century was the prototypical pig, having a large subcutaneous layer of fat. Moreover, fat marbled the pork. The fat gave pork from this breed excellent flavor, and it was popular in Europe and the United States. The Berkshire pig is still kept in the United Kingdom and Australia, but its meat is no longer the pork of choice. An animal of the meatpacking industry, the Berkshire pig was itself a victim of industry. As the machine age, particularly the invention and spread of the automobile, made people less active, they began to demand leaner cuts of pork. The Berkshire pig would no longer suffice. Scientists turned to other breeds, crossing them to achieve an ever-leaner animal so that today the average pig has less fat than the average American.

consumed meat, beating even beef. Pork thus must have changed the world by helping to fuel the dramatic population increase of the last century or two. In fact, thanks to pork and other foods, humans may be tottering at a precipice. With a global population of 7 million people, many scientists fear that the food supply cannot expand to feed many more people. In the 18th century, British economist Thomas Malthus was among the first to warn of these dangers. Because of this prescience, the phenomenon by which the human population outruns its food supply is know as the Malthusian Crisis.

Pork encompasses a range of foods: the tenderloin, pork chop, ham, and bacon perhaps being the most popular. In the West, ham rivals turkey as a holiday meat, though strictly turkey is poultry rather than meat. Some families serve both ham and turkey on Thanksgiving and Christmas, underscoring the bounty of their table.

Pork and the Rise of the Corn Belt

Pork has been particularly important in the American Midwest. Since colonial times, the pig was a common animal on the family farm. Its versatility came from its willingness to eat anything, even the excrement from humans and other animals. By the 19th century, pig and pork production began to cluster in the Midwest. The region was ideal because it produced the lion's share of America's corn. This moment arose at a time when many Americans were reducing their consumption of corn, though it is true that many African Americans continued to eat several dishes based on a foundation of corn. Given these circumstances, what was a Midwesterner to do with his or her bounty of corn? The answer was to feed it to pigs. With millions of pigs devouring corn, the farmer planted ever more corn, making the Midwest into the Corn Belt, a designation it retains today even though soybeans are at least as important as corn in many regions of the Corn Belt. Pork thus made the Corn Belt possible.

Pork and the Industrialization of Meat Production

With demand for pork high, Americans had to figure out how to butcher pigs and transport cuts of pork throughout the United States and other nations. Geography was critical because the Corn Belt was the pork kingdom. In the 19th century, western and southern Ohio were essential parts of the pork kingdom. Well situated was Cincinnati to the pork lands of western and southern Ohio, and it grew into the nation's pork-producing capital by 1840, when it was known as Porkopolis. The city's reign was brief. By the 1860s, Chicago, able to draw on the colossal scale of pig raising in Illinois and Iowa, emerged as the new pork capital. Long before

American automaker Henry Ford, Chicago butchers invented, if not the assembly line, then the disassembly line. Rather than moving workers, each of whom specialized in removing a certain cut of pork, from station to station, the pork producer moved a pig's carcass to a succession of workers. What had been a full carcass at the outset of the disassembly line became by the end little more than a skeleton. Because each worker did only a small, discrete task, he could not claim special skills. Indeed, he appeared to be more robot than human. Anyone could be trained to do a single job, making workers of little value. Meatpackers responded by paying workers next to nothing, the 19th-century capitalist solution to whatever ailed business, and an idea very much alive today. Poor pay and dismal working conditions motivated prolific American author Upton Sinclair in 1905 to investigate Chicago's meatpacking industry. The resulting expose, *The Jungle*, received widespread coverage. President Theodore Roosevelt may even have read it. Although Sinclair had hoped that *The Jungle* would awaken Americans to the suffering of workers, readers came instead to interpret the book as a compendium of filth and disease. It was demanded that government must make pork and other meats safe for consumption. Accordingly, in 1906, Congress passed and President Roosevelt signed the Pure Food and Drug Act and the Meat Inspection Act. Pork had expanded the role of the federal government. Moreover, Henry Ford toured a disassembly line, from which he derived the assembly line. One wonders whether the Model T would have been possible without pork.

Pork Is Too Fat

Pork had long been noted for its high fat content. This circumstance had satisfied consumers for centuries because fat enhanced pork's flavor. By the 1930s and 1940s, matters were beginning to change. Americans were more sedentary than their forbearers. They walked little and bicycled even less. The automobile took them wherever they wanted to go without any exertion. Labor-saving devices began to lighten the burden of housework. Mechanization made farm and factory life less strenuous. In short, Americans were burning fewer calories than their ancestors had. Amid these circumstances, Americans took aim at pork. Once a delight, its fat was now a calorie-laden drawback. Consumers began to demand leaner cuts of pork. Again, government had the solution. Federal and state funding spurred livestock breeders at the U.S. Department of Agriculture (USDA), the land-grant universities, and the agricultural experiment stations to act. Often these ventures were cooperative. Among the earliest efforts was the establishment of a hog improvement center in Columbus, Ohio, at which scientists gathered from The Ohio State University and the Ohio Agricultural Experiment Station (today the Ohio Agricultural Research and Development Center) around 1940. The progress in artificial insemination was the key to success. Scientists collected sperm from only the leanest male pigs, inseminating only the leanest females. Repeating the process over several generations, progress was rapid. Today, one can enter any Walmart to buy ham with only 3 percent fat. The average pig today is leaner than the average human. This is a case where pork did not so much change the world as the world changed pork. Yet matters are not easy to sort out. While Americans continue to demand lean cuts of pork, they continue to seek sources of fat, accounting for the huge rise in the consumption of junk food. Americans might eat a lean ham at the same time that they indulge in fattening pizza, potato chips, french fries, chocolate chip cookies, and many other permutations of foods that one ought not to eat, at least not in abundance.

Pork and Fat: A Second Take

Although Americans say they want lean cuts of pork, they also indulge in less-healthy alternatives. Pork is often the leading ingredient in hot dogs and other types of sausage. These items remain popular. Who goes to a baseball game without eating a hot dog? Sausage of all types is a staple of Fourth of July cookouts. Consumers do not appear to know exactly what parts of a pig are in hot dogs and sausage, but they do not seem to care. The parts of a pig that do not end up in hot dogs and sausage often make dog food. It turns out that in dietary terms, not much separates humans from dogs. In parts of the United States, Europe, Asia, and Africa, humans still use pig fat to fry other foods. Obviously the low-fat impulse may not be as strong as one might wish. The use of pork fat appears to be particularly strong in China. This fact seems paradoxical. The Chinese appear to consume liberal amounts of pork fat but as a group are leaner than Americans.

The Maximization of Pork

In modernity one tends to worry little about the stability of the food supply, though one should be anxious in light of the Malthusian Crisis. In earlier times, the food supply varied. This variability was true of pork. In this context, humans sought to maximize the supply of pork. A finite number of pigs of course provided a finite amount of pork. If a group of humans could not eat all the pork from a single butchering, they needed to preserve the rest for lean times. Pork, along with fish, was one of the first items that humans salted. The strategy worked because salt, absorbing water, dried the pork, making it less subject to decay. Although they cannot have known it at the time, the use of salt as a preservative meant that humans ate pork and other foods too laden with salt. Although one cannot blame pork alone, it is clear that many people consume too much salt. According to one account, the average American eats 11 pounds of salt per year when less than one pound suffices. Even in modernity, thanks to methods of preservation and preparation, pork still has too much salt. The result is an increase in the incidence of high blood pressure and cardiovascular disease. Humans pay a price for eating pork and other salty foods. From an early date, humans stretched their pork supply through other methods of drying and smoking. Even today, methods of preservation remain important. Worldwide, less than one third of pork is cooked fresh. The rest is processed and preserved as ham, bacon or filling for hot dogs and sausages.

Pork and Status

For centuries, pork was a measure of status. Choice cuts went to the elites. Commoners had to make do with what was left. The Afro-European Caribbean was a classic case. Europeans came to the Caribbean after Italian Spanish explorer Christopher Columbus's voyages to establish sugarcane and coffee estates. When other sources of labor faltered, Europeans enslaved Africans to toil in tropical America. The master assigned a black woman the job of cook. For his family she prepared the best cuts of pork. Even though she had cooked the meal she was not entitled to any of it. Often she and other slaves made do with little more than the pig's snout. The lack of pork, and the lack of nourishment in general, tormented slaves. Often masters were so cruel that they deliberately underfed their slaves while expecting their full exertions in the field. The result was slow starvation. Pork thus underscored the chasm between slave and master.

Further Reading

Rogers, Katharine M. *Pork: A Global History*. London: Reaktion Books, 2012.

Potato

People in the English-speaking world call the potato, a perennial grown as an annual, the "white potato" or "Irish potato" to distinguish it from the sweet potato. Although superficially similar, the two are only distantly related. The Peruvians called the potato *papa* or *papus*, meaning "root," in the mistaken belief that the tuber is a swollen root. In fact, the potato is an enlarged stem. The Spanish confused the term *papa* with the word *batata*, meaning sweet potato, yielding the

An indigene of the Andes Mountains in South America, the potato has become a world staple in the temperate zone. Even subtropical regions like Florida grow potatoes as a winter crop. (Sever180/Dreamstime.com)

word *patata*, or *potato* in English. The term *potato* refers to both plant and tuber. The potato excited the curiosity and caution of Europeans because, unlike grain, it produced its edible parts underground, similar to the production of turnips and carrots. Europeans were right to focus on the production of tubers because the potato is an efficient converter of sunlight into biomass, yielding more than three-quarters of its biomass in tubers. By contrast, grain yields only about one-third of their biomass in edible seeds.

A member of the Nightshade family, the potato plant produces toxic foliage. For this reason, its vegetation cannot be fed to humans or livestock. Some wild potato plants produce poisonous tubers, an evolutionary adaptation that deters predators. Tubers exposed to sunlight turn green, producing the toxin solanine. A cook must peel away the green flesh if people are to eat sun-exposed potatoes. As a member of the Nightshade family, the potato is related to the tomato, peppers, tobacco, petunia, and the poisonous belladonna.

Although it has less protein than grains, the potato yields high-quality protein with all the essential amino acids. The quality of potato protein ranks second only to the protein in egg whites. Potato protein is even superior to soy protein and much better than the protein in corn and wheat. One medium potato has nearly half the recommended daily allowance of vitamin C, 18 percent of potassium, 10 percent of vitamin B_6, and thiamine, riboflavin, folic acid, niacin, magnesium, phosphorus, iron, zinc, and fiber. Potato fiber may reduce the risk of colon cancer and diabetes and does lower cholesterol and triglycerides.

Luther Burbank

Born in 1849, Luther Burbank achieved renown as an American amateur botanist. But it is too much to claim him a scientist because he opposed Darwinism and lacked formal scientific training, though over the course of his career Burbank greeted many Americans who had traveled to California to see him at work. American oil baron John D. Rockefeller and American automaker Henry Ford made a pilgrimage to Burbank's farm. Throughout a career that exceeded more than 50 years, Burbank developed more than 800 new crop varieties. He was particularly proud of his work with tree fruits, but his fame appears to rest on the Burbank potato, now known as the Russet Burbank or Idaho potato. The potato is long, relatively spherical, and uniform. Because of its uniformity the variety is used to make french fries and potato chips. The Burbank potato thus underpins the fast food industry.

The Potato's Reception in Europe

The Spanish encountered the potato in the Andes mountains in the 1530s, but it did not begin to sink roots into Europe's soils until the late 16th century. Even then, it did not gain popularity until the 18th and 19th centuries. Several factors account for the slowness of adoption. Europeans were suspicious of the potato because of its membership in the Nightshade family. Because it was strangely shaped, the potato was thought to cause leprosy, a terrible disease that afflicted Europe's poor. The potato was also thought to be an aphrodisiac. This supposition cut both ways. It was a boon to lovers, but the many Protestant sects that glorified self-control

Vitamin C

It is curious that humans appear to be the only primate that cannot synthesize vitamin C in the way that they can synthesize vitamin D from sunlight. Vitamin C was discovered only in the 20th century, though it was important to humans for millennia. Our lineage appears to have eaten a diet rich in fruits containing vitamin C and so lost the ability to synthesize the vitamin. The consumption of vitamin C has thereafter become essential. Without sufficient vitamin C humans can develop scurvy, a fatal disease. Fortunately, a number of foods are rich in vitamin C. A medium potato, for example, has half the recommended daily allowance of vitamin C. Other foods rich in this vitamin are pineapple, citrus fruits, and cabbage. Because the vitamin is water soluble and thus excreted in urine, one must consume the vitamin every day.

urged their congregants not to eat potatoes. Others branded the potato insipid and would not eat it. Still others, nurtured on bread, thought the potato a poor substitute. An important factor was the potato's initial difficulties in Europe. Coming from tropical America, though at elevations that made the potato a fine crop for temperate zones, it had evolved in an area with 12 hours of daylight year round. But in northern Europe, summer days were much longer, causing the potato to yield abundant foliage but small tubers. Only careful selection, which took time, remedied this problem. The potato's demographic effects would ultimately make it one of the world's most important foods.

An Antiscurvy Agent

From its establishment in Europe and to a lesser degree in cool regions of Asia and Africa, the potato changed the world in important ways. It appears to be well known that sailors on long-distance voyages often suffered from scurvy, from the poverty of their diet. Although humans would not know about vitamins until the early 20th century, a paucity of vitamin C in the diet causes scurvy. Interest has focused on citrus fruits and pineapple as antiscurvy agents, but they were not alone.

In 1784, a U.S. private ship, the *Empress of China*, left New York City for China, in the most ambitious voyage the United States had attempted. It would be the first American ship to reach China. The *Empress* carried enough food for at least 14 months. The ship would have no citrus fruits or pineapple until the crew gathered oranges at the Cape Verde Islands off the coast of Africa. Instead, their diet was a monotonous fare of salted beef and pork, bread, and potatoes. How did they manage to fend off scurvy? The potato is the answer. One medium potato, as noted earlier, has half the recommended daily allowance of vitamin C and so has been an unsung but important antiscurvy agent. As much as citrus fruits and pineapple, the potato made long-distance voyages possible in the early modern era and beyond. In this regard, potatoes were particularly important for temperate ocean crossings. One could not hope to stop at Greenland for citrus fruits or pineapple, which do not grow in temperate locales.

Potatoes and Corn

Perhaps nothing has been so important to the potato's conquest of northern Europe as its nutritional profile. Many Europeans, especially the poor, had little but the potato to eat, and they were healthy. By the mid-18th century, nearly half of all Irish subsisted on little more than potatoes, plus an occasional cabbage and milk. Even though they were destitute, they were probably much healthier than today's average American, who often suffers from obesity, diabetes, and other ailments. Acre for acre, the potato provides four or five times more calories than any grain. Herein was the secret of Europe's demographic revolution. Given the potato's superior nutrition, it serves as a contrast to corn. A diet of little but corn leads to pellagra, a disease of dietary deficiency. Pellagra was an enormous problem in the U.S. South in the early 20th century, when many poor people were reduced to eating little more than corn. Scientists puzzled over this disease until the U.S. Department of Agriculture (USDA) fingered corn as the culprit. Both American indigenes, potatoes and corn, have been important foods worldwide, but there is little doubt that potatoes yield superior nourishment.

Warfare

In its own way, the potato revolutionized warfare in early modern Europe. The notion that an army would maintain a supply line of food was little evident at this time. Instead, soldiers lived off the land, meaning that they stole food from nearby peasant families. A year's harvest of grain might disappear into the stomachs of hungry plunderers, leaving a family to starve during the winter. In this context, as so often, war meant disaster for all. The potato improved the fate of peasants. Because the tuber resided below ground, soldiers seldom stopped long enough to dig them. A family that lost its grain to war still had potatoes that would allow them to survive.

The Thirty Years' War (1618-1648) demonstrated the value of the potato and, toward the end of the 17th century, militarist Prussian king Frederick William ordered all farmers to plant potatoes or risk losing their ears and noses. In the 18th century, Prussian king Frederick II (Frederick the Great) continued this policy, dispatching free seed potatoes throughout the kingdom. The potato had saved Prussia from ruination during the Seven Years' War (1756-1763). In 1778, war erupted between Prussia and Austria. Each combatant tried to destroy the opponent's potato fields as a way of terrorizing civilians and undermining morale. So important was the potato that this conflict became known as the "potato war." A few years earlier, Empress Catherine the Great, following developments to her west and so recognizing the potato's importance in warfare and in averting famine, ordered her peasants to plant potatoes. Poland, the Netherlands, Belgium, and Scandinavia followed this example. The potato had conquered northern and eastern Europe. The more Europeans fought one another the more important became the potato.

Demography and Disaster

The potato's density of calories and nutrients caused Europe's population to soar. Between 1750 and 1800, Europe's population increased from 140 to 190 million.

By 1850, Europe bulged with 266 million people, and the number reached 400 million in 1900. Nowhere were these effects more evident than in Ireland. In 1600, Ireland had at most 1.5 million people. In 1700, the population reached 2 million; in 1800, 5 million; and in 1845, 8.5 million.

The potato and people fared so well not only because the climate and soils favored potatoes, but also because the land tenure system was so flawed. English landlords owned Ireland and demanded such high rents in grain that the poor had to plant nearly all their land to grain or leave it as pasture for livestock. They could maintain themselves on only a small parcel of land on which they grew potatoes. Dysfunctional though it was, the system worked initially. Two or three acres were enough to feed even a large family with potatoes left over to feed a pig. By one account the potato enabled the Irish peasant to eat better than his counterpart on the continent, who subsisted on bread. One historian estimated that the average adult Irishman ate 10 pounds of potatoes per day. Supplementing this monotonous fare with cabbage, turnips, and milk, when available, he consumed some 4,000 calories per day, a high figure by contemporary standards.

The first evidence that the system could not be sustained came in 1740 and 1741, when a long, frigid winter killed the potato crop. By one estimate, hundreds of thousands of people starved and only the apparent willingness of English landlords to let the peasants keep some of the grains, notably oats, prevented the famine from killing more. From this disaster and others like it, British clergyman Thomas Malthus concluded that population tends to outrun its food supply. He understood that the potato had allowed the population to increase in Ireland and throughout northern Europe. Ireland and other countries did not have jobs for all those extra people, so that wages decreased. Many people had no alternative to an existence as landless laborers. The potato had not improved living standards. It had only allowed more people to live in a state of misery. Between 1800 and 1845, 114 commissions reported that Ireland's poor were on the verge of starvation, yet England did nothing to ameliorate conditions. The final precondition to disaster came in the early 19th century when scientists derived a new potato variety, the Lumper. It had little to recommend it beyond high yield. It was insipid, less nourishing than the old varieties, and vulnerable to disease. Because the Irish planted the Lumper to the exclusion of other varieties, they had a genetically uniform crop. A disease that killed one plant would likely kill many more.

Warning came in 1843 when a fungus struck potato plants near Philadelphia. In 1844, the fungus spread to lands near Lakes Erie and Ontario. In 1845, it reached the Mississippi River. By that year it had spread in Europe to Belgium, Denmark, the United Kingdom, France, northern Italy, Spain, Norway, and Sweden. The fungus and the damage it caused were not therefore a local event. The fungus was an epidemic that attacked a vulnerable crop.

In Ireland, the year 1845 seemed promising at the outset. The Irish planted a few million acres to potatoes, a 6 percent increase over the previous year, and expected a harvest of tens of millions of tons. Summer bathed the potato plants in sun but in September the rains and overcast skies brought a fungus to Ireland. As one might have expected of a genetically uniform crop, the fungus swept through the potato fields, killing the entire crop in only weeks. The fungus turned a potato plant black and withered it. When an anxious farmer dug up the tubers he found them rotten. In cases where a farmer had an intact potato, he celebrated his luck but it, too, rotted. The entire crop was lost. In 1846 the fungus returned, repeating the tragedy. Bereft of their potatoes, the poor had nothing to eat. Some were reduced to eating acorns and tree bark in an attempt to satiate hunger.

The masses might have eaten some of the grain that they had grown, but the British landlords took it all as rent. Acting selfishly, they worsened the crisis. The U.K.'s Parliament was slow to act. Its members did nothing to help the Irish in 1845. Reformers, roused at last, targeted the Corn Laws as part of the problem. The laws placed a duty on grain imported to the British Isles, raising its price. Because imported grain was costly, domestic growers could keep prices above market value, ensuring that the poor could not afford bread. Repealing the Corn Laws in 1846, Parliament made possible the importation of cheaper grain to Ireland. Parliament even sent a shipment of corn from the United States to Ireland to feed the poor, but these measures were not enough. Between 1845 and 1849, 1 million died and 1.5 million left Ireland for the United States and Canada.

Scientists could not initially agree on the cause of this catastrophe. In 1845, Belgian clergyman and amateur scientist Edouard van den Hecke made a promising start, using a microscope to identify a fungus on the leaves of diseased plants. Botanist Rene van Oye, using Hecke's discovery, asserted that the fungus had killed the potato plants. British surgeon Alfred Smee disagreed, countering that the fungus had arisen from putrefying plants. The fungus was therefore a result, not a cause of the malady. Others thought that excess water in the soil, rather than a fungus, had rotted the potatoes. These attacks did not put the supporters of the fungal hypothesis off the track. In 1846, clergyman and amateur scientist Miles Joseph Berkeley published a detailed study of the fungus, once more fingering it as the culprit. Finally, in 1861, German botanist Heinrich Anton de Bary took the decisive step, putting the fungus on healthy plants. They all succumbed, proving the fungal hypothesis. De Bary named the fungus *Phytophthora infestans*, a moniker it retains today. De Bary's work marked the foundation of the new science of plant pathology. Through the perverse agents of disease and death, the potato had advanced science.

To Mars

The National Aeronautics and Space Administration (NASA) has in the 21st century explored the possibility of planting potatoes on rockets and space stations. The plants would yield oxygen for the crew and the tubers would provide an ideal source of nourishment, being rich in so many vitamins and minerals. Even the protein content, though not large, is of the highest quality. The potato and little else sustained generations of northern Europeans. It may now be poised to take humans to Mars, a goal that President George W. Bush wished to achieve by 2040. True, Mars is an alien land. Humans will not be able to plant potatoes in its ground, but the potato will nonetheless be momentous in value.

Further Reading

Donnelly, James S. Jr. *The Great Irish Potato Famine*. Gloucestershire, UK: Sutton Publishing, 2001.

Gallagher, Carole. *The Irish Potato Famine*. Philadelphia: Chelsea House Publishers, 2002.

Johnson, Sylvia A. *Tomatoes, Potatoes, Corn, and Beans: How the Foods of the Americas Changed Eating Around the World*. New York: Atheneum Books, 1997.

McNeill, William H. "How the Potato Changed the World's History." *Social Research* 66 (March 1999): 67–83.

Meltzer, Milton. *The Amazing Potato: A Story in Which the Incas, Conquistadors, Marie Antoinette, Thomas Jefferson, Wars, Famines, Immigrants, and French Fries All Play a Part*. New York: HarperCollins Publishers, 1992.

Reader, John. *Potato: A History of the Propitious Esculent*. New Haven, CT: Yale University Press, 2008.

Rodger, Ellen. *The Biography of Potatoes*. New York: Crabtree Publishing, 2007.

Salaman, Redcliffe. *The History and Social Influence of the Potato*. Cambridge: Cambridge University Press, 1985.

Schumann, Gail L. *Plant Diseases: Their Biology and Social Impact*. St. Paul, MN: APS Press, 1991.

Potato Chip

The potato chip is among America's most popular snack foods. The story of its creation has become a popular legend that probably contains much truth. The trouble with the potato chip is its contribution to obesity. To be sure, it is not the sole culprit. Lack of exercise and other poor dietary habits are also to blame, but the potato chip has certainly not improved matters. From a business perspective, the potato chip is a hallmark of all the ingredients of American capitalism: uniformity, standardization, mass production, and mass consumption. The potato chip is thus a microcosm of the American and the global economy.

Not All Potatoes are Suitable for Making Potato Chips

The potato, a world staple and highly nutritious food, has its spin-off in the highly prized but unhealthy potato chip. As a rule, potatoes suitable for baking are often poor for making chips. Even the Russet Burbank potato, of American amateur botanist Luther Burbank fame, is unsuitable for making potato chips, though it is entirely appropriate for slicing into fries. The traditional baking potato yields about 22 percent biomass for frying. Today's varieties, like Snowden, are an improvement, but the yield is still only about 30 percent.

American company Frito-Lay buys potatoes in bulk and demands consistency, standardization, and year-round mass production and mass consumption that are the hallmarks of American capitalism. Indeed, the potato chip industry shares its operational insights with the meatpackers and automakers that have made fortunes catering to consumers. Every potato chip must look and taste the same. The combination of starch, fat, and salt make the potato chip an evil necessity because humans are biologically predisposed to crave sugar, fat, and salt, with the potato chip supplying two of these three.

Potatoes that might otherwise be ideal for making potato chips may sprout during storage, forcing farmers to sell them as cattle feed. In the drive toward standardization Frito-Lay once bought potatoes from Ohio, but since 1990 has turned to Michigan and North Dakota, where irrigation produces the perfect chipping potato. Ohio has had to turn to niche potato chip companies in Pennsylvania. Florida has captured the off-season chip market, planting potatoes in January. By April, Florida's potatoes are sold to chippers. Florida, given its warmth, is not suitable for potatoes and so is not a big producer. But in the chip industry timing is everything.

Note that potatoes come in a diversity of colors, but chippers and American consumers in general want only white potatoes, a fact Burbank had sensed in the 19th century. Brown or green potato flesh, the result of fungi or sun exposure, is not suitable for making potato chips, nor should they be. As chippers have cut costs they have paid less for potatoes. It was possible to earn $25 per 100 pounds of potatoes in the 1980s. Today the pay is as little as $2 per 100 pounds. With this decline, potato farms have had to amass economies of scale, another feature of American capitalism, by buying their struggling neighbors. About 2000, Florida had some 300 potato farms. Today the number has dwindled to no more than 50. The decline has been even steeper in Ohio.

The Origin of the Potato Chip

Although the potato is a South American domesticate, the potato chip is a U.S. invention. Not all historians believe the Creation story, but it is so ubiquitous that there must be some truth to it. In the mid-19th century, Moon's Lake House in Saratoga Springs, New York, was a favorite retreat for America's industrial barons. In 1853, George Crum, of African American and Native American ancestry, joined the restaurant as chef. He prepared food flawlessly but had a temper. One dared not send food back to the kitchen for additional preparation. That year, according to all accounts, railroad magnate Cornelius Vanderbilt, among America's richest men, did the unthinkable by returning a plate of fried potatoes with the complaint that they were not sufficiently crunchy. Outraged, Crum determined to humiliate Vanderbilt. He chopped and fried potatoes in such thin strips that Vanderbilt would be forced to eat them by hand, something no one of status did. Crum failed. Vanderbilt so liked these chips that he ordered a second helping. Because of the connection to Saratoga Springs, the chips were known as Saratoga chips. Perhaps Crum should have patented his invention, but he never did, dying in virtual obscurity in 1914. Accounts hold that presidents Chester A. Arthur and Grover Cleveland indulged in Saratoga chips.

Creation of an Industry

Soon potato chips were sold in glass containers or, more popularly, in bags. The intent was to make potato chips a portable snack in the same way that the cone had made ice cream a portable product. Stores throughout the eastern United States filled barrels with potato chips, inviting customers to bag their own. Grocers began selling potato chips. About 1900, Snack Food Association member William Tappenden began to mass-produce potato chips in Cleveland, Ohio. At the same time, Ohio Chip Association leader Harvey Noss began selling potato chips and pretzels, promoting the salty appeal of both. Pennsylvania entrepreneurs followed this example, creating the largest number of potato chip companies in the United States. Prohibition boasted sales as speakeasies served them with alcohol, knowing that a salty snack would make a patron want a drink, in this case an alcoholic beverage. The Great Depression led Americans untraumatized by events to create small potato chip companies. After World War II, the potato chip became a national phenomenon, growing to be among America's prized snack foods.

Herman Lay, who sold peanuts at baseball games, made his fortune with the potato chip. With a Ford Model A, he toured the United States, selling potato chips wherever he stopped. In 1938, Lay built his first chip factory. In 1945, Lay merged in all but name with Elmer Doolin's company Fritos, which sold corn chips, to create a snack empire. The two formally merged in 1962. Frito-Lay advertised heavily on television, as did iconic Coca Cola and automakers. Magazine ads merged sex appeal with potato chips. Then as now, sex sells. As Microsoft has, Frito-Lay bought small competitors to create a virtual monopoly, the desideratum of the business model in a Darwinian context.

In the 1970s, American company Procter & Gamble launched Pringles, which became quickly popular. Contrary to traditional potato chips, Pringles were stacked in cans. Pringle's competitors, chiefly Frito-Lay, believed that this departure in shape and texture disqualified them from being a true potato chip. This contentious context provided the fodder for marketing wars and lawsuits. When the dust settled, Pringles retained the right to call themselves a potato chip product, a compromise that did not satisfy all litigants. Since the 1970s, competition has been cutthroat.

The Potato Chip and Obesity

Internecine warfare was only one problem that beset the potato chip. As the automobile and other accoutrements of modern existence took hold, Americans found themselves less engaged in strenuous work or exercise. In this environment, a diet high in fat, calories, and sugar led to obesity. It was clear to physicians and dieticians that the high-fat potato chip was part of the problem. The initial solution, conceived in the 1970s, was to fry potato chips in olestra, a large chemical compound that the human stomach could not digest. Yet it had the texture and taste of fat. Here, at last, one could eat something akin to a fat-free potato chip. Olestra was the result of 25 years of research and development and Food and Drug Administration (FDA) testing. The FDA approved the chemical in 1996. Yet because it could not be digested, olestra caused diarrhea and stomach and intestinal cramps in some people. In retrospect, it seems surprising that the FDA, after nine years of testing, approved the compound despite these problems. Later findings surfaced indicating that olestra reduced the body's ability to absorb vitamins. Fat-soluble vitamins D and E passed through the body. Again, the FDA should have been alert to this danger.

Not only was the potato chip not nourishing, it was now an obstacle to the absorption of nutrients from other foods. Perhaps most damning was the fact that the potato chip degraded the nutritious potato into junk food. Partly in response to criticism, Frito-Lay announced in 2006 that it would fry potato chips in sunflower oil rather than cottonseed oil to reduce the content of saturated fat. The U.S. Department of Agriculture (USDA), eager to protect potato farmers, issued an announcement that implied that potato chips were as healthy as apples, an irresponsible statement. Outraged apple growers forced the USDA to retract this distortion.

Manufactures returned to the offensive, claiming that potato chips were the largest contributors of vitamin C to the human diet. Even if such statements were true, they ignored the high fat content of potato chips. Medical concerns might consign the potato chip to the fridge.

Further Reading

Burhans, Dirk. *Crunch!: A History of the Great American Potato Chip*. Madison, WI: Terrace Books, 2008.

R

Rice

Today, half the world's population eats rice as the primary source of nourishment. Because so much rice is grown, it supplies more calories than any other food. Several percent of all farmland is planted to rice, a larger percentage than to any other crop. Unlike corn, farmers grow rice principally for human consumption. So important is rice that the ancients believed it to have been a divine gift. Probably because women did much of the work of growing rice, the rice deity was thought to be a goddess: the Rice Goddess or Rice Mother. The ancients believed that rice sustained the body like no other food can. Because humans ate rice, it must be a component of body and soul. Like humans, the rice plant, people conjectured, had a soul. Rice growers elaborated rituals to propitiate rice spirits, thereby ensure an abundant harvest. Rice contains carbohydrate, thiamine, riboflavin, niacin, vitamin D, calcium, iron, and fiber. Rice has little fat and sodium and no cholesterol or gluten. Rice fiber may protect one against cancer. Rice contains eight of the nine essential amino acids.

Asia

Authorities disagree about when and where humans domesticated rice. One scholar believes that humans first domesticated rice in the Yellow River valley about 8000 BCE. Alternatively, humans may have first domesticated rice in northeastern India and southwestern China, perhaps along what is now the border between India and China, about 7000 BCE. Another account identifies the Yangtze River valley around the same time as the cradle of rice culture. One account dates the origin of rice farming in India to 6500 BCE, whereas another points to 4000 BCE as the proper date. By 5000 BCE, according to one scholar, rice was grown in China, India and Southeast Asia. The earliest efforts to grow rice were on rainfed lands. Before farmers grew rice in paddies, dryland agriculture prevailed in Thailand, Laos, Vietnam, and southwestern China. As people migrated along the Mekong and Chao Phraya

Rice is the staff of life. Worldwide, more people derive the bulk of their calories from rice than from any other food. For this reason rice is arguably the world's most important grass. (Narathip Ruksa/Dreamstime.com)

Rivers, they brought rice to Indochina. From the Brahmaputra and Ganges Rivers, people brought rice into the heartland of India. From India, rice was taken across the Bay of Bengal to Malaysia and Indonesia. From Indonesia, rice spread to the Philippines, and from there, to Taiwan and Japan. Rice is the staff of life in Asia and is grown from India and Sri Lanka in the west to Southeast Asia and the islands of South Asia and to China, Korea, and Japan in the north. By 1000 CE, farmers were growing rice in all these areas. In Japan, farmers took great pride in their rice fields, earning the islands the moniker "the land of vigorous rice plants."

African Rice

There are two species of rice, one native to Africa and the other to east and south Asia. In principle, the two are easy to distinguish. The polished Asian kernel is long, cylindrical, and white. The African species presents two types of kernel, one short and white and the other long and red. The people of West Africa began cultivating rice about 4000 BCE. This rice was important during the Columbian Exchange. In the late 17th century, slaves brought African rice into South Carolina, intensifying slavery in North America, where rice planters became some of the richest and most influential Americans during the 18th century.

In Asia and elsewhere, water serves two purposes in rice culture. First, plant roots take up water. Although all plants use water, rice requires more water than any other grain. The second purpose of water is to flood land, suffocating weeds. Farmers in Asia cultivated both rainfed and paddy rice. A minority of farmers in Laos and Borneo and half the farmers in India rely on rain. The rest of the farmland is paddy. In some cases, throughout India for example, irrigation supplements the water that rice plants derive from rain.

Because rice is a labor-intensive crop, it required the effort of an entire community to grow it. The need for labor led communities to centralize their leadership, for someone had to determine when to plant, weed, and harvest rice. The aggregation of communities into larger units led to the creation of civilization, and in China, to dynastic rule. Rice therefore made possible the organization of Asia into hierarchical states. Curiously, in China, rice culture took root in the south whereas the dynasties flourished in the north. Consequently, the first Chinese states did not elevate rice culture to the status of a quasireligious activity. Nonetheless, the empire could not have survived without abundant harvests of rice, which fed people in both south and north.

In south China farmers from an early date put fish eggs in rice paddies. The fish that developed from these eggs ate insect larvae, lessening the damage insects did to rice. Because of this practice, people throughout Asia referred to south China as "the land of rice and fish." Innovations in China and Vietnam intensified the growing of rice. In the second century CE the Chinese began raising seedlings in nursery beds, transplanting them into the field as they matured. Although this practice demanded more labor than simply seeding the land, it increased yields. Sometime in antiquity, farmers in Vietnam derived a rapidly maturing cultivar that made possible the growing of more than one crop per year in temperate climates. In the 11th century, Chinese farmers adopted this cultivar, the Champas variety. Along the Guangong-Vietnam border, farmers raised two crops of rice per year and one crop of sweet potatoes. In the lower Yangtze River valley, farmers rotated rice with wheat. In parts of Cambodia, farmers raised as many as four rice crops per year, and even temperate locales could produce two or three crops of rice in a year. Over the millennia, Asian farmers have grown more than 120,000 varieties of rice, each with its own characteristics. The fast-maturing varieties ripen in as little as two-and-a-half months, whereas the full-season varieties take nine months to mature. From its inception rice has been the foundation of the civilizations of China, Southeast Asia, and India.

Africa

Some Africans believe that the rain god gave them rice in the mythic past. The Niger River valley may have been the center of rice cultivation in West Africa, where farmers domesticated rice between 4500 and 3000 BCE. Another account puts the origin of rice culture in West Africa at 1500 BCE. From the Niger River valley, rice spread to Senegal, if the first dates are correct, between 1700 and 800 BCE, and to East Africa in the ninth century CE. In addition to the Niger River valley, farmers independently domesticated rice along the Guinea coast between 1000 and 1200 CE. African rice, however, is not an iteration of Asian rice but a separate subspecies. Its grains are either short and white or long and red.

As early as 1000 BCE, merchants may have brought varieties of Asian rice to Madagascar, from which they spread to East Africa. Alternatively, merchants in East Africa may have imported rice from South Asia. According to one account, Arabs brought Asian rice to Africa between the sixth and 11th centuries. Another source holds that Africans did not know about *Oryza sativa* until the era of the slave trade. Despite its advantages, Asian rice did not supplant African rice, at least not everywhere, because Asian rice does not compete well with African weeds. Nevertheless, where farmers irrigated their land, Asian rice yielded well and displaced indigenous varieties. Yet Asian rice spread only slowly. Only in the 19th century did Asian rice spread from Mozambique to the Congo. Farmers cultivated rice, likely African varieties, in deep water basins, water holes, hydromorphic soils in the forest, on drylands in the hills of West Africa and in mangrove swamps along the Guinea coast. In the 16th century, African farmers began to grow rice on the Cape Verde Islands. Farmers grew rice as far north as Morocco.

In West Africa, farmers practiced three systems of cultivation: rainfed agriculture, paddy agriculture in inland swamps, and floodplain agriculture. In the last, farmers along the Guinea coast took advantage of the fact that the tide pushes freshwater upriver ahead of saltwater. They used this source of freshwater to flood lowlands on which they had planted rice. The advent of the slave trade opened a new market for African rice: ship captains bought it to feed slaves on the Middle Passage. Because it was cheap, slavers bought unmilled rice, which female slaves milled and cooked aboard ship to feed the rest of the slaves. African rice would influence the growth of rice and slavery in the Carolinas.

Rice and the Green Revolution

Perhaps no collection of scientific breakthroughs, known as the Green Revolution, did more to make rice the world staple capable, along with other foods, of feeding 7 billion people. Thanks to Green Revolution rice, science has for now averted the Malthusian Crisis. The India of the Green Revolution planted 125 million hectares to grains, an amount that is three-quarters of the nation's arable land. Of these 125 million hectares, about one-third is planted to wheat and legumes, one-third to rice, and one-third to sorghum and millet. Most of India's rice, as is true of much of south, east, and Southeast Asian rice, is paddy, not the dryland varieties that have had some success in parts of Africa and the United States. In 1970, Indian farmers planted 15 percent of their rice land to high-yielding varieties (HYVs). By 1980, the figure had more than doubled to one-third. Yield gains have been dramatic, ranging between 1,000 and 1,300 kilograms of rice per hectare during this period. Yet closer analysis reveals problems. Between 1961 and 1976, rice yields in India grew only 1.1 percent per year because 60 percent of rice lands were rainfed, suffering from non-uniform distribution, with floods alternating with dry spells.

In some ways, Japan, with a growing population and limited land, was a precursor to the Green Revolution. In the 20th century, Japan labored to breed HYVs of rice. The use of fertilizers in Japan had only limited success because the extra nitrogen caused a plant to elongate its stalk, which then lodged under the weight of heavy grains. Japanese scientists were among the first to understand that dwarf rices were necessary in any breeding program that wished to prevent lodging. The United States took notice of these dwarfs, acquiring them for its seed banks. As early as 1911, Japan shared these dwarfs with France and Italy. Japan experimented with crossing these dwarfs with U.S. and Korean rice varieties. A few of the offspring were important to the launching of the Green Revolution.

The Central Rice Research Institute concentrated on breeding HYVs of rice, crossing the japonica varieties from Japan with the indica varieties of India to yield progeny with a yield between five and six metric tons per hectare, whereas indica varieties yielded no more than two metric tons per hectare. Some of the offspring of these crosses were grown in Malaysia between the 1960s and 1990s. Green Revolution rice breeding began in India, spreading to the Philippines and the rest of Southeast Asia. In 1949, the Food and Agriculture Organization (FAO) established a rice-breeding center in Cuttack, India, which began to screen germplasm for dwarfs. Scientists crossed dwarf japonica varieties from Japan with tall indica varieties that were suited to the tropics and subtropics. The results were ADT-27 and Mahsuri, which yielded well and were widely adapted to India. ADT-27 was especially popular in India. In 1960, the Ford and Rockefeller Foundations established the International Rice Research Institute (IRRI) in the Philippines. IRRI scientists screened more than 10,000 rice varieties worldwide in search of novel genes. Collecting dwarfs, they began shuttle breeding as American agronomist Norman Borlaug had done with wheat. In 1962, IRRI breeder Peter Jennings crossed 38 varieties from seed banks. The eighth cross, between the Chinese dwarf Dee-geo-woo-gen and the tall Indonesian Peta, yielded a single plant with 130 precious seeds, the basis for IR 8. Jennings planted the F1, allowing the progeny to cross. One-quarter of the F2 were dwarfs, the typical Mendelian segregation for a single recessive gene. These offspring were crossed over several additional generations. The F5 contained a single promising plant, IR 8. It matured in 130 days, whereas traditional varieties needed 160 to 170 days. It yielded five metric tons per hectare without fertilizer, five times the average yield of traditional varieties. With fertilizer, IR 8 yielded 10 metric tons per hectare. The president of the Philippines visited India to see IR 8 and presumably took seeds home. In Pakistan IR 8 yielded 11 metric tons per hectare. The IRRI crossed IR 8 with 13 other varieties to derive IR 36, which matured in 105 days and was disease and insect resistant. In 1990, IR 72 yielded even more grain than IR 8 and IR 36. In the 1970s and 1980s alone, 11 Asian countries, mostly in South and Southeast Asia, increased yields 63 percent. By 1982, one-third of rice land in Latin America was planted to HYVs. In 1992, Asia yielded 460 million metric tons of paddy rice on 140 million hectares. Two-thirds of this land was planted to HYVs. Asia planted HYVs on 91 percent of its rainfed rice lands for consumption by 2.7 billion people. CGIAR admitted, however, that most of these gains accrued to affluent farmers.

Golden Rice

Since the discovery of vitamins in the early 20th century, scientists have been eager to improve the nutritional value of foods, particularly the staples on which the world depends. One example concerns vitamin A. By way of clarification, only animals are capable of synthesizing vitamin A from dietary sources. Plants do not provide vitamin A, but rather beta-carotene, the chemical that the body readily converts to vitamin A. Scientists have long noted the severity of vitamin A deficiency in the developing world. Where rice is the staple, this problem persisted into the 21st century. Rice does contain beta-carotene, but only in the husk. Milling discards the husk. Even where the husk is retained, it would only cause rice to decay soon after the harvest. A deficiency of vitamin A causes blindness, particularly in children. Every year 250,000 people go blind for want of vitamin A. A lack of vitamin A exacerbates diarrhea, respiratory ailments, and measles, all of which can cause debility or death. An improvement in vitamin A levels might cut the death rate 30–50 percent in the developing world.

Noting the importance of vitamin A, in 2000 biotechnologist Ingo Potrykua of the Swiss Federal Institute of Technology in Zurich approached rice through the process of genetic engineering (GE), sometimes known as genetic modification (GM). This science is an improvement over conventional breeding. In conventional breeding, one crosses varieties of plants within a species. Genetic engineering, however, breaks the species barrier by making possible the insertion of genes from one species to another. Because no rice variety contained beta-carotene, conventional breeding was not helpful. Rather Potrykua inserted genes from daffodil and a bacterium into rice that stimulated the variety to produce enhanced levels of beta-carotene. Potrykua crossed this variety by traditional breeding techniques with a variety of rice with a high content of iron. The product was known as Golden Rice, though properly speaking it was Golden Rice 1.

Environmentalists, having visceral dislike of genetic modification, began in 2001 to criticize Golden Rice 1 as "fool's gold." Meanwhile, the International Rice Research Institute in the Philippines began crossing Golden Rice 1 with innumerable local varieties to make beta-carotene and iron-rich rice varieties throughout Asia and parts of Africa. Potrykua followed the success of Golden Rice 1 by engineering Golden Rice 2, which had even more beta-carotene. Yet criticism continued to mount, causing many governments to reject Golden Rice 1 and 2 for fear that they could not export rice to GE-phobic Europe and the United States. Only in 2012 and 2013, was the transition to Golden Rice 2 complete. Potrykua may build on his triumphs because his techniques should be feasible with cassava, another staple, particularly in Africa.

Further Reading

Halford, Nigel G. *Genetically Modified Crops*. 2nd ed. Rothamsted, UK: Imperial College Press, 2012.

Hamilton, Roy W. *The Art of Rice: Spirit and Sustenance in Asia*. Los Angeles: UCLA Fowler Museum of Cultural History, 2003.

Harlan, Jack R. *Crops and Man*. Madison, WI: American Society of Agronomy, 1992.

Schiebinger, Londa, and Claudia Swan, eds. *Colonial Botany: Science, Commerce, and Politics in the Early Modern World*. Philadelphia: University of Pennsylvania Press, 2007.

Sharma, S. D., ed. *Rice: Origin, Antiquity and History*. Enfield, NH: Science Publishers, 2010.

Smith, C. Wayne, and Robert H. Dilday, eds. *Rice: Origin, History, Technology, and Production*. Hoboken, NJ: John Wiley, 2003.

Rice Liquor

Rice may be fermented and distilled into a potent beverage with much more alcohol than wine or beer. For centuries, the beverage had been popular in many rice-growing regions of Asia, particularly Southeast Asia and southern China. Curiously, it seems to have been unknown in India, another important rice producer. Africa and parts of the Americas after European contact also grew rice without making alcohol from it. From an early date, peasants in Southeast Asia and southern China made rice liquor as part of their household activities, revering the beverage for its various utilitarian and symbolic uses. The French attempt in the 19th and 20th

centuries to wrest control of making and selling rice liquor from traditional manufacturers to colonial authorities provoked a variety of reactions from the Vietnamese.
Intellectual, nationalist, and communist leader Ho Chi Minh was an early opponent
of French interference in traditional methods of making rice liquor. He would lead
a war of resistance against the French and, ultimately, the United States.

Traditional Rice Liquor Production and Consumption

Because the peasant relied on rice liquor for a variety of reasons, he or she often
drank it throughout the day, perhaps as a way of minimizing the discomfort of
fatigue and the ardor of his or her work. Because traditional rice liquor contained
20 percent alcohol, it is hard to imagine that the peasant drank it in full force.
Serious inebriation would surely have resulted. More likely would have been the
practice of diluting rice liquor with water, as the Greeks and Romans had diluted
wine. Because rice was ubiquitous in Southeast Asia and southern China, it must
have long been the food of choice for distillation. Before the French incursion, not
every peasant still made rice liquor. Rather, larger producers had arisen in the
north, what would for a time be North Vietnam, to specialize in the production of
rice liquor, which would then be sold throughout the countryside. Here one
glimpses a rural-urban divide, as the people who lived in the countryside drank
much more rice liquor than urbanites. In what would become South Vietnam for a
time, the Chinese manufactured much of the south's rice liquor. Villagers who
continued to make rice liquor traded it for polished rice, salt, and other essentials.
So prestigious was rice liquor that the emperor in Hue received gifts of the finest
liquor from both north and south. In this context, rice liquor was the beverage of
elites and commoners and must have been an egalitarian and unifying product.

In some regions of Vietnam, rice liquor was thought to be an aphrodisiac and
so was the beverage of brothels and weddings. In this context, popular lore credited rice liquor with fortifying the libido of men and women. It was the beverage
of poets, artists, and other creative people. Rice liquor was especially important in
celebrating the numerous religious festivals throughout the year. Hospitality demanded that a host present a gift of rice liquor to a guest. Rice liquor was omnipresent at funerals and agricultural festivals. One could not honor the spirits of the
dead without rice liquor. In this context, it was appropriate to pour the beverage on
burial grounds to satiate these spirits.

French Interference

In the 19th century the French conquest of Southeast Asia, then known as French
Indochina, disrupted the traditional role that the Vietnamese and Chinese had

played in distilling and consuming rice liquor. French intervention seems to have drawn its motives from the crass desire for profit. By outlawing Vietnamese and Chinese production of rice liquor, France could monopolize the market. French sales of rice liquor would amass such profits that Indochina would, in effect, pay the cost of French occupation. The Vietnamese had traditionally distilled liquor from the highest quality and highly prized varieties of sticky rice that imparted an appealing flavor and aroma to the beverage. So ubiquitous was this product that the Vietnamese called rice liquor simply "alcohol." It was the only alcoholic beverage the Vietnamese knew. The French discarded these traditions, using the cheapest grades of rice to cut cost. Proud of its own traditions in making wine, France nonetheless refused to accept Vietnamese traditions of making rice liquor. The result was an inferior imitation.

The French considered Vietnamese and Chinese rice liquor primitive, believing that their imitation reached the heights of sophistication and science. In distilling rice liquor, the French boasted that they had brought to Indochina the factory system and the science and technology of making alcohol. The Vietnamese thought such talk demeaning. As shown, rice liquor had many utilitarian and symbolic uses. To the Vietnamese, the French attempt to monopolize the production and sale of rice liquor threatened their way of life because the beverage was one of the foods that defined Vietnam. Some Vietnamese poets and intellectuals came to the view that one should prefer to die than drink France's bland rice liquor. The French, they belived, were nothing more than barbarians, parasites who sucked Vietnam dry. French rice liquor became a symbol of oppression and exploitation. To oppose French rice liquor was to resist French occupation. In this way, rice liquor became a symbol that united the Vietnamese in opposition to France.

To drink good rice liquor was to assert oneself as a true citizen of what would become Vietnam. To drink insipid rice liquor was to align oneself with the French. The French paid no attention to the growth in opposition. In the 1890s, they began to tax rice liquor, imagining that they would recoup tremendous revenues. When the tax yielded disappointing results, France monopolized rice liquor's production and sale. French physician Albert Calmette, a pupil of French microbiologist Louis Pasteur, refined the production of 45-percent-alcohol rice liquor for about the cost of the 20-percent-alcohol rice liquor that the Vietnamese and Chinese produced. Halving the alcoholic content of the French beverage with the addition of water, Calmette could produce rice liquor at half the cost of the Vietnamese and Chinese product. By undercutting the price of traditional rice liquor, France felt sure of driving everyone else out of business. In the south, Chinese producers were furious. Some had large enough businesses to defy France, though the French countered by buying out competitors, as Microsoft did software makers in late-20th-century America. Between 1900 and 1903, the number of Chinese distillers fell from 47 to 14. In a propaganda campaign, France extolled its rice liquor as the pinnacle of applied science, contrasting it with the primitive beverage of Vietnam and China.

As would happen in the United States during prohibition, the Vietnamese and Chinese continued to produce rice liquor in violation of law. Soon Vietnam had its own speakeasies. As Vietnamese resistance crystallized, Ho Chi Minh and other intellectuals advocated attacks against French officials and police. Minh also criticized Vietnamese, usually urbanites, who drank French wine rather than Vietnamese rice liquor. Minh understood that Vietnamese resistance was strongest in the countryside and would launch a war of resistance in agrarian Vietnam. To attack French rice liquor was to question the legitimacy of French rule. Much of this opposition came from the Chinese in the south, but they always had the support of rural Vietnam, north and south. Vietnamese and Chinese opposition crippled the French. Between 1903 and 1906, sales of French rice liquor faltered. French authorities stepped up policing, arresting 622 bootleggers in 1903 and 1,287 in 1906. Accordingly, the animus toward the police heightened. Joined by the Chinese, many Vietnamese refused to buy the French beverage. Newspapers averred that French rice liquor was nothing more than poison, that only the irresponsible and unhealthy would consent to drink it. Newspapers also promoted the fact that the French added corn and sugar to their product, adulterations that were foreign to the Vietnamese palate. Even some French, though admittedly a small minority, opposed the government's heavy-handedness. One French Catholic missionary declared that the Vietnamese did not sin by producing and consuming their own rice liquor. By the first decade of the 20th century, one senior French official admitted that Vietnamese resistance might lead to war. To try to placate the countryside, the French bribed village elders in return for an end to resistance. On the other hand, some French commanders in the provinces permitted bootleggers to supply the locals. Meanwhile, French soldiers loyal to the government raided homes to search for illegal rice liquor and paid informants to betray their neighbors.

Rice liquor was not the only grievance that divided the Vietnamese and the French, but it was an important one in dragging both sides into war. The French never really learned how to fight a war of attrition against an enemy it could seldom pinpoint, in a terrain that was forbidding, and in a climate that sapped one's energies. Ho Chi Minh asked two U.S. presidents for aid against the French, but the logic of the Cold War prevented any alliance between the United States and Vietnam. In fact, the defeat of France in 1954 caused the United States to sink into the morass. Encountering the same difficulties as had France, the United States lost its first war with the unification of North and South Vietnam in 1975. The conflict over rice liquor had helped Vietnam dethrone the French and defeat the world's superpower.

Further Reading

Peters, Erica J. *Appetites and Aspirations in Vietnam: Food and Drink in the Long Nineteenth Century*. Lanham, MD: Rowman & Littlefield, 2012.

Rye

An annual grass, rye is a member of the Gramineae or Poaceae family and is related to other grains, prominent among them corn, rice, wheat, oats, and barley. Among the grains, rye has the eighth largest yield, trailing wheat, corn, rice, barley, sorghum, oats, and millet. Humans consume rye as bread and whiskey, though some of the harvest feeds livestock. Most varieties of cultivated rye are members of the species *Secale cereale*, though farmers in southwestern Asia grow some *Secale fragile*, a species of rye related to *Secale cereale*.

Origin and Diffusion

The wild annual grass *Secale vavilovii* may be the progenitor of cultivated rye. Alternatively, the perennial grass *Secale montanum* may be the ancestor of domesticated rye. Whereas *Secale vavilovii* is native to southwestern Asia, *Secale montanum* is indigenous to southern Europe and Central Asia. Because rye appears to have originated in southwestern Asia, *Secale vavilovii* may be the better candidate as progenitor. Rye retains two features of its wild relatives. First, like corn, it cross-pollinates.

U.S. Department of Agriculture (USDA)

The Republican Party, rising as a national party in the 1850s, promised economic reforms including the application of science to solve the problems of American agriculture. The Democratic Party, then the party of conservatism and the South, opposed the idea of economic reform, but their exit from both houses of Congress during the Civil War left the Republicans free to enact their agenda. Among its enactments was the creation in 1862 of the U.S. Department of Agriculture (USDA). In its early years the USDA was a clearinghouse of information in an era when farmers did not have access to the latest science. It had an experimental outlook, undertaking trials among several varieties of wheat and other crops and testing fertilizers to ensure truth in labeling. With the years its agenda has enlarged to develop and disseminate to farmers the latest agricultural applications from the sciences of genetics, molecular biology, chemistry, plant and animal physiology, entomology, pathology, and a variety of other fields.

Most other grains—wheat, barley, and oats, for example—self-pollinate. Second, rye shatters. That is, the grain disperses its seed when mature. The dispersal of seed is basic to the survival of a plant in the absence of human intervention.

Like oats, rye may have arisen as a weed in barley and wheat fields. Like these grains, humans probably harvested stands of wild rye before they domesticated it. Domestication may have followed from the observation that rye tolerates extreme cold and poor soils better than do wheat and barley. Into modernity, farmers grew rye in fields of wheat or barley, creating a mixture of crops. The sowing of rye ensured the harvest of a crop even if wheat or barley failed. In this context, rye was a famine crop. In Syria, Iraq, Iran, the Balkans, Turkey, Caucasia, and Transcaucasia, farmers planted rye with wheat for fear that cold or dry weather might claim their wheat. The practice of intercropping rye and wheat persisted in Europe, where farmers named the mixture *maslin*, meaning "mixed." Between the 14th and 17th centuries, maslin was the most common crop in Europe.

Rye may have originated in eastern Turkey and Armenia, though the earliest evidence of rye comes from northern Syria, where scientists have dated rye grains to 8500 BCE, a date that may be too early for the cultivation of rye. These kernels were found with einkorn wheat, suggesting that people harvested both grains and that wild rye and wheat grew together. Scientists have dated rye to 6600 BCE in Turkey, though these carbonized grains likely derived from wild rye. Humans domesticated rye comparatively late, possibly in the fourth millennium, when farmers grew it in Poland and Romania. Farmers then grew more wheat and barley than rye, raising the latter as a minor crop. About 2000 BCE, humans domesticated rye in Turkey, an event that may have been independent of the domestication of rye in Poland and Romania. Between 1800 and 1500 BCE, rye culture spread to the Czech Republic and Slovakia. At the end of the second millennium, farmers grew rye in Iran. Later, farmers grew admixtures of rye and wheat in Moldavia, Ukraine, Germany, Denmark, and the Crimea. The Romans grew rye along the Rhine and Danube Rivers and in Gaul and Britain. Roman encyclopedist Pliny the Elder knew of rye but he had a low opinion of it. Rye was suitable only as a famine food and had a bitter taste, he believed.

Despite its prevalence in western Asia and Northern Europe rye was unknown in ancient Egypt, the Aegean, Greece, Bulgaria, and Yugoslavia. Its absence in southern Europe leads one to suspect that rye must not have come to Europe from the Mediterranean but instead across the Caucasus Mountains. From Turkey, rye may have migrated north to Russia and then west to Poland and Germany. By another route, rye may have spread from Turkey to the Balkans and then into northern and central Europe.

If rye was a minor crop in antiquity, its popularity grew in the Middle Ages. In medieval Europe and western Asia farmers planted 40 percent of their grain land to rye, a much larger proportion than is common today. Rye bread was the staple of peasants and the poor. In the early modern era, peasants ate as much as three pounds of rye per day. In contrast, prosperous urbanites ate wheat bread. In the 16th and 17th centuries, Europeans introduced rye into North America. In the 17th century, for example, the French planted rye in Nova Scotia. In New England and Virginia, farmers intercropped rye with oats, barley, or corn. The 16th and 17th centuries witnessed the migration of rye from Russia to Siberia. In the 19th and 20th centuries, farmers grew rye in Argentina, southern Brazil, Uruguay, Australia, and South Africa.

Modernity, Rye, and the Columbian Exchange

The English and Dutch brought rye to North America, probably in the 17th century. It was an important crop on the Great Plains and in the Midwest into the early 20th century. In 1930, for example, Minnesota alone planted 7.2 million acres to rye. By 1989, the figure had fallen to 32,000 acres. That year, Wisconsin ceded only 6,000 acres to rye. As production has declined, yield has increased. Whereas yield per acre in the United States stood at 17, it doubled by 1989. Less than half the U.S. rye crop feeds humans. The rest goes to livestock, is exported, or produces whiskey. Midwestern rye typically is made into bread for human consumption. In this context, rye is often mixed with wheat flour. Today, rye is grown in all 50 states. It has, however, outcrossed with a weed in California. The offspring are troublesome weeds in northern California. Northern California and the Pacific Northwest are important regions of rye culture today. In modernity, the production of rye has declined as farmers have grown corn for feed and wheat for bread. Today, rye is a minor crop, being grown on one acre for every 20 acres of wheat, rice, and corn. Production has fallen worldwide and in the United States. Despite these discouraging numbers, one authority predicts an increase in the number of acres to rye in the northern Great Plains, an area in which farmers now grow wheat and barley. Among the states, the leading producers are Oklahoma, Georgia, North Dakota, and South Dakota. In Oregon, farmers grow rye for forage. As a forage, crop rye is often grown with vetch and clover. Rye is planted for forage in Argentina. In some cases, farmers permit livestock to graze immature fields. Removing the animals, farmers then allow the rye to mature, harvesting it in spring or summer. Canada is among the leading rye exporters.

Rye and Ergotism

The worst disease of rye is ergot, not for the damage it does rye but for its toxicity to humans and livestock. Rye and ergotism would set the stage for a religious shock in Europe and New England. Ergot, caused by the fungus *Claviceps purpuru*, afflicts about 170 species of grasses, including triticale, wheat, and barley, but it is most common and most severe in rye. Ergot settles inside the flowers of these plants. Because wheat and many other grasses self-pollinate, their flowers do not open to receive ergot spores. Their infection rate is accordingly low. Rye flowers, however, open to pollinate and so are a target of ergot fungi. Once ergot has infiltrated one flower, insects feeding on the flower get ergot fungi on their legs and so transmit them to other flowers. In one study, hybrid rye was more susceptible to ergot than were traditional varieties. In this study, ergot afflicted one-third of hybrids in a field. Having hijacked a flower for their own use, ergot fungi grow in place of the kernel. The result is a purple cockspur that is easily identifiable.

Ergot is a disease of cool locales and so was prevalent in northern Europe, probably since antiquity. Before people connected the ingestion of contaminated rye with the onset of ergotism they were helpless against the disease. Ergotism impairs the circulatory system, causing gangrene. Other symptoms include hallucinations, insanity, and convulsions. The worst cases are fatal.

Because people did not know the cause of ergotism they called it "Holy Fire," apparently believing that it was God's punishment for sin. The first mention of Holy Fire dates to the eighth century CE, though the disease is surely older. In the Rhine valley an outbreak of ergotism, possibly the first epidemic, killed thousands in 857 CE. In the eleventh century, the Order of Saint Anthony established hospitals to treat the victims of ergotism, and so the disease came to be known as "Saint Anthony's Fire." In 1581, the first case of ergotism arose in Germany. In 1722, ergotism killed tens of thousands of men and cavalry horses in Russian czar Peter the Great's army, halting his invasion of Turkey.

In 1670, a French physician made the connection between contaminated rye and ergotism. Intrigued by the fact that affluent urbanites did not contract the disease but that the poor and rural folk fell victim to it, he visited the homes of several families in the countryside. Noting the presence of loaves of rye bread in their homes, he focused on the rye grown in farmers' fields. Observing purple cockspurs in some of the plants, the doctor, in a flash of insight, drew the connection between ergotism and contaminated rye. In 1676, Frenchman Denis Dodert published the first medical report on the disease, but the first American reference to it came only in 1807. In 17th-century America, as in Europe, some people ascribed ergotism to the malevolence of witches. Some scholars believe that the witchcraft hysteria in Salem, Massachusetts, derived from ergotism.

From 1640, rye was a common crop in New England. The warm, rainy spring and summer of 1691 were ideal for the onset and spread of ergot in rye fields. The colonists planted spring rather than winter rye, an important circumstance because ergot infects spring rye more readily than winter rye. Moreover, the curious circumstance that ergotism appears to have afflicted more women than men throughout history may explain why the accusers in Salem were eight girls. Their behavior—incoherent speech, strange posture and gestures, and convulsions—mimicked the symptoms of ergotism. The girls reported sensations of choking, biting, pinching, and pricking, all symptoms in accord with ergotism. The rye that they must have eaten had probably been threshed in November 1691 and consumed thereafter, a chronology that fits with the onset of the girls' behavior in December. At the witchcraft trials witnesses testified to having had hallucinations, another symptom of ergotism. The connection between ergotism and witchcraft must have been close. In the 17th century, French officials and physicians puzzled over the question of whether one might cause the other, and German clerics wondered whether ergotism might be mistaken for witchcraft. Other scholars, however, doubt that ergotism was at the root of the witchcraft trials in Salem. They note that whole families did not display the symptoms of ergotism, though one should have expected this circumstance because a family would have shared the same contaminated loaf of bread.

Rye and the French Revolution

Bread is commonly made from wheat or rye, the only two grains with sufficient gluten, a protein, to allow the bread maker to form dough. Of the two, wheat has been more important to the people of western Asia, but for centuries rye bread was a staple of the European masses because it was cheap and there were few alternatives to it. This fact would shape French history. In France, wheat bread had long been a luxury that only the elites could afford, leaving the masses to subsist on rye bread. There was therefore a kind of social and economic stigma attached to the consumption of rye bread. This social and economic situation, though tilted heavily toward the plutocrats, was manageable so long as the masses could afford rye bread. The dynamic changed in the 1780s, when a series of poor harvests made wheat and rye scarce. The situation for wheat was not consequential. It was already too expensive and the subsequent rise in the price meant nothing to the masses. The price of rye bread, however, also leapt to levels that the masses could no longer afford. The situation might have been different had the French made the same commitment to the potato that the Irish had. To be sure, several French authorities understood that the potato was nourishing and yielded more calories per acre than either wheat or rye, but by the 1780s, the potato had not taken root as a staple of the masses. With bread unaffordable, the French masses rioted in Paris, as the Russians later would in Russia. The French monarchy, never sympathetic to the masses, refused to make reforms. A radical new government convened, executing the king and queen and instituting a reign of terror that cost many ordinary and prominent French persons their lives, perhaps the most renowned being the French chemist Antoine Lavoisier. Out of this tumult emerged French general and later emperor Napoleon Bonaparte, who launched a war across Europe. The radicalized French Revolution unleashed misery and death throughout Europe. The dearth of rye bread had created a European-wide revolution.

Further Reading

Abdel-Aal, Elsayed, and Peter Wood. *Specialty Grains for Food and Feed*. St. Paul, MN: American Association of Cereal Chemists, 2005.

Bushuk, Walter, ed. *Rye: Production, Chemistry, and Technology*. St. Paul, MN: American Association of Cereal Chemists, 2001.

Carefoot, G. L., and E. R. Sprott. *Famine on the Wind: Plant Diseases and Human History*. London: Angus and Robertson, 1967.

Levack, Brian P. *Possession and Exorcism*. New York: Garland Publishing, 1992.

Martin, John H., Richard P. Waldren, and David L. Stamp. *Principles of Field Crop Production*. Upper Saddle River, NJ: Pearson, 2006.

Zohary, Daniel, and Maria Hopf. *Domestication of Plants in the Old World: The Origin and Spread of Cultivated Plants in West Asia, Europe and the Nile Valley*. Oxford: Oxford University Press, 2000.

S

Salsa

Although there may be several, the essential ingredients in salsa are tomatoes and pepper. Because this is so, the invention of salsa does not predate the Columbian Exchange, though the Aztecs made a tomato-based sauce. If salsa, or at least protosalsa, can claim deep historical roots, it is better known in its modern incarnation, and only since World War II has it commanded a vast market and glittering revenues. Indeed, the revenues from salsa now exceed those of ketchup, what was once America's principal condiment.

The Rise of Salsa

Mexicans and Americans share a taste for hot foods, with salsa perhaps topping the list. Salsa, as shown, outsells ketchup, mustard, and mayonnaise, the condiments of an earlier era. Mustard remains an important condiment at the baseball park when one hankers for a hot dog, and salsa and ketchup share an intimate relationship because both trace their lineage to the Amerindian tomato, a fruit that is now a global food. The comparisons appear to end here because first, salsa outsells ketchup in revenues even though by volume ketchup remains the leader. Second, salsa makes a greater claim to wholesomeness. It is not loaded with salt and sugar, as is ketchup. Moreover, salsa needs no preservatives, and the tomatoes, peppers, and pepper are wholesome, nourishing foods. The tomato in salsa in particular adds vitamin C and antioxidants to the diet. Even tomato seeds are nutritious. The move toward salsa thus has shaped history and daily life by offering the consumer a healthful alternative to ketchup. Salsa, a food with ingredients from both the Americas and the Old World, has toppled New World ketchup and Old World mustard.

Salsa comes in many forms, "from red-colored water to lava capable of demolishing concrete" (Arellano 2012, 215). Austin, Texas, may be the U.S. salsa capital, though Los Angeles, California, is important. Austin restaurants hold salsa-tasting competitions. Salsa is an important item in the restaurants of this city. The newspaper the *Austin Chronicle* sponsors an annual Hot Sauce Festival, an event that includes music and Mexican food of all descriptions, including salsa, of course. Salsa is thus important because it brings the community of Austin together for food and festivities. Tents line a park, each serving salsa with other foods. Some salsas are the familiar red varieties, whereas others are green. Some salsas include fruits (of which tomatoes are a part) as ingredients, and others tomatillos and pepper. It bears repeating that salsa thus unifies New and Old Worlds with its combination of tomatoes and pepper. Some salsas have so much pepper that they are known as "pepper sauces." The formal judging at the Hot Sauce Festival includes about 30 food critics, farmers, and business leaders, all prominent members of the community.

Salsa makers pride themselves on elaborate preparations and hours of cooking to impart a smoky flavor. Some roast tomatoes and pepper to achieve a smoky, tangy taste. By its nature as a condiment, salsa demands other foods, adding a kick to salty tortilla or corn chips. In this context, salsa is part of a snack food industry. Although salsa may be nutritious on its own, its coupling with salty, fried chips does no one any favors. In fact, it appears to enhance the junk food industry in a nation already suffering from heart disease, diabetes, and obesity. By tagging along with junk food, salsa has shaped history and daily life by imperiling the health of many Americans.

Some salsas even bear a flavor akin to citrus. Here, like pepper, is another link to the Old World, because the orange, lemon, and all other citrus fruits except the grapefruit originated in tropical Asia. The presence of these fruits in South Florida, California, Texas, and Arizona obscures for many Americans their Old World origins. Some Texans do not consider breakfast complete without eggs and salsa. Salsa's connection with pepper is important to understand how it shaped history. Europeans long desired pepper and Italian Spanish explorer Christopher Columbus crossed the Atlantic Ocean in search of it. In this way, salsa, more particularly its ingredient pepper, has shaped the world in ways that are difficult to overstate.

The Leap to Prominence

The Spanish who encountered Aztec tomato-based sauce found it flavorful. Curiously, in contrast, the Spanish, particularly Columbus himself, disliked cocoa because of its spiciness. This fact may imply that the Aztec sauce may not have been all that hot. It must have been the Europeans who stoked its flavor by adding pepper. Salsa has existed since at least 1800 and became popular in Mexico during the 1860s. American firms began to sell salsa in the 1880s. In 1908, the Omega

Company of Los Angeles began canning salsa to widen its distribution. After World War II, sales grew in the United States, with rapid gains in the American Southwest. The rise of the taco piqued Americans' interest in Mexican food, and so salsa gained market share. The taco demanded a condiment, a need salsa met in quantity. In 1948, the Mountain Pass Canning Company of El Paso, Texas, began marketing salsa under the name "taco sauce." At first it was not as potent as Mexican salsas, but many Americans appreciated a condiment that was not too fiery to eat. Americans knew this variant of salsa as "Old El Paso sauce." The rise of Taco Bell franchises widened the appeal of salsa, bringing it outside the American Southwest.

As more Mexicans came to the United States the demand for salsa increased, especially in the 1980s, though other factors must have been involved because salsa sales increased rapidly among Americans of European ancestry. Salsa was no longer a regional food. Part of the reason salsa sales mushroomed must have stemmed from a surging interest in ethnic foods, a natural state of affairs for a nation of immigrants. Ambitious homeowners were not content with the occasional meal at a Mexican restaurant but wanted to make their own salsa, or at least buy what the grocer carried. Salsa grew rapidly into a large enterprise with economies of scale, mass production, and mass consumption, all hallmarks of American capitalism and now the global economy. Campbell's Soup launched its own line of salsas. Salsa sold in six-packs with $20 million advertising campaigns. Salsa makers secured government contracts to supply the condiment to the U.S. military. Heinz, a company famous for its ketchup, also sold salsa in recognition of its profitability. In 1988, 16 percent of U.S. households purchased salsa. In 1992, the figure had risen to one-third. In 1994, Campbell's bought Texas firm Pace for more than $1 billion to become the dominant salsa maker in the United States. Campbell's retained the name Pace to assure consumers that it would continue the company's legacy. Even firms in New York City, far from the Southwest, made salsa, though Texans tended to dismiss any salsa made outside Texas.

No longer was it necessary or even desirable to import salsa from Mexico. Texas' salsa more than satisfied the American palate. At the same time, Los Angeles continued to be the Pacific coast's hub of salsa production. From the city arose Tapario salsa in the 1970s. That decade, the company offered its salsa in modest five-ounce packages. In 1988, the size doubled to 10-ounce containers. The next year, the company offered 32-ounce containers, and in 1999 came gallon jugs of salsa. The name Tapario attracted Mexican immigrants who had settled in Los Angeles because it referred to the place in Mexico from which many of them had come. In 2010, Kraft Foods bought a share in the company, ensuring its future. The next year, Frito-Lay began buying Tapario sauce and bought the right to sell Tapario-flavored Fritos, Doritos, Ruffles, and Lay's potato chips. Aging celebrities, including the late actor Paul Newman, Aerosmith guitarist Joe Perry, Van Halen's Michael Anthony, and singer Patti LaBelle also marketed their own brands of salsa. Salsa has come a long way from its Aztec and European roots.

Further Reading

Arellano, Gustavo. *TACO USA: How Mexican Food Conquered America*. New York: Scribner, 2012.

Salt

A salt is a type of chemical compound. A partial tour of the periodic table is helpful at this point. At the far left of the table are the alkali metals. Each element in this group, after lithium, contains an additional electron, meaning that these elements have one electron more than the octet of electrons necessary to produce the most stable atom. These elements will donate this extra electron to another element in hopes of acquiring the octet of stability. To the far right of the periodic table are the noble gases, which are inert, reacting with no other element. To the immediate left of the noble gases are the halogens. Each halogen has seven electrons in its outermost shell, one short of the desideratum of the eight electrons of an octet. One may easily see that the combination of an alkali metal and a halogen is a perfect pairing. The alkali metal donates its one electron to the halogen, forming the perfect octet. Because the alkali metal has given its extra electron, it acquires a positive charge. The halogen, a beneficiary of this extra electron, acquires a negative charge. These opposite charges attract one another, forming a tight durable bond. Sodium is a prime example of an alkali metal. Fluorine is an ideal example of a halogen. Together they form the compound sodium fluoride which, when added to toothpaste, protects against tooth decay. The compound, known as an ionic compound, most familiar to us is the pairing of sodium and chlorine to make sodium chloride, which we know as common table salt. Like all salts, sodium chloride dissociates in water into its component atoms, explaining why it is difficult to see table salt crystals once they dissolve in water. This ability to dissociate in water will become important to humans.

Salt and Basic Biology

All animals, including humans, are biologically predisposed to crave salt. Even insects crave salt. This craving is natural because sodium and chlorine are

A camel caravan arrives on the salt pan of Ethiopia's Danakil depression near Dallol volcano. Generations of Afar salt merchants haul blocks of salt along treacherous caravan routes from the depression to the Tigray highlands. (STR/Reuters/Corbis)

necessary to the proper functioning of the body. The body uses a complex series of ion replacements, which include sodium and chlorine, to maintain the proper amount of water and ions in each cell. This craving must therefore be an evolutionary adaptation, though here the trail goes cool. The food plants that humans consume have sufficient sodium and chlorine in them so that it should never be necessary to need additional salt in the diet. Perhaps this craving predated the eating of plants by some distant human ancestor. Perhaps the craving for salt arose in an environment where strenuous labor was the norm. When a person perspires he or she releases sodium and chlorine from the body. Perhaps perfuse sweating requires the ingestion of additional sodium and chlorine in the form of table salt.

Salt as a Preservative

The desire for salt may have led humans in prehistory to add salt to fish and other perishable foods. Though they did not know the chemistry behind the process, the addition of salt preserved food. The method worked because of the process known as osmosis. Osmosis is the diffusion of water. That is, water moves from an area of greater concentration to an area of lesser concentration. The addition of salt to fish, for example, draws water out of the cells in the fish, taking water from an area of greater concentration (inside the fish) to an area of lesser concentration, the salt, which has no water. The water that comes out of the fish causes the salt, as already shown, to dissociate, creating a brine that holds water outside the fish. The fish, bereft of water, cannot serve as the host of bacteria, which need water to survive. The salted fish, then, decays very slowly, whereas fish not thus preserved are bacteria-ridden in only days. The use of salt thus changed the world by making foods last longer. The combination of salt and pepper has been common since antiquity.

The salting of fish is an ancient process. The Romans made a fish sauce, garum, that included salt, chopped pieces of fish, wine, and perhaps olive oil. They added garum to an array of foods: pork, beef, more fish, and vegetables of all kinds. In short, garum was the staff of life in Roman antiquity. Garum probably tasted like anchovies and the odor may not have been pleasant, but these factors did not deter the Romans. Turkey, part of the Roman world in antiquity, still prepares its own variant of garum. So close was the connection between salt and sauce that the Roman word for sauce also means "salty." In fact the Romans and other ancients salted a variety of foods: fish, ham, beef, other cuts of pork, and sausage, which may have been made from pork, beef, or both. So ubiquitous was the use of salt that food manufacturers began to add sugar to disguise the taste of salt. The addition of sugar must have been a modern activity because sugar was scarce in most parts of the Old World before the discovery of the Americas. Only with the creation of sugarcane plantations in tropical America did sugar become cheaper and more abundant.

The salting of herring, probably first accomplished in the 14th century, was an example of how the process worked. The people of Flanders may have been the first to adopt the procedure. One cut a fish to remove the gills, bronchia, heart, and viscera. Blood drained from the wound. The gutted fish were placed in a barrel of salt to cure over time. The mythology that surrounds salt curing attributes the invention to Willem Benkelsz. His name is spelled many ways. The dates of his birth and death are not fixed and it is not clear that he actually lived. Nonetheless, his putative hometown erected a church in his honor. A stained-glass window shows him in the process of salting herring. Holy Roman Emperor Charles V visited the church to honor Benkelsz and his achievements. This method of salt curing spread throughout northern Europe, though it is hard to believe that Mediterranean Europe did not make similar progress.

The famed Russian Cossacks who peopled Russian novelist Fyodor Dostoyevsky's novels may have been the first to preserve sturgeon and sturgeon eggs (caviar) in the 19th century. The Cossacks were fortunate to live in a salt-rich region and so sold salted sturgeon and caviar. A single such fish could command 400 rubles in the 19th century at a time that the average Russian earned just that amount in a year. This wealth enabled the Cossacks to pay the czar to allow them to maintain their traditional lifeways. Salt, then, was the key to virtual independence. Northern Scotland salted cod, which it sold throughout the British Isles. Merchants as far away as Germany came to buy Scottish cod. So ubiquitous was salted food in Poland that its people called the act of sharing a meal as "to have eaten a cask of salt with someone." Salt was thus a social lubricant. It brought people together to share food. Guests in a Polish household received bread and salt as a gesture of hospitality. The Poles built friendships on the foundation of salt and salted foods.

There is a curious similarity between salt and the story of Saint Nicholas, and the more ancient one about the Egyptian goddess Isis and her brother and husband Osiris. The legend about Saint Nicholas concerns three boys whom a butcher killed, chopped up, and salted in hopes of selling what was left of their bodies as meat. Saint Nicholas somehow learned of their fate, found their body parts in a barrel of salt, put them back together and raised them from the dead. Although the Isis-Osiris myth does not involve salt, it is nonetheless similar. An enemy killed Osiris, cut up his body, and flung the pieces into the Nile River. Isis recovered all body parts, put Osiris together, and resurrected him. This story seems fundamental to understanding Christianity, in which a god is killed and later resurrected.

Today, sausage, ham, and canned foods are still salted. In fact, it is difficult to find foods that are not salted. Consider the importance of salt to potato chips, crackers, pretzels, french fries, cheese, peanuts, corned beef, and many other foods.

The Salt Trade

The nomads of Africa and Asia established caravan routes so that either they had enough salt with them or could stop along the way to extract or buy salt. Indeed, these caravan routes made possible the salt trade across even inhospitable lands. Greek historian Herodotus may have been the first to link these nomads with the salt trade. One wonders whether the need for salt was acute in the hot desert because humans must have sweated profusely. Herodotus understood that what had once been inland seas had evaporated through desertification, leaving salt outcroppings in the Sahara Desert. In the seventh century CE, Arabs introduced the camel as the means of desert transportation par excellence. They used it to carry salt, four cakes per animal. The people of Ghana, so desperate for salt, were willing to pay gold for it. The people of Morocco sent salt south through the desert to get this gold. So important was salt that one could buy a slave with it. Thanks to the salt trade, Timbuktu emerged as a commercial power in Africa. The salt trade was profitable but not always safe. In 1805, a party of merchants left Timbuktu.

Heading north through the Sahara Desert, they became lost. Thirst killed 2,000 men and 1,800 camels. Because the desert tends to look the same no matter where one looks, many parties must have suffered this fate.

Roman emperor Augustus built roads to salt deposits in various parts of the empire, using sheep to carry salt back to Rome. By the 19th century, the railroads had arisen to further the salt trade. In the 20th century the truck was the vehicle of choice, though even today the camel, though slow, is cheaper to maintain than a truck. By the 18th century, Lubeck, in what is today Germany, was a center of northern Europe's salt trade. The city's wealth attracted luminaries such as organist Dietrich Buxtehude. In 1705, Johann Sebastian Bach, then just 20 years old, walked 200 miles to hear Buxtehude. Inspired, Bach returned home to compose what is arguably some of the world's finest music.

Further Reading

Laszlo, Pierre. *Salt: Grain of Life*. New York: Columbia University Press, 2000.

Sandwich

A sandwich consists of two slices of bread between which are stuffed a variety of foods, both meats and vegetables. The Vietnamese, for example, make sandwiches from herbs and pickles, though the pickle strictly derives from a fruit. The same is true of the addition of the tomato to sandwiches. The Oreo cookie looks akin to a sandwich because it has a filling and a top and bottom made from wheat flour. But it is not a sandwich because top and bottom are not bread. This is not to imply that the sandwich must be of wheat bread. Rye is perfectly suitable and in some places preferred to wheat bread. Endlessly adaptable, the sandwich has become popular nearly worldwide and for that reason has shaped history and daily life. Today, the sandwich may be the most popular and ubiquitous food on the planet. Think of the ubiquity worldwide of the Big Mac to appreciate the significance of the sandwich. Part of its popularity is doubtless due to the fact that the sandwich requires no utensil, not even a plate if one does not wish. The sandwich is not a pretentious food but rather the embodiment of the ordinary, at least today. It is quick and satisfying. The sandwich is the perfect lunchtime food or snack. With the exception of people who do not eat bread, everyone is a potential sandwich consumer, though not everyone eats sandwiches. The sandwich is versatile, accommodating a variety of ingredients. Or the sandwich may be standardized and mass-produced like the Big Mac, which has aped the industrial methods of the meatpackers and

The sandwich is a democratic food and a staple on the lunchtime menu. British historian Edward Gibbon was among its admirers. (Jennifer Pitiquen/Dreamstime.com)

automakers and so has a firm place in the annals of American capitalism. Schools often serve sandwiches for lunch. What would a picnic be without a sandwich? It is eaten in hospitals and prisons. The sandwich may be the quickest, most convenient way to prepare a meal. The sandwich bears an intimate relationship with the rise of urban, industrial Europe and the United States, in which office and factory workers had little time for lunch, a circumstance that surely propelled them toward the sandwich. The hamburger arose in the 19th century as the prototype of the sandwich, a position it retains today. The sandwich is important in history and daily life because of its variety of ingredients, convenience, inexpensiveness, and ability to satiate.

The Putative Invention of the Sandwich

In the 18th century, British nobleman John Montagu, the fourth Earl of Sandwich, gave his name to the sandwich. Often too busy for dinner, he asked his chef to prepare a slice of beef between two pieces of bread. This moment not only marked the sandwich's official creation myth but also pointed it in the direction of becoming a hamburger, an important development in daily life. His friend, British

Edward Gibbon

Born May 8, 1737, in Great Britain, Edward Gibbon would rise to become among the notable historians of his era. He focused on Roman history, and his landmark publication, *The History of the Decline and Fall of the Roman Empire*, a six-volume work, set the standard for scholarship in his day. In addition to his scholarship, Gibbon served several years in Parliament. He made eminent, wealthy friends, among them the Fourth Earl of Sandwich, credited as the creator of the sandwich. Gibbon took particular pleasure in eating sandwiches, sprinkling his diary with notes of his fondness for the new food. He died on January 16, 1794, the victim of an infection that had set in after surgery for a testicular problem.

historian Edward Gibbon, appears to have been the first to use the term "sandwich," in a 1762 diary entry. Gibbon was exceedingly fond of these beef sandwiches, which probably accounted for his girth.

Yet it is difficult to credit either Montagu or Gibbon with the invention of the sandwich. For centuries, French farm laborers had eaten meat between two slices of bread, either whole wheat or, perhaps more likely, rye, given the importance of this grain to France. In fact, the preference for meat sandwiches seems to have been common to peasant communities throughout Europe well before Montagu was born. Curiously, no one had thought of naming this food, perhaps because it was too common to warrant a label. Though the sandwich was not a new food, the Earl of Sandwich deserves credit for bringing it into public consciousness so that by the 1770s the term "sandwich" was firmly entrenched in the English language. In some ways, the story of the too-busy-to-eat-anything-but-a-sandwich Montagu bears a peculiar resemblance to a more famous Englishman, the polymath Isaac Newton, who was to have been so immersed in thought that he forgot to eat anything for days. Perhaps the earl was in a similar position, though he never forgot to eat. The first English cookbook to cite a recipe for a sandwich dates to 1773, well within Montagu's lifetime and well after Gibbon coined the term. The naming of the sandwich after Montagu was no anomaly. English captain James Cook named the Sandwich Islands after him.

The early sandwich must, at least in 18th-century England, have had connections to nobility and scholarship. It was eaten at or after dinner and after attending the theater. It cannot then have been the democratic item it apparently was earlier and remains today. In 2003, a descendent of Montagu founded Earl of Sandwich, a chain of restaurants that had outlets in Walt Disney World in Florida and the Detroit Airport in Michigan. These restaurants claim to use Gibbon's original 1762 recipe: roast beef, cheese, and horseradish on bread, likely white.

All the focus on Montagu may be overkill. Some historians trace the roots of the sandwich to the Roman snack *offala*. Others disagree, though the Romans were passionate about bread and meat, especially pork. Perhaps they ate pork sandwiches of some sort. Jews may have eaten something akin to a sandwich during Passover, a religious festival. They ate herbs between two slices of unleavened bread. In the first century BCE, rabbi Hillel the Elder may have eaten lamb and herbs between two pieces of unleavened bread. These ingredients have religious significance to Jews. The lamb was the animal whose blood saved the Hebrews from death during Yahweh's vengeance against the Egyptians. The herbs, being bitter, remind Jews of the torment of slavery in Egypt. To the Jews, then, the sandwich is a religious and cultural symbol and for that reason has shaped history and daily life. Yet the Jewish sandwich remained a ritual meal and does not appear to lead to the modern sandwich.

The Ubiquity of the Sandwich in Daily Life around the World

According to food historian Andrew F. Smith, people throughout the world eat sandwiches. By 1986, Americans ate 1 billion sandwiches per year, or nearly 200 sandwiches per person per year. That year, the United Kingdom recorded the same quantity of consumption. In the United Kingdom, the sandwich derives more than five times the revenues of pizza. The United Kingdom estimates that Brits now consume 2.7 billion sandwiches at shops and an incalculable number at home. Many other countries do not publish such statistics, making difficult the calculation of worldwide sandwich consumption, though the figure must be enormous. The sandwich is a food for the television age. One may eat a sandwich with one hand and surf channels with the other. Similar feats may be possible with the computer and telephone, but one cannot master the keyboard with one hand and it is impolite to speak with one's mouth full.

The British sandwich could be a meal on its own, stuffed with veal, egg yolks, scrambled eggs, cheese, and anchovies. Over time, meat and cheese appear to have been the central ingredients. In the 16th century, Protestants accused Catholics of making something akin to a sandwich with rat meat. The accusation doubtless stemmed from the animosity between these groups. In the 17th century, the Dutch may have eaten something that resembled a sandwich. One senses that the sandwich then must have been a food of the elite and middle class in northern Europe, because evidence suggests that the masses were turning to the potato rather than bread, a trend that accelerated in the 18th and 19th centuries. One historian supposes that everyone ate sandwiches even before Montagu. This attempt to democratize that sandwich in the 18th century is probably incorrect. As shown earlier, the people of northern Europe ate potatoes, and the inhabitants of southern Europe,

Italians in particular, ate pizza and pasta. With Montagu and Gibbon eating sandwiches, the food must have been elitist in the 18th century, though one might make a case for the sandwich as a democratic food if the stories of peasants eating it are true. In fact, accounts from the 18th and 19th centuries note the ubiquity of sandwiches among the nobility and monarchs. There is no doubt, however, that in industrial and urban America the sandwich was a democratic food that sank roots in the working class. Nineteenth-century British novelist Charles Dickens suggested that the English masses ate sandwiches. In the 19th century, train stations sold sandwiches in the United States and Britain. During World War I, soldiers could expect free sandwiches at the train stations. Into the 20th century the sandwich retained its position as a snack food eaten between meals or perhaps before bed. Venues for athletic contests served sandwiches to spectators. In the 1920s, hikers began carrying sandwiches for instant nourishment. That decade, the invention of sliced bread boosted the popularity of the sandwich. In the 20th century, the sandwich gained traction as a food of children, fit for the school lunch box. In the United States, the television characters Scooby Doo and Shaggy were voracious sandwich eaters.

In the 19th century, France introduced the sandwich to Southeast Asia, though it was not until the 1940s that it emerged as a popular food. Doubtless the Vietnamese resented the sandwich for a long time as a foreign food, the food of a conqueror. The Vietnamese prefer mayonnaise and onions as toppings. Peppers, cucumbers, pickles, and herbs are popular ingredients. The Vietnamese who have come to the United States have introduced their sandwiches. Poles in New York City hanker for Vietnamese sandwiches. Greeks eat sandwiches with tomato and onion. The Portuguese favor ham, sausage, cheese, and beer sauce. The people of Uruguay eat sandwiches of steak, bacon, mayonnaise, and olives. The Finns eat sausage sandwiches. The New Zealand sandwich is made with cheddar cheese, possibly an approximation of the grilled cheese sandwich popular in the United States. The people of the Dominican Republic eat sandwiches of pork and cabbage. Yet the sandwich is foreign to Russia, the Baltic States, and parts of Scandinavia. In parts of Asia, rice and noodles trump bread so that sandwiches are uncommon. South Korea and Japan, however, have adopted the sandwich, but their ingredients do not lure the Western palate. In Japan, bean sandwiches are popular, though the source of the beans is unclear. Soybeans would probably be the bean of choice, but one cannot exclude the *Phaseolus* beans of the Americas. Subway and its sandwiches are popular in China. The sandwich is truly a global food.

Further Reading

Wilson, Bee. *Sandwich: A Global History*. London: Reaktion Books, 2010.

Sorghum

A perennial grass, sorghum is grown as an annual in lands that are too hot and dry for corn. Worldwide, sorghum is the fourth most widely grown crop, trailing corn, rice, and wheat. Sorghum competes with millet for dry land acreage in Africa and Asia, though in the United States farmers prefer sorghum to millet. The people of Africa and Asia eat much of the sorghum they grow, though in the United States sorghum feeds cattle, pigs, and poultry. Rich in starch, sorghum has nearly all the feed value of corn. In the United States only corn surpasses sorghum as a livestock feed. U.S. farmers grow sorghum, a versatile crop, for hay and pasturage in addition to feed. Despite its importance, sorghum has in the United States always been in the shadow of corn. Corn, the American indigene, has resisted the encroachment of alien sorghum. One cup of sorghum has 2,370 calories, 25 grams of protein, 118 grams of carbohydrate, 18.5 grams of water, 3.4 grams of ash, 24.7 grams of fiber, 24.7 grams of starch, 4.2 grams of fat, 18.6 international units of beta-carotene, 0.5 milligrams of thiamine, 0.4 milligrams of riboflavin, 7.2 grams of niacin, 0.5 milligrams of vitamin B_6, 2.2 milligrams of vitamin E, 101 micrograms of folic acid, 10 micrograms of vitamin K, 2.5 milligrams of pantothenic acid, 55.8 milligrams of calcium, 0.8 milligrams of copper, 4.5 milligrams of iron, 204 milligrams of magnesium, 4.5 milligrams of manganese, 632 milligrams of phosphorus, 446 milligrams of potassium, 60 milligrams of selenium, 10 milligrams of sodium, and 6.3 milligrams of zinc.

Origin and Diffusion in the Old World

The progenitor of sorghum may have arisen in southern Asia, but sorghum arose as a cultivated plant in Africa. Russian agronomist Nikolai Vavilov placed the early cultivation of sorghum in northeastern Africa. The Wadi Kubbaniya of Sudan may have been among the first to grow sorghum, planting it in damp beds that retained floodwater from the Nile River. Migrants, they planted sorghum, leaving it to mature while they wandered and returning in time to harvest it. The Mande of the Niger River valley may have planted sorghum as early as 5000 BCE. The Mande may have borrowed sorghum, or at least agriculture, from others. One school of thought holds that agriculture arose in western Asia and through human migration spread to Africa between 12,000 and 7000 BCE. Once in Africa, agriculture moved west between 10,000 and 6000 BCE, when the climate was wet in the Sahara and Sahel. Thereafter, the climate dried. The Sahara desert expanded, forcing farmers south, where they encountered the Mande who, borrowing agriculture from them, began to cultivate sorghum. If, as one hypothesis holds, Africans grew sorghum in the Saharan Fertile Crescent as early as 6100 BCE, then the Mande cannot have been the first to cultivate the grain. Alternatively Ethiopians may have been among the early cultivators of sorghum. From Ethiopia, sorghum spread west to Lake Chad and then to the Niger River, where the Mande presumably adopted it. Other early cultivators may have been the Hamites, a Caucasian people who migrated into northeastern Africa around 7000 BCE. Harvesting wild sorghum that grew in this region, the Hamites domesticated the grain before 1000 BCE. In the process of domestication the mutation of two genes transformed sorghum from a shattering to a non-shattering plant. Because sorghum could no longer disperse seeds on its own, it held its seeds until humans harvested them. Benefiting from the non-shattering habit, humans selected for this mutation. By 1000 BCE, the Hamites had spread sorghum south to Kenya and Tanzania. Around the time of Christ, the Bantu, who must have adopted sorghum earlier, migrated to the Congo and then further south, taking sorghum with them. By 500 CE they reached East Africa. As they migrated they established the culture of sorghum in central and southern Africa. By the 10th century the Bantu carried sorghum to Botswana, and by the 14th century, to Zimbabwe. Sorghum has long been a staple in Africa and so has shaped the continent's history and the daily lives of its peoples.

From Africa, sorghum spread to Asia. India may have cultivated sorghum as early as 1500 BCE, though the source of this early introduction is unknown. The Arabs, who had established trade between Africa and India across the Indian Ocean, provisioned their ships with sorghum. From these stores may have come the introduction of sorghum into India 2,000 years ago. One authority dates the cultivation of sorghum in India to the first century CE. Another scholar believes that humans independently domesticated sorghum in India and Africa. From Africa, sorghum migrated to western Asia. A carving of a sorghum plant dates its cultivation in Assyria no later than 700 BCE. From India, sorghum spread to Iran, though the date of this transfer is unclear. About 600 CE, China adopted sorghum from Arabia or India. The people of Africa, India, and Arabia traded sorghum, certainly by the first millennium CE. Around 60 CE the Romans grew sorghum, and first-century Roman encyclopedist Pliny the Elder wrote the first description of the plant. Again, the prominence of sorghum in parts of Asia and the Mediterranean Basin heightens its influence on three continents and the daily lives of their peoples.

The Attributes of Sorghum and Its Central Role to Agriculture

Sorghum's outstanding attribute is its drought tolerance. With a root system twice as extensive as that of corn, sorghum extracts 90 percent of the water and nutrients available from the soil. Some sorghum roots penetrate to a depth of six feet, deriving water at depth. Most sorghum roots are shorter than 10 inches and derive water from the upper layer of soil. During drought, sorghum becomes dormant, resuming growth when the rains return. When rain is scarce, sorghum leaves curl up, exposing less surface area to transpiration. Moreover, the leaves and stalk have a waxy coating that minimizes the loss of water. Sorghum tolerates drought best between 20 and 40 days after planting. During flowering, the need for water is greater, and a sorghum plant may absorb 0.2 inches of rain per day. Overall, sorghum survives with as little as 15 inches of rain per year. Of the grains, only millet can cope with less rain, though sorghum better tolerates a prolonged drought. Sorghum's drought tolerance makes it a crop of the arid regions of Texas and Oklahoma.

A tropical crop, sorghum will not tolerate frost. Photosensitive, sorghum flowers with 12 hours of daylight. Sorghum will grow from sea level to 9,800 feet. It germinates between 50°F and 95°F. The optimal growing temperature is 86°F, though sorghum can tolerate temperatures above 100°F. Sorghum needs at least 130 days to mature and so cannot be grown at latitudes higher than 45° north or south. Adapted to both acidic and basic soils, sorghum will tolerate a pH between 6.2 and 7.8. Throughout much of the world, farmers grow sorghum in soils with a pH between 7 and 8.3, that is, in slightly alkaline soils. Where farmers irrigate sorghum the soil may become too saline. Like sugarcane, rice, and millet, sorghum will regenerate after the harvest, though the second crop will yield only half the grain of the first crop.

Sorghum is a tall plant. African cultivars exceed eight feet, and early American varieties were also tall. Because early sorghum varieties were so tall, they sometimes lodged. One account holds that U.S. sorghum growers could harvest their plants only by standing on a wagon. Because of its height, sorghum is still harvested by hand in much of Africa. In the United States, tall cultivars persisted so long because, grown in the South, sorghum did not benefit from the mechanization of agriculture in the North and West in the 19th century. The desire to mechanize the harvest prompted scientists to breed short cultivars suitable for machine harvest. Farmers began to adopt these varieties in the 1940s. Texas farmers harvested all sorghum by combine in 1945.

Sorghum extracts nitrogen, phosphorus, potassium, sulfur, calcium, magnesium, iron, zinc, manganese, copper, boron, molybdenum, and chlorine from the soil. Sorghum absorbs more nitrogen, phosphorus, and zinc than corn but less potassium and iron. Sorghum growers add potassium and phosphorus to the soil before planting. Farmers plant and fertilize with nitrogen in a single operation. As a rule, they apply half the nitrogen at planting and the other half 10 to 25 days later. Sorghum is so efficient at extracting nutrients from the soil that, when grown in rotation, farmers must fertilize their soil before the next crop so that it has enough nutrients.

In the United States, many farmers rotate sorghum with other crops. On the Great Plains, farmers let land lie fallow after a sorghum crop and then rotate with wheat. In other instances, farmers do not fallow land but instead alternate sorghum and wheat in a two-year rotation. In the South, farmers rotate sorghum with cotton.

A sorghum-cotton rotation is common in Texas. Sorghum is suitable for this rotation because it reduces the population of the pathogens that cause cotton root rot and verticillium wilt. In some regions, farmers rotate sorghum with vegetables and sugarbeets. In arid regions, farmers alternate sorghum and fallow. In the North, farmers rotate winter wheat and sorghum. In the Southeast, farmers double-crop sorghum and a winter grain. In other instances, farmers in the Southeast rotate sorghum and soybeans, cotton, or peanuts. In the Midwest, farmers rotate sorghum with soybeans, though they are more apt to rotate corn and soybeans. In some cases, farmers flood their sorghum fields, raising crawfish in the muck.

Sorghum is a self-pollinator, though 4–8 percent of pollen fertilizes another flower. Each panicle has more than 20 million pollen grains, more than enough to pollinate an entire field, were sorghum a crossbreeder. Excessive heat reduces the rate of pollination, though sorghum does tolerate high temperatures. The discovery that some sorghum produced no pollen led to its use as the female line in hybrid crosses and so made hybrid sorghum a reality. Although farmers rapidly adopted hybrid sorghum, early hybrids were vulnerable to insects and diseases. In the 1970s, scientists incorporated insect and disease resistance into elite lines. Curiously, this decade witnessed a retreat from sorghum. In western Ohio, where farmers had grown sorghum for decades, they switched to soybeans.

In Sudan, Ethiopia, Yemen, and Nigeria people eat sorghum as a type of bread known as *injere* in Ethiopia, *rison* in Yemen, and *masa* in Nigeria. In Ethiopia, people roast and eat immature sorghum grains. In India, Bangladesh, China, Ethiopia, Kenya, Botswana, and Nigeria, people boil and eat sorghum, which has the consistency of boiled rice. Indians eat popped sorghum as a snack, much as Americans eat popcorn. The people of India, Botswana, Uganda, and Nigeria make sorghum into porridge. In India, people eat boiled sorghum with meat and vegetables. Indians eat popped sorghum with syrup, butter, milk, and sugar.

By 1920, U.S. farmers grew sorghum on several million acres. Acreage declined during the 1930s as machines replaced draft animals, reducing the demand for sorghum as feed. After 1940, sorghum rebounded and in the 1950s was cultivated on a larger number of acres. By the 1980s, farmers grew sorghum on even more acres, but acreage fell during the 1990s. In paying farmers not to plant crops on marginal land, the federal government inadvertently caused sorghum acreage to decline. Moreover, the derivation of drought-tolerant corn hybrids gave dryland farmers an alternative to sorghum.

As early as 1935, Kansas, Oklahoma, and Texas produced the vast majority of all U.S. sorghum. By 1998, these states plus Nebraska and Missouri yielded nearly all sorghum grown in the United States. Kansas was the leading producer, followed by Texas and Nebraska. Farmers grew sorghum from Georgia to California and from Texas to South Dakota. In 2000, the United States was the world's leading producer of sorghum. In addition to the United States, El Salvador, Mexico, and Nicaragua produce hundreds of thousands of tons of sorghum. In South America, Argentina produced the most sorghum in 2000, followed by Brazil. In Africa, Nigeria was the leading producer in 2000, followed by Sudan, Burkina Faso, and Ethiopia. In Asia, China and India totaled more than 90 percent of the continent's sorghum production in 2000. Other Asian producers are Pakistan, Saudi Arabia, Thailand, and Yemen.

Conscious of sorghum's importance, the townspeople of Butler County, Kansas, held an annual Butler County Kafir Corn Carnival in 1911 and for several years thereafter. Carnival organizers sponsored an essay contest, soliciting the best prose about the value of kafir to the local economy. The carnival featured a kafir-ville arch, which was ablaze in electric lights. The information booth had a telephone, which was a novelty in rural America. The carnival featured a parade with floats and automobiles. Analogous to the corn shows of the Midwest, the Kafir Corn Carnival promoted civic pride and the virtues of rural living.

Further Reading

Bennett, William F., Billy B. Tucker, and A. Bruce Maunder. *Modern Grain Sorghum Production*. Ames: Iowa State University Press, 1990.

Dendy, David A. V. *Sorghum and Millets: Chemistry and Technology.* Saint Paul, MN: American Association of Cereal Chemists, 1995.

Doggett, Hugh. *Sorghum*. New York: Longman Scientific and Technical, 1988.

Leslie, John F., ed. *Sorghum and Millets Diseases*. Ames: Iowa State Press, 2002.

Lupien, J. R. *Sorghum and Millets in Human Nutrition*. Rome: Food and Agriculture Organization, 1995.

Smith, C. Wayne. *Crop Production: Evolution, History, and Technology*. New York: John Wiley and Sons, 1995.

Smith, C. Wayne, and Richard A. Frederiksen. *Sorghum: Origin, History, Technology, and Production*. New York: John Wiley and Sons, 2000.

The World Sorghum and Millet Economies: Facts, Trends and Outlook. Rome: International Crops Research Institute for the Semi-Arid Tropics and Food and Agriculture Organization, 1996.

Soup

Soup may be the world's most ubiquitous collection of foods, and for that reason alone has shaped the world. It may date to 100,000 years ago, making it an early food. Its roots may trace to the Neanderthals (sometimes rendered Neandertals)

Neanderthals

Excluding our own species, no human has been as closely studied as Neanderthals. These humans may have evolved in Africa, or perhaps in Europe, being an offshoot of an early human ancestor, *Homo heidelbergensis*. Between perhaps 600,000 years ago and 28,000 years ago, Neanderthals inhabited Europe and the Levant. Beginning about 45,000 years ago, Neanderthals and anatomically modern humans encountered one another in these regions, probably regularly. Given the 19th-century tendency to denigrate Neanderthals as primitive and unintelligent, paleontologists believed for decades that anatomically modern humans would have wanted nothing to do with these creatures. In fact, recent evidence has confirmed that all humans have some Neanderthal DNA. This is only possible if the two had children. Indeed, modern reconstructions of Neanderthals, particularly women, reveal a people of great beauty. It is hard to deny the inevitability that anatomically modern men would have found Neanderthal women attractive. This encyclopedia has emphasized that Neanderthals appear to have been the first humans to eat soup. Neanderthals appear to have become extinct about 28,000 years ago.

rather than to anatomically modern humans. The essence of soup lies in the boiling of meat. The juices that drip into a container from this meat are broth. To this broth one may add a number of ingredients, but whatever the ingredients, one has soup. The ingredients vary from culture to culture, though there is an overarching similarity in the foods used to make the simplest soups.

The Origin and Importance of Soup

Soup has become an ubiquitous food and for that reason has shaped human communities. Many cultures do not eat bread, potatoes, fish, or any of a number of foods, but all share in common the consumption of soup, though the ingredients vary from culture to culture. Since antiquity, soup may have been the only truly global food, though one might counter that the same is true of coffee, tea, and chocolate. The pease porridge of the Middle Ages was almost certainly a type of soup, though at the time this food was known as either "porridge" or "pottage." By all accounts, pea soup was the staple of the masses in the Old World and a vital source of protein for people too poor to afford meat or fish. In sustaining the masses, then, pea soup shaped history and daily life. When available, it was common to serve bread with soup to make the bread, perhaps stale, moist, and flavorful. In some cases, soup was nothing more than bread and broth. In the 17th century, the English coined the term "soup" to refer to what had been called "pottage."

The origin of soup may date to 100,000 years ago and may have been a Neanderthal invention. Much controversy surrounds Neanderthals. Those controversies will not be entertained here, but it is likely that Neanderthals and anatomically modern humans were of the same species, interbred to produce children, and exchanged knowledge and other parts of culture. Neanderthals cooked meat from a very early date. Once they began to boil meat in a container they could make broth, to which they added meat and perhaps edible plants. The "container" may have been no more elaborate than a hole in the ground. Nonetheless, if Neanderthals invented soup they must have been every bit as intelligent as we are. The supposition that Neanderthals went extinct because they were somehow inferior is not convincing. Soup shaped history by forcing modern humans to reevaluate their relationship with Neanderthals.

The indigenes of the Americas and Australia both made soup in holes in the ground. Pieces of bark, bamboo, and shells all served as soup containers in different regions of the world. Shells would have been available only along the coastlines. Bamboo would have been available in the tropics. In the 19th century, British naturalist Charles Darwin and the crew of the *Beagle* used large tortoise shells from the Galapagos Islands as soup containers. Darwin expressed delight at the taste of tortoise meat in soup. The Plains Amerindians cooked soup in bison stomachs extracted from a kill. The Mongols cooked soup in goats' heads. Now aluminum is the container of choice. The Romans ate several types of soup. Soup was not quite a democratic food because the plebeians ate simple soups with a small number of ingredients, whereas the patricians loaded their soups with a bounty of foods. The soup of a poor person would not have impressed the rich. A typical patrician soup might include broth, wine, lettuce, eggs, and pepper. The poor made do with a soup of barley and peas or barley and lentils. One supposes that barley and chickpeas were a possibility because several Roman authors, notably Columella, wrote about the importance of chickpeas in the diet. A soup of chickpeas must have been popular in India, which remains a large chickpea consumer. Another soup, surely for elites, contained broth, chickpeas, lentils, peas, barley, leafy vegetables, leeks, cabbage, coriander, dill, fennel, fennel seeds, oregano, and lovage.

The English had a special soup, made with almond milk, for Lent. One supposes that fish soups must have been important during Lent. Soup was therefore flexible enough in pagan and Christian settings. The Germans made soup with beans, though because these recipes date to the 14th century the bean of choice must have been the fava bean. Europeans did not yet know about the many varieties of beans native to the Americas. One assumes that after *Phaseolus* beans (American beans) appeared in Europe they must have supplanted fava beans, because American beans are much easier to prepare than fava beans. Indeed, the only bean soups that Americans know contain *Phaseolus* beans. The Germans added fava beans, beer, caraway seeds, leeks, almond milk, rice, and carrots to broth. Soup with such ingredients points to a large trade network because rice, for example, could have come only from Africa or Asia. It could not have been grown in what is today Germany. This trade network would only spread during the Columbian Exchange. Another German soup recipe called for goose, garlic, saffron, milk, and egg yolks. The soup must have been calorie dense. The French made even more elaborate recipes for soup. The Spanish amassed their soup recipes from the Moors who had conquered parts of Spain in the Middle Ages.

By the 17th century, the average cookbook devoted about 20 percent of its recipes to soups. For all this diversity, throughout the world the basis of soup has clustered on seeds as the principal ingredient, that is, either legumes or grains. Peas, beans, and lentils have played an essential role in the making of the simplest soups. Among grains, corn and rice have been important. In India, soups often contain chickpeas or lentils. Egyptian soups favor fava beans, a puzzling circumstance given the availability of American beans. Moroccan soups have chickpeas. Black bean soup is a staple throughout the Caribbean islands, also known as the West Indies. England, Sweden, Finland, and the Netherlands favor pea soup. Cabbage soup is important in France, Germany, Eastern Europe, and Russia. African slaves made soup from tomatoes and corn, both American foods. Today the tomato may be the chief ingredient in soups worldwide. In the 1840s, tomato soup was among the first canned foods. Today, American company Heinz sells tomato soup worldwide. With the Columbian Exchange, corn chowder became a worldwide soup, though the Amerindians had made corn soup long before European contact. Featuring okra, gumbo is popular in the American South. The people of Philadelphia eat soup made with tripe, perhaps an Italian import.

Soup Kitchens

One important spin-off from soup is the soup kitchen, a charitable center that feeds the poor and unfortunate. One thinks of soup kitchens as an American innovation, and there have been times in American history that soup kitchens have been indispensable. Yet the religiously inspired trace the roots of soup kitchens much deeper in history. They focus on soup kitchens as an outgrowth of the western Asian sentiment that people should aid strangers and the less fortunate. The Old Testament called the Hebrews to feed strangers, orphans, and widows. The New Testament also undergirded the notion of helping people through food. According to the canonical gospels, Jesus put a poor beggar, Lazarus, in heaven and the rich man who did not tend his needs in hell. Moreover, Jesus may have divided people into two types. Those who fed the hungry, cared for the sick, and visited those in prison would receive heaven as their reward. The other type, who ignored the hungry, sick, and imprisoned, were destined for hell. The Judeo-Christian tradition may have been the basis of the modern soup kitchen.

Soup kitchens were particularly important during the post-Civil War depressions, when the United States was transforming from a rural into an urban nation. In a rural setting, one can always hope to find food to eat, but an urban industrial economy will always have cycles of boom and bust. During down times, the unemployed need soup kitchens to survive. One cannot think of the depressions of 1873 to 1877, 1893 to 1897, and 1929 to 1939 (the Great Depression) without reminding oneself of the importance of soup kitchens in serving the masses of unemployed Americans. Mobster Al Capone even opened soup kitchens in Chicago and New York City during the Great Depression to feed the unemployed.

Aside from individual effort, Catholic and Protestant churches have been in the forefront of establishing soup kitchens in the United States, Europe, Asia, and parts of Africa. A 1994 study found that 97 percent of U.S. Presbyterian churches operate or support a soup kitchen. These churches encourage high school and college students to volunteer in soup kitchens, which often marks their first encounter with poverty. Such experiences can go a long way toward quickening the development of empathy and compassion. As public funds cannot entirely alleviate poverty, churches and private philanthropy must feed the poor, often through soup kitchens. In this sense, soup kitchens symbolize charity and community. Since the 19th century, the Salvation Army, both in Europe and the United States, has played an important role in operating soup kitchens. The organization, as many religious groups do, couples food with evangelism.

In Atlanta, soup kitchens multiplied during the Great Depression. As a railroad and now airline hub, Atlanta has long attracted drifters who eat at the soup kitchens. The Atlanta Holding Mission, now the Atlanta Union Mission, operates the city's primary soup kitchens, though it is certainly not alone. By 1956, these soup kitchens served 300 meals per day. The mission claims to have served Protestants, Catholics, and Jews. One wonders where agnostics and atheists were to go. By 1976, the mentally ill represented an increasing number of clients at the soup kitchens. In the 1980s, young unemployed men and drug addicts came to Atlanta's soup kitchens. Accordingly, the kitchens had to expand to include substance abuse counseling. In the 21st century the homeless make up a large proportion of soup kitchen clients.

Further Reading

Clarkson, Janet. *Soup: A Global History*. London: Reaktion Books, 2010.

Sack, Daniel. *Whitebread Protestants: Food and Religion in American Culture.* New York: St. Martin's Press, 2000.

Soybeans and Their Foods

The soybean is among humankind's most important world crops, feeding livestock and people. The soybean is a seed from a plant in the Leguminosae or Fabaceae family. In this regard it is a true bean, though it is unfamiliar in the West to people accustomed to the many and nutritious *Phaseolus* beans from the Americas. Like all other beans, peas, chickpeas, lentils, cowpeas, and peanuts, soybeans are a legume, a unique category of plants whose definition follows later. In the West, soybeans are primarily used to feed livestock, the protein-rich meal being an additive to livestock feed. In parts of Asia and Africa, the soybean in all its variety is a dietary staple, though one should add that the market for soy foods is growing in the United States. The U.S. market is nonetheless immature by Asian standards.

Soybeans and Their Foods in the United States

The story of the soybean does not begin in the United States, but because this narrative targets readers of English, it will be more familiar than the compelling events in Asia. The soybean appears to have come to the United States from China, with Europe as the intermediary, in the 18th century. Its value in feeding livestock was realized quickly. Unlike current practices, soybeans were fed to livestock as hay. That is, livestock consumed the whole plant. Because the bean itself was not as valuable as the plant, stockmen did not need a plant that produced large beans. This state of affairs began to change in the late 19th century. In 1898, the U.S. Department of Agriculture (USDA) sent an expedition of scientists to Japan and China, one of the first of its kind, to gather soybeans with large pods and beans. These plants would become the foundation of the U.S. effort to breed ever-larger soybeans. By World War II, plants with large beans had supplanted the hay varieties. The future of the soybean in the United States was assured.

The soybean rapidly emerged as an important complement to corn in the Corn Belt of the American Midwest. The soybean was valuable because of its status as a legume. As is true of all legumes, soybeans have specialized roots that contain nodules. These small spaces attract and are a haven for nitrogen-fixing bacteria. This relationship is symbiotic. The soybean roots provide safety and a home for these bacteria. In turn, the bacteria convert atmospheric nitrogen, oxygen, and hydrogen to create vital ions like nitrate ions and ammonium ions. Plant roots

Often prized for their versatility as livestock feed and in the making of industrial products, soybeans retain their importance as food throughout Asia. Tofu and other soybean derivatives provide a bounty of nutrients. (Envision/Corbis)

cannot absorb gaseous nitrogen, oxygen, and hydrogen directly, but can readily uptake these ions. A soybean root, in short, has its own fertilizer factory. Not only does the soybean benefit from this arrangement, but also the corn that follows soybeans in rotation derives the leftover nitrogenous ions. In this context, soybeans shaped the world by making the Corn Belt possible. The entire livestock industry could not exist in its present form without corn and soybeans. Without soybeans, life in the West would be dramatically, and perhaps drastically, different.

The soybean does not only prop up the Corn Belt. It is becoming a food among the peoples of North America. In Mexico, the United States, and Canada, the

Semidwarf Soybeans

The Green Revolution revealed that short (semidwarf) cultivars of wheat and rice yielded more grain than their taller counterparts. This revelation led scientists to apply these breeding techniques to other crops, among them soybeans. From the standpoint of nutrition, soybeans and their products have the same properties whether tall or short. In the 1980s, U.S. Department of Agriculture agronomist Richard Cooper bred several semidwarf soybean varieties with quaint names: Elf, Pixie, Gnome, and other such appellations. On research farms these varieties yielded well, but they were ill-suited to cultural methods. The beauty of soybeans, from the standpoint of farming, lies in their ability to be planted at the same width as corn seeds (kernels), necessitating no new planting equipment, but semidwarf soybeans required close spacing that made traditional planters obsolete. The beans (seeds) also hung low to the ground so that they were difficult to harvest by machine. Never a fit for the corn and soybean belt of the American Midwest, these soybeans have fallen from view.

appetite for soy foods is not large but is nonetheless growing at 30 percent per person per year. The rise of health-conscious consumers is fueling what may become a food revolution. Soy milk, sometimes flavored with vanilla, is marketed throughout North America. Vegetarians eat tofu. Soy yogurt, frozen soy treats, and soy "cheese," though not truly cheese, may gain market share. Some breads contain pulverized soybeans, which are not really flour. Processed soybean meal may contain 70–90 percent protein and is suitable for addition to baked products, whipped cream, lunch meats, ground beef, breakfast cereals, weight-loss products, and so-called energy bars, and in the making of dairy and meat substitutes. Perhaps these uses are particularly impressive because many Americans are eating foods that contain soy protein without realizing it. In this case, soybean consumption

1898 Expedition

In 1898, the U.S. Department of Agriculture, committed to making the soybean an important American crop, dispatched two scientists, Charles Piper and William Morse, to China and Japan to collect new soybean varieties. Most were suitable for feeding livestock, but about 40, producing large seeds, formed the basis for the U.S. soybean breeding program. All current U.S. varieties trace their lineage to these 40 lines. In the meantime, the soybean has gained importance in many regions of the United States and throughout the rest of the Americas. In the United States, the Midwest has emerged as a land of corn and soybeans.

must be larger than most Americans appreciate. Even baby foods contain soy protein. In one sense, these are new developments and trends, though American automaker Henry Ford anticipated them by hiring scientists to prepare soybean products that resembled hamburgers, steak, chicken, hot dogs and other sausages, and bacon.

East Asia Emerges as the Principal Consumer of Soy Foods

The story of soybeans really begins in China. The wild species *Glycine soja* may have given rise to *Glycine max*, the domesticated soybean, sometime in antiquity. *Glycine soja* grows wild in parts of China, Taiwan, Japan, Korea, and Russia. This transformation from perennial to annual occurred without human intervention. Compared with the grains, soybeans were domesticated late, about 2800 BCE, in northern China. In 2207 BCE, a Chinese agriculturalist wrote a treatise on, among other topics, the cultivation of soybeans. During the Shang and Chou dynasties (1700–700 BCE), farmers spread soybeans throughout China. In the 11th century BCE, a Chinese book of verse mentioned the soybean and its uses. One poem noted that people boiled soybeans before eating them. Another poem implied that the Chinese ate soybean leaves as a vegetable and fed them to livestock. A fifth-century-BCE Chinese text classed the soybean as one of five grains, though it is really a legume. Despite this textual evidence, one archaeological site dates soybean culture to only 700 BCE. A second site dates soybeans even later, to 300 BCE.

In the first century CE, the soybean migrated to Manchuria and Korea. Following land and oceanic trade routes, soybeans spread to Japan, Indonesia, the Philippines, Vietnam, Thailand, Malaysia, Myanmar, Nepal, and India between the first and 15th centuries. In Asia, farmers planted soybeans with rice, a nutritious combination. Whereas rice provided carbohydrates, soybeans nourished humans with a balance of amino acids and oil. Farmers repeated this combination of a grain and a legume in Eurasia, where they planted wheat and peas, and in the Americas, where they planted corn and beans.

As this narrative suggests, soybeans were an important component in the diet of east and Southeast Asians for millennia. The Japanese eat immature soybeans in the pod, in the way that Americans eat green beans. Because both seeds and pods are tender, they are edible. The Japanese also eat soybean sprouts, newly germinated plants. These tender, nascent plants are germinated in the dark. China and Japan make soy milk by pulverizing and heating soybeans in the presence of water. The liquid is filtered to derive its present form. The Chinese and Japanese consume soy milk in the way that much of the world drinks Coca-Cola, though soy milk is not carbonated. Heated soy milk forms *yuba*, a film of protein on the surface of the liquid. Skimmed off, yuba is sold in sheets to upscale restaurants. The Chinese and Japanese prize it as a delicacy. Tofu also derives from soy milk. One heats the liquid until it forms curds, from which the whey is extracted and salted. The whey is tofu. A versatile food, tofu may be frozen, freeze-dried, fried or grilled to yield different textures and flavors. The method of preparation also affects the quantity and quality of nutrients. Once soy milk has been filtered, the remaining solid is known as *okara*. It is sometimes pickled. In other cases it is cooked with meat to make a nourishing stew. The roasted soybean is a soy nut and serves as a snack in the way that Americans eat peanuts at baseball games. When pulverized, soybeans are added to pastries in China and Japan. Japan and Indonesia pair soybeans with rice, an ancient tradition.

Asia has also fermented soy foods and beverages to provide an alcoholic kick. Fermented tofu is known as sofu or Chinese cheese, though it is not, as we have seen, derived from milk. Okara, too, may be fermented. Fermentation is not simply about the derivation of alcohol. The products have a high quality and quantity of nutrients. Because alcohol is present, it destroys harmful microbes, so that fermented products have a long shelf life. Fermentation, as one might expect, enhances the flavor of soy foods and beverages. Sometimes East Asians ferment a paste of soybeans with wheat, barley, or rice. Soy sauce, a product of fermented soybeans and wheat, is a tempting addition to a number of foods. Fermented soybean nuggets are known as "salted black beans," though strictly speaking the black bean is an American rather than an Asian bean. In this case, language confuses rather than clarifies. Popular in Indonesia, soy nuggets may be formed into a "cake," though this is not a cake in the way that the West has defined cake. The soy cake is rich in B vitamins. The Japanese often eat a fermented food made from soy sauce, mustard, and rice at breakfast or dinner.

The United Nations Food and Agriculture Organization (FAO) recently published data on the consumption of protein. The per capita leaders are North Korea, Japan, Indonesia, South Korea, and China. Although not posting robust numbers, Libya, Uganda, Nigeria, and Costa Rica are all eating more soy protein than in the past. U.S. consumption is small, but we have seen the rapidity of current growth. Soybean protein deserves special mention because it is a much more efficient source of protein than beef, pork, and chicken. Soybeans shaped civilizations in east and Southeast Asia for millennia. Moreover, soy protein may be the best way of averting the Malthusian Crisis, and in this sense soybeans are destined to play an even larger role in the future.

Also important is soybean oil. In its natural state the oil is unsaturated and so a healthy oil. Regrettably, its short storage life has led chemists to hydrogenate it so that soybean oil is much less healthy than in its natural state. Like soy protein, soybean oil is in a variety of foods: soups of all kinds, breakfast cereals, sausages, ice cream, and many other foods. In fact, the more processed the food, the more likely it is to contain a vegetable oil of some kind, with soybean oil the leader, though soybeans are not strictly vegetables. Soybean oil also has a number of industrial uses. Cosmetics and paint are only two of many products to contain soybean oil.

Further Reading

Boerma, H. Roger, and James E. Specht, eds. *Soybeans: Improvement, Production and Uses*. Madison, WI: American Society of Agronomy, 2004.

Du Bois, Christine M., Chee-Beng Tan, and Sidney W. Mintz, eds. *The World of Soy*. Urbana: University of Illinois Press, 2008.

Gunstone, Frank D. *Oils and Fats in the Food Industry*. Oxford: Wiley-Blackstone, 2008.

Heatherly, Larry G., and Harry F. Hodges, eds. *Soybean Production in the Midsouth*. Boca Raton, FL: CRC Press, 1999.

Liu, KeShun. *Soybeans: Chemistry, Technology, and Utilization*. New York: Chapman and Hall, 1997.

Smith, C. Wayne. *Crop Production: Evolution, History, and Technology*. New York: Wiley, 1995.

Spam

The American meatpacker Geo. A. Hormel & Co. (today Hormel Foods Corporation) conceived of Spam during the Great Depression, when it was a food of the poor and unemployed. From this modest beginning Spam grew to supply American and allied troops during World War II. After the war, thanks to America's global military presence, Spam became a worldwide food, being especially popular in parts of Asia. The reception the meat has received in these regions outshines American perceptions of Spam as the food of the poor and unsophisticated. In this respect, Spam, at least in the United States, never shed its association with the deprivation of the Great Depression and World War II. Because of its importance during World War II, Soviet premiere Nikita Khrushchev credited Spam with saving his army from starvation. In this sense, Spam shaped history by assuring the allied victory over Nazism, fascism, and imperial Japan.

A Wartime Food

Perhaps more than any other American food, Spam came to the fore during World War II. During the war, the U.S. military bought 90 percent of Hormel's canned

A dish of Musabi Spam. Before deciding that Spam is not for you, consider that President Barack Obama enjoyed it during a visit to Hawaii during his presidency. With the highest per capita consumption of Spam, Hawaiians consider the well-known processed meat a staple item. (AP Photo/Larry Crowe)

meats, including Spam, a term that is short for "spiced ham," although it was really only part ham. The rest of Spam was derived from the shoulders of a pig, so that Spam was a polyglot meat. Hormel advertised Spam as "Hormel's new miracle meat in a can." There was, of course, nothing miraculous about Spam. It was similar to the meat products that Hormel and the other meatpackers had been producing for about a century. During and immediately after the war, Hormel diversified Spam to include Spam fritters, soup, sandwiches, salad, stew, meatballs, chop suey, Spam and macaroni, Spam and dehydrated eggs, and Spam and dehydrated potatoes. These products must have been appealing because Hormel sold more than 100 million pounds of Spam and other products per year during World War II. Spam fat lubricated guns, soothed skin, and was made into candles. The tin can was made into pots, pans, and the stills to distill whiskey and other potent beverages. Soldiers no longer referred to "Uncle Sam" but to "Uncle Spam." In the United Kingdom, civilians ate Spam. French restaurants served Spam. The French erroneously believed that Spam was an acronym for "specially prepared american meat." The Soviet army marched on Spam. After the war, the Red Cross distributed Spam to the masses of hungry refugees. After the war, Nikita Khrushchev recollected that the Soviet army would have starved without Spam. In this respect, Spam was essential to the allied war effort. Spam shaped history as a food that helped assure the victory over Germany, Italy, and Japan. Not only the U.S. military but also American civilians subsisted on Spam during the war. For many Americans of the World War II generation, Spam is a reminder of the deprivations of the Great Depression and world war. In this context, many Americans dislike Spam.

Spam in the West

The Western palate tends to equate Spam with the meat equivalent of junk food, though it is far more nourishing than potato chips, donuts, Twinkies, and many other true junk foods. In 1937, Minnesota meatpacker Hormel introduced Spam in the United States. In the midst of the Great Depression this inexpensive meat must have attracted impoverished Americans. Hormel was clever enough to create a product with salt, sugar, and fat, all three of which humans are biologically predisposed to crave. Spam may be likened to a type of canned meatloaf. Most American consumers agree that Spam is bland but for the salt. Bowing to pressure from nutritionists and physicians, in 1986 Hormel reduced the salt content of a Spam spinoff, though the company continues to market its original high-salt product. In 1992, Spam Lite offered the consumer fewer calories than the original product. In 1999, Hormel offered a product made of turkey but marketed as Spam.

After the United States lifted wartime restrictions at the end of World War II, Spam sales decreased in the United States as Americans hankered for better cuts of beef and pork. The military has had fewer options. Spam has been the meat of choice (or compulsion) in every American war since World War II. To many Americans, Spam is an artless food that symbolizes a lack of refinement and sophistication. One would never, for example, serve Spam at an American wedding. Other Americans, however, recognize Spam as an authentic item of Americana. It is part and parcel of the history of the 20th century. Nonetheless, U.S. history text-books omit Spam. It is possible and perhaps desirable that U.S. colleges and universities graduate men and women who know something about Greek philosopher Plato's dialogues, German composer Johann Sebastian Bach's music, and Russian author Fyodor Dostoyevsky's novels, but nothing about Spam. The meat may be more an item of popular culture than of history. Some Americans, now in their 50s and 60s, recall Spam as a food of their childhood but certainly not of their mature years. Spam does not accommodate the adult palate, according to this line of thought. Some Americans cast Spam alongside Ramen noodles as foods of the poor. Others state the obvious, that Spam is a processed food and so not really worthy of the label "meat." In short, Spam aspires to be something that it is not: a meat of distinction. Perhaps to its credit, Hormel makes few elevated claims about Spam. Nonetheless, where it is used, Spam is often a substitute for ham.

Spam in the Philippines and Other Parts of Asia and the Pacific Islands

Since 1937, Hormel has sold billions of tins of Spam worldwide. The company expects to surpass the 7 billionth sale sometime in the 2010s. Hormel makes Spam in the United States, Australia, Denmark, the United Kingdom, Japan, the Philippines, South Korea, and Taiwan. More than 50 countries worldwide import Spam from these facilities. Few U.S. foods have dominated the Filipino market as has Spam. At the end of World War II, American troops gave Filipino civilians tins of Spam. The food quickly rose to prominence. In the Philippines and other islands of Southeast Asia, Spam is a popular food in ways that surprise Americans, who have tended to take it for granted. Spam is part of the burgeoning fast food industry in East Asia and the Pacific. In this sense, Spam is among the most successful foods in modernity. People worldwide recognize the 12-ounce tin can that contains the meat. Spam has achieved its success partly through its inexpensiveness, long shelf life, and adaptability to a range of recipes. Spam transcends national and economic boundaries and is truly a democratic food. Because Spam need not be refrigerated, it is ideal as a source of protein for the developing world, where many people lack electricity. Spam may be heated in its tin or served cold, depending on the preference of the consumer. It is versatile enough to be the main course, a side dish, or an ingredient in an elaborate recipe. Moreover, Spam may be eaten for breakfast, lunch, dinner, or a snack. It is convenient because it requires little, if any, preparation.

Spam retains its military associations. Wherever U.S. forces have occupied land—Guam, South Korea, Okinawa, and the Philippines, for example—Spam has remained popular and not just among soldiers. As a rule, Asians have a much more favorable view of Spam than do Americans. Filipinos feel an attachment to Spam. For them it is an authentic meat. Both Christian and Muslim Filipinos like Spam. Muslims eat turkey Spam, abiding by dietary laws that appear to have originated among the Hebrews indicating that one must not eat pork. In the Philippines, all classes consume Spam. There is no association, as there is in the West, between Spam and the poor and unsophisticated. Filipinos pair Spam with rice, deriving protein from Spam and carbohydrates from rice. The traditional afternoon snack, *merienda*, may include a tin of Spam, often eaten as a sandwich with ketchup and mayonnaise, admittedly giving one too much fat. Filipinos often fry Spam, again augmenting the fat content. Filipinos consider Spam a delicacy, surpassing sardines and corned beef in sales. Spam is popular enough to command nearly the price of ham, ounce for ounce. Filipinos give one another gifts of Spam. It is the meat families use when they reunite with kin who have returned from abroad.

Further Reading

Civitello, Linda. *Cuisine and Culture: A History of Food and People*. Hoboken, NJ: John Wiley and Sons, 2011.

Williams-Forson, Psyche, and Carole Counihan, eds. *Taking Food Public: Redefining Foodways in a Changing World*. New York and London: Routledge, 2012.

Sugar

For millennia, humans relied on honey as the principal sweetener. It remains popular today, even though sugar dwarfs it in sales. The term "sugar" may be misleading because several types of sugars, all products of plants, exist. For example, when one eats a strawberry, an apple, a banana, or some other fruit, one derives sweetness from the sugar fructose. The sugar with which humankind is most familiar is sucrose, a sweet, crystalline molecule. In fact, ounce for ounce sucrose is sweeter than honey. For millennia, sugarcane has been the principal source of sucrose, which will be called sugar throughout the remainder of this essay. Through a tedious process, sugar is extracted from the pith in the stems of sugarcane plants. Sugarcane is a grass of the tropics and subtropics. For centuries, humans in temperate locales have sought their own source of sugar. Through careful selection and breeding they derived—one is tempted to say invented—the sugar beet, a plant only distantly related to sugarcane. Unlike sugarcane, sugar beet amasses its sugar in its extensive taproot, not from a stem. By 1900, the sugar beet achieved such promise that it accounted for half the world's supply of sugar. Thereafter,

Sugar has emerged as among history's most important foods, a fact that may seem strange when one considers that sugar is little more than empty calories. Sugar is nothing more than sucrose, a carbohydrate. Sugar has no nutrients of any kind. (Fei Li/Dreamstime.com)

sugarcane took command as yields jumped, thanks to hybridization. By 1950, sugarcane produced more than 75 percent of the world's sugar, leaving sugar beet with less than one quarter of the global harvest. Sugar beet producers have made this decline a political issue, demanding government subsidies for an industry that appears to be moribund.

Powered Sugar

Like sugar, powdered sugar is crystalline sucrose, a sugar that humanity has prized for millennia. That is, there is in this context no chemical difference between sugar and powdered sugar. The difference is one of size, with powered sugar being much smaller and finer than sugar. In this respect, powdered sugar has one additional chemical to prevent it from forming clumps. Confectioners often use powdered sugar to make icing for cakes, cupcakes, and a number of other baked goods.

Sugar Stimulates Trade

The people of Papua New Guinea probably were the first to covet sugar and for this reason cultivated sugarcane as early as 9000 BCE. From there, sugar spread throughout the tropics of the Old World, and with it spread the trade in sugar to almost global dimensions, a position that the Columbian Exchange would begin to realize in the late 15th century. From Papua New Guinea, sugar spread east and then north through a swath of Polynesian islands, culminating in its conquest of Hawaii in about 1100 CE. To the west, sugar swept into mainland Asia by two primary routes. From Papua New Guinea sugar reached Southeast Asia, including Borneo, Indonesia, and the Philippines. Another line traced sugar's exit from Papua New Guinea to India about 1000 BCE. These waterborne journeys must have fueled a shipbuilding industry early in antiquity. Curiously, sugar does not appear to have moved north from Southeast Asia to China. Rather, China likely acquired sugar from India about 200 CE. The overland route from India to China appears to have traversed the eastern terminus of what would become the Silk Road. Sugar thus played an important role in the formation and use of the Silk Road, really a network of roads that stretched from China to the Levant. To the west, sugar spread from India to Persia (today Iran) in about 500 CE and to Egypt within the next 200 years. From humble beginnings, sugar became an important item of trade in Asia and Africa long before Europeans were sweetening coffee and tea with sugar, though there appears to be literary evidence that Greek historian Herodotus and Greek conqueror Alexander the Great knew that India was a source of the sugar trade.

Sugar and the Formation of Religions

Sugar also changed the world by helping to form religions in antiquity. The ancients offered sugar to the gods, sometimes burning the juice derived from the pith of sugarcane stems, along with other offerings. Sugar, honey, milk, cheese, and butter may have been among the earliest offerings to the gods. The Indian deity Durga was the goddess of sugar and sugarcane. During fortunate years, she assured the bounty of the harvest. Perhaps through these religious rituals, humans discovered that the burning of cane juice allowed the sugar to crystallize, probably the most important insight in the processing of pith into sugar. Sugar thus became the sweetener with which nothing else could compete. Indeed English renders the Indian word for sugar as "candy," probably because of its ubiquity as a sweetener, at least in Asia.

Sugar Conquers the Mediterranean Basin

In the seventh and eighth centuries, the Muslims brought sugar to North Africa and southern Spain, its westernmost outpost before the Columbian Exchange. Muslims favored sugar from Egypt rather than India, probably because Egypt rather than India was within Islam's orbit. Egypt prided itself on producing the purest, whitest sugar crystals devoid of the liquid that is prominent in the pith. By the Middle Ages, Italians, particularly the Venetians, entered the sugar trade, bringing the sweetener at last to parts of Europe. In addition, Sicily grew sugarcane, providing a source of sugar close to home. Yet it is easy to exaggerate the importance of sugar in medieval Europe. The sweetener was almost unknown in northern Europe and the British Isles. This near absence probably stemmed from the high price that the Venetians charged for sugar. Europeans also tended to think of sugar in medicinal rather than culinary terms, an idea that was not unknown in antiquity.

Sugar, the New World, and the Sugar-Slave Complex

The dynamic expansion of sugar into the Americas began when Italian Spanish explorer Christopher Columbus planted sugarcane on the Caribbean island of Hispaniola (today Haiti and the Dominican Republic) in 1493. As sugarcane culture expanded, labor emerged as a problem. The Amerindians might have been coerced to work the sugar estates, but they died in large numbers from European and African diseases. Plantation owners had little more success with indentured servants. The work was intensive, deterring whites from toiling in the cane fields. Planters turned to an old institution, but with a new and ominous feature. By enslaving Africans to work the cane plantations, the planters made race the cardinal feature of modern slavery. One's African heritage, once a source of pride, became a vexation in the crucible of sugar and slavery. Race became a mark of inferiority. Whites thought blacks primitive in every way, believing that they lacked intelligence and self-control. These traits were particularly worrisome to whites because they meant that people of African descent could not control their libido. Even the suspicion that a black man might desire a white woman was enough to execute him. Whites likewise feared that a black temptress might seduce a white man. The reality was otherwise. White elites raped their female slaves. Though the children were his, he nonetheless demoted them to slavery. This slave-sugar model swept the Caribbean, South America, Central America, Mexico, and even the Louisiana territory, then owned by France. In what would become the United States, slavery and racism saturated the American South. Rice, cotton, indigo, and tobacco all borrowed the slave-sugar model. The split between a free but largely racist North and a slave-owning South led to the Civil War. Sugar and the labor it spawned culminated in the deadliest war in U.S. history.

It is difficult to overstate the suffering that sugar has caused. Europeans, largely the Portuguese, Spanish, Dutch, and English, sent some 10 million slaves to the Caribbean, Brazil, and other centers of sugarcane culture. Many perished in transit and were unceremoniously tossed into the ocean. Those who reached the Americas knew no respite. They toiled in the heat and humidity of tropical America. The average slave seldom survived longer than 10 years past the date of his or her arrival. Disease and undernourishment killed slaves. Slave owners were unwilling to feed slaves enough to do the arduous work that sugarcane demanded. All this anguish was meant only to entice the sweet tooth of Americans and Europeans.

Treatment was so brutal that slaves had little alternative but to revolt. Most rebellions failed, with the execution of large numbers of blacks, most of them men. At the end of the 19th century, however, the slaves on Saint Domingue, the jewel in the French sugar crown, launched what may be history's only successful slave rebellion. They burned the sugar estates and killed the French army that Emperor Napoleon Bonaparte had sent to restore order. Perhaps frightened, Napoleon sold the Louisiana territory to the United States, more than doubling the nation's size. Sugar had thus set America on the course of Manifest Destiny. The Haitian revolution also sickened third U.S. president Thomas Jefferson, a prominent slave owner. Jefferson feared that a similar revolt might grip the United States, ending the old dichotomy between slave and master, black and white. He feared an influx of Haitians into the United States. They would be sure to light the torch of freedom that Jefferson promised to extinguish. Sugar thus hardened racial attitudes in the United States.

One should note that the end of slavery in the United States did not cut the connections between sugar, racism, and coercion. As early as the 1920s, the National Association for the Advancement of Colored People (NAACP) began to investigate sugar planters in South Florida. The planters recruited African Americans throughout the South, promising them free transportation and food and a wage of $8 per day. These were empty promises. The transportation and food were not free and pay was less than $1 per day. Because the men had no money, they assumed a debt that could be worked off only as cane cutters. Armed guards shot anyone attempting escape. These circumstances were slavery in fact, if not in name. Yet the federal government refused the NAACP's request to prosecute these planters.

Elsewhere, sugar inspired repression. Poor Chinese and Japanese who had no means of earning a living at home sold themselves to planters on Hawaii. When this labor did not suffice, the United States imported Filipinos to fill the gap. As these groups began to agitate for better wages and working conditions, planters abandoned them for Korean immigrants. Indians and Chinese came even as far as the Caribbean to work the cane estates. In short, the demand for sugar appears to have created a permanent underclass. Middle class people in the temperate zone demand sugar that comes from the sweat and fatigue of the poor in the tropics.

Sugar has also inspired heroic leadership in the midst of injustice. Mohandas K. Gandhi, born in India, received his legal training in the United Kingdom. He settled in Natal, a village in what is today South Africa, where many Indians labored on the sugar estates. Gandhi first rose to prominence by defending these workers against the abuse of the sugar system. Gandhi articulated the obvious: the sugar system of South Africa was no better than slavery had been in the Americas. For his experiences in South Africa, Gandhi emerged as one of the 20th century's principal voices for peace, justice, and nationalism.

Sugar and Science

Sugar has also inspired advances in the sciences. For decades, scientists had been skeptical about the prospect of improving sugar yields because sugarcane plants produce so few flowers. But the success of hybrid corn and the remarkable spread of hybrids in the 1930s and 1940s prompted scientists in the tropics to hybridize varieties of sugarcane. The phenomenon of heterosis (hybrid vigor), pronounced in corn, propelled sugarcane to yield ever-larger quantities of sugar. Competition from sugar beet became irrelevant as cane yields soared. Today, Americans buy sugar from South Florida and Mexico. Little comes from beet growers in the American West. Even with this abundance of sugar, scientists have looked for substitutes, making saccharine in 1879. Perhaps the greatest threat to sugar, and a boon to the Midwest, has been the derivation of high fructose corn syrup (HFCS) since 1967. HFCS has made advances in the beverage industry, but sugar retains a foothold wherever aesthetics are important. The presence of appetizing sugar crystals in cookies and on breakfast cereals surely boosts the appeal of sugar. Sugar has even more uses. Scientists in Brazil are running automobiles on ethanol derived from sugar, much as the United States derives ethanol from corn.

Further Reading

Abbott, Elizabeth. *Sugar: A Bittersweet History*. New York: Duckworth Overlook, 2008.

Aronson, Marc, and Marina Budhos. *Sugar Changed the World: A Story of Magic, Spice, Slavery, Freedom, and Science*. Boston and New York: Clarion Books, 2010.

Dunn, Richard S. *Sugar and Slaves: The Rise of the Planter Class in the English West Indies, 1624–1713*. Chapel Hill: University of North Carolina Press, 1972.

Macinnis, Peter. *Bittersweet: The Story of Sugar*. Crows Nest, Australia: Allen and Unwin, 2002.

O'Connell, Sanjida. *Sugar: The Grass that Changed the World*. London: Virgin Books, 2004.

Sweet Potato

The term *sweet potato* refers to both the perennial vine and the swollen root. Despite its name, the sweet potato is not a potato. It does not develop from an underground stem, as does the potato, but from a root. The tendency to refer to the sweet potato as a yam is also incorrect. The two are in different genera and are not closely related despite superficial similarities. Yet southerners persist in calling the sweet potato a yam. The U.S. Department of Agriculture has further complicated matters by allowing farmers to market their crop as sweet potato yams. In the Arawak language of the Caribbean, *batatas* means "sweet potato," giving the roots its species name. The indigenes of Peru called the sweet potato *apichu* or *kumara* depending on its moisture content. The people of Paraguay know the sweet potato as *yety*. The sweet potato is known as *chaco* in Venezuela, *camote* in Bolivia, Chile, and Ecuador, *boniato* in Uruguay, and *batata-douce* in Brazil. In China the sweet potato is known as the "red potato," "red creeper," "white potato," "mountain taro," "red taro," "ground melon," and "foreign potato." Africans call the sweet potato the "local potato" or the "traditional potato." A member of the Convolvulaceae family, the sweet potato is related to morning glory. Scientists know the sweet potato as *Ipomoea batatas*.

The sweet potato is 70 percent water and 30 percent dry matter. It has a greater proportion of dry matter than other crops. Seventy-five to 90 percent of the dry matter is carbohydrate. An ideal food for health conscious consumers, the sweet potato has only 0.4 percent fat. It has beta-carotene, the vitamin A precursor, vitamin C, riboflavin, vitamin B_6, vitamin E, potassium, copper, manganese, and iron. Orange flesh varieties have more beta-carotene than white flesh cultivars. With 1.5–2.5 percent protein, the sweet potato compares favorably to vegetables and fruits but poorly to grains and legumes. The sweet potato is low in sulfur, bearing

Africa

A continent, Africa boasts many ethnicities, climates, and foods. Egypt and North Africa originally contained people of Mediterranean descent, as the tomb paintings in Egypt revealed. But in the seventh century CE, Muslim Arabs conquered the region. South of the Sahara Desert lie the tropics, which black Africans inhabit, and which include a variety of foodways. One thesis holds that sub-Saharan Africa had a poverty of food plants, leading its people to borrow heavily from the crops of the Columbian Exchange. Accordingly, sweet potatoes, cassava, corn, and peanuts are all important.

amino acids. In Southeast Asia, people eat leaves, petioles, and stem tips as greens. These parts of the plant have vitamins A and C, and more protein than roots. Compared with the potato, the sweet potato has more dry matter, starch, sugar, fiber, and fat, but less protein. Because of its nutritional profile, especially the presence of beta-carotene, the sweet potato has aided the developing world, where vitamin A deficiency is endemic. The root crop has therefore shaped history, health, and daily life.

Origin and Diffusion

The genus *Ipomoea* has 400 species, most of them diploids, though the sweet potato is a hexaploid. Scientists are not certain of the steps that transformed a diploid ancestor into a hexaploid sweet potato. A New World crop, the sweet potato may have originated between the Yucatán peninsula and the Orinoco River in Venezuela and Colombia. Panama, northern South America, and the Caribbean have all been proposed as the place of origin. Central America has the greatest diversity of sweet potato varieties and so may be the site of origin. The closest relative of the sweet potato, *Ipomoea trifida*, grows wild in Mexico, making it a possible location of origin. Another relative, *Ipomoea tiliacea*, is native to the Caribbean, strengthening the assertion that it may be the ancestral homeland of the sweet potato. The remains of the sweet potato date to 6000 BCE, in a Peruvian cave, though scientists do not know whether the ancient Peruvians had domesticated the plant by this date. The people of tropical America domesticated the sweet potato at least 5,000 years ago. In pre-Columbian America the Maya grew the sweet potato in Central America, and the Inca cultivated it in Peru.

By one account, farmers grew the sweet potato in New Zealand as early as 1000 CE, having gotten the root possibly from Peru or Polynesia. From Central America the sweet potato reached Oceania, though humans may not have been involved in this transfer. The sweet potato of Papua New Guinea differs from that of Peru, ruling out the latter as the source of the root in the former. In 1492, Spanish explorer Christopher Columbus brought the sweet potato from the Caribbean to Spain. Around 1600, the Portuguese introduced the sweet potato to West Africa, Southeast Asia, and the East Indies. Later, the root migrated to India, China, and Japan, though not everyone supports a late date for China. It is possible that farmers in the Philippines and Polynesia grew the sweet potato before European contact. One authority believes that the sweet potato may have originated in the Philippines and Polynesia, though this school of thought is difficult to reconcile with the antiquity of cultivation in the Americas. Alternatively, migrants or ocean currents may have spread the sweet potato from Central America and Mexico to the Philippines, and from Peru to the Pacific Islands before the arrival of Europeans. Differences between the sweet potato in the Caribbean and in the Philippines and Polynesia rule out the West Indies as the source of the root in these islands. Another possibility is that the Spanish brought the sweet potato from Mexico to the Philippines in the 16th century.

The United States

Explorers in Mexico and the Caribbean brought the sweet potato to the American colonies. As early as 1648, farmers grew the sweet potato in Virginia, in 1723 in Carolina, and in 1764 in New England. A crop of the South, sweet potatoes were grown for home use. In the 18th century farmers grew the sweet potato in eastern North Carolina, South Carolina, and Georgia. The yield was then 100 to 200 bushels per acre, though farmers reported up to 1,000 bushels per acre. The sweet potato was a staple during the American Revolution and the Civil War. Slaves ate the root. By 1909, Delaware, Maryland, Virginia, and New Jersey emerged as the center of sweet potato culture. Per person consumption was 31 pounds in 1920. During the Great Depression, the sweet potato emerged as a subsistence crop. Between 1930 and 1937, the land planted to the crop increased 200,000 acres, but the yield decreased because farmers had little money for fertilizer. Because the price of sweet potatoes halved during the Depression per person consumption hovered at 25 pounds per year. In the 1930s, Louisiana established a program to breed improved varieties. After World War II, scientists in North Carolina, Maryland, South Carolina, Georgia, Mississippi, Virginia, and Oklahoma began breeding sweet potatoes. With the return of prosperity after World War II the production and consumption of sweet potatoes declined as Americans spent money on meat and milk rather than sweet potatoes. In the 1960s, Louisiana and California emerged as important producers. Since the 1970s, per-person consumption of sweet potatoes lingered at four-and-a-half pounds per year, a steep reduction from the amount early in the century. Between 2000 and 2003, the United States averaged hundreds of thousands of tons of sweet potatoes on tens of thousands of acres for a yield of tens of thousands of pounds per acre. In 2007, the leading producers were North Carolina, Louisiana, Mississippi, California, Alabama, Arkansas, New Jersey, and Texas. In the United States the majority of sweet potatoes are eaten fresh, with the rest to chips, fries, canned products, and feed. Cookies and pet food contain sweet potato flour. In the United States, farmers harvest sweet potatoes in August in the South, in September in New Jersey, and in October in California. The harvest occurs before or immediately after the first frost. Although most of the world depends on rainfall, California irrigates virtually all its sweet potato crop. Farmers grow the sweet potato from Florida to southern Ontario.

China

According to one account, Chinese businessman Zhenlong Chen brought the sweet potato from Luzon in the Philippines to Fujian, China, sometime in the 16th century. The date remains unknown because the merchants of Zhangzhon, the port of Fujian, kept this information secret. Chen's son presented the sweet potato to the governor of Fujian, and either father or son introduced the root to Zhejiong, Shandong, and Henan provinces. The introduction of the sweet potato must have occurred before 1594 because the governor of Fujian, familiar with the crop, ordered peasants to plant it to avert famine that year. One account holds that the peasants of Myanmar introduced the sweet potato to Tali, China, in 1563. Another account maintains that the sweet potato spread from Vietnam to Dongyuan, China, in 1582. Another possibility is that the sweet potato migrated from India to China. From the south of China, the sweet potato spread to Quanzhou, Putian, and Changle counties.

In the 1950s and 1960s, farmers increased the production of sweet potatoes to feed a growing population. In 1961, farmers planted sweet potatoes on record acreage. By 1985, the area had fallen as farmers switched to rice, wheat, and corn. Since 1985, the land planted to sweet potato has steadied at several million acres. In China, the sweet potato ranks fifth behind rice, wheat, corn, and soybeans in the size of the harvest. Farmers grow sweet potatoes from Hainan in the south to Inner Mongolia in the north and from Zhejiang in the east to Tibet in the west. The Yellow and Yangtze River valleys are the centers of sweet potato culture. The leading producers are Sichuan, Hanan, Chengzing, Anhui, Guangdong, and Shandong provinces. Stockmen feed sweet potato stems and leaves to pigs, cows, and goats. China's soils are often deficient in phosphorus, leading farmers to fertilize their sweet potatoes to ensure an abundant harvest.

Africa

During the era of the slave trade, the Portuguese brought the sweet potato to Africa. Farmers first grew sweet potatoes in West Africa about 1520. By the end of the 17th century, the sweet potato was widely cultivated in the region. There farmers grow sweet potatoes with cassava and yams. The sweet potato is not the most important crop in West Africa because farmers prefer to grow yams, cassava, rice, cowpeas, cocoyams, and acha. West Africa and East Africa account for the majority of Africa's sweet potato harvest. In Ghana, sweet potatoes rank third in acreage, trailing cassava and yams. The people of Ghana boil, fry, or roast sweet potatoes.

In sub-Saharan Africa, farmers adopted the crop from an early date, often planting it in preference to yams. So long has the sweet potato been in cultivation that some Africans erroneously assume it to be a native crop. In 2001 and 2002,

Africa yielded a few tons of sweet potato per acre. The poor grow sweet potatoes, a subsistence crop, on small farms. With little investment in fertilizer and technology these farmers have nonetheless managed to increase production of sweet potato at a faster rate than other crops. African farmers grow the sweet potato from sea level to 7,500 feet. The sweet potato is an important crop in Africa because it requires less labor and fertilizer than other crops. The root has made gains where cassava and banana disease have limited these crops, especially in land near Lake Victoria. Farmers often plant sweet potato and cassava on adjoining plots. Where cassava fails, farmers plant sweet potato. Where the size of farms has decreased farmers have increased the proportion of land planted to sweet potato in order to derive the maximum calories and nutrients from the soil.

Government policies have favored the cultivation of sweet potato in Africa. At the end of colonialism, governments subsidized corn growers to encourage subsistence agriculture. These subsidies have proven too costly, and in the early 21st century, governments, especially in southern Africa, have ended them, leading corn growers to plant sweet potatoes for subsistence. The AIDS epidemic, in depopulating the countryside, has led single-parent households, seeking to minimize labor and costs, to plant sweet potatoes. Where farmers have opted for a less capital-intensive agriculture they have switched from coffee and banana to sweet potato. In Africa, sweet potatoes, planted where other crops have failed, are a famine food.

In sub-Saharan Africa, 23 countries produce virtually all the region's sweet potatoes. Uganda and Nigeria total one-third of sub-Saharan Africa's sweet potato yield. In Uganda and Nigeria the most densely populated areas produce the most sweet potatoes. Uganda, Rwanda, Burundi, and Malawi harvest hundreds of pounds of sweet potato per person. The lowest producers are the Congo, Ethiopia, South Africa, Côte de Ivoire, Niger, and Burkina Faso. Not as productive as the United States and China, sub-Saharan Africa yields 1.8 tons of sweet potatoes per acre. In South Africa, prosperous farmers use irrigation and fertilizers to produce several tons of sweet potatoes per acre. In eastern and parts of southern Africa, farmers grow sweet potatoes as a secondary crop with corn, banana, and plantain being the primary crop. In parts of Africa, sweet potatoes are planted after a grain or cash crop. In Uganda, farmers dry sweet potatoes so they can be stored for five months. Ugandans grind sweet potatoes to make a porridge known as *atapa*. Throughout Africa women tend sweet potatoes, giving rise to the association between the root, women, and poverty.

India

In India, the sweet potato ranks third among tuber and root crops, trailing the potato and cassava. The sweet potato is cultivated everywhere in India except Jammu,

Kashmir, Himachal Pradesh, and Sikkim. In comparison with other countries, India ranks fifth in the yield of sweet potatoes per acre, eighth in sweet potato production and 12th in acreage to sweet potatoes. The sweet potato is a rainfed crop in Orissa, West Bengal, Uttar Pradesh, Bihar, and Jharkhand. These states account for the majority of India's sweet potato acreage and a large fraction of production. In India, the average farm has only a few acres of sweet potatoes. In Bihar, farmers cultivate sweet potatoes year round. Elsewhere sweet potatoes are grown in the rainy season between September and January and in summer. The yield in Bihar is modest. In Orissa and Jharkhand, where the soil is poor, the yield is meager.

As incomes have risen in India, as in the United States, people have eaten fewer sweet potatoes. Accordingly, farmers have switched from sweet potatoes to grain. In India, the majority of sweet potatoes are eaten fresh. Indians roast, bake, or boil the root. Many Indians believe that sweet potatoes and milk are a healthy addition to the diet but that sweet potatoes alone are unwholesome. Stockmen feed the vast majority of sweet potato vines to animals, saving the rest for next year's planting. In Bihar, farmers rotate sweet potatoes with corn, wheat, and onions. In Orissa, sweet potato follows corn or rice. In West Bengal farmers rotate moong, taro, and sweet potatoes. In Andhra Pradesh, sweet potatoes follow corn and pre-cede vegetables. In Chhattigarh, Uttar Pradesh, and Maharashtra farmers rotate sweet potatoes with cowpeas.

South America

In South America, the sweet potato ranks third among tubers and roots, trailing cassava and potato. Between 2005 and 2007, Brazil, ranking first among South American countries, averaged hundreds of thousands of tons of sweet potatoes. Argentina ranked second; Peru, third; and Paraguay, fourth. Among South American nations, Brazil devotes the greatest acreage to sweet potatoes. Argentina ranks second; Paraguay, third; and Peru, fourth. Peru recorded the greatest yield. Guyana ranked last in yield per acre. In Guyana, farmers intercrop sweet potatoes with coffee, citrus, and avocado. Unlike much of the developing world, farmers in South America grow sweet potatoes for the market. In South America, most sweet potatoes are eaten fresh. Smaller amounts produce starch, flour, canned products, and chips. In 2007, South American farmers harvested millions of tons of sweet potatoes. South America yields half the New World's sweet potatoes. In South America, farmers favor the sweet potato because it requires little labor or cost, yields well in infertile soils, and tolerates heat and drought. In the central coast of Peru, which has little ranch land, stockmen feed roots and vines to animals. In Argentina and Uruguay, manufacturers make sweet potatoes into sweets.

Brazil, Argentina, Peru, Paraguay, and Uruguay produce virtually all South America's sweet potatoes. In Argentina, Uruguay, and Chile, the sweet potato ranks behind only the potato as a tuber or root crop. In Paraguay and Guyana it trails only cassava. The continent's largest exporter, Brazil, sends little of its crop to foreign buyers. In South America, per-person consumption of sweet potato trails that of Asia, Africa, Oceania, and the Caribbean. Paraguay and Uruguay have the continent's highest per-person consumption of sweet potato. In Paraguay, sweet potato rivals cassava as a staple. In Uruguay and Argentina, people eat sweet potatoes primarily during winter. Brazilians eat sweet potatoes when other crops fail. In the Yungas region of Peru, sweet potato rivals potato as a staple. People in the countryside eat more sweet potatoes than do urbanites.

Further Reading

Loebenstein, Gad, and George Thottappilly, eds. *The Sweetpotato*. Dordrecht, Netherlands: Springer, 2009.

Martin, John H., Richard P. Waldren, and David L. Stamp. *Principles of Field Crop Production*. Upper Saddle River, NJ: Pearson-Prentice Hall, 2006.

Onwueme, I. C. *The Tropical Tuber Crops: Yams, Cassava, Sweet Potato, and Cocoyams*. New York: John Wiley and Sons, 1978.

Rubatzky, Vincent E., and Mas Yamaguchi. *World Vegetables: Principles, Production, and Nutritive Values*. New York: Chapman and Hall, 1997.

Woolfe, Jennifer A. *Sweet Potato: An Untapped Food Resource*. Cambridge, UK: Cambridge University Press, 1992.

T

Taco

Originally a Mexican food, the taco spread to the United States in the 1920s and became a global commodity in the late 20th century. The taco is a variant of the tortilla. Made from corn flour, the tortilla destined to be a taco is usually fried to give it a hard texture. As it is fried, the taco assumes a U shape capable of holding other ingredients, particularly beef, in the way that two slices of bread hold meats and other ingredients. In function, then, the taco is not far removed from the sandwich. The taco shares with the sandwich and other foods ease of preparation and so can be made quickly to cater to a busy lunch crowd. The taco has shaped history and daily life by helping to introduce Americans to Mexican foods, by its link to sexuality, by its movement toward standardization, which had been part of Fordism, by embracing the factory system, by sinking roots in the history of Los Angeles, California, and by its rise to global prominence. Today the taco is likely the prominent Mexican food.

The Taco and Its Origins

The popular fried taco shell is known as a *dorado* and may be eaten at breakfast, lunch, dinner, or as a snack. Its use at breakfast may be faltering because Taco Bell has recently expanded its breakfast menu well beyond the taco. The taco may be a full meal or a snack depending on its contents. Some people eat tacos along with simpler tortillas. Popular taco ingredients may include salsa, cilantro, and onions. The earliest use of the word "taco" to mean a taco dates to the late 19th century, though the term had earlier been employed for a different purpose. The taco is popular in Mexico, the United States, Sweden, and Japan. It is a global commodity.

The taco was a relative latecomer to the United States. The enchilada, frijoles, tamale, and Mexican beef stew all predated the taco as migrants to the United

States, particularly California and the American Southwest. The original taco held spicy meats. Indeed, Americans expected Mexican foods of all descriptions to be spicy. In this sense, the taco and other Mexican foods conditioned the American palate to enjoy spicy foods and thereby expanded American cuisine, a move that shaped history and daily life. In the 1920s, the taco debuted in the United States, staking claim to California and Texas. In the 1930s, the taco was part of American cuisine, to judge from its appearance in American cookbooks. In the 1960s, Taco Bell and its imitators made tacos widespread, first throughout the United States and then worldwide. Mexicans thought the Americanized taco a cheap and bland imitation of the Mexican taco, but Americans ate tacos en masse nonetheless. Today, Americans think of the taco first when they think of Mexican food. Even Irish restaurants serve corned beef tacos during Cinco de Mayo, a Mexican celebration. The slogan of the day is that the Irish are Mexicans too. Here one sees the taco's international reach.

Los Angeles and San Bernardino, California, early adopted the taco. Food vendors sold tacos to the lunchtime crowd. Consumers had only a brief respite for lunch and so needed something quick to eat. The taco filled this need, as did the hamburger, hot dog, and sandwich. In this sense, the taco adapted to, and shaped, the people who worked in factories or on farms. One popular taco, Beautiful Little Heaven, had beef, salsa, avocado, and chili peppers. One could purchase two for $3. California in the 1930s was in the midst of a population boom, attracting tourists and settlers with the promise of sweet oranges, fresh tacos, and recreation. The taco had become a full partner in California cuisine. Los Angeles transformed Olvera Street, one of the city's oldest roads, into a series of restaurants and craft stores to attract tourists. Restaurants served Mexican fare, especially the taco. Having sunk its roots into the city's soil, the taco had become part of Los Angeles's history.

By 1901, Los Angeles had more than 100 street vendors, most of whom sold Mexican food. The police were sometimes suspicious of them, thinking these vendors akin to vagrants. In the 1920s, the vendors began selling tacos to the influx of Mexican immigrants fleeing the instability of the Mexican government. These vendors expanded, selling not only tacos but also goat stew, tripe soup, and permutations of chicken, pork, and beef. According to one journalist, nothing compared to the taco in giving one the authentic flavor of Los Angeles. The taco had become a civic booster. Mexican immigrants tended to prefer fresh grilled soft tacos, whereas whites preferred the fried hard-shelled tacos loaded with meat, typically beef. "Taco houses," restaurants that made their livelihood selling tacos and other Mexican foods, expanded throughout southern California. The tendency to fry tacos and the meats used as stuffing contributed to the inclination to view the taco as a kind of junk food. Certainly it was fast food long before the rise of Taco Bell.

By the 1930s, taco houses had expanded to New York City, many of them decorated with images of the Aztec goddess of beauty, combining sexuality and the taco. The link between sex and various foods has been constant throughout history and an important aspect of our understanding of food. The link between sex and wine is another example and goes back to the early inhabitants of the Mediterranean Basin. Magazine ads urged housewives to prepare tacos for their families. In the 1950s, a family could buy its own fryer to prepare and shape tacos.

Taco Bell

Glen Bell, the founder of Taco Bell, used a similar fryer, though on a large scale, and must have borrowed heavily from his predecessors. Bell acquired skills as a cook for the U.S. Marine Corps during World War II. Herein he developed his interest in food service. After the war he frequented McDonald's franchises, where the idea must have been born to create a taco franchise. The car culture in which Americans were immersed and the widespread homage of consumerism created the environment in which Bell would rise to prominence. In 1948, he opened Bell's Hamburger and Hot Dogs in San Bernardino. Selling the restaurant the next year, he opened a second, with an eye on the Mexican restaurants in the city. He understood the taco's changing demographics. More and more whites were eating tacos. In 1950, Bell opened a third restaurant, Bell's Burgers. Only a block from a tortilla factory, he began buying and shaping them into tacos. The idea of Taco Bell was born in fact if not yet in name. As McDonald's had done, Bell standardized ingredients: fried taco shells, ground beef, shredded lettuce, cheese, and chili sauce. Bell understood that Americans should have the same experience no matter which Taco Bell they visited. Standardization is at the heart of the American experience. American inventor Thomas Edison's light bulb and American automaker Henry Ford's Model T were models of standardization. The taco was no different.

By 1962, Taco Bell had expanded well beyond California. By 1969, Bell was opening two new franchises per week throughout the United States. Texas, the Midwest, and Florida were all converts to Taco Bell. In 1978, the year Taco Bell merged with PepsiCo, Bell counted more than 800 Taco Bells in the United States with annual revenues topping $1 billion.

Imitators abounded. In 1960, U.S. Navy veteran Ron Fraedrick opened Taco Time in Eugene, Oregon. Near the University of Oregon, it attracted college students in large numbers. In the 1980s, Taco Time opened its first franchise in Japan. Worldwide, Taco Time has more than 300 restaurants. Other imitators succeeded in similar ventures in Texas, Oklahoma, and the Midwest. The taco had become a global food.

With its 21st-century headquarters in Irvine, California, Taco Bell and its competitors have spread the taco worldwide. Affiliated with Pizza Hut and Kentucky Fried Chicken (KFC), Taco Bell sells a variety of foods in the United States and throughout the globe. Curiously, company employees can no longer eat at the headquarters, but must venture to the nearest Taco Bell three miles distant. There, they can load their tacos with Korean barbecue, Argentine sausage, tofu, or jackfruit. The taco itself is an international food depending on what one puts in it.

Further Reading

Arellano, Gustavo. *TACO USA: How Mexican Food Conquered America*. New York: Scribner, 2012.

Chavez, Denise. *A Taco Testimony: Meditations on Family, Food and Culture*. Tucson, AZ: Rio Nuevo Publishers, 2006.

Pilcher, Jeffrey M. *Planet Taco: A Global History of Mexican Food*. Oxford and New York: Oxford University Press, 2012.

Wilson, Scott. *Tacos: Authentic, Festive and Flavorful*. Seattle, WA: Sasquatch Books, 2009.

Tea

A perennial tree, tea is an ancient plant. *Homo erectus*, the forbearer of modern humans, may have encountered tea in Asia 500,000 years ago. Like several other crops, tea is grown in developing countries for consumption in the developed world. Tea is adapted to a range of climates and may be grown in the tropics and in temperate locales. Known by many names, tea is *te* in Catalan, Latvian, Malay, Norwegian, Danish, Hebrew, Italian, Spanish, and Swedish; *tee* in Afrikaans, Finnish, German, and Korean; *the* in French, Icelandic, Indonesian, and Tamil; *thee* in Dutch; *cha* in Greek, Hindi, Japanese, Persian, and Portuguese; *chai* in Russian; *chey* in Albanian, Arabic, Bulgarian, Croatian, Czech, Serbian, and Turkish; and *tea* in English and Hungarian. In the parlance of science, Swedish naturalist Carl Linneaus placed tea in the genus *Thea* in 1753, though second thoughts led him to assign it instead to the genus *Camellia*. In 1905, the International Code of Botanical Nomenclature named cultivated tea *Camellia sinensis*, an appellation it retains today. Linneaus believed that there were two species of tea, one that yielded green tea and the other black tea. This is incorrect. The method of preparation yields either green or black tea. British adventurer Robert Fortune, visiting China in disguise in the 19th century, learned that only one species of tea is capable of producing green or black tea.

Tea may span hundreds of thousands of years if *Homo erectus* really did boil the leaves or perhaps chew them. Other than coffee, it is difficult to think of a more popular beverage than tea. (Rawpixelimages/Dreamstime.com)

The Prehistory and Antiquity of Tea

Tea may have originated in Southeast Asia, where most of the 82 extant species reside. Alternatively, tea may have arisen in Central Asia or in the land that is the border between India and China. Some varieties of tea may have originated in southern China, Indonesia, and Assam. According to one authority, tea may have originated in the region where southwestern China, Myanmar, and Laos meet. Wild tea still grows in Yunnan, China. Tea must have been among the earliest plants to elicit the curiosity of humans, if the conjecture is correct that *Homo erectus* came across tea in what is today Yunnan, China. *Homo erectus* mastered fire and may have been adept at boiling water. Into this water he may have placed tea leaves, consuming the beverage, perhaps for its caffeine. Another account of the origin of tea concerns the emperor Shen Nung, possibly a legendary figure, who was said to rule China between 2737 and 2697 BCE. Boiling water, Nung used the branches from a tea tree to stoke the fire. By chance, a gust of wind blew a tea leaf into the water. Nung tasted the brew, finding it flavorful. Committing this discovery to paper, he supposedly wrote the *Pen Ts'ao*, a book on medicinal herbs in which Nung extolled tea. He supposedly wrote that tea "quenches the thirst, lessens the desire for sleep and gladdens and cheers the heart." Yet the earliest edition

Homo erectus

A possible ancestor of modern humans, *Homo erectus* appears to have evolved in Africa about 1.8 million years ago. This species of human was the first to venture outside Africa, tracing its way east along the southernmost coast all the way to the Indonesian island of Java. Adapted to the tropics, *Homo erectus* appears to have prospered in tropical Asia. A powerfully built species, *Homo erectus* had large bones and must have had large muscles to move them. Its robust physique must have been accustomed to vigorous activity. *Homo erectus* must have been more muscular than modern humans. When anatomically modern humans moved into Asia, they encountered *Homo erectus,* as was the case with Neanderthals in Europe. The result must have been the same. Anatomically modern humans likely had children with *Homo erectus*. The descendants of these unions may have been the early colonists of China and Australia. It is unlikely, however, that scientists will ever have *Homo erectus* DNA to match with the DNA of modern humans. This encyclopedia has suggested that *Homo erectus* may have been the first to taste tea.

of the *Pen Ts'ao* dates to the first century CE, long after Nung had died. Moreover, this edition is silent about tea. Only in the seventh century did someone add a reference to tea. In any case, tea must have been one of the building blocks of civilization in east, south and Southeast Asia. For this reason, one can scarcely overvalue tea as an agent in the construction of human societies.

Tea and the Rise of Buddhism

Foods and beverages have been important to religions. Bread, fish, and wine, for example, were prominent in the rise of Christianity, and Islam stimulated the consumption of coffee. Tea played a similar role in the rise of Buddhism. According to one legend, tea originated in a gruesome way. In 520 CE, Buddhist monk Bodhidharma, traveling from India to China, sought refuge in a cave, where he vowed to stay awake in meditation for nine years. Despite his resolve, he fell asleep. When he awoke Bodhidharma was so angry with himself that he cut off his eyelids and cast them to the ground. From this spot grew the first tea tree. Thereafter, monks have consumed tea to stay awake so that they would not suffer Bodhidharma's fate. This story explains why tea leaves are shaped like eyelids. Although Bodhidharma's story is doubtless myth, it explains the importance of tea to Buddhism. One does not need to stretch the imagination to conceive of the possibility that Buddha drank tea just as Jesus apparently drank wine and ate fish and bread. In this context, religions are not simply systems of doctrines. They exist in a world of foods and beverages and take on those that advance their purposes. In this way, tea advanced the cause of Buddhism, which remains a major world religion.

Tea as an Addiction

Because of its caffeine, tea may be the world's oldest addictive beverage. Yet the addiction gives pleasure and by most accounts does not undermine one's health. Tea has become so ubiquitous that it has become almost as essential to life as water or oxygen. By 1500, more than half the world's population drank tea. By the 1930s, the world consumed some 200 cups of tea per person per year. Today the world drinks billions of cups of tea per year. Although coffee had been popular in Britain since the opening of plantations in tropical America in the 16th century, tea has largely displaced it. Today, the average Brit imbibes 40 percent of his or her liquid nourishment in the form of tea. On its own, tea commands a larger segment of the world's population than coffee, cocoa, soft drinks, and alcohol combined. As in China, tea has become one of the building blocks of modernity. One can scarcely imagine a world bereft of tea, so important has the beverage become. In this context, tea may have been the first global commodity, though one might make an argument on behalf of coffee.

Tea and the Vietnam War

This is not the place for a detailed examination of the Vietnam War. One should note, however, that the people of Vietnam had a long history of resisting invaders, notably the Chinese. In the 19th century, France became the latest imperial power, once more arousing the Vietnamese to resistance. As early as the Paris peace talks that ended World War I, Ho Chi Minh, an intellectual, a nationalist, and a communist, sought American assistance in freeing Vietnam from France. U.S. President Woodrow Wilson refused even to meet him. In the context of the Cold War, the French collapse in 1954 led the United States to become the de facto foreign power in Vietnam, again arousing Vietnamese resistance. The Vietnamese had triumphed over countless invaders and the United States would fare no better. As the war expanded to no discernable purpose, Americans began to turn against it. At the height of American involvement Ho Chi Minh made a bold declaration, announcing that U.S. President Lyndon Johnson was welcome to meet him in Hanoi to seek peace. If the United States chose to continue fighting, Vietnam would resist it for 1,000 years, but if America sought peace, Minh and Johnson could share a cup of tea. In this way, Minh elevated tea to a symbol of peace. A prized beverage in Vietnam, Minh would serve the best brew to President Johnson.

Regrettably the president rejected the offer. The man who had accomplished so much domestically became known to some as the villain who embroiled the United States in a horrific war. In 1969 Minh died, never to realize the victory he sought.

Tea and Diseases

In prehistory, human populations were small and the land sparsely settled. Diseases appear not to have plagued humans at this early stage. The establishment of dense populations and the rise of civilization changed matters. Now the diseases that have caused so much suffering—malaria, smallpox, influenza, cholera, plague, and a host of others—became endemic. How to combat these perils emerged as an important challenge. Part of the problem was that water, essential to human life, could easily become polluted. The microbe that causes cholera, for example, is waterborne. Milk was no better an alternative because its nutrients and fat benefit the replication of harmful bacteria. Alcohol was a promising alternative because the alcohol killed bacteria. When the content of alcohol was low, it was possible to get through the day in a mild state of intoxication. To combat the problem of inebriation, the Greeks and Romans diluted their wine with water. The Romans also supplied their soldiers with vinegar to drink because it was an abiotic beverage, though the experience of consuming it must have been unpleasant. In this context, tea showed its value. One Chinese emperor credited the beverage with saving his life.

Tea may have improved the health of people in the early modern era. One account holds that after 1730 the incidence of dysentery diminished in Britain, and in 1796 one commentator remarked that waterborne diseases were "almost unknown in London." In the early 19th century, physicians attributed this improvement in public health to tea, which is an abiotic drink. The tannic acid in it kills the bacteria that cause cholera, typhoid, and dysentery, though it is also true that the boiling of water to make tea would have killed microbes. Because tea was free of pathogens it was safer to drink than water or beer. Because tannic acid passes into breast milk, it may have protected infants from diseases and so lowered infant mortality. One writer believes tea increased longevity in early modern Europe and Asia. Because of tea's antimicrobial properties one army physician urged soldiers in 1923 to fill their canteens with tea to prevent typhoid. By killing pathogens, tea reduced the incidence of diarrhea and lessened the rate of infection from influenza. Tea combated the growth of bacteria in the mouth and so improved oral health. Had 19th-century Russian composer Peter Tchaikovsky imbibed tea rather than water he might not have succumbed to cholera, a disease that truncated a brilliant career.

A Universal Stimulant

Tea was not always a beverage. Mammals have long chewed tea leaves, probably for their caffeine. It seems reasonable to assume that humans, migrating into Asia, witnessed and imitated this behavior. The tea leaves provided a boost, heightening concentration and alertness, qualities that must have been valuable in a hostile world. Tea leaves, and later the beverage, may have given humans an important survival and reproductive advantage. The growth of human populations must have owed something to tea, both as a stimulant and an abiotic liquid. Fortified with tea, or perhaps just tea leaves, humans developed the cognitive capacity to design and improve tools, to build simple dwellings, and, ultimately, to create civilization. Homo sapiens's rise to prominence must stem at least partly from tea.

Further Reading

Faulkner, Rupert, ed. *Tea: East and West*. London: V & A Publications, 2003.

Heiss, Mary Lou, and Robert J. Heiss. *The Story of Tea: A Cultural History and Drinking Guide*. Berkeley, CA: Ten Speed Press, 2007.

Hohenegger, Beatrice. *Liquid Jade: The Story of Tea from East to West*. New York: St. Martin's Press, 2006.

Macfarlane, Alan, and Iris Macfarlane. *The Empire of Tea: The Remarkable History of the Plant That Took over the World*. New York: Overlook Press, 2003.

Mair, Victor H., and Erling Hoh. *The True History of Tea*. London: Thames and Hudson, 2009.

Martin, Laura C. *Tea: The Drink That Changed the World*. Tokyo: Tuttle Publishing, 2007.

Mitscher, Lester A., and Victoria Dolby. *The Green Tea Book: China's Fountain of Youth*. New York: Avery, 1998.

Standage, Tom. *A History of the World in 6 Glasses*. New York: Walker and Company, 2005.

Tomato

A member of the unfairly treated Nightshade family, the tomato is a perennial vine grown as an annual in the temperate zone. Related to the potato, peppers, eggplant, tobacco, and the poisonous belladonna, the toxic foliage of the tomato cannot be fed to humans or livestock. Although doubts persisted for centuries in Europe, the tomato is safe to eat. Far from toxic, the tomato is much more nourishing than European critics believed. One hundred milligrams of tomato contain 40 of the recommended daily allowance of vitamin C, 30 percent of vitamin A, and

Italian cuisine is unthinkable without the tomato, even though the tomato is not native to Italy. Rather the tomato came to Italy from South America and through Spanish efforts. (Amy Nicolai/Dreamstime.com)

potassium, calcium, iron, and the B vitamins thiamine and riboflavin. Controversy has attended the debate over whether the tomato is a fruit or vegetable. The debate climaxed in the 1890s and again in 1981. In the second instance, President Ronald Reagan convinced Congress to cut funding for school lunches. To make sure that schools did not appear to skimp on vegetables, Reagan ordered the U.S. Department of Agriculture (USDA) to classify ketchup as a vegetable. French fries and ketchup were nutritious after all. In the 20th and 21st centuries the tomato has emerged as the most popular item in the home garden. Gardening books, with advice on how to grow tomatoes, proliferate. Some gardeners spend 25 cents per tomato seed for a variety of heirloom tomato, some of which trace their lineage to the 19th century. One gardener facetiously wrote that it cost him $64 to grow a single tomato. Others, spade in hand, enrich the soil with leaves, grass clippings, pine needles, and other organic matter. All this effort and expense is worthwhile because the harvest is so tasty.

American Origins

The tomato grows wild in Peru, Ecuador, Bolivia, Chile, and Colombia, suggesting an origin in South America. The fact that the people of South America took no

Tomato Soup

A versatile food, tomato soup may be served hot or cold. The texture may be smooth or contain chunks of chopped tomatoes. Tomato soup may even be served with chunks of chicken or vegetables. Tomato soup remains popular in the United States and Poland. Tomato soup may have been invented around 1872, though it gained popularity in 1897 when American entrepreneur Joseph A. Campbell condensed and canned it. It is a leading product of the Campbell Soup Company.

note of the tomato is clear from the absence of a word for tomato in the languages of these people. Possibly birds took the tomato to the Galapagos Islands, Central America, and Mexico. The Maya of southern Mexico and Guatemala domesticated the tomato sometime in prehistory. They named it *xtomatl* or *tomatl*, from which we derive the word *tomato*. The Maya selected tomatoes for size and flavor. Mayan selection is responsible for the range in sizes and colors. Using slash-and-burn agriculture, the Maya planted tomato seeds in clearings. Each Mayan household may have grown tomatoes in the family garden. The Maya planted tomatoes with chili peppers. The descendants of the Maya appear to have favored the yellow tomato, which they traded with the Aztecs. In this way, the Aztecs came to cultivate the fruit.

Curiously, the tomato did not migrate north from Mesoamerica to North America as one might have expected. Rather, like the potato and turkey, the tomato made two transatlantic crossings: east to Europe and then west from Europe to Spanish and British North America. In 1710, the people of the Carolinas were growing tomatoes. A written account that year marked the first reference to the tomato in North America, though it seems strange that Spanish Florida did not earlier adopt the tomato. Third U.S. president Thomas Jefferson, an able gardener, credited physician John de Sequayra with planting the first tomato in North America about 1750, but this date is too late if the people of the Carolinas had planted the fruit 40 years earlier. Later still is the assertion of Mary E. Cutler, a member of the Massachusetts Historical Society, that a man from Bermuda planted the first tomato in North America in 1802. The tomato appears to have been grown in the Caribbean from an early date. African women, slaves and cooks, brought the tomato to the attention of their masters. In the 18th century, the Spanish planted the tomato in California, then part of Mexico, and the French did likewise in Alabama and Louisiana. In the 1760s, prominent rice planter and slave owner Henry Laurens grew tomatoes on his South Carolina plantation and Jefferson grew them in his garden, though again, slaves did the real work.

The Tomato Shapes World Cuisine and Science

If one considers the tomato a vegetable, its consumption worldwide is second only to that of the potato. This statement may be misleading because neither is truly a vegetable. The tomato, as botanists have long recognized, is a fruit, and the potato is a tuber. The tomato's ubiquity is a recent phenomenon. The Spanish, the first Europeans to encounter the tomato, did not eat it, at least not initially. Many factors influenced the Spanish. Historian Madeleine Ferrieres suggests that the Spanish, reckless and bold in so many ways, were conservative when it came to food. She suggests that New World foods like the tomato might have frightened them. Moreover, was it proper for Christian Spaniards to eat heathen foods?

The Italians may have been the first Old World people to embrace the tomato. They doubtless got it from Spain, which then had conquered parts of southern Italy, a region ideal for tomato culture. One may place tomatoes into two rough categories for the purposes of this discussion. One class ripens to a rich red while the second ripens to a golden yellow. Other colors are possible, but they are not widely grown. The Italians appear to have favored yellow tomatoes in the 16th and 17th centuries. They prepared these tomatoes simply and in imitation of their preparation of eggplant and edible mushrooms. Italians sliced and fried tomatoes, probably in olive oil, a world commodity, and added salt and pepper. By the 17th century the tomato was an addition to salads, eaten raw and fresh from the vine. Probably in that century the Italians invented tomato sauce, a worldwide commodity with many uses. The Italians used tomato sauce to flavor meat and fish and finally pizza and pasta. Interestingly, one cannot trace a straight line from sauce to pizza, because Italians first made pizza with slices of tomato, as one might add a slice of tomato to a hamburger. Only in the 19th century did tomato sauce begin to replace tomato slices on pizza, though even today the use of tomato slices on pizza is not unusual. Indeed, so important is the tomato that one cannot conceive of pasta, particularly spaghetti and meatballs, and pizza without generous helpings of tomato sauce. In some Italian and Italian American households, the family and friends judge the matron of the home by her ability to make a flavorful tomato sauce. Mainland Italy was not alone in using tomatoes in their cuisine. Sicilians prided themselves on creating recipes for tomato sauce that differed from those on the peninsula. The use of tomatoes was one way Sicily declared figurative independence from peninsular Italy. By their own reckoning, Sicilians were the truest of Italians, a circumstance that the tomato confirmed. Sicilians may have been the first to add basil to tomato sauce.

By the 18th century the tomato must have traveled north, at least to some degree, because Swedish naturalist Carl Linnaeus (sometimes rendered Carl von Linné) knew that it was edible. He likened it to a type of peach, probably on the basis of color and shape, though the two are not closely related, as even Linnaeus must have known. Yet not everyone in northern Europe had access to tomatoes because the fruit is perishable and could not withstand the rough handling of transit. Moreover, not everyone in northern Europe wanted to eat the tomato. It was a food of southern Europe, a region that northern Europeans considered backward and inferior. By the late 18th century, however, fashionable restaurants in Paris and elsewhere in France served tomatoes as an ingredient in several dishes. The exclusiveness and expensiveness of these establishments suggest that the tomato had gained an allure to the wealthy. It seems likely that the influence of wealthy Parisians motivated Thomas Jefferson, who was then minister to France, to add the tomato to his cuisine and, when he returned home to Monticello in Virginia, to plant tomatoes in his extensive gardens. The tomato was popular in France at just the moment when potato flowers were conquering the monarchy and aristocracy. One is tempted to draw a connection because tomatoes and potatoes are closely related, both belonging to the Nightshade family. The French, following the Italian example, made tomato sauces. They also chopped and added tomatoes to soup with rice, ate tomatoes as a side dish, and even stuffed them with meat.

In this context it seems surprising that the tomato, native to South America, made slow progress in North America. The American South and possibly the Southwest were the first regions of North America to embrace the tomato. In the early 19th century, the people of Louisiana were the first to make ketchup from tomatoes. Previously, ketchup had been a fish sauce. By the late 19th century the tomato had become so important that it had prompted the U.S. Supreme Court to protect it. The issue concerned the tomato's status as fruit or vegetable. Tomato growers wanted the court to declare it a vegetable so it would enjoy the protection of a tariff against the import of cheap vegetables, that is, tomatoes, from Mexico. Although the tomato was, in the judgment of botanists, a fruit, the court declared that the tomato was really a vegetable. Tomato growers were jubilant that the court had made an economic rather than a scientific ruling. Even today most people think of the tomato as a vegetable.

The tomato has been an important subject of scientific advancement and for that reason has also shaped history. It was among the first plants to be hybridized, an achievement that predated the spectacular success of hybrid corn. About 1920, seedsmen sold the first hybrid tomato seeds, an advancement given that tomatoes are not ideal for hybridization. Unlike corn, the exemplar of hybrid breeding, the tomato has perfect flowers. That is, each flower contains both male and female parts. A scientist must declare one flower as female, meaning that he or she must remove the anthers, which contain the pollen, from the flower. Tweezers are necessary because the anthers are small and close to the female pistil. The scientist must then collect the pollen from these anthers, dusting them onto the pistil of a "female" flower to create a hybrid. For maximum benefit the cross will be between two different varieties of tomatoes to ensure the phenomenon of heterosis or hybrid vigor.

After World War II, the tomato spawned a greenhouse industry in the northern United States and parts of Europe, allowing people to have tomatoes year round. Restaurants bought these tomatoes in bulk and the system worked well until the early 1970s, when the energy crisis that decade saw the price of natural gas soar. Greenhouse growers could no longer afford to heat their structures during winter and the industry collapsed in the United States. Nonetheless, the greenhouse industry produces about 90 percent of France's tomatoes.

Another problem centers on what one might call the flavor crisis. Supermarket tomatoes are insipid. Perhaps no other fruit displays such disparity. A supermarket tomato cannot boast anything like the flavor of a fresh, vine-ripened tomato. Why is the difference so pronounced? The answer lies in the practices of industrial agriculture. Because a vine-ripened tomato cannot withstand rough handling and is perishable, supermarkets generally cannot and will not buy them. Instead the grower, seeking a tough, durable fruit for shipment, picks his or her tomatoes green and then sprays them with ethylene gas to feign the process of ripening. But because these tomatoes have not been allowed to ripen, they have none of the flavor or nutrients of a real tomato. In the end, the consumer suffers for the sins of agribusiness. In the 1990s, American biotechnology company Calgene attempted to solve this problem, bioengineering a tomato, known as the Flavr Savr, that ripened on the vine but had greater shelf life in the supermarket than a traditional vine-ripened tomato. One might have expected gratitude from consumers, but success eluded Calgene. Americans were and continue to be hostile to genetically engineered foods. Apparently it is fine to feed genetically modified (GM) corn to pigs but not GM tomatoes to humans.

Outside the United States, the tomato appears subject to fewer hang-ups. The people of Mali regard the tomato as a symbol of fertility. Couples share one before having sex.

Further Reading

Alexander, William. *The $64 Tomato*. Chapel Hill, NC: Algonquin Books of Chapel Hill, 2006.

Bloch-Dano, Evelyne. *Vegetables: A Biography*. Chicago and London: The University of Chicago Press, 2008.

Culter, Karen Davis. *Tantalizing Tomatoes: Smart Tips and Tasty Picks for Gardeners Everywhere*. Brooklyn, NY: Brooklyn Botanical Garden, 1997.

Foster, Nelson, and Linda S. Cordell, eds. *Chilies to Chocolate: Food the Americas Gave the World*. Tucson and London: The University of Arizona Press, 1992.

Goodman, Amy. *The Heirloom Tomato: From Garden to Table*. New York: Bloomsbury, 2008.

Johnson, Sylvia A. *Tomatoes, Potatoes, Corn, and Beans: How the Food of the Americas Changed Eating around the World*. New York: Atheneum Books, 1997.

Smith, Andrew F. *Souper Tomatoes: The Story of America's Favorite Food.* New Brunswick, NJ: Rutgers University Press, 2000.

Smith, Andrew F. *The Tomato in America: Early History, Culture, and Cookery.* Urbana: University of Illinois Press, 2001.

Tortilla

The tortilla, made from the American grass corn, is a staple of Mexican cuisine. It is the foundation of the taco, burrito, enchilada, nachos, and tortilla and corn chips. Latinos brought their cuisine, including the tortilla, to the United States, just as Italian immigrants brought pizza and spaghetti and meatballs to the United States in the 19th century. The tortilla thus was part of the globalization of food, a process that has been ongoing for centuries. The tortilla and its spin-offs, the tortilla chip and corn chip, have created food empires not just in the American Southwest but also throughout the United States. The tortilla is thus part of American capitalism.

The Tortilla and Essence of Mexico

The tortilla originated in prehistoric Mexico long before the era of European contact. The tortilla of Mexican tradition is thin, perhaps no thicker than the width of a quarter. It is traditionally fried, though the oil of choice is unknown. Lard may be a possibility, except that the Amerindians had few domesticated animals. The tortilla, traditionally made from corn flour, may also be made from wheat, and even spinach. The tortilla is a marker of ethnicity, class, and even beauty. It is "the essence" of Mexico, uniting all parts of the nation. For the poor, a tortilla and salt may make a meal. Without the tortilla, Mexican cuisine would not exist. The tortilla gives Mexican food its identity. The tortilla and Mexican foods in general have come with immigrants to the United States. In 2009, the tortilla was a $3.2 billion industry in the United States, triple the amount just of 12 years earlier. The Tortilla Industry Association disagrees, estimating that the tortilla is an $8 billion industry in the United States. This figure excludes the income from tortilla chips, tostadas, and corn chips. One can only guess the income from these derivatives of the tortilla. The art of making a tortilla is in decline. Instead of undergoing the laborious process of making one from scratch, Latinos and other Americans simply buy tortillas at the grocer. Gone is the tradition that a woman is not ready for marriage until she can prepare a tortilla from scratch.

The tortilla is a basic food throughout Latin America. Immigrants brought the tortilla to the American Southwest, from where it has become an important food throughout the United States. (Joshua Resnick/Dreamstime.com)

The Tortilla and Inferiority

As early as the 1870s, a group of intellectuals and politicians asserted that Mexico would remain poor and backward as long as it continued to cling to corn and its primary product, the tortilla. Had not the Mexican-American War proved the inferiority of Mexican arms, soldiers, and commanders? Among the tortilla's detractors, Francisco Bulnes divided the world into three quasiracial categories on the basis of food. People were of three types: consumers of corn, wheat, and rice. This simple system ignored the contribution of root and tuber crops and was based solely on an accounting of grain crops. Conflating race with food preference, Bulnes asserted that the race that ate wheat was superior to the races that ate corn and rice. Corn and tortillas had prevented the Amerindians from becoming civilized. Bulnes made a number of errors. Many biologists today dismiss the attempt to divide humans into races. There simply is not sufficient genetic diversity to justify racial categories. Moreover, corn and the tortilla were not impediments to civilization. The civilizations of the Maya and Aztecs owed their origin and development to corn. These civilizations would not have been possible without corn and its product the tortilla. Bulnes further entangled himself in error by referring to the Spanish conquest. Had not the Spanish proven superior to the Aztecs? They had not. Their success largely came from a stroke of epidemiological luck. Spain, like the rest of Europe, had for centuries traded with Africa and Asia. Along these trade routes came diseases like smallpox, influenza, plague, measles, and other killers. In contact with these diseases over centuries, Europeans evolved partial immunity to them. The Amerindians, outside this commerce, lacked this immunity. The Aztec empire fell because of disease, not because Spain was in any way superior.

The Tortilla in Its Iterations Conquers the United States

As early as the 1890s, U.S. cookbooks featured recipes for tortillas. Yet many of the recipes departed from Mexican traditions and seem designed to minimize preparation time. In the early 20th century, food manufacturers spun-off the tortilla chip and corn chip from the tortilla. These fried, heavily salted foods remain a snack favorite in the United States. The tortilla chip is strategically shaped as a triangle to hold salsa or dip. San Antonio, Texas, was the birthplace of the tortilla chip, though it does not receive proper credit for this innovation. In the 1940s, Los Angeles opened its first tortilla chip factory to such fanfare that many food historians forgot San Antonio's contribution. By 1950, *Popular Mechanics* magazine referred to Los Angeles as the home of the tortilla chip. In the 1990s, the Tortilla Industry Association credited Los Angeles innovator Rebecca Carranza with inventing the tortilla chip, giving her the Golden Tortilla award. Those who knew the true history of the tortilla chip resented that the award had gone to a white person rather than the rightful Mexican innovator. In this case, the tortilla rose to significance in allowing whites to expropriate the achievements of people of color, composing the comforting narrative of white supremacy that remains alive with many bigots and misguided people.

Another white person, Elmer Doolin, the inventor of Fritos, took credit for inventing the corn chip. In fact, he had expropriated it from a Mexican restaurant he frequented. Doolin purchased the right to sell corn chips for just $100 from Gustavo Olguin, who wished to return to Mexico without the encumbrance of business obligations in the United States. In 1934, Doolin filed for and received trademark protection for Fritos corn chips. Two years later a patent followed. Despite the Great Depression Doolin prospered, opening factories in Dallas, Texas, and Tulsa, Oklahoma. With success in the Southwest, Doolin pushed for national recognition after World War II, advertising in *Life* magazine and other national periodicals. In 1948, Doolin introduced Cheetos. Made from corn, one might consider the Cheeto a distant cousin to the tortilla. When Doolin partnered with Walt Disney, both master marketers, to sell Fritos at Disneyland, Doolin achieved his greatest triumph. The corn chip was thus a success of American capitalism. Tragically, and perhaps fittingly, Doolin, the promoter of fried foods, died of a heart attack at age 56.

The Tortilla in Folk Religions

In October 1977, New Mexico maid and Mexican immigrant, Maria Rubio, set out to prepare a burrito for her husband. For this task she had assembled pinto beans, scrambled eggs, chili peppers, and of course a tortilla, that is, an unleavened piece of bread made from corn flour. As she fried the tortilla, she gasped, believing that she saw an image of Jesus's face in it. The fact that she could make an association between Jesus and a tortilla was only possible because the Spanish had centuries earlier forced Mexico's indigenes to convert to Catholicism. Showing her tortilla to her daughter and a neighbor, Rubio gained the consensus that the apparition was real. A priest blessed it, though he stopped short of agreeing that the tortilla contained the image of anyone or anything. The story nonetheless spread. Soon Rubio's house was a pilgrimage destination for thousands of Christians, many of who brought flowers to honor Jesus. Letters came to Rubio from around the world. Convinced that a miracle had occurred, Rubio quit her job, and her husband stopped drinking alcohol. People donated money so that Rubio could build a shrine, but the Archdiocese of Santa Fe denied permission. Instead, Rubio converted her shed into a shrine, placing the tortilla there. In just a few years she found herself the guest on national television shows. The press worldwide clamored to interview her. The Jesus tortilla made Rubio a celebrity. The press christened it the "miracle tortilla." *The Simpsons* television show even referred to it in one of its broadcasts. Yet matters came to a bad end. While sharing the tortilla with school-children Rubio let them hold it. One child dropped it. The miracle tortilla shattered. Despite Rubio's faith, it is easy to see the miracle tortilla as a widespread experiment in mass self-delusion. People respond to what they are conditioned to believe. This Mexican woman did not see an Aztec god but Jesus because of her partly, and surely accidental, Eurocentric upbringing.

Further Reading

Arellano, Gustavo. *TACO USA: How Mexican Food Conquered America*. New York: Scribner, 2012.

Turkey

The turkey traces its roots to a wild bird that lived 23 million years ago in Central and North America. The Amerindians tamed it, using the bird for many purposes. In European hands, the turkey became the source of major feasts, notably Christmas and, later, Thanksgiving. Among Europeans, the English appear to have been particularly attached to the turkey. As an important part of the economy, the turkey has been and remains a subject of scientific research. After the chicken, the turkey is the world's most numerous livestock. The name *turkey* may be confusing because there may not be a connection between turkeys and the Muslim nation Turkey in western Asia.

The Turkey

A curious bird, the turkey displays several Darwinian traits. Notably, the male is larger than the female, meaning that females have preferred to breed with large males, a trait that some other birds and many mammals, including humans, share.

Thanksgiving

Thanksgiving, an American celebration, may trace its roots to a communal meal between English colonists and Native Americans in the 17th century. It is difficult to know what the groups shared at this meal or even whether it occurred. The timeworn image of the turkey as the main course is probably fanciful. In 1789, President George Washington declared a national day of "thanksgiving," but it became a national holiday only during the presidency of Abraham Lincoln. The tradition of eating turkey on Thanksgiving appears to be nearly ubiquitous in the United States. In this sense, the turkey is the national bird, a position that American polymath Benjamin Franklin appears to have favored early in American history.

The male is also more colorful than the female, suggesting that females have sought out males with colorful plumage for breeding. British naturalist Charles Darwin labeled such traits and behaviors as the product of sexual selection, an idea that was part of and even an extension of natural selection. Early in its evolution, the wild turkey was an able flier. Domestication ended this ability as humans selected for ever-larger turkeys. In fact, scientific breeding got the turkey into trouble during the 1980s. The demand of consumers for turkeys with ever-larger breast meat led to the breeding of turkeys that were so massive that they could not sustain their large breasts. This work involved not only conventional genetics but also artificial insemination. The simple act of walking broke turkey's legs because they could not bear the weight of their heavy breasts. Scientists, particularly those at the U.S. agricultural experiment stations, might have scaled back the size of turkeys, but instead bred them for larger legs with stouter leg bones. The result was an even larger bird that could at least sustain its own weight. After the experience with the Dodo, humans appear to have understood that they must perpetuate large flightless birds if they are to benefit from them.

New World Origins

The turkey, as shown above, is ancient to the Americas. It had been part of the biota for 23 million years before the Maya domesticated it in Central America about 2 million years ago. From Central America, the turkey spread north into Mexico and was a staple of Aztec cuisine. This scenario is contested. The Amerindians may have domesticated the turkey only during the last 2,500 years in Mesoamerica. The Amerindians associated the turkey with good fortune and even divinity. At the very least, the turkey was a conduit between humans and the gods. The Amerindians adorned themselves with turkey feathers and ate both turkey meat and eggs.

The Holiday Tradition Begins

The Spanish exported the turkey from Mexico to Europe. The British mistook it for a "turkey fowl." The name "turkey" stuck. There is also speculation that the nation of Turkey did import turkeys from the Americas, though this conjecture remains just that. The British may have been the first to associate turkey with major religious festivals, notably Christmas. The traditional Christmas feast in Britain included turkey, chestnuts, sausage, stuffing, gravy, potatoes, brussels sprouts, and carrots. This tradition appears to have predated British settlement of North America. As early as the 16th century, British taverns served turkey, and the homemaker prepared turkey as an everyday item that need not be confined to holidays. King Henry VIII ate turkey on Christmas. It is interesting that Europeans adopted a New World bird for Christmas, a festival of an Old World religion. Indeed, Jesus could not have known of the turkey. By the late Victorian era, the turkey had surpassed even the goose as a holiday food. The turkey has also become the Christmas bird of choice in Australia.

Back in the Americas

When the British settled North America they brought turkeys with them, in a reversal of the Columbian Exchange. The British may not have known that the turkey was a New World domesticate. The original Thanksgiving feast in the Americas, if it happened, may have occurred in 1619 in Virginia or in 1621 in Massachusetts. The story has a mythic quality, and it is worth noting that the British had by then eaten turkey for more than 100 years, so the bird cannot have been foreign to them. It may be that the British amplified a simple meal by adding turkey to convey a British culinary context to the feast. There appears to be no doubt that the first European settlers needed help from the Amerindians. Most of the Europeans were not farmers and had little familiarity with Native American farming methods and crops. It seems plausible that some Amerindians may have helped the British and the two may even have shared meals together on occasion. It is possible that turkey was a dish at these meals. The idea of a first thanksgiving is, however, difficult to pinpoint because only during the 1860s did President Abraham Lincoln establish it as a national holiday. The holiday story may tell us more about the symbolic role of turkey in the origins of British North America. If one is to believe the account, the British and Native Americans must have coexisted peacefully. We know this opinion to be false. The Europeans who came to the Americas spread diseases, sometimes purposefully, that may have killed 90 percent of Native Americans, who had no immunity to Old World diseases. Europeans also appear to have been violent against the Amerindians and accounts exist to verify the fact that European men sometimes raped Native American women. In this respect, the act of eating turkey on Thanksgiving reflects a more idyllic view of American history than a realistic one.

By one account, founding father Benjamin Franklin was the lone dissenter against the bald eagle as the national bird. Instead, he favored the turkey. Perhaps indulging in hyperbole, Franklin asserted that the turkey would attack any British soldier who dared trespass on an American farm. Because of the connection between turkey and Thanksgiving, many Americans know the feast as "turkey day." The American iteration of Thanksgiving includes turkey, stuffing, mashed potatoes, sweet potatoes, gravy, cranberry sauce, corn, squash, and pumpkin pie. In his context, Thanksgiving is a Euro-Amerindian event tethered to turkey and other American foods. The tradition originated in the culinary and cultural tradition of both the Old World and the Americas, though it pointed the way to the Europeans' future in the New World.

Turkeys are Part of Agribusiness

The U.S. production of turkeys year round suggests that the turkey is no longer simply a holiday food. Americans eat turkeys in a variety of contexts throughout the year. Part of the growth in the consumption of turkeys stems from their nutritional profile. Nutritionists favor the turkey because it is a low-fat source of protein. In this respect, it fills that same role in the diet as do chicken and fish. This is not to say that turkeys are low in calories. Ounce for ounce, the breast contains the fewest calories, but the legs have lots of carbohydrates from the glycogen that the turkey had stored in its leg bones while alive. The consumer generally has two choices if he or she wishes to purchase a whole turkey. The turkey hen generally weighs between 14 and 18 pounds, and is the favorite of consumers because the nuclear family can eat only so much turkey. A large gathering may prefer a tom, which weighs 26 to 32 pounds. As noted above, the tom, being a male, is inherently larger than the female because of the phenomenon of sexual dimorphism. Where the tom is not sold whole it is processed into smaller cuts and different products. Most turkeys come from Virginia and the Carolinas, though Arkansas remains an important producer. The United States consumes about 8 billion pounds of turkey per year, though not all, we have seen, as whole birds. One may buy turkey meat including turkey bologna, ground turkey, turkey sausage, turkey bacon, and other products.

Further Reading

Chaline, Eric. *Fifty Animals that Changed the Course of History*. Buffalo, NY: Firefly Books, 2011.

Damron, W. Stephen. *Introduction to Animal Science: Global, Biological, Social, and Industry Perspectives*. 5th ed. Boston: Pearson, 2013.

Scanes, Colin. *Fundamentals of Animal Science*. Australia: Delmar, 2011.

Turnip

Perhaps the simplest definition of a plant is an organism with a root and shoot. The root is the underground portion of the plant and the shoot is all the above-ground portions. The roots absorb water and nutrients from the soil. In some cases, roots store nutrients, as is true of the sweet potato, cassava, carrot, and turnip. These nutrients, requiring space, cause the root to swell. This process must be an evolutionary adaptation to lean times, when the shoot had to use the stored nutrients to survive. When one thinks of a turnip, one almost always thinks of the swollen root, but one should not neglect the shoot, particularly the stem and leaves. The leaves are edible and highly nutritious. The turnip is an important plant because nearly all parts of it are edible. One may enjoy the fruits of a tomato plant but the leaves are inedible because they are toxic. The same is true of the potato plant. The tubers are perfectly nutritious but the foliage is toxic. In the Brassicaceae or Cabbage family, the turnip (*Brassica rapa* ssp. *rapitera*) is related to rutabaga, which is a hybrid between turnip and cabbage. A biennial grown as an annual, turnip fills its hypocotyl, what many people mistake as a root, in the first year, and flowers and seeds in the second. The person who harvests the turnip root at the end of the first growing season will not have the pleasure of eating the leaves in the second. Turnips shaped history and daily life because they were one of the foods that stood between the masses and famine. Before the arrival of the potato in Europe, the failure of the grain crop left the peasants desperate for food. Turnips were one of a handful of foods that the masses could rely on for sustenance. The pea was another such crop. Turnips were also part of the livestock industry, which provided humans with meat.

Turnip Greens

The leaves of the turnip plant are known as turnip greens. The taste is a bit bitter due to the high calcium content. Indeed, ounce for ounce turnip greens have four times the calcium of the turnip's relative the cabbage plant. Even mustard greens, renowned for their calcium content, have only half the calcium of turnip leaves. Scientists aim to breed less bitter turnip greens, but this would necessarily reduce the amount of calcium in the leaves. This trade-off may not make nutritional sense. A cruciferous crop (like cabbage, kale, mustard, cauliflower, and broccoli), turnip greens rival and even surpass their peers in nutrition. Turnip leaves contain glucosinolate, a chemical thought to prevent some types of cancer. One cup of turnip greens have just 29 calories but nearly six times the recommended daily allowance of vitamin K, 61 percent of beta carotene (the precursor of vitamin A), 53 percent of vitamin C, 42 percent of folic acid, 40 percent of copper, 25 percent of manganese, 20 percent of calcium, 18 percent of vitamin E, and smaller amounts of vitamins B_1, B_2, B_3, B_6, pantothenic acid, potassium, phosphorus, magnesium, and iron. Turnip greens even have small amounts of protein and omega 3 fatty acids, the fat found in fish and a wholesome addition to the diet. Turnip greens also have fiber, though they appear to lack vitamin D, the focus of research and media coverage.

The Turnip Root

The turnip may have arisen independently in the Mediterranean Basin and eastern Afghanistan and Pakistan. One writer posits an origin in Europe or western Asia about 2000 BCE. A third pinpoints northeastern Europe or Asia as the cradle of the turnip. Turkey, Iran, and Transcaucasia may have been a secondary center of origin. Wild species may be found in Russia, Siberia, and Scandinavia. The Celts and Germans may have been the first to cultivate turnip. By the time of Christ, the Greeks and Romans grew turnip. The Romans preferred the flavor of turnip to that of carrot. Legend holds that a Roman general refused to give his meal of turnips to the enemy in exchange for a bag of gold. The Romans introduced the turnip into Britain and France. Before the Columbian Exchange brought the potato to Europe, turnip was the staple, especially in the Middle Ages. Because the masses ate turnips, the wealthy thought them fit only for commoners. Although many aristocrats refused to eat turnips, the Duke of Orleans, France, served them to his guests in 1690. The advent of the potato in Europe left turnip a famine food. Because of its association with hard times and poverty, turnip was known as "poor man's food."

The root was probably picked wild in prehistory, though it appears not to have been cultivated until about 2000 BCE. The existence of wild turnips in western Asia and Europe suggests that domestication may have occurred on one continent with the crop spreading to the other, or that turnips were domesticated separately in western Asia and Europe. It would make sense to favor Europe in this regard because the Greeks and Romans were strong proponents of the crop. From an early date, humans favored turnip roots not merely for their own sustenance but also to feed livestock, in turn supplying people with meat. Turnips likely made meat more available and in this way shaped history and daily life. Given the tendency of early stockmen to let their animals graze, it is difficult to know how prevalent turnips were in the diet of livestock.

Europeans, including first-century-CE Roman encyclopedist Pliny the Elder, classified turnip roots as a vegetable. This definition holds for the leaves but not the roots, which by definition are a root crop like carrots, sweet potatoes, and cassava. American root crops like sweet potatoes and cassava were unknown to Europeans before the Columbian Exchange. Even then the sweet potato and cassava were more important to Asia and Africa than to Europe. Pliny was fond of the turnip, regarding it as among the chief foods of Rome. He believed that the turnip's importance rivaled those of grains and fava beans, which are not related to the *Phaseolus* beans of the Americas. Like the potato, the turnip does best in a cool climate. Yet by the 18th century the turnip was in partial retreat. Although it had been a staple of the Middle Ages, it could not compete with the American potato in northern Europe and in the northern United States. The turnip nonetheless persisted as a crop of the American South, probably grown in very early spring or late autumn. In southern Europe, the turnip may have persisted as a winter crop.

Eighteenth-century British agriculturalist Charles "Turnip" Townshend was not ready to jettison the turnip. He turned a critical eye to stockmen. Because hay was expensive, stockmen could afford to keep few animals through winter. Consequently, they butchered much of the herd in autumn, leaving them with a glut of meat, much of which spoiled in an era before refrigeration. Townshend thought this practice wasteful and proposed to feed turnips to livestock through winter. His idea gained adherents and a new role for the turnip. Today stockmen still feed turnips to their animals. British stockmen feed turnips to sheep and pigs. Moreover, turnip has not ceased to be food. People still eat it in Britain, Germany, Poland, Russia, and the Czech Republic. They eat turnip with potatoes or add it to soup and stew. In addition, turnip is used in roasts, casseroles, and salad, or cooked as a side dish.

Just as the Columbian Exchange brought the potato to Europe, it carried turnip to the Americas. Canada received the turnip in 1540, Mexico in 1586, Virginia in 1610, and New England in 1628. Admittedly, the turnip is not popular in the United States, though Southerners still prize it for its leaves. The United States, Britain, and Japan have amassed collections of turnip varieties, but these countries are making little effort to breed new cultivars. Japan plants hybrids but the United States has been slow to adopt them. Hybrids yield large hypocotyls and a large number of leaves.

As a rule, some turnip varieties produce a small, fairly compact root, though the end of the taproot is long and narrow. Other varieties produce large roots. The small roots tend to nourish humans whereas the large roots feed livestock. The small roots tend to be tender whereas the large roots are fibrous. Because of the close relationship to other crucifers, turnips may be crossed with cabbage to yield the rutabaga, sometimes known as the "yellow turnip" in the United States and the "swede" in England and other parts of northern Europe.

Further Reading

Coulter, Lynn. *Gardening with Heirloom Seeds: Tried-And-True Flowers, Fruits, and Vegetables for a New Generation.* Chapel Hill: University of North Carolina Press, 2006.

Hughes, Meredith Sayles, and Tom Hughes. *Buried Treasure: Roots and Tubers.* Minneapolis: Lerner Publications, 1998.

Kalloo, G., and B. O. Bergh. *Genetic Improvement of Vegetable Crops.* Oxford: Pergamon Press, 1993.

Singh, P. K., S. K. Dasgupta, and S. K. Tripathi, eds. *Hybrid Vegetable Development.* Binghamton, NY: Food Products Press, 2004.

V

Vanilla

Vanilla is a type of orchid native to Africa, Asia, and the Americas. Only the American species of vanilla produces edible fruits. Because these fruits look like large green beans, it has become fashionable to term the fruit of a vanilla flower a bean. This is incorrect. The true beans are all legumes and a supremely important source of protein. The vanilla fruit, by contrast, as we have seen, is an orchid. Orchids and beans are only distantly related. Because of the antiquity of orchids, one may be confident that, among flowering plants, vanilla and bean are among the least related of plants. This entry will not refer to the vanilla fruit as a bean or cite as legitimate "vanilla bean" ice cream.

Vanilla Is an Orchid

Among orchids, vanilla has conquered the world with its aroma and flavor. As an orchid, vanilla must be among the oldest flowering plants, having arisen perhaps 90 million years ago, an early date for the evolution of a flowering plant. Curiously though, flowering plants are latecomers to the world's flora. By the standards of ferns, orchids, and vanilla in particular, they are not exceedingly ancient. Indeed, the tenure of plants on earth is much older than the evolution of the vanilla orchid. Orchids are the largest family of flowering plants. Vanilla and all orchids are related to asparagus, amaryllises, daffodils, irises, onions, agaves, and yucca.

Vanilla comprises about 150 species, all of them tropical plants. Some grow in Africa and Asia, but they are inedible. Only American vanilla is edible, and in fact only two species of American vanilla are commercially cultivated worldwide. Like many agronomic plants, vanilla is propped up on a narrow genetic base. The vanilla fruit ripens in six to nine months, a long duration compared to many other food plants. Potatoes, for example, yield their tubers in only a few months. In the Americas, vanilla is native from southern Mexico to Nicaragua in Central America,

Vanilla Ice Cream

Among the beloved varieties of ice cream, vanilla ice cream became possible only after the discovery of the Americas brought Europeans into contact with the vanilla orchid. From an early date, vanilla ice cream was authentic in containing real vanilla. Now one is apt to find no trace of vanilla in vanilla ice cream, but rather a list of artificial ingredients. These imitation ice creams are often of low quality. One can still find real vanilla ice cream on the market, however, though the price may be a bit higher.

though the plant does well in large areas of South America, Brazil prominent among them. Vanilla is also grown in the Caribbean (sometimes known as the West Indies).

Vanilla and the Amerindians

The Amerindians used vanilla for religious and ceremonial purposes as early as the 13th century CE. In this respect, vanilla was a latecomer to cultivation. The plant was used for the aroma of its flowers. Vanilla was initially a fragrance rather than a food, in contrast to the major agronomic foods of the Americas: corn, beans, squash, cassava, potatoes, sweet potatoes, tomatoes, peppers, peanuts, and other American indigenes. The Amerindians believed that vanilla had medicinal properties. The Maya may have used vanilla in various beverages. The Maya thought of vanilla as the "perfume of the world." To the north, the Totanecs of Mexico claimed to have domesticated vanilla.

The European Encounter with Vanilla

As early as 1502, the Spanish brought vanilla from Cuba to Spain. Spanish conquistador Hernán Cortés likewise carried vanilla from Mexico to Spain. Vanilla was thus an early item of the Columbian Exchange. At first a luxury in Europe, vanilla was not at all the democratic food that the potato would become. Vanilla was not a food or flavoring of the masses, at least not at the outset. Vanilla was thus a mark of distinction. It drew a line of demarcation between rich and poor and in this way shaped history as a marker of class in a world that was class conscious above all else. Because of its expensiveness, vanilla helped launch Spain's golden age, a period when it may have been Europe's richest nation. Perhaps because of its religious roots in the Americas, vanilla was an item that Catholic priests favored in Spain. As in the Americas, vanilla assumed the status of a medicine in Europe.

Europeans early used vanilla to flavor cocoa, the product of the cacao tree, another American indigene. The Spanish and Italians were avid consumers of vanilla-flavored cocoa. Jews in Spain and Portugal emerged as vanilla merchants. Their status in this regard is an important reminder that Catholic Europe did not permit Jews, the killers of Jesus, as Christians believed, to own land. Without land, Jews could not farm, so they had no alternative but to turn to commerce. European anti-Semitism was virulent. One finds it in German composer Richard Wagner's prose and in many other places. Wealthy Jewish vanilla merchants were envied, faced high taxes, and were never safe from scrutiny.

Vanilla in the New United States

An accomplished gardener, third U.S. president Thomas Jefferson emerged as a champion of vanilla in a nation foreign to it. As minister to France in the 1780s, Jefferson copied French culinary habits, among them the drinking of vanilla-flavored cocoa. Because this was the drink of France's aristocracy, Jefferson beheld it as a food of civilized and enlightened consumers. It was part of wholesome living and refined taste that was, he thought, important to building a prosperous nation at home. When Jefferson returned to the United States at the outbreak of the French Revolution he could not find vanilla in any market, so he ordered it from France and the Netherlands, both of which had tropical colonies. So focused was Jefferson on acquiring vanilla from Europe that he may not have known that the plant was native to tropical America. He probably could have gotten vanilla much cheaper from Cuba than from the Netherlands.

The Rise of Empires

By the 19th century, Europeans had planted vanilla worldwide throughout the tropics. In 1898, the U.S. Department of Agriculture (USDA) announced that vanilla was a plant of empire and enormous wealth. As a crop of empire, vanilla was a measure of European power, conquest, and capitalism. Vanilla was thus important as the leading edge of European colonialism that transformed the world, not always for good. The French planted vanilla on Tahiti. By the 19th and 20th centuries, vanilla production had increased, bringing down prices. What had been a commodity of elites was now affordable to everyone. As a mass commodity, it had become, by a curious route, similar to the appeal of the potato as a mass food. Vanilla became the most important flavoring for ice cream and so gave rise to an important snack and dessert food. Druggists used vanilla to mask the unpleasant taste of medicines. As sugarcane had much earlier, vanilla became, because of its popularity, a plantation crop. Once more, a crop of poor people of color in the tropics enriched whites in the temperate zone. Sugarcane, coffee, tea, cacao, and others all manifest this flow of wealth and food, from tropics to temperate zone. Islands in the Indian Ocean, Indonesia, and Tahiti supplied Europe and the United States, though Mexico, Central America, and the Caribbean remained important exporters. In some areas of the tropics, vanilla was actually more profitable than sugarcane.

Candy makers combined vanilla and chocolate to create a new snack industry almost overnight. One often thinks of the connection between peanuts and chocolate, though the link between vanilla and chocolate has been just as important. Coca-Cola and Dr Pepper were both early adopters of vanilla in their soft drinks. Other manufacturers combined vanilla and maple syrup. In 1796, New York City opened the first ice cream shop. By the mid-19th century, vanilla was the leading ice cream flavor. In the 1850s, Maryland entrepreneur Jacob Fussell was the first to mass-produce and standardize vanilla ice cream in the way that the meatpackers and automaker Henry Ford would mass-produce and standardize the production of meat and Model Ts, respectively. Because vanilla ice cream was a Sunday treat, it lent itself to the phenomenon of the ice cream sundae, another staple of the food industry. About the time of the 1904 St. Louis World's Fair, someone invented the ice cream cone. Vanilla ice cream and other flavors were now portable in the way that a cup of coffee or tea or a bottle of Coca-Cola was portable. By 1909, the consumption of vanilla ice cream topped that of alcoholic beverages in New York City. The Eskimo Pie of 1919 was another vanilla ice cream treat. By 1921, Americans bought 2 million Eskimo Pies per day. By 1924, the average American ate nearly 7 pounds of ice cream, most of it vanilla, per year. The spread of the refrigerator and freezer in the 1930s and 1940s allowed homeowners to store and eat ice cream whenever they wished. Today, 30 percent of Americans list vanilla as their favorite ice cream flavor. Chocolate is a distant second at just 8.9 percent. In the 20th century, Illinois' Nielsen-Massey Vanillas emerged as the world's largest producer of vanilla extract. Here, as elsewhere, vanilla distinguished itself in an economy of mass production, mass consumption, and economies of scale, all at the heart of American capitalism. The first Dairy Queen served vanilla ice cream. Prohibition quickened the sale of vanilla-flavored soft drinks. This interlude witnessed the rise of the root beer float with its iconic scoop of vanilla ice cream. As had happened with the rise of margarine in the butter industry, chemists invented artificial vanilla flavoring to compete with real vanilla.

The Plantation Economy Quickens

In the meantime, vanilla plantations expanded to Madagascar, Mauritius, the Seychelles islands, and the Comoros islands. In all these areas, vanilla rivaled sugarcane. In some places, investors, averse to risk, chose vanilla as the safe and steady cash crop. Madagascar grew rapidly. Between 1900 and 1915, the island's production of vanilla leapt from 15 to 233 tons. By 1929, Madagascar produced 80 percent of the world's vanilla. In the 20th century, vanilla culture was so robust on Tahiti that it attracted Chinese immigrants in what is part of the story of human migration, one of history's most durable themes. During the late 20th century, the Indonesian island of Java rose to prominence because of the flavor and aroma of its vanilla. Other Indonesia islands have been important into the 21st century, including Sumatra, Sulawesi, and Flores.

Further Reading

Cameron, Ken. *Vanilla Orchids: Natural History and Cultivation*. Portland, OR: Timber Press, 2011.

Foster, Nelson, and Linda S. Cordell. *Chilies to Chocolate: Food the Americas Gave the World*. Tucson, University of Arizona Press, 1992.

Frenkel, Donna H. *Handbook of Vanilla Science and Technology*. Indianapolis: Wiley, 2011.

Rain, Patricia. *Vanilla: The Cultural History of the World's Most Popular Flavor and Fragrance*. New York: Penguin Group, 2004.

Vitamin Pill

The vitamin pill grew into a daily supplement after the discovery of vitamins in the early 20th century. Vitamins are micronutrients. That is, they are essential to health but necessary in only small quantities. One tends to think of a vitamin as something to be consumed, and the notion of the efficacy of vitamin pills exploits this belief. In part, it is true. One may consume vitamin C by eating citrus fruits, pineapple, potatoes, cabbage, and a number of other foods. Fruits are a particularly good source of this vitamin. Sweet potatoes and carrots are good examples of foods that contain vitamin A. Fish supplies vitamin D, though in this instance consumption is unnecessary in the case of exposure to sunlight because the body can manufacture vitamin D in the presence of sunlight. This fact reveals that not every vitamin must be consumed, though most do. As a historical matter, vitamins are the most recently discovered nutrients. Only in the 20th century did scientists pinpoint them, well after they had established the necessity of protein, carbohydrates, fatty acids, and minerals. Iron, calcium, magnesium, and manganese, for example, are all minerals, though they should perhaps be better known as elements, most of them metals, on the periodic table. The periodic table, as with it the discovery of minerals, was complete by the 1860s.

The Discovery of Vitamins

Taking the long view, several occurrences predated the discovery of vitamins. The Egyptians may have known that the consumption of an animal's liver prevented blindness due to insufficient consumption of vitamin A, though they had no idea of the relationship among liver, blindness, and vitamin A. One might note that only meat can supply vitamin A. From plants like carrots and sweet potatoes, one received beta-carotene, the precursor to vitamin A, which the body converts into vitamin A. One may therefore consume beta-carotene and vitamin A in a number of ways. The same may be said about vitamin C. The age of exploration in the early modern era exposed sailors to diseases of dietary deficiency because their diets were not varied. In the 1740s, Scottish physician James Lind demonstrated that the consumption of lemon juice prevented and cured scurvy, one such disease of nutritional deficiency. That is, Lind had discovered an antiscurvy agent, but he had no notion of vitamin C, the vitamin that prevented scurvy. Additional research confirmed that other citrus fruits, the potato, cabbage, and pineapple were all anti-scurvy agents. In the 19th century, scientists discovered that the consumption of fish, notably its fat, prevented rickets, another disease of dietary deficiency, in this case of vitamin D. These discoveries heightened interest in the science of nutrition, but they did not lead directly to the discovery of vitamins.

Rapid progress came in the early 20th century. In 1910, Japanese scientist Umetaro Suzuki discovered a water-soluble micronutrient, which he called aberic acid. In an article, he heralded the discovery of a new nutrient, and in this context he merits credit as the discoverer of the first vitamin. The study of science in the United States tends to award priority to University of Wisconsin agricultural scientist Elmer V. McCollum who, in 1914, after feeding trials with rats, announced the discovery of vitamin A. Because "A" is the first letter of the alphabet, it has become the standard story in the history of American science that McCollum discovered the first vitamin. Suzuki and McCollum's discoveries were not the same. Suzuki had discovered a water-soluble B vitamin whereas McCollum's vitamin A is fat-soluble. Several additional discoveries followed, each carrying a Nobel Prize in medicine or physiology.

The Vitamin Pill

Americans have had a long fascination with nutritional supplements. In the 19th century, for example, the tomato pill was in vogue. It contained an extract from the fruit of the tomato plant, but this was not a vitamin pill. The discovery of vitamins led, by the 1940s, to the growth of a vitamin supplements industry. At the time, the industry promoted the vitamin pill as a once-daily supplement. For accuracy, perhaps, one might refer to the vitamin pill as the multivitamin and mineral pill, because most vitamin pills contained several vitamins and minerals. In addition, as the industry has branched out, vitamin pill manufacturers have targeted some supplements for children, others for men, others for women, others for pregnant women, others for men over age 50 or 60, depending on the label, and others for women over age 50 or 60. In addition to this diversity, one may purchase a vitamin pill with only a single vitamin. In the 20th century, American chemist and two-time Nobel laureate Linus Pauling advocated the consumption of high doses of vitamin C. The vitamin industry, capitalizing on Pauling's renown, sold pills with high doses of vitamin C. The extra vitamin C probably does no harm because, being water soluble, what the body does not absorb passes through the urine. Fat-soluble vitamins, like A, D, and E, are another matter. The body stores them so that a megadose of vitamin D, for example, may build to toxic levels over time.

Thanks to supplementation, the vitamin industry perhaps oversimplified nutrition. Americans became tempted to believe that by taking a multivitamin and mineral tablet once per day, they were free from dietary concerns. In this sense, vitamin pills shaped history and daily life by deluding the gullible to believe that they could eat anything they wanted without fear of deficiency by taking a magic bullet of sorts. One could eat junk food, so this line of thinking ran, and be healthy simply by ingesting a vitamin pill once per day. This logic, or abuse of logic, may be behind the fact that more than 10 million Americans take vitamin supplements every day. To be sure the vitamin pill industry has done its part to make vitamin pills seductive. Some industry marketers claim that vitamin pills may improve the immune system and protect against colon cancer and heart disease, though these statements are medical claims that physicians must evaluate. It is tempting but untrue to regard vitamin pills as a cure-all.

The truth is that vitamin pills, except in certain cases, cannot substitute for a balanced diet of lean meats and fish, vegetables, fruits, whole grains, and dairy products. A person who eats a balanced diet does not need vitamin supplementation. In fact, vitamin supplements may be counterproductive. We have seen the risk of vitamin toxicity with the fat-soluble vitamins. The claim that vitamin pills provide energy is false unless the pill contains calories. Vitamin pills provide the vitamins that help the body metabolize the calories it has absorbed. The claim that vitamin pills help one lose weight is also untrue. Only the regulation of one's diet, coupled with daily vigorous exercise, can accomplish this goal. Arithmetic, rather than the vitamin pill, is the answer. To lose weight, the body must burn more calories than it consumes.

The Vitamin Pill in Its Iterations

As shown above, manufacturers make vitamin pills for all groups of people. Vitamin pills for men have less iron, strictly a mineral, than those for women because men need less of it. Here, again, the vitamin pill cannot substitute for a good diet. Meat, potatoes, legumes, and oysters are all good sources of iron. Some vitamin pills for men omit iron, though they likely contain extra selenium, also a mineral, and vitamin E to protect the prostate. Women need extra iron and, among the B vitamins, extra folic acid. The inclusion of folic acid in a vitamin pill is important for pregnant women. Vitamin pills for pregnant women also contain extra vitamin A. Children are also a target of the vitamin pill industry. Who has not taken a Flintstones multivitamin tablet during childhood? These pills are seldom necessary because much of what children eat, breakfast cereals for example, already contain extra vitamins and minerals. The exception is vitamin D. Because children are growing they need more vitamin D than adults, and here a supplement may be desirable. During the summer, plenty of outdoor activity provides vitamin D. After age 60, the vitamin pill becomes more important because the body loses the ability efficiently to absorb vitamins. Vitamins, in this context B_{12} and K, are essential in a multivitamin pill for older adults. Adults on blood thinners may not react well to large doses of vitamin K. When in doubt, adults should consult a physician. Older adults may not, however, need much iron in their supplements. Vegetarians and vegans need supplements with vitamins D and B_{12} and the minerals iron, magnesium, selenium, calcium, and zinc. One should beware, except in the case of pregnant women, of vitamin pills that contain megadoses of folic acid, which might put one at risk of developing prostate and colon cancer.

Consumer advocates note that less than half the vitamin pills in the United States and Canada contain the nutrients on the label. At least one brand of vitamin pill contained lead, a toxic metal that has no place in the human diet. The manufacturer is no longer in business. Another pill, Hero Nutritionals Yummi Bears, aimed at children, had nearly three times the amount of vitamin A that the label claimed. Because vitamin A is fat soluble, it can accumulate in the body in toxic levels, diminishing the growth of bones in children. Where they are necessary, however, vitamin pills have shaped history and daily life by providing the body with the nourishment it needs.

Further Reading

Blake, Joan Salge. *Nutrition and You*. 2nd ed. Boston: Benjamin Cummings, 2012.

Watermelon

An annual vine, the aptly named watermelon (*Citrullus lanatus*) is 92 percent water. In addition to containing water, watermelon is 6 percent sugar; 14 percent vitamin C; 4 percent pantothenic acid; 3 percent vitamin A, thiamine, vitamin B_6, and magnesium; 2 percent iron, phosphorus, and potassium; and 1 percent riboflavin, niacin, folic acid, calcium, and zinc. One hundred grams of watermelon contain only 30 calories, 0.4 grams of fiber, 0.15 grams of fat and 0.61 grams of protein. Watermelon has more lycopene, an antioxidant that may prevent cancer, than any other fruit or vegetable, including the tomato. The Bushmen of the Kalahari Desert in southern Africa called watermelon *tsamma*. Watermelon is a cucurbit, or gourd. Controversy attends the question of whether watermelon is a fruit or vegetable. In 2007, Oklahoma adopted watermelon as the state vegetable, provoking a debate about its status. Indeed, several vegetable books include a section on watermelon. In the United States, 44 states produce watermelon. Georgia, Florida, Texas, California, and Arizona are the leading producers. The Chinese roast and salt watermelon seeds, eating them as a snack, much as Americans eat peanuts. The Vietnamese eat watermelon seeds during Tet, their New Year.

Origin and History

In the 1850s, British explorer David Livingstone discovered wild watermelons in the Kalahari Desert. He found them to be less sweet than cultivated watermelon, but this discovery nonetheless led others to suppose that watermelon originated in this inhospitable land. It may seem strange that a plant so dependent on water might have originated in a desert, but the vine is adept at absorbing even small amounts of water, and the thick rind minimizes evaporation. In 1882, French botanist Alphonse de Candolle, perhaps incredulous at the suggestion that a water-loving plant could have originated in the desert, proposed tropical Africa as the

Indigenous to the Kalahari Desert in southern Africa, the watermelon is a marvelous adaptation to aridity. The fruit evolved as an organ to store water against the desert's lean times. (Theo Allofs/Corbis)

homeland of watermelon. From the tropics, if this hypothesis is correct, watermelon spread both north and south. French explorers proposed yet a third possibility. Because they found Native Americans growing watermelon in the Mississippi River valley, they supposed that it had originated in the New World. Another possibility, of course, is that watermelon spread throughout the New World ahead of European settlement, in which case the Native Americans were cultivating an African rather than American indigene.

The Egyptians may have been the first to cultivate watermelon, a possibility that accords with the hypothesis that it originated in the tropics and migrated north. Alternatively, a northern migration from the Kalahari Desert was also possible. It is much harder to envision a migration from the New World to Egypt in antiquity. The date of cultivation is open to debate. One hypothesis holds that the Egyptians cultivated watermelon as early as 3000 BCE. Another pinpoints 2000 BCE as the earliest date of cultivation, whereas a third proposal points to the second millennium BCE, of which 2000 BCE would have marked the beginning. This range of dates may stem from the difficulty in identifying the ancient remains of watermelon. One authority notes that ancient watermelon seeds resembled cucumber seeds, complicating their identification. Some scholars believe that the Egyptians put watermelon seeds in 14th-century-BCE pharaoh Tutankhamun's tomb. Others suspect that those seeds belonged to cucumber.

From Egypt, watermelon spread to the Middle East, Greece, Rome, India, and China, though in the latter two locales it was not widely cultivated until 800 CE and 1000 CE, respectively. The identification of Greece and Rome as early adopters may be problematic. The ancient Greek and Latin sources are silent about watermelon, and it does not appear to have spread throughout the Mediterranean Basin in antiquity, a fact that is surprising given the supposition that Rome had cultivated watermelon. The Arabs and Berbers in North Africa and the Moors in Spain cultivated watermelon, having doubtless acquired it from Egypt. From Spain, watermelon spread throughout the Mediterranean during the Middle Ages.

The introduction of watermelon into the New World owes much to the efforts of the Spanish, British, and Africans. The Spanish may have been the first to act, bringing watermelon to the Americas, probably in the 16th century. The slaves who populated the New World brought watermelon with them, possibly around the time of the Spanish introduction. In 1628, the British brought watermelon to the Massachusetts Bay Colony, from where it spread to Virginia and Florida. In the 18th century, Spanish missionary Francisco Garces introduced watermelon to the Amerindians of the lower Colorado River valley. As shown, Native Americans were eager adopters of watermelon, and they spread it from the Colorado River valley to the Pacific coast. In the 19th century, watermelon crossed the Pacific Ocean to Hawaii.

In the American South, African Americans made watermelon a part of their cuisine. Malevolent whites denigrated blacks as "watermelon eaters," but the fruit's popularity did not wane. Today, African Americans near Lake Okeechobee, Florida still sell watermelon at roadside stands. This brand of culinary racism also permeates Russia, whose inhabitants mock the people of Central Asia for eating watermelon. Despite this prejudice, Russia imports watermelon from Central Asia. Russians make beer from watermelon.

Toward Today's Watermelons

A watermelon may be a diploid, having two sets of chromosomes; a triploid, having three; or a tetraploid, having four. The cross between a tetraploid female flower and a diploid male flower yielded a sterile triploid plant. The sterile plant had fertile female flowers but lacked pollen, so that a plant could not pollinate itself. (A watermelon plant has male and female flowers on the same plant in a ratio of 13 male flowers to one female flower, but it does not have perfect flowers that can self-pollinate.) The sterile plant is desirable because it produces seedless watermelon, which consumers prefer to watermelon with seeds. Because the sterile triploid does not produce pollen, a traditional pollen-bearing cultivar must fertilize it to yield fruit. Accordingly, the farmer or gardener must plant a triploid and either a diploid or a tetraploid to obtain seedless watermelon. The ratio of fertile to sterile plants should be one to three, to ensure the production of enough pollen. Honeybees and bumblebees are the principle pollinators. Raised in the United States since the late 1980s, Tri-X 313 is a triploid with a tough rind, small fruit, a vigorous vine, disease resistance, and slow spoilage. Tri-X 313 is now grown throughout North America, Europe, and Israel.

An open pollinated variety, Moon and Stars, has a mysterious origin. Mennonite immigrants from Russia may have introduced it into the United States, possibly in the 19th century. It was apparently poorly known, and in 1926 the Peter Henderson seed company of New York claimed to have bred the variety. It was not popular in the early 20th century because, being round, it did not stack well. It was well-known enough and at the same time rare enough that Seed Savers Exchange determined to find it, tracing a handful of seeds to gardener Merle Van Doren of Macon, Missouri. The exchange maintains the variety, which derived its name from its exterior being speckled with small spots akin to stars and a large yellow blotch akin to the moon.

Another open pollinated variety, Rattlesnake, is known as Southern Rattlesnake and Gypsy Oblong. As the last appellation suggests, Rattlesnake is oblong and easily stacked in truck and railroad cars. Dating to the 1830s in Georgia, the variety has dark green lines along its exterior that some gardeners liken to the outlines of rattlesnakes. Others think the lines resemble a tiger's stripes. Maturing 90 days after planting, a ripe melon may weigh as much as 45 pounds.

In 1881, the seed company W. Atlee Burpee introduced the open-pollinated variety Cuban Queen. It produces long vines, a trait that it shares with many watermelon varieties. Melons, containing red flesh, grow larger than 70 pounds.

A 19th-century open-pollinated variety, Ice Cream, is named because its white seeds and white flesh resemble vanilla ice cream. Maturing in 82 days, it is suitable for the short growing seasons of the North, though as a rule watermelon grown in the North is not as sweet as watermelon grown in warm locales. In 1876, Americans ate a variety of watermelon known as Ice Cream during the centennial celebration. Having pink flesh and black seeds, however, it was not the real Ice Cream, whose seeds are today difficult to obtain.

About 1940, U.S. Department of Agriculture (USDA) horticulturist Charles Andrus bred the popular Charleston Gray, a variety that was disease resistant, did not wilt, bruise, or crack, and was slow to spoil. Being oblong rather than round, it was easy to stack. A number of varieties trace their lineage to Charleston Gray.

As the family has gotten smaller, Americans have come to prefer a small watermelon and breeders complied. Burpee markets the Fordhook Hybrid, which produces 12- to 14-pound melons. At six to eight pounds, Burpee's Sugar Bush yields even smaller melons. Grocers have also adjusted to the desire for small melons, selling melons by the half, quarter, or even slice.

Within the past 25 years, hybrids have supplanted open-pollinated varieties, leaving the cultivation of the latter to heirloom enthusiasts. Although hybrid seed is more expensive than open-pollinated seed, farmers found that the high yield of hybrids justified their cost. The adoption of hybrids changed farming practices. Because open pollinated seed was cheap, farmers did not worry about a late frost. If frost killed their plants they simply replanted. Hybrid seed, however, was too expensive to risk a late frost. Farmers turned to germinating hybrid seed not in the field, where it was at the mercy of the weather, but in a greenhouse, transplanting seedlings in the field only when the danger of frost had passed. Hybrids yield 40–60 percent more fruit than open pollinated varieties and produce more uniform fruit. China plants nearly all of its 5 million acres to hybrids, and the figure is also high in Japan and Korea. U.S. breeding programs focus almost exclusively on hybrids.

Further Reading

Coulter, Lynn. *Gardening with Heirloom Seeds: Tried-and-True Flowers, Fruits, and Vegetables for a New Generation.* Chapel Hill: University of North Carolina Press, 2006.

McNamee, Gregory. *Movable Feasts: The History, Science, and Lore of Food.* Westport, CT: Praeger, 2007.

Singh, P. K., S. K. Dasgupta, and S. K. Tripathi, eds. *Hybrid Vegetable Development.* Binghamton, NY: Food Products Press, 2004.

Weight Loss Products

People in the developed world inhabit a medicinal culture in which a pill is thought to exist for any ailment or condition, whether a vitamin pill to augment one's nutrition or an antibiotic to cure a bacterial infection. The diet pill is part of this worldview, and in this sense has shaped history and daily life, and has become important only in the 20th and 21st centuries because of important changes in daily life. The automation and the introduction of labor-saving devices, not least of all the automobile, has led people in the car culture of much of the world to exert less energy than had earlier generations of people who had to walk wherever they wished to go. The trend toward less activity in the developed world has caused people to metabolize fewer calories over the course of a day. At the same time, food is plentiful in the developed world, which has a robust junk food industry, so that at a time when people are less active they eat more food. The result has been an increase in overweight and obese people. Living in a pill-for-everything culture, they naturally, perhaps even reflexively, turn to diet pills to solve their problems. Herein lays the power of the diet pill to shape history and daily life.

The Current State of the Diet Pill

In the early 21st century the market for diet pills and other weight loss products has been robust. The promise of a quick fix, alluring to a population that has packed on extra fat, can be bought over the counter. One can be one's own diet coach. There is no need, one might suppose, to consult a physician or other health care provider. Because not all Americans have medical coverage, the diet pill is a real alternative to unaffordable medical care. People who have tried to diet but failed may be more tempted to resort to diet pills. The Hollywood effect also comes into play. Hollywood saturates the mind with images of lean, ruggedly attractive men and women. The consumer wishes to possess that body and so takes diet pills. This syndrome can be quite serious. Women, more than men, suffer from anorexia and other eating disorders. These women may take diet pills to maintain too low a weight. In such cases, the ingestion of more food and fewer diet pills would be beneficial. Others seek the same effect by exercising to excess in the same battle over body image. Some people take two diet pills when the dosage should be one, in an attempt to hasten weight loss.

The Components of Diet Pills

It is unnecessary to give space to all the brands of diet pills, but it is worthwhile to examine the ingredients that many have in common. Caffeine is often a primary ingredient. Athletes have known for decades that caffeine stimulates to body to burn fat preferentially. That is, the body on caffeine is more likely to metabolize fat than glycogen, a sugar stored in muscles, or muscles themselves. Caffeine also helps one cope with fatigue and heightens alertness, all desirable qualities. The presence of caffeine in diet pills is curious, given its availability in coffee or tea. The fact that coffee consumption and obesity are high in the United States suggests that there may be no ironclad correlation between the consumption of caffeine and the loss of weight. Nonetheless, the U.S. Food and Drug Administration (FDA) has approved the presence of caffeine in diet pills for Americans above age

11. The use of caffeine in clinical trials has produced worrisome results in some cases, as it tends to elevate blood pressure and heart rate. A stimulant, caffeine may also cause insomnia. One set of trials, however, showed a reduction in the weight of participants over two months. By the third month, the body had reached stasis with no further reductions. Other studies have shown that participants may lose weight while ingesting caffeine over six months. The average loss totaled nearly 18 percent of participants' mass. At the end of this trial, weight loss was significant enough to reduce blood pressure in the participants. One should note that clinical trials use higher doses of caffeine than one tends to find in a diet pill. The average diet pill has less caffeine than three cups of coffee, though this is not a trivial amount.

Tea extracts are also commonly found in diet pills, but the primary effect of these extracts appears, again, to introduce caffeine into the body. It is interesting to note the prevalence of tea and leanness among Asians, though the effect may stem more from lifestyle and diet than from any of tea's properties. Some researchers believe that one compound in tea, epigallocatechin gallate (EGCG) may stimulate the body to burn fat in preference to glycogen in muscle or muscle tissue itself. We have observed this effect in caffeine. This phenomenon makes it difficult to know whether EGCG or caffeine, or both, cause the body to burn fat. Researchers have pointed to the fact that caffeine alone does not reduce weight as much as EGCG and caffeine together. Some synergy must be at work. The consumption of EGCG and caffeine appear to cause the body to metabolize an extra 80 calories per day. One might achieve a similar result by eliminating the consumption of one can of soft drink per day, reducing one's calorie intake about 100 calories.

Diet pills may also contain hydroxyciatric acid, a compound found in the rind of the obscure brindall berry. The acid may block human cells from synthesizing excess sugars into fat molecules. The nucleus of a cell directs this synthesis, which occurs outside the nucleus in the cytoplasm. One trial determined that men and women lost about 5 percent of their mass after ingesting the acid over two months. A second study found no effect on weight, and a third strikes me as less valuable because in addition to the ingestion of the acid, participants had to modify their diet by eating less fat and more fiber. Such a diet should reduce weight irrespective of any contribution from hydroxycitric acid. Even so, participants lost little weight. Diet pills may also contain a salt of calcium and other ions. In rats the salt appears to reduce weight, but human trials have shown little benefit.

Diet pills are also likely to contain chromium picolinate, a compound that bodybuilders use in the final weeks of dieting in the belief that they will lose only fat, preserving their massive muscles. The compound appears to make insulin more effective. One trial suggests that women athletes who take chromium picolinate are particularly successful in losing fat and increasing muscle mass. The implication for overweight and obese people is unclear, because the athletes burn hundreds of additional calories per day through the rigorous training they undertake as part of preparing for competition. Such athletes cannot be stand-ins for the consumers of diet pills, who are largely sedentary. Curiously, obese women who take diet pills with chromium picolinate, according to one study, actually gained weight, though the additional mass was muscle rather than fat. It seems clear that such diet pills will not work without modifications in diet and exercise. Other studies have shown no weight gain in other obese people, men as well as women.

The Diet Pill Re-examined

There may be other ingredients in diet pills, but their efficacy is less well known. In fact, physicians wish to study these compounds but lament the lack of external funding for such research. This is a common complaint that stems from the conservative agenda of diminishing the size and scope of the federal government. Federal grants are accordingly less plentiful and more difficult to obtain. Physicians caution that, as an enterprise, the diet pill industry is not regulated as strictly as is the production and testing of new pharmaceuticals. Several prescription medicines appear to reduce weight better than the over-the-counter diet pill. This fact raises the central issue by which diet pills masquerade as pharmaceuticals, complete with putative clinical studies and graphs that appear to document weigh loss. It is difficult for the layperson to gauge the value of what is really advertising. If diet pills work, the results of such studies should be open to peer review. In the meantime, the pretense of scientific objectivity, if such a quality is truly possible, doubtless causes people to anticipate wondrous result from diet pills. In this context, diet pills have shaped history and daily life by surrounding themselves in the mystique of science, by promising consumers a Hollywood body, and by making it appear possible to be thin amid a junk food culture. The reality appears to be otherwise.

Further Reading

Bessesen, Daniel H., and Robert Kusher. *Evaluation and Management of Obesity*. Philadelphia: Harley and Belfus, 2002.

Blake, Joan Salge. *Nutrition and You*. 2nd ed. Boston: Benjamin Cummings, 2012.

Lillis, Jason, Joanne Dahl, and Sandra M. Wineland. *The Diet Trap: Feed Your Psychological Needs and End the Weight Loss Struggle Using Acceptance and Commitment Therapy*. Oakland, CA: New Harbinger Publications, 2014.

Whiskey

Whiskey was among the early alcoholic beverages to be distilled. In this respect, it differed from beer and wine. Beer, the product of a grain, usually barley, and wine, the product of grapes, are both fermented. That is, the grain or fruit are allowed to stand in the presence of yeast, which converts the sugar in barley or grapes into alcohol. Whiskey is initially prepared in a similar way. A grain, though barley and other cereals are acceptable, is fermented to produce alcohol. The next step, however, was revolutionary. The beverage is boiled and allowed to cool to the point of condensation. The process of boiling releases water vapor (steam) into the air. The condensate has a high proportion of alcohol so that a distilled beverage like whiskey is far more potent than beer or wine. The important implications of distillation on social and daily life will be discussed below.

Origins

According to one account, the Muslims may have invented the distillation process in the early Middle Ages, spreading it with their conquests throughout Asia, North Africa, and Spain. In fact, the term "alcohol" derives from the Arabic *al-kohl*. Thereafter, the process of distillation must have moved north, ultimately to the British Isles, though the date of arrival may be speculative. Other than the Muslims, alchemists in Europe may have been among the first to take an interest in distillation. They may have been the first to ferment and distill grains, making the first whiskeys. At this juncture, one must remember that corn could not yet have been an ingredient because the American grass was then unknown in the Old World. Antiquated references to "corn" use the term as a generic for grain of any kind, not for the Amerindian grain that 18th-century Swedish naturalist Carl Linnaeus (his name is sometimes rendered as Carl von Linné) classified *Zea mays*.

Some people point to Ireland as the place where whiskey originated. This conjecture comes from the notion that Irish Catholic missionaries encountered the process of distillation when they visited Muslim lands in hopes of winning converts. Another thesis pinpoints the origin of whiskey in Europe, in Wales, where the first batch of the beverage was distilled in 1329. The earliest use of the term "whiskey" dates to Dublin, Ireland, in 1753. There were other variants. The *Oxford English Dictionary* coined the term "whiskie" in 1715, "whisky" in 1716, and "whiskee" in 1753. If whiskey was invented earlier, as seems likely, the terminology took many years to catch up.

Some scholars seek an even earlier date for the origin of whiskey. The book of proverbs uses the laconic phrase "strong drink," differentiating it from wine. No further commentary illuminates what this drink was. One cannot even be certain that the beverage was alcoholic, although its association with wine suggests an alcoholic drink of some type. It also seems likely that this strong drink was not beer because the Hebrews were familiar with beer and likely would have mentioned it by name. Fourth-century-BCE Greek philosopher and pupil of Plato, Aristotle, described the process by which one might distill wine. Aristotle did not write that he had performed the procedure. Even if he did, Aristotle did not invent whiskey because wine derives from grapes not grains, which must be the case for beer and whiskey. In any case, it would seem strange for whiskey to have been present in a land so devoted to wine. Others believe that the Egyptians invented the process of distillation by the first century CE. By then, Egypt was the personal property of the Roman emperors, so Rome should have known about this process. But none of Rome's historians, not even Tacitus, mentioned it. In the 18th century, British historian Edward Gibbon traced the process of distillation to the nomads of the Asian steppe.

The earliest interest in whiskey, wherever or whenever it was invented, stemmed from the belief that it had medicinal value. Along this line of thought, King James I of England thought whiskey a curative agent and gave the Guild of Surgeon Barbers in Edinburgh, Scotland, where he was James VI, a monopoly on the production of whiskey. Scottish tradition holds that the Scots were the first to make whiskey, in 1434. Before the movement toward standardization in the 20th century it was difficult to know what whiskey contained. Depending on what foods were available, whiskey might be made from potatoes, sugar, oats, turnips, honey, thyme, anise, or mint.

The Classification and Characteristics of Whiskey

To derive whiskey one must have fermentation, distillation, and aging, at a minimum. To be whiskey, the beverage must be aged in a wooden cask. Oak is common for this purpose. The way whiskey is aged separates it from other important distilled spirits, like the rice liquor of Vietnam. Rice liquor receives treatment in another entry. Here it suffices to note rice liquor's role in polarizing relations between the colonial French and the oppressed Vietnamese.

Although whiskey may be defined simply, as done above, the reality is a bit different. A brand of whiskey may change over time. Despite the constancy of ingredients, whiskey experts agree that a 2010 bottle of Bruichladdich Scotch (Scotch is a type of whiskey) does not taste the same as a 1930 bottle of the same product. In this sense, whiskey has evolved and is evolving as a beverage, perhaps through the agencies of artificial selection and technological change. Whiskey has shaped politics, economics, and the culture at large. One might define culture as all the nonbiological material and ideas that humans pass from one generation to the next. The music of Bach, a bottle of whiskey, the prose of French novelist André Malraux, and the ideas of British naturalist Charles Darwin are all parts of culture.

The principal ingredients of whiskey may be barley, corn, oats, rye, wheat, rice, or another cereal. Many factors affect the flavor: the quality and quantity of water, yeast, the grain or grains, the type of still, and the number of distillations to which whiskey is subject. The more distillations, the higher the alcohol content. Also important are the cask in which the beverage is aged and the microclimate of the warehouse in which the whiskey is stored. As a rule, the production of whiskey requires five stages: the preparation of the grain, fermentation, distillation, aging, and bottling and sale. Though simple in conception, the production of whiskey is akin to a science and must conform to exacting standards. Homemade whiskey is apt to be terrible. The attempt to familiarize oneself with whiskey by reading the label on a bottle may confuse rather than clarify because the label is full of jargon that puts off those without specialized knowledge of whiskey. Perhaps one might do best by seeking the country of origin. As a rule, U.S. whiskeys tend to be sweet and Canadian whiskeys tend to taste like fruits. Scotch has a smoky flavor. In Irish whiskeys, the taste of alcohol may be all but overpowering.

Society and Work: The Effects of Whiskey on Daily Life

Whiskey probably arose sometime before the 15th century CE. It seems likely that it grew in popularity only slowly and must for a time have had difficulty competing with beer in northern Europe and wine in the Mediterranean Basin. Because of distillation, whiskey, as noted, had far more alcohol than beer or wine. Compared to less than 5 percent alcohol for beer, whiskey, and the rice liquor that the French produced in the 19th century, had about 40 percent alcohol. The percent is sometimes expressed as "proof," though the proof of an alcoholic beverage is twice the percentage. Eighty proof whiskey, therefore, contains 40 percent alcohol.

The percentage, or proof, of alcohol shaped work patterns and daily life. In the rural world of antiquity, whiskey was unknown. The choices of an alcoholic beverage were beer or wine. In the agrarian world of antiquity, farming did not require the use of potentially dangerous machinery. Accordingly, one could drink beer or wine throughout the day. In fact, Greece and Rome diluted their wine with water to make it even less intoxicating. One could thus work through the day with a slight buzz to lessen the perception of fatigue that came from arduous work. Collapse from intoxication was unlikely because of the low alcohol levels. This pattern of daily life was not possible with whiskey, which could not be consumed throughout the day without inebriation severe enough to impair one's work and mental faculties. The only solutions were to abstain, to switch to beer or wine, or to dilute whiskey to the point that it was no longer whiskey. Whiskey thus complicated the working lives of Europeans and later Americans and so had a dark side. It is too potent a beverage for some, ruining families and leading to destruction.

American playwright and Nobel laureate Eugene O'Neill almost wrecked his career with whiskey and other potent beverages. He appears to have drunk heavily during his one term at Princeton University. Thereafter, he continued to drink until he contracted tuberculosis. Settling at a sanatorium, O'Neill vowed that if he recovered he would become a dramatist. Even in maturity, however, he did not steer entirely clear of whiskey, and his great work *A Long Day's Journey into Night* tells us something about his encounter with whiskey. The play concerns a dysfunctional family. The mother is a morphine addict and the father and both sons are alcoholics. They play on one another's fears and memories until the audience understands that there can be no redemption for this family.

Toward the 21st Century

In the 20th and 21st centuries, whiskey became a global product. By the mid-20th century, Japan made a type of whiskey that resembled Scotch. In the 1990s, Australia produced quality whiskeys, though the tradition may date to the English settlement of the continent. Today the Czech Republic, Germany, New Zealand, Spain, Turkey, and Sweden are all renowned for their whiskeys. For a time, Thailand marketed cobra whiskey, made from rice, ginseng, peppers, and a dead cobra. The degree of globalism is evident in the fact that an Italian company owns a Kentucky distiller that claims roots in antebellum America. A Minnesota company owns a brand of whiskey produced in Ireland. One still speaks of Irish whiskey and Scotch even when the beverage is produced elsewhere. Crisp single cask whiskey has a gay clientele. The trend toward inclusiveness, of which this whiskey is part, is shaping the world in profound ways. The fans of the University of Kentucky drink a limited edition of Maker's Mark Bourbon, a type of whiskey. Some whiskeys, perhaps aiming for a young audience, produce flavors akin to soft drinks. Some whiskey makers have diversified to produce sauces for steak or chicken wings. Jim Beam makes salsa, beef jerky, and clothes. Twenty-first-century whiskeys are in the process of redefining themselves and their markets.

Further Reading

Kosar, Kevin R. *Whiskey: A Global History*. London: Reaktion Books, 2011.

Wine

Wine is an agricultural product. Although dates were probably the first fruit to be fermented into wine, the beverage has a long association with a single species of grape, *Vitis vinifera*, which is the wine grape par excellence. The wine grape is superior because of its high sugar context. About 30 percent of the grape is sugar in the form of fructose. Yeast, existing naturally on the skins of grapes, when given access to the sugar, converts it into alcohol. The alcohol in wine made it the most potent drink in antiquity. If care is not taken, however, and wine is set out in the presence of air for some time, it will oxidize, turning into vinegar. Roman records suggest that soldiers drank vinegar, though the experience must have been unpleasant, and vinegar never rivaled wine as a beverage. Under proper storage, wine may retain its characteristics for more than 100 years.

Since antiquity, wine has been the alcoholic beverage of choice in the Mediterranean Basin. Although the first wine may have been made from dates, the grape is now the fruit of choice in making wine. (Ilfede/Dreamstime.com)

Wine in the Roman World

In Roman antiquity, wine was the most potent beverage and the drink of the god Bacchus, the Roman rendering of the Greek god Dionysus. Wine was the beverage of merriment and the universal sexual lubricant. It was the beverage of bars and brothels. Aristocratic women and commoners alike served their lovers wine. On the other hand, wine was the beverage of the Hebrews and Christians, both religions on the margins of Roman life. Wine was particularly important in Christianity, in which it symbolized the blood of Jesus.

The Origins of Wine and Its Significance from an Early Date

Humans may have made wine as early as roughly 6000 BCE. The mountains of Persia (today Iran) may have been the source of the earliest experiments in wine-making. The spread of *Vitis vinifera* to the Mediterranean world led wine to assume a prominent place in Egyptian civilization. The pharaoh Tutankhaman's tomb contained 26 amphorae of wine. Some of the tomb's wine had come from Syria, demonstrating the importance of trade in this region. Perhaps so much wine was necessary to please him in the afterlife. Here, wine was intertwined with religion, and not for the last time in a society obsessed with death, preservation, and the afterworld. Wherever civilization arose—Egypt, Greece, Rome, and North Africa—wine played a prominent role. The agricultural treatises that have survived, those of the Romans Cato the Elder, Columella, and Varo all concerned themselves with the production of wine and its commerce. Wine was the beverage of kings, pharaohs, and warriors. At the same time, wine was the social lubricant of the masses. No one went without wine.

In the context of Greece and Rome, wine emerged as a symbol of vulgarity and refinement. It became the beverage of Western civilization. For centuries, wine, the most expensive agricultural item, spurred the Roman economy and was, in some respects, a foundation for the grandeur that was Rome. Wherever the Romans went they planted grapevines—throughout the Mediterranean Basin, Gaul (today largely France), Britain, and parts of what is today Germany. Rome could not conceive of civilization without wine. Wine certified one's status as a true Roman even if he or she lived far from the capital. The Roman passion for wine in Italy and Gaul spanned the centuries to the present. Wine remains an indispensable component of Italian and French life. The Italians, French, and other peoples of Europe often drink wine with meals.

Wine assumed such importance partly because of the poor state of medical knowledge. In antiquity, no one knew of the existence of pathogens and no city-state sanitized its potable water. The careless pollution of water with animal and human waste led bacteria and other pathogens to multiply in water. Cholera, a wholly waterborne disease, is an example of the danger contaminated water poses. If one could not trust the water, what could one drink? Wine was the answer because its alcohol killed dangerous microbes. In antiquity, the people of the Mediterranean Basin drank wine every day because it was safer than water. Most people followed the Greek and Roman practice of diluting wine with water to avoid excessive intoxication and make the wine last longer. Once in contact with the wine, the alcohol sterilized the added water, making the entire mixture safe to drink. One imagines that most people went through the day with a slight buzz from the consumption of diluted wine. The experience may have been pleasurable. Because of its abiotic properties, wine must have saved many lives that contaminated water would otherwise have truncated.

Wine and Religions

The importance of wine in the formation of religions in antiquity has elevated the beverage to worldwide importance. The origins of the intersection between wine and religion are difficult to trace, but it is clear that by the time of the Greeks and Romans, wine was ensconced in religious rituals. Both peoples had a god of wine. The Greeks had Dionysus and the Romans, Bacchus. The characteristics of these gods were identical, and it appears that the Romans simply borrowed Dionysus from the Greeks, renaming him Bacchus. These gods ensured that the grape harvest would be abundant and that the quality and quantity of wine would be excellent. But there was much more to these gods and their relationship to wine. Because wine is intoxicating, Dionysus and Bacchus were the gods of revelry, animal instinct, and sexual excess. From the outset, the Greeks and Romans recognized that wine lowered inhibitions, facilitating intercourse between men and women, men and men, and women and women. Prostitutes throughout the Greco-Roman world served wine to their customers. As a beverage bound up with the gods, wine was also the earthly beverage of lustful men and women. Wine was a sexual lubricant of sorts, and the Greeks and Romans at once accepted wine as a beverage that was both vulgar and at the pinnacle of religious intensity.

Those who followed the Greeks and Romans might easily have stigmatized wine as a vice. Instead they joined them in elevating wine into a religious symbol. The Hebrews gave wine a prominent place in the record of their relationship with Yahweh. According to Genesis, Yahweh commanded Noah to build an ark. After extirpating all life but what resided in the ark, Yahweh allowed the floodwaters to recede. Once on land, one of Noah's first acts was to plant a vineyard. The wine it produced made Noah drunk. His behavior during his intoxication is unclear, but he seems to have performed a deviant sexual act. Here, again, one finds the connection between wine and sex, if unseemly in this context. It is unclear from this passage whether the writer wished to devalue or elevate wine, though its presence throughout the Old Testament suggests wine's importance in the development of Judaism.

The relationship between wine and the rise of Christianity appears to be more intimate. The canonical gospels cleanse wine of its sexual intimations, positioning it as Jesus's beverage of choice. Apparently aware that death was imminent, Jesus gathered his apostles for a final meal, what the gospel writers termed the Last Supper. The fare must have been simple. The gospels mention only bread and wine, though other foods may have been present. Bread is the subject of another entry. Here wine is the focus. The gospels indicate that Jesus drank some wine at this meal, entreating his apostles to do likewise. Jesus is to have said that the apostles should continue the practice of sharing wine in remembrance of him. He also, in astonishing fashion, told them that in drinking the wine, the apostles were drinking the blood that he was about to shed for them. Wine was not just a symbol of Jesus; it was actually his blood if the stories about him are to be believed. The Christian Church arose to commemorate these events. Congregants believed that they were drinking Jesus's blood when they shared wine. The Romans found this practice abhorrent and a relic of cannibalism. Although it is easy to overstate the extent and frequency of persecution, Roman authorities long maintained a poor opinion of Christianity. In the 13th century, Italian priest Thomas Aquinas explained how the miracle of wine changing into blood occurred. According to Aquinas, the substance, what a thing is, ordinarily does not change. A block of wood remains a block of wood for all eternity, unless, of course, it rots. Similarly, wine is ordinarily just wine. In the case of the reenactment of the Last Supper, God changes the substance of wine into blood, although it continues to taste and smell like wine. Aquinas termed this process transubstantiation.

An Old World Problem, A New World Solution

It has long been possible to graft the stems of one plant onto the rootstock of another plant, often a closely related species. A famous case involved the grape industry of 19th-century Europe, particularly France. An apparent introduction of the grape phylloxera, a type of aphid, from the Americas to Europe about 1860, nearly ruined the French wine industry because the aphid, spreading widely in its new environment, devoured grape roots, killing the plant. Much credit for ending this catastrophe goes to American entomologist Charles Valentine Riley, one of the world's most eminent scientists in his day. Riley understood that the aphid, being native to the Americas, must once have caused losses to the grape varieties native to the Americas. He reasoned that over time and through natural selection (Riley early embraced Darwinism in contrast to some of his contemporaries) American grapes had evolved resistance to the phylloxera. European grapes, not being previously exposed to the aphid, had no immunity to it. The solution, as Riley saw it, lay in grafting European grapes on the rootstocks of American grapes. Although labor intensive—the French had to replant more than 1 million acres— grafting saved the wine industry. Through this program, Riley helped avert ruin- ation. A grateful French government showered honors on him. This success was one of several accomplishments that elevated him to worldwide fame before a bi- cycle accident truncated his career. This incident did much to elevate the status of science in general and of entomology in particular. Because of Riley's work, ento- mology has emerged as an agro-economic science. Popular in the 20th and 21st centuries has been the quip that all entomology aims to benefit agriculture and the economy at large. Wine has thus played a role in the expansion in the range and importance of science and in this sense helped change the world.

Wine Conquers California

Wine has formed one of the pillars of wealth in California. Although citrus fruits and nuts remain important, the Golden State is known for its vintages. The begin- nings of the wine industry in California were inconspicuous. The Spanish, finding a New World, planted vineyards in Mexico, Peru, Chile, Argentina, Uruguay, and southern California, then part of Mexico. The first planting of *Vitis vinifera* in southern California probably dates to roughly 1772. A U.S. state in 1850, California production soared as grapevines migrated north into San Francisco. Southern California's Mediterranean climate was and is ideal for grape culture. By 1890, California had more than 800 wineries. Today, California alone produces more wine than many other nations. California vintages have attained renown world- wide. Once a Mediterranean commodity, wine is today part of the global economy.

Global Warming and Climate Change

Some people deny global warming and climate change, but both appear to be oc- curring. As the climate has warmed, it has hastened the ripening of grapes, produc- ing vintages with more alcohol and less acidity. Some people find such wines less aromatic and so less pleasing. As temperatures rise at higher latitudes, the centers of wine production are likely to move farther from the equator. Canada may emerge as the new southern California. Other nations to the north in the Northern Hemisphere and to the south in the Southern Hemisphere appear likely to see their fortunes as wine producers increase. Part of the problem is that the climate, as it warms, will become more volatile. Torrential rains may deluge some areas and drought may ravage another. Such events are sure to impair the quantity and quality of wine. Global warming should also favor the growth and reproduction of insects that feed on grapevines, erecting another barrier to viticulture and winemaking.

Further Reading

Creasy, G. L., and L. L. Creasy. *Grapes*. Cambridge, MA: CABI, 2009.

Henderson, J. Patrick, and Dellie Rex. *About Wine*. New York: Thomson Delmar Learning, 2007.

Millon, Marc. *Wine: A Global History*. London: Reaktion Books, 2013.

Yam

A crop primarily of the tropics and subtropics, the yam is a perennial tuber. During the rainy season, a tuber produces a vine, which in turn generates one or more tubers. At the end of the rainy season the vine dies and the farmer, treating the plant as an annual, harvests the tubers. Left in the ground, however, a tuber will produce a new vine during the next rainy season, displaying its perennial habit. The yam is like the potato in yielding a tuber, and unlike the sweet potato and cassava, which do not produce tubers but rather swollen roots. The distinction between the yam and the sweet potato is lost on many Americans, who mistakenly call the sweet potato a yam. The "yam belt" of the southern United States is really an area of sweet potato culture. Worldwide, people confuse the yam with the cocoyam (*Xanthosoma*), taro, eddoe, and arrowroot. Some people assume erroneously that the cocoyam is a type of yam. The elephant yam of India is not a yam but a relative of the cocoyam. The term *yam bean* refers to a legume, not the yam.

The term *yam* is properly applied only to members of the *Dioscorea* genus, which is, in turn, part of the Dioscoreaceae family. The yam, depending on the species, is 63–83 percent water, compared to 68–82 percent for the potato and 58–81 percent for the sweet potato. The yam is a rich source of carbohydrates, though they have fallen into disfavor among some nutritionists. The yam is 15–38 percent carbohydrate, whereas the potato is 14–27 percent and the sweet potato 17–43 percent. Ninety-nine percent of the yam's carbohydrates are starch. Low in fat, the yam contains only 0.03–1.1 percent lipids, compared to 0.02–0.18 percent for the potato and 0.18–1.66 percent for the sweet potato. The yam is not a rich source of protein, containing 1.02–2.78 percent protein, compared to 1.14–2.98 percent for the potato and 0.18–1.66 percent for the sweet potato. Although the yam cannot boast an abundance of protein, it has more protein than cassava does. The yam contains the minerals calcium, iron, and phosphorus. Some varieties of yam have six milligrams of vitamin A per 100 grams of flesh, though other

Like cassava and sweet potatoes, the yam is an important root crop. In parts of the Old World tropics yams must compete with sweet potatoes for acreage. (Caroline Penn/Corbis)

varieties have no vitamin A. Of the B vitamins, the yam has thiamine, riboflavin, and niacin. The yam has 4.5–21.5 milligrams of vitamin C per 100 grams of tuber. The species *Dioscorea alata* and *Dioscorea trifida* lose more than half their vitamin C when stored just a few weeks. *Dioscorea rotunda* loses 20 percent of its vitamin C in four months' storage. Little vitamin C is lost during cooking. A little over two pounds of yam supply 33 percent of the recommended daily allowance of calories, 23 percent of protein, 19 percent of calcium, 84 percent of iron, 84 percent of thiamine, 17 percent of riboflavin, 33 percent of niacin, and more than 100 percent of vitamin C. Because people derive an adequate amount of vitamin C from yams, scurvy is rare in yam-producing countries. Although the yam is a staple in the diets of the people of Africa, Asia, South America, and the Caribbean, it is not consumed alone. People eat it with meat, fish, and vegetables.

Origin and History

Dioscorea is an ancient genus. By the end of the Cretaceous period (65 million years ago), *Dioscorea* was distributed worldwide. By the Miocene epoch (23 million years ago), the yams of Africa and Asia had split into separate lineages. Although *Dioscorea* contains more than 500 species, only about 60 are edible, and of these, only 10 are widely cultivated. In 1886, French botanist Alphonse de Candolle supposed that *Dioscorea opposita* and *Dioscorea japonica* originated in China and *Dioscorea alata* in Indonesia. He doubted that the Caribbean had indigenous species of yam but instead adopted the species that Europeans imported. One authority avers that *Dioscorea cayenensis*, *Dioscorea rotundata*, and *Dioscorea dumeturum* originated in West Africa; *Dioscorea alata, Dioscorea pentaphylla, Dioscorea esculenta*, and *Dioscorea bulbifera* in Southeast Asia; *Dioscorea opposita* and *Dioscorea japonica* in southern China; and *Dioscorea trifida* in the Caribbean.

One school of thought proposes independent domestication of the yam in Southeast Asia, southern China, West Africa, the Caribbean, and South America about 3000 BCE. One hypothesis holds that the yam originated in India and Myanmar and migrated to Southeast Asia, Indonesia, and Thailand by 100 BCE. From Indonesia, the yam spread to New Guinea, the Solomon Islands, Fiji, Samoa, Polynesia, and the rest of the tropical Pacific. The yam did not gain a foothold in New Zealand, which was too far south of the equator. One authority proposes Myanmar and Thailand as the original centers of cultivation. The people of Southeast Asia cultivated the yam at least 2,000 years ago, and possibly in prehistory. One hypothesis holds that fishermen gathered wild yams to diversify their diet. Those they did not eat sprouted and were planted. Focusing on Asia as the continent of cultivation, Russian agronomist Nikolai Vavilov asserted in the 20th century that the species *Dioscorea alata, Dioscorea esculenta, Dioscorea hispida, Dioscorea pentaphylla, Dioscorea bulbifera, Dioscorea opposita*, and *Dioscorea japonica* originated in several regions of Asia. Alphonse de Candolle asserted that the Chinese used the yam for medicine before 2000 BCE. In the third century CE, the Chinese cultivated *Dioscorea esculenta*. Around 600 CE, an Indian text noted that farmers grew the yam in the Ganges River Basin. The tuber was then widespread as a food. In Asia, foraging pigs ate the tubers near the surface of the soil. Under this pressure, *Dioscorea alata* evolved the habit of developing its tubers deep in the soil.

Given an Asia-first hypothesis, the yam must have migrated to Africa in prehistory. One hypothesis holds that Malaysians brought the yam from Asia to Africa when they settled Madagascar. Yet Madagascar had indigenous species of yam, which the inhabitants cultivated before the arrival of Malaysians in the first or second century CE. From the island the yam spread to East Africa and then west through the tropics. Yet the yams grown in East Africa originated in Africa, not Asia, weakening this hypothesis. Another hypothesis asserts that a "pre Negro people" from Southeast Asia brought the yam to Africa, possibly overland through Iran and Arabia, though these areas are bereft of the yam. This hypothesis supposes that people brought *Dioscorea batata*, a Chinese species, to Africa, yet this species is little cultivated in Africa.

In West Africa, people may have harvested the tubers from wild yams. Noting the ability of a plant to generate a new tuber to replace the one taken, people may have visited the plant later for a second harvest. Humans protected these plants from injury and transplanted them in their gardens, marking the beginning of yam cultivation in Africa. Africans cultivate *Dioscorea alata*, an Asian cultigen, but they also grow *Dioscorea cayenensis* and *Dioscorea rotundata*, which appear to be indigenous to Africa. In some areas of Africa, farmers may use only wooden implements to cultivate the yam, suggesting that yam culture predated the Iron Age, some 2,000 years ago. Yam cultivation arose independently in Central and South America and the Caribbean. The people of the Caribbean cultivated the yam before the arrival of Columbus. The Amerindians probably began cultivating the yam before the rise of the Maya. The Amerindians cultivated the native *Dioscorea trifida*, which Europeans and Africans adopted when they settled the Caribbean.

Africans may have begun to cultivate the yam around 5000 BCE. Despite the early cultivation of the yam in Africa, the ancient Egyptians appear not to have grown it. The same appears to be true of the people of Mesopotamia (now Iraq) and the Near East. The yam was unknown in the Mediterranean Basin, where winters were too cold. The yam was also unknown in Arabia. In the 16th century, Portuguese explorer Pacheco Pereira observed the cultivation of yams in Guinea, western Ghana, and eastern Nigeria.

The Portuguese learned that Indians and Malaysians provisioned their ships with yams. Adopting this practice, the Portuguese introduced the yam to Elmina, Ghana, and São Thomé, Brazil. Portuguese ships laden with yams disembarked in Africa, taking on new provisions. Old yams that had been dumped to make room for new provisions may have sprouted and been taken into cultivation. Slavers carried yams as provision because they were a food that Africans would eat. The people of the Caribbean, taking surplus rations of *Dioscorea rotundata* and *Dioscorea cayenensis*, planted them for food. As early as 1522, the Amerindians of the Caribbean may have cultivated African species. By the mid-17th century the Asian cultigen *Dioscorea alata* was widely grown in the Americas. Europeans must have brought *Dioscorea esculenta* to the Caribbean, though it does not store well and so was unsuitable for ocean crossings. From the Americas, the Portuguese took *Dioscorea trifida* to Sri Lanka, where it was grown in the 16th and 17th centuries. In the 19th century, the Japanese introduced *Dioscorea opposita* and *Dioscorea japonica* to Hawaii, though the yam never emerged as an important crop in the islands. Queensland, Australia, grew *Dioscorea alata*, though it was never widespread.

The Columbian Exchange brought the potato, sweet potato, cassava, and cocoyam, all American indigenes, to the Old World, where they competed with yams. In many parts of Africa and Asia, sweet potato replaced yams. In other areas, cocoa replaced yams. By the end of the 19th century, cassava competed against the yam in Africa and Asia. Cassava was cheaper and easier to prepare than yam. A world food, the yam has shaped the history and daily lives of people throughout the globe.

The Importance of Yams

West Africans celebrate the planting and harvesting of yams. The New Yam Festival marks the harvest and is the greatest celebration of the year in some villages in West Africa. Priests, officials, or village elders take charge of the festival. On the day of the festival, the people harvest yams from sacred soil and offer them to the gods. After this offering, the people eat these yams. Having fasted before eating the yams, West Africans consider it sinful to eat yams before the first offering has been made to the gods. According to one authority, some people starved rather than consume yams before the festival. The prohibition against eating yams before the festival may have arisen because millennia ago some yams may have been toxic when young and edible when mature. Alternatively, the prohibition may have arisen from the desire to avoid damaging a young plant by harvesting a tuber too soon.

The Ibo of Nigeria worship Ajokuji, the "Great Spirit of the Yam." The priests of Ajokuji determined when to plant and harvest yams. So important is the yam to many Africans that parents give it to infants as a first food. The Ibo deem the theft of yams as more serious than the theft of other items. Adultery, if committed in a yam field, is a crime, whereas adultery in other places is merely a civil offense; it is believed that adultery corrupts the soil, leaving it to yield a poor crop. In this instance, Ajokuji may cause misfortune as punishment for the defilement of a yam field. The people of Malaysia and Indonesia believe the species *Dioscorea pentaphylla* to be sacred. Some Malaysians put yam juice in the mouth of an infant at its naming ceremony.

Further Reading

Coursey, D. G. *Yams: An Account of the Nature, Origins, Cultivation and Utilisation of the Useful Members of the Dioscoreaceae*. London: Longmans, 1967.

Rubatzky, Vincent E., and Mas Yamaguchi. *World Vegetables: Principles, Production, and Nutritive Values*. New York: Chapman and Hall, 1997.

Bibliography

Albala, Ken. *Beans: A History*. Oxford: Berg, 2007.

Albala, Ken. *Nuts: A Global History*. London: Reaktion Books, 2014.

Albala, Ken. *Pancakes: A Global History*. London: Reaktion Books, 2008.

Anderson, Heather Arndt. *Breakfast: A History*. Lanham, MD: Rowman & Littlefield, 2013.

Arellano, Gustavo. *TACO USA: How Mexican Food Conquered America*. New York: Scribner, 2012.

Bloch-Dano, Evelyne. *Vegetables: A Biography*. Chicago and London: The University of Chicago Press, 2008.

Cecla, Franco La. *Pasta and Pizza*. Chicago: Prickly Paradigm Press, 2007.

Chaline, Eric. *Fifty Animals that Changed the Course of History*. Buffalo, NY: Firefly Books, 2011.

Chang, Shu-Ting, and Philip G. Miles. *Mushrooms: Cultivation, Nutritional Value, Medicinal Effect, and Environmental Impact*. Boca Raton, FL: CRC Press, 2004.

Civitello, Linda. *Cuisine and Culture: A History of Food and People*. Hoboken, NJ: John Wiley and Sons, 2011.

Clarkson, Janet. *Soup: A Global History*. London: Reaktion Books, 2010.

Coe, Andrew. *Chop Suey: A Cultural History of Chinese Food in the United States*. Oxford: Oxford University Press, 2009.

Dickie, John. *Delizia!: The Epic History of the Italians and Their Food*. New York: Free Press, 2008.

Du Bois, Christine M., Chee-Beng Tan, and Sidney W. Mintz, eds. *The World of Soy*. Urbana: University of Illinois Press, 2008.

Food and History. www.foodandhistory.me.

"Food History." The Kitchen Project. kitchenproject.com/history.

Food History. www.world-foodhistory.com.

Food Timeline. www.foodtimeline.org.

Harlan, Jack R. *Crops and Man*. Madison, WI: American Society of Agronomy, 1992.

Helstosky, Carol. *Pizza: A Global History*. London: Reaktion Books, 2008.

Hillocks, R. J., J. M. Thresh, and A. C. Bellotti, eds. *Cassava: Biology, Production and Utilization*. New York: CABI Publishing, 2002.

Hughes, Meredith Sayles. *Glorious Grasses: The Grains*. Minneapolis: Lerner Publications, 1999.

Hughes, Meredith Sayles. *Spill the Beans and Pass the Peanuts: Legumes*. Minneapolis: Lerner Publications, 1999.

Hughes, Meredith, and Tom Hughes. *Buried Treasure: Roots and Tubers*. Minneapolis: Lerner Publications, 1998.

Humble, Nicola. *Cake: A Global History*. London: Reaktion Books, 2010.

Janer, Zilkia. *Latino Food Cultures*. Food Cultures in America, edited by Ken Albala. Westport, CT: Greenwood Press, 2008.

Janik, Erika. *Apple: A Global History*. London: Reaktion Books, 2011.

Johnson, Sylvia A. *Tomatoes, Potatoes, Corn, and Beans: How the Foods of the Americas Changed Eating around the World*. New York: Atheneum Books, 1997.

Katz, Solomon H., ed. *Encyclopedia of Food and Culture*. Detroit, MI: Thomson and Gale, 2003.

Koeppel, Dan. *Banana: The Fate of the Fruit that Changed the World*. New York: Hudson Street Press, 2008.

Kostioukovitch, Elena. *Why Italians Love to Talk about Food*. New York: Farrar, Straus and Giroux, 2006.

Kraig, Bruce. *Hot Dog: A Global History*. London: Reaktion Books, 2009.

Krampner, Jon. *Creamy and Crunchy: An Informal History of Peanut Butter, the All-American Food*. New York: Columbia University Press, 2013.

Lanza, Fabrizio. *Olive: A Global History*. London: Reaktion Books, 2011.

Laszlo, Pierre. *Citrus: A History*. Chicago and London: The University of Chicago Press, 2007.

Laszlo, Pierre. *Salt: Grain of Life*. New York: Columbia University Press, 2000.

Loebenstein, Gad, and George Thottappilly, eds. *The Sweetpotato*. Dordrecht: Springer, 2009.

McWilliams, Mark. *The Story behind the Dish: Classic American Foods*. Santa Barbara, CA: Greenwood Press, 2012.

Miller, Adrian. *Soul Food: The Surprising Story of an American Cuisine, One Plate at a Time*. Chapel Hill: The University of North Carolina Press, 2003.

Millon, Marc. *Wine: A Global History*. London: Reaktion Books, 2013.

Moss, Sarah, and Alexander Bodenoch. *Chocolate: A Global History*. London: Reaktion Books, 2009.

Percy, Pam. *The Complete Chicken: An Entertaining History of Chickens*. New York: Crestline, 2011.

Reader, John. *Potato: A History of the Propitious Esculent*. New Haven, CT: Yale University Press, 2008.

Rimas, Andrew, and Evan D. G. Fraser. *Beef: The Untold Story of How Milk, Meat, and Muscle Shaped the World*. New York: William Morrow, 2008.

Sack, Daniel. *Whitebread Protestants: Food and Religion in American Culture*. New York: St. Martin's Press, 2000.

Schiebinger, Londa, and Claudia Swan, eds. *Colonial Botany: Science, Commerce, and Politics in the Early Modern World*. Philadelphia: University of Pennsylvania Press, 2007.

Shaffer, Marjorie. *Pepper: A History of the World's Most Influential Spice*. New York: St. Martin's Press, 2013.

Sharma, S. D., ed. *Rice: Origin, Antiquity and History*. Enfield, NH: Science Publishers, 2010.

Smith, Andrew F. *Hamburger: A Global History*. London: Reaktion Books, 2008.

Smith, Andrew F. *Peanuts: The Illustrious History of the Goober Pea*. Urbana: University of Illinois Press, 2002.

Smith, Andrew F. *Souper Tomatoes: The Story of America's Favorite Food*. New Brunswick, NJ: Rutgers University Press, 2000.

Smith, Gavin D. *Beer: A Global History*. London: Reaktion Books, 2014.

Toops, Diane. *Eggs: A Global History*. London: Reaktion Books, 2014.

Warman, Arturo. *Corn and Capitalism: How a Botanical Bastard Grew to Global Dominance*. Chapel Hill and London: The University of North Carolina Press, 2003.

Warner, Melanie. *Pandora's Lunchbox: How Processed Food Took over the American Meal*. New York: Scribner, 2012.

Weiss, Laura B. *Ice Cream: A Global History*. London: Reaktion Books, 2013.

Williams-Forson, Psyche, and Carole Counihan, eds. *Taking Food Public: Redefining Foodways in a Changing World*. New York and London: Routledge, 2012.

Wilson, Bee. *Sandwich: A Global History*. London: Reaktion Books, 2010.

Young, Allen M. *The Chocolate Tree: A Natural History of Cacao*. Gainesville: University Press of Florida, 2007.

Index

About the Author

CHRISTOPHER CUMO holds a PhD in history and has taught at Walsh University, the University of Akron, and Kent State University. He is the editor of *Encyclopedia of Cultivated Plants: From Acacia to Zinnia* (ABC-CLIO, 2013), and the author of *Science and Technology in 20th-Century American Life* (Greenwood, 2007), *Seeds of Change* (2000), and *A History of the Ohio Agricultural Experiment Station, 1882–1997* (1997). He has also written numerous encyclopedia entries, magazine articles, and book reviews.